Optimization Techniques
in Engineering

Scrivener Publishing
100 Cummings Center, Suite 541J
Beverly, MA 01915-6106

Sustainable Computing and Optimization

Series Editor: Prasenjit Chatterjee, Morteza Yazdani and Dilbagh Panchal

Scope: The objective of "Sustainable Computing and Optimization" series is to bring together the global research scholars, experts, and scientists in the research areas of sustainable computing and optimization from all over the world to share their knowledge and experiences on current research achievements in these fields. The series aims to provide a golden opportunity for global research community to share their novel research results, findings, and innovations to a wide range of readers, present globally. Data is everywhere and continuing to grow massively, which has created a huge demand for qualified experts who can uncover valuable insights from data. The series will promote sustainable computing and optimization methodologies in order to solve real life problems mainly from engineering and management systems domains. The series will mainly focus on the real life problems, which can suitably be handled through these paradigms.

Publishers at Scrivener
Martin Scrivener (martin@scrivenerpublishing.com)
Phillip Carmical (pcarmical@scrivenerpublishing.com)

Optimization Techniques in Engineering

Advances and Applications

Edited by

Anita Khosla
Prasenjit Chatterjee
Ikbal Ali
and
Dheeraj Joshi

Scrivener
Publishing

WILEY

This edition first published 2023 by John Wiley & Sons, Inc., 111 River Street, Hoboken, NJ 07030, USA and Scrivener Publishing LLC, 100 Cummings Center, Suite 541J, Beverly, MA 01915, USA
© 2023 Scrivener Publishing LLC
For more information about Scrivener publications please visit www.scrivenerpublishing.com.

Wiley Global Headquarters
111 River Street, Hoboken, NJ 07030, USA

For details of our global editorial offices, customer services, and more information about Wiley products visit us at www.wiley.com.

Limit of Liability/Disclaimer of Warranty
While the publisher and authors have used their best efforts in preparing this work, they make no representations or warranties with respect to the accuracy or completeness of the contents of this work and specifically disclaim all warranties, including without limitation any implied warranties of merchantability or fitness for a particular purpose. No warranty may be created or extended by sales representatives, written sales materials, or promotional statements for this work. The fact that an organization, website, or product is referred to in this work as a citation and/or potential source of further information does not mean that the publisher and authors endorse the information or services the organization, website, or product may provide or recommendations it may make. This work is sold with the understanding that the publisher is not engaged in rendering professional services. The advice and strategies contained herein may not be suitable for your situation. You should consult with a specialist where appropriate. Neither the publisher nor authors shall be liable for any loss of profit or any other commercial damages, including but not limited to special, incidental, consequential, or other damages. Further, readers should be aware that websites listed in this work may have changed or disappeared between when this work was written and when it is read.

Library of Congress Cataloging-in-Publication Data

ISBN 978-1-119-90627-8

Cover image: Pixabay.Com
Cover design by Russ Richardson

Set in size of 11pt and Minion Pro by Manila Typesetting Company, Makati, Philippines

Printed in the USA

10 9 8 7 6 5 4 3 2 1

This book is dedicated to the Editors' parents, life partners, children, students, scholars, friends, and colleagues

Contents

Part 2: Decision Science and Simulation-Based Optimization

Preface

Optimization is a precise method that allows the planner to identify the best solution to a problem by using design restrictions and criteria. Optimization techniques have been used to solve a variety of practical problems in a variety of fields. These optimization methods have existed since the time of Newton, Lagrange and Cauchy. The contributions of Leibnitz and Newton to calculus are responsible for the growth of differential calculus approaches for optimization. Optimization techniques are useful tools for obtaining the required design parameters and operational conditions. They direct the experimental effort and lower the design and operations risk and cost. Finding the values of decision variables that correspond to and give the maximum or minimum of one or more specified objectives is referred to as optimization. An optimization algorithm is a process that compares numerous solutions iteratively until an optimum or satisfying solution is identified. Thus, optimization has become a feature of computer-aided design activities since the invention of computers. The formulation of goal functions and the optimization technique chosen determine the reliability of optimal solutions. A mathematical model that characterizes and predicts the process behavior is required for optimization. An optimization search could aid in the estimation of unknown parameters in complex nonlinear processes. In dynamic processes, robust optimization can be used to find uncertainty variables. Optimization can also be used to aid in the development of scale-up methodologies and the design of multiphase reactors and flow systems. Manufacturing and engineering activities currently being used will not be as efficient until design and operations are optimized. The purpose of design optimization might simply be to reduce production costs or to increase production efficiency. Optimization is particularly important in companies since it helps to cut costs, which can lead to increased earnings and success in a competitive environment.

There are two types of optimization approaches used: traditional and soft computing-based. Traditional optimization techniques can be used to identify the best solution or unconstrained maxima and minima of continuous and differentiable functions. These are mathematical methods that use differential calculus to get the best solution. Optimization can decrease readability and introduce code that is only needed to boost performance. This might make programs or systems more difficult to maintain and debug. As a result, performance tweaking or optimization is frequently done near the conclusion of the development stage. Customer experience optimization is critical since it boosts customer satisfaction and helps organizations improve their key performance indicators. More revenue and growth are frequently associated with satisfied customers and improved key performance indicators. Performance optimization is the practice of altering how a system functions to increase its efficiency and effectiveness. Debugging the optimization solution is more complex than debugging the rule-based simulation solution. It could be a mix of numerous limitations and input data from multiple places and time steps. Many fields have used optimization theory and methodologies to solve various practical challenges. Soft computing is the application of approximation computations to difficult computer problems to produce "mushy" but usable outcomes. The method produces results for issues that are either unsolvable or take too long to solve using traditional methods.

An optimization algorithm is a process that compares numerous solutions iteratively until an optimum or satisfying one is identified. It follows particular rules when moving from one solution to the next. Many fields of study employ optimization methods to find solutions that maximize or minimize certain study parameters, such as minimizing expenses in the manufacture of a thing or service, maximizing earnings, minimizing raw materials in the development of a good, or maximizing productivity.

The goal of optimizing an objective function is to identify a set of inputs that results in a maximum or minimal function evaluation. Many machine learning algorithms, from fitting logistic regression models to training artificial neural networks, are based on this concept. The purpose of the optimization process is to find choice variable values that result in an objective function's maximum or minimum. Optimization issues are characterized as linear, nonlinear, geometric, or quadratic programming problems based on the nature of the expressions for the objective function and constraints. An optimization model is a representation of the key features of the business problem being addressed. The objective function, decision variables, and business constraints are the three components of the model.

The purpose of optimization is to find the best design possible based on a set of prioritized criteria or constraints. These include, among other things, boosting productivity, strength, reliability, lifetime, efficiency, and utilization. Many fields have used optimization theory and methodologies to solve various practical challenges; and optimization techniques have become increasingly important and popular in various engineering applications as computing systems have advanced.

The aim of this book is to present some of the recent developments in the area of optimization theory, methods, and applications in engineering. It focuses on the metaphor of the inspired system and how to configure and apply the various algorithms. The book is organized into two parts: Part I – Soft Computing and Evolutionary-Based Optimization; and Part II – Decision Science and Simulation-Based Optimization, which contains application-based chapters. A brief description of each of the chapters is presented below:

Part I: Soft Computing and Evolutionary-Based Optimization

- Chapter 1 attempts to realistically represent the existing grey wolf optimizer in order to increase the algorithm's efficiency. Unlike grey wolf optimizers, the modeling of prey in this study is considered dynamic. To solve a dynamic economic dispatch problem with electric vehicle profiles, dynamism is added to the prey using the Levy flight distribution function.
- Chapter 2 presents an object detection approach devised for detecting plastics. To apply transfer learning, the algorithm is written in tensor flow. The two most commonly used object identification approaches, YOLO and Faster R-CNN, are compared.
- Chapter 3 strives to increase the use of real power in relation to reactive power in order to improve the power factor. The power factor is corrected closer to unity with the help of a smart power factor correction device. The power factor controller swaps the appropriate capacitor blocks in steps depending on the load and power factor of the network to raise the power factor to almost 0.95. MATLAB software is used to simulate the system.
- Chapter 4 focuses on the design and analysis of a solar-fed cascaded boost converter with a maximum power point tracking (MPPT) algorithm based on neural networks (NN), which is used for electric vehicle (EV) applications.
- Chapter 5 proposes modeling of a single and multi-junction solar cell with maximum power point tracking (MPPT)

using an intelligent fuzzy logic algorithm (FLA) for maximum productivity.

- Chapter 6 discusses the utility of particle swarm optimization (PSO), as well as the weaknesses in the algorithm. The latest developments and improvements to the PSO parameters are also highlighted. Finally, it explores its hybridization with other notable algorithms and applications in a variety of disciplines and contexts during the last few decades.

- Chapter 7 delves into the uniformity subfields of sensor networks, as well as energy-efficient sensor networks, which actively investigate the use of genetic algorithms (GAs) as a fundamental component in developing deployment strategies and routing protocols. Since manual garbage collection is a time-consuming technique that cannot keep up with the ever-increasing demands of city rubbish, sensor networks can be used in garbage collection as the first step toward proper plastics treatment and recycling for a more environmentally friendly future.

- Chapter 8 presents several machine learning methods, such as random forests, linear regression, XGBoost, and support vector machine (SVM), that aid in the estimation of delamination factor based on known inputs such as feed rate, point angle, and spindle speed.

- Chapter 9 attempts using a differential evolutionary algorithm to perform sand elevation categorization of sand deposits acquired with a drone camera in a desert location. However, the results are unsatisfactory, prompting the development of an evolutionary algorithm-based contour identification approach for accurate elevation categorization.

- Chapter 10 mainly discusses promoting energy efficiency while maintaining a sustainable minimum spectral efficiency requirement. By obtaining the Pareto optimal solution set, the joint user clustering and multi-objective particle swarm optimization (MOPSO) method has been proposed for downlink non-orthogonal multiple access (NOMA). The simulation results reveal that the proposed MOPSO approach outperforms the existing systems in terms of parametric efficiency.

- Chapter 11 uses the Amazon fine food reviews dataset to automatically analyze product reviews and classify them as good or terrible. Four distinct types of classifiers were employed to identify the reviews as positive or negative: logistic regression, support vector machine (SVM), random forest, and XGBoost.

- Chapter 12 primarily determines the best cutting conditions for turning operations. Rake angle, entry angle, and cutting speed were used as cutting parameters during the turning operation in this investigation. Different cutting forces, such as primary cutting force and feed force, have been used as machining variables at the same time. A variety of cutting settings were chosen as inputs, and all machining variables were monitored as outputs. With the use of Minitab software, the effects of cutting parameters on cutting forces were identified as a regression equation. In this chapter, single objective optimization and multi-objective optimization approaches have been used for optimization. For optimization, a genetic algorithm (GA) has been applied as an evolutionary computation approach.

- Chapter 13 uses a genetic algorithm (GA) with modified mutation and crossover to address the classification problem on the hate speech detection problem in social media.

- Chapter 14 investigates load frequency control (LFC) based on a neural network for increasing the power system dynamic performance of a single area thermal power plant.

Part II: Decision Science and Simulation-Based Optimization

- Chapter 15 uses the Fuzzy VIKOR (VIse Kriterijumska Optimizacija I Kompromisno Resenje) method to choose non-powered industrial trucks based on several conflicting criteria. Subjective weighting of criteria and alternative performance ratings are made based on the experience, perception, and opinion of experts and decision makers participating in the process.

- Chapter 16 introduces new concepts for continuous function in neutrosophic topological spaces.

- Chapter 17 identifies mental health risk factors, such as the unique stressors that farmers face, based on an exhaustive assessment of the literature and discussions with farmers and agricultural professionals. Then, the ELECTRE technique, one of the most recent multi-criteria decision-making techniques, was chosen to address the increased concern over farmers' mental health issues.

- Chapter 18 proposes a scientific and mathematically based multiple objective and subjective criteria evaluation technique (MOSCET) to assist decision makers in industrial organizations in making the most appropriate decision based on objective and subjective criteria in situations where the human brain is incapable of finding the right solution.
- Chapter 19 employs an analysis of variance (ANOVA) measure of signal-to-noise ratio (S/N ratio) to see if environmental variables such as lighting, humidity, and other elements had a significant impact on worker output in an Indian manufacturing plant.
- Chapter 20 focuses on rural tourism in an attempt to identify critical characteristics that could help India's rural tourism grow. Sub-determinants of the top three primary factors were also ranked in order to learn more about contributing sub-factors by allocating both local and global weights to the success of rural tourism. Several factors and sub-factors were found and prioritized using the analytic hierarchy process (AHP).
- Chapter 21 uses a cost minimization technique to construct an economic order quantity (EOQ) model based on environmental contamination. By mixing the demand rate and all cost elements of the inventory management system as triangle dense fuzzy numbers, the fuzzy model parameters create a triangular dense fuzzy mathematical model.
- Chapter 22 considers a total of ten major factors responsible for aging and uses the analytic hierarchy process (AHP) to sift through and choose the best of these factors based on their priority order, which are extremely, strongly, and least accountable for aging.
- Chapter 23 uses the analytic hierarchy process (AHP) in an attempt to identify and rank e-waste management concerns according to their importance.
- Chapter 24 suggests employing the k-means method to identify different groupings of primary energy household emissions in Indian states.
- Chapter 25 proposes using the fast Fourier transform (FFT) algorithm to detect and remove the noise from the

transmitted signal to reduce misinterpretation in the exploration of hydrocarbon in shallow water environments.

- Chapter 26 explores the linear and nonlinear portions of an active suspension system using a quarter vehicle model. Nonlinearity in the plant must be considered to ensure resilience of the specified control technique in various operating situations. Proportional–integral–derivative (PID) and state feedback methodologies are used to investigate the performance of the suggested quarter vehicle model. The simulation results for a passive, active, and linearized quarter vehicle system are compared.
- Chapter 27 examines various peak-to-average power ratio (PAPR) reduction techniques for 5G communication systems.
- Chapter 28 explores the rebound phenomena for an electromagnetic V-bending test based on the time-bearing disparity between the sheet metal displacement and the power amplitude. The loose coupling strategy is studied using a numerical simulation method.
- Chapter 29 presents a new class of compandors-based peak-to-average power ratio (PAPR) reduction approach. Nonlinear compandors are applied to orthogonal frequency division multiplexing (OFDM) signals to attenuate the high signal peaks more than the rest of the signal, lowering the PAPR.
- Chapter 30 proposes a novel multi-criteria group decision-making approach for supplier selection. This method can take into account various subjective criteria and their sub-criteria that are in conflict.

The Editors
February 2023

Acknowledgment

The editors would like to thank everyone who helped them edit this book by providing vital feedback, support, constructive recommendations, and assistance.

The editors would like to express their gratitude to all of the authors for their outstanding contributions to the book's intellectual substance.

Simple words cannot describe the editors' thanks to Scrivener Publishing's complete editing and production teams, notably Mr. Martin Scrivener, for his unwavering support, encouragement, and direction throughout the publishing process. Without his enormous contributions, this work would not have been feasible.

The editors want to express their gratitude to the reviewers who generously donated their time and expertise to help shape such a high-quality book on such a topical issue.

During the book's preparation, the editors would like to thank their families for their love, understanding, and support.

Finally, the editors would like to thank all of the readers for their support and hope that this book will continue to inspire and guide them in their future endeavours.

The Editors

Part 1

SOFT COMPUTING AND EVOLUTIONARY-BASED OPTIMIZATION

Improved Grey Wolf Optimizer with Levy Flight to Solve Dynamic Economic Dispatch Problem with Electric Vehicle Profiles

Anjali Jain[1]*, Ashish Mani[1] and Anwar S. Siddiqui[2]

[1]Department of Electrical and Electronics Engineering, Amity University Uttar Pradesh, Noida, Uttar Pradesh, India
[2]Department of Electrical and Electronics Engineering, Jamia Milia Islamia, Delhi, India

Abstract

Meta-heuristic algorithm plays an important role in solving nonconvex, nondifferentiable complex problems. One such complex problem in the power system is dynamic economic dispatch (DED), which is difficult to solve while considering transmission losses and ramp-rate limits. The purpose of dynamic economic dispatch is to find power generated by different generating units for the given specified load while fulfilling the operational constraints along with ramp rate limit and also optimizing the cost of generation as well. Moreover, the problem considered in this chapter is of 15 generator test cases for 24 hours along with three distinct profiles of electric vehicles. Here, in this chapter, an improved version of the Grey wolf optimizer is utilized to optimize the cost objective function. In this variant, grey wolf optimizer prey position is modeled with the help of Levy probability distribution, which makes the modeling of prey dynamic in nature and, hence, showcases the more realistic modeling of the grey wolf hunting process. The selection of parameters for Levy flight is done with the help of experimentation conducted on different benchmark functions. After finalizing the parameters for Levy flight, an improved grey wolf optimizer with Levy flight demonstrated its efficacy for nonconvex and nondifferentiable functions. The numerical results shown with the help of Benchmark solution and 15 bus generators showcase the efficiency of the algorithm. The results produced

*Corresponding author: anjalijain.121@gmail.com

Anita Khosla, Prasenjit Chatterjee, Ikbal Ali and Dheeraj Joshi (eds.) Optimization Techniques in Engineering: Advances and Applications, (3–36) © 2023 Scrivener Publishing LLC

by this algorithm are compared with other state-of-the-art algorithms, which prove that the algorithm is giving either better or competitive results.

Keywords: Charging scenario, electric vehicle profile, dynamic economic dispatch, Levy flight, probability distribution function

1.1   Introduction

Static economic dispatch problem determines the optimal schedule of the different committed units to meet the load demand at the given time with minimum operating cost while meeting the operational cost. On the other hand, dynamic economic dispatch is defined to schedule the generators in such a way for the given time taking into consideration of operational constraints along with ramp rate limits. It can be understood in this way that the DED problem is dividing the dispatch period into smaller time intervals wherein the SED problem is just to find the power generated by each unit in such an individual interval. Hence, we can say, DED is an extension of the SED problem.

DED problem has been noticed by many researchers in the 1980s, wherein several algorithms have been proposed by different researchers from time to time. DED problem has been discussed for various test cases in Jain *et al.* [1]. Chen *et al.* [2] showed its application to analyze both distribution and transmission systems. The classical methods to solve such problems are Lambda iterative method [3], Lagrangian method [4] and interior point method [5]. But this type of methods does not work well for the nonsmooth and nonconvex objective function. Hence, these solutions do not work for DED objective function, which itself is a nonsmooth and nonconvex optimization problem. To overcome this problem, evolutionary algorithms are proposed from time to time to solve DED problems.

Some of the meta-heuristic techniques, which have been explored to find the solution for such a nonsmooth and nonconvex optimization problem are genetic algorithm [6], grey wolf optimizer [7], biogeography based optimization [8], differential evolution [9], simulated annealing [10], gravitational search algorithm [11], firefly algorithm [12], self-learning teaching learning-based algorithm [13], etc. These algorithms utilize an initially generated population of individuals, which represents the solution for the said problem and then iterated and evolved to find the better solution.

Moreover, the trend of using a single heuristic technique has been shifted to a hybrid meta-heuristic, so that the hybrid solution will be able to give better results by mitigating its limitations and employing its strengths. The authors from time to time used a hybrid algorithm to solve complex problems [14, 15].

Here, in the proposed work, an effort has been made to realistically model the existing grey wolf optimizer so that the efficiency of the algorithm is improved. The modeling of prey in this work is considered to be dynamic, unlike grey wolf optimizers. The dynamism has been added to the prey with the help of the Levy flight distribution function. Also, the tuning of parameters of probability distribution has been done with the help of experimentation by taking a different combination of variable parameters. The performance of the different parameters is tested on different benchmark function, and hence, the optimum variables are selected as per their performance. Since it is the improved version of grey wolf optimizer, and it is utilizing Levy flight probability distribution function for modeling of prey position, hence, the name proposed for the algorithm is improved grey wolf optimizer with Levy flight, i.e., improved GWOLF. The algorithm is modeled using the MATLAB platform and is run for a 15-unit DED problem without electric vehicles and with electric vehicles for different load profiles.

Dynamic economic dispatch problem is itself a complex problem, wherein the inclusion of renewable energy sources will further make the power system more dynamic. The intermittent power generated by renewable energy sources can be taken care of with the help of plug-in electric vehicles. Moreover, the charging of electric vehicles adds to increased load in the grid. Three different profiles of plug-in electric vehicles have been used to analyze the performance of improved GWO to solve the DED problem. The charging probability distribution of these electric vehicle profiles has been shown in Figure 1.1. The different profiles considered in this chapter are EPRI, off-peak, and stochastic profiles [13].

Section 1.2 discusses problem formulation of DED problem, Section 1.3 elaborates the proposed algorithm, i.e., improved grey wolf optimizer with Levy flight along with the brief introduction to grey wolf optimizer. Section 1.4 talks about simulation and results, and the chapter is concluded in Section 1.5.

1.2 Problem Formulation

Dynamic economic dispatch (DED) is a well-known power system complex problem. The mathematical modeling of the cost function is considering the cost of thermal generators along with valve-point effect [1] as under,

$$F_{cost} = \sum_{t=1}^{T} \sum_{i=1}^{N_g} (a_i + b_i P_{i,t} + c_i P_{i,t}^2) + \left| e_i \sin(f_i(P_{i\ min} - P_{i,t})) \right| \quad (1.1)$$

Here in Eq (1.1), a_i, b_i and c_i are the fuel coefficients, e_i and f_i represents valve point parameters to model the ripples produced in the cost curve. N_g represents the maximum number of generating units in the test case, T is the total time interval in hours for which objective function is calculated, $P_{i\,min}$ is the minimum powergeneration by i^{th} generator and is the power generation by i^{th} generator in t^{th} interval

The different constraints accompanying DED are [1]:

1.2.1   Power Output Limits

Power generated by a specific unit should be within its minimum and maximum limits.

$$P_{i\,min} \leq P_{i,t} \leq P_{i\,max} \qquad (i = 1,2,\ldots\ldots,N_g) \qquad (1.2)$$

where $P_{i\,min}$, $P_{i\,max}$ are the minimum and maximum of power generation bygenerator.

1.2.2   Power Balance Limits

Power generated must be equal to the algebraic sum of power demand and losses at all times. Since in the test case, we have electric vehicles as well, which are also acting as the load for the system. Hence, the power balance equation is written as

$$\sum_{i=1}^{N_g} P_{i,t} = P_{D,t} + P_{L,t} + L_{pev,t}, \quad (t = 1,2,\ldots\ldots,T) \qquad (1.3)$$

Here, $P_{D,t}$ is the power demand in t^{th} interval, t is the time interval, $P_{L,t}$ is the transmission losses in t^{th} interval and $L_{pev,t}$ is load added because of charge probability distribution given by different electric vehicle profiles. Transmission losses are defined with the help of Kron's formula,

$$P_{L,t} = \sum_{i=1}^{N_g}\sum_{j=1}^{N_u} P_{i,t}B_{ij}P_{j,t} + \sum_{i=1}^{N_u} B_{0i}P_{i,t} + B_{00} \qquad (1.4)$$

where loss coefficients are defined as B_{ij}, B_{0i}, and B_{00}

1.2.3   Ramp Rate Limits

The change in power generation during any time interval cannot occur abruptly. Hence the change in power is defined with the ramp rate limits as under,

$$P_{i,t} - P_{i,t-1} \leq UR_i, P_{i,t-1} - P_{i,t} \geq DR_i \tag{1.5}$$

UR_i and DR_i represents the ramp-up and ramp-down rate limit of the ith generator respectively. $P_{i,t}$ of the ith generator in the tth time interval should be limited by the previously dispatched power $P_{i,t-1}$ of the ith generator in the $(t-1)^{th}$ time interval within ramp-up and ramp-down rate limits UR_i and DR_i.

1.2.4   Electric Vehicles

Greenhouse gas emission by conventional locomotives is the main reason for the increased use of electric vehicles. The increased use of electric vehicles leads to added load on the generators. Hence, these electric vehicles in this chapter are treated as load and the profile for different test cases such as EPRI, off-peak and stochastic are considered in this chapter [13].

Figure 1.1 represents the charging probability distribution function of different electric vehicle profiles. These profiles are adding extra load $L_{pev,t}$ to the system, and this has been shown in Eq. (1.3).

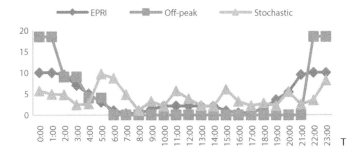

Figure 1.1 Charging probability distribution by different profiles.

1.3   Proposed Algorithm

1.3.1   Overview of Grey Wolf Optimizer

The behavior of *Canis lupus* wolves is the source of inspiration to model the grey wolf optimization algorithm. This algorithm is modeled based on the social hierarchy and hunting behavior followed by different wolves in the pack [7]. The alpha (α) wolves are at the top of the pack and are considered to be leaders of the pack. Beta (β) wolves act as the advisors of α wolves wherein δ wolves are following α and β wolves. Omega (ω) wolves have the function of scapegoats only. The positions vectors of different wolves are updated to model the encircling behavior of the wolves in the $(t + 1)^{th}$ iteration as under,

$$\vec{X}(t+1) = \overrightarrow{X_p}(t) - \vec{A}.\left|\vec{C}.(\overrightarrow{X_p}(t) - \vec{X}(t))\right| \tag{1.6}$$

where,
  $\vec{X}(t)$: position vector of a *Canis lupus* wolf in iteration
  t: the index for the current iteration
  $\vec{X}_p(t)$: position vector of the prey

$$\vec{A} = 2\vec{a}.\vec{r_1} - \vec{a} \tag{1.7}$$

$$\vec{C} = 2.\vec{r_2} \tag{1.8}$$

$$a(t) = 2 - \frac{2t}{MaxIter} \tag{1.9}$$

where
  $\vec{A}, \vec{C}$: coefficient vectors
  $\vec{r_1}, \vec{r_2}$: random vectors lies in [0, 1]
  $\vec{a}$: parameter from 2 to 0 over the course of iterations,
  MaxIter: maximum number of iterations.

The positions of the other wolves are updated according to the positions of α, β, and δ as follows [7]:

$$\vec{X_1} = \overrightarrow{X_\alpha}(t) - \overrightarrow{A_1}.\overrightarrow{C_1}.(\overrightarrow{X_\alpha}(t) - \vec{X}(t)) \tag{1.10}$$

$$\vec{X}_2 = \overrightarrow{X_\beta}(t) - \overrightarrow{A_2}.\overrightarrow{C_2}.(\overrightarrow{X_\beta}(t) - \vec{X}(t)) \tag{1.11}$$

$$\vec{X}_3 = \overrightarrow{X_\delta}(t) - \overrightarrow{A_3}.\overrightarrow{C_3}.(\overrightarrow{X_\delta}(t) - \vec{X}(t)) \tag{1.12}$$

where
$\overrightarrow{X_\alpha}$: position of α wolves,
$\overrightarrow{X_\beta}$: position of β wolves,
$\overrightarrow{X_\delta}$: position of δ wolves

The next generation will be generated as under,

$$\vec{X}(t+1) = \frac{\vec{X}_1 + \vec{X}_2 + \vec{X}_3}{3} \tag{1.13}$$

1.3.2   Improved Grey Wolf Optimizer with Levy Flight

The Exploration and exploitation behavior of the algorithm is defined by the values of $\vec{A}$ and $\vec{C}$ [7]. $\vec{A}$ lies in $[-2a, 2a]$, where the elements are linearly decreasing from 2 to 0. Grey wolf optimizer is modified by adding one more hierarchal level, which leads to better exploitation capability and modeling prey position with the help of Levy flight distribution, which improves the exploration capability.

Addition of one more level of hierarchy
The exploitation capabilities of GWO is enhanced by adding one more hierarchal level comprised of Kappa (say κ wolves). One more level is added in *Canis lupus* hierarchy as shown in (1.14) as discussed in the previous section so that exploitation is further enhancement,

$$\vec{X}_4 = \overrightarrow{X_\omega}(t) - \overrightarrow{A_4}.\overrightarrow{C_4}.(\overrightarrow{X_\omega}(t) - \vec{X}(t)) \tag{1.14}$$

where $\overrightarrow{X_\omega}$: position of ω wolves
The next generation of wolves will be produced by taking the average of all positions and will be updated as under for one more hierarchal level [16].

$$\vec{X}(t+1) = \frac{\vec{X}_1 + \vec{X}_2 + \vec{X}_3 + \vec{X}_4}{4} \tag{1.15}$$

The proposed algorithm also uses Levy flight to mimic the behavior of prey, which was considered to be static in Mirjalili *et al.* [7], wherein it is taken dynamic as per Mani and Jain [16].

1.3.3 Modeling of Prey Position with Levy Flight Distribution

As per the proposed methodology, prey is moving, and hence, it is not realistic to assume the position of prey static. The random behavior of prey needs to be incorporated to give a realistic mimicking of the hunting process. Hence, in this chapter, the Levy probability distribution function has been tried to find out the best fit for modeling the prey position.

The term Levy flight has been used to model random walks. A random walk may be appropriate to model the animal motions more realistically. The following equations define the Levy distribution [17]:

$$L(s) \sim |s|^{-1-\beta}, \qquad 0 < \beta < 2 \qquad (1.16)$$

Here, s represents a variable, β represents an index for stability control.

$$L(s,\gamma,\mu) = \begin{cases} \dfrac{\gamma}{2\pi} \exp\left[-\dfrac{\gamma}{2(s-\mu)} \right] \dfrac{1}{(s-\mu)^{3/2}} & 0 < \mu < s < \infty \\ 0 & s \leq 0 \end{cases} \qquad (1.17)$$

Here, μ and γ represent the shift and scale parameters, respectively.

Here, the Mantegna strategy [18] is being used to obtain Levy distribution in the search process. The inclusion of Levy flight distribution in the modeling of prey position improves the exploration capability of the algorithm.

The above subsection talks about the modification in the original GWO. These changes when incorporated with the original GWO improve the exploration and exploitation capabilities of the proposed algorithm. This dynamic behavior is modeled with the help of Levy distribution, and hence, the proposed algorithm is named improved grey wolf optimization with Levy flight (IGWOLF) [19]. Figure 1.2 shows the hierarchy of *Canis lupus* or grey wolves as per the proposed algorithm.

In the proposed algorithm, alpha wolves will try to get hold of prey. Hence, alpha wolves are updated as per the prey position wherein the prey

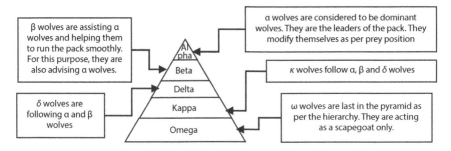

Figure 1.2 Social Hierarchy of wolves and their characteristics in improved GWOLF.

is not static and hence it is modeled with the help of Levy distribution [19]. The rest of the wolves are updating themselves as per [7]

$$\overrightarrow{X_p} = \overrightarrow{X_\alpha}(t) + a' \oplus Levi(b) \tag{1.18}$$

where a': step size and lies in between (0,1), b: power-law index, which lies in between (0,2). Equation (1.8) is modified as

$$\vec{X}_1 = \overrightarrow{X_\alpha}(t) - \overrightarrow{A_1}.\overrightarrow{C_1}.(\overrightarrow{X_p}(t) - \vec{X}(t)) \tag{1.19}$$

The rest of the wolves will be following the same strategy to update their equation as per eq. no. (1.11, 1.12) and (1.14).

The new position of rest wolves will be given as

$$\vec{X}(t+1) = 0.4 * \vec{X}_1 + 0.3 * \vec{X}_2 + 0.2 * \vec{X}_3 + 0.1 * \vec{X}_4 \tag{1.20}$$

The pseudo-code for the algorithm as under:

Step 1: Initialize the population of grey wolves Xi
Step 2: Initialize parameters
Step 3: Generate random population
Step 4: Calculate fitness function
Step 5: Order position of alpha, beta, modified delta, kappa, and omega wolves as per hierarchy
Step 6: Calculate prey position
Step 7: Update each search agent
Step 8: Update parameters

Step 9: Calculate fitness of all search agent
Step 10: t=t+1
Step 11: Return alpha score if the termination condition is met.

Figure 1.3 shows the flowchart of GWOLF algorithm.

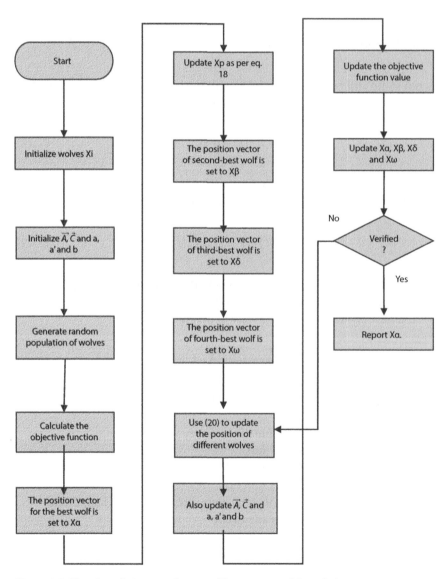

Figure 1.3 Flowchart for improved grey wolf optimizer with levy flight.

1.4   Simulation and Results

For fixing the parameters utilized in different distribution functions, the proposed algorithm is investigated for 23 benchmark test systems as defined in CEC2005 [19]. The platform used for the evaluation of these experiments is MATLAB R2017b on a Windows 10 Lenovo PC with i5-CPU@1.60GHz, RAM of 8 GB, x64-based processor, and 64-bit operating system. 23 benchmark test functions of CEC2005 are solved with the help of different variants of improved GWO including Levy probability distribution functions and ranked as per their performance for different benchmark functions.

Now the question comes, what should be the selected values of μ and γ as mentioned in Heidari and Pahlavani [17]. Hence, different combinations for μ and γ are used as shown in Appendix I, and the response to benchmark function using these Levy distribution parameters in improved GWOLF has been shown in Appendix II.

It has been found when the value of μ is changed from 1 to 2, the rank increases, hence μ is kept to 1. Moreover, when γ is increased from 1 to 2, it decreases wherein when it is further increased rank increases and hence the value of μ and γ is kept to 1 and 2, respectively, for getting the best results for optimum function. It has been assumed that using these parameters the proposed algorithm will give better results to the DED problem also.

Random walks generated by Levy flight distribution for $\gamma = 1$, and $\mu = 2$ have been shown in Figure 1.4 using MATLAB.

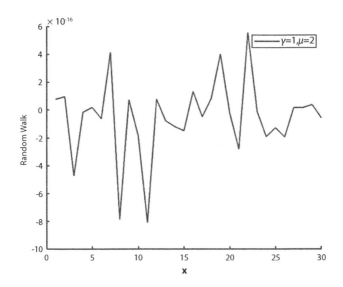

Figure 1.4 Random walk by Levy distribution for Levy probability distribution.

1.4.1 Performance of Improved GWOLF on Benchmark Functions

The best value for 23 benchmark problems obtained by improved GWO with prey position modeled as per different variants of Levy distribution for different parameters in Appendix I is shown in Appendix II. The rank shown in Appendix II for different variants of Levy distribution evaluated that if the prey position is modeled as per LEVY12, it is producing better results for most of the benchmark problems among all the Levy variants. Hence, the LEVY12 variant is utilized for modeling prey position.

Grey wolf optimizer with Levy Flight has been verified on the benchmark problems, as well as real-time dynamic economic dispatch problem. The value of the power law index chosen for GWOLF is $b = 2$. The number of steps is defined by n, which is taken as 1. The value of a' is taken as 2.

Tables 1.1 to 1.3 show the performance of GWO and improved GWO with Levy flight and it can be easily seen that improved GWO with Levy flight gives better results for most of the functions for unimodal, multimodal high-dimension, and low-dimension benchmark function.

1.4.2 Performance of Improved GWOLF for Solving DED for the Different Charging Probability Distribution

The proposed algorithm is used to solve the DED problem, which has 15 generators along with electric vehicle loads as per Figure 1.1 for EPRI load, off-peak and stochastic load. The test case for 15 generators has been shown in Yang *et al.* [13]. The generation by 15 generators for different load cases has been shown in Tables 11.4 to 11.6. The cost incurrent per day for 24 hours for dynamic economic dispatch of power for EPRI load, Off-peak load, and stochastic load is $780828.88, $780784.83, and $780681.29, respectively, as shown in Table 1.7. The transmission losses for different loads, i.e., EPRI load, off-peak load, and stochastic load are 809.76 MW, 812.52 MW, and 822.90 MW, respectively.

Table 1.1 Description of Unimodal Benchmark Problems with the Performance of GWO [7] and Improved GWOLF.

Fun	Formulation	D	Calculation	GWO	IGWO+ Levy
F1	$F_1(x) = \sum_{i=1}^{n} x_i^2$	30	Average	5.712E-28	5.846E-32
			St. Dev.	7.989E-28	1.480E-31
			Best (Min)	2.210E-29	1.268E-34
F2	$F_2(x) = \sum_{i=1}^{n} |x_i| + \prod_{i=1}^{n} |x_i|$	30	Average	8.490E-17	5.331E-20
			St. Dev.	8.509E-17	5.275E-20
			Best (Min)	1.240E-17	1.690E-20
F3	$F_3(x) = \sum_{i=1}^{n} \left(\sum_{j-1}^{n} x_j \right)^2$	30	Average	2.307E-05	4.843E-05
			St. Dev.	9.217E-05	1.568E-04
			Best (Min)	1.770E-09	4.394E-11
F4	$F_4(x) = \max\{|x_i|, 1 \leq i \leq n\}$	30	Average	7.111E-07	1.274E-07
			St. Dev.	1.164E-06	2.139E-07
			Best (Min)	7.566E-08	4.680E-09

(Continued)

Table 1.1 Description of Unimodal Benchmark Problems with the Performance of GWO [7] and Improved GWOLF. (*Continued*)

Fun	Formulation	D	Calculation	GWO	IGWO+ Levy
F5	$F_5(x) = \sum_{i=1}^{n-1} \{100(x_{i+1} - x_i^2)^2 + (x_i - 1)^2\}$	30	Average	2.696E+01	2.719E+01
			St. Dev.	6.759E-01	6.028E-01
			Best (Min)	2.610E+01	2.620E+01
F6	$F_6(x) = \sum_{i=1}^{n-1} ([x_i + 0.5])^2$	30	Average	6.997E-01	8.195E-01
			St. Dev.	2.994E-01	3.967E-01
			Best (Min)	6.520E-05	2.500E-01
F7	$F_7(x) = \sum_{i=1}^{n-1} ix_i^4 + random(0,1)$	30	Average	1.749E-03	1.666E-03
			St. Dev.	8.517E-04	9.517E-04
			Best (Min)	4.230E-04	1.077E-04

Table 1.2 Description of multimodal, high dimension benchmark problems with the performance of GWO [7] and improved GWOLF.

Fun	Formulation	D	Calculation	GWO	IGWO+ Levy
F8	$F_8(x) = \sum_{(i=1)}^{n} -x_i \sin(\sqrt{\lvert x_i \rvert})$	30	Average	−6.117E+03	−5.794E+03
			St. Dev.	6.656E+02	6.989E+02
			Best (Min)	−7.860E+03	−7.755E+03
F9	$F_9(x) = \sum_{(i=1)}^{n} [x_i^2 - 10\cos(2\pi x) + 10]$	30	Average	3.113E+00	1.201E-01
			St. Dev.	3.902E+00	6.578E-01
			Best (Min)	0.000E+00	0.000E+00
F10	$F_{10}(x) = -20\exp(0.2\sqrt{\dfrac{1}{n}\sum_{i=1}^{n} x_i^2} - \exp(\dfrac{1}{n}\sum_{i=1}^{n}\cos(2\pi x) + 20 + e$	30	Average	9.859E-14	3.395E-14
			St. Dev.	1.377E-14	5.767E-15
			Best (Min)	7.550E-14	2.220E-14
F11	$F_{11}(x) = 2.5 \times 10^{-4} \sum_{i=1}^{n} x_i^2 - \prod_{i=1}^{n}\cos\left(\dfrac{x_i}{\sqrt{i}}\right) + 1$	30	Average	4.050E-03	2.227E-03
			St. Dev.	8.575E-03	5.919E-03
			Best (Min)	0.000E+00	0.000E+00

(Continued)

Table 1.2 Description of multimodal, high dimension benchmark problems with the performance of GWO [7] and improved GWOLF. (*Continued*)

Fun	Formulation	D	Calculation	GWO	IGWO+ Levy
F12	$F_{12}(x) = \dfrac{\pi}{n}\{10\sin(\pi y_i) + \sum_{i=1}^{n-1}(y_i-1)^2 [1+10\,sin^2(\pi\,y_{i+1})] + (y_n-1)^2\} + \sum_{i=1}^{n} u(x_i,10,100,4),\ y_i = 1+\dfrac{x_i+1}{4},\ u(x,a,k,m)$ $= \begin{cases} k(x_i-a)^m & x_i < a \\ 0 & -a < x_i < a \\ k(-x_i-a)^m & x_i < -a \end{cases}$	30	Average	1.665E-03	9.380E-02
			St. Dev.	9.516E-04	1.305E-01
			Best (Min)	1.080E-04	1.230E-02
F13	$F_{13}(x) = 0.1\{\sin^2(3\pi x_i) + \sum_{i=1}^{n}((x_i-1)^2[1+sin^2(3\pi x_i+1)] + (x_n-1)^2[1+sin^2(2\pi x_n)])\} + \sum_{i=1}^{n} u(x_i,5,100,4)$	30	Average	5.772E-01	8.148E-01
			St. Dev.	1.915E-01	2.509E-01
			Best (Min)	1.920E-01	2.980E-01

Table 1.3 Description of multimodal, low dimension benchmark problem with performance of GWO [7] and improved GWOLF.

Fun	Formulation	D	Calculation	GWO	IGWO+ Levy
F14	$F_{14}(x) = \left(\dfrac{1}{500} + \sum_{j=1}^{25} \dfrac{1}{j + \sum_{i=1}^{2}(x_i - a_i)^6} \right)^{-1}$	2	Average	3.846E+00	4.076E+00
			St. Dev.	3.795E+00	3.864E+00
			Best (Min)	9.980E-01	9.980E-01
F15	$F_{15}(x) = \sum_{i=1}^{11}\left[a_i - \dfrac{x_1(b_i^2 + b_i x_2)}{b_i^2 + b_i x_3 + x_4} \right]^2$	4	Average	4.432E-03	1.152E-03
			St. Dev.	8.124E-03	3.645E-03
			Best (Min)	3.080E-04	3.070E-04
F16	$F_{16}(x) = 4x_1^2 - 2.1\,x_1^4 + \dfrac{1}{3}x_1^6 + x_1 x_2 - 4x_2^2 + 4x_2^4$	2	Average	-1.030E+00	-1.032E+00
			St. Dev.	4.517E-16	2.537E-08
			Best (Min)	-1.030E+00	-1.032E+00
F17	$F_{17}(x) = \left(x_2 - \dfrac{5.1}{4\pi^2}x_1^2 + \dfrac{5}{\pi}x_1 - 6\right)^2 + 10\left(1 - \dfrac{1}{8\pi}\right)cos x_1 + 10$	2	Average	3.980E-01	3.979E-01
			St. Dev.	1.694E-16	2.308E-06
			Best (Min)	3.980E-01	3.979E-01

(Continued)

Table 1.3 Description of multimodal, low dimension benchmark problem with performance of GWO [7] and improved GWOLF. (*Continued*)

Fun	Formulation	D	Calculation	GWO	IGWO+ Levy
F18	$F_{18}(x) = [1 + (x_1 + x_2 + 1)^2 (19 - 4x_1 + 3x_1^2 - 14x_2 + 6x_1 x_2 + 3x_2^2)] \times$ $[30 + (2x_1 - 3x_2)^2 \times (18 - 32x_1 + 12x_1^2 + 48x_2 - 36x_1 x_2 + 27x_2^2)]$	2	Average	3.000E+00	3.000E+00
			St. Dev.	6.128E-05	0.000E+00
			Best (Min)	3.000E+00	3.000E+00
F19	$F_{19}(x) = -\sum_{i=1}^{4} c_i exp\left(-\sum_{j=1}^{3} a_{ij}(x_j - p_{ij})^2\right)$	3	Average	-3.861E+00	-3.861E+00
			St. Dev.	2.557E-03	2.916E-03
			Best (Min)	-3.863E+00	-3.863E+00
F20	$F_{20}(x) = -\sum_{i=1}^{4} c_i exp\left(-\sum_{j=1}^{6} a_{ij}(x_j - p_{ij})^2\right)$	6	Average	-3.264E+00	-3.235E+00
			St. Dev.	7.393E-02	8.279E-02
			Best (Min)	-3.320E+00	-3.320E+00
F21	$F_{21}(x) = -\sum_{i=1}^{5} [(X - a_i)(X - a_i)^T + c_i]^{-1}$	4	Average	-1.040E+01	-9.870E+00
			St. Dev.	1.807E-15	1.616\E+00
			Best (Min)	-1.040E+01	-1.040E+01

(*Continued*)

Table 1.3 Description of multimodal, low dimension benchmark problem with performance of GWO [7] and improved GWOLF. (*Continued*)

Fun	Formulation	D	Calculation	GWO	IGWO+ Levy
F22	$F_{22}(x) = -\sum_{i=1}^{7}[(X - a_i)(X - a_i)^T + c_i]^{-1}$	4	Average	−1.040E+01	−9.870E+00
			St. Dev.	1.807E-15	1.616E+00
			Best (Min)	−1.040E+01	−1.040E+01
F23	$F_{23}(x) = -\sum_{i=1}^{10}[(X - a_i)(X - a_i)^T + c_i]^{-1}$	4	Average	−1.036E+01	−9.724E+00
			St. Dev.	9.787E-01	2.148E+00
			Best (Min)	−1.054E+01	−1.054E+01

Table 1.4 Power generated by 15 generators for 24 hours for EPRI load.

T(h)	Pg1	Pg2	Pg3	Pg4	Pg5	Pg6	Pg7	Pg8	Pg9	Pg10	Pg11	Pg12	Pg13	Pg14	Pg15
	Generated Power (MW)														
1	398.9146	223.3647	87.7046	84.0739	271.0811	376.0081	439.977	191.2899	45.5259	55.96	45.3707	53.9169	44.3988	41.0733	19.2083
2	424.0488	218.6065	101.6196	125.6949	262.621	382.4968	438.4194	109.8916	53.9181	44.7934	43.9315	68.7951	51.4122	29.9027	20.7352
3	417.0363	215.7712	89.2077	109.3408	320.6617	384.1065	380.2997	109.4939	70.4024	38.2216	52.2145	46.1026	53.2209	39.7394	33.5307
4	342.0848	238.313	116.1375	114.4893	287.4338	355.2541	424.4876	124.4706	72.3992	60.5982	49.0911	53.2048	46.3548	26.241	30.7593
5	373.1583	289.7006	84.1937	93.8615	263.7959	340.2352	429.3159	121.9349	77.8843	88.0003	54.2625	63.5202	40.7722	29.7035	31.1872
6	437.3401	298.6813	115.5867	100.2986	210.5674	366.4477	424.3257	78.136	80.4048	61.2879	53.6998	54.6374	37.0999	30.6587	24.0184
7	364.6624	331.6262	118.2367	99.932	155.4007	429.7924	400.6732	100.0034	69.3088	84.3499	64.7041	52.3575	35.0519	28.9539	30.9506
8	387.2359	397.279	109.3632	93.6801	208.3718	400.497	437.9567	104.6841	69.6601	63.7372	52.9067	34.5208	50.0654	29.7375	32.9144
9	436.1706	416.5205	116.5483	88.3356	261.2698	450.772	419.422	100.4592	79.2555	55.7666	66.4421	40.3484	50.7849	37.5368	44.178
10	409.3004	416.3521	128.4026	115.2068	321.613	448.5031	436.4217	115.8294	61.5536	104.6089	41.1455	61.8368	59.0806	30.9223	26.7162
11	388.5255	437.2707	115.1696	100.022	355.6866	411.7337	442.3922	154.5432	80.5575	121.5017	53.0742	61.9425	61.1581	36.2551	27.7618
12	443.9739	420.7602	95.7329	121.0308	408.3902	456.3702	418.5733	83.6373	63.131	129.6522	59.6325	31.247	47.0528	36.2678	33.1452
13	447.6652	448.4579	121.1437	121.3296	387.0881	451.6323	312.4449	62.0474	89.1817	136.0724	75.6377	46.758	37.3183	54.029	52.9739
14	389.65	434.2301	118.8063	114.3248	391.8739	413.1756	458.5302	124.6997	86.2752	133.8654	37.0077	65.3481	67.9012	35.4851	25.1025
15	398.661	417.1559	114.3455	120.5734	456.1936	449.0109	449.7727	112.5165	133.1465	120.3827	60.5331	71.2817	59.5037	47.77	31.4293

(Continued)

Table 1.4 Power generated by 15 generators for 24 hours for EPRI load. (*Continued*)

T(h)	Generated Power (MW)														
	Pg1	Pg2	Pg3	Pg4	Pg5	Pg6	Pg7	Pg8	Pg9	Pg10	Pg11	Pg12	Pg13	Pg14	Pg15
16	441.8877	428.5356	122.2905	122.9937	395.3337	433.2153	408.1304	155.2116	140.5022	134.9071	39.8504	72.5274	37.8603	45.6289	32.4854
17	429.5284	411.7488	105.9648	106.953	436.1248	396.7481	452.8118	136.3067	107.648	132.709	56.7552	57.7561	42.8528	37.1475	44.1516
18	441.0582	386.2966	92.4561	102.5215	411.8586	365.9486	455.1434	158.7887	116.5771	85.9639	67.6637	56.5486	48.2493	34.0205	29.4054
19	394.4352	402.4473	107.3843	116.4003	361.0756	374.8697	385.4966	172.9241	70.2212	85.0488	67.2784	44.5971	62.8387	24.7646	39.8557
20	438.7107	419.2449	71.5015	103.9836	320.2064	400.9271	406.0241	140.3589	41.7199	88.5178	47.0223	66.0087	42.9493	40.4196	29.8912
21	431.4542	378.0526	120.5969	81.89	260.8214	422.5748	387.8428	103.1815	38.1953	58.4221	55.7935	57.3614	49.9847	34.0511	36.8957
22	419.8605	408.5051	109.7268	81.0517	327.6593	349.915	358.5093	86.0584	50.1675	48.3584	59.4431	49.1484	26.6884	40.9118	30.5625
23	379.3132	351.8351	119.8885	117.0915	335.0742	258.5051	399.2535	94.1867	49.3007	65.8945	57.2308	38.8298	60.5861	36.9116	37.4889
24	429.6692	368.4981	57.7212	85.7553	344.4595	311.588	351.8059	96.6334	89.1434	78.9413	38.8532	36.4155	44.2413	33.3589	28.9341

Table 1.5 Power generated by 15 generators for 24 hours for off-peak load.

T(h)	Pg1	Pg2	Pg3	Pg4	Pg5	Pg6	Pg7	Pg8	Pg9	Pg10	Pg11	Pg12	Pg13	Pg14	Pg15
	Generated Power (MW)														
1	393.6588	342.8855	93.4255	101.165	335.8991	375.7757	386.4761	90.1122	82.8435	82.4433	41.1752	51.3849	43.1093	25.4002	27.7559
2	347.845	374.1893	82.3758	87.1962	362.3005	398.4447	366.9629	97.7747	53.3971	96.3048	65.2792	47.7031	33.2689	34.0892	31.4442
3	368.2252	337.3901	86.3982	82.5609	385.0657	385.8975	357.1292	85.6219	43.1639	46.0328	30.6628	44.579	34.4006	38.3185	30.0471
4	353.7115	361.0737	82.8143	127.0129	338.8231	277.4974	347.178	84.5597	61.6368	91.8871	53.7605	70.8846	54.6829	25.4127	33.5777
5	363.1364	314.2088	99.1899	93.9397	268.196	352.6588	391.4821	131.2288	47.5008	95.7681	23.3184	49.7232	59.4523	39.8235	40.8275
6	308.0521	345.5846	89.504	94.5512	308.0271	357.8113	316.1814	157.9934	51.0526	121.9707	49.546	76.0811	48.3425	29.0476	37.7635
7	307.8884	365.9865	83.8806	105.7937	349.4861	340.6498	387.8696	107.0833	45.5479	67.2044	40.9104	47.4468	34.485	45.3196	29.4861
8	367.1452	321.8015	100.4882	114.6433	288.6827	402.655	430.5997	81.8597	80.1384	54.3351	65.1331	48.2755	50.4027	33.0047	30.3978
9	415.6947	328.5936	126.8899	103.1877	334.3895	438.7695	441.7328	123.0501	74.4917	63.0974	54.1163	61.8217	40.1355	35.584	21.1741
10	417.7893	407.6128	123.7024	123.143	364.5094	422.9691	450.734	99.0852	76.956	49.4031	64.8696	61.609	43.8007	28.231	27.9529
11	388.53	416.671	118.2291	102.0653	396.176	412.34	456.6942	105.7307	57.0744	115.7853	65.1366	67.5318	40.3682	42.0423	36.9481
12	421.6805	378.6319	111.8313	75.9395	431.9528	395.5421	431.89	163.0039	75.7701	96.9863	53.8038	57.3877	43.6028	51.5345	38.6727
13	433.0972	423.702	103.7094	77.7994	373.7429	428.3721	431.3117	109.6436	79.2067	109.2025	58.4522	56.6474	52.2817	39.9355	40.8731
14	428.6805	430.4888	116.5958	123.5623	408.539	446.1906	407.9616	123.8469	65.5349	116.3221	44.5976	60.9813	40.8333	28.1157	28.9072
15	444.8013	439.082	122.4769	102.4037	437.1047	413.2862	432.0676	148.6088	94.2925	140.4618	68.8911	66.8623	48.4443	28.0738	31.5529

(Continued)

Table 1.5 Power generated by 15 generators for 24 hours for off-peak load. (*Continued*)

T(h)	Generated Power (MW)														
	Pg1	Pg2	Pg3	Pg4	Pg5	Pg6	Pg7	Pg18	Pg9	Pg10	Pg11	Pg12	Pg13	Pg14	Pg15
16	426.4855	446.4964	102.4232	126.6652	435.9978	433.9143	453.5525	143.5167	79.0661	99.9959	61.2713	61.97	51.5598	37.3103	35.3186
17	446.0316	454.5726	107.5761	114.8306	435.6225	438.1414	438.9415	89.1551	87.468	99.8757	56.9953	51.4341	50.5477	39.6352	33.5465
18	442.9637	406.3211	102.9747	102.5952	408.7502	372.2962	425.4259	96.9851	116.2783	133.0002	55.923	59.6468	58.8422	28.0188	35.073
19	430.7841	431.9473	105.9519	108.4713	303.5446	421.6144	407.7898	77.2084	62.4238	95.8616	51.3614	57.7152	59.7056	37.2016	30.2455
20	349.6578	405.1945	102.5964	110.4224	348.5678	384.2658	448.1285	124.9781	80.9335	82.6456	41.257	53.8221	30.6172	31.8954	23.3657
21	374.8704	349.9952	83.9852	121.0848	248.2995	356.2409	380.7452	108.6672	93.2555	96.4937	64.2512	53.0993	52.3753	44.7878	32.6793
22	333.5138	340.2555	83.3352	78.7665	301.2133	334.2009	443.0082	98.441	75.0397	43.9797	52.1658	49.9198	42.9086	26.1087	34.5929
23	405.2106	348.7715	104.4974	92.7098	303.8343	348.3163	416.9774	104.2259	93.8578	60.0077	35.8603	56.5003	60.2709	30.0755	37.0144
24	404.1337	320.3498	91.3456	104.3069	300.8022	362.486	422.4674	97.0953	99.5917	83.2116	63.8253	39.0789	40.9616	42.0768	20.337

Table 1.6 Power generated by 15 generators for 24 hours for stochastic load.

T(h)	Generated Power (MW)														
	Pg1	Pg2	Pg3	Pg4	Pg5	Pg6	Pg7	Pg8	Pg9	Pg10	Pg11	Pg12	Pg13	Pg14	Pg15
1	407.7283	303.1505	94.1986	113.8869	275.5872	419.2052	290.6166	128.8909	60.4688	50.8358	41.5486	34.2217	31.3886	43.0169	31.4334
2	371.1830	290.6089	121.4625	96.9989	222.9607	369.0879	350.2448	129.7254	64.6454	65.2790	58.9663	65.9912	45.5314	34.0595	32.5967
3	378.4830	286.2391	114.8799	99.6194	227.5176	428.0879	312.9765	108.5949	68.4261	88.3418	41.2791	47.0487	48.2929	27.8281	26.4032
4	364.2762	327.3283	79.8887	110.9551	228.1957	385.5858	337.9169	106.3294	54.2722	79.5414	42.2327	63.2315	41.5854	38.9051	25.8644
5	334.7144	337.8315	102.1970	119.2782	216.1140	402.2249	380.1320	122.9110	44.8887	81.2538	40.6558	66.2008	44.4877	34.7105	24.1281
6	381.0476	416.6593	122.1914	118.8398	190.6949	416.4595	347.9799	75.0016	75.5118	96.7614	43.6699	56.8411	50.4183	34.0350	24.3526
7	419.0725	385.6592	125.1822	72.0076	226.1470	357.8365	371.2234	130.0697	78.1978	101.8058	33.5659	42.3352	59.2664	27.3510	28.3132
8	420.6200	332.8160	110.1309	103.1375	250.3332	401.4384	382.0207	129.5165	89.0191	97.5889	39.1818	47.3961	59.6493	27.4767	37.3115
9	397.6199	379.1468	115.8991	105.6977	304.1034	426.9933	428.9862	115.7678	121.0357	90.4546	31.9150	65.0009	39.3044	30.4251	24.8447
10	434.6636	410.0341	103.2855	122.2115	334.4047	445.6370	436.9564	119.4380	84.9185	80.3528	57.0279	42.8175	61.4368	36.5048	30.5156
11	428.2251	414.3267	101.0289	104.2461	361.0435	450.1701	406.3581	141.5219	119.2930	112.8267	56.5678	46.8821	44.5828	33.3373	28.4151
12	415.3852	437.3831	114.7303	105.8368	368.0140	452.0447	444.1652	132.8087	122.2410	73.4315	55.4413	56.8983	49.2866	31.4607	30.6201
13	423.7384	449.5063	100.3539	104.1909	419.9147	435.6533	438.2120	176.6348	59.6362	61.7838	49.8259	53.7464	41.0024	27.8944	23.2560
14	429.1913	391.3539	107.2176	120.3237	449.1341	436.3744	444.3233	108.5322	97.2056	89.1978	50.4448	62.8661	50.0338	29.4967	31.8418
15	447.8393	428.1463	123.0166	112.1459	459.7212	451.6062	451.4469	112.4516	130.8050	96.7196	55.8164	64.7703	44.3180	39.7068	22.9594

(Continued)

Table 1.6 Power generated by 15 generators for 24 hours for stochastic load. (Continued)

T(h)	Generated Power (MW)														
	Pg1	Pg2	Pg3	Pg4	Pg5	Pg6	Pg7	Pg8	Pg9	Pg10	Pg11	Pg12	Pg13	Pg14	Pg15
16	438.3298	446.6645	115.5626	116.7406	445.8064	445.1271	428.9675	144.7066	121.9007	126.3056	64.6518	59.1967	57.1215	32.2506	25.8739
17	431.6707	445.4424	124.8555	109.8598	449.4489	449.5045	411.7622	105.0111	99.0114	137.9153	57.9638	58.2687	42.1340	35.1895	26.3943
18	424.6676	406.9127	121.9297	105.4255	390.3509	449.9811	437.0178	121.3279	93.5414	86.3268	47.3400	63.5418	48.1465	34.2114	36.7464
19	428.0311	406.4808	94.7059	100.2326	437.9782	430.6229	400.4577	65.6351	89.5684	80.4194	48.3356	42.2526	41.5012	28.7772	24.9576
20	440.5316	333.7743	64.9793	117.8083	389.0208	436.3532	426.9712	85.8626	63.6792	104.9872	42.0356	46.0909	36.2244	24.8762	30.3887
21	387.4071	323.4986	74.2282	75.6089	393.7925	392.0350	363.0938	92.4076	94.9388	118.7308	50.3108	51.4708	45.2772	26.8253	38.8972
22	369.0788	332.2955	96.3327	86.4714	370.7157	343.3517	377.4819	74.2002	55.1389	61.9380	40.5196	59.8139	47.3968	26.3015	26.1909
23	368.2121	245.2601	100.0047	94.3361	401.8596	349.9030	347.4599	66.8176	61.2682	94.0716	66.7259	44.4558	31.4069	25.9126	31.9430
24	339.6308	286.0807	103.4765	88.8067	373.5462	341.7668	414.3256	96.1648	65.4784	58.2716	56.1692	44.0963	46.0089	23.9174	37.2923

Table 1.7 Cost incurred by 15 generators for meeting different load distribution.

Type of load	Algorithm							
	wPSO	PSO-CF	DE	TLBO	eTLBO	mTLBO	SL-TLBO	Improved GWOLF
EPRI Load	783004.14	784391.24	784354.55	781644.49	782323.93	781562.91	781001.23	780828.88
Off-peak Load	783650.51	784532.96	784313.52	783002.47	782320.70	781179.19	780862.82	780784.83
Stochastic Load	784610.33	785491.74	785273.31	783962.29	783280.51	782138.87	781459.24	780681.29

1.5   Conclusion

Dynamic dispatch problem has, for quite a while, been a determining issue for power system engineers and the unpredictability is ever-growing with new participants like renewable energy sources, electric vehicles, etc. being added to the system. In this chapter, the effect of electric vehicles has been incorporated as a load with which the varied generation by different generators has also been tabulated. This chapter has the hierarchy strategy of *Canis lupus* wolves to model the algorithm with the prey being dynamic with the help of Levy flight distribution. The Levy flight parameters are tuned by carrying a different combination of γ, μ values and it has been found Levy flight distribution shows the best performance for $\gamma = 1$, $\mu = 2$ for most of the benchmark functions and hence IGWOLF with $\gamma = 1$, $\mu = 2$ is used to solve solved the problem for dynamic economic dispatch for network comprised of 90000 electric vehicles. The algorithm investigated the DED problem with better or competitive results with state of art algorithms present in literature as shown in Table 1.6. Additionally, it has been seen that the stochastic charging case gives the best outcome with this calculation. Even though, in past writing, it has been discovered that cost function is limited for off-peak charging situations though, in this section, the stochastic charging situation which is viewed as nearer to the truth is giving the least cost function when contrasted with different cases with improved GWOLF calculation. The mathematical results show that the improved GWOLF calculation is most appropriate for handling tremendous extension dynamic dispatch issues and beats other notable heuristic strategies in the test for DED issues with genuine parameter tuning. The future scope of work includes the inclusion of renewable energy sources, energy storage devices along demand response.

Appendix I Parameters of optimizers.

Description of algorithm	Parameter	Description of algorithm	Parameter
LEVY11	$\gamma = 1, \mu = 1$	LEVY22	$\gamma = 2, \mu = 2$
LEVY12	$\gamma = 1, \mu = 2$	LEVY13	$\gamma = 1, \mu = 3$
LEVY21	$\gamma = 2, \mu = 1$		

Appendix II Best solution and rank of LEVY variant for benchmark function.

Fun	Parameter	LEVY11	LEVY12	LEVY21	LEVY22	LEVY13
F1	Best value	2.3551E-06	7.2244E-34	1.0692E-05	1.7112E-18	6.5861E+04
	Rank	3	1	4	2	5
F2	Best value	3.6753E-03	5.4322E-20	1.0444E-02	1.0030E-10	2.4206E+11
	Rank	3	1	4	2	5
F3	Best value	1.0844E+00	2.9190E-07	4.8644E+00	1.6319E+00	1.7850E+05
	Rank	2	1	4	3	5
F4	Best value	3.6377E-02	2.0111E-08	2.0053E-01	1.5811E-03	9.0908E+01
	Rank	3	1	4	2	5
F5	Best value	2.8086E+01	2.7947E+01	2.8623E+01	2.6041E+01	3.1247E+08
	Rank	3	2	4	1	5
F6	Best value	1.7933E+00	8.4232E-01	2.0392E+00	6.6007E-05	6.5617E+04
	Rank	3	2	4	1	5

(Continued)

Appendix II Best solution and rank of LEVY variant for benchmark function. (*Continued*)

Fun	Parameter	LEVY11	LEVY12	LEVY21	LEVY22	LEVY13
F7	Best value	2.2079E-02	2.0124E-03	2.2378E-02	1.1846E-02	1.1279E+02
	Rank	3	1	4	2	5
F8	Best value	-6.6781E+03	-7.1590E+03	-7.5686E+03	-6.8627E+03	-1.5429E+03
	Rank	4	2	1	3	5
F9	Best value	4.9698E+01	5.6843E-14	5.9431E+01	4.2908E+01	4.2811E+02
	Rank	3	1	4	2	5
F10	Best value	1.0306E-03	4.3521E-14	9.1909E-04	5.2026E-08	2.0366E+01
	Rank	4	1	3	2	5
F11	Best value	1.6865E-07	0.0000E+00	2.7109E-02	2.5607E-02	5.4615E+02
	Rank	2	1	4	3	5
F12	Best value	1.1971E-01	3.3140E-02	1.7133E+00	1.3206E-01	6.1614E+08
	Rank	2	1	4	3	5

(*Continued*)

Appendix II Best solution and rank of LEVY variant for benchmark function. (*Continued*)

Fun	Parameter	LEVY11	LEVY12	LEVY21	LEVY22	LEVY13
F13	Best value	1.1340E+00	8.6441E-01	8.5920E-01	1.0483E-01	1.0529E+09
	Rank	4	3	2	1	5
F14	Best value	9.9800E-01	9.9800E-01	9.9800E-01	9.9800E-01	1.5881E+02
	Rank	1	1	1	1	5
F15	Best value	4.1355E-04	3.1375E-04	5.4917E-04	3.8958E-04	1.5752E-01
	Rank	3	1	4	2	5
F16	Best value	1.0316E+00	−1.0316E+00	−1.0316E+00	−1.0316E+00	1.4543E-01
	Rank	1	1	1	1	5
F17	Best value	3.9789E-01	3.9789E-01	3.9789E-01	3.9790E-01	5.1557E+00
	Rank	1	1	1	4	5
F18	Best value	3.0000E+00	3.0000E+00	3.0002E+00	3.0000E+00	3.2914E+01
	Rank	1	1	4	1	5

(*Continued*)

Appendix II Best solution and rank of LEVY variant for benchmark function. (*Continued*)

Fun	Parameter	LEVY11	LEVY12	LEVY21	LEVY22	LEVY13
F19	Best value	-3.8607E+00	-3.8618E+00	-3.8616E+00	-3.8621E+00	-3.3605E+00
	Rank	4	2	3	1	5
F20	Best value	-3.1534E+00	-3.3220E+00	-3.1335E+00	-3.2024E+00	-1.6398E+00
	Rank	3	1	4	2	5
F21	Best value	-1.0151E+01	-1.0151E+01	-1.0151E+01	-1.0153E+01	-1.2189E+00
	Rank	2	4	3	1	5
F22	Best value	-1.0402E+01	-1.0400E+01	-1.0401E+01	-1.0401E+01	-5.8508E-01
	Rank	1	4	3	2	5
F23	Best value	-1.0535E+01	-1.0535E+01	-1.0535E+01	-1.0535E+01	-8.7607E-01
	Rank	4	1	3	1	5
OVERALL RANK		3	1	4	2	5

References

1. Jain, A., Mani, A., Siddiqui, A.S., Solving dynamic economic dispatch problem with plug-in electric vehicles using GWOLF. *2020 IEEE International Conference on Computing, Power and Communication Technologies*, October 2-4, 2020.

2. Chen, Z., Chuangxin, G., Shufeng, D., Ding, Y., Mao, H., Distributed robust dynamic economic dispatch of integrated transmission and distribution systems. *IEEE Trans. Ind. Appl.*, 57, 5, 4500–4512, 2021.

3. Granelli, G.P., Marannino, P., Montagna, M., Silvestri, A., Fast and efficient gradient projection algorithm for dynamic generation dispatching, in: *IEE Proceedings C (Generation, Transmission and Distribution)*, vol. 136, IET Digital Library, pp. 295–302, September 1989.

4. Hindi, K.S. and Ab Ghani, M.R., Dynamic economic dispatch for large scale power systems: A Lagrangian relaxation approach. *Int. J. Electr. Power Energy Syst.*, 13, 1, 51–56, 1991.

5. Vargas, L.S., Quintana, V.H., Vannelli, A., A tutorial description of an interior point method and its applications to security-constrained economic dispatch. *IEEE Trans. Power Syst.*, 8, 3, 1315–1324, 1993.

6. Rezaei, N., Uddin, M.N., Amin, I.K., Othman, M.L., Marsadek, M., Genetic algorithm-based optimization of overcurrent relay coordination for improved protection of DFIG operated wind farms. *IEEE Trans. Ind. Appl.*, 55, 6, 5727–5736, 2019.

7. Mirjalili, S., Mirjalili, S.M., Lewis, A., Grey wolf optimizer. *Adv. Eng. Software*, 69, 46–61, 2014.

8. Ma, H., Simon, D., Siarry, P., Yang, Z., Fei, M., Biogeography-based optimization: A 10-year review. *IEEE Trans. Emerg. Top. Comput. Intell.*, 1, 5, 391–407, 2017.

9. Wu, G., Shen, X., Li, H., Chen, H., Lin, A., Suganthan, P.N., Ensemble of differential evolution variants. *Inf. Sci.*, 423, 172–186, 2018.

10. Delahaye, D., Chaimatanan, S., Mongeau, M., Simulated annealing: From basics to applications, in: *Handbook of Metaheuristics*, pp. 1–35, Springer, Cham, 2019.

11. Rashedi, E., Rashedi, E., Nezamabadi-Pour, H., A comprehensive survey on gravitational search algorithm. *Swarm Evol. Comput.*, 41, 141–158, 2018.

12. Ray, P.K., Paital, S.R., Mohanty, A., Foo, Y.E., Krishnan, A., Gooi, H.B., Amaratunga, G.A., A hybrid firefly-swarm optimized fractional order interval type-2 fuzzy PID-PSS for transient stability improvement. *IEEE Trans. Ind. Appl.*, 55, 6, 6486–6498, 2019.

13. Yang, Z., Li, K., Niu, Q., Xue, Y., Foley, A., A self-learning TLBO based dynamic economic/environmental dispatch considering multiple plug-in electric vehicle loads. *J. Mod. Power Syst. Clean Energy*, 2, 4, 298–307, 2014.

14. Chaudhari, K., Ukil, A., Kumar, K.N., Manandhar, U., Kollimalla, S.K., Hybrid optimization for economic deployment of ESS in PV-integrated EV charging stations. *IEEE Trans. Ind. Inform.*, 14, 1, 106–116, 2017.

15. Słowik, A. and Cpałka, K., Hybrid approaches to nature-inspired population-based intelligent optimization for industrial applications. *IEEE Trans. Ind. Inform.*, 18, 1, 546–558, 2021.

16. Mani, A. and Jain, A., Towards realistic mimicking of grey wolves hunting process for bounded single objective optimization, in: *2020 IEEE Congress on Evolutionary Computation (CEC)*, IEEE, pp. 1–8, July 2020.

17. Heidari, A.A. and Pahlavani, P., An efficient modified grey wolf optimizer with levy flight for optimization tasks. *Appl. Soft Comput.*, 60, 115–134, 2017.

18. Mantegna, R.N., Fast, accurate algorithm for numerical simulation of levy stable stochastic processes. *Phys. Rev. E*, 49, 5, 4677, 1994.

19. Suganthan, P.N., Hansen, N., Liang, J.J., Deb, K., Chen, Y.P., Auger, A., Tiwari, S., Problem definitions and evaluation criteria for the CEC 2005 special session on real-parameter optimization, in: *KanGAL Report, 2005005(2005)*, 2005.

Comparison of YOLO and Faster R-CNN on Garbage Detection

Arulmozhi M.[1]*, Nandini G. Iyer[1], Jeny Sophia S.[2], Sivakumar P.[2], Amutha C.[2] and Sivamani D.[1]

[1]Department of Electronics and Communication Engineering, Rajalakshmi Engineering College, Chennai, India
[2]Department of Electrical and Electronics Engineering, Rajalakshmi Engineering College, Chennai, India

Abstract

The huge garbage management is becoming a challenging task in India. Major parts of them are plastics, which are found in beaches and seashores. Proper treatment and recycling of such plastics is very crucial to compensate for the ever-growing demands of waste management. Garbage collection is the first step toward it. Traditional manual garbage collection is a labor-intensive process and is unable to match the ever-growing demands of city garbage. For this detection of plastics, an object detection technique has been developed. The algorithm is developed in tensor flow to make use of transfer learning. A comparison is made between the two major object detection techniques YOLO and Faster R-CNN. Faster R-CNN though comparatively slower, is found to be more accurate, hence is chosen to fit the requirement. This project further aims to develop an autonomous robot, which collects the garbage without any human intervention and increase the efficiency of garbage collection.

Keywords: Machine learning, faster R-CNN, You Only Look Once (YOLO)

2.1 Introduction

About three decades ago, the manufacturing of plastic containers of various shapes and sizes were started and now the society very much depends

---

*Corresponding author: arulmozhi.m@rajalakshmi.edu.in

Anita Khosla, Prasenjit Chatterjee, Ikbal Ali and Dheeraj Joshi (eds.) Optimization Techniques in Engineering: Advances and Applications, (37–50) © 2023 Scrivener Publishing LLC

on plastics for everyday use for packing and carrying a variety of items but now we have come to a stage of dumping the entire ecosystem in plastics. Solid waste management is the need of the time, solid waste collection and proper disposal are the key steps toward it. By the end of this century, garbage will be collected at a rate of 11 million tons per day throughout the world [1], more than three times the current rate. It suggests that the generation of the garbage that amounted to 4.5 million tons per day in 2019 will become 7.5 million tons per day by 2025. At present, the population of India produces around 62 million tons of solid waste [2].

Annually, out of this, 45 million tons of garbage are not treated and disposed of by civic agencies in an unscientific way [3]. There is a dire need for an efficient, less hazardous way to dispose of garbage. Many of the upcoming technologies have a must contain objective for garbage collection solution provision. All countries are aiming at reducing the garbage rate all the way they can. Garbage management in all countries tries every best solution to counter the garbage collection problem. We are now entering into an era of artificial intelligence, where the implementation of large scale fully autonomous vehicles will soon become a reality. The algorithm will detect the presence of garbage by using object detection techniques. The model can further be used accordingly in autonomous vehicle to collect the garbage. In various attempts to overcome the garbage management, many technologies have been used to clear the garbage problem. A paper proposed railway track cleaning bot makes use of specially designed retractable wheels, an optimized height adjustable sweeper roller, chlorination unit, bot retracting mechanism and Global Positioning System (GPS - Global System for Mobile Communication (GSM) module interfaced via AT commands. But found to be not manually controlled and not autonomous [4]. Few projects due to later development of robotics ensure the working robots incorporated with brushes, scrubbers or other cleaning equipment that could traverse across a specific surface in a spiral pattern thereby ensuring the surface is cleaned completely.

Infrared sensors were used to avoid the obstacles in the path and helped the robots to travel continuously. Similarly, a project was implored into creating an autonomous robot with IR Sensors. This work involves creation of a simple household cleaning robot based on IR Sensors, which is not suitable to pick garbage but to clean the surface [5]. Projects have been done on routine collection problems and efficiency in the garbage collection system. This physical device uses an ultrasonic sensor to be aware of a dustbin's current content level. The method of unsupervised learning utilized is K Means Clustering [6] to sort the collected garbage, but not to pick them selectively [7]. Similarly, a project [8] to get accurate grabbing of objects was done using Region Position Generation (RPN).

Faster Region-based Convolutional neural network (R-CNN) was pre-trained with ImageNet to obtain accurate object detection on malaria images [9]. CNN is deployed for various applications by using transfer learning technique, the ability of a CNN network to learn increases with increase in its non-linear parameters and this project makes of such CNN for garbage detection [10]. To overcome all these disadvantages and to make robots completely autonomous, the following project is proposed by using a pre-trained COCO model to detect and collect the garbage.

2.2 Garbage Detection

The process of classifying and locating the presence of garbage or an object in an image is called garbage detection or object detection. A classifier is needed to distinguish a target object from all the other categories and to make the representations more hierarchical, semantic, and informative for visual recognition. The classified object is then localized using a bounding box usually using a regressor [11].

2.2.1 Transfer Learning-Technique

Transfer learning is a popular approach in deep learning where pre-trained models are used as the starting point on computer vision and natural language processing tasks given the vast compute and time resources required to develop neural network models on these problems and from the huge jumps in skill that they provide on related problems. Transfer learning involves using optimization of the skills learned from the first task and making use of it in the next task effectively. Thousands of parameters including their weights and parameters are transferred from one model to another one.

2.2.2 Inception-Custom Model

Inception is preferred over all the other models because of its processing speed and the low percentage top -1 error rate. %Top −1 error is a metric where the most confident prediction of the model is tested for is correctness. There is a tradeoff between error rate and the model performance always, depending on the project requirement tradeoff is made. The following Figure 2.1 [11] is general architecture of the inception model.

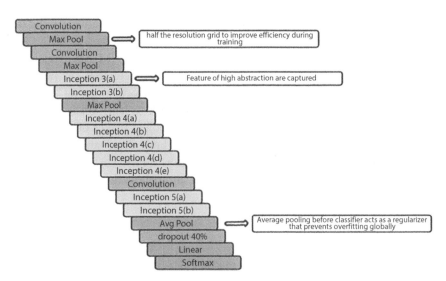

Figure 2.1 Architecture of inception model.

This project uses Inception model to detect the objects. Inception models trained on COCO dataset are used as the starting point and to transfer the learning to our Machine Learning model. Each block in the above architecture is explained below with their block diagram.

2.2.2.1 Convolutional Neural Network

Convolutional Neural Network (CNN) is a class of deep neural networks basically used for visual imagery applications. CNNs are regularized versions of fully connected networks which means that each neuron is connected to all neurons in the next layer. CNN consists of a number of input and output layers with a lot of layers which is dormant in between. Those dormant layers convolve with a multiplication or dot product. Unlike other methods the features are not pre-defined to a particular formation. They are learnt in the training phase using the filters or kernel which is added within. They are initialized and back propagated to update the parameters using gradient descent. The architecture of CNN in Figure 2.2 depicts an input and an output layer with a filter or kernel explaining the convolution operation.

Here, convolution happens on the input images just like a torch light is hovered over the image to scan all the features from top left till bottom right. The output has all the required features and is called "Feature map".

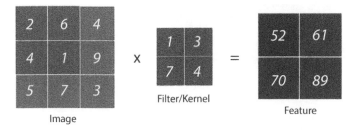

Figure 2.2 Architecture of inception model.

2.2.2.2   *Max Pooling*

Max pool layer filters the unwanted values and selects only those that have large weights. And helps reduce the computation by decreasing the dimension of the input to the next layer, and thereby giving importance to the most required feature, shown in Figure 2.3.

2.2.2.3   *Stride*

When a filter like average pooling or max pooling is applied then the filter is slide over the previous layer in particular order from left to right and also from top to bottom filtering the entire image. This movement of filter on the image is termed as stride. Depending on the input size stride dimension is designed, here examples are shown with stride dimensions being (2,2).

2.2.2.4   *Average Pooling*

Average pool layer makes the model less variant for minuscule changes in the input image and reduces the dimension by averaging all the values in

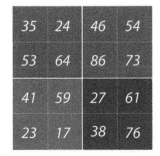

Figure 2.3 Input and output of Max pool layer.

35	24	46	54
53	64	86	73
41	59	27	61
23	17	38	76

44	64
35	50

Figure 2.4 Input and output of average layer.

the 2*2 window as shown in Figure 2.4. Thereby, by giving focusing on the required features.

2.2.2.5   Inception Layer

Each inception module is made up of a fundamental inception block as in Figure 2.5 [12]. A fundamental inception block contains layers of convolutions which are then filtered and compared to the previous layer. They all perform based on the principle "The neurons that fire together wire together" i.e., when a neuron is triggered the corresponding neuron of close proximity is also fired together and using this principle inception makes use of the previous layer to compute the next layer and efficiently learn the features.

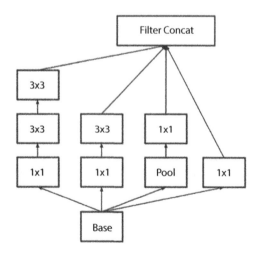

Figure 2.5 Fundamental inception block.

2.2.2.6   3*3 and 1*1 Convolution

Two 3*3 convolution is used in inception v2 architecture instead of a single 5*5 block as in inception v1, since they give the same output but, in a par, efficient manner. Each 3*3 convolution block learn a different set of features and constitute a new feature same as given by 5*5 layers. The 1*1 layer is used to reduce the number of channels from the previous layer and is added before the max pooling. All together inception makes a total of 27 layers to extract the feature map from the input image.

2.2.2.7   You Only Look Once (YOLO) Architecture

On top of the inception layer, the feature learnt in the inception is used in YOLO. YOLO is an object recognition technique that when applied to the image takes a look into the image only once and breaks down the image into many regions using equally spaced grids. It is a real time object detection technique used popularly because it can achieve high accuracy compared to other object recognition techniques. It "looks only once" because the algorithm passes through the neural network only once to complete the object recognition. YOLO has a generalized approach to object detection as it generalizes an object by its shape, color or any other features of the object and it remembers it to recognize the object presented to it and uses it for comparison. The following are the steps involved in a YOLO algorithm.

- YOLO looks into the image once and feeds it to the neural network.
- The image is then broken into several equal fragments using a grid.
- Garbage classification and garbage location is done to each grid as obtained from the feature map in the previous layer, Figure 2.6 represents the approximate grids formed as boxes in the image.
- After garbage detection, Non-Max Suppression technique is further used to improve the overall performance.
- It first looks at the probabilities associated with each detection and takes the largest one.
- The boxes, which have high Intersection over Union (IoU) with the current box, are suppressed.
- The box with highest probability is then selected for comparison with another box, the above 2 steps are iterated until the final bounding box.

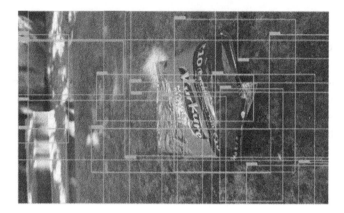

Figure 2.6 YOLO output after first stage detection, prior non-max suppression.

Training parameters of YOLO:

- Batch size: 2
- Training images: 100
- Test images: 20
- Number of steps: 1000

2.2.2.8 Faster R-CNN Algorithm

The first part of the three sections in a Faster R-CNN architecture is CNN network. Inception as described in the above section involves various filters and CNN layers which extract the feature from the input image and filter is run over the test image to obtain the feature map.

Region Proposal Network (RPN) is the second section in Faster R-CNN. RPN is a fully CNN for generating object proposals that will be fed to the next stage.

The next part is the Fast R-CNN, they refine the proposals from the previous section by using region of interest (RoI) pooling layer. The predictions along with their bounding boxes are taken by passing the above to a softmax layer. In Faster R-CNN, the key to high accuracy is making use of the same CNN for both RPN and Fast R-CNN layer [13].

Training parameters of YOLO:

- Batch size: 2
- Training images: 100
- Test images: 20
- Number of steps: 1000

Figure 2.7 graph plotted for global step per second shows the global steps taken for each second. Each global second refers to a batch updating the weights for object detection during back propagation. Figure 2.8 and Figure 2.9 depict the loss associated with classification, localization, RPN, and total loss.

Classification loss refers to the loss calculated for the classification of the object in the final prediction. Similarly, localization loss refers to the loss calculated for bounding box over the classified object. Together, they calculate the overall total loss.

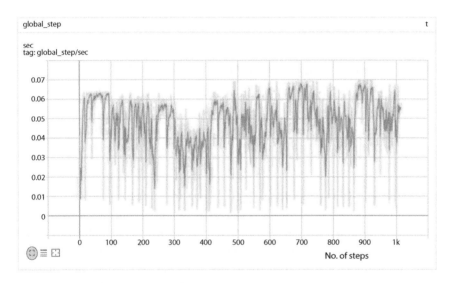

Figure 2.7 Global steps per second.

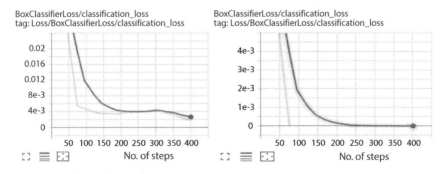

Figure 2.8 Classification and localization loss.

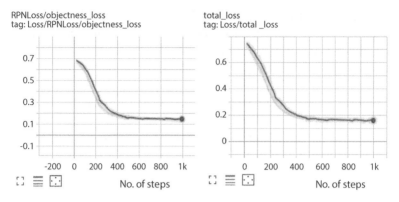

Figure 2.9 RPN and total loss.

2.2.2.9   *Mean Average Precision (mAP)*

mAP is an evaluation metric used for evaluating both classification and localization, where the average of precision and recall is calculated. Precision refers to the percentage of prediction, whereas recall corresponds to the measure of ability to find all the positive cases in the image.

2.3   Experimental Results

The image obtained from webcam is used as the test image. The test image is compared to the trained images for similarities. If the test image matches with the features learnt from the trained images, it is then identified as garbage.

2.3.1   Results Obtained Using YOLO Algorithm

By using the YOLO algorithm, the results obtained were fast enough but it is found to be having less accuracy. The accuracy obtained was around in the range of 40 to 50% accuracy. Figure 2.10 shows the test image accuracy obtained by using the YOLO algorithm.

2.3.2   Results Obtained Using Faster R-CNN

Faster R-CNN algorithm has better accuracy than YOLO algorithm but it is a little slower than YOLO algorithm. The accuracy for Faster R-CNN trained images were found in the range of 80% to 90%. Figure 2.11 and Figure 2.12 represent the test output images used in Faster R-CNN algorithm.

Figure 2.10 Test image for YOLO.

Figure 2.11 Test image for faster R-CNN 1.

Figure 2.12 Test image for faster R-CNN 2.

Table 2.1 Comparison of YOLO and Faster R-CNN.

Framework	Train image	Test image	Accuracy in %	Platform
You Only Look Once	100	20	50%	TensorFlow
Faster R-CNN	100	20	89%	TensorFlow

A comparison of the two algorithms is presented in Table 2.1 in terms of the number of training images and the number of test images as well as the accuracy of the algorithm. A deviation of 0.39% from YOLO indicates Faster R-CNN provides a good level of accuracy.

2.4   Future Scope

The piece of garbage is identified by the algorithm as trained. The garbage can then be lifted by the mechanical arms of a robot and disposed of in the proper way. The robot is capable for mass production and can be applied everywhere when properly monitored. It is an autonomous robot so it does not require any manual intervention in doing its job. To make the robot more precise and work in all circumstances considering edge cases, we require advanced cameras, Lidar, sensors and efficient processing units.

2.5   Conclusion

A real-time image of a Kurkure packet is obtained from the webcam and is tested on the trained model. The boundary boxes are drawn for the recognized parts of the image, and the amount of accuracy achieved is also seen on the boundary box. The images are tested for both YOLO and Faster R-CNN algorithms. As the Faster R-CNN algorithm is more accurate than YOLO, faster R-CNN is made use in recognizing the garbage. This model is made to be used in a robot, which collects the garbage autonomously.

References

1. Dutta, S., Disposing Waste Scientifically: How Scientific Landfills Can Change The Waste Disposal Scenario in India, 2017, Retrieved from https://

swachhindia.ndtv.com/disposing-waste-scientifically-how-scientific-land-fills-can-change-the-waste-disposal-scenario-in-india-8159/

2. Francis, N.R., Design, modelling and fabrication of railway track cleaning bot. *Procedia Comput. Sci.*, 133, 526–536, 2018.

3. Hoornweg, D., Bhada-Tata, P., Kennedy, C., *Global Waste on Pace to Triple by 2100*, 2013, Retrieved from https://www.worldbank.org/.

4. Hung, J. and Carpenter, A., Applying faster R-CNN for object detection on malaria images, in: *Proceedings of the IEEE conference on Computer Vision and Pattern Recognition Workshops*, pp. 56–61, 2017.

5. Lahiry, S., India's challenges in waste management, 2019. Retrieved from https://www.downtoearth.org.in/blog/waste/india-s-challenges-in-waste-management-56753.

6. Jiang, H. and Learned-Miller, E., Face detection with the faster R-CNN, in: *2017 12th IEEE International Conference on Automatic Face & Gesture Recognition*, pp. 650–657, 2017.

7. Kumar, N., Swamy, C., Nagadarshini, K.N., Efficient garbage disposal management in metropolitan cities using VANETs. *J. Clean Energy Technol.*, 2, 258–62, 2014.

8. Gupta, P.K., Shree, V., Hiremath, L., Rajendran, S., The use of modern technology in smart waste management and recycling: Artificial intelligence and machine learning, in: *Recent Advances in Computational Intelligence*, pp. 173–188, Springer, Cham, 2019.

9. Szegedy, C.V., Rethinking the inception architecture for computer vision, in: *Proceedings of the IEEE Conference on Computer Vision and Pattern Recognition*, pp. 2818–2826, 2016.

10. Yashwanth, A., Shammer, S., Sairam, R., Chamundeeswari, G., A novel approach for indoor-outdoor scene classification using transfer learning. *IJARIIT*, 5, 1759, 2019.

11. Szegedy, C., Liu, W., Jia, Y., Sermanet, P., Reed, S., Anguelov, D., Erhan, D., Vanhoucke, V., Rabinovich, A., Going deeper with convolutions, in: *Proceedings of the IEEE Conference on Computer Vision and Pattern Recognition*, pp. 1–9, 2015.

12. Zhao, Z.Q., Zheng, P., Xu, S.T., Wu, X., Object detection with deep learning: A review. *IEEE Trans. Neural Netw. Learn. Syst.*, 30, 3212–32, 2019.

13. Zhihong, C., Hebin, Z., Yanbo, W., Binyan, L., Yu, L., A vision-based robotic grasping system using deep learning for garbage sorting, in: *2017 36th Chinese control conference (CCC)*, pp. 11223–11226, 2017.

## 3

Smart Power Factor Correction and Energy Monitoring System

Amutha C.[1]*, Sivagami V.[1], Arulmozhi M.[2], Sivamani D.[2] and Shyam D.[2]

*[1]Department of Electrical and Electronics Engineering,
Rajalakshmi Engineering College, Chennai, India
[2]Department of Electronics and Communication Engineering,
Rajalakshmi Engineering College, Chennai, India*

Abstract

The power factor has been an increasingly important concern in all industries. Poor power factors can result in many problems and financial loss for industries. This work aims at improving the power factor by increasing the usage of real power in relation to reactive power. In the system, relay switching is used in conjunction with a capacitor to sense any drops in the power factor and switch the capacitor whenever requires. The addition of capacitor will help to improve power factor and also the demand of electricity on utility side will be reduced. With the help of a smart power factor correction unit, the power factor is corrected closer to unity. Depending on the load and power factor of the network, the power factor controller switches the necessary blocks of capacitors in steps to improve the power factor nearly 0.95. The system is simulated by using MATLAB software.

Keywords: Power factor, relay switching, smart power factor correction unit, capacitors

3.1 Introduction

Alternating current circuits, in contrast to direct current circuits, does not rely solely on resistance to regulate the flow of current. Various aspects of the circuit can be compared to resistance; however, these do not consume

*Corresponding author: amutha.c@rajalakshmi.edu.in

Anita Khosla, Prasenjit Chatterjee, Ikbal Ali and Dheeraj Joshi (eds.) *Optimization Techniques in Engineering: Advances and Applications*, (51–58) © 2023 Scrivener Publishing LLC

any power. Just as in DC circuits, multiplied by voltage, current equals watts, here it only equals Volt Amperes (VA). Reactance is caused by either inductance or by capacitance [1]. The inductance current lags the voltage, while that of the capacitance leads it. Since most domestic loads are inductive in nature, they draw a lagging current, thereby overloading the system without performing any useful work [2]. Loading the system with capacitors wipes out the capacitive currents since they are leading in nature. A lower power factor translates to a more problematic situation [3]. In many cases, consumers are penalized if they fail to improve their load power factor [4]. The power factor can be improved by reducing the lag between the supply voltage and supply current. By introducing reactive power in the opposite sign of the load's inductive and capacitive effects, power factor correction brings the power factor of an AC power circuit closer to 1 [5]. Whenever they are switched on or off, reactive elements can cause voltage fluctuations and harmonic noise [6]. Regardless of whether any corresponding load is nearby, they will supply or sink reactive power, thus increasing the system's no-load losses [7].

At worst, reactive elements can create resonant conditions and cause severe overvoltage fluctuation and system instability [8]. The power factor can be enhanced with automatic power factor correction units. Power factor correction units are generally made up of capacitors. They are switched using contactors. Normally, these contactors are controlled by a regulator that measures power factor in a network. The regulator measures one phase's current using a current transformer in order to measure the power factor. Based on the load and power factor of the network, the power factor controller will switch the necessary blocks of capacitors in steps to ensure the power factor remains above a predefined level, for example, 0.95. The use of the series active filter is a low-cost approach to power factor correction [9].

Compared to AC to DC PFCs, the proposed PFC has lower device requirements that reduces cost, boost efficiency, and reduces electromagnetic interference. The interest in power factor correction circuits has increased due to new recommendations and future standards, this paper examines the most promising solution for single phase and low power applications [10]. Capacitor banks used to obtain power factor correction to generate locally the reactive energy necessary for the transfer of electrical power, which provides a better and more rational technical-economical management of the plants. Power factor of medical industries has increased from 0.85 to 0.90 through automatic power factor correction device. Power factor compensation contributes to reduction in current-dependent losses and increase energy efficiency while expanding the reliability of planning for future energy network [11]. It consists of controller, which determines the power factor value, if the power factor is low, the capacitor bank is improved. The primary point of the model is to retain the power factor as high as possible, which builds the proficiency of the framework [12].

3.2 Block Diagram

This system uses a microcontroller for switching the capacitor bank connected at the end of the main power supply. The smart power factor correction unit consists of capacitors connected to the load terminal of the main supply, relays connected in series with capacitors and controller. The controller reads the system power factor, voltage, and current. Then based on the uploaded program, the controller decides the number of capacitors to be inserted for bringing up the required power factor, thereby the main supply is compensated with shunt technique.

The energy readings are stored in a database. The consumer can monitor the data through internet in real time. The data can be shared to the power supplier for load predicting. In Figure 3.1, initially, voltage is stepped down with the help of voltage transformer and converted into DC voltage using rectifier. The output of rectifier is given to zero crossing detector. The same is done for current using current transformer. The output of zero crossing detector is sent to Arduino. Arduino calculates the energy and power factor, depending on the output of zero crossing detector. Based on the calculated power factor, the required capacitor banks are switched using relay module until the required power factor is obtained. After the process is completed, the obtained power factor is displayed with the help of LCD.

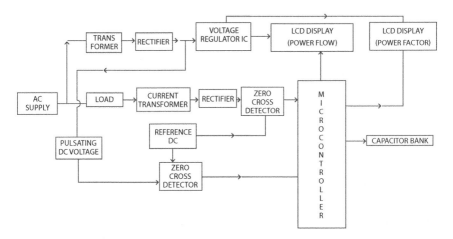

Figure 3.1 Block diagram of proposed system.

3.2.1   Power Factor Concept

Power factor (PF) is the ratio of real power, measured in kilowatts (kW), to apparent power, measured in kilovolt amperes (kVA). Apparent power, also known as demand, is the amount of power used to run machinery and equipment during a certain period. To calculate power factor, you need a power quality analyzer that measures both real power (kW) and apparent power (kVA), and to calculate the ratio of kW/kVA. The power factor formula can be expressed from Eq. (3.1) to Eq. (3.5) where f, frequency of AC supply and ΔT, time difference between voltage and current waveform.

$$\text{Power Factor, Cos } \emptyset = (\text{True power}) / (\text{Apparent power}) \quad (3.1)$$

$$\text{Phase Angle, } \emptyset = 360° \times f \times \Delta T \quad (3.2)$$

$$\text{Real Power, } P = V \times I \times \cos(\emptyset) \quad (3.3)$$

$$\text{Reactive Power, } Q = V \times I \times \sin(\emptyset) \quad (3.4)$$

$$\text{Apparent Power, } S = V \times I \quad (3.5)$$

3.2.2   Power Factor Calculation

Consider motor input, P (kW)

Power factor before correction = $\cos \emptyset_1$
Desired power factor = $\cos \emptyset_2$

The required capacitor kVAR to improve the PF is shown in Eq. (3.6)-Eq. (3.8). From this formula, calculation of desired capacitor size can be found.

$$\text{Required power factor, } QC = P(\tan \emptyset - \tan \emptyset_0) \quad (3.6)$$

$$\text{Required Capacitive Reactance, } XC = V^2 / QC \quad (3.7)$$

$$\text{Required Capacitance, } C = 1 / (2\pi f X_C) \quad (3.8)$$

3.3   Simulation

In Figure 3.2, initially, input voltage is fed into the current and voltage transformer. The output voltage and current are taken to the power measurement block where real power (P) and reactive power (Q) is found. Using divider block, the value of P/Q is found. By taking the tan inverse for the obtained value, the value of Φ is found. By taking the value of Φ to cos block, the power factor of the system is obtained.

Depending on the power factor, the capacitor will be added in the circuit to get the required power factor. In Figure 3.3, current lagging the voltage can be seen. After connecting the capacitors to circuit, the current runs almost at the same phase as voltage. In Figure 3.4, the power factor

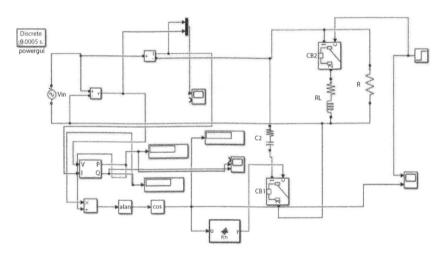

Figure 3.2 Simulation diagram using MATLAB.

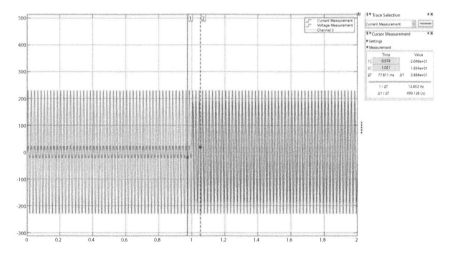

Figure 3.3 Output voltage and current.

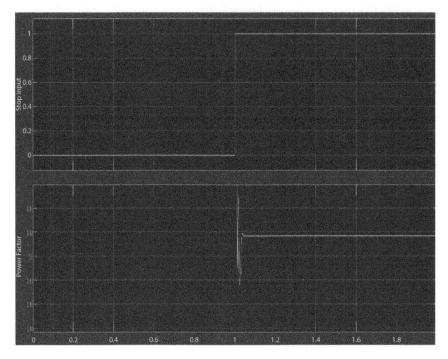

Figure 3.4 Power factor output.

is dropped when the inductive load is connected. After sensing the low power factor, the relays are switched which connects the capacitors to the circuit, thus improving the power factor.

3.4 Conclusion

This automatic power factor correction technique improves the power factor in an economical way. This system uses capacitor when the power factor is less. Otherwise, the capacitor is removed from the line. Thus, it not only improves the power factor but also increases the life time of capacitor. The power factor of the line can be increased with the small rating of capacitor. The power factor of the system can be increased and make the system stable by increasing its efficiency. The techniques of this work could be applied to design power factor improvement for smooth regulation of the load power factor.

References

1. Sree, B.L. and Umamaheswari, M.G., A Hankel matrix reduced order SEPIC model for simplified voltage control optimization and MPPT. *Sol. Energy*, 170, 280–292, 2018.

2. Nazarali, A., Premkumar, K., VishnuPriya, M., Manikandan, B.V., Tamizhselvan, T., Design and development of realistic PV emulator adaptable to the maximum power point tracking algorithm and battery charging controller. *Int. Sol. Energy Soc.*, 220, 473–490, 2014.

3. Nazarali, A., Sivamani, D., Jaiganesh, R., Pradeep, M., Solar powered air conditioner using BLDC motor. *IOP Conf. Ser. Mater. Sci. Eng.*, 623, 1–10, 2019.

4. Premkumar, K. and Shyam, D., Design and development of n-level symmetrical multilevel inverter topology with reduced switches. *J. Circuit. Syst. Comput.*, 30, 11, 2150197, 2021.

5. Salas, V., Olias, E., Barrado, A., Lazaro, A., Review of the maximum power point tracking algorithms for stand-alone photovoltaic systems. *Sol. Energy Mater. Sol. Cells*, 90, 11, 1555–1578, 2006.

6. Sangari, A. and Umamaheswari, R., Analysis of impedance source inverter topologies for grid integration of PV inverters. *Int. J. Power Electron. Drive Syst.*, 6, 4, 797–807, 2015.

7. Sangari, A., Umamaheswari, R., Umamaheswari, M.G., A novel SOSMC based SVPWM control of Z-source inverter for AC microgrid applications. *Microprocess. Microsyst.*, 75, 103045, 2020.

8. Shyam, D., Sivamani, D., Jaiganesh, R., Narendiran, S., Solar PV fed parallel SEPIC converter for highly efficient multilevel inverter integration. *Int. Trans. Power Energy Syst.*, 1, 1, 1–17, 2021.

9. Sivamani, D., Ramkumar, R., Ali, A.N., Shyam, D., Design and implementation of highly efficient UPS charging system with single stage power factor correction using SEPIC converter. *Mater. Today Proc.*, 45, 1809–1819, 2021.

10. Sivamani, D., Shyam, D., Ali, A.N., Premkumar, K., Narendiran, S., Alexander, S.A., Solar powered battery charging system using optimized pi controller for buck boost converter. *IOP Conf. Ser. Mater. Sci. Eng.*, 1055, 1, 012151, 2021.

11. Thamizhselvan, T., Ramalingam, S., Premkumar, K., Maximum power point tracking algorithm for photovoltaic system using supervised online coactive neuro fuzzy inference system. *J. Electr. Eng.*, 17, 270–286, 2017.

12. Venkatesh, V., Nazar Ali, A., Sivaraman, P.R., Remkumar, K.P., Shyam, D., Performance enhancement of elementary additional series positive output super lift converter fed PMBLDC drive. *Int. J. Sci. Technol. Res.*, 9, 1, 4018–4022, 2020.

4

ANN-Based Maximum Power Point Tracking Control Configured Boost Converter for Electric Vehicle Applications

Sivamani D.*, Sangari A., Shyam D., Anto Sheeba J., Jayashree K. and Nazar Ali A.

Department of Electrical and Electronics Engineering,
Rajalakshmi Engineering College, Chennai, India

Abstract

This chapter focuses on the design and analysis of a solar-fed cascaded boost converter with a maximum power point tracking (MPPT) algorithm based on neural networks (NN) for electric vehicle (EV) applications. For changes in irradiation and temperature conditions, the maximum power is extracted from the solar panel using a NN-based MPPT algorithm. The regulated output voltage is obtained from the cascaded boost converter using a proportional integral (PI) controller. The two switches in the cascaded boost converter are controlled by two different controllers. The first controller employs an NN-based MPPT algorithm to generate PWM pulses for switch 1. The second controller utilizes PI controller to produce the PWM pulse for switch 2. The simulation results show that the NN-based MPPT converter can extract the maximum power from the solar panel for changes in irradiation and temperature conditions. The output voltage is regulated by a PI controller in response to changes in irradiation, temperature, and load conditions.

Keywords: Neural network, maximum power point tracking, proportional integral, pulse width modulation

4.1 Introduction

Environmental change caused by deforestation is causing people all over the world to promote green energy. The availability of energy is greater

---

*Corresponding author: sivamani.d@rajalakshmi.edu.in

Anita Khosla, Prasenjit Chatterjee, Ikbal Ali and Dheeraj Joshi (eds.) *Optimization Techniques in Engineering: Advances and Applications,* (59–72) © 2023 Scrivener Publishing LLC

in fossil fuels, and pure energy does not pollute the environment. Solar power panels have the advantages of producing renewable energy, being highly reliable, and operating at a high efficiency [1]. The output voltage of a PV panel is affected by the temperature and irradiance falling on it. PV panels are used to transform photons into electricity [2]. No fuel is used in the PV panel, no emissions are generated, all parts are stationary, and there are no wear and tear losses [3]. The performance of the PV panel is DC voltage, which is very low and is boosted to our required range using a DC-DC converter. The amount of DC power produced is affected by variable irradiation and variable ambient temperature [4]. It is observed that the DC voltage of a PV panel varies with the load. Using MPPT, the maximum power point of a specific point is chosen for constant V-I characteristics [5, 6]. At the maximum point, the PV array produces the most electricity. MPPT is tracked using an artificial neural network (ANN) soft computing technique [7, 8]. The ANN-based MPPT is trained to extract the maximum power. The output voltage is regulated by a converter [9]. A DC-DC Boost converter, which consists of power electronic switches with inductance and capacitance. The boost converter's output voltage is held constant. The operation of switching devices is non-linear [10–12]. The dynamic response of the converter is required by the PI controller. PI controller is required to operate the converter in dynamic response [11–13].

4.2   Block Diagram

Figure 4.1 shows the block diagram and closed loop implementation of the proposed system. It consists of ANN controlled boost converter.

A. Solar Panel
The key theme of absorbing the sun's energy is the use of photovoltaics. Photovoltaic (PV) technology generates electricity by using photons from the sun. In general, photovoltaic (PV) arrays turn sunlight into electricity. The amount of DC power produced is determined by the brightness of the star and the temperature of the surrounding atmosphere, both of which are variable. It also varies in accordance with the amount of load. A PV array exhibits a V-I characteristics called maximum power point under uniform irradiance and temperature, which is where the PV array generates the most output power. The maximum power point tracking (MPPT) algorithm is important for PV arrays in order to supply maximum power to load.

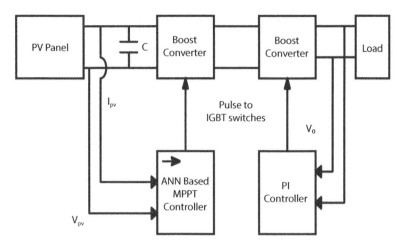

Figure 4.1 Block diagram.

B. MPPT technique

A maximum power point tracker is a DC to DC electronic converter that optimizes the match between the solar array (PV panels) and the load. Panel monitoring denotes that the panels are mounted on a track that tracks the light.

The MPPT controls the converters to continuously detect the PV array's maximum power. It is very essential to extract the maximum power from the boost converter at various temperature and Irradiance conditions also in varying load condition.

Figure 4.2 shows the variable irradiance fall on PV panel versus the variations of voltage, current and power.

Figure 4.3 shows the voltage Vs current and voltage Vs power for various irradiance conditions. It is observed that the MPPT algorithm can extract the maximum power from the solar panel.

C. Boost Converter

Boost converter is a DC-to-DC converter and is used to increase the output voltage. It utilizes IGBT switch to control the output. When the IGBT switch is ON, the inductor L is connected to the PV panel, and L stores energy during ON period, Ton. Hence, diode D reverses biased and isolates the output stage. When the IGBT switch is OFF, the output stage receives energy from L, as well as from PV panel. The current now flows through L,

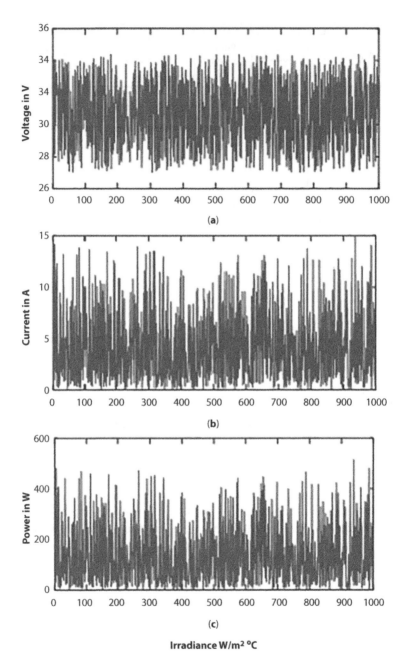

Figure 4.2 (a) Variable irradiance vs voltage. (b) Variable irradiance vs current. (c) Variable irradiance vs power.

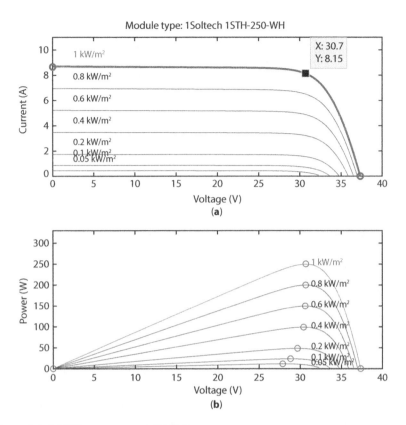

Figure 4.3 (a) Voltage vs current. (b) Voltage vs power.

D, C, and resistive load. Boost converter parameters are designed by using the following specifications: output power: 250 W, output voltage Vo: 80 V, load resistance R: 25 Ω, switching frequency fs: 20 kHz, duty ratio do: 0.7, ripple current in the inductor ΔI: 1 % of Io, ripple voltage across the capacitor ΔVC: 3% of VC. The inductors L and C values are designed by using the above specifications as,

$$L = \frac{V_C * d_o}{\Delta I * f_s} = 350 \mu H \tag{4.1}$$

$$C = \frac{I_o * d_o}{\Delta V_C * f_s} = 500 \mu F \tag{4.2}$$

The parameters of boost converter are shown in Table 4.1.

Table 4.1 Parameters of boost converter.

Parameter	Value
Power	250 W
Output voltage	80 V
Switching frequency	25 kHz
Inductor	350 μH
Capacitor	500

4.3   ANN-Based MPPT for Boost Converter

In the proposed system, ANN based MPPT is used to extract the maximum power from the PV panel.

A. Artificial Neural Network (ANN)
Artificial neural networks (ANNs) are efficient computational structures made up of several basic computing elements linked together to perform tasks similar to those performed by biological brains. The ability of NN to learn and generalize to new situations from a collection of training data is one of their most important features. They change the weights of the connections between neurons to ensure that the final output activations are accurate. They are extremely fault tolerant. There is a variety of ANN architectures. Figure 4.4 depicts a standard neuron structure.

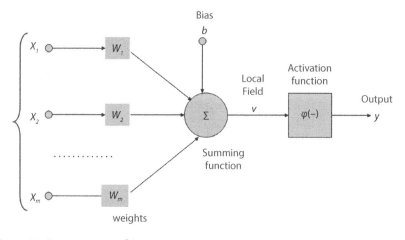

Figure 4.4 Basic structure of ANN.

The neuron is the basic information processing unit of a NN. It consists of a) A set of links, describing the neuron inputs, with weights W_1, W_2, ..., W_m. b) An adder function (linear combiner) for computing the weighted sum of the inputs:

$$v = \sum_{j=1}^{m} wjxj$$

Activation function (sigmoidal function) for limiting the amplitude of the neuron output.

$$y = \phi(u+b).$$

Simulink structure of ANN is shown in Figure 4.5. It consists of three layers namely an input layer, output layer and the hidden layer. For the proposed system, the number of nodes in the input layer is 2. The input nodes are used to collect the Vpv and Ipv from solar panel also to transmit the data to the hidden layer. The hidden layer consists of 10 neurons. Every node in the hidden layer performs sigmoidal function and sigmoidal function is used as the membership function in ANN. The number of nodes in the output layer is 1. It is used to give reference voltage for MPPT. The connections between the input to hidden layer and output to hidden layer have associated with weights. Weights are modified during training and it increases the signal strength. The training of NN is done using backpropagation training. The training data is exactly matched with the target data, which are shown in Figure 4.6.

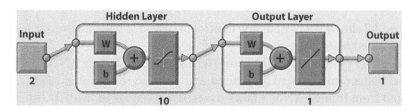

Figure 4.5 SIMULINK structure of ANN.

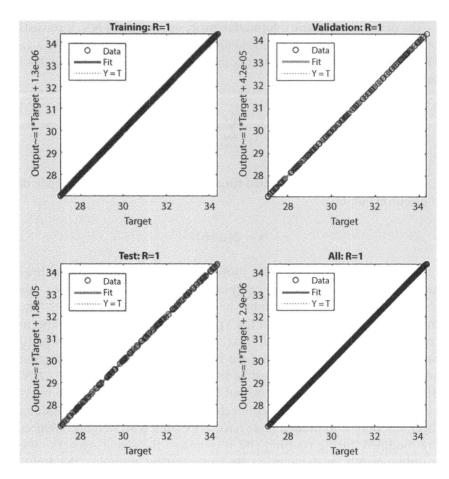

Figure 4.6 Output of trained NN.

4.4   Closed Loop Control

Figure 4.7 shows the closed loop control of cascaded boost converter using ANN based MPPT algorithm.

The duty cycle of the boost converter 1 is generated using ANN. The PV panel voltage and current are sensed and given to the input of ANN. The output from trained ANN is taken as reference voltage for MPPT. This reference voltage is compared with the PV panel voltage and the error is given to the input of PI controller. The output from PI controller is compared with the carrier signal of switching frequency 20 kHz. Then switching pulses are produced and given to the input of IGBT switch 1 present in the boost converter 1. The output voltage Vo is compared with the reference voltage

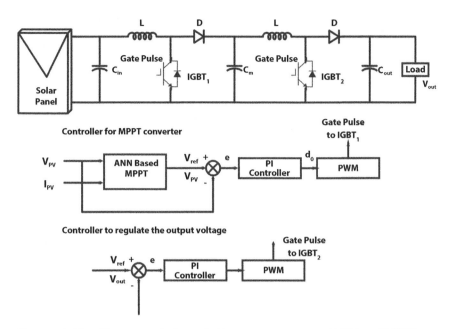

Figure 4.7 Closed loop control of cascaded boost converter using ANN-based MPPT.

and the error is given to the input of PI controller. The output from PI controller is compared with the carrier signal of switching frequency 20 kHz. Then switching pulses are produced and given to the input of IGBT switch 2 presents in the boost converter 2.

4.5   Simulation Results

The simulation results of the proposed system are discussed in this section. Figures 4.8 (a) and (b) depict the input and output power for various irradiations for NN based boost converter. Results show that that the NN based boost converter can track a maximum power for various irradiations. Figure 4.9 depicts the PV voltage for various irradiations for NN based boost converter. Figure 4.10 depicts the PV current for various irradiations for NN based boost converter. Figure 4.11 shows output voltage and output current of proposed system for change in temperature.

Figure 4.12 shows the output voltage and output current for change in load conditions. The 40% increase in load is introduced at 1 sec. From the simulation results, it is reveals that the proposed system can provide the regulated output voltage for 40% increase in load.

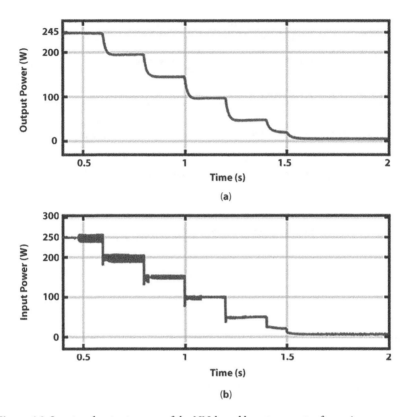

(a)

(b)

Figure 4.8 Input and output power of the NN-based boost converter for various irradiations.

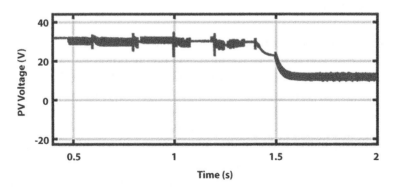

Figure 4.9 PV voltage of NN-based boost converter for various irradiations.

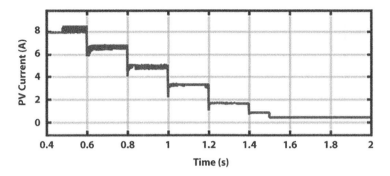

Figure 4.10 Output voltage and output current of proposed system for change in irradiations.

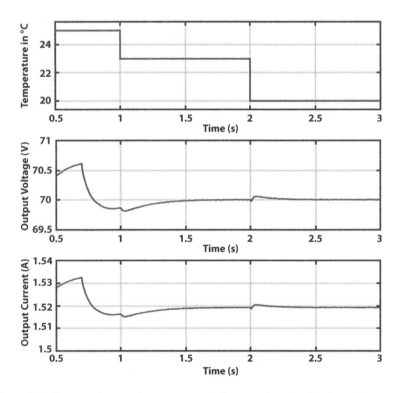

Figure 4.11 Output voltage and output current of proposed system for change in temperature.

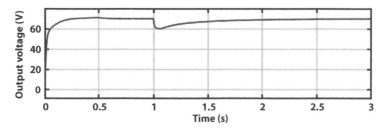

Figure 4.12 Output voltage and output current for change in load condition.

4.6   Conclusion

In this proposed work, closed loop implementation of solar-fed cascaded boost converter with a maximum power point tracking (MPPT) algorithm based on neural networks (NN) was carried out for electric vehicle (EV) applications. From the simulation results, it is observed that the NN-based MPPT converter can extract the maximum power from the solar panel for changes in irradiation and temperature conditions. The cascaded converter's output voltage is regulated by a PI controller in response to changes in irradiation, temperature, and load conditions. The proposed system is well suited for EV applications.

References

1. Thamizhselvan, T., Ramalingam, S., Premkumar, K., Maximum power point tracking algorithm for photovoltaic system using supervised online coactive neuro fuzzy inference system. *J. Electr. Eng.*, 17, 1, 270–286, 2017.
2. Salas, V., Olias, E., Barrado, A., Lazaro, A., Review of the maximum power point tracking algorithms for stand-alone photovoltaic systems. *Sol. Energy Mater. Sol. Cells*, 90, 11, 1555–1578, 2006.
3. Lee, H.H., Phuong, L.M., Dzung, P.Q., Vu, N.T.D., Khoa, L.D., The new maximum power point tracking algorithm using ANN-based solar PV systems, in: *Proceedings of the IEEE Region 10 Conference (TENCON '10)*, Fukuoka, Japan, pp. 2179–2184, November 2010.
4. Khan, M.J. and Mathew, L., Fuzzy logic controller-based MPPT for hybrid photo-voltaic/wind/fuel cell power system. *Neural Comput. Appl.*, 31, 1–14, 2018.
5. Sree, B.L. and Umamaheswari, M.G., A Hankel matrix reduced order SEPIC model for simplified voltage control optimization and MPPT. *Sol. Energy*, 170, 280–292, 2018.

6. Sangari, A. and Umamaheswari, R., Analysis of impedance source inverter topologies for grid integration of PV inverters. *Int. J. Power Electron. Drive Syst.*, 6, 4, 797–807, Dec. 2015.

7. Shyam, D., Premkumar, K., Thamizhselvan, T., N. Ali, A., V. Priya, M., Symmetrically modified laddered H-bridge multilevel inverter with reduced configurational parameters. *Int. J. Eng. Adv. Technol.*, 9, 1, 5525–5532, 2019.

8. Garrigos, A., Marroqui, D., Garcia, A., Blanes, J.M., Gutierrez, R., Interleaved, switched-inductor, multi-phase, multi-device DC/DC boost converter for non-isolated and high conversion ratio fuel cell applications. *Int. J. Hydrogen Energy*, 44, 25, 12783–92, 2019.

9. Ali, A.N., Premkumar, K., Priya, M.V., Manikandan, B.V., Tamizhselvan, T., Design and development of realistic PV emulator adaptable to the maximum power point tracking algorithm and battery charging controller. *Int. Sol. Energy Soc.*, 473–490, 1–9, 2014.

10. Sivamani, D., Shyam, D., Ali, A.N., Premkumar, K., Narendiran, S., Alexander, S.A., Solar powered battery charging system using optimized pi controller for buck boost converter. *IOP Conf. Ser. Mater. Sci. Eng.*, 1055, 1, 012151, 2021.

11. Sivamani, D., Ramkumar, R., Ali, A.N., Shyam, D., Design and implementation of highly efficient UPS charging system with single stage converter. *Mater. Today Proc.*, October 10 2020.

12. Ali, A.N., Ganesh, R.J., Sivamani, D., Shyam, D., Solar powered highly efficient seven-level inverter with switched capacitors. *IOP Conf. Ser. Mater. Sci. Eng.*, 906, 17578981, 1757899X, Aug 2020.

13. Ali, A.N., Sivamani, D., Jaiganesh, R., Pradeep, M., Solar powered air conditioner using BLDC motor. *IOP Conf. Ser. Mater. Sci. Eng.*, 623, 1–10, Oct 2019.

## 5

Single/Multijunction Solar Cell Model Incorporating Maximum Power Point Tracking Scheme Based on Fuzzy Logic Algorithm

Omveer Singh[1]*, Shalini Gupta[2] and Shabana Urooj[3]

[1]Electrical Engineering Department, Gautam Buddha University, G.B. Nagar, India
[2]C&S Electricals Pvt. Ltd., G.B. Nagar, India
[3]Electrical Engineering Department, Princess Nourah Bint Abdul Rahman University, Riyadh, Saudi Arabia

Abstract

In the present chapter, modeling of a single and multijunction solar cell with maximum power point tracking (MPPT) utilizing intelligent fuzzy logic algorithm (FLA) for maximum productivity is proposed. The circuit model of the single/multijunction solar cell considers the scale of every subcell. It considers the temperature changes effect on energy gap of every subcell. The solar cells behaviors are also analyzed through the fill factor value. The MPPT scheme is also implemented with perturb and observe method (P&O) and FLA. This proposed FLA-based MPPT method is also matched with traditional, and P&O-based MPPT method in the MATLAB software. This FLA technique gives ameliorated dynamic performance to pursue the MPPT. Additionally, it has been found that the FLA gives better dynamic response characteristics than other techniques, and also it improves the efficiency of the solar photovoltaic (PV) cell.

Keywords: Single/multijunction, photovoltaic, solar cell, MPPT, perturb & observe, fuzzy logic algorithm

*Corresponding author: omveers@gmail.com

Anita Khosla, Prasenjit Chatterjee, Ikbal Ali and Dheeraj Joshi (eds.) Optimization Techniques in Engineering: Advances and Applications, (73–94) © 2023 Scrivener Publishing LLC

5.1   Introduction

Electricity plays a very vital role in day to day life of people. Generally, it is generated from different sort of conventional fossil fuels (sources) in the most of the geographical regions of the world. Earlier days these sources were available in abundant amount on the earth but now days, these energy sources are going to be reduced and unfortunately, increasing pollution level for living creatures. However, pollution level on the earth is the major menace to the rising growth of people in the living societies. It reflects impurity summation to the nature. The nature substitutes that balance its equation are water, air, plants, humans, and animals. If they disturbed/polluted, then the existence of the life word can be ends from earth environment or can be hampered. Therefore, the need of green and clean other alternate energy sources are raised in the whole world. The renewable energy sources (RESs) can be a name of the alternate energy sources. RESs include solar, wind, hydro, tidal, biogas and biomass, etc. which would be the futuristic solution for fulfilling the electricity demands without increasing pollution level index of the world with enhancement of clean and green culture toward environment.

Recent adequate incremental contribution through the solar energy source reflects that it would be a beautiful and economic facilitator and easy provider of electricity locally as well as globally. Solar energy can also be counted as the prominent source of energy as it is the green and clean energy source and can also provide enough amount of energy for electricity production. Thus, to protect the atmosphere in the world, it is very important to switch on from conventional energy sources to non-conventional RESs.

The best alternative solution to this issue is use of solar energy in a significant way. Solar energy can be created from solar thermal storage scheme or solar PV cell scheme but the efficient and economical way of using solar energy to generate electricity is through solar PV cells. The PV solar cells are nonpolluting. The solar PV technology is cost-effective and needs no maintenance for longer period. This technology is reliable and does not have any fluctuating losses in itself [1–3]. Other relevant facts and advancements are examined in Sathya and Natarajan [4].

A solar cell is a tool, which allows direct conversion of incident sunlight energy into electricity [2]. The single-junction solar cells mainly consist of one junction, made up of semiconductor materials, like silicon. The single-junction cells are less efficient as compared to the multijunction solar cells. Multijunction solar cells consist of higher than one junction in order to increase the number of absorbed photons and utilize the entire spectrum.

In the present time, solar cells utilizing a variety of materials instead of silicon have been grown to enhance the changing quality and getting more efficiency with multijunction solar cells. It is a concept of the priority in photovoltaic investigations [3].

Developments in this area have been gained through the combined form of many junctions utilizing diverse materials to realize layer of stack solar cells with higher than one junction so that a solar radiation over a maximum spectrum can be transferred into electric energy. Rather than high transfer efficiency, multijunction tools have other beneficial qualities like superior material symptoms, stability, radiation harness, and tenability of energy band gap [4]. These solar cells are very much efficient in uses where the operational result is more needed than the price, such as engineering utilizations [5].

The tandem cells can also be designed based on category of solar absorber combined forms [6]. The limitation of tandem cells may include the resistive losses. Also, when the solar irradiation increases, the losses occur due to series resistance, which results in decrease in fill factor and the efficiency. In this article, the value of series resistance is considered negligible, hence enhancing the competence of the solar cell.

The multijunction solar cells' performance can be improved by using MPPT scheme as it can optimize the output power of the cells. The P&O- and FLA-based MPPT schemes are applied to calculate and optimize the output power of the solar cells. It has been observed that the FLA-based MPPT method has better optimizing quality than the P&O-based MPPT technique.

In the present chapter, several sections have been presented. Section 5.1 presented introduction, as well as literature survey about single-junction and multijunction solar cells development stages with recent MPPT techniques. Further, section 5.2 demonstrated modeling of single-junction/ multijunction solar cells architecture on MATLAB/Simulink platform by the help of their equations. This section also explains proportionate circuit structure of the single/multijunction solar cell. Next, P&O and FLA-based MPPT schemes are designed and examined in section 5.3. Moreover, section 5.4 reflected the dynamic plots, results with their effective analysis. All key points of this proposed work is written and mirrored in the section 5.5.

5.2   Modeling Structure

5.2.1   Single-Junction Solar Cell Model

The modeling of single-junction solar cell is presented in this section. The equivalent circuit of solar PV cell is as exhibited in Figure 5.1:

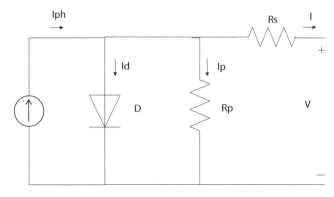

Figure 5.1 The proportionate circuit of a solar cell.

By implementing Kirchhoff's Current Law, current is evaluated as [6, 7]:

$$I = I_{ph} - I_d - I_p \tag{5.1}$$

I_{ph} = photocurrent, I_d is diode current which is identical to the saturation current I_o.

The I_d is reflected through the below equation:

$$I_d = I_o \left[\exp\{V / (A.N_s.V_T)\} \right] - 1] \tag{5.2}$$

V = voltage applied on the diode; A = ideality factor, N_s = count of solar cells interconnected. Thermal voltage V_T is given by:

$$V_T = k\, T_c / q \tag{5.3}$$

I_o = reverse saturation current of the diode (A), T_c = temperature (K) of practical cell, k = Boltzmann constant 1.381×10^{-23}J/K, q = electron charge (1.602×10^{-19}C).

The I_{ph} rely upon irradiance and temperature and is represented by:

$$I_{ph} = (G/G_{ref}) \{I_{sc} + \mu_{sc}. (T_c - T_{cref})\} \tag{5.4}$$

G: Irradiance (W/m²), G_{ref}: Irradiance at STC= 1000 W/m², T_{cref} = temperature of cell at STC = 25+ 273 = 298 K, μ_{sc} = coefficient temperature of short circuit current (A/K).

The reverse saturation current I_o is given through expression (5.5):

$$I_o = I_{sc}\{(T_c/T_{cref})^3\} \left[\exp\{q\, \varepsilon_o / Ak\} \{(1/T_{cref}) - (1/T_c)\} \right] \tag{5.5}$$

ε_0: Material band gap energy (eV) i.e. 1.12 eV for Si. Thus, substituting the value of I_{ph}, I_d and I_p from expressions (5.2), (5.4) and (5.5) in expression (1), the resulting current I of a solar cell is provided by:

$$I = (G/G_{ref})\ \{I_{sc} + \mu_{sc}.(T_c - T_{cref})\} - I_o[\exp\{(V + IR_s)/a\}-1]$$

$$- [(V + IR_s)/R_p] \tag{5.6}$$

The single-junction solar cell transfer function model is enhanced by using the above expressions and then simulated in the MATLAB/Simulink scenario.

Fill factor
Fill factor is claimed as the ratio in between the larger amount of power and the multiplication of open circuit (O.C.) voltage and short circuit (S.C.) current. The expression of fill factor is written as:

$$FF = P_{max}/(I_{sc} \times V_{oc}) \tag{5.7}$$

Fill factor indicates the level of the cell. The more the value of fill factor to hundred percent, the cell quality is considered the best. Fill factor is an extremely helpful idea for characterizing and contrasting two PV cells in terms of efficacy and outcome.

5.2.2   Modeling of Multijunction Solar PV Cell

Multijunction solar PV cells arranged one over the other which is separated by junctions. Multijunction, i.e., triple-junction solar cell has two junctions. The triple-junction solar cells are characterized by the materials which are used to construct the subcells. The subcells are made with the help of different materials, which are characterized by the value of their band gap energies. The band gap energy of the materials activates the essential character in increasing the efficiency of the cells as compared to the single-junction solar cells. The materials with the maximum band gap energy are placed at the top most layers so that it can absorb maximum photons. The modeling of multijunction solar cells has same basic criteria which must be fulfilled. The three criteria are: lattice matching, band gap energy matching and current matching [8]. In this chapter, the appropriate materials used for the subcells are InGaP, InGaAs and Ge. The similar circuit layout of multijunction solar PV cell is as presented in Figure 5.2.

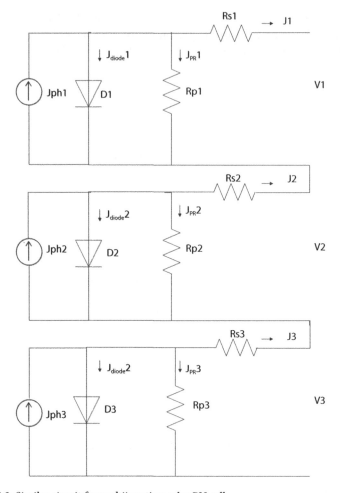

Figure 5.2 Similar circuit for multijunction solar PV cell.

By applying Kirchhoff's current law, the current density J_i for particular cell is obtained by [5]:

$$J_i = J_{phi} - J_{diode} - J_{PR} \qquad (5.8)$$

Photon current density J_{phi} is given by:

$$J_{phi} = (G^*K_c) \{J_{sci} + \mu_{sc} \cdot (T_c - T_{cref})\} \qquad (5.9)$$

J_{diode} is calculated by the below expression:

$$J_{diode} = J_{oi} [\exp \{q(V_i + J A R_{si})/(n_i K_b T)\} - 1] \qquad (5.10)$$

where J_{oi} = diode's reverse saturation current density in A/cm², q = charge constant (1.602×10⁻¹⁹C), A = cell area in cm², n_i is a constant, K_b = Boltzmann constant (1.38064852 × 10⁻²³J/K), T = operating temperature in K, R_s = series resistance, K_c = concentration constant.

The diode's reverse saturation current is provided through the below expression:

$$J_{oi} = K_i * (T)^{(3+\gamma i/2)} * \exp[(-q\, \varepsilon g_i/n_i\, Kb\, T)] \qquad (5.11)$$

where γ_i is a constant, and ε_g is the band gap energy in eV. The value of R_{PR} is large and shunt current density J_{PR} is very less, hence, it is omitted.

$$J_{PR} = (V_i + JAR_{si})/(AR_{shi}) \qquad (5.12)$$

where V_i is the voltage beyond the individual junction in V, R_{sh} is shunt resistance.

Band gap energy for different materials varies due to the different arrangements of interatomic spacing of materials. The value of band gap energy has an inverse relation to operating temperature.

The band gap energy and temperature is correlated as [9]:

$$Eg_i = Eg_i(0) - [(\alpha_i \times T^2) / (T+\beta_i)] \qquad (5.13)$$

where $Eg_i(0)$ is band gap energy at 0°C, α, and β are constants.

For a multijunction cell, each subcell is made with the help of different materials. The materials used for each junction can be pure or an alloy. Due to the different composition of alloy while manufacturing, the issues like differences in band gap energy value may occur even if the materials are identical. Hence, to avoid this problem, the band gap energy value for semiconductors' alloys can be calculated by the consecutive expression in [10].

$$Eg(A_{1-x}B_x) = (1 - x)Eg(A) + xEg(B) - x(1 - x)P \qquad (5.14)$$

$A_{1-x}B_x$ is the alloy combination and P (eV) is an alloy reliant parameter.

The top two subcells used are made of alloys in this chapter. Hence, expression (5.14) is used to obtain the equivalent band gaps of the individual alloys.

In multijunction solar cell, each subcell acts as a current source and all the subcells are interconnected in series. Hence, the resultant current is limited to the smallest current carried by the subcell [11]. So, the resultant current density of a multijunction cell is given by following expression:

$$J = \min(J_{top}, J_{mid}, J_{bottom}) \tag{5.15}$$

where J_{top}, J_{mid}, and J_{bottom} are the current density of the top, middle and bottom subcell, respectively.

The O.C. voltage of each subcell is given by following:

$$V_{oci} = [\{(n_i\ Kb\ T)/q\}\ \ln\{(J_{sci}/J_{oi}) + 1\}] \tag{5.16}$$

The largest recoverable voltage in a solar cell is its O.C. voltage. For multijunction solar cell, the O.C. voltage is considered to be equal to the sum of O.C. voltage of each junction and is stated by following equation:

$$V_{oc} = V_{top} + V_{mid} + V_{bottom} \tag{5.17}$$

where V_{top}, V_{mid}, and V_{bottom} are the voltage across the top, medium and bottom subcell, respectively.

5.3   MPPT Design Techniques

The design techniques for MPPT-based solar PV cell are very important and crucial for the designers and operators. They have to take up number of limitations whenever design/operation is going on practical path. Authors have also incorporated and attempted to take up them in the suitable form. Some of the design criterions are illustrated below:

5.3.1   Design of MPPT Scheme Based on P&O Technique

The P&O-based MPPT scheme is using fixed step size checking for maximum power point. That's the main limitation of this scheme. So, researchers move toward more promising techniques i.e. FLA. In this path, FLA technique is one of them for acquiring better maximum power point in solar PV cell.

The P&O algorithm is based on the hill climbing search methodology. In series to obtain largest output power from the solar cell, it is important to trace persistently the maximum power point, for a given set of operating conditions [12]. The power is given as the input to the algorithm. In the counted scheme, the power is moved in the direction of maximum power. The electric energy is varied through a little value and then the variation in power is checked. If the change in power is advantageous, then the next upgradation is done in the same direction else in the opposite way. This procedure is implemented until the maximum power point is achieved. This method is easy and convenient to implement. This algorithm helps in extracting maximum power for long time period so that the efficiency is improved. The flowchart of P&O scheme is exhibited in Figure 5.3.

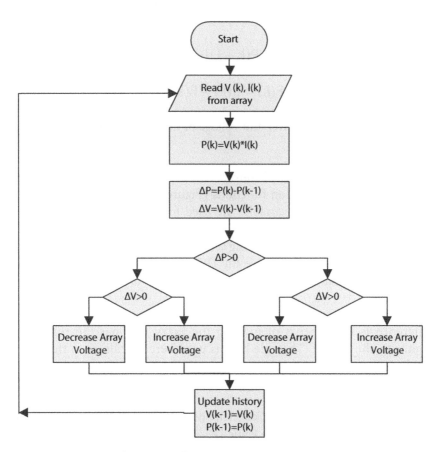

Figure 5.3 Flowchart of P&O algorithm.

5.3.2   Design of MPPT Scheme Based on FLA

The FLA-based MPPT scheme is designed to find out better dynamic results than that of P&O algorithm. FLA-based tracker deals with uncertain data sources, it need not require an exact arithmetic framework and this can deal with nonlinearity well [13]. The FLA-based tracker handles the vagueness of the system and exhibits immense potential for effective solving of the uncertainties in the problem. The FLA fabricates by the below mentioned steps:

1. Fuzzification
2. Inference
3. Defuzzification

In the proposed chapter, two inputs i.e. Error (E) and variation in the error (ΔE) are used, which are computed by following [14]:

$$E(k) = [P(k) - P(k - 1)]/[V(k) - V(k - 1)] \qquad (5.18)$$

$$\Delta E(k) = E(k) - E(k - 1) \qquad (5.19)$$

where P and V are the power and voltage of the solar cell, respectively.

Fuzzification
Fuzzification is the process of converting crisp value into fuzzy set. This is represented by membership functions (Figure 5.4). These are mainly the linguistic variables. Five variables are used for developing the fuzzy rule base.
These are as follows: Negative Big (NB), Negative Small (NS), Zero (ZE), Positive Small (PS) and Positive Big (PB). The relation of these variable components is mainly responsible for the behavior of FLA.

Inference
Inference is the process of making the fuzzy rule base to relate the inputs to the output. The rule base is used here as follows in the given Table 5.1.

Defuzzification
Defuzzification is the turn back activity of fuzzification. It is the process of converting fuzzy set to a crisp value [15–17]. This is done by the center of gravity method.

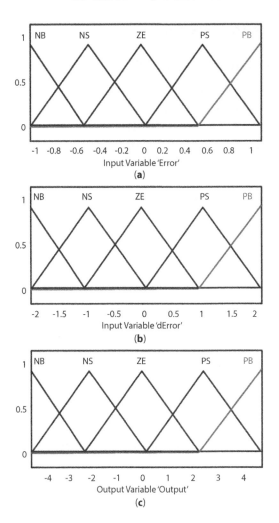

Figure 5.4 Membership function patterns for (a) input$_1$ (b) input$_2$ (c) output.

Table 5.1 Fuzzy rule base.

E\ΔE	NB	NS	ZE	PS	PB
NB	PS	PS	NB	NB	NS
NS	PS	PS	NS	NS	NS
ZE	ZE	ZE	ZE	ZE	ZE
PS	NS	NS	PS	PS	PS
PB	NS	NB	PB	PB	PS

5.4   Results and Discussions

5.4.1   Single-Junction Solar Cell

The V-I and P-V behavioral patterns of single-junction solar PV cell at standard test condition (STC), i.e., T=25°C and G=1000W/m² is as presented in Figures 5.5 and 5.6, respectively.

All the investigations are performed strictly on the STC. Each and every variable are completely following STC for the sake of actual simulation results. The dynamic curves are in the same fashion as per expectations from single-junction solar cell.

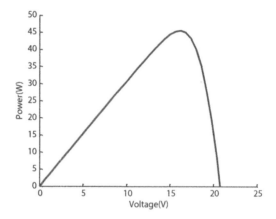

Figure 5.5 P-V behavioral patterns of single-junction solar PV cell.

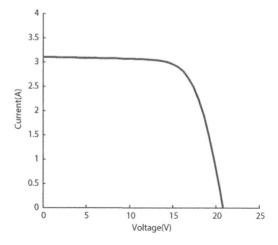

Figure 5.6 V-I behavioral patterns of single-junction solar PV cell.

The V-I characteristics indicates the value of O.C. voltage and S.C. current, whereas the P-V behavioral patterns give the value of maximum power which is generated by the cell which are useful in finding the fill factor amount.

With the help of the above P-V and V-I graph, fill factor is calculated as 67.11% for single-junction solar cell using expression (7).

Figure 5.7 shows the V-I behavioral patterns of a single-junction solar cell at different temperatures (°C) and constant irradiance levels, i.e., G=1000W/m². It is seen that on increasing the temperature, the O.C. voltage of the cell is reduced and the S.C. current slightly increases.

Figure 5.8 presents the V-I behavioral patterns of single-junction solar cell at different irradiance levels (W/m²) and constant temperature, i.e., T=25°C. It is reflected that on increasing the irradiance level, the S.C. current of the cell increases and the O.C. voltage has a momentary impression.

Figures 5.9 and 5.10 presented the V-I behavioral patterns of single-junction solar cell at different series and shunt resistances (Ω), respectively. It is seen that O.C. voltage and S.C. current is slightly affected by varying series and shunt resistance. Only the shape of the curve is slightly changed when the series resistance is decreased. The effect of changing the shunt resistance is negligible as its value is kept quite high.

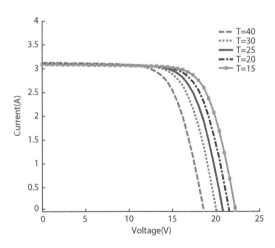

Figure 5.7 V-I behavioral patterns of single-junction solar PV cell at different temperatures (°C).

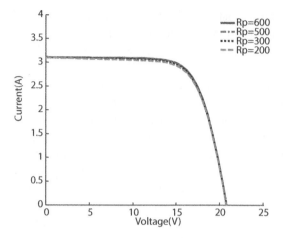

Figure 5.8 V-I behavioral patterns of single-junction solar PV cell at different irradiance levels (W/m²).

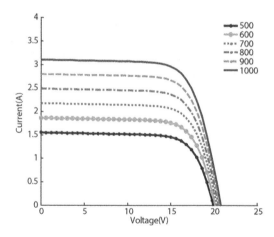

Figure 5.9 V-I behavioral patterns of single-junction solar PV cell at different series resistance (Ω).

5.4.2 Multijunction Solar PV Cell

The V-J and P-V characteristics of multijunction solar cell at T=313K and G=500W/cm² is as presented in Figures 5.11 and 5.12, respectively.

The V-J behavioral patterns indicates the value of O.C. voltage and S.C. current density, whereas the P-V characteristics give the value of maximum power, which is generated by the cells that are useful in finding the value of fill factor. Fill factor plays an important character in the designing

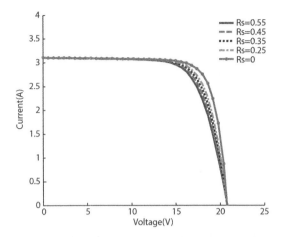

Figure 5.10 V-I behavioral patterns of single-junction solar PV cell at different shunt resistance (Ω).

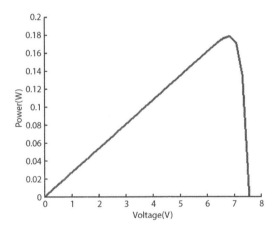

Figure 5.11 P-V behavioral patterns of multijunction solar cell.

of solar PV cell, and its value can enhance or reduce the performance of solar PV cell.

With the help of the above P-V and V-J graph, fill factor is calculated as 88.98% for multijunction solar cell using expression (5.7).

Figure 5.13 shows the V-J behavioral patterns of triple-junction solar cell at various irradiance levels (W/cm²) and constant temperature, i.e., T=313K and Figure 5.14 presents the V-J behavioral patterns of triple-junction solar cell at different temperatures (K) and constant irradiances, i.e., G=500W/cm². It is seen that on increasing the irradiance level, the

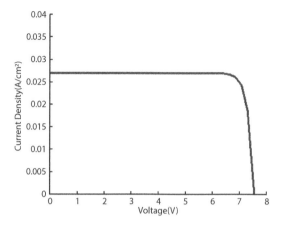

Figure 5.12 V-J behavioral patterns of multijunction solar cell.

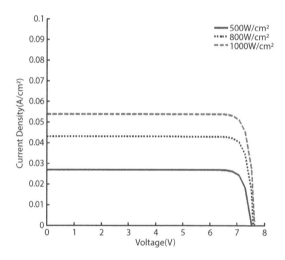

Figure 5.13 V-J behavioral patterns of multijunction solar cell at different irradiance levels (W/cm²).

S.C. current density increases while O.C. voltage has a slight effect. Also, it is also observed that O.C. voltage has an inverse relation with temperature, hence, on increasing the temperature, O.C. voltage is reduced and vice versa.

Figure 5.15 justifies the expression (17) and shows that the sum of the O.C. voltage of a multijunction solar cell is equal to the sum of O.C. voltage of every junction.

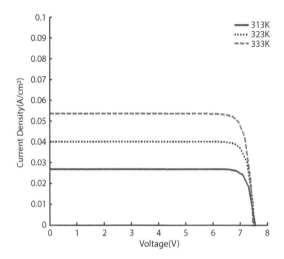

Figure 5.14 V-J behavioral patterns of triple-junction solar cell at different temperatures (K).

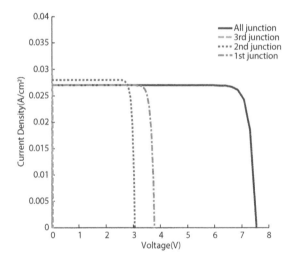

Figure 5.15 V-J behavioral patterns of all junctions individually.

Figure 5.16 prints the P-V behavioral patterns of cells when the single, double, and triple junctions are considered. It is examined that the power obtained through triple junction is greater than that of single and double junctions. Hence, it is noted that triple-junction solar cells are better than single-junction solar cells.

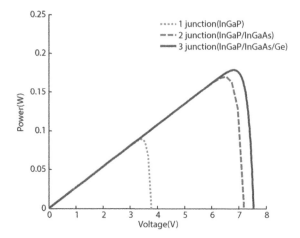

Figure 5.16 P-V behavioral patterns of 1-, 2-, and 3-junction solar cell.

5.4.3   Implementation of MPPT Scheme Based on P&O Technique

P&O algorithm maintains the maximum power point for longer period so that the efficiency is increased.

The output power obtained after implementing P&O scheme at different temperatures and irradiance levels are shown in Figures 5.17 and 5.18, respectively. It is investigated that the power increases on increasing both temperature, as well as irradiance levels and the power remains constant for longer duration as compared to the conventional method.

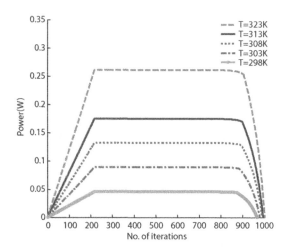

Figure 5.17 Power obtained by P&O-based MPPT scheme at different temperatures (K).

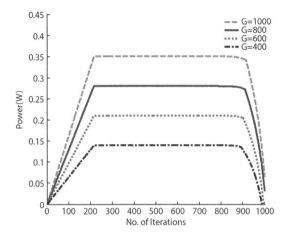

Figure 5.18 Power curve obtained by P&O-based MPPT scheme at different irradiance levels (W/cm²).

5.4.4   Implementation of MPPT Scheme Based on FLA

The FLA-based MPPT is designed on MATLAB/Simulink platform. The output power obtained after implementing proposed tracker at different temperatures and irradiance levels are shown in Figures 5.19 and 5.20, respectively.

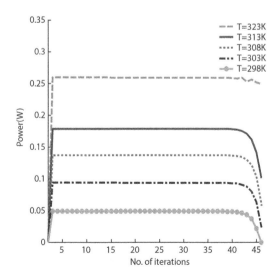

Figure 5.19 Power curve obtained by FLA-based MPPT scheme at different temperatures (K).

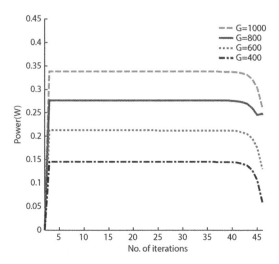

Figure 5.20 Power curve obtained by FLA-based MPPT scheme at different irradiance levels (W/cm²).

It is identified that the obtained power curve has less or reduced number of iterations in itself, which presents faster response than conventional, as well as classical P&O method.

It is investigated from Figure 5.21 that the power curve obtained by P&O algorithm-based MPPT is efficient than that of conventional (without MPPT) method. Also, the power obtained by using FLA is more efficient than that of both conventional and P&O-based MPPT schemes.

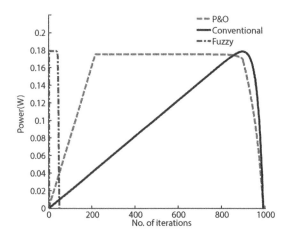

Figure 5.21 Comparative study of power obtained by conventional, P&O-, and FLA-based MPPT.

Hence, by utilizing FLA, the performance rate is higher. Moreover, the simulation outcomes exhibit that the FLA can achieve maximum power point quicker as compared to that of P&O-based MPPT scheme. Dynamic curves taken from FLA-based tracker also proves its quality in the operating time.

5.5 Conclusion

The modeling of single-junction and multijunction solar cells has been implemented to get the desired specific outcomes. The single-junction and multijunction solar cells performance is also compared with fill factor effect. The implementation of P&O and FLA-based MPPT presents that the output power can be optimized to get better results from the solar PV cell.

The solar PV cell efficiency is improved by using both the MPPT schemes but it has been observed from the test cases that the FLA is better as compared to the conventional, and P&O technique due to its faster response and easy to find out maximum power point on solar cell.

The FLA gives the more accurate tracking than the P&O scheme and also has better optimizing quality.

In this chapter, the air mass coefficient is kept constant. The irradiance changes with change in air mass coefficient, which affects the efficiency, and in the future, it can be considered to observe its effect.

References

1. Islam, H. *et al.*, Performance evaluation of maximum power point tracking approaches and photovoltaic systems. *Energies*, 11, 2–24, 365, 2018.
2. Das, N., Wongsodihardjo, H., Islam, S., Modeling of multi-junction photovoltaic cell using MATLAB/simulink to improve the conversion efficiency. *Renew. Energy*, 74, 917–924, 2015.
3. Catelani, M., Ciani, L., Kazimierczuk, M.K., Reatti, A., MATLAB PV solar concentrator performance prediction based on triple junction solar cell model. *Measurement*, Elsevier, 88, 310–317, 2016.
4. Sathya, P. and Natarajan, R., Numerical simulation and performance measure of highly efficient GaP/InP/Si multi-junction solar cell. *Int. J. Energy Res.*, John Wiley & Sons, 41, 1211–1222, 2017.
5. Hussain, A.B. *et al.*, Modeling and simulation of single and triple junction solar cell using MATLAB/SIMULINK. *Int. J. Ambient Energy*, Taylor & Francis, 38, 6, 613–621, 2016.

6. Davidson, L., Haque, K.A.S., Toor, F., Analytical model for simulating thin-film/wafer-based tandem junction solar cells. *Sol. Energy*, 150, 287–297, 2017.

7. Bellia, H., Youcef, R., Fatima, M., A detailed modeling of photovoltaic module using MATLAB. *NRIAG J. Astron. Geophys.*, 3, 53–61, 2014.

8. Das, N., Alghadeer, A., Islam, S., Modeling and analysis of multi-junction solar cells to improve the conversion efficiency of photovoltaic systems. *Australasian Universities Power Engineering Conference, AUPEC-2014*, Curtin University, Perth, Australia, 2014.

9. Amine, A., Mir, Y., Zazoui, M., Modeling of dual-junction solar cells including tunnel junction. *Adv. Condens. Matter Phys.*, Hindawi Publications, 2013, 1–5, 2013.

10. Segev, G., Mittelman, G., Kribus, A., Equivalent circuit models for triple-junction concentrator solar cells. *Sol. Energy Mater. Sol. Cells*, 98, 57–65, 2012.

11. Akter, T. *et al.*, In$_x$Ga$_{1-x}$N-based multi-junction solar cell: modeling and performance analysis using MATLAB/SIMULINK. *3rd International Conference on Energy Systems and Technologies*, Cairo, Egypt, pp. 159–169, 2015.

12. Femia, N. *et al.*, Optimization of perturb and observe maximum power point tracking method. *IEEE Trans. Power Electron.*, 20, 4, 963–973, 2005.

13. Bounechbaa, H. *et al.*, Comparison of perturb & observe and fuzzy logic in maximum power point tracker for PV systems. *The International Conference on Technologies and Materials for Renewable Energy, Environment and Sustainability, TMREES14, Energy Procedia*, 50, 677–684, 2014.

14. Bouchafaaa, F., Hamzaouia, I., Hadjammara, A., Fuzzy logic control for the tracking of maximum power point of a PV system. *Energy Procedia*, 6, 633–642, 2011.

15. Rezvani, A., Esmaeily, A., Etaati, H., Mohammadinodoushan, M., Intelligent hybrid power generation system using new hybrid fuzzy-neural for photovoltaic system and RBFNSM for wind turbine in the grid connected mode. *Front. Energy*, 13, 1, 131–148, 2019.

16. Awais, M. *et al.*, Nonlinear adaptive neuro-fuzzy feedback linearization based MPPT control schemes for photovoltaic system in microgrid. *Plos One*, 15, 6, e0234992, Open Access 2020.

17. Saluel, J.L. and Saleme, S., II, Robust digital control strategy based on fuzzy logic for a solar charger of VRLA batteries. *Energies*, MDPI Publishers, 14, 4, 2–27, 2021.

6

Particle Swarm Optimization: An Overview, Advancements and Hybridization

Shafquat Rana, Md Sarwar*, Anwar Shahzad Siddiqui and Prashant

Department of Electrical Engineering, Faculty of Engineering and Technology, Jamia Millia Islamia, New Delhi, India

Abstract

Particle swarm optimization (PSO) has gained its importance over last 20 years and has been proven successful in many domains and disciplines of science and technology, as well as in other fields. It has shown its ability in optimizing various complex problems in a simpler way. Due to its simplicity and worldwide applications, the latest breakthroughs in PSO, as well as their applications in various fields are stated in this chapter. Its significance, algorithm and working mechanism along with the pseudo-code are presented in this chapter. The utility of PSO has been addressed and the flaws in the algorithm have been recognized. The recent advancements and modifications of PSO in terms of its parameters are also discussed. Finally, its hybridization with other illustrious algorithms and applications in multiple disciplines and domains over the last decades are discussed. The motivation for all hybrid optimization techniques is examined for real-world challenges. It has been noticed that PSO can be hybridized with other algorithms and parallel applications.

Keywords: Particle swarm optimization, swarm intelligence, evolutionary arithmetic, intelligent agents, optimization, limitation of PSO, hybrid algorithms, metaheuristic search, applications of PSO system

*Corresponding author: msarwar@jmi.ac.in

Anita Khosla, Prasenjit Chatterjee, Ikbal Ali and Dheeraj Joshi (eds.) Optimization Techniques in Engineering: Advances and Applications, (95–114) © 2023 Scrivener Publishing LLC

6.1 Introduction

Optimizing of problems to get the desired results and benefits is one of the oldest techniques of humankind. Optimization is used in many disciplines, including physics, biology, engineering, economics, and business. The idea behind Optimization is to obtain the desired results or ultimate goals either by minimizing the efforts required or maximizing the desired results. The efforts required or desired benefits in any practical situations can be expressed as objective function with certain decision variables therefore Optimization can be defined as the process of finding the maxima or minima of function through the optimal conditions [1]. Optimization Techniques has discerned unprecedented advancements not only in the field of computational Intelligence but also in research operations, numerical analysis, mathematical economics, game and control theories and several other domains. While optimizing any problem three fundamental elements are taken care [2]. The first is objective function, which is to be maximized or minimized. The second element include the sets of variables, whose values need to be exploited to obtain the best solution out of objective functions. The third element being the number of constraints or the restrictions on the second element to get the optimal solution of the problems. Optimization include three important classes namely linear programming, nonlinear programming and stochastic programming, where in linear programming linear objective functions are maximized (or minimized) whose variables are sets of real numbers that are manipulated to satisfy the linear equalities and inequalities, whereas the objective functions and some of constraints of nonlinear programming includes complex numbers, products of variables or trigonometric functions with real number variables. While stochastic programming solve problems with random variables and optimal solution is obtained using probabilistic approach. There are, however, several cons and limitations of classical optimization techniques that only local optimal values can be located using them with problem in solving complex algorithms and discrete optimization problems, which has led to extensive studies and developments focusing on resolving the same.

In this chapter, an overview and developments of PSO with their applications in different domains are reported. Its significance and working mechanism along with the pseudo-code and flaws in algorithm are presented. The recent advancements and modifications of PSO over last two decades are also discussed with emphasis on its hybridization with other illustrious algorithms.

The rest of the chapter is organized sequentially as follows: Section 6.2 contains an overview and significance of Particle Swarm Optimization, Section 6.3 provides the information about the PSO algorithms and working mechanisms along with the pseudo-code, section 6.4 reviews the developments and modifications in PSO over the last decades, section 6.5 detail perspectives on hybridization of PSO with other illustrious algorithms, Section 6.6 presents the applications of PSO in different disciplines and domains and finally, section 6.7 concludes the chapter.

6.2   The Particle Swarm Optimization: An Overview

Nature has continually galvanized and impelled folks to unravel their complicated issues with unembellished techniques. Organisms who are behaviorally unsophisticated, perform their complicated task beside ease provides with one such inspiration. Species like ants, bees, and termites perform their all tasks like searching or gathering of food and building of complex structures by formation of swarms, whereas species of birds flock together and fish form schools to finish their works. The term swarms is employed to outline such teams and might vary in size from handful to millions. The rationale behind formation of swarms among these organisms is to unravel the matter by collective intelligence, which further coined the term swarm intelligence. Swarm intelligence refers to the property of system wherever collective behaviors of unsophisticated agents, which belong to similar teams, act and coordinate in their native surroundings in such the way that makes solutions to troublesome tasks and helps in determination real-world issues. This can be created doably through many low-level objectives that once met result in aborning behavior from these ostensibly preposterous and insignificant singular agents.

The initial inspiration is derived from Reeves' introduction of particle systems in computer-based animation at Lucasfilm Ltd (1993) on the topic of modeling natural objects like clouds, fireplace, and water [3]. According to Reeves, such a model is accustomed and represents the dynamics and totally different kinds of natural environments and ready to replace classical surface, primarily based representations [1]. Later, in 1986, for the first time, flocking behavior of birds was simulated on computer by Craig Reynolds. The Boid Model describes the low-level behavior of boids (bird-oid objects), which they follow to administer rise to aborning behavior [4]. One among the vital features of birds, that facilitate them in locating their food is vision. It is conjointly famous that birds have one amongst the foremost extremely developed sense of vision within the animal kingdom. Consequently, the developed vision owing to larger eye size and its alignment with head provide them a large space read, for instance, pigeons will see three hundred degrees while not turning their heads, that facilitate them in their strategies. The best food searching strategies to follow the nearest bird when one does not have prior knowledge of food locations. The flying bird continually changes its positions and velocity looking on previous expertise and feedback from neighbours. As a result, Reynolds put together three unique rules of flocking for a particle to follow, which is known as cohesion, alignment, and separation in literature. Here, each solution is considered as bird and represented as "Particle" not "Points," the reason being velocity and acceleration are more appropriately applied to particles according to Kennedy and Eberhart. The cohesion principle permits particles to remain close the flock members and alignment and separation principle necessitate directional update and avoid occurrence of any collision between particles respectively. The case where every boid is aware of the whereabouts of each alternative boid has $O(n^\wedge)$ quality creating it computationally impossible. However, Reynolds propositioned a neighborhood model with data exchange among boids in a general vicinity, thereby reducing the quality to $O(n)$ and rushing up the algorithmic implementation [1].

The particle swarm optimization model was formally introduced by Russell Eberhart, an electrical engineer, along with James Kennedy, a social psychologist in 1995, which was an extension of Reynold's work. Particle swarm optimization is one the advance global optimization paradigms, which has gained its importance in the last two decades because of its simple representation and adjustable parameters that results in easy solving of complex multidimensional problems and still there is area for future advancements and enhancements.

6.3 PSO Algorithms and Pseudo-Code

6.3.1 PSO Algorithm

The PSO algorithm consists of a swarm of particles that seek optimal solution by multidimensional search and update its velocity and position. Here, each particle represents a potential solution, which is influenced by itself and neighbors. The feasible solutions in PSO algorithm are represented by (p1, p2, ... pn) and known as particles, whereas the population of feasible solutions or particles is known as swarm and represented by P (p1, p2, ... pn). These particles are uniformly distributed over space. The particle's update its previous position if the present position is better than former. The equation for updating particles' velocity and position is given by equation (6.1) and equation (6.2), respectively.

$$V_{id}(t+1) = V_{id}(t) + C_1 R_1 (p_{id}(t) - X_{id}(t)) + C_2 R_2 (p_{gd}(t) - X_{id}(t))$$
(6.1)

$$X_{id}(t+1) = X_{id}(t) + V_{id}(t+1)$$
(6.2)

where

- V_{id} represents the velocity of i_{th} particle in the d_{th} dimension, and t denotes the iteration counter.
- X_{id} represents the position of the i_{th} particle in the d_{th} dimension [present x].
- p_{id} represents the best position of ith particle in the d_{th} dimension in the past [pBest].
- P_{gd} represents the position of the global best particle of swarm [gBest].
- R_1 and R_2 are random numbers (n-dimensional vectors)
- C_1 and C_2 are called cognitive and social parameters respectively and known as weighting parameters.

The velocity update equation in equation (6.1) has following three principal parts:

i. The first term, $V_{id}(t)$ guarantees that there is no sudden change in the velocity of each particle and sometimes also referred as "habit," "inertia," or "momentum."

ii. The second term, $(p_{id}(t) - X_{id}(t))$, which is the "cognitive" part of the equation, represents the self-learning phenomenon of particle from their own experience.

iii. The third term, $(p_{gd}(t) - X_{id}(t))$, which is the "social" part of the equation, represents the group learning experience.

The working mechanism of the PSO algorithm can be summarized with the flowchart shown in Figure 6.1.

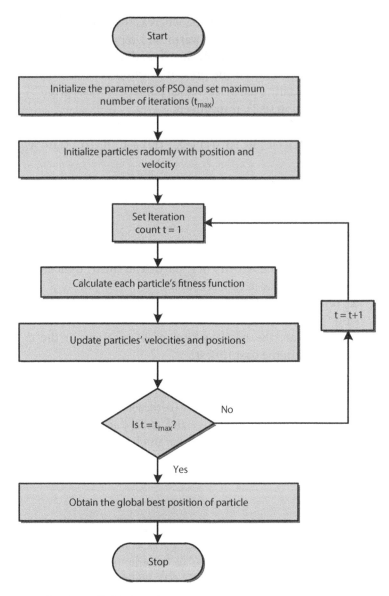

Figure 6.1 Flowchart of PSO algorithm.

6.3.2 Pseudo-Code for PSO

The PSO algorithm pseudo-code is as below:

For each particle (i)
   Initialize with position vectors (x_i) and velocity vectors (v_i)
End
Do
  For each particle (i)
  Calculate the value of fitness function (f)
  If the fitness function value is better than the individual particle best
fitness value (p_{best}) in history
   Set the current fitness value as p_{best}
  End
  Select the particle with the best fitness function value among all the
particles as the g_{best}
  For each particle (i)
  Update particle velocity (v_i)
  Update particle position (x_i)
  End for
  while maximum iteration or stopping criteria is achieved.

6.3.3 PSO Limitations

Although PSO proves to be an effective optimization technique in solving the complex problems, it has certain limitations too which are as follows:

a) PSO fails to figure if the matter illustration provides a transparent way to unambiguously outline what successive and former particle positions are to search within the solution area.

b) The original PSO fails to find the multiple optima, since the thought of original PSO was to regulate the swarm direction nearer to the swarm's world best particle to guide the whole swarm to converge to one optimum.

c) The original PSO assumes all particles of the whole swarm area unit utterly homogenous, and thus employs a similar worth settings of inertia weight, cognitive and social parameters for the whole swarm. This assumption, however, ignores the interior variations among birds of a similar swarm in reality, like ages, catching skills, flying experiences, and muscles' stretching. It conjointly neglects the relative flying position at intervals the swarm.

6.4   Advancements in PSO and Its Perspectives

Since the introduction of PSO in 1995, the algorithm of PSO has been through numerous extensions and improvements in order to achieve the ultimate goal and lessen the shortcomings of the process by making it convergent and improving diversity.

Some of the areas of extension are:

6.4.1   Inertia Weight

When the initial velocity is zero, the particles' initialization is critical in reaching the optima. Although the pBest and gBest intelligently help in searching the neighbourhood of the initial centre but they do not participate in exploration of new regions in the space search [1]. The velocity of swarm particles helps to achieve these goals but still need appropriate clamps on the velocity to avoid the divergence of the particles. There is also need of selecting suitable maximum velocity Vmax to ensure the control as inappropriate selection can further lead to serval uncertainty. Therefore an "inertia weight" w is suggested as a controlling variable for the swarm particle's velocity by Shi and Eberhart [5], henceforth making the modulation of particles' momentum possible by using constant, linear time-varying dependencies [6]. But inertia weight is not the complete solution and still urge for velocity clamping [7]. Therefore, in order to maintain the equilibrium between exploration and exploitation, the values of inertia weights should be chosen with care. However, the value of inertia weight equal or greater than one can result into swarm divergence whereas the values less than one can reduce the acceleration of swarm [1]. A constant value was used during early works on the inertia weight for entire iterations but subsequent improvements has made possible to use the dynamically changing values for the same.

Following are some of the efforts to dynamically change the inertia weight.

6.4.1.1   Random Selection (RS)

The selection of inertia weight in each iteration is possibly done from an underlying distribution with standard and mean deviation of choice [1]. However, convergent behavior of the particles must be taken care.

6.4.1.2   Linear Time Varying (LTV)

The LTV inertia weight can be expressed by equation (6.3) [8, 9]:

$$w_t = ((w_{max} - w_{min})\,(t_{max} - t)/t_{max}) + w_{max} \qquad (6.3)$$

where

- t represents the current iteration
- w_t represents the value of inertia weight in the t-the iteration
- t_{max} represents no. of iterations

According to the standard convention, wmax and wmin as 0.9 and 0.4, respectively.

6.4.1.3   Nonlinear Time Varying (NLTV)

The nonlinear time varying inertia weight proposed by Naka *et al.* is given by equation (6.4) [10]:

$$w_{(t+1)} = (w_t - 0.4)\,(t_{max} - t)/t_{max} + 0.4 \qquad (6.4)$$

where $w_{t=0} = 0.9$ is the initial choice of w

However, the relative improvement concept of the swarm in developing an adaptive inertia weight was introduced by Clerc [11], where the relative improvement k_t^i is estimated by equation (6.5):

$$k_t^i = f(lbest_t^t) - f(x_t^t)/\,f(lbest_t^t) + f(x_t^t) \qquad (6.5)$$

Inertia weight, updated by Clerc, can be expressed by equation (6.6):

$$w_{(t-1)} = w_0 + (w_{tmax} - w_0)\,(e^{mi(t)} - 1/\,e^{mi(t)} + 1) \qquad (6.6)$$

where $w_{tmax} = 0.5$ and $w_0 < 1$.

6.4.1.4   Fuzzy Adaptive (FA)

By the use of fuzzy sets and membership rules, dynamically updates in inertia weight can be done as in [12].

6.4.2   Constriction Factors

Constriction co-efficient was developed by Clerc from eigenvalue analyses of computational swarm dynamics [13]. Therefore, the velocity update equation changes to as given in equation (6.7):

$$vx[][] = \lambda \times (vx[][] + \mu_1 \times rand(\ ) \times (p_{Best}[][] - presentx[][]$$

$$+ \mu_2 \times rand(\ ) \times (_{Best}[][g_{Best}] - presentx[][])) \qquad (6.7)$$

where λ is shown by equation (6.8):

$$\lambda = \frac{2v}{\left|2 - \mu - \sqrt{\mu(\mu - 4)}\right|} \qquad (6.8)$$

$$\mu = \mu_1 + \mu_2 \qquad (6.9)$$

Note: μ_1 and μ_2 given in by equation (6.9) can be divided as products of social and cognitive acceleration coefficient, which is C_1 and C_2 times the random noise r_1 and r_2.

6.4.3   Topologies

As the term suggests, it is a measure of the degree of connectivity of swarm particles to one another. There are two topologies related to original PSO that led to two different algorithms: local Best (lBest) PSO and Global Best (gBest) PSO. In lBest PSO structure, there is multiple best particles, which consequently led to multiple social attractor that create the condition, where swarm is attracted to a group of subswarm bests instead of being attracted to single global best [1]. In gbest structure, all the swarm particles simultaneously influence the social component of velocity update which results into increase of convergent speed and a potential stagnation to local optima in case the true global optima are not where the best particle of the neighbourhood is.

6.4.4   Analysis of Convergence

Below is the review of constraints for convergence of the swarm to an equilibrium point. Van den Bergh, Engelbrecht and Trelea acknowledged the parameters for the convergence of an individual particle's trajectory. The condition is given by equation (6.10) [14–16].

$$1 > w > \frac{\mu_1 + \mu_2}{2} - 1 > 0 \qquad (6.10)$$

The stochastic factors given in equation (6.10) can be replaced with the acceleration coefficients C_1 and C_2 as presented in equation (6.11) to simplify the above equation.

$$1 > w > \left(\frac{C_1 + C_2}{2} \right) - 1 > 0 \qquad (6.11)$$

6.5   Hybridization of PSO

The hybridization of PSO with evolutionary algorithms has helped in overcoming the weakness of traditional methods and also helped in achieving the optimal goal of intelligent exploration-exploitation. Hybrid PSO algorithms is growing fast and gaining its importance in the field. Following are some of the notable works under this:

6.5.1   PSO Hybridization with Artificial Bee Colony (ABC)

The artificial bee colony (ABC) is one of the optimization techniques based on the intelligent behaviors of honey bee swarm in search of food which was proposed by Dervis Karaboga and Basturk [17]. In 2010, an integrated model based on parallel working of PSO and ABC algorithms was proposed by Shi *et al.* by exchanging information between the colony of bee and swarm particles [18]. The author El-Abd proposed a hybrid ABC-SPSO algorithm for continuous function optimization in 2011 [19], in which he combined the artificial bee colony with standard particle swarm optimization for updating the personal best in Standard PSO using ABC at each iteration and further applied it in continuous optimization. Xiang *et al.* in 2014 introduced a particle swarm inspired multielitist artificial bee colony algorithm for real parameters optimization, i.e., to enhance the strategy of exploitation of artificial bee colony by modification of food source parameters for spectators [20]. Vitorino *et al.* used a mechanism based on artificial bee colony to generate diversity in particle swarm optimization [21].

Lin and Hsieh [22] came up with the hybrid evolutionary algorithms working on the principle of an endocrine-based particle swarm optimization and artificial bee colony algorithms for classification of medical datasheet using SVMs. Zhou and Yang [23] proposed PSO-DE-PABC and PSO-DE-GABC based on particle swarm optimization, differential evolution and artificial bee colony to overcome the drawbacks of ABC. There are several other proposed models developed by different authors in hybridization of PSO and ABC and still the work for its extension is continued.

6.5.2 PSO Hybridization with Ant Colony Optimization (ACO)

Ant colony optimization (ACO) was proposed by Marco Dorigo in 1991 based on the idea of ant colonies use to communicate among them [24]. In later years, for improved continuous optimization, Shelokar *et al.* introduced particle swarm and ant colony optimization [25], in which the algorithm's first part works with PSO to generate initial solutions, while the positions updates of the particles are done by ACO in the next part. The strategy proved to give almost optima for highly nonconvex problems. Kaveh *et al.* came up with a particle swarm ant colony optimization for truss structure with discrete variables, which later on proved to be a fast algorithm with high convergence speed [26, 27]. On the other hand, Niknam and Amiri [28] introduced a combined efficient approach with fuzzy adaptive PSO, Ant Colony Optimization and the K-Means for clustering analysis and obtained improvement.

Chen *et al.* [29] proposed a genetic simulated annealing ant colony system with particle swarm optimization techniques for solving the travelling salesman problems. Mandloi *et al.* [30] presented a hybrid algorithm infused with a novel probabilistic search method by integrating the distance search approach practiced by ants in reaching the food and returning back to their colonies (ACO) and velocity-oriented search mechanism adopted by swarm particles in PSO, thereby replacing the pheromone update of ACO with velocity update of PSO. The algorithm uses sigmoid function to obtain heuristic values from transformation of distance and velocity thereby ensuring less complexity, fast convergence and avoidance of stagnation in local optima [1]. There are further many works acknowledge by various authors in its expansion by the time.

6.5.3 PSO Hybridization with Genetic Algorithms (GA)

Hybridization of PSO and GA can be done using two perspectives, the first being in parallel and the other sequentially. Yet another way is to use GA operators, such as reproduction, mutation, as well as selection within the PSO framework [1]. Robinson *et al.* [31] employed different terminating criterion and a single algorithm to reach there then uses the final solution in other algorithm for the purpose of fine tuning. The condition when one algorithm fails to improve upon past results over a selected number of iterations, they also used a switching method between algorithms. Yang *et al.* [32] introduced a PSO-GA based hybrid evolutionary algorithm, where the process of evolution of particles is spur by PSO and diversity is maintained by GA. The author used this method to optimize three constrained and three unconstrained problems. Valdez *et al.* proposed an evolutionary method combining GA and PSO using fuzzy logic for decision making [33]. Benvidi *et al.* [34] introduced spectrophotometric determination of synthetic colorants using PSO-GA-ANN. Similarly various works have been recorded in this domain by hybridization of particle swarm optimization and genetic algorithms.

There are several other metaheuristic algorithms which by hybridization with PSO give popular and effective solutions for solving global optimization problems. Some of the other approaches are as follows

- Hybridization of PSO Using Differential Evolution.
- Hybridization of PSO Using Simulated Annealing.
- Hybridization of PSO Using Cuckoo Search.

Some other familiar techniques include artificial immune systems (AIS), bat algorithm (BA), firefly algorithm (FA), glow worm swarm optimization (GSO), etc.

6.6   Area of Applications of PSO

PSO has found its application in almost every field as the need to attend the optima is always required is each process. The growing importance of PSO has also urged the chance of improvements and extensions. By the time PSO has been evolved with many other developments and in parallel with other algorithms and has modified its structure, resulting into better results.

In 2002, PSO-GA and GA-PSO algorithms were introduced by Robinson *et al.* in the area of engineering design optimization [31] and life cycle model by Krink and Lovbjerg for unconstrained global optimization [35], as well as SMNE by Conradie *et al.* in neural networks applications [36]. Grimaldi *et al.* introduced GSO for electromagnetic applications in 2004 [37]. By the time the authors had found the applications of GA-PSO in feature selection, spectrophotometric determination of synthetic colorants, estimation of energy demand and for constrained optimization [38–40]. While the area of unconstrained global optimization has found SDEA and DEPSO useful [41, 42]. DEPSO algorithms has found it wide area of applications as acknowledged by many authors in rigid-body multimodal image registration [43], linear phase FIR filter design [44], power dispatch [45], clustering [46], mobile robot localization [47], PID controller [48], photovoltaic power generation [49], and transmission expansion planning [50]. SA-PSO has also gained its importance in the field of global optimization [51], dynamic optical power flow [52], non-linear model predictive control [53], k-mean clustering [54]. Luzzus *et al.* has introduced PSO+ACO application as interaction parameters on phase equilibria in 2016 [55].

A different algorithm has been used with modification and improvement in the same field to minimize the weakness and maximize the outcome with ease. Several hybrid models have been tested in different domain to get favourable results and have been proven successful making it more explorable in order to get better outcomes. Further applications of PSO for different problems are listed in Table 6.1.

Table 6.1 Applications of PSO.

Area of Applications	Algorithms	Author(s)
Medical image registration	PSO-BA	Manoj *et al.* [56]
Multiobjective vehicle routing problem	PS-ABC	Sedighizadeh and Mazaheripour [57]
Real parameter optimization	PS-MEABC	Xiang *et al.* [20]
Linear phase multiband stop filters	ICSP ICSPSO	Dash *et al.* [58]
Artificial neural network	PSOCS	Chen *et al.* [59]
Travelling salesman problem	PSO, ACO and K-Opt Algorithm	Indadual *et al.* [60]
Hybrid clustering	TAPC	Xiong and Wang [61]
Truss structure with discrete variable	DHPSACO	Kaveh and Talatahari [26]
Job-shop scheduling	Hybrid PSO with SA operator	Ge *et al.* [62]
Unconstrained global optimization	Breading Swarm	Settles and Soule [63]

6.7   Conclusions

Optimization techniques have found its applications and modification accordingly by-passing time and have given the desired results. In this chapter, the inspiration behind optimization of any technique has been discussed, along with evolution of swarm intelligence and algorithm in real-life problems. The importance of PSO in different fields and its improvements in term of social and cognitive parameters, inertia weight and convergence have also been the focus. The perspectives of hybridization of PSO with different algorithms and its work with parallel applications have also been highlighted. Applications of PSO in different domains are noted and various hybrid models of PSO have been shown. There are certain limitations to the reported methods which need to be improved and provides area for future expansions. For example, the improvements in multidimensional optimization problems and the sensitivities of constraints variables can be done to overcome the limitations.

References

1. Saptarshi, S., Basak, S., Peters, R.A., Particle swarm optimization: A survey of historical and recent developments with hybridization perspectives. *Mach. Learn. Knowl. Extr.*, 1, 157–191, 2018.
2. Wright, S.J., Optimization, in: *Encyclopedia Britannica*, 2021.
3. Reeves, W.T., Particle systems—A technique for modelling a class of fuzzy objects. *ACM Trans. Graph.*, 2, 91–108, 1983.
4. Reynolds, C.W., Flocks, herds, and schools: A distributed behavioral model. *ACM Comput. Graph.*, 21, 25–34, 1987.
5. Shi, Y. and Eberhart, R.C., Parameter selection in particle swarm optimization. *International Conference on Computation Programming VII*, 1998.
6. Shi, Y. and Eberhart, R., A modified particle swarm optimizer. *IEEE International Conference on Evolutionary Computation Proceedings, IEEE World Congress on Computational Intelligence*, pp. 69–73, 1998.
7. Eberhart, R.C. and Shi, Y., Particle swarm optimization: Developments, applications and resources. *IEEE Congress on Evolutionary Computation*, vol. 1, pp. 27–30, 2001.
8. Suganthan, P.N., Particle swarm optimizer with neighborhood operator. *IEEE Congress on Evolutionary Computation*, pp. 1958–1962, 1999.
9. Ratnaweera, A., Halgamuge, S., Watson, H., Particle swarm optimization with self-adaptive acceleration coefficients. *International Conference on Fuzzy Systems and Knowledge Discovery*, pp. 264–268, 2003.

10. Naka, S., Genji, T., Yura, T., Fukuyama, Y., Practical distribution state estimation using hybrid particle swarm optimization. *IEEE Power Engineering Society Winter Meeting*, vol. 2, pp. 815–820, 2001.

11. Clerc, M., *Think Locally, Act Locally: The Way of Life of Cheap-PSO, an Adaptive PSO*, 2001. (http://clerc.maurice.free.fr/pso)

12. Shi, Y. and Eberhart, R.C., Fuzzy adaptive particle swarm optimization. *IEEE Congress on Evolutionary Computation*, vol. 1, pp. 101–106, 2001.

13. Clerc, M. and Kennedy, J., The particle swarm-explosion, stability and convergence in a multidimensional complex space. *IEEE Trans. Evol. Comput.*, 6, 58–73, 2002.

14. van den Bergh, F., *An Analysis of Particle Swarm Optimizers*, Ph.D. Thesis, Department of Computer Science, 2002.

15. van den Bergh, F. and Engelbrecht, A.P., A study of particle swarm optimization particle trajectories. *Inf. Sci.*, 176, 937–971, 2006.

16. Trelea, I.C., The particle swarm optimization algorithm: Convergence analysis and parameter selection. *Inf. Process. Lett.*, 85, 317–325, 2003.

17. Karaboga, D. and Basturk, B., A powerful and efficient algorithm for numerical function optimization: Artificial bee colony (ABC) algorithm. *J. Glob. Optim.*, 39, 459–471, 2007.

18. Shi, X., Li, Y., Li, H., Guan, R., Wang, L., Liang, Y., An integrated algorithm based on artificial bee colony and particle swarm optimization. *International Conference on Natural Computation (ICNC)*, vol. 5, pp. 2586–2590, 2010.

19. El-Abd, M., A hybrid ABC-SPSO algorithm for continuous function optimization. *IEEE Symposium on Swarm Intelligence*, pp. 1–6, 2011.

20. Xiang, Y., Peng, Y., Zhong, Y., Chen, Z., Lu, X., Zhong, X., A particle swarm inspired multi-elitist artificial bee colony algorithm for real-parameter optimization. *Comput. Optim. Appl.*, 57, 493–516, 2014.

21. Vitorino, L.N., Ribeiro, S.F., Bastos-Filho, C.J., A mechanism based on artificial bee colony to generate diversity in particle swarm optimization. *Neurocomputing*, 148, 39–45, 2015.

22. Lin, K. and Hsieh, Y., Classification of medical datasets using SVMs with hybrid evolutionary algorithms based on endocrine based particle swarm optimization and artificial bee colony algorithms. *J. Med. Syst.*, 39, 119, 2015.

23. Zhou, F. and Yang, Y., An improved artificial bee colony algorithm based on particle swarm optimization and differential evolution, in: *International Conference on Intelligent Computing Theories and Methodologies*, Springer International Publishing, pp. 24–35, 2015.

24. Colorni, A., Dorigo, M., Maniezzo, V., Distributed optimization by ant colonies. *Première Conférence Européenne sur la vie Artificielle*, Elsevier Publishing, pp. 134–142, 1991.

25. Shelokar, P.S., Siarry, P., Jayaraman, V.K., Kulkarni, B.D., Particle swarm and ant colony algorithms hybridized for improved continuous optimization. *Appl. Math. Comput.*, 188, 129–142, 2007.

26. Kaveh, A. and Talatahari, S., A particle swarm ant colony optimization for truss structures with discrete variables. *J. Constr. Steel Res.*, 65, 1558–1568, 2009.

27. Kaveh, A. and Talatahari, S., Particle swarm optimizer, ant colony strategy and harmony search scheme hybridized for optimization of truss structures. *Comput. Struct.*, 87, 267–283, 2009.

28. Niknam, T. and Amiri, B., An efficient hybrid approach based on PSO, ACO and k-means for cluster analysis. *Appl. Soft. Comput.*, 10, 183–197, 2010.

29. Chen, S.M. and Chien, C., Solving the traveling salesman problem based on the genetic simulated annealing ant colony system with particle swarm optimization techniques. *Exp. Syst. Appl.*, 38, 14439–14450, 2011.

30. Mandloi, M. and Bhatia, V., A low-complexity hybrid algorithm based on particle swarm and ant colony optimization for large-MIMO detection. *Exp. Syst. Appl.*, 50, 66–74, 2016.

31. Robinson, J., Sinton, S., Rahmat-Samii, Y., Particle swarm, genetic algorithm, and their hybrids: Optimization of a profiled corrugated horn antenna. *IEEE Antennas and Propagation Society International Symposium and URSI National Radio Science Meeting*, vol. 1, pp. 314–317, 2002.

32. Yang, B., Chen, Y., Zhao, Z., A hybrid evolutionary algorithm by combination of PSO and GA for unconstrained and constrained optimization problems. *IEEE International Conference on Control and Automation*, pp. 166–170, 2007.

33. Valdez, F., Melin, P., Castillo, O., Evolutionary method combining particle swarm optimization and genetic algorithms using fuzzy logic for decision making. *IEEE International Conference on Fuzzy Systems*, pp. 2114–2119, 2009.

34. Benvidi, A., Abbasi, S., Gharaghani, S., Tezerjani, M.D., Masoum, S., Spectrophotometric determination of synthetic colorants using PSO-GA-ANN. *Food Chem.*, 220, 377–384, 2017.

35. Krink, T. and Løvbjerg, M., *The LifeCycle Model: Combining Particle Swarm Optimisation, Genetic Algorithms and HillClimbers*, pp. 621–630, 2002.

36. Conradie, E., Miikkulainen, R., Aldrich, C., Intelligent process control utilizing symbiotic memetic neuro-evolution, in: *Proceedings of the IEEE Congress on Evolutionary Computation*, vol. 1, pp. 623–628, 2002.

37. Grimaldi, E.A., Grimacia, F., Mussetta, M., Pirinoli, P., Zich, R.E., A new hybrid genetical—Swarm algorithm for electromagnetic optimization, in: *Proceedings of the International Conference on Computational Electromagnetics and its Applications*, pp. 157–160, 2004.

38. Ghamisi, P. and Benediktsson, J.A., Feature selection based on hybridization of genetic algorithm and particle swarm optimization. *IEEE Geos. Rem. Sens. Lett.*, 12, 309–313, 2015.

39. Yu, S., Wei, Y.-M., Wang, K.A., PSO–GA optimal model to estimate primary energy demand of China. *Ener. Polic.*, 42, 329–340, 2012.

40. Garg, H., A hybrid PSO-GA algorithm for constrained optimization problems. *Appl. Math. Comput.*, 274, 292–305, 2016.
41. Hendtlass, T., A Combined Swarm differential evolution algorithm for optimization problems, in: *Lecture Notes in Computer Science, Proceedings of 14th International Conference on Industrial and Engineering Applications of Artificial Intelligence and Expert Systems*, vol. 2070, Springer Verlag, pp. 11–18, 2001.
42. Zhang, W.J. and Xie, X.F., DEPSO: Hybrid particle swarm with differential evolution operator, in: *Proceedings of the IEEE International Conference on Systems, Man and Cybernetics (SMCC)*, pp. 3816–3821, 2003.
43. Talbi, H. and Batouche, M., Hybrid particle swarm with differential evolution for multimodal image registration. *IEEE International Conference on Industrial Technology*, vol. 3, pp. 1567–1573, 2004.
44. Luitel, B. and Venayagamoorthy, G.K., Differential evolution particle swarm optimization for digital filter design. *Congress on Evolutionary Computation (IEEE World Congress on Computational Intelligence)*, pp. 3954–3961, 2008.
45. Vaisakh, K., Sridhar, M., Linga Murthy, K.S., Differential evolution particle swarm optimization algorithm for reduction of network loss and voltage instability. *Proceedings of the IEEE World Congress on Nature and Biologically Inspired Computing*, Coimbatore, India, pp. 391–396, December 9–11, 2009.
46. Xu, R., Xu, J., Wunsch, D.C., Clustering with differential evolution particle swarm optimization. *IEEE Congress on Evolutionary Computation*, pp. 1–8, 2010.
47. Junfei, H., Liling, M.A., Yuandong, Y.U., Hybrid algorithm based mobile robot localization using DE and PSO. *International Conference on Control and Automation*, pp. 5955–5959, 2013.
48. Sahu, B.K., Pati, S., Panda, S., Hybrid differential evolution particle swarm optimization optimized fuzzy proportional–integral derivative controller for automatic generation control of interconnected power system. *IET Gen. Trans. Distr.*, 8, 1789–1800, 2014.
49. Seyedmahmoudian, M., Rahmani, R., Mekhilef, S., Oo, A.M.T., Stojcevski, A., Soon, T.K., Ghandhari, A.S., Simulation and hardware implementation of new maximum power point tracking technique for partially shaded PV system using hybrid DEPSO method. *IEEE Trans.Sust. Ener.*, 6, 850–862, 2015.
50. Gomes, P.V. and Saraiva, J.T., Hybrid discrete evolutionary PSO for AC dynamic transmission expansion planning. *IEEE International Energy Conference (ENERGYCON)*, 2016.
51. Shieh, H.-L., Kuo, C.-C., Chiang, C.-M., Modified particle swarm optimization algorithm with simulated annealing behavior and its numerical verification. *Appl. Math. Comput.*, 218, 4365–4383, 2011.
52. Niknam, T., Narimani, M.R., Jabbari, M., Dynamic optimal power flow using hybrid particle swarm optimization and simulated annealing. *Int. Trans. Elect. Ener. Syst.*, 23, 975–1001, 2013.

53. Sudibyo, S., Murat, M.N., Aziz, N., Simulated annealing particle swarm optimization (SA-PSO): Particle distribution study and application in neural wiener-based NMPC. *Asian Control Conference*, Kota Kinabalu, Malaysia, 2015.

54. Wang, X. and Sun, Q., The study of k-means based on hybrid SA-PSO algorithm. *9th International Symposium on Computational Intelligence and Design (ISCID)*, pp. 211–214, 2016.

55. Lazzus, J.A., Rivera, M., Salfate, I., Pulgar-Villarroel, G., Rojas, P., Application of particle swarm+ant colony optimization to calculate the interaction parameters on phase equilibria. *J. Engin. Therm.*, 25, 216–226, 2016.

56. Manoj, S., Ranjitha, S., Suresh, H.N., Hybrid BAT-PSO optimization techniques for image registration. *International Conference on Electrical, Electronics, and Optimization Techniques (ICEEOT)*, pp. 3590–3596, 2016.

57. Farmer, J.D., Packard, N.H., Perelson, A., The immune system, adaptation, and machine learning. *Phy. D: Nonlin. Phen.*, 22, 187–204, 1986.

58. Dash, J., Dam, B., Swain, R., Optimal design of linear phase multi-band stop filters using improved cuckoo search particle swarm optimization. *Appl. Sof. Comput.*, 52, 435–445, 2017.

59. Chen, J.F., Do, Q.H., Hsieh, H.N., Training artificial neural networks by a hybrid PSO-CS algorithm. *Algorithms*, 8, 292–308, 2015.

60. Indadul, K., Maiti, M.K., Maiti, M., Coordinating particle swarm optimization, ant colony optimization and k-opt algorithm for traveling salesman problem. *Third International Conference International Conference on Mathematics and Computing*, Springer, pp. 103–119, 2017.

61. Xiong, W. and Wang, C., A novel hybrid clustering based on adaptive ACO and PSO. *International Conference on Computer Science and Service System (CSSS)*, pp. 1960–1963, 2011.

62. Ge, H., Du, W., Qian, F., A hybrid algorithm based on particle swarm optimization and simulated annealing for a periodic job shop scheduling. *Third International Conference on Natural Computation*, pp. 715–719, 2007.

63. Settles, M. and Soule, T., Breeding swarms: A GA/PSO hybrid. *Genetic and Evolutionary Computation Conference*, pp. 161–168, 2005.

## 7

Application of Genetic Algorithm in Sensor Networks and Smart Grid

Geeta Yadav[1]*, Dheeraj Joshi[2], Leena G.[1] and M. K. Soni[1]

[1]Department of Electrical Engineering, Manav Rachna International Institute of Research and Studies, Faridabad, India
[2]Department of Electrical Engineering, Delhi Technical University, Delhi, India

Abstract

This chapter describes the usage of genetic algorithms (GAs) in multiple real-time applications. The subarea of wireless sensor networks is explored with the help of a GA to get the best possible trajectory planning. Along with that, another major application of the smart grid is used to get a deeper understanding of GA optimization strategy to get the best possible reliability and availability of micro-grids. After characterizing the kind of different strategies motivating this approach, a brief overview of the GA is present. Three major approaches to using GA for optimum deployment of wireless sensor networks and reliability/availability assessment of microgrid is explained in detail along with some sample programs. Finally, the assessment of the strength and weaknesses of these approaches to these two major applications is provided. The area of genetic operators, fitness function, and hybrid algorithms are discussed concerning these applications. The optimization discussed with meta-heuristic, cross-over, mutation, and selection, variant of the GA along evolution using GAs.

Keywords: Wireless sensor networks, genetic algorithm, smart grid, reliability, availability

7.1 Introduction

This chapter describes the coverage and uniformity as subfields of sensor networks and energy-efficient sensor networks that actively explore the

---
*Corresponding author: gt.yadav@gmail.com

Anita Khosla, Prasenjit Chatterjee, Ikbal Ali and Dheeraj Joshi (eds.) Optimization Techniques in Engineering: Advances and Applications, (115–138) © 2023 Scrivener Publishing LLC

use of genetic algorithms (GAs) as a key element in designing deployment strategies and routing protocols. In addition, this chapter covers the reliability and availability subfields of using GAs in smart microgrid policy design. After describing the different types of methods used to assess reliability, availability in microgrid, and the uniformity and coverage of sensor networks that drive this approach, a brief overview of GAs is given [1]. Two main applications of using GAs in various fields are described, and examples of their use through programs are given. Finally, the advantages and disadvantages of this approach to deploying sensor networks and smart grids are evaluated. Science, engineering, and business are among the common fields that use GAs mostly. The GA idea has been carried out to lots of engineering problems, together with navy packages for surveillance of enemy forces, surveillance of pleasant forces and equipment, navy theater or battlefield surveillance, goal location, fight harm assessment, chemical, biological, radiological, and nuclear (CBRN) assault detection, and many more. It may be utilized in environmental packages like microclimates, wooded area hearthplace detection, flood detection, and precision agriculture. Among different things, those may be utilized in fitness packages for far-flung tracking of physiological data, monitoring, and tracking of medical doctors and sufferers in hospitals, medicinal drug management, and aged assistance. It may be applied in domestic software like domestic robots, instrumented weather, automatic meter perusing or commercial enterprise programs for weather manipulation in cutting-edge locations of commercial enterprise, inventory manipulation, automobile following and location, site visitors move reconnaissance, and so forth [2].

7.2   Communication Sector

7.2.1   Sensor Networks

The wireless sensor networks are the monitoring devices used to monitor or sense information and then process and communicate with another connected node in the network in a small amount of time [3]. A single sensing mote includes transceiver, microcontroller, external memory, power source, and multiple converters and sensors. Sensors are hardware devices that produce measurable responses to change in any physical condition like temperature, moisture, pressure, stress, strain, etc. Sensors sense the physical data of the area to be monitored. These analog signals can be changed to digital using converters. These wireless sensing nodes are randomly deployed to the application field by airdropping [4]. These sensors can be randomly deployed and multiple deployment schemes are employed to arrange them uniformly in the field so that optimum data can be collected from these sensors and accurate actions have been done in multiple applications like in agriculture to get the knowledge of the moisture of soil, in military applications to monitor inimical forces, military-theater or battlefield surveillance, targeting, battle damage assessment, nuclear, biological, and chemical attack detection, and environment applications like microclimate, forest fire detection, flood detection, and health applications like remote monitoring of physiological data, tracking and monitoring of doctors and patients inside a hospital, drug administration, and home appliances like home automation, automated meter reading, and commercial applications like environment control in industrial and office buildings, inventory control, vehicle tracking and detection, traffic flow surveillance, etc.

After random deployment, these sensors have to do movement using distributed self-spreading algorithm. The force which moves the nodes is received from the nearest node and the field area is also fixed. These nodes move based on two criteria: stable status limit and oscillation limited. The nodes should be optimally distributed based on expected density, stability check, and oscillation checks to place the node in the correct location to share the correct data. The problem is getting the optimum deployment of these sensing nodes to get optimal coverage and uniformity in minimum time and consuming minimum energy.

The challenges and hurdles of wireless sensor networks are deployment, network lifetime, communication bandwidth, scalability, and power management. There are multiple issues with the wireless sensor networks, these are problems with the size, limited functional capabilities, power factors, node cost, environment factors, transmission channel factors, topology management complexity and node distribution, standard versus proprietary solutions, scalability concerns, etc. The quality of communication and quality of service is optimized here using the best deployment and network lifetime. These points are best solved using a GA.

7.3   Electrical Sector

7.3.1   Smart Microgrid

The smart microgrid adds digital, control, advanced operations, and resources to the electrical grid. A lot of changes are needed in the existing legacy electrical grid by adding renewable resources from generation to adding smart appliances at consumption along with the addition of new technologies, like IoT, scheduling, cronjobs, etc. The smart grid needs to be energy efficient, reliable, and secure same as the existing electrical grid with the new changes as new technologies and optimizations. This two-way flow of information enhances the need for a wireless sensor network on the transmission and distribution side. The technology applied for the smart grid is still in the process of implementation. There are a lot of challenges to its implementation like the two-way flow of information, adding renewable resources, adding smart appliances at the consumer side, reliable and cost-effective way of the flow of information, self-healing, etc. The communication n is a leading component within n smart grid optimizing the use of electrical energy from financial perspective and reliability of systems.

The idea to replace the existing system with a new improved optimized smart power grid infrastructure rejuvenates multiple challenges and threats to effectively integrate smartness without impacting the use of the existing grid. The various indices for visualizing the performance of the integrated system are energy-efficient system reliability, security, and flexibility. A protocol for the smart grid needs to be designed which manages demand and supply as per customer needs and the use of renewable energy. Markov process and Poisson's method can be used for two-way communication and the educing average cost of energy production at the main grid. The electricity generation at the consumer end from renewable sources is stored in batteries and used when required and sent back to the main grid if excess. The average cost of power production is calculated, and appropriate action is suggested to increase the efficiency of the entire system. In this chapter, the two main areas considered as performance indices are energy efficiency reliability and availability of smart microgrid using GAs.

7.4   A Brief Outline of GAs

Many AI problems can be viewed as searching a space of legal alternatives for the best solution one can find within reasonable time and space limitations. Path planning for data flow from deployed wireless sensor networks in the control center and move selection to gather maximum information in military and agriculture applications are familiar examples. What is required for such problems are techniques for rapid location of high-quality solutions in search spaces of sufficient size and complexity to rule out any guarantees of optimality? When sufficient knowledge about such search spaces is available a priori, one can usually exploit that knowledge to develop problem-specificity strategies capable of rapidly locating "satisficing" solutions. If, however, such a priori knowledge is unavailable, acceptable solutions are typically only achieved by dynamically accumulating information about the problem and using that knowledge to control the search process. Problems of this character are not hard to find. Optimum deployment of wireless sensor networks in multiple applications is an unstructured environment and applications whose strategies involve identifying and exploiting the characteristics of any party are excellent examples. Inferring an acceptable set of classification rules from training examples without a significant amount of domain knowledge is a familiar example from classical learning problems.

GAs are global optimization techniques developed by John Holland in 1975. They are one of several techniques in the family of evolutionary algorithms—algorithms that search for solutions to optimization problems by evolving better and better solutions. A GA begins with a population of solutions and then chooses parents to reproduce. During reproduction, each parent is copied, and then parents may combine in an analog to natural cross-breeding, or the copies may be modified, in an analog to a genetic mutation. The new solutions are evaluated and added to the population, and low-quality solutions are deleted from the population to make room for new solutions. As this process of parent selection, copying, crossbreeding, and mutation is repeated, the members of the population tend to get better. When the algorithm is halted, the best member of the current population is taken as the solution to the problem posed.

One critical feature of a GA is its procedure for selecting population members to reproduce. Selection is a random process but a solution member's quality biases its probability of being chosen. Because GAs promote the reproduction of high-quality solutions, they explore neighboring solutions in high-quality parts of the solution search space. Because the process is randomized, a GA also explores parts of the search space that may be far from the best individuals currently in the production. In the last 20 years, GAs has been used to solve a wide range of optimization problems. There are many examples of optimization problems in the electronics and electrical industries for which GAs are well suited. In sensor networks, in addition to the deployment of WSNs, coverage calculation, uniformity, network lifetime, energy efficiency optimization, device scheduling, and facilities design have been addressed with GAs. In the electrical sector, GAs have been used in reliability evaluation, availability evaluation, cost optimization, usage of renewable resources optimization, and controlling demand/supply balance while satisfying failure rate and repair rate constraints.

7.5   Sensor Network's Energy Optimization

The wireless sensor organization (WSN) is made out of an assortment of sensor hubs, which are little energy compelled gadgets. Wireless sensor network has been broadly utilized in the field of climate checking, military and shrewd home, and so on. WSNs can be used to monitor physical phenomena over a large geographical area with acceptable accuracy and dependability. Temperature, pressure, humidity, salinity, metallic items, and motion are all monitored by the sensors. Deployment, network longevity, communication bandwidth, scalability, and power management are all issues with sensor networks. One of the most essential problems is energy efficiency for extending network lifetime [3]. Sensor nodes are likely to be battery-powered, and changing or charging the batteries for these nodes can be tricky. The challenge of extending the network lifetime of these nodes is essential. Topology control is the most efficient way to utilize the energy of sensor nodes while also extending the network lifetime.

This chapter discusses an energy-efficient technique for obtaining data between sensor nodes and communicative nodes for transmission to the base station. The major goal is to extend the network's lifetime and maintain a balanced energy consumption among nodes. To limit the amount of data sent to the base station, localized information is employed, as well as data fusion.

The assumptions are:

- Each node regularly observes its immediate surroundings and wishes to relay its data to a base station at a fixed location.
- Sensor nodes are homogenous and have a limited amount of energy.
- Both the sensor nodes and the base station are at rest position.

The distributed approach is used to describe an energy-efficient strategy for wireless sensor networks. The goal is to send all of the data to the base station as quickly as possible so that the network's lifetime is maximized in terms of rounds, where a round is defined as the process of collecting all of the data from sensor nodes and sending it to the base station, regardless of how long it takes [3]. Direct transmission is a straightforward solution to this problem, in which each node sends its data to the base station. If the base station is too far away, however, the cost of transferring data to it becomes too high, and the nodes will quickly perish.

Two elegant methods, the low-energy adaptive clustering hierarchy (LEACH) and Power-Efficient Gathering in Sensor Information Systems (PEGASIS) [5], were proposed to tackle this problem. The main goal of LEACH is to limit the number of nodes that communicate with the base station directly. The protocol accomplishes this by self-organizing a small number of clusters, each of which receives data from nodes in its cluster, fuses it, and delivers the result to the base station. When compared to straight transmission, LEACH exploits randomness in the cluster-head selection and produces up to an 8× improvement. PEGASIS takes it a step further and reduces the number of nodes talking directly with the base station to one by constructing a chain that connects all nodes and allows each node to receive and transmit data from the nearest available neighbor. Starting at each endpoint of the chain, data is collected until the randomized endpoint is reached. Each time the data passes from one node to the next, it is fused. The final data must be transmitted to the base station via the specified head node. A new protocol is explained and optimized using a GA that integrates the ideas of both LEACH and PEGASIS protocols. This technique extends the network's total lifespan significantly.

Initially, N nodes are randomly dispersed in a 100×100 region. In this area, there are now five clusters. Starting with the farthest node, a chain is constructed. A distinct chain is produced in each cluster. The first layer chain generated within the cluster members is used to transmit data within the clusters. The farthest node in the chain initiates data transmission in each cycle of communication for data collecting. Except for the farthest node in the chain, data fusion is conducted at each node. Each node takes data from one of its neighbors, fuses it with its own, and sends it to the next node in the chain. This is done for each of the chains that form within each of the clusters. After the data has been collected at the cluster heads, the data is not sent directly to the base station as it is in LEACH. However, the data from the cluster heads in the chain is sent to the cluster heads' leader node once more. The data is transmitted to the base station by each cluster head in turn. The formula (r mod n) is used to choose a leader among the cluster heads, where r is the number of rounds and n is the total number of cluster heads. This selection is made in each round, decreasing the cluster heads' energy dissipation. When the residual energy of any of the cluster heads falls below K^*E in each round of communication, it broadcasts within its chain to find a replacement, with the node with the highest residual energy in that cluster becoming the new cluster head and the previous cluster-head becoming a normal node in the chain. This is done to prevent a node with the least amount of leftover energy from becoming a cluster-head. In this study, we defined network lifetime as the number of rounds until the first node dies [6].

The pseudocode is explained below:

1. Initially, 100 random nodes are selected and the base station is located far away around 2 times away from the location of nodes.
2. Starting from the farthest node, five clusters are constructed, with chains forming inside each cluster.
3. The transformer and receiver circuitry of a radio dissipates 50nJ/bit. For transformer amplifier, a radio dissipates $(100 \text{ pJ/bit/m})^2$. The packet length is 2000 bits, and k is the length of the packet. The cost of data dispersion is 5 nJ/bit/message. Every node has initial energy of 0.25 J. The bare minimum of energy is necessary to maintain an active node. Energy is calculated in joules in the below equation [1].

$$E_e = (2 \times 50 \times 10^{(-9)} \times 2000) + (100 \times 10^{(-12)} \times 100)$$

$$+ (5 \times 10^{(-9)} \times 2000) \tag{7.1}$$

4. Then header node is selected in step 4. Header node should have energy greater than or equal to k × Es; here k=0.5
5. Selection of leader nodes from cluster heads.
6. Deletion of the dead node. Display the number of runs when 1st node, 20 nodes, 50 nodes, or 100 nodes failure occurs.

Starting from step 1, hundred nodes are randomly deployed to a 100 × 100 square meter area where the base station is located 100 meters away at (50,100) meters as shown in Figure 7.1. WSNs have been simulated using randomly distributed hundred node networks to test the performance of a network lifespan.

In a 100 m × 100 m field, the base station is located at (50,300). The radio model utilized is the same as the LEACH protocol. Radio in this model uses E_{elec} = 50 nJ/bit to power the transmitter and receiving electronics, and E_{amp} = 100 pJ/bit/m2 to power the transmitter amplifier. In data fusion, there is additionally a cost of E_{diff} = 5 nJ/bit/message for 2000-bit messages. Each node starts with the same amount of energy (0.25 joule) [3].

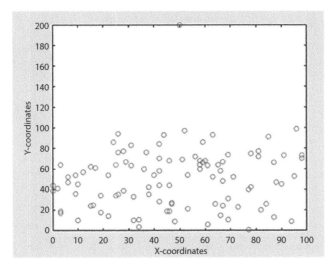

Figure 7.1 Hundred random node topologies.

The first 20 nodes transfer data from the farthest node to the 20th node as shown in Figure 7.2. From the 20th node to the next 40th node, chaining is performed as shown in Figure 7.3.

Similarly, chaining is done in the 4th, 5th, and 6th clusters too as shown in Figure 7.4, Figure 7.5, and Figure 7.6, respectively.

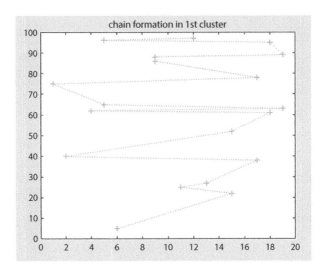

Figure 7.2 Chain creation in the first cluster.

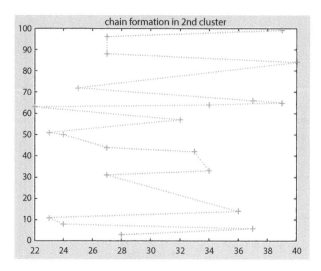

Figure 7.3 Chain creation in the second cluster.

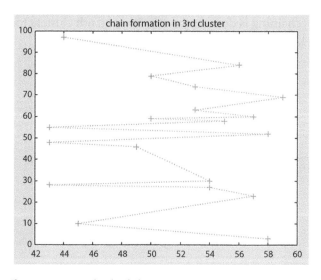

Figure 7.4 Chain creation in the third cluster.

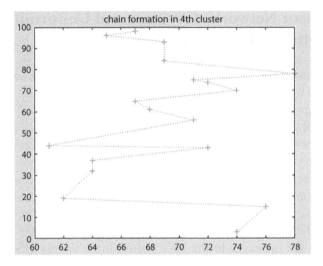

Figure 7.5 Chain creation in the fourth cluster.

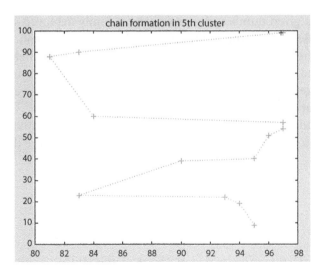

Figure 7.6 Chain formation in the 5th cluster.

7.6 Sensor Network's Coverage and Uniformity Optimization Using GA

Many visions of the future include people immersed in an environment surrounded by sensors and intelligent devices, which use smart infrastructures to improve the quality of life and safety in emergencies. The concept of sensing physical phenomena has been inspired by biological living creatures. Sensors have been in existence for a few decades now and are being used in everyday life. A sensor network is a collection of communicating sensing devices or nodes. All of the sensor nodes are not necessarily communicating at any particular time, and nodes can only communicate with a few nearby sensor nodes. The network has a routing protocol to control the routing of data messages between sensor nodes. The routing protocol also attempts to get messages to the base station in an energy-efficient manner. Typical examples include traffic monitoring of vehicles, cross-border infiltration-detection and assessment, military reconnaissance and surveillance, target tracking, habitat monitoring, and structure monitoring, to name a few.

The algorithms start with random deployment. Assume a two-dimensional sensor field is the target area of surveillance. In the initial condition, a given number of sensors are randomly deployed such as air-dropping. Because of the randomness in initial deployment, very likely the sensor field will not be fully covered. Part of the sensor field might be overcrowded with the sensors. Such unbalanced deployment brings difficulty in target detection and tracking and increases the interference during communications [7].

After random deployment of WSN nodes, the nodes distribute based on a partial force for the movement of sensor nodes during the deployment process:

$$f_n^{i,j} = \frac{D}{\mu^2}(cR - |p_n^i - p_n^j|)\frac{p_n^i - p_n^j}{|p_n^i - p_n^j|} \tag{7.2}$$

Communication range is denoted by the letter cR [2],

$$\mu(cR) = \frac{N.\pi.cR^2}{A} \tag{7.3}$$

μ is called the expected density [7].

The Algorithm is shown below:

Step 1: Random Deployment of Sensors:
   The nodes are initially randomly deployed. The sensing range, communication range, and initial node location is estimated based on the number of iterations and number of sensors that are not oscillating and are in a region of the stable.
Step 2: Force and Expected density calculation:
   Based on the temporary position, partial force is calculated using the above formula (7.2).
Step 3: Oscillation check:

$$\left| P_{n-1}^i - P_{n+1}^i \right| < t_1 \qquad (7.4)$$

$$\text{If} \left(\left| P_{n-1}^i - P_{n+1}^i \right| < t_1 \right) \qquad (7.5)$$

where t_1 is the threshold. Increase oscillation count by 1 and again check if oscillation limit is greater than oscillation count, If so, then update the next location to the temporary position and also update the local density denoted as D.
   Else, sensors move to the centroid of oscillating points and update local density till sensing node i's movement stops.
   Else, update the next location to the temporary position and update local density D.
Step 4: Stability Check

$$\text{If} \left(\left| P_{n+1}^i - P_n^i \right| < t_3 \right) \qquad (7.6)$$

where t_3 is the threshold for stability check.
Increase stability count one by one and check, if the stability count is less than the stability limit, go the while loop else stop sensing node's movement, else go the wile loop and end. This will continue until all the sensor nodes are stable and several iterations are completed. There are two while loops are used starting with several iterations and another one is for several sensors completely covered.

The coverage of a sensor network has been approximated using a random deployment method [1]. The GA toolbox of Matlab is used for simulation.

The sensing range and communication range are varied from 0 to 2 and 0 to 4, respectively. Figure 7.8 shows the GA toolbox's result when 30 nodes are deployed with 100 iterations. Sensor data can be collected within the sensing range, and communications between nodes are possible within the communication range [3, 8]. GA-based optimum deployment of WSN gives an improvement over other existing algorithms named as distributed self-spreading algorithm (DSSA), modified distributed self-spreading algorithm (MDSSA), and generalized reduced gradient (GRG) algorithms.

Figure 7.7 shows the coverage with several generations. It is observed from the figure that the coverage using GA is better in comparison to DSSA [1] and GRG [14]. In [14] DSSA gives 85%, GRG algorithm 89%, reduced DSSA is giving 91%, and reduced GRG algorithm 93%, whereas GA gives 96% [14].

Three operators make up a simple GA that produces good results in a variety of practical problems:

1. Reproduction
2. Adaptation
3. Variation.

Individual strings are copied according to their objective function values in the reproduction process (biologically call this function as the fitness function) [9]. The function f might be thought of as a measure of profit, usefulness, or virtue that we wish to maximize intuitively. When you copy strings based on their fitness values, strings with a higher value have a better chance of producing one or more offspring in the next generation. This operator, of

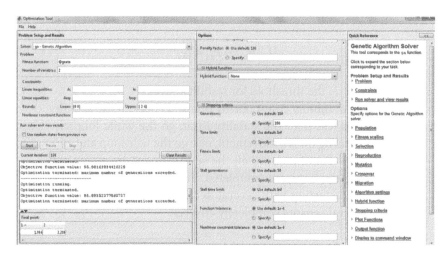

Figure 7.7 Results of applications of GAs.

course, is a Darwinian survival of the fittest among string animals, an artificial version of natural selection [9]. In natural populations, a creature's capacity to withstand predators, pestilence, and other obstacles to adulthood and subsequent reproduction determines its fitness [10]. The objective function is the final arbitrator of the string-life creature's death in an artificially manufactured situation. Algorithms begin with a random distribution. Assume the surveillance target is a two-dimensional sensor field. In the beginning, a set number of sensors is dropped at random, similar to airdropping [11, 12].

Coverage with 100 iterations (Figure 7.8), and with several nodes (Figure 7.9).

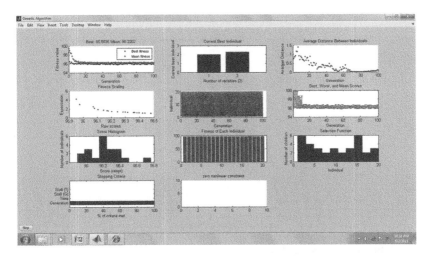

Figure 7.8 Coverage with 100 iterations.

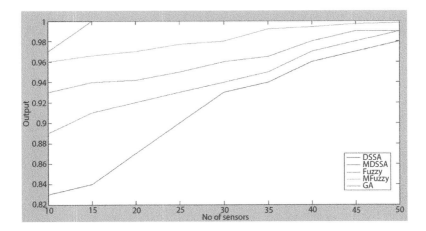

Figure 7.9 Coverage with several nodes.

Coverage is plotted with several iterations with a fixed number of nodes as 10, which is shown in Figure 7.10.

Coverage vs. number of iteration for 20 numbers of nodes is in Figure 7.11.

The results are: mutation rate, 0.01; crossover rate, 0.9071; number of sensors deployed, 30; number of iteration, 30.

The population considered is a double vector, since we have considered integer constraints because we need to move evenly using a random integer

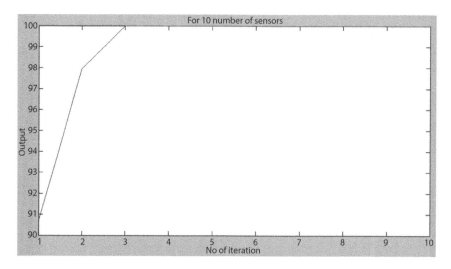

Figure 7.10 Coverage vs. number of iterations.

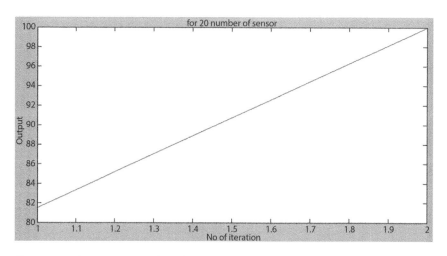

Figure 7.11 Coverage vs. number of iterations (with 20 numbers of nodes).

Table 7.1 Simulation results.

	Coverage	Uniformity	Time	Outage probability	Energy
Random	Less	Less	No time	Less	Less
DSSA	√	√	√	√	
GRG Algorithm	√	√	√	√	√ √
RDSSA	√	√	√	√	
RGRG Algorithm	√ √	√ √ √	√ √	√√	√ √ √
GA based Deployment	√ √ √	√ √ √	√	√ √ √	√ √ √

less than the step size, the selection is stochastic uniform. The creation of children in a new generation is determined by reproduction. The crossover fraction is between 0 and 1, and the elite count is a positive integer.

The comparison has been given in Table 7.1. In Table 7.1, after random deployment of sensors, how much area is covered by the sensor is defined as coverage, and these sensors should be placed uniformly to cover the entire area is defined as uniformity. The time of deployment should be quick and outage probability is the probability to have lesser oscillations. These nodes should be energy efficient. Coverage is calculated as union of covered areas of node to the complete area of interest.

7.7 Use GA for Optimization of Reliability and Availability for Smart Microgrid

The smart grid sends electricity in an efficient manner same as the legacy grid with digital optimization in every component and the use of renewable resources. The components used in microgrid incl PV panels, converters, breakers, transformers, and consists load also. All these need to be connected to the utility. Evaluating the reliability of each component and then merging the best components, makes the smart grid an optimal one. The reliability of the microgrid can be computed with other performance parameters like mean time to failure (MTTF), mean time to repair (MTTR), and availability. The components considered can be repairable components or nonrepairable components. It represents the expected operational lifetime of repairable or nonrepairable components. Higher the MTTF, lower the downtime of the system. Similarly, the meantime to repair is a measure of time elapsed in the repair of a component and restoration of the component to full functionality [13]. MTTR includes repairing time, testing time, and reenergization. MTTR can be minimized by tracking spare inventory and performing condition-based maintenance. MTTR can be calculated as total maintenance time concerning the total number of repairs.

Performing a reliability study on a microgrid is primarily an analytical problem that involves a combination of both statistical and engineering aspects. The reliability of the smart grid can be computed with a reliability block diagram, Markov modeling, fault tree analysis, failure mode effect analysis, Monte Carlo simulations, etc. Along with these methods, the reliability should be increased by considering the reliability of every component. The multiple component reliability can be optimized by using optimal values of failure rate and repair rate of the different components. Consider the specific configuration of the components, such as series, parallel, series-parallel combination, hybrid combination, and bridge linked configuration of PV panels, to improve the system's reliability and availability [14]. The overall reliability is computed using Matlab and the GA toolbox is used to get the optimized value.

In the overall architecture of the microgrid, the PV panels are the first components. The PV panels can be connected in multiple configurations like series configuration, parallel configuration, series-parallel configuration, Total cross-tied configuration, bridge-linked configuration, etc. When the reliability is evaluated for these systems, the best configuration is considered based on the operational lifetime of the networks. The operational lifetime is maxed when a cross-tied array has been used. So we have used a total cross-tied connection between solar cells. The mathematical equations are shown below for solar PV panels:

$$R(t) = e^{-\int_0^\infty \lambda(t)dt} \tag{7.7}$$

The converters are utilized between the PV panels and the transformer, and subcomponents of the converters are used to estimate the overall reliability of the smart grid using an optimal failure rate and repair rate. The overall dependability is calculated after the subcomponent level reliability. When the oil pump and cooling fans are running, the transformer is loaded to its maximum capacity [14]. However, if one or both of these pumps or cooling fans fail, transformers can still run at a lower load. As a result, a parallel reliability structure for the cooling system's reliability model is constructed, which computes reliability when both the pump and the fan are operating normally or when one of these components fails [14]. The component wise reliability of transformer with respect to different failure modes is shown in Table 7.2.

The entire cooling system reliability (RCS) is calculated as follows:

$$R_{CS} = 1 - (1 - R_P R_{CF})(1 - R_P)(1 - R_{CF}) \qquad (7.8)$$

Table 7.2 Component wise reliability of transformer.

S. no	Component name	Failure modes
1	Transformer core	The core lamination, core joints, and lamination gaps were found to be the most common causes of transformer core failure [14].
2	Winding	A typical winding failure occurs when the insulation on the winding fails to owe to widespread or local overheating.
3	Tank	The high pressure in a transformer's tank caused by gases, as well as corrosion caused by moisture and aging, are the main causes of the tank's failure [14].
4	Oil insulation	The main causes are partial discharge and moisture infiltration; other causes include suspended particles in oil and arcing.
5	Solid insulation	Insulation failure is primarily caused by short circuiting or cellulose aging, according to the electrical survey.
6	Bushing	Overheating and insulation failure cause failure due to dust, water infiltration, and effects on the bushing [14].
7	Tap-changer	Its operation is mechanical, which means it could break down. Other problems could be caused by motor drives or contact cooking [14].
8	Cooling pump	
9	Cooling fan	

Finally, the expression for total transformer reliability (RTXR) is as follows:

$$R_{TXR} = R_{MAN}R_{CS}R_{TC} \tag{7.9}$$

The reliability of the microgrid is calculated concerning time using Markov modeling. The total time considered is 200 years and simulation iterations are considered as 5000 so the delta per iteration is time per division. At moment t = 0, corresponding to A(0) which is supposed to be the normal state (GG) of the system then A(0) is:

$$S(0) = [1\,0\,0\,0\,0\,0\,0\,0\,0]^{T} \tag{7.10}$$

$$At\ t = n.\Delta t,\ S(nt) = A^{n}\,I(0) \tag{7.11}$$

The optimum value of the failure rate and repair rate is calculated based on the reliability formula, and as shown in Figure 7.12, the values of repair rate are optimized as 0.002 for a microgrid. The Markov modeling used for getting the reliability and optimum value of reliability can be achieved

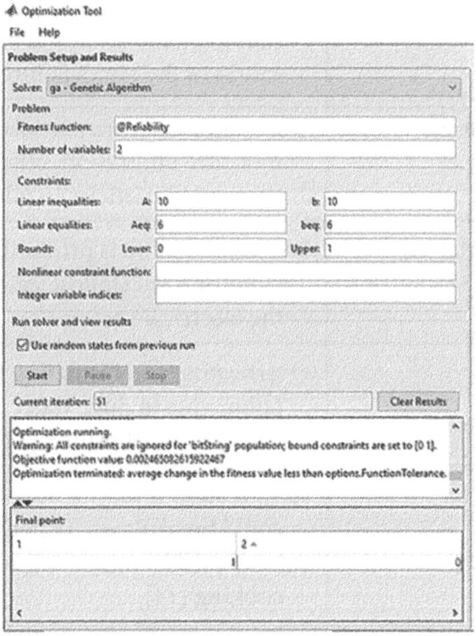

Figure 7.12 GA.

by following values of the reliability failure rate of components and repair rates shown below:

Failure rate	Repair rate	MTTF (failures/years)
0.02	1/12.50	26 years
1/5.2	0.002	
0.2	0.02	

7.8   GA Versus Traditional Methods

GAs deal with the parameter set's coding rather than the parameters themselves. A GA looks for a group of points rather than a single point. GAs use payoff information rather than derivative or auxiliary knowledge, and they use probabilistic rather than deterministic transition rules [15].

Calculus-based, enumerative, and random research methods are the three basic types of research methods. These are further divided into two categories: indirect and direct. The indirect method finds local extrema by solving a non-linear set of equations that results from putting the goal function's gradient to zero. Finding a probable peak in a smooth, unconstrained function begins with limiting the search to places with slopes of zero in all directions. Direct (search) approaches, on the other hand, look for local optima by hopping on the function and traveling in the direction of the local gradient. This is the basic concept of hill climbing: to locate the best local option, one climbs the function in the steepest direction possible [16].

Both calculus-based approaches are local in scope: the best near the current point are sought. Beginning the search in the vicinity of the lower peak will result in our missing the main event (the higher peak). Furthermore, once the lower peak has been attained, additional progress must be sought through random restart or other deception. Another issue with calculus-based approaches is that they rely on the existence of derivatives (well-defined slope values). This is a serious flaw, even if we allow for the numerical approximation of derivatives [17]. The real world of search is full of discontinuities and large multimodal (i.e., numerous "hills") noisy search spaces; approaches that rely on rigid constraints of continuity and derivative existence are inadequate for all but a small subset of problem domains [15].

Enumerative schemes come in a variety of shapes and sizes. The concept is simple: within a finite search space, the search algorithm begins by examining objective function values at each point in the space one by one. Although the algorithm's simplicity is appealing, and enumeration is a highly human sort of search, such systems have uses where the number of options is limited. On issues of moderate size and complexity, even the much-praised enumerative approach, dynamic programming, fails [12].

Random walks and random schemes that search and save the best, in the long run, can be expected to do no better than enumerative schemes. The GA is an example of a search procedure that uses random choice as a tool, to guide a highly exploitative search through the coding of parameter space. Using random choice as a tool in a directed search process seems strange at first but nature contains many examples.

The GA describes a large number of successful applications, but there are also many cases in which GAs performs very poorly. Given a potential application, how do we know if a GA is a good method to use? There is no rigorous answer, though many researchers share the intuitions that if the space to be searched is large, it is known not to be perfectly smooth and unimodal, or it is not well understood; or if the fitness function is noisy; and if the task does not require a global optimum to be found—i.e., if quickly finding a sufficiently good solution is enough—a GA will have a good chance of being competitive or surpassing other methods. If the space is not large, it can be searched exhaustively by enumerative search methods, and one can be sure that the best possible solution has been found, whereas a GA might give only a "good" solution. A gradient ascent algorithm will be much more efficient than a GA if the space is smooth and unimodal. If the space is well understood, search methods using domain-specific heuristics can often be designed to outperform any general-purpose method, such as a GA. If the fitness function is noisy, a one-candidate solution at a time search method such as a simple hill climbing night be irrecoverably led astray by the noise; but GAs, since work by accumulating fitness statistics over many generations, are thought to outperform robustly in the presence of the small amount of noise.

7.9   Summaries and Conclusions

GAs solve many difficult problems that took a long time to solve. It has been used in various real-life applications like artificial creativity, data processing, electronics circuit design, data warehouses, etc. These algorithms have better intelligence than random search algorithms since they use historical data to take the search to the best-performing values within the solution space.

The goal of this chapter is to understand how GAs might be used for real-world problems. The approach has been to visualize different applications of different fields with different performance parameters evaluated using GAs. Wireless sensing nodes are used for multiple applications, and the problems can be restated as one of the searching the space of parameter changes for instances that achieve the desired objectives. Without requiring significant amounts of domain knowledge, GAs have been used to rapidly search spaces for each of the categories listed above.

References

1. ur Rehman, Z. Fatima, M., Khan, A. *et al.*, Energy optimization in a smart community grid system using genetic algorithm. *Int. J. Commun. Syst.*, e4265, 2019.

2. Pahuja, G.L. and Yadav, G., Energy efficient double chain clustered communication protocol for WSN. *MIT Int. J. Electr. Instrum. Eng.*, 1, 2, 76–79, 2011.

3. Hsu, H.-L. and Liang, Q., An energy-efficient protocol for wireless sensor networks. *2005 IEEE 62nd Vehicular Technology Conference VTC-2005-Fall*, vol. 4, pp. 2321–2325, 2005.

4. Heo, N. and Varshney, P.K., A distributed self-spreading algorithm for mobile wireless sensor networks, in: *2003 IEEE Wireless Communications and Networking, WCNC 2003*, vol. 3, pp. 1597–1602, 2003.

5. Lindsey, S. and Raghavendra, C.S., PEGASIS: Power-efficient gathering in sensor information systems. *Proceedings, IEEE Aerospace Conference*, pp. 3–3, 2002.

6. Gandham, S., Dawande, M., Prakash, R., *An Integral Flow-Based Energy-Efficient Routing Algorithm for Wireless Sensor Networks*, 2004.

7. Shu, H., Liang, Q., Gao, J., Distributed sensor networks deployment using fuzzy logic systems. *Int. J. Wirel. Inf. Netw.*, 14, 3, 163–173, Sep. 2007.

8. Heo, N. and Varshney, P.K., *A Distributed Self Spreading Algorithm for Mobile Wireless Sensor Networks*, 2003.

9. Zomaya, A.Y. and Olariu, S., Special issue on parallel evolutionary computing guest editors' introduction. *J. Parallel Distrib. Comput.*, 47, 1, 1–7, 1997.

10. Takahashi, Y., Convergence of simple genetic algorithms for the two-bit problem. *Biosystems*, 46, 3, 235–282, 1998.

11. Perillo, M., Cheng, Z., Heinzelman, W., On the problem of unbalanced load distribution in wireless sensor networks, in: *GLOBECOM-IEEE Global Telecommunications Conference*, pp. 74–79, 2004.

12. Mohamed, F.A. and Koivo, H.N., Online management genetic algorithms of microgrid for residential application. *Energ. Convers. Manage.*, 64, 562–568, 2012.

13. Yu, Y. and Wei, G., *Energy Aware Routing Algorithm Based on Layered Chain in Wireless Sensor Network*, 2007.

14. Singh, A., Patil, A.J., Tripathi, V.K., Sharma, R.K., Jarial, R.K., Reliability modeling and simulation for assessment of electric arc furnace transformers, in: *2020 IEEE International Conference on Computing, Power and Communication Technologies, GUCON 2020*, pp. 239–244, 2020.

15. Vasant, P., A novel hybrid genetic algorithms and pattern search techniques for industrial production planning. *Int. J. Model. Simul. Sci. Comput.*, 3, 4, 1250020, 2012.

16. Joshi, D. and Sandhu, K.S., Excitation control of self excited induction generator using genetic algorithm and artificial neural network. *International Journal of Mathematical Models and Methods in Applied Sciences*, 3, 68–75, 2009.

17. Joshi, D., Sandhu, K.S., Bansal, R.C., Steady-state analysis of self-excited induction generators using genetic algorithm approach under different operating modes. *Int. J. Sustain. Energy*, 32, 4, 244–258, 2013.

8

AI-Based Predictive Modeling of Delamination Factor for Carbon Fiber–Reinforced Polymer (CFRP) Drilling Process

Rohit Volety and Geetha Mani*

School of Electronics Engineering, Vellore Institute of Technology, Vellore Campus, Tamil Nadu, India

Abstract

Carbon fiber reinforced plastic (CFRP) materials have played an important part in the domains of aerospace, sports, etc because of its various characteristics like better modulus, specific, fatigue strength, and also tensile strength, CFRP Drilling is one of the crucial processes in the making of components of CFRP. Delamination can be said to be one of the greatest challenges in the machining process because of its major effect on the structural integrity of CFRP and its application. The delamination factor may decrease the load-carrying ability of the joint. Often, this damage is not detected upon visual inspection because of the nature of the material. Traditional methods of estimation of delamination which is using lab instruments like optical microscopy, digital scanning, ultrasonic C-scan, X-ray have proven to be highly inefficient as these instruments take a long time to measure components and are also subject to human errors. Moreover, these instruments are expensive and very difficult to maintain. Another major disadvantage is that some of the instruments cannot be taken in the field for testing. Machine learning has made a mark in every industry and the machining industry is no different. Machine learning approaches can help optimize the process. This chapter presents several machine learning algorithms like Random forests, linear regression, XGBoost, and Support Vector Machine (SVM), which can help make the process of estimating delamination factor more efficient based on known inputs like Feed Rate, Point angle, and spindle speed,

Keywords: CFRP, delamination factors, linear regression, XGBoost, random forests, SVM

---

*Corresponding author: geetha.mani@vit.ac.in

Anita Khosla, Prasenjit Chatterjee, Ikbal Ali and Dheeraj Joshi (eds.) Optimization Techniques in Engineering: Advances and Applications, (139–154) © 2023 Scrivener Publishing LLC

8.1   Introduction

Carbon fiber reinforced plastic (CFRP) is being used in a lot of industries because of its lightweight and high strength characteristics. For example, to decrease the amount of fuel consumption carbon fiber reinforced plastic is being used for airframe structural application [1–5]. Another application that sees a high usage of CFRP is sports. A major amount of CFRP is being used for clubs, badminton rackets, etc. [6–8]. Because of its static properties, dynamic properties, thermal properties, and chemical properties, CFRP also finds major uses in domains of machine tools, structures of transportation, and increasing the strength of shear walls in regions that are seismically active [9]. CFRP is also heavily employed to increase the performance of components of structures responsible for carrying load, ductility, stiffness, and execution in cyclic loading and also environmental durability. CFRP materials are non-homogenous and also behave aniso-tropically, CFRP materials have been known to cause major problems in their machining [10]. It is a known fact that there are a lot of defects that are accompanied by the drilling process of CFRP, the most hazardous ones are considered to be micro cracking, fiber breakage thermal damage delamination, and matrix cratering. In all the above-mentioned defections, delamination is one of the crucial faults that affect the use case of CFRP. Over the years there has been a significant amount of work done in the prediction of delamination. Three types of solutions have been proposed for estimation of delamination, measurement methods using instruments, modeling analysis methods, and data analysis methods. Davis *et al.* came up with an approach to identify the cutting parameters which use a combination of Taguchi techniques and ANOVA for damage-free drilling [11]. A. Krishnamoorthy *et al.* give an artificial neural network for predicting delamination which gives a max error of 0.81% and the least error of 0.03% [10]. Jiacheng Cui *et al.* propose a novel method that is based on multi-sensor data for predicting delamination. XGBoost-ARIMA model is proposed which includes regression and a sequential part that is made for the use of rolling prediction. Yun Zhang *et al.* propose a method based on Gaussian process regression for the prediction of the delamination factor [21]. Offline methods point toward estimating delamination using instruments after the drilling process to get their shape, size, and position data [12]. These geometric features can provide an approximate estimation of delamination damage. There are many different delamination image acquisition techniques. These include optical microscopy [13, 14], digital scanning [15, 16], ultrasonic C-scan [17, 18], X-ray [19, 20], etc.

These techniques can be used to estimate the delamination with high accuracy but the instruments used in the process are very expensive. Also, these instruments take a long time to measure the factor. The biggest concern is that these methods cannot be used in the onsite measurement.

Machine learning algorithms have made a mark in every domain in the industry. The machining industry is no exception. Delamination factors can be predicted using these machine learning techniques. In this paper, several machine learning approaches have been used for predicting the delamination factor. These algorithms have been chosen for their quick computation, less error, and high accuracy. The paper will compare XGBoost, decision tree, linear regression, random forests, and SVM. Based on several evaluation metrics like accuracy, R^2 value, MSE, RMSE, etc, the best model will be chosen for the task of predicting the delamination factor.

This research chapter is presented as follows: section 8.2 gives a detailed view of the proposed methodology of the entire experiment. It elaborates on the data preprocessing techniques used, dataset, testing, and training metrics, and the models used. The input parameters and the output parameter are also defined. Section 8.3 gives us a brief introduction to each of the models used along with the required mathematical equations. Also, designed model parameters for each of the ML models are provided. Section 8.4 gives the performance indices used in the paper to evaluate the ML models. Multiple performance indices have been used to evaluate the developed ML model. Section 8.5 provided the results and discussions. As mentioned, multiple metrics have been used to evaluate the model. The training and testing metrics have been given. Also, the predicted vs actual values are plotted for each of the ML models. The paper ends with a conclusion summarizing the results and inferences.

Use of traditional algorithms over techniques like neural networks
Neural networks and Fuzzy techniques have long been used for predictive analytics. Because of high yielding accuracy, it has often been the most popular choice for predictive modeling of real-time applications. But neural networks and Fuzzy techniques have their own disadvantages because of which traditional models have been used. Some of the disadvantages are:

1. Black Box
   The outputs of neural networks are very difficult to explain. Most recent research has been able to make some progress in explaining neural networks and their outputs but it is still very much behind explainability of traditional machine learning algorithms. Simply put, outputs of traditional

machine learning algorithms can be explained far more accurately than that of a neural network.

2. Resource-Oriented

Training neural networks take a lot of time. The models that they output are dependent on the iterations that they are run through. Models that are trained on a larger dataset can take weeks of training to output a model capable of any type of predictive analytics

3. Data-Oriented

Neural networks need a lot of data to train as they have a lot of parameters. A model with too many constraints will underfit the small training dataset, whereas an under-constrained model will likely overfit the training data. Both of these result in poor performance. Too little test data will result in an optimistic and high variance estimation of model performance.

8.2   Methodology

CFRP can permit redeveloping well-maintained metallic structures like manipulators for decreasing their weight and increasing their performance. During the drilling process, the delamination factor is very important as it affects the property of the hole which has been drilled. Traditional methods like x-ray, optical microscopy, etc cannot be used indefinitely because of various reasons like cost, long measurement time, etc. Hence a need for a system that is very accurate and fast is felt. The block diagram can be seen in Figure 8.1. This work elaborated on how to utilize machine learning algorithms for the efficient prediction of delamination factors. The dataset has been split into two parts: train and testing. The input arguments are feed rate, spindle speed, and point angle. The output parameter to be predicted is the delamination factor. The dataset has been taken from [22]. The experiments were conducted on this dataset. Data preprocessing has been applied to remove outliers and to standardize the parameters. The test set is 20% of the entire dataset. Each of the models is applied to it. The models chosen are linear regression, XGBoost, decision trees, and random forests. These models are trained on train data and then evaluated on the unseen testing data. The metrics that are used to evaluate the test data set are R^2, MSE, and RMSE. Furthermore, cross-fold validation has been done for further evaluating the models.

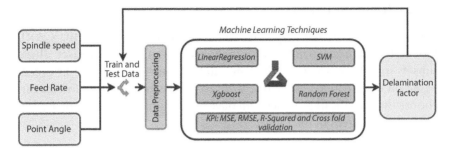

Figure 8.1 Proposed methodology block diagram.

8.3 AI-Based Predictive Modeling

8.3.1 Linear Regression

It is a type of model in the supervised mode of machine learning. The linear regression model has a predictor variable and a dependent variable which is linearly related to each other. The objective is to find the relationship between independent variables and corresponding dependent variables. This may be seen in the form of:

$$y_i = \alpha_0 + \alpha_1 x_{i1} + \alpha_2 x_{i2} + \ldots + \alpha_p x_{ip} + \varepsilon \qquad (8.1)$$

The line of regression goes through the mean of the independent variable, also the mean of the dependent variable. The line minimizes the sum of squared differences between observed values and predicted values. Table 8.1 shows the model coefficients for linear regression.

$$y_i = 3.3366\text{e-}05x_{i1} + 1.0449\text{e}+00x_{i2} + 1.4229\text{e-}03x_{i3} + 1.0829$$

where y_i = independent variable
x_i = dependent variable

Table 8.1 Model parameters of linear regression ML model.

Model	α_1	α_2	α_3	α_0
Linear regression	3.3366e-05	1.0449e+00	1.4229e-03	1.0829

8.3.2   Random Forests

Here, more than 1 tree is grown rather than only one tree in the CART model. Trees are constructed from the subsets of an original dataset. These subsets may have a part of the rows and columns. To classify an object based on the attribute, every tree will give a classification. The forests can choose the classification which will have the maximum votes compared to the rest of the trees in the forest.

It works in the following way:

- N rows in the train set can be assumed. A part of n < N rows will be taken with replacement at random. This part is used as the train set to grow the tree.
- M input variables are considered where an integer m < M is taken so at every node, m variables have been chosen at random from M. The best splitting on this m can be utilized for splitting the node. The value of m is the same but the forest is grown.
- Every tree has grown and without any pruning.
- Prediction of new data by taking all the predictions of n tree

For each tree, Scikit-learn will get the importance of the node utilizing Gini Importance, with the assumption that there are only two child nodes:

$$ni_j = w_j C_j - w \qquad (8.2)$$

$ni_{(j)}$ = node j importance
$w_{(j)}$ = samples reaching node j weighted number
$C_{(j)}$ = the value of impurity of node j
$left_{(j)}$ = child node in the left splitting on node j
$right_{(j)}$ = child node in the right splitting on node j

Table 8.2 shows the random forests model parameters.

Table 8.2 Model parameters of random forests ML model.

Model	Maximum feature	Minimum number of observations to split	Number of estimator
Random Forests	auto	2	100

8.3.3   XGBoost

XGBoost is an addition to the gradient boosting machine. XGBoost applies parallel processing and is very fast when compared to GBM. It is known that each tree can be made only after the previous one, but all the cores of the system are used to make a tree. XGBoost permits its users to define custom optimization objectives and evaluation criteria. It utilizes the function to make trees by minimization of:

$$\mathcal{L}(\phi) = \sum_i l(\hat{y}_i, y_i) + \sum_k \Omega(f_k) \qquad (8.3)$$

$$\text{where } \Omega(f) = \gamma T + \frac{1}{2}\lambda\|w\|^2 \qquad (8.4)$$

Here, the first part of the equation will be the loss function which will calculate the pseudo residuals of predicted value Yi with hat and true value yi in each leaf. The final part has lambda (λ) which is a regularization term, *it intends to reduce* the insensitivity of prediction to individual observations and w is leaf weight.

T-terminal nodes

gamma- penalty

Table 8.3 shows the XGBoost model parameters.

Maximum depth—It is utilized to drive the overfitting with a higher depth, which will allow the model to be taught relations particular to a sample.

Gamma—it tells the least loss reduction for making a splitting.

Learning rate—controls the weighting of the new trees.

Several estimators—This dictates the number of estimators. Having a high value can be computationally expensive.

Table 8.3 XGboost model parameters.

Model	Gamma	Learning rate	Maximum depth	Number of estimators
Xgboost	0	0.1	3	100

8.3.4 SVM

It is an algorithm that is utilized for regression and classification purposes. It is a powerful machine learning algorithm for classification, regression, and detecting outliers. It can be seen as a nonprobabilistic binary linear classifier.

SVM can be utilized for linear classification purposes in Despite High-dimensional feature spaces.

An example of the function of SVM using the logistic regression cost function log loss and also using the l2 regularization:

$$J(\theta) = C\left[\sum_{i=1}^{m} y^{(i)}Cost_1(\theta^T(x^{(i)})) + (1 - y^{(i)})Cost_0(\theta^T(x^{(i)}))\right] + \frac{1}{2}\sum_{j=1}^{n}\theta_j^2$$

(8.5)

n = number of features
m = number of samples
$\theta^T x$ = raw model output

Table 8.4 shows SVM model parameters.

Table 8.4 SVM model parameters.

Model	C	Kernel
SVM	1	linear

C- Adds a penalty for every misclassified data point.

Kernel- Dictates the kernel type to be utilized in the calculation. Some examples are linear, poly, etc.

8.4   Performance Indices

8.4.1   Root Mean Squared Error (RMSE)

It is popularly utilized for regression purposes and can be seen as the root of the average square difference between the target value and the predicted value

$$\frac{1}{N}\sum_{i=1}^{n}(\text{actual values} - \text{predicted values})^2$$

(8.6)

8.4.2   Mean Squared Error (MSE)

It is the average of the square difference between the target value and the predicted value

$$\frac{1}{N}\sum(y-\hat{y})^2 \tag{8.7}$$

8.4.3   R² (R-Squared)

The metric gives the comparison of our model with a baseline which is constant. This baseline is selected by taking the average and drawing a line at the mean. The R^2 will always be either 1 or lesser than it.

$$R^2 = 1 - \frac{SS_{Res}}{SS_{tot}} \tag{8.8}$$

where SS_{Res} is the residual sum of squares and SS_{tot} is the total sum of squares.

8.5   Results and Discussion

The drilling process of (CFRP) is important for the complete specifications of the final assembly. In spite of the good characteristics of composites, it is difficult to be machined as they are very tough. Peel-up and push-out delamination damages often present themselves during the process of machining. Many penetration angles drilling have also been researched to know the impact of delamination.

Delamination factor [23] can be expressed as:

$$\frac{A_o}{A_{hole}} \tag{8.9}$$

where the diameter of the drill is represented by A_{hole} in mm² and the area between the hole circle and the maximum delamination zone is represented by Ao in mm² and equivalent factor of delamination diameter is expressed as

$$\left[\frac{4(A_d + A_o)}{\pi}\right]^{0.5} \tag{8.10}$$

where De is equivalent delamination diameter and D is the hole diameter, respectively; its delamination area is expressed as Ad, and the area of the hole is expressed as Ao.

8.5.1 Key Performance Metrics (KPIs) During the Model Training Phase

It can be seen from Table 8.5 that XGBoost has the highest R^2 values. A high R^2 value indicates good model performance. A low R^2 value indicates bad performance. The score is highest for XGBoost also. MSE and RMSE are the lowest in XGBoost, which shows less tendency toward errors.

8.5.2 Key Performance Index Metrics (KPIs) During the Model Testing Phase

It can be seen from Table 8.6 that XGBoost has the highest R^2 values for the test set. A high R^2 value indicates good model performance on the test set. A low R^2 value indicates bad performance. MSE and RMSE are the lowest in XGBoost, which shows less tendency toward errors. The second highest R^2 value seems to be that of Random forests.

Table 8.5 KPIs of the training phase.

Model	Score	MSE	RMSE	R^2
Linear Regression	0.713	8.215	2.866	0.678
Random Forests	0.938	1.857	1.362	0.927
XGboost	0.952	1.167	1.080	0.951
SVM	−0.039	23.760	4.874	0.069

Table 8.6 Testing metrics.

Model	MSE	RMSE	R^2
Linear Regression	21.238	4.608	0.584
Random Forests	20.151	4.489	0.605
XGboost	13.863	3.723	0.728
SVM	31.452	5.608	0.384

8.5.3   K Cross Fold Validation

a. Metric-R^2

The set has been divided into 5 equal parts. And then each of the parts has been used for testing purposes. For each split, the R^2 value has been calculated. As mentioned, a higher R^2 value indicates a higher model performance. It is observed from Table 8.7 that XGBoost gets the highest R^2 digit from split 3 among all the models. This is closely followed by Linear regression in split 3.

b. Metric negative mean squared error

A negative mean square error metric has been used to evaluate the model performance for each of the splits in Table 8.8. It can be observed that XGBoost gets the lowest Negative mean square error. This is consistent with our observation that XGBoost performed well among all the models.

c. Metric negative root mean squared error

This error has been used in each of the splits in this section and presented in Table 8.9. As is consistent with all our previous observations, the XGBoost model has the lowest Negative root mean squared error for split 1.

Table 8.7 K cross-fold validation of R^2.

Models	Split 1	Split 2	Split 3	Split 4	Split 5
Linear Regression	0.337	0.446	0.768	0.359	0.686
Random Forests	0.492	0.443	0.728	−0.222	0.677
XGboost	**0.708**	**0.553**	**0.794**	**−0.001**	**0.729**
SVM	3.156	0.664	0.275	−1.060	0.461

Table 8.8 K cross-fold validation of negative mean squared error.

Model	Split 1	Split 2	Split 3	Split 4	Split 5
Linear Regression	−0.0018	−0.0018	−0.0026	−0.0021	−0.0017
Random Forests	−0.00144192	−0.0017	−0.0031	−0.0034	−0.0017
XGboost	**−0.0008328**	**0.0015**	**0.0023**	**0.0033**	**0.0015**
SVM	−0.01189409	−0.0055	−0.0083	−0.0068	−0.0030

Table 8.9 K cross-fold actual validation of Metric negative root mean squared error.

Models	Split 1	Split 2	Split 3	Split 4	Split 5
Linear regression	−0.043	−0.043	−0.051	−0.046	−0.042
Random forests	−0.0402	−0.039	−0.055	−0.058	−0.040
XGboost	**−0.028**	**−0.038**	**−0.048**	**−0.0575**	**−0.039**
SVM	−0.109	−0.074	−0.091	−0.082	−0.055

Figure 8.2 presented the predicted value vs actual values of the delamination factor of four ML techniques like linear regression, random forests, XGBoost, and SVM during the model training phase. Figure 8.3 shows the predicted versus actual value of the delamination factor for the model testing phase of the aforementioned ML techniques. From the obtained results, it was inferred that during the training process, XGBoost emerges with the lowest RMSE and MSE. Also, it gets the highest R^2 value. Similar kinds of observations can be seen when the model has passed the test and from the cross-validation results. This gives us the observation that

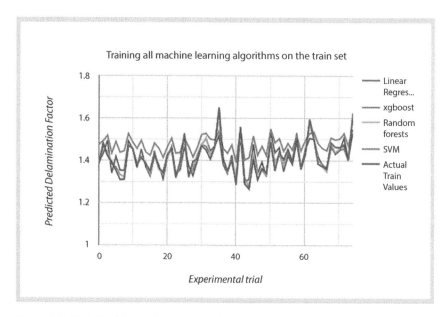

Figure 8.2 Training all machine learning algorithms on the train data set.

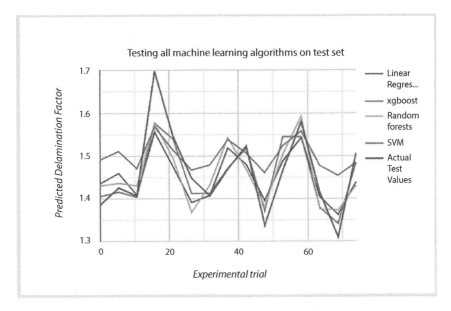

Figure 8.3 Testing all machine learning algorithms on the test data set.

XGBoost has the best performance compared with all on the provided dataset among all the models.

8.6 Conclusions

CFRP is known to be utilized in the aerospace, marine, sports industry because of its thermal, dynamic, and static properties. High load-carrying capacity and lightweight is what makes CFIR an extremely popular material for industries. Delamination factor is seen in the drilling process and is a major reason for decreased load-carrying capacity. As mentioned, using instruments for estimating delamination factors has several disadvantages like long measurement time, being incapable of being used in onsite areas, and being too expensive to maintain. Hence, in this paper, several machine learning techniques have been applied for the task of predicting the delamination factor. Models like linear regression, XGBoost, Random forests, and SVM have been compared and evaluated based on various KPIs. Out of all the models, XGBoost gave the optimal prediction and confirmed the same with the help of various KPIs. Random forests are closely followed by the XGBoost model in terms of performance. It was concluded that the XGBoost was chosen as the best machine learning model for accurate prediction of the delamination factor when the spindle speed, Feedrate, and Point angle feed as input parameters for the CFRP drilling process.

References

1. Rahim, E.A. and Sasahara, H., High performance machining of carbon fiber-reinforced plastics, in: *Sustainable Composites for Aerospace Applications*, pp. 211–226, Woodhead Publishing, 2018.
2. J. Schwartz, C.C. Koch, Y. Zhang, X. Liu, Formation of bismuth strontium calcium copper oxide superconductors. U.S. Patent US9773962B2, September 26, 2017.
3. Zhang, Y., Johnson, S., Naderi, G., Chaubal, M., Hunt, A., Schwartz, J., High critical current density Bi2Sr2CaCu2O x/Ag wire containing oxide precursor synthesized from nano-oxides. *Supercond. Sci. Tech.*, 29, 9, 095012, 2016.
4. Zhang, Y., Koch, C.C., Schwartz, J., Formation of Bi2Sr2CaCu2O x/Ag multifilamentary metallic precursor powder-intube wires. *Supercond. Sci. Tech.*, 29, 12, 125005, 2016.
5. Zhang, Y., Koch, C.C., Schwartz, J., Synthesis of Bi2Sr2CaCu2Ox superconductors via direct oxidation of metallic precursors. *Supercond. Sci. Tech.*, 27, 5, 055016, 2014.
6. Inagaki, M., *New Carbons-Control of Structure and Functions*, Elsevier, Hokkaido University, Japan, 2000.
7. Wang, Y., Chan, W.K., Schwartz, J., Self-protection mechanisms in no-insulation (RE) Ba2Cu3Ox high temperature superconductor pancake coils. *Supercond. Sci. Tech.*, 29, 4, 045007, 2016.
8. Wang, Y., Weng, F., Li, J., Souc, J., Gömöry, F., Zou, S., Zhang, M., Yuan, W., No-insulation high temperature superconductor winding technique for electrical aircraft propulsion. *IEEE Trans. Transp. Electrification*, 6, 4, 1613–1624, 2020.
9. Motavalli, M. and Flueler, P., Characterization of unidirectional carbon fibre reinforced plastic laminates. *Mater. Struct.*, 31, 3, 178–180, 1998.
10. https://core.ac.uk/download/pdf/26972982.pdf
11. Davim, J.P. and Reis, P., Study of delamination in drilling carbon fiber reinforced plastics (CFRP) using design experiments. *Compos. Struct.*, 59, 4, 481–487, 2003.
12. https://www.researchgate.net/profile/Jiacheng-Cui-2/publication/349573980_A_novel_method_for_predicting_delamination_of_carbon_fiber_reinforced_plastic_CFRP_based_on_multi-sensor_data/links/606a7a3c299bf1252e-2bad33/A-novel-method-for-predicting-delamination-of-carbon-fiber-reinforced-plastic-CFRP-based-on-multi-sensor-data.pdf
13. Su, F., Zheng, L., Sun, F., Wang, Z., Deng, Z., Qiu, X., Novel drill bit based on the step-control scheme for reducing the CFRP delamination.

J. Mater. Process. Technol., 262, 157–167, 2018. https://doi.org/10.1016/j.jmatprotec.2018.06.037.

14. Xu, J., Li, C., Mi, S., An, Q., Chen, M., Study of drilling-induced defects for CFRP composites using new criteria. *Compos. Struct.*, 201, 1076–1087, 2018. https://doi.org/10.1016/j.compstruct.2018.06.051.

15. Durão, L.M.P., Tavares, J.M.R.S., de Albuquerque, V.H.C., Gonçalves, D.J.S., Damage evaluation of drilled carbon/epoxy laminates based on area assessment methods. *Compos. Struct.*, 96, 576–583, 2013. https://doi.org/10.1016/j.compstruct.2012.08.003.

16. Silva, D., Teixeira, J.P., Machado, C.M., Methodology analysis for evaluation of drilling-induced damage in composites. *Int. J. Adv. Manuf. Technol.*, 71, 9-12, 1919–1928, 2014. https://doi.org/10.1007/s00170-014-5616-y.

17. Jia, Z., Chen, C., Wang, F., Zhang, C., Analytical study of delamination damage and delamination-free drilling method of CFRP composite. *J. Mater. Process. Technol.*, 282, 116665, 2020. https://doi.org/10.1016/j.jmatprotec.2020.116665.

18. Nagaraja, R. and Rangaswamy, T., Drilling of CFRP G-833 composite laminates to evaluate the performance of K20 and one shot solid carbide step drill K44. *AIP Conference Proceedings*, vol. 2247, AIP Publishing LLC, p. 050017, 2020.

19. Haeger, A., Schoen, G., Lissek, F., Meinhard, D., Kaufeld, M., Schneider, G., Schuhmacher, S., Knoblauch, V., Non-destructive detection of drilling-induced delamination in CFRP and its effect on mechanical properties. *Procedia Eng.*, 149, 130–142, 2016. https://doi.org/10.1016/j.proeng.2016.06.647.

20. Saoudi, J., Zitoune, R., Gururaja, S., Salem, M., Mezleni, S., Analytical and experimental investigation of the delamination during drilling of composite structures with core drill made of diamond grits: X-ray tomography analysis. *J. Compos. Mater.*, 52, 10, 1281–1294, 2018. https://doi.org/10.1177/0021998317724591.

21. Zhang, Y. and Xu, X., Predicting the delamination factor in carbon fibre reinforced plastic composites during drilling through the Gaussian process regression. *J. Compos. Mater.*, 55, 15, 2061–2068, 2021.

22. Wang, Q. and Jia, X., Multi-objective optimization of CFRP drilling parameters with a hybrid method integrating the ANN, NSGA-II and fuzzy C-means. *Compos. Struct.*, 235, 111803, 2020.

23. Tsao, C.C. and Hocheng, H., Evaluation of thrust force and surface roughness in drilling composite material using Taguchi analysis and neural network. *J. Mater. Process. Tech.*, 203, 1-3, 342–348, 2008.

Performance Comparison of Differential Evolutionary Algorithm-Based Contour Detection to Monocular Depth Estimation for Elevation Classification in 2D Drone-Based Imagery

Jacob Vishal, Somdeb Datta, Sudipta Mukhopadhyay, Pravar Kulbhushan, Rik Das*, Saurabh Srivastava and Indrajit Kar

Siemens Advanta, Siemens Technology and Services Pvt. Ltd. Bengaluru, India

Abstract

Processing of drone-based land imagery is an open research area since it is meant to offer assorted real-time solutions. The images captured using drone cameras comprise of rich descriptor details to leverage content-based image classification. However, the land images captured using drone are two-dimensional in nature, which poses significant challenge in depth estimation for elevation classification of the image content. Moreover, absence of any prior scale (for example, Lidar data, etc.) for estimating the elevation makes the task even more nonconventional. There are state-of the-art techniques existing for understanding the depth of image content using monocular depth estimation of images captured from ground level. This chapter primarily attempts to apply the same technique to carry out sand elevation classification of sand deposits in desert area captured using a drone camera. Nevertheless, the results are not encouraging, which has led to proposition of an evolutionary algorithm-based contour identification method for efficient elevation classification. The structural similarity index (SSIM) to the ground truth scores high for the proposed technique of classification in comparison to the state-of-the-art technique. The test bed is prepared by extracting image frames from an open-source drone video. The research outcomes are encouraging and have outclassed the categorization efficiency of state-of-the-art model for elevation classification.

Corresponding author: rikdas78@gmail.com

Anita Khosla, Prasenjit Chatterjee, Ikbal Ali and Dheeraj Joshi (eds.) Optimization Techniques in Engineering: Advances and Applications, (155–168) © 2023 Scrivener Publishing LLC

Keywords: Drone camera, image classification, depth estimation, elevation classification, contour identification, structural similarity index

9.1   Introduction

The last couple of years have observed high popularity of drone cameras for capturing aerial images and videos under various tropical and subtropical latitude interfaces [1]. This is because of the technological development of lightweight drones. It provides high resolution images compared to satellite imagery with lesser price, elasticity, and low altitude coverage. It can hold various sensors that help in efficient and relevant data collection [2]. Regardless of its utility, depth estimation for elevation classification remains a challenge because of flight altitude, image overlapping, camera pitch, and weather conditions in desert regions. Additionally, elevation detection from aerial view is a difficult task since the images captured with drones are two-dimensional, and there is dearth of reference data available to estimate the depth of such images.

Efficient depth estimation is carried out using learning-based methods in recent times [3]. However, majority of recent approaches have considered supervised techniques for addressing the depth estimation challenge and hence resulted in requirement of bulky training data [4]. This in turn enhances the time for computation which corresponds to increased computational overhead. Nevertheless, the outcomes of the techniques are satisfactory and have revealed impressive precision in identifying the depth of contents for a given image. The work in Zhao *et al.* [5] has predicted single image depth using monocular depth estimation. Investigation of the long tail property resulted in proposing an attention-based model for depth estimation in [6]. Additionally, it is observed that understanding of contour plays a vital role in estimating the depth [7]. Attention-based reconstruction of occluding contour is seen to produce perfect estimation of depth for an image [8].

However, most of the existing depth estimation models for elevation classification is applied on ground level images. Two-dimensional images captured from an altitude using drone cameras are seldom analysed for depth estimation. The authors have identified the dearth of depth estimation techniques for drone-based two-dimensional image and have attempted to address the same using the proposed technique. Hence, the objectives of the research are to:

- Explore the possibility of elevation classification for two-dimensional drone imagery

- Comparing performance of proposed evolutionary algorithm-based contour detection technique to deep learning–based state-of-the-art elevation classification model

The state-of-the-art pretrained monocular depth estimation model-based approach is prepared using computation expanding across six GPU months [9]. Assorted image sources are considered for training purpose and pertinent training modality is maintained to create the architecture. The resultant output has carried out elevation classification of sand deposits of medium and high altitude as well as plain land in the desert area. However, the outcomes are not satisfactory when compared to ground truth. This has resulted in proposition of a differential evolutionary algorithm-based contouring technique for elevation classification. The output images with proposed technique showing boundaries of classified elevations has resulted in statistically significant structural similarity index (SSIM) ground truth comparison scores in contrast to the elevation boundaries revealed in images using existing pretrained model for monocular depth estimation.

9.2   Literature Survey

The autonomous flying drone hovers in the air and moves in the right path avoiding the objects with the help of computer vision. A deep learning technique of depth estimation-based crack detection in bridges using unmanned arial vehicles (UAVs) with vision sensors is discussed by the authors in Kim *et al.* [10]. In French *et al.* [11], a software-based simulator is deployed for base station-equipped unmanned aerial vehicles (UAVs) in a cellular network. Here, the drawbacks are in the approximation of buildings with irregular shapes, like buildings with rounded sides. Singh *et al.* [12] propose the use of drones for track detection and gauge elevation by resizing and cropping the still images from the drone followed by Gaussian smoothing to remove noise. Depth is a key requisite for computer vision specially to perform multiple tasks such as navigation, perception, navigation, and scene understanding. In Mertan *et al.* [13], the work is carried out using various convolution neural networks (CNNs), and in Eigen *et al.* [14], the problem is tackled using supervised regression. The framework consists of two neural networks, namely a coarse and fine network. For learning depth and pose information, two different neural networks, one for depth and other one for pose, are trained jointly using monocular video frames [15]. Improvement in forecasting the depth map is carried out by predicting it using reconstruction method [14]. Pixels are resampled by the 2D displacement field around the occlusion boundaries for sharper reconstruction [16]. This method can be applicable for the output of any type of depth estimation method to make it fully differentiable and enable it for end-to-end training. Object Detection and Segmentation using drones has been extensively utilized in ground object surveillance and supervising [17, 18]. However, the dramatic scale changes and complex backgrounds of images come up from drone usually result in weak feature representation of small entities, which makes it challenging to achieve high-precision object detection. Aiming to improve small objects detection, cross-scale knowledge distillation method can be used, which enhances the features of small objects in a manner like image enlargement. First, based on an efficient feature pyramid network structure, the teacher and student network are trained with images in different scales to introduce the cross-scale feature [17, 19]. In Shoukat *et al.* [20], the depth estimation is carried out by cluster-based approach. In Xu *et al.* [21], a two-stage framework is designed to estimate the depth and semantic segmentation. An attention map is developed using the feature maps of intermediate output and are gated with the feature maps generated from the encoder. Euclidean loss is used for estimation of depth, cross-entropy is used for the contour detection, soft-max loss for semantic segmentation. The neural network architecture is trained with a linear combination of these losses. A very famous approach named structure -from-motion (SFM) is used to recover the 3D shape of an object from multi frame images. To factor the observation matrix into a shape matrix and a motion matrix the singular value decomposition (SVD) technique is used in Chandar and Savithri [22]. Blind source optimization (BSS) is introduced [23] to estimate the maximized posterior shape from the observations which were considered as missing signals. Applications in several use cases have made differential evolution (DE)–based algorithm as a very significant form of optimization algorithm. The control parameters are less, and the optimization is robust to noise with comparison to Genetic Algorithm (GA) [24]. Since the invariance of 3D models are with the changes like illumination, background clutter and occlusion, an efficient 3D reconstruction algorithm is proposed to reconstruct a 3D model from single 2D image [25]. The pose and depth estimation from the 2D feature points of the respective images is fixed as optimization goal and differential evolution optimization is used to get the optimal solution. Simple model integration method is introduced to predict the estimation accuracy of the 3D imagery.

A generative model for the multivariate data is defined as iterative soft thresholding algorithm (ISTA) in Berisha and Nagy [23]. Improved iterative soft thresholding algorithm (IISTA) is proposed in Kothapelli and Tirumala [25] combined with basic differential evolutionary (DE) algorithm to get the optimal solution for extracting important features from 2D images global continuous optimization problem [26].

The existing literature has nurtured the thought of applying evolutionary algorithm-based contour detection technique in this research work for elevation classification of sand deposits captured with drone images. The research outcomes have exhibited significant improvement in output image generation with statistical significance.

9.3   Research Methodology

The authors have proposed a customized selection of threshold by means of a differential evolution-based metaheuristic search algorithm for initiating contour detection for elevation classification. The optimized selection of threshold for contour detection is carried out with this algorithm by iterative improvement of a candidate solution which is based on an evolutionary process.

The differential evolution (DE) is a population-based direct search method that starts working by generating the population randomly over the solution space [27, 28]. The iterated process of reproduction of the population continues until the maximum iteration or other stopping criterion is met. Genetic operator mutation, crossover and selection are performed to estimate the new solution for next generation in reproduction process. Three random indices are chosen in mutation operation and by (9.1) a new solution is generated:

$$m_{i,G+1} = V_{r_1,G} + F * (V_{r_2,G} - V_{r_3,G}) \qquad (9.1)$$

F denotes a constant number lying between 0 and 2. To get the mutant vector $m_{i,G+1}$, difference between to parameter vectors $V_{r_2,G}, V_{r_3,G}$ is added to a third one $V_{r_1,G}$. This is known as rand/1/ mutation strategy. To generate the mutant vector, crossover operation is performed. Either parameters of trial vectors can be randomly chosen from mutant vector or parameter vectors are called as target vector.

$$c_{ji,G+1} = \begin{cases} m_{ji,G+1} \ if \ (rand \ p(j) \leq CR) \ or \ j = rnbr(i) \\ V_{ji,G+1} \ if \ (rand \ p(j) > CR) and \ j \neq rnbr(i) \end{cases} \qquad (9.2)$$

j = 1, 2,...,D (D dimensional parameter is taken).

The selection operation of crossover is calculated from equation (9.2). *rand p(j)* is the jth evaluated value from uniform random generator *rand p(j)* and its value lies between 0 and 1. CR is the user defined crossover constant lying between 0 and 1. Randomly chosen index rnbr(i) where i belongs to {1, 2,...,D} helps $c_{ji,G+1}$ to achieve at least one parameter from $m_{i,G+1}$. Hence, the trial vector is formed by taking account both the current and mutant vector parameters. The individual solutions are ranked according to their fitness value for each iteration. This process is termed as selection on DE. A new generated parameter vector can be calculated using:

$$V_{i,G+1} = \begin{cases} c_{i,G+1} & \text{if fitness } (c_{i,G+1}) < \text{ fitness } (V_{i,G+1}) \\ V_{i,G} & \text{otherwise} \end{cases} \quad (9.3)$$

The Entropy Yen fitness function is used for determining two different optimal threshold values. Based on the threshold values the contouring is carried out.

A flowchart for the proposed technique is given in Figure 9.1.

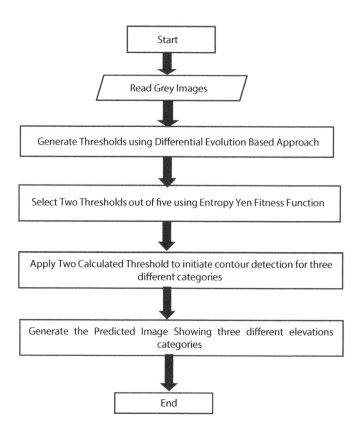

Figure 9.1 Proposed technique.

9.3.1 Dataset and Metrics

The dataset is created by generating images from an open-source video [29]. The images in the dataset are captured in a desert area using drone camera.

A sample image dataset is given below in Figure 9.2.

Structural Similarity Index (SSIM) is used to find the similarity between the ground truth images and the images processed from both the methods: monocular estimation and Evolutionary method. SSIM is calculated using the equation:

$$SSIM(x, y) = \frac{(2\mu_x\mu_y + c_1)(2\sigma_{xy} + c_2)}{(\mu_x^2 + \mu_y^2 + c_1)(\sigma_x^2 + \sigma_y^2 + c_2)} \tag{9.4}$$

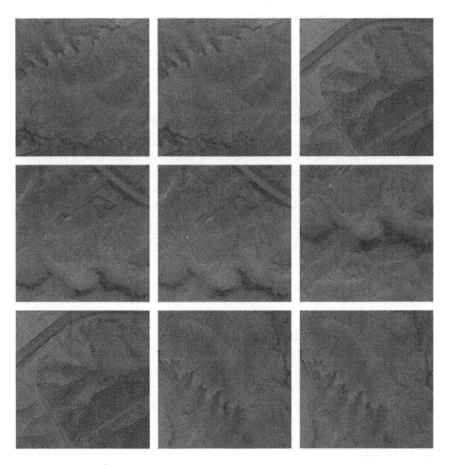

Figure 9.2 Image dataset.

where x and y are images in form of an array, μ_x is the average of x, μ_y is the average of y and σ_x^2, σ_y^2 are variance of x and y respectively and σ_{xy} is the covariance of x and y.

Further, a paired t test is carried out to estimate the statistical significance of the calculated results using the proposed technique to that of the state-of-the-art technique.

9.4   Result and Discussion

All the experiments were carried out on a Windows system with Intel i7 processor paired with 32 GBs of RAM. Elevation classification is carried out for different heights of sand deposits as well as plain land present in the images of the dataset. Different levels of elevations are represented with three different colors, namely red, green, and blue.

The classification task is primarily carried out using the proposed technique that has implemented a differential evolution-based algorithm with Entropy Yen as Fitness Function to determine two different thresholds to guide optimal contouring for elevation classification.

Further, a state-of-the-art monocular depth estimation technique is used on the dataset. The method implements prediction of disparity between pixels by taking the help of a pool of shift and scale independent dense losses. Let p be the parameter of the prediction model and Z implies the number of pixels in an image with valid ground truth. Let $x^* \in M^Z$ be the disparity in ground truth and $x = x(p) \in M^Z$ be the corresponding prediction of the disparity. Subscripts are used to index singular pixels.

The method defines the shift and scale independent dense losses for a single sample as:

$$\varphi_{ssi}(\hat{x}, \hat{x}^*) = \frac{1}{2Z} \sum_{i=1}^{Z} \sigma(\hat{x}_1, \hat{x}_1^*) \tag{9.5}$$

where $\hat{x}^*$ and $\hat{x}$ are shifted and scaled versions of the ground truth and predictions and defines the loss function of a particular category.

Let $a: M^Z \rightarrow M_+$ and $b: M^Z \rightarrow M$ denote estimators of the scale and transition. A logical necessity for shift and scale independent loss is that the ground truth and prediction should be appropriately in sync with respect to their scale and shift, which means, $a(\hat{x}) \approx a(\hat{x}^*)$ and $b(\hat{x}) \approx b(\hat{x}^*)$.

First, based on least squares criterion, the prediction is aligned the ground truth.

$$(a, b) = \arg min_{s,t} \sum_{i=1}^{Z} (ax_i + b - x_i^*)^2 \tag{9.6}$$

$$\hat{x} = ax + b, \quad \hat{x}^* = x^*$$

Subsequently, if the above equation can be represented as a typical least squares problem:
Let

$$\vec{x_i} = (x_i, 1)^T \ and \ d = (a, b)^T,$$

and hence,

$$d^{opt} = \arg min_d \sum_{i=1}^{Z} (\vec{x_i}^T d - x_i^*)^2 \tag{9.7}$$

Then Structural Similarity Index (SSIM) is the evaluation metric estimate the similarity between the ground truth images and the output images produced using the state-of-the art technique, as well as the proposed technique. A sample illustration of the outcomes with proposed technique and the state of the art is shown in Figure 9.3.

The closer the SSIM output to 1 the greater is the similarity of the two images. The results shown in Figure 9.4 clearly reveal that our proposed method has outclassed the state of the art (monocular depth estimation for elevation classification).

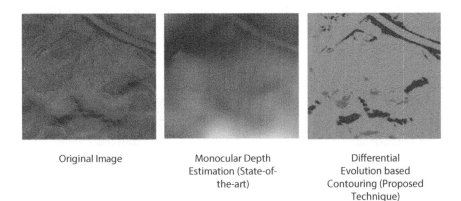

| Original Image | Monocular Depth Estimation (State-of-the-art) | Differential Evolution based Contouring (Proposed Technique) |

Figure 9.3 Output images state-of-the-art vs proposed techniques.

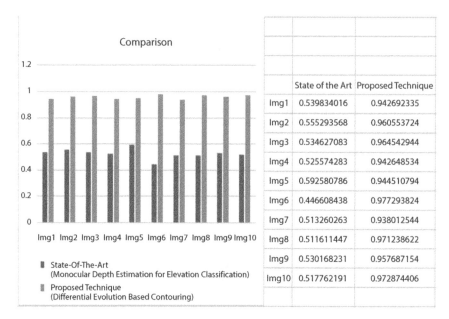

Figure 9.4 Comparison of similarity index of outputs of both methods vs ground truth value.

Henceforth, the authors have carried out a two-tailed, paired *t-test* to evaluate the statistical significance of the proposed technique over the state of the art. The p-value computed for the existing state-of-the-art with respect to our proposed technique is shown in Table 9.1.

H0: There is no significant difference in SSIM values of the state-of-the-art technique to that of the proposed technique when compared to ground truth images

H1: There is significant difference in SSIM values of the state-of-the-art technique to that of the proposed technique when compared to ground truth images

Table 9.1 *Paired t-test for* significance of precision value.

Comparison	*t-calc*	*p-value*	Significance of difference value
Monocular depth estimation	29.4051	0.0001	Significant

The p value shows strong evidence against the null hypothesis $H0$. Hence the proposed technique has outperformed the existing state-of-the-art monocular depth estimation technique and has shown significant improvement in performance. Thus, the research objective of carrying out improvement in elevation classification for two-dimensional drone imagery is successfully achieved using the proposed method of evolutionary algorithm-based optimized contouring technique.

9.5   Conclusion

This work has carried out a comparison of the proposed differential evolution-based contour detection technique to that of existing state-of-the-art model of monocular depth estimation for the task of elevation classification in two-dimensional drone imagery. The research outcomes have established the superior performance of proposed model over existing deep learning-based approach. Compared to the existing models, the proposed approach in this work is more efficient in identifying different levels of elevation. The authors have used SSIM as the metric for evaluating the proposed algorithm. The computed values of the metric on ten different images achieve improved results compared to monocular depth estimation algorithm. The proposed model can be helpful in analyzing the images captured using unmanned aerial vehicles (UAV) for military surveillance, e-commerce, track detection, and various other agricultural use cases.

References

1. Mishra, B., Garg, D., Narang, P., Mishra, V., Drone-surveillance for search and rescue in natural disaster. *Comput. Commun.*, 156, 1–10, 2020.
2. Caillouet, C., Giroire, F., Razafindralambo, T., Efficient data collection and tracking with flying drones. *Ad Hoc Netw.*, 89, 35–46, 2019.
3. Sarfraz, F., Arani, E., Zonooz, B., Knowledge distillation beyond model compression, in: *2020 25th International Conference on Pattern Recognition (ICPR)*, IEEE, pp. 6136–6143, January 2021.
4. Cho, J.H. and Hariharan, B., On the efficacy of knowledge distillation, in: *Proceedings of the IEEE/CVF International Conference on Computer Vision*, pp. 4794–4802, 2019.
5. Zhao, C., Sun, Q., Zhang, C., Tang, Y., Qian, F., Monocular depth estimation based on deep learning: An overview. *Sci. China Technol. Sci.*, 63, 1612–1627, 2020.

6. Jiao, J., Cao, Y., Song, Y., Lau, R., Look deeper into depth: Monocular depth estimation with semantic booster and attention-driven loss, in: *Proceedings of the European Conference on Computer Vision (ECCV)*, pp. 53–69, 2018.

7. Weili, D., Yong, L., Wenfeng, W., Xiuyan, C., Depth estimation of urban road image based on contour understanding. *Acta Opt. Sin.*, 34, 7, 0715001, 2014.

8. Ramamonjisoa, M. and Lepetit, V., Sharpnet: Fast and accurate recovery of occluding contours in monocular depth estimation, in: *Proceedings of the IEEE/CVF International Conference on Computer Vision Workshops*, 2019.

9. Ranftl, R., Lasinger, K., Hafner, D., Schindler, K., Koltun, V., Towards robust monocular depth estimation: Mixing datasets for zero-shot cross-dataset transfer, in: *IEEE Transactions on Pattern Analysis and Machine Intelligence*, vol. 44, no. 3, pp. 1623–1637, 2019.

10. Kim, I.H., Jeon, H., Baek, S.C., Hong, W.H., Jung, H.J., Application of crack identification techniques for an aging concrete bridge inspection using an unmanned aerial vehicle. *Sensors*, 18, 6, 1881, 2018.

11. French, A., Mozaffari, M., Eldosouky, A., Saad, W., Environment-aware deployment of wireless drones base stations with google earth simulator, in: *2019 IEEE international conference on pervasive computing and communications workshops (PerCom Workshops)*, IEEE, pp. 868–873, March 2019.

12. Singh, A.K., Swarup, A., Agarwal, A., Singh, D., Vision based rail track extraction and monitoring through drone imagery. *ICT Express*, 5, 4, 250–255, 2019.

13. Mertan, A., Duff, D.J., Unal, G., Single image depth estimation: An overview. *Digit. Signal Process.*, 123, 1051–2004, 2021.

14. Eigen, D., Puhrsch, C., Fergus, R., Depth map prediction from a single image using a multi-scale deep network. *Adv. Neural Inf. Process. Syst.*, 2366–2374, 2014.

15. Madhuanand, L., Nex, F., Yang, M.Y., Self-supervised monocular depth estimation from oblique UAV videos. *ISPRS J. Photogramm. Remote Sens.*, 176, 1–14, 2021.

16. Ramamonjisoa, M., Du, Y., Lepetit, V., Predicting sharp and accurate occlusion boundaries in monocular depth estimation using displacement fields, in: *Proceedings of the IEEE/CVF Conference on Computer Vision and Pattern Recognition*, pp. 14648–14657, 2020.

17. Chen, G., Choi, W., Yu, X., Han, T., Chandraker, M., Learning efficient object detection models with knowledge distillation, in: *Advances in Neural Information Processing Systems*, vol. 30, 2017.

18. Chanduri, S.S., Suri, Z.K., Vozniak, I., Müller, C., CamLessMonoDepth: Monocular Depth Estimation with Unknown Camera Parameters, 2021, https://doi.org/10.48550/arXiv.2110.14347.

19. Wang, Y., Li, X., Shi, M., Xian, K., Cao, Z., Knowledge distillation for fast and accurate monocular depth estimation on mobile devices, in: *Proceedings of the IEEE/CVF Conference on Computer Vision and Pattern Recognition*, pp. 2457–2465, 2021.

20. Shoukat, M.A., Sargano, A.B., Habib, Z., You, L., An automatic cluster-based approach for depth estimation of single 2D images, in: *2019 13th International Conference on Software, Knowledge, Information Management and Applications (SKIMA)*, IEEE, pp. 1–8, August 2019.

21. Xu, D., Ouyang, W., Wang, X., Sebe, N., Pad-net: Multi-tasks guided prediction-and-distillation network for simultaneous depth estimation and scene parsing, in: *Proceedings of the IEEE Conference on Computer Vision and Pattern Recognition*, pp. 675–684, 2018.

22. Chandar, K.P. and Savithri, T.S., 3D face model estimation based on similarity transform using differential evolution optimization. *Procedia Comput. Sci.*, 54, 621–630, 2015.

23. Berisha, S. and Nagy, J.G., Iterative methods for image restoration, in: *Academic Press Library in Signal Processing*, vol. 4, pp. 193–247, Elsevier, Emory University, Atlanta, GA, USA, 2014.

24. Mirjalili, S., Dong, J.S., Sadiq, A.S., Faris, H., Genetic algorithm: Theory, literature review, and application in image reconstruction, in: *Nature-Inspired Optimizers*, pp. 69–85, 2020.

25. Kothapelli, P.C. and Tirumala, S.S., Depth estimation using hybrid optimization algorithm. *J. Comput. Inf. Syst.*, 11, 19, 7103–7112, 2015.

26. Kopf, J., Rong, X., Huang, J.B., Robust consistent video depth estimation, in: *Proceedings of the IEEE/CVF Conference on Computer Vision and Pattern Recognition*, pp. 1611–1621, 2021.

27. Şahin, C. and Kuvvetli, Y., Differential evolution based meta-heuristic algorithm for dynamic continuous berth allocation problem. *Appl. Math. Modell.*, 40, 23-24, 10679–10688, 2016.

28. Dhal, K.G., Abdulazeez, A.M., Nishad, S., Enhancement of UAV-aerial images using weighted differential evolution algorithm. *International Journal of Scientific Research in Computer Science, Engineering and Information Technology (IJSRCSEIT)*, 7, 2, 196–206, 2021.

29. https://dronemapper.com/sample_data/ (last accessed: 20-11-2021).

10

Bioinspired MOPSO-Based Power Allocation for Energy Efficiency and Spectral Efficiency Trade-Off in Downlink NOMA

Jyotirmayee Subudhi* and P. Indumathi

Department of Electronics Engineering, MIT campus, Anna University, Chennai, India

Abstract

For its excellent spectrum efficiency, nonorthogonal multiple access (NOMA) has lately been examined as a viable radio access technique for 5G mobile communication. Green radio (GR), which concentrates on energy efficiency (EE), is quickly gaining a popular trend. We have regarded the advantage of NOMA for multiuser downlink 5G networks, where spectral efficiency (SE) is the metric which demonstrates how many information bits can be delivered within a unit of time and system bandwidth and energy efficiency (EE) is represented as the ratio of achievable sum rate and overall power consumption of the system which contains circuit power and transmission power. As there being a nontrivial trade-off between the EE and SE, it should be considered while developing resource allocation algorithms in communication systems. Motivated by this issue, we have focused on the downlink NOMA network in this paper, where the base station operates multiuser deployed randomly. The primary goal of this research is to increase energy efficiency while keeping a minimal SE need that is sustainable. The joint user clustering and multiobjective particle swarm optimization (MOPSO) method have been suggested for downlink NOMA by reaching the Pareto optimal solution set. The mathematical results obtained by simulation show that the suggested MOPSO method dominates the existing systems based on parametric efficiency.

Keywords: EE-SE tradeoff, nonorthogonal multiple access, power allocation, PSO

Corresponding author: jyotirmayee.subudhi@mitindia.edu

Anita Khosla, Prasenjit Chatterjee, Ikbal Ali and Dheeraj Joshi (eds.) Optimization Techniques in Engineering: Advances and Applications, (169–186) © 2023 Scrivener Publishing LLC

10.1 Introduction

To satisfy the expectations of next-generation networks for larger capacity, faster data rates, and higher service quality, energy-efficient designs must be used. The benefit of NOMA for multiuser downlink 5G networks, where spectral efficiency (SE) is the metric that shows how many information bits can be delivered within a unit of time and system bandwidth and energy efficiency (EE) is the ratio of achievable sum rate. Overall power consumption of the system, which includes both circuit and transmission power, has been considered. Generally, the optimum EE is often directed to lower SE and vice versa. So, there is a need to study the SE-EE trade-off in NOMA [1]. Limiting consumed power or equivalently increasing EE while decreasing SE are conflicting goals that may be connected via trade-offs. Since this is a nontrivial trade-off between the EE and SE must be considered while designing power allocation algorithms in wireless systems.

Under user-rate fairness and NOMA design, the spectral efficiency (SE) improvement issue has restrictions and constraints. Increasing the SE unilaterally results in increased energy consumption, which raises the total cost of system operation. The total energy efficiency (EE) is severely reduced by utilizing as much power as feasible to enhance SE [4]. SE and EE are critical factors that improve resource efficiency in communication networks by decreasing energy costs per bit transferred while increasing user data rate. However, all EE and SE measures are generally contradictory, meaning that increasing one leads to a reduction in the other, and vice versa [5]. As a result, a superior optimizing technique requires addressing the trade-off between SE and EE variables through the use of a multiobjective optimizing formulation [7]. Similarly, some recent papers in the research have been devoted to solving multiobjective optimization problems in communications systems.

Ni *et al.* [6] address the EE-NOMA optimizing problem with finding the minimum overall power necessary to obtain a certain fair rate for each user. The authors evaluate these variables for each user and show which one has the best resource efficiency (RE) in the system based on the EE-SE trade-off optimization issue with optimum fairness. The present contribution differs from Ni *et al.* [6] in that we adopt a multiobjective PSO technique with a specific number of users in each cluster [8]. Takeda and Higuchi [9] investigated the EE-SE trade-off in DL NOMA-based heterogeneous networks. The EE-SE trade-off problem is modeled as a biobjective optimization (BOO) problem. Both EE and SE are optimized to meet the maximum transmit power for small cell users (SUEs) and the lowest rate constraints. To maintain the multiobjective problem computable, it is converted into a single objective problem using a weighted sum technique, allowing network operators to dynamically modify the weight factor to adapt to different EE and SE design requirements. Song *et al.* [2] developed an enhanced particle swarm optimization (PSO) technique with faster convergence over normal PSO to maximize the SE-EE tradeoff in a down-link NOMA network using the quasi-concave function and QoS requirements. Al-Obiedollah *et al.* [3] investigated a multiobjective optimization strategy for the SE-EE tradeoff in a downlink NOMA system. The authors used a weighted sum approach with the flexibility to change the weight as needed to maximize SE while limiting power consumption (PC). Subudhi and Indumathi [11] proposed a single-objective optimization approach in a downlink NOMA network to maximize the EE while adhering to the strictest QoS constraints. Finally, Mahrach *et al.* [12] developed a power allocation issue solution in downlink NOMA systems to optimize the SE-EE trade-off utilizing fairness concerns.

To the best of our understanding, this is the first study to address the user pairing and multiobjective PSO technique in downlink NOMA networks and discover the Pareto optimal solution sets compared to multiple suggestions for the SE-EE tradeoff optimization. The objective is to maximize the EE and SE parameters by pairing users and allocating power to maintain the EE and SE. In consequence, various circumstances impose varying communication requirements on the network. As a result, it is more vital to improve SE during high traffic hours, while outside of peak hours, it is most important to consider EE. For this reason, describing the Resource efficiency issue as a multiobjective optimization process is essential.

In this paper, we explain the trade-off between energy efficiency and spectral efficiency in downlink NOMA using bio-inspired multiobjective PSO optimization (PPSO) and analyze the performance of the proposed system model with existing works. The contribution of work is explained here.

i.   Our study provides a comprehensive methodology in clustering users and optimizing power allocation for the trade-off between SE and EE in multiuser power domain downlink NOMA network to address the gap.

ii. For downlink NOMA in 5G, we present an efficient and low-complexity Joint user clustering where users are paired in the groups by their channel gains.

iii. To tackle this challenging trade-off issue, we propose a unique solution that optimizes the EE by maximizing the SE under optimal power allocation. This solution considers the multiobjective PSO algorithm for power optimization in the system model.

iv. We conducted comprehensive analysis and numerical simulations to establish our proposed multiobjective PSO method (PPSO). Simulation outcomes show that the PPSO approach has a higher and enhanced system performance than other existing methods, demonstrating the influence of NOMA in diverse 5G communication environments.

The remainder of this work is structured as follows. The downlink NOMA system model is detailed in Section 10.2. Section 10.3 provides a formulation of the low complexity user pairing for the NOMA system. Section 10.4 develops solutions to the EE-SE trade-off problem, outlining the primary aspect of increasing EE while keeping a minimum SE need. Finally, section 10.5 presents comprehensive numerical findings, while Section 10.6 summarizes the paper.

10.2   System Model

Consider a downlink multiuser NOMA network with a single base station (BS) and a single antenna located in the middle of a hexagonal cell. In the coverage region, N users are allocated at random. This must be noted that in this NOMA system, several users could be assigned to the single spectrum resource in a specific SIC order and decode their signals using the SIC technique. After eliminating all signals from the weakest users with lower gain levels, the strongest user having the greatest gain value generally decodes its signal. Users with greater channel knowledge may minimize or lessen disruption caused by users with lower channel information. The SIC process for the downlink NOMA is explained in the Figure 10.1.

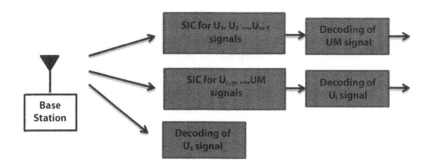

Figure 10.1 SIC process in downlink NOMA transmission with N users.

Bs denotes the accessible system bandwidth, subdivided into frequency available bandwidth. Let us denote x1, x2, ...,xN denoted as the messages transferred to the users. The number of clusters might range between 1 and N/2 depending on the value of n. The maximum BS transmit power is PT, while the maximum downlink NOMA per cluster transmission power value is Pt.

Hence the NOMA signals can be expressed as

$$x_{NOMA} = \sqrt{P}(\sqrt{\alpha_1}x_1 + \sqrt{\alpha_2}x_2 + \cdots + \sqrt{\alpha_N}x_N) \tag{10.1}$$

where α1, α2 and αN are the fractional coefficients of power.

$$\alpha_1 > \alpha_2 > \cdots > \alpha_N \tag{10.2}$$

$$\alpha_1 > \alpha_2 + \alpha_3 + \cdots + \alpha_N \tag{10.3}$$

$$\alpha_1 + \alpha_2 + \cdots + \alpha_N = 1 \tag{10.4}$$

the noma equation can be re-expressed as

$$x_{NOMA} = \sqrt{P}\sum_{i=1}^{N}\sqrt{\alpha_i}x_i \tag{10.5}$$

The signal received at the ith user may be represented as

$$y_{i,NOMA} = h_i x_{NOMA} + z_i \tag{10.6}$$

where $h_i = g_i.PL^{-1}(d)$ are the Rayleigh channel coefficient, PL-1(d) represents the path loss function among the BS, and the user over distance d, and gi is considered Rayleigh fading channel gain. In addition, N0 denotes the noise power spectral density.

The above equation (10.6) is represented as

$$y_{i,NOMA} = h_i\sqrt{P}(\sqrt{\alpha_1}x_1 + \sqrt{\alpha_2}x_2 + \cdots + \sqrt{\alpha_N}x_N) + z_i \tag{10.7}$$

At the far user, the received vector is given by

$$y_{1,NOMA} = h_1\sqrt{P}(\sqrt{\alpha_1}x_1 + \sqrt{\alpha_2}x_2 + \cdots + \sqrt{\alpha_N}x_N) + z_1 \tag{10.8}$$

Direct decoding will be performed to estimate x1.
The SINR for decoding far user signal is given by

$$\gamma_{1,NOMA} = \frac{\alpha_1 P |h_1|^2}{\alpha_2 P |h_1|^2 + \alpha_3 P |h_1|^2 + \cdots + \alpha_N P |h_1|^2 + \sigma^2} \tag{10.9}$$

At the second user, the recived signal can be expressed as

$$y_{2,NOMA} = h_2 \sqrt{P}(\sqrt{\alpha_1} x_1 + \sqrt{\alpha_2} x_2 + \cdots + \sqrt{\alpha_N} x_N) + z_2 \tag{10.10}$$

The concept of SIC is applied to get

$$y'_{2,NOMA} = h_2 \sqrt{P}(\sqrt{\alpha_2} x_2 + \cdots + \sqrt{\alpha_N} x_N) + z_2 \tag{10.11}$$

SINR for decoding the second user signal is given by

$$\gamma_{2,NOMA} = \frac{\alpha_2 P |h_2|^2}{\alpha_3 P |h_2|^2 + \alpha_4 P |h_2|^2 + \cdots + \alpha_N P |h_2|^2 + \sigma^2} \tag{10.12}$$

The ith SINR is given by

$$\gamma_{i,NOMA} = \frac{\alpha_i P |h_i|^2}{\alpha_{i+1} P |h_i|^2 + \alpha_{i+2} P |h_i|^2 + \cdots + \alpha_N P |h_i|^2 + \sigma^2} \tag{10.13}$$

or

$$\gamma_{i,NOMA} = \frac{\alpha_i P |h_i|^2}{P |h_i|^2 \sum_{j=i+1}^{N} \alpha_j + \sigma^2} \tag{10.14}$$

The achievable total rate is written by using Shannon's capacity equation.

$$R_{i,NOMA} = log_2(1 + \gamma_{i,NOMA}) \tag{10.15}$$

The sum rate of all NOMA users is expressed by

$$R_{NOMA} = \sum_{i=1}^{N} R_{i,NOMA} \qquad (10.16)$$

Equation (10.16) can be rewritten as

$$R_{NOMA} = B_s \sum_{i=1}^{N-1} \log_2 \Sigma \left(1 + \frac{\alpha_i P |h_i|^2}{P |h_i|^2 \sum_{j=i+1}^{N} \alpha_j + \sigma^2} \right)$$
$$+ \log_2 \left(1 + \frac{\alpha_N P |h_N|^2}{\sigma^2} \right) \qquad (10.17)$$

10.3   User Clustering

To investigate traditional near–far pairs in NOMA, the topic is limited to the simplest scenario of two users in pairs. It is preferable to group users from the cell centre (high CQI) and cell edge (low CQI) into pairs to preserve the highest channel gain differential between these users [10]. Cell mid users who therefore remain unpaired must also be handled. The channel gain variation between these in-pair users is quite small when mid cell users are grouped. This mentioned pairing case is shown in Figure 10.2.

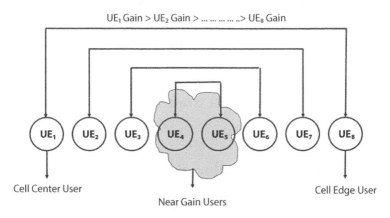

Figure 10.2 Near far user pairing in NOMA.

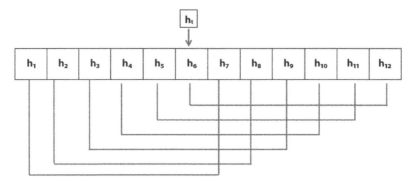

Figure 10.3 User pairing for 12 users.

Since the inverse relationship between channel gains and allotted powers, the proximity in assigned powers among these cell mid-in-pair users caused significant interference. The capacity reduction in these central cell pairings may be attributed to two factors: greater noise at low-gain users and SIC imperfection at strong users. These challenges are caused by the strong correlation between channel gains and assigned powers. Due to their limited mobility, cell mid users' gain difference might become minimal if they are still paired. This produces extremely high interference among in-pair users, necessitating their un-pairing and re-pairing with the other users. This causes constant un-pairing and re-pairing, increasing computing complexity, signaling overhead, and transmitter time delays. Though near–far pair effectively produces capacity enhancements for cell-edge users, difficulties for intermediate and high-gain users remain a major subject of concern.

A high difference in the channel gain between users is required for mitigating the interference between the users in the pair. This is the key point in the pairing strategy depicted in Figure 10.3. 12 users in the cell for the simulation point of view has been assumed. In this proposed static user pairing, the Rayleigh fading channel gain for each user has been found. Then one threshold value has been fixed for the channel gain for users is described. Here the average of the channel gain has been decided as the threshold value.

10.4　Optimal Power Allocation for EE-SE Tradeoff

Consider the EE metric, which is generally characterized as the ratio of the attainable data rate over total energy usage, represented as follows:

$$EE = \frac{R_{NOMA}}{p_c + p_t} \tag{10.18}$$

where transmission power is denoted as pt and constant circuit power as pc, it should be noted that the overall data rate R is connected to the SE parameter using the formula R=SE*Bs. The EE–SE tradeoff is mathematically formulated as an optimization problem with various restrictions. The primary concept is to enhance EE by setting a minimum SE to be fulfilled, RMin. Let us define the related minimal desired rate RMin.

$$max \ EE = \frac{\sum_{i=1}^{N} R_{NOMA}}{\sum_{i=1}^{N} p_i + p_c} \tag{10.19}$$

$$\text{Subject to } C1: p_t \geq 0 \tag{10.20}$$

$$C2: \sum_{i=1}^{N} p_i \leq P \tag{10.21}$$

$$C3: R_{NOMA} \geq R_{min} \tag{10.22}$$

$$C4: R_{NOMA} \geq R_i^{min} \tag{10.23}$$

where C1 is the nonnegative assigned power of users. C2 imposes the transmitted power restriction with the highest total power available at the BS, P. In this scenario, the minimum SE is an input in constraint C3, which must be met while assigning the radio resource. C4 guarantees that users are subjected to the minimal data rate limits specified by QoS.

10.4.1 Multiobjective Optimization Problem

In general, a multiobjective optimization problem (MOP) is made up of a number of objective functions as well as certain restrictions [18]. For example, a MOP with m objective functions and n deciding variables may be defined below without losing generality.

$$min \; \Sigma \; f(x) = (f_1(x), f_2(x), \cdots, fn(x)) \qquad (10.13)$$

with some equality and inequality constraints.

10.4.2   Multiobjective PSO

Pareto, an Italian economist, developed the Pareto optimum solution. Multiobjective mathematics programming may be used to define a rigorous Pareto optimum solution. Considering that multiple objectives are being achieved at the same time, these objectives are unrelated to one another and cannot be balanced and combined. To tackle such a challenge, a new optimization concept is required. In general, when one sub-objective is enhanced, another sub-objective is sacrificed. As a result, it is challenging to enhance all sub-goals at the same time. The Pareto optimum solution is also known as the nondominated solution. Owing to circumstances such as conflict and incomparability between many different sub-objectives. A solution in a multiobjective optimization process is often the finest in one sub-objective and could be the very worst others; if there is only one answer, enhancing any sub-objective feature will invariably degrade at least one other sub-objective function, which is identified as a nondominated solution or Pareto optimal solution. The Pareto optimum solution set comprises all Pareto optimal solutions, then mapped by the objective function to generate the Pareto optimal front.

PSO is an optimization approach based on bird flocking behavior [13]. Before the optimized result is reached, a large population (swarm) of ideal solution (parts) is positioned at randomly initialized positions and transported around the search space. Particles see their separate best solutions, in addition to the best solution discovered so far. The advantage of using PSO is that it can search for the best solution in a large solution space by studying the objective function. Every particle searches the swarm. During the search, every particle does have its memories to recall the best location and share the information obtained to neighbouring particles in the swarming to suitably upgrade their position and velocity. Because each particle in the PSO algorithm is analogous to a bird in the population, each particle has its speed and location. The particles travel in the solution space to achieve the global optimum via self and social learning [14]. This procedure is repeated until there is no change in the location of any of the particles. The fundamental formula of the PSO shall be represented by

$$v_i^{k+1} = v_i^k + \triangle v_i^k \qquad (10.24)$$

$$\Delta v_{i,k}^k = w v_{i,k}^k + c_1 \bullet rand() \bullet (pbest_{i,k}^k - s_i^k) + c_2 \bullet rand() \bullet (gbest^k - s_i^k)$$

$$(10.25)$$

where v_i^{k+1} is the position of particle P at (k+1)th iteration, whereas v_i^k is the position of particle P at kth iteration. Δv_i^k is the velocity of a particle at kth iteration. c1 and c2 are the inertia weights. $pbest_{i,k}^k$, pbest is the best solution achieved to date by that particle, and gbestk is also the finest particle obtained to date by any particle in the area of the particle.

The gbest is particularly significant in a MOPSO algorithm since it directly impacts convergence and capability. In MOPSO, the size of the population is constant, and particles are not eliminated from the population; nevertheless, the particle's location in the population must be modified to change pbest and gbest. In multiobjective circumstances, gbest is often found in a group of noninferior solutions rather than a distinct gbest location. When gbest and pbest are not dominant, each particle can have multiple pbest (as a result, the proper procedure must be used to choose pbest and the gbest). The most important aspect of the MOPSO is the selection of Pbest. Pbestki, k is employed to store the nondominated solutions of the particles in the evolutionary process and preserve their positions. The updating formula for pbest is

$$pbest_{i,k}^k = \begin{cases} pbest_{i,k}^k \ \text{if} \ (f(pbest_{i,k}^k) < f(s_i^k)) \\ s_i^k \ \text{if} \ (f(pbest_{i,k}^k) \geq f(s_i^k)) \end{cases} \quad (10.26)$$

where $pbest_{i,k}^k$ is the optimum location of the i -th particle in the previous k generations and s_i^k is the best position of the I -th particle in the k-th generation. The inertia weight and the learning variables c1 and c2 in the MOPSO approach significantly impact the population's capacity to explore in the target area. The inertia weight specifies the previous generation particle's effect on the present velocity (an adequate modification rule may successfully balance the algorithm's exploitation and exploration). If w = 0, the particle speed is decided by the present location, and the particle has no connection to the preceding generation's speed, hence, the algorithm is easily prone to falling into the local optimum. If w ≠ 0, the bigger inertial weight can improve global search capacity, while the lower inertial weight can improve local search capability. The learning factor governs the impact of self-learning and social-learning abilities on particle motion throughout the search phase, indicating the information flow level among particles.

10.4.3 MOPSO Algorithm for EE-SE Trade-Off in Downlink NOMA

input: Population of users, Iteration numbers, the Fitness function
    output: The Energy Efficiency of downlink NOMA and the power allocation coefficients of users, i.e., α.

1. Set the group's location and speed to zero. Specify the number of iterations, population size, and process parameters.
2. Determine each particle's fitness value as per equation (10.3). Here the fitness value is the EE of the downlink NOMA system.
3. Generate a nondominating solution set according to dominating relation.
4. Upgrade the individual ideal position; if this is the initial generation, use the starting location of each particle as the individual optimum point; otherwise, use the Pareto dominance relation to modify.
5. Keep personal pbest and global gbest up to date.
6. Revise the speed equation. When the particle velocity vi exceeds Vmax, then let vi equal vmax. Whereas if particle velocity vivmax is greater than the particle velocity vivmin, then vi=vmin.
7. Updating the location of each particle's next iteration.
8. Check whether the condition (the maximum number of iterations) has been reached and stop the loop. Otherwise, go to Step 2 to complete the iteration.

10.5   Numerical Results

This section displays the simulation analysis and result discussion, in which the proposed MOPSO technique for optimum power allocation is modeled and compared to the existing state of the art. At the BS, the channel state information is expected to be perfect. The wireless communication channel is made up of separate Rayleigh Channels. The path loss exponent is fixed to 3, and the AWGN power spectral density is -174 dBm/Hz. We assume each user has the exact Rmin = 2 Mbps, minimum data rate requirement. PC = 20 dBm is the circuit power consumption, while Pmax = 35 dBm is the maximum transmission power of the BS. Unless otherwise specified, the simulation settings are presented in Table 10.1, and they are premised on the third-generation partnership project (3GPP) LTE standard and associated literature. The proposed MOPSO algorithm (PPSO) is assessed

Table 10.1 Simulation parameters.

Parameters	Configuration
Cell radius	1000 m
Distance between users	200 m
Distance between BS and user	100 m
Path loss exponent (α)	3
Maximum transmission power	40 dBm
Bandwidth	5 MHz
Noise power spectral density	−147 dBm
User number per cell	30
Base station power	20 dBm
PSO population size	50
Inertia weight	0.9–0.4
Maximum iterations	100

and compared to current approaches, namely proportional channel and power allocation (PCPA) [15], gain ratio power allocation (GRPA) [16], and fractional transmission power allocation (FTPA) [17].

In Figure 10.4, it is evident that progressively boosting the transmission power may improve the achievable sum-rate (hence the SE) since greater transmission power provides users with more coverage, which improves their capacity to combat unfavourable channel circumstances. The MOPSO-based approach, in particular, delivers power allocation performance that is extremely near to the optimum power allocation technique.

Figure 10.5 depicts the energy efficiency performance for the downlink NOMA systems with various ranges of transmission power. This data also demonstrates that raising transmission power is inefficient to enhance EE, particularly beyond a particular power level. Since raising the transmission power increases the sum rate, it simultaneously increases the power consumption, as shown in (10.5); consequently, energy efficiency is lowered. Because of the multiuser-diversity advantage provided by NOMA, it is apparent that EE rises monotonically with the number of users. The NOMA multiuser diversity advantage is produced due to the flexibility of power allocation systems that optimally leverage variances in the channel gains of the users.

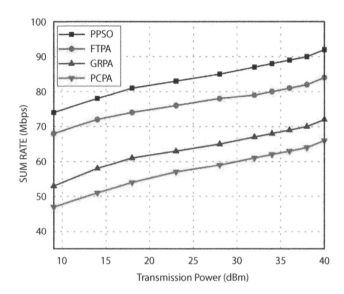

Figure 10.4 Sum rate vs transmission power.

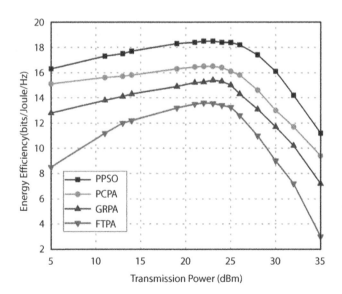

Figure 10.5 Energy efficiency vs transmission power.

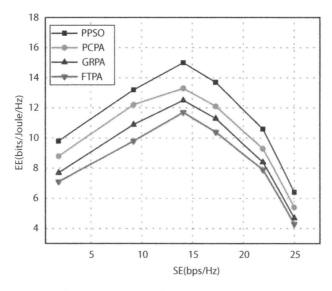

Figure 10.6 Energy efficiency vs spectral efficiency.

Figure 10.6 plots the EE versus SE of all the studied schemes at 40 dBm transmission power. This graph shows the comparative effectiveness of the suggested MOPSO schemes versus the already existing methods in downlink NOMA. The EE-SE curve in Figure 10.6 demonstrates that it is feasible to raise the EE and SE jointly in the lowest SE range, and there is no trade-off in this regime. But EE begins to deteriorate at a particular operational point as SE grows, illustrating its trade-off. It is clear from Figure 10.5 that raising the SE corresponds to expanding the transmission power, and Figure 10.6 demonstrates that improving the transmission power resulted in a decrease in the EE. As a result, there is a fundamental trade-off between the EE and the SE. This graph also demonstrates that NOMA is much more cost-efficient than OFDMA since it enables consumers to utilize the whole bandwidth.

10.6 Conclusion

Future networks must be designed to be energy efficient to mitigate the high energy consumption caused by the expected increase in traffic demand. The EE and the relationship between the EE and the SE of a downlink-multiuser NOMA system were explored in this work. We formulated the EE-SE trade-off like an optimization issue, besides maximizing EE while meeting a minimal SE requirement. Downlink NOMA has discussed the proposed combined user clustering and MOPSO-based power allocation strategy. The findings also validated the efficacy of the suggested strategy and the efficiency of the proposed MOPSO scheme in regard to SE and EE when contrasted to existing NOMA methods. So, in the future, it is essential to expand on this study by taking into account imperfect and statistical CSI in various homogeneous and heterogeneous 5G networks.

References

1. Jacob, J.L., Martinez, C.A.P., Martinez, A.L.M., Abrão, T., Non-linear biobjective EE-SE optimization for NOMA-MIMO systems under user-rate fairness and variable number of users per cluster. *AEU-Int. J. Electron. Commun.*, 138, 153870, 2021.
2. Song, Z., Ni, Q., Navaie, K., Hou, S., Wu, S., Sun, X., On the spectral-energy efficiency and rate fairness tradeoff in relay-aided cooperative OFDMA systems. *IEEE Trans. Wirel. Commun.*, 15, 9, 6342–6355, 2016.
3. Al-Obiedollah, H.M., Cumanan, K., Thiyagalingam, J., Tang, J., Burr, A.G., Ding, Z., Dobre, O.A., Spectral-energy efficiency trade-off-based beamforming design for MISO non-orthogonal multiple access systems. *IEEE Trans. Wirel. Commun.*, 19, 10, 6593–6606, 2020.
4. Guo, Y.X. and Li, H., A power allocation method based on particle swarm algorithm for NOMA downlink networks. *J. Phys. Conf. Ser.*, IOP Publishing, 1087, 2, 022033, September 2018.
5. Xiao, H., Wang, Y., Cheng, Q., Wang, Y., An improved PSO-based power allocation algorithm for the optimal EE and SE tradeoff in downlink NOMA systems, in: *2018 IEEE 29th Annual International Symposium on Personal, Indoor and Mobile Radio Communications (PIMRC)*, IEEE, pp. 1–5, 2018.
6. Ni, D., Hao, L., Qian, X., Tran, Q.T., Energy-spectral efficiency tradeoff of downlink NOMA system with fairness consideration, in: *2018 IEEE 87th Vehicular Technology Conference (VTC Spring)*, IEEE, pp. 1–5, 2018.
7. Glei, N. and Chibani, R.B., EE-SE trade-off optimization for downlink NOMA systems, in: *2020 17th International Multi-Conference on Systems, Signals & Devices (SSD)*, IEEE, pp. 799–802, July 2020.
8. Zhang, S., Zhang, N., Kang, G., Liu, Z., Energy and spectrum efficient power allocation with NOMA in downlink HetNets. *Phys. Commun.*, 31, 121–132, 2018.
9. Takeda, T. and Higuchi, K., Enhanced user fairness using non-orthogonal access with SIC in cellular uplink, in: *2011 IEEE Vehicular Technology Conference (VTC Fall)*, IEEE, pp. 1–5, September 2011.

10. Shahab, M.B., Kader, M.F., Shin, S.Y., A virtual user pairing scheme to optimally utilize the spectrum of unpaired users in non-orthogonal multiple access. *IEEE Signal Process. Lett.*, 23, 12, 1766–1770, 2016.

11. Subudhi, J. and Indumathi, P., Joint user clustering and salp based particle swarm optimization algorithm for power allocation in MIMO-NOMA. *J. Intell. Fuzzy Syst.*, 40, 5, 9007–9019, Jan. 1, 2021.

12. Mahrach, M., Miranda, G., León, C., Segredo, E., Comparison between single and multi-objective evolutionary algorithms to solve the knapsack problem and the travelling salesman problem. *Mathematics*, 8, 11, 2018, 2020.

13. Srinivas, N. and Deb, K., Muiltiobjective optimization using nondominated sorting in genetic algorithms. *Evol. Comput.*, 2, 3, 221–248, 1994.

14. Li, Y.L., Shao, W., You, L., Wang, B.Z., An improved PSO algorithm and its application to UWB antenna design. *IEEE Antennas Wirel. Propag. Lett.*, 12, 1236–1239, 2013.

15. Long, K. *et al.*, Spectrum resource and power allocation with adaptive proportional fair user pairing for NOMA systems. *IEEE Access*, 7, 80043–80057, 2019.

16. Cai, W. *et al.*, Subcarrier and power allocation scheme for downlink OFDM-NOMA systems. *IET Signal Process.*, 11, 1, 51–58, 2017.

17. Parida, P. and Das, S.S., Power allocation in OFDM based NOMA systems: A DC programming approach. *2014 IEEE Globecom Workshops (GC Wkshps)*, IEEE, 2014.

18. Emmerich, M. and Deutz, A.H., A tutorial on multiobjective optimization: Fundamentals and evolutionary methods. *Nat. Comput.*, 17.3 585–609, 2018.

11

Performances of Machine Learning Models and Featurization Techniques on Amazon Fine Food Reviews

Rishabh Singh[1]*, Akarshan Kumar[2] and Mousim Ray[1]

[1]Department of Computer Science & Engineering, Siksha 'O' Anusandhan Deemed to be University, Odisha, India
[2]Department of Information Science & Technology, BMS Institute of Technology and Management, Bengaluru, India

Abstract

In this technologically advanced world, the existence of online stores, which makes products available to the consumers on their fingertips, it is important for retailers to take feedback on their products by the consumers. Reviewing a product also gives other customers an idea about how good or bad a product could be. Reviews will help the retailers improve their service or their product. Our work aims to automatically analyze the reviews and classify if a review is good or bad using amazon fine food reviews dataset. To classify the reviews as positive or negative, four different kind of classifiers such as logistic regression, support vector machine (SVM), random forest and XGBoost were used. Each classifier was used along with four different vectors such as bag of words, TFIDF, average of word2vec, and a combination of TF-IDF and word2vec. The paper proposes a framework to automate the text analysis of reviews for polarization of its sentiment. The work also emphasizes that for certain datasets, simpler models and simpler featurization gives higher accuracy and performance compared to complex models.

Keywords: NLP, machine learning, sentiment analysis, tokenization, vectorization

*Corresponding author: rsrishi10@gmail.com

Anita Khosla, Prasenjit Chatterjee, Ikbal Ali and Dheeraj Joshi (eds.) Optimization Techniques in Engineering: Advances and Applications, (187–200) © 2023 Scrivener Publishing LLC

11.1 Introduction

In the era of digitization, the advent of electronic commerce platforms for making products available online to all consumers has brought a revolutionary change commercially. The rising demand of such platforms has given opportunities to people to come up with innovative ways to improve the customer experience for the consumers. Reviews are one such feature that allows consumers to decide the most suitable product for them. The use of ratings and reviews also helps sellers to make suitable improvements to their products. Customers often tend to compare products based on their reviews and ratings whether a product has negative or positive reviews. It can be seen how much of an influence can reviews have on the decisions of a consumer in buying a product. It is important to make best use of this feature and build a systematic model to further enhance the ability of this feature to cater to the consumers and sellers efficiently. One such method is sentiment analysis.

Sentiment analysis is among the important tasks of natural language processing (NLP) that has gained a momentum in recent years. It is also known as opinion mining. Sentiment as we know is an expression of a thought. Sentiment represents the emotion of a person toward a particular entity. Analyzing the sentiment of the reviews posted by consumers helps us understand how satisfied they are with the product. It helps us to compute the review to be either positive, negative, or neutral. With the advancement of technology, these forms of text analysis, which can detect polarities like if an opinion is positive or negative within a word, phrase, paragraph or sentence help companies build products according to the needs of the customers. There have been many approaches to build a system that automatically analyses customer feedbacks and social media interactions. Kumar, Kolla and Rao [7] in their paper performed classification and sentimental analysis on amazon reviews. Fang and Zhan [8] and Shivaprasad and Shetty [9] also performed sentimental analysis using product review data.

This paper aims at analyzing the polarity of sentiment to be positive or negative for comments and reviews of customers on a sentence level. An approximate way to determine the polarity of review is to observe the rating of a product. If the rating of an item is 4 or 5 it can be considered as a positive review likewise if the rating is 1 or 2 it can be assumed to be a negative review. A rating of 3 can be considered as neutral. We have ignored such reviews in our analysis. The dataset for our work was chosen on the basis that compared to other datasets the reviews are streamed data representing actual true reviews.

11.1.1   Related Work

Recently, there have been a vast number of developments in research related to sentiment analysis on product reviews. The developments have significantly helped the retailers in improving their products and customers to make better choices while buying online. The sentiment analysis performed by Jagdale, Shirsat and Deshmukh [10], Singla, Randhawa and Jain [11] and Chen, Xue and Zhao [12] using machine learning and neural network techniques has contributed to the improvement in customer experiences. Vineet Jain and Mayur Kambli [1] had performed experiments on amazon product review dataset for both classification and extraction of narratives using logistic regression (LR) achieving an accuracy of 89% with bag of words (BOW). In their work, Johar and Mubeen [2] built a prototype to classify the reviews into positive and negative using Naïve Bayes and Support Vector Machine (SVM). They used BOW and term frequency and inverse document frequency (TF-IDF) for vectorization. Nguyen *et al.* [3] presented a comparative study of text sentiment analysis using TF-IDF in both lexicon-based approaches and supervised machine learning algorithm. They used three types of supervised learning algorithms, namely LR, SVM and gradient boosting. To compare the machine learning algorithms with lexicon-based approaches Valence Aware Dictionary and Sentiment Reasoner (VADER), SentiWordNet and Pattern. Consequently, it was seen that all the machine learning algorithms performed better than the lexicon-based techniques where LR gave the highest accuracy of 90%. Haque *et al.* [4], in their work, polarized reviews into positive and negative by extracting features using BOW and TF-IDF. They compared the results obtained from various classifiers, such as Linear SVM, Multinomial Naïve Bayes, Stochastic Gradient Descent, Random Forest, Logistic Regression, Decision Tree. Linear SVM gave the highest accuracy of 93.52% with 10-fold cross-validation and 91.72% accuracy with 5-fold cross validation. Jyoti Budhwar and Sukhdip Singh [5] in their paper proposed a hybrid approach for analyzing sentiment on reviews from amazon. The dataset was trained using long short-term memory (LSTM) after which the data were grouped with the help of k-nearest neighbor (KNN) followed by Naïve Bayes for classification. The research was conducted to provide a better solution for sentiment analysis. The experiment conducted by Thakkar *et al.* [6] showed that logistic regression with an accuracy of 93.7% using Bi gram for featurization gave the best results for the automatic analysis of sentiments for the corpus.

11.2   Materials and Methods

The work was carried out for the polarization of customer's reviews to be positive or negative. Figure 11.1 illustrates the proposed framework. The first step in the framework was to clean the dataset of any duplications and pre-process the data to make it suitable to feed it into the network. In the next step, feature extractions were applied for information retrieval. Four different types of feature extraction process were applied for each classifier namely bag of words, TF-IDF, average of word2vec and by combining TF-IDF and word2vec. Lastly, the reviews were polarized using a classifier. The experiment was conducted using four different kinds of classifiers that were logistic regression, support vector machine, random forest, and xgboost.

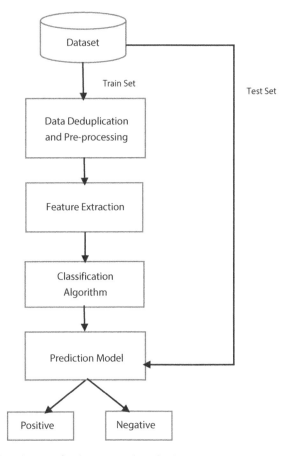

Figure 11.1 Flow diagram for the proposed method.

11.2.1   Data Cleaning and Pre-Processing

The dataset used for our work was Amazon fine food reviews dataset from Kaggle. The dataset used contains approximately 500,000 reviews on fine food products. The information of the users and products are present in the dataset along with the ratings and reviews in plain text. The dataset includes 568,454 reviews, 256,059 users and 74,258 products. Noticeably, 260 users had reviews more than 50. It was observed that the dataset contained some duplicate data. In order to remove the duplicate data, the dataset was sorted in order of the product ID, then the first row among the similar one was kept, and others were deleted. This ensured that only one record for each product was maintained.

The first step taken toward the preprocessing of the data was removal of any unwanted tags, special symbols (? / " : < > | ^ *, etc) and web links. So first, the html tags were removed. Any punctuations or a limited set of special characters were also removed. The words were then checked for the presence of any alphanumeric after which they were converted into lowercase.

Removal of stop words: The irrelevant words that are of no significance in text mining are commonly known as the stop words. Therefore, these words are ignored to optimize the performance and enhance the accuracy. Stop words vary depending on the languages.

From the lowercase words, the stop words were removed.

Tokenization: The process of splitting a collection of strings individually into words, phrases, symbols or even a whole sentence from a paragraph is known as tokenization. The punctuation marks are generally removed during tokenization as they are redundant. These tokens are used as inputs for text mining.

For the reduction of the words to their word stem, snowball stemming was used.

11.2.2   Feature Extraction

Using the below approach, the preprocessed dataset was split into training and test set and each set was vectorized using these techniques individually with each classifier.

Bag of words: A process for text modelling by counting the number of times each word appears. It is a basic model but is frequently used for NLP tasks. In this process, the arbitrary texts are converted into fixed-length vectors by count the occurrence of each word. The reason for this technique being frequently used is its simplicity, the ease of understanding and implementation. Bag of words tries to learning about the meaning of a document assuming that documents having similar content are similar to each other.

TF-IDF: TF-IDF is an information retrieval technique, which extracts features on the basis of the weighs of the term frequency (TF) and inverse document frequency (IDF). Each word having their own weighs of TF and IDF. Term frequency (TF) implies the number of times the word occurs in the corpus. Inverse document frequency defines the measure of significance of the word in the corpus. Calculating the product of TF and IDF gives the TF-IDF score, the higher the score more is the relevancy of the word in that document.

In Bag of Words and TF-IDF vectorizations, we have seen that the output matrix/vectorization is very sparse in nature. On top, these vectorizations do not have any semantic values to them other than what is statistically apparent. So, to deal with this, we might want some vectorization techniques, which reduces the dimensionality of the vectors, as well as mathematical implications to represent the semantic relations of the tokens in their vectorization form. These semantic relations represented in mathematical forms can be leveraged by the ML models to enhance their performance. The average of word2vec and the combination of TF-IDF and word2vec are individually used on each classifier to reduce the dimensionalities.

Average of word2vec: Word2vec is a NLP model which uses a feed forward neural networks to encode and decode textual data (of large size) to a vector form with more semantic similarity and compact nature of output (depending upon the number of activation units used). If two words are semantically similar then the vector (n-dim) corresponding to them are also geometrically close in an n-dimension space, and away from a third vector which is the representation of a word not semantically related to the other two words. As word2vec are pretrained models, in this paper we are just downloading the model and using it to fetch word wise vectorization. For a sentence vectorization, we get all the w2v vectors of words in the sentence and take the mean of it to represent the sentence vector. This representation of word2vec sent vector is posited here as average of word2vec. The implementation of the featurization can be seen in the snippet below (Figure 11.2).

TF-IDF and word2vec: As for TF-IDF word2vec, in the above process we get Tf-idf weights of words as well and final representation of sentence is a weighted average (instead of simple mean) of word2vec of words with their Tf-idf weights multiplied to them. Following snippets of code given in Figure 11.3 is more comprehensive for understanding purposes.

```
# average Word2Vec
# compute average word2vec for each review.
sent_vectors = []; # the avg-w2v for each sentence/review is stored in this list
for sent in tqdm(list_of_sentance): # for each review/sentence
    sent_vec = np.zeros(50) # as word vectors are of zero length 50, you might need to
    cnt_words =0; # num of words with a valid vector in the sentence/review
    for word in sent: # for each word in a review/sentence
        if word in w2v_words:
            vec = w2v_model.wv[word]
            sent_vec += vec
            cnt_words += 1
    if cnt_words != 0:
        sent_vec /= cnt_words
    sent_vectors.append(sent_vec)
print(len(sent_vectors))
print(len(sent_vectors[0]))
```

Figure 11.2 Snippet of code for featurization using average of word2vec.

```
# TF-IDF weighted Word2Vec
tfidf_feat = model.get_feature_names() # tfidf words/col-names
# final_tf_idf is the sparse matrix with row= sentence, col=word and cell_val = tfidf

tfidf_sent_vectors = []; # the tfidf-w2v for each sentence/review is stored in this li
row=0;
for sent in tqdm(list_of_sentance): # for each review/sentence
    sent_vec = np.zeros(50) # as word vectors are of zero length
    weight_sum =0; # num of words with a valid vector in the sentence/review
    for word in sent: # for each word in a review/sentence
        if word in w2v_words and word in tfidf_feat:
            vec = w2v_model.wv[word]
#           tf_idf = tf_idf_matrix[row, tfidf_feat.index(word)]
            # to reduce the computation we are
            # dictionary[word] = idf value of word in whole courpus
            # sent.count(word) = tf valeus of word in this review
            tf_idf = dictionary[word]*(sent.count(word)/len(sent))
            sent_vec += (vec * tf_idf)
            weight_sum += tf_idf
    if weight_sum != 0:
        sent_vec /= weight_sum
    tfidf_sent_vectors.append(sent_vec)
    row += 1
```

Figure 11.3 Snippet of code for featurization using combination of TF-IDF and word2vec.

11.2.3   Classifiers

Application of each feature extraction technique mentioned above was followed by a classification algorithm to classify the comments into positive and negative reviews. Four types of classification models were used namely logistic regression, support vector machine (SVM), random forest and XGBoost. To avoid over-fitting logistic regression and svm model were regularized using L1 and L2 regularization.

11.3   Results and Experiments

Confusion matrix is one of the significant metrics for the evaluation of a model's performance. The measure of accuracy alone is not enough to determine how good a model is, confusion matrix helps us evaluate other metrics for the model. The results obtained from the experiments were evaluated using the confusion matrix.

Confusion matrix represents four types of cases: true positive (TP), false positive (FP), true negative (TN), false negative (FN).

Accuracy: Accuracy is the ratio of correct predictions to total number of predictions. It can be defined as

$$Accuracy = \frac{TP + TN}{TP + FP + TN + FN}$$

Precision: The ratio of correctly identified positives to all predicted positives. High precision implies less false positives, on the other hand low precision implies more false positives. It can be defined as

$$Precision = \frac{TP}{TP + FP}$$

Recall: The ratio of actual positives that got correctly identified as positives. Higher recall implies less false negatives while lower recall implies high false negatives. It can be shown as

$$Recall = \frac{TP}{TP + FN}$$

F-Measure: The weighted harmonic mean of precision and recall is known as the F-measure. It is defined as

$$F = 2\frac{P * R}{P + R}$$

where P is precision and R is recall. The evaluation metrics for logistic regression with L1, logistic regression with L2, SVM with L1, SVM with L2, random forest, XGBoost are given in Table 11.1, Table 11.2, Table 11.3, Table 11.4, Table 11.5 and Table 11.6 respectively.

Table 11.1 Evaluation metrics for logistic regression with L1.

LR-L1	Accuracy	Precision	Recall	F1-score
BOW	89.36%	97.52%	89.59%	93.39%
TFIDF	88.47%	97.59%	88.44%	92.79%
AVG W2v	84.22%	95.96%	84.75%	90.01%
TFIDF-W2v	80.88%	95.33%	81.19%	87.69%

Table 11.2 Evaluation metrics for logistic regression with L2.

LR-L2	Accuracy	Precision	Recall	F1-score
BOW	86.84%	96.71%	87.28%	91.76%
TFIDF	86.84%	96.99%	87.01%	91.73%
AVG W2v	84.18%	95.97%	84.69%	89.98%
TFIDF-W2v	85.46%	97.01%	85.29%	90.77%

Table 11.3 Evaluation metrics for SVM with L1.

SVM-L1	Accuracy	Precision	Recall	F1-score
BOW	77.61%	95.42%	76.99%	85.22%
TFIDF	75.32%	95.79%	73.81%	83.38%
AVG W2v	78.90%	96.59%	77.57%	86.04%
TFIDF-W2v	79.49%	94.99%	79.75%	86.71%

Table 11.4 Evaluation metrics for SVM with L2.

SVM-L2	Accuracy	Precision	Recall	F1-score
BOW	85.46%	95.70%	86.58%	90.91%
TFIDF	83.97%	83.98%	99.99%	91.29%
AVG W2v	82.70%	95.63%	83.20%	88.98%
TFIDF -W2v	78.67%	95.53%	78.26%	86.04%

Table 11.5 Evaluation metrics for random forest.

Random forest	Accuracy	Precision	Recall	F1-score
BOW	88.51%	96.95%	89.12%	92.87%
TFIDF	88.56%	97.04%	89.09%	92.90%
AVG W2v	81.93%	96.11%	81.79%	88.37%
TFIDF-W2v	80.52%	95.34%	80.74%	87.44%

Table 11.6 Evaluation metrics for XGBoost.

XGBoost	Accuracy	Precision	Recall	F1-score
BOW	82.06%	96.10%	81.93%	88.45%
TFIDF	81.13%	96.00%	80.87%	87.79%
AVG W2v	77.74%	95.82%	76.80%	85.27%
TFIDF-W2v	79.41%	95.08%	79.57%	86.63%

Table 11.7 Heatmap for accuracies of different classifiers with different featurization.

Accuracy	BOW	TFIDF	AVG W2v	TFIDF W2v
LR – L1 regularization	89.36%	88.47%	84.22%	80.88%
LR – L2 regularization	86.84%	86.84%	84.18%	85.46%
SVM-L1 regularization	85.46%	83.97%	82.70%	78.67%
SVM-L2 regularization	88.51%	88.56%	81.93%	80.52%
Random forest	77.61%	75.32%	78.90%	79.49%
XG Boost	82.06%	81.13%	77.74%	79.41%

Table 11.8 Heatmap for f-measure of different classifiers with different featurization.

F1-score	BOW	TFIDF	AVG W2v	TFIDF W2v
LR – L1 regularization	93.39%	92.79%	90.01%	87.69%
LR – L2 regularization	91.76%	91.73%	89.98%	90.77%
SVM-L1 regularization	90.91%	91.29%	88.98%	86.04%
SVM-L2 regularization	92.87%	92.90%	88.37%	87.44%
Random forest	85.22%	83.38%	86.04%	86.71%
XG Boost	88.45%	87.79%	85.27%	86.63%

11.4   Conclusion

From the heat maps above (Tables 11.7 and 11.8), we can see all the end results acquired from all the model runs. The heat map shows higher accuracy and F1 score resides on the left and top side of chart. This is the part of chart where we can find simpler models and simple featurization, while part of charts where complex featurization and models reside show a lower performance. This rather seems pretty counterintuitive where the theoretical matters lie.

First interpretation can be describing as follows for the bottom part of the chart. The model in this part are based on decision trees that work better with categorical data. While the work deals with textual data and the featurization of this kind of data produces continuous variables at large. Provided the fact that NLP vectorizations are of continuous form, this should be expected of decision tree models.

Second interpretation can be laid as such for the right side of Chart. The featurization from Avg Word2Vec and TF-IDF Word2Vec produces vectors that have good semantic relations and are represented in a compact form of 50 dim instead of 5000 dims from vanilla Tf-idf and BOW.

This might proliferate a caveat as linear models might not be good enough to extract the semantic relation from this vectorization and are left with only 50 most useful dimensions to work with, and decision tree-based models still suffer the same fate as described in the above expositions but now with even smaller data at hand.

The performance of the models incentivizes that the work should extend upon the notion that deep learning models such as LSTM, CNN and state of the art Bert models have potential to outperform these already great results or the work could furcate into studies with categorical data. As we know decision tree-based models work good with categorical data, and we also know that linear models can also work with this kind of data pretty well. Hence, with this kind of data, we might see higher performance scores at the bottom of the chart unlike the one presented above. The above themes can be developed for the future work on this proposed methodology.

References

1. Jain, V. and Kambli, M., *Amazon Product Reviews: Sentiment Analysis*, 2020.
2. Johar, S. and Mubeen, S., Sentiment analysis on large scale amazon product reviews. *IJSRCSE*, 8, 1, 7–15, 2020.
3. Nguyen, H., Veluchamy, A., Diop, M., Iqbal, R., Comparative study of sentiment analysis with product reviews using machine learning and lexicon-based approaches. *SMU Data Sci. Rev.*, 1, 4, 7, 1–22, 2018. Available at: https://scholar.smu.edu/datasciencereview/vol1/iss4/7.
4. Haque, T., Saber, N., Shah, F., *Sentiment Analysis on Large Scale Amazon Product Reviews*, 2018.
5. Budhwar, J. and Singh, S., Sentiment analysis based method for Amazon product reviews. *Int. J. Eng. Res. Technol.*, ICACT–2021 9, 9, 8, 2021.
6. Thakkar, K., Sidharth, S., Ujjwal, C., Gupta, C., Sentimental analysis on Amazon fine food reviews. *International Journal of Scientific Research & Engineering Trends*, 6, 1, 318–324, 2020.
7. Kumar, N.V., Kolla, M., Rao, H.V.R., Amazon review classification and sentimental analysis on mobile products with R. *AIP Conf. Proc.*, 2358, 110004, 2021. https://doi.org/10.1063/5.0057939.
8. Fang, X. and Zhan, J., Sentiment analysis using product review data. *J. Big Data*, 2, 5, 2015. https://doi.org/10.1186/s40537-015-0015-2.
9. Shivaprasad, T.K. and Shetty, J., Sentiment analysis of product reviews: A review. *2017 International Conference on Inventive Communication and Computational Technologies (ICICCT)*, pp. 298–301, 2017.
10. Jagdale, R.S., Shirsat, V.S., Deshmukh, S.N., Sentiment analysis on product reviews using machine learning techniques, in: *Cognitive Informatics and Soft Computing. Advances in Intelligent Systems and Computing*, vol. 768, P. Mallick, V. Balas, A. Bhoi, A. Zobaa, (Eds.), Springer, Singapore, 2019, https://doi.org/10.1007/978-981-13-0617-4_61.

11. Singla, Z., Randhawa, S., Jain, S., Sentiment analysis of customer product reviews using machine learning. *2017 International Conference on Intelligent Computing and Control (I2C2)*, pp. 1–5, 2017.

12. Chen, X., Xue, Y., Zhao, H. *et al.*, A novel feature extraction methodology for sentiment analysis of product reviews. *Neural Comput. Appl.*, 31, 6625–6642, 2019. https://doi.org/10.1007/s00521-018-3477-2.

## 12

Optimization of Cutting Parameters for Turning by Using Genetic Algorithm

Mintu Pal* and Sibsankar Dasmahapatra

*Department of Mechanical Engineering, Kalyani Government College,
West Bengal, India*

Abstract

Every manufacturing process should be operated with optimum machining conditions to achieve the goal of less machining time, less cost, as well as better quality of the product. The main objective of this research work is to find out the optimum cutting condition for turning operation. In this study, rake angle, entering angle and cutting speed have been considered as cutting parameters during turning operation. At the same time, different cutting forces, such as main cutting force, feed force have, been taken as machining variables. Different combination of cutting parameters selected as input and all the machining variables have been observed as output. The effects of cutting parameters on the cutting forces have been recognized as regression equation with help of Minitab software. For the optimization purpose, single objective optimization and multiobjective optimization techniques have been adopted in this chapter works. Genetic algorithm has been used as an evolutionary computation technique for the optimization purpose. The best fitness values and the curves of corresponding output have been presented in this work. The pareto optimal solution has been tabulated, and the pareto front has been represented as graphical form for the multiobjective optimization solution in this present work. The pareto optimal in this work reveals that higher rake angle and higher cutting speed can help the operator to reduce the generated cutting forces in turning operation.

Keywords: Turning, genetic algorithm (GA), best fitness value, multiobjective optimization, pareto optimal solution

---

*Corresponding author: palmintu1997@gmail.com

Anita Khosla, Prasenjit Chatterjee, Ikbal Ali and Dheeraj Joshi (eds.) Optimization Techniques in Engineering: Advances and Applications, (201–214) © 2023 Scrivener Publishing LLC

12.1   Introduction

Turning is one of the most important material removal process. In this machining process, materials are detached from the work piece in the form of chips. When cutting tool comes in contact to the rotating work piece, different cutting forces, such as main cutting force, feed force, and thrust force, are generated. To reduce the amount of cutting forces as less as possible, the turning process should be operated with optimum cutting parameters, like rake angle, entering angle, depth of cut, feed, cutting speed [1].

Different algorithms are available which can be used to get the optimum cutting condition for economic machining. Genetic algorithm (GA) is one of the most widely applied approach, which is able to identify the suitable optimum condition that is required to succeed economic machining [2]. Through optimization technique, it is possible to converge the fitness value of objective function. In case of turning operation speed, feed and depth of cut have been considered as cutting parameters and maximization of materials removal rate and minimization of surface roughness have been consider as objective function [3]. By providing the importance to the complexity of the problem, GA can also be used along with other optimization tools like simulated annealing (SA) to get the optimum value of cutting force, power constraints and tool tip temperature [4]. The parameters required to develop the controllers as Fuzzy-PI, PID [5–7] can be optimized with help of this optimization technique. To compare the ability of GA for optimization, response surface methodology (RSM) has been parallelly applied to optimize cutting temperatures, tool life. Reddy *et al.* [8] applied Taguchi method and GA tool to predict the response variables in turning of EN19 steel. The online adaptive parameters [9–11] can also be adjusted through GA. For a production-based industry, machining time or production rate and production cost have great impacts. To optimize these response variables, nondominated sorting genetic algorithm (NSGA-II) has been applied [12]. The multiple parameters to control the parallel manipulator [13–15] can also be optimized by this optimization technique.

The optimization of the output variables for the corresponding input parameters are becoming an emerging research work. The single objective optimization and multiobjective optimization [16, 17] both are necessary for the turning operation to find out the optimum set to get the better performances. The optimization with GA is one of the main important research objective to find out the optimum solution to optimize and predict the cutting parameters for turning for the better and accurate performances. In this study, GA has been used to point out the optimum value of cutting forces and corresponding cutting parameters. In the next section, GA has been discussed along with frame work followed by the discussion of the design of objective functions. The results and discussions section shows the optimal solutions.

12.2 Genetic Algorithm GA: An Evolutionary Computational Technique

Genetic algorithm (GA) is a population-based probabilistic search and optimization technique. This technique follows the biological behavior of living beings and works based on the mechanism of natural genetics and natural evolution. So it is a natural inspired algorithm [18]. The steps followed by the GA to reach to the next generation has been depicted in Figure 12.1.

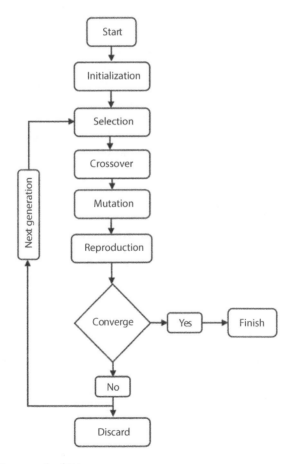

Figure 12.1 Framework of GA.

The first step of GA is to initialization of initial population which is randomly selected with in the valid range. Then "parents" are chosen based on the given selection from initialized population function. The "parents" go through the crossover, mutation and produce new population called offspring. This new generations inherit all the characteristics from parents [19]. The offspring provides the optimal or near-optimal solutions. If the fitness value of given objective function converges to the optimal value then the process will be stop. Otherwise, the weak offsprings are deleted from the tournament and remaining offspring will be considered as new generation. From this new generation again, selection will be done based on selection criteria, and remaining process will be continued till the best fitness is not achieved.

12.3 Design of Multiobjective Optimization Problem

In this section, details of the multiobjective optimization problem have been presented. The real-time experimental data [20] of turning operation have been used for optimization problem. In this experimental work, cutting parameters have been considered as rake angle, entering angle and cutting speed whereas the machining variables are main cutting force, feed force, thrust force and tool tip temperature. In this research work, the optimization problem has been formulated and solved with help of multiobjective genetic algorithm (MOGA).

12.3.1 Decision Variables

To study the optimum condition, three different cutting parameters have been considered as decision variables. These decision variables are rake angle, entering angle, and cutting speed.

12.3.2 Objective Functions

In this research work, minimization of main cutting force and feed force has been considered as two different objectives. In this section, the regression equations have been constructed to make the objective function. The regression equations have been formulated with the help of Minitab software. These corresponding objectives have been given as next.

12.3.2.1   Minimization of Main Cutting Force

Minimization of main cutting force is one of the objective of this recent problem. The objective function for F_m has been formulated in (12.1). The corresponding equation is given as

$$F_m = 560.8 - 7.852*\alpha - 0.744*\theta - 0.3381*v_c \qquad (12.1)$$

where
F_m = Main cutting force,
α = Rake angle,
θ = Entering angle,
v_c = Cutting speed.

12.3.2.2   Minimization of Feed Force

The second objective of this optimization problem is minimization of feed force. The expression given in (12.2) has been used as an objective function for feed force. The equation is as

$$F_f = 259.9 - 9.92*\alpha + 1.381*\theta - 0.862*v_c \qquad (12.2)$$

In this equation, F_f represents feed force and other terms α, θ, v_c represent the same thing as represented in (12.1).

12.3.3   Bounds of Decision Variables

During the construction of the optimization, problem lower bound (L.B) and upper bound (U.B) should to be declared. The lower bound is basically the lower limit of selected cutting parameters. Similarly, upper bound is the upper limit of selected cutting parameters. In this work, the corresponding limiting values of L.B in (12.3) and U.B in (12.4) have been mentioned as

$$L.B = [\alpha_1 \; \theta_1 \; v_{cl}] = [0 \; 45 \; 75] \qquad (12.3)$$

where α_1, θ_1, and v_{cl} represent the lowest value of α, θ, and v_c, respectively

$$U.B = [\alpha_u \; \theta_u \; v_{cu}] = [12 \; 75 \; 160] \qquad (12.4)$$

where α_u, θ_u and v_{cu} represent the highest value of α, θ and v_c respectively.

12.3.4 Response Variables

In this chapter, the response variables that have been considered are main cutting force and feed force. The effect of changes in input cutting parameters can be observed as finite changes in response variable.

12.4 Results and Discussions

In this research work, the optimization problem has been solved by GA tool available in Matlab package. In this section, all the collected results from the GA tool have been depicted and elaborately discussed. Initially, GA has been implemented as a single objective optimization tool for optimization of main cutting force and feed force separately. The corresponding best fitness values of each objective in (12.1) and (12.2) have been also mentioned in this section. Multiobjective genetic algorithm has been also applied here to achieve the pareto optimal solutions of the objectives mentioned in (12.1) and (12.2).

12.4.1 Single Objective Optimization

Single objective optimizations for minimization of main cutting force and feed force have been depicted in Figure 12.2 and Figure 12.3, respectively. These figures represent the fitness value for the corresponding generation. The best fitness value has been represented as dotted line of black color, whereas the mean fitness value has been represented as dotted line of blue colour in both Figure 12.2 and Figure 12.3. The fitness value for the corresponding force has been started from an initial value and converged towards a best fitness value to solve the optimization process.

Figure 12.2 depicts best fitness plot corresponds to the objective function given in (12.1) for minimization of main cutting force. Figure 12.2 illustrates that the curve converges toward best fitness value as 356.681 N from the initial value of 425 N approximately. This converging profile of best fitness curve denotes that the designed problem for optimization works have been done properly. GA algorithm stops after 125 generations, whereas it can be observed that approximately after 55 generations, the fitness curve makes a linear profile. The best fitness value for the main cutting force provided by GA tool is 356.681 N and the value of corresponding decision variables are rake angle = 12°, entering angle = 75° and cutting speed = 159.99 m/min.

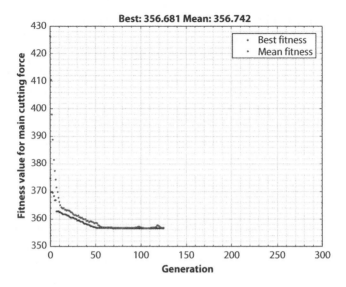

Figure 12.2 Best fitness plot for main cutting force.

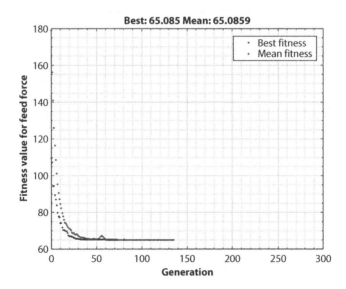

Figure 12.3 Best fitness plot for feed force.

The best fitness plot for feed force has been depicted in Figure 12.3 for minimization of feed force objective function mentioned in (12.2). Figure 12.3 shows that the fitness function value has been initially shown as approximately 180 N, then it gradually converges toward best fitness value. After approximately 40 generations, it has started to make a linear profile, and GA has been stopped to produce new generation after 135 generation. The GA tool provides the best fitness value of feed force as 65.085 N and the corresponding each decision variables are rake angle = 12°, entering angle = 45° and cutting speed = 160 m/min.

12.4.2   Results of Multiobjective Optimization

Now both the objectives in (12.1) and (12.2) have been taken into consideration, and MOGA has been applied to solve the problems. The MOGA provides a set of pareto optimal solutions of both the cutting forces and value of corresponding cutting parameters, which have been tabulated in Table 12.1.

From the listed data in Table 12.1, it has been observed that for different sets of optimal solution, the variation in rake angle is very small as well as in case of cutting speed also. For all the set of pareto optimal solution in Table 12.1, it can be observed that rake angle and cutting speed value either equal to or near equal to their upper limit. So it can be said that operation with higher rake angle and higher cutting speed can help the operator to reduce the generated cutting forces in turning.

The variations of main cutting force and feed force with respect to input decision variables have been depicted in Figures 12.4 to 12.6. Figures 12.4 and 12.6 depict the variation of optimal solution corresponding to rake angle and cutting speed, respectively. Both the rake angle and cutting speed provide very small range of variation for all the optimal solutions, whereas Figure 12.5 shows that for different set of pareto optimal solution for entering angle. The variation of the entering angle in Figure 12.5 is shown as 45° to 75°.

Figure 12.7 depicts the pareto front of the main cutting force and feed force mentioned in (12.1) and (12.2). Different sets of optimum solutions have been represented in Figure 12.7 as pareto front in the graphical form. Figure 12.7 reveals that the value of main cutting force increases when the feed force has been decreased.

Table 12.1 Pareto optimal solution and corresponding decision variables.

Sl. no.	Main cutting Force, F_m (N)	Feed force, F_f (N)	Rake angle, α (°)	Entering angle, θ (°)	Cutting speed, v_c (m/min)
1	356.68	106.51	12.00	75.00	160.00
2	357.57	104.90	12.00	73.82	159.99
3	358.78	103.12	11.98	72.39	159.99
4	359.31	101.88	11.99	71.57	160.00
5	360.00	100.95	11.98	70.79	159.99
6	360.34	99.83	12.00	70.12	159.98
7	361.35	97.94	12.00	68.76	159.99
8	362.79	95.64	11.98	66.98	159.99
9	362.85	95.12	12.00	66.73	160.00
10	363.64	94.51	11.96	66.03	159.98
11	363.78	93.53	11.99	65.54	159.98
12	363.85	93.27	12.00	65.39	159.99
13	364.38	92.31	12.00	64.69	159.98
14	364.53	91.95	12.00	64.45	160.00
15	365.01	91.10	12.00	63.82	159.98
16	365.94	89.76	11.98	62.74	159.98
17	366.48	88.47	11.99	61.89	159.99
18	367.76	85.96	12.00	60.11	160.00
19	368.23	85.10	12.00	59.48	160.00
20	369.12	83.54	12.00	58.33	159.98
21	369.38	83.01	12.00	57.95	159.96
22	370.13	81.70	12.00	56.98	159.98
23	370.37	81.17	12.00	56.62	160.00

(*Continued*)

Table 12.1 Pareto optimal solution and corresponding decision variables. (*Continued*)

Sl. no.	Main cutting force, F_m (N)	Feed force, F_f (N)	Rake angle, α (°)	Entering angle, θ (°)	Cutting speed, v_c (m/min)
24	371.95	78.65	11.98	54.68	159.99
25	372.39	77.82	11.98	54.08	160.00
26	373.30	75.71	12.00	52.68	160.00
27	373.90	75.10	11.98	52.08	159.98
28	374.13	74.18	12.00	51.57	159.99
29	374.48	73.59	12.00	51.12	160.00
30	375.57	71.48	12.00	49.62	160.00
31	376.97	68.87	12.00	47.73	160.00
32	377.38	68.11	12.00	47.19	159.99
33	378.22	66.73	11.99	46.13	160.00
34	378.53	66.00	12.00	45.65	160.00
35	379.00	65.09	12.00	45.00	160.00

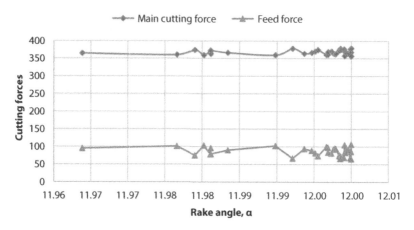

Figure 12.4 Variation of cutting forces with respect to rake angle.

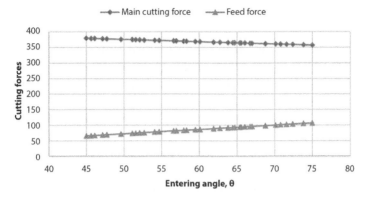

Figure 12.5 Variation of cutting forces with respect to entering angle.

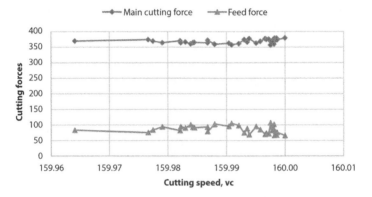

Figure 12.6 Variation of cutting forces with respect to cutting speed.

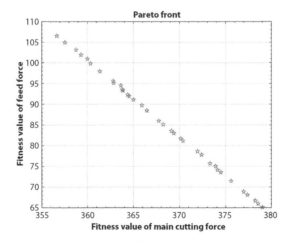

Figure 12.7 Pareto front for the optimal solutions.

12.5   Conclusion

The present study in this work has been based on GA as an optimization tool. This tool has been implemented to minimize the main cutting force and feed force in turning operation for the corresponding decision variables as rake angle, entering angle and cutting speed. GA has been used here to solve single objective, as well as to solve multiobjective optimization problems. The performances of the GA have been carefully observed in both the cases. For single objective optimization problem, GA is able to provide an optimum value of fitness function, and a particular set of decision variable has been found out to which machine should to be operate to get the optimum condition. In case of multiobjective optimization problem, a set of optimum solutions and the corresponding input variables has been generated. The pareto optimal in this work reveals that higher rake angle and higher cutting speed can help the operator to reduce the generated cutting forces in turning operation. It can also be concluded from the present work that the main cutting force increases when the feed force decreases for the given set of input variables.

The output parameters of the turning operation as thrust force, tool tip temperature, tool wear rate, and input parameters as depth of cut, feed can also be taken into consideration for optimization process in further study. The concepts of single and multiple objective optimizations using GA can be implemented in other machining process as optimization in abrasive jet machining, surface grinding, universal drilling, slotting, surface finishing, milling. The other optimization algorithms, such as artificial bee colony (ABC) and particle swarm optimization (PSO), can be used and compared with the existing results.

References

1. Bhuiyan, T.H. and Ahmed, I., Optimization of cutting parameters in turning process. *SAE Int. J. Mater. Manuf.*, 7, 1, 233–239, 2014.
2. Jameel, A., Minhat, M., Nizam, M., Using genetic algorithm to optimize machining parameters in turning operation: A review. *Int. J. Sci. Res. Publ.*, 3, 5, 1–6, 2013.
3. Sarvanakumar, K., Kumar, P., Dawood, A.K.S., Optimization of CNC turning process parameters on INCONEL 718 using genetic algorithm. *IRACST–Eng. Sci. Technol. An Int. J.*, 2, 4, 532–537, 2012.
4. Saravanan, R., Asokan, P., Vijayakumar, K., Machining parameters optimization for turning cylindrical stock into a continuous finished profile using

genetic algorithm and simulated annealing. *Int. J. Adv. Manuf. Technol.*, 21, 1–9, 2003.

5. Dasmahapatra, S., Chaudhuri., S., Mandal., P., Mookherjee., S., Saha., R., Fuzzy-PI control of motion tracking by an electrohydraulic system with multiple nonlinearities. *Proceeding of Michael Faraday IET International Summit: MFIIS-2015*, 2015.

6. Dasmahapatra, S., Saha, R., Sanyal, D., Sengupta, A., Bhattacharyya, U., Adaptive PID control for angular motion tracking by linear electrohydraulic actuation. *Proceeding of IEEE First International Conference on ICPEICES*, 2016.

7. Dasmahapatra, S., Saha, D., Saha, R., Sanyal, D., Lahiri, D., Singh, J.P., Analysis of 6-DOF motion with PI controller in electrohydraulic Stewart platform. *Proceeding of IEEE First International Conference on CMI*, 2016.

8. Reddy, V.V., Krishna, N.J., Bhaskar, N., Optimization of cutting parameters in turning of EN-19 by using taguchi and genetic algorithm. *IJETR*, 5, 797–799, 2016.

9. Dasmahapatra, S., Saha., R., Mookherjee., S., Sanyal., D., Designing an input-linearized adaptive sliding mode coupled nonlinear integral controller. *IEEE/ASME Trans. Mechatron.*, 23, 2888–2895, 2018.

10. Dasmahapatra, S., Saha., R., Chatterjee., A., Mookherjee., R., Sanyal., D., Design of an adaptive-fuzzy-bias-SMC and validation for a rugged electrohydraulic system. *IEEE/ASME Trans. Mechatron.*, 20, 2708–2715, 2015.

11. Dasmahapatra, S., Saha., R., Sanyal., D., Sengupta., A., Snyal., S., Designing sliding mode with integral control for angular rotation of a link by linear electrohydraulic actuation. *Proceeding of 12th IEEE India International Conference of INDICON*, 2015.

12. Ganesan, H. and Mohankumar, G., Optimization of machining techniques in CNC turning centre using genetic algorithm. *Arab J. Sci. Eng.*, 38, 1529–1538, 2013.

13. Dasmahapatra, S., Saha, S., Saha, R., Sanyal., D., Lahiri., D., Singh., J.P., Analysis of 6-DOF motion with PI controller in electrohydraulic Stewart platform. *Proceeding of IEEE First International Conference on CMI*, 2016.

14. Dasmahapatrta, S. and Ghosh., M., Workspace identification of stewart platform. *Int. J. Eng. Adv. Technol.*, 9, 1903–1907, 2020.

15. Mullick, S.H. and Dasmahapatra, S., Combined motion generation by electro-hydraulic stewart platform for manufacturing industries. *ICIMSAT 2019, LAIS*, vol. 12, Springer Nature Switzerland AG, pp. 596–604, 2020.

16. Gadagi., A. and Adake., C., A constrained multi-objective optimization of turning process parameters by genetic algorithm and particle swarm optimization techniques. *Mater. Today Proc.*, 42, 1207–1212, 2021.

17. Vukelic, D., Simunovic, K., Kanovic, Z., Saric, T., Tadic, B., Simunovic, G., Multi-objective optimization of steel AISI 1040 dry turning using genetic algorithm. *Neural Comput. Appl.*, 33, 12445–12475, 2021.

18. D'Addona, D.M. and Teti, R., Genetic algorithm-based optimization of cutting parameters in turning processes. *Forty Sixth Conference on Manufacturing Systems*, pp. 323–328, 2013.

19. Sardinas, R.Q., Santana, M.R., Brindis, E.A., Genetic algorithm-based multi-objective optimization of cutting parameters in turning processes. *Eng. Appl. Artif. Intell.*, 19, 127–133, 2006.

20. Saglam, H., Yaldiz, S., Unsacar, F., The effect of tool geometry and cutting speed on main cutting force and tool tip temperature. *Mater. Des.*, 28, 101–111, 2007.

## 13

Genetic Algorithm-Based Optimization for Speech Processing Applications

Ramya.R[1]*, M. Preethi[2] and R. Rajalakshmi[2]

*[1]Department of Electronics and Communication Engineering,
Sri Ramakrishna Engineering College, Coimbatore, India
[2]Department of Information Technology, Sri Ramakrishna Engineering College,
Coimbatore, India*

Abstract

Optimization techniques are meant to solve optimization of smooth problems where it follows to find gradient of the functions. Gradients look into minima value unfortunately local minima can be a hindrance. Genetic algorithm (GA) follows biological evaluation that provides fittest solution to smooth problems and many times even to discontinue functions. GA integrated with neural network enhances its learning capabilities and input selection. This integration can be a fathom to a variety of speech processing applications, like automatic speech recognition (ASR), speech emotion recognition (SER), hate speech detection, and many other. GA plays a good role in selecting the fittest parameter set in voice activity detection, feature selection, phonetic decoding of ASR. In SER, GA improves the accuracy by using clustering-based fitness function for choosing the elementary population. Modified mutation and crossover in GA model is drawn on to solve classification problem in despise speech detection problem in social media.

Keywords: Genetic algorithm optimization, automatic speech recognition, speech emotion recognition, hate speech detection

13.1 Introduction to GA

The best solutions behind many technologies are evolved from principles of nature. GA is one such algorithm that solves optimization problem

---

*Corresponding author: ramya.ece@srec.ac.in

Anita Khosla, Prasenjit Chatterjee, Ikbal Ali and Dheeraj Joshi (eds.) Optimization Techniques in Engineering: Advances and Applications, (215–230) © 2023 Scrivener Publishing LLC

based on biological evolution and survival of fittest principle. GA attempts to solve a function on a set of randomly chosen points in the function's variable space. It solves in an iterative manner which mimics the biological evolution and also less prone to local minima. Now consider an example of maximization of a function with variable n given by [1],

$$f(x_1, x_2,...., x_n): R^n \to R \tag{13.1}$$

After GA optimization we will get,

$$f(x_1^*, x_2^*,...., x_n^*) \geq f(x_1, x_2,...., x_n) \tag{13.2}$$

where $(x_1^*, x_2^*,...., x_n^*)$ is the solution vector in the function search space.

GA first choose a random population, represented as a string of p binary digits using binary encoding procedure. This is formed as a matrix n rows and pm rows. Now, the commonly used genetic operators, like selection, crossover, and mutation, are applied.

Selection refers to select the best individual to give the next generation. Deciding the best individual may be based on elite model, ranking model and roulette wheel procedure. Elite model uses top individual, where ranking model assigns rank based on its fitness value. In roulette wheel method, each individual is given a probability, and after which, the cumulative probability is calculated. In crossover phase, genes of two parents combine to form the child of similar genotype. During mutation, the allele of the child changes in a random manner.

13.1.1   Enhanced GA

The enhanced GA provide optimum solutions compared to traditional GA. hybrid GA and interval GA are discussed here.

13.1.1.1   Hybrid GA

Traditional GA finds difficult to solve the problems with exact constraints. In hybrid GA, it solves the initial design variables avoiding the trail process. As in traditional GA, after mutation operation new population $t + 1$, an initial design variable Z is obtained. Until the algorithm gets converged, the design variable gets updated [2].

13.1.1.2   *Interval GA*

In manufacturing, it is not always easy to find the exact design variables due to inaccuracy in measurement. Interval analysis helps to solve this by providing upper and lower bound in this error. The interval can be in complex plane in the form of a rectangle or circle. Interval GA gives optimum interval parameters [2].

13.1.1.3   *Adaptive GA*

In traditional GA, all the genetic operators are fixed where all the individuals in the population may get similar values. This may not help to achieve the optimum global value. The average square deviation (ASD) is measured to know the difference in individual values. When ASD is less, more individuals will be the same, and for getting global optimal solution, mutation probability should be increased [3].

The average fitness function f_v for the tth generation with N individual is given by [3],

$$f_v = \frac{1}{N} \sum_{i=1}^{N} fit(x_t^i) \qquad (13.3)$$

$fit(x_t^i)$ gives the evaluation function of individual x^i
ASD of the population is given as

$$ASD_t = \frac{1}{N} \sqrt{\left(\sum_{i=1}^{N} fit_t^i - f_v \right)^2} \qquad (13.4)$$

Depending on ASD value mutation probability P_n is varied, and their relationship is given as

$$P_n = M_a * \left(1 + \frac{f_{max} - ASD_t}{f_{max} + ASD_t} \right) \qquad (13.5)$$

Here f_{max} is the maximum fitness value of present generation.

13.2   GA in Automatic Speech Recognition

In recent years, voice-controlled–based application, like web search, navigation systems, health care applications, are growing and are in greater demand. ASR suffers from variation effects like speaking style, speaker characteristics, channel characteristics like background noise, room acoustics, and interfering speakers.

13.2.1   GA for Optimizing Off-Line Parameters in Voice Activity Detection (VAD)

ASR uses microphone array for voice communication, needs optimization methods to fix the parameters set, thereby improving the ASR accuracy. VAD algorithm finds the voice activity from noise corrupted signal using the first formant of the speaker as an energy feature [4]. This feature is normalized using other features obtained from the noise signal. VAD decides the voice activity by using two thresholds obtained from the normalized energy feature. GA optimizes VAD performance by increasing the F1 score.

The objective function of VAD is based on F1 score given by [4],

$$F1 = 2 \times \frac{precision \times recall}{precision + recall} \tag{13.6}$$

The precision and recall are defined in terms of true positive rate (TPR), false negative rate (FPR), and false negative rate (FNR).

$$precision = \frac{TPR}{TPR + FPR} \tag{13.7}$$

$$recall = \frac{TPR}{TPR + FNR} \tag{13.8}$$

From this, we can understand that GA optimizes the decision threshold. GA gives an F1 score of 98.5% after 10 generations.

Speech enhancement in front end includes VAD, multichannel Wiener filter, compression or expansion and finally equalization. GA is involved to determine the parameter sets for improving the ASR accuracy [5]. The character error rate (CER) of ASR $\mathfrak{I}_{CER,I}$ is kept as the GA fitness function.

$$\mathfrak{S}_l = \left(1 - \mathfrak{S}_{CER,l}\right)^{i_{gen}} \tag{13.9}$$

i_{gen} is the generation number and power law scaling is used here.

13.2.2   Classification of Features in ASR Using GA

Recognition of Arabic word–based ASR extracts features from speech frames by applying discrete wavelet transform along with Haar transform. Magnitude of each feature is determined and subjected to classification using GA. An initial population is chosen, and fitness values are calculated over the individual. The objective function is framed as the mean square error (MSE) between the word to be recognized and word in the database. For N number of input blocks, the Euclidean distance is evaluated between the test feature vectors A and reference data B. Also the fitness value (Fitness) in equation (13.11) is determined based on MSE [6].

$$\text{Euclidean distance} = \frac{1}{N} \sum_{i=1}^{n} \sqrt{(A - B)^2} \tag{13.10}$$

$$Fitness = \frac{1}{1 + MSE} \tag{13.11}$$

Elitist model is used for selection, crossover probability is fixed as 0.7, and mutation probability is 0.001. Evolution is completed once the word is recognized. Speech recognition models like hidden Markov model HMM, Gaussian mixture model (GMM) combined with GA shows improved results in word error rate [7].

13.2.3   GA-Based Distinctive Phonetic Features Recognition

ASR uses acoustic features like melfrequency cepstral coeffificients (MFCCs), spectrogram, short time energy, short time autocorrelation, and phonetic features. Distinctive phonetic features uses the acoustic and articulatory nature of phoneme utterance. They are represented as binary vectors, and each bit denotes the presence and absence of phoneme. GA helps in selecting the appropriate feature vectors [8]. GA-based approach is employed to reduce the feature vectors in phoneme recognition as shown in Figure 13.1.

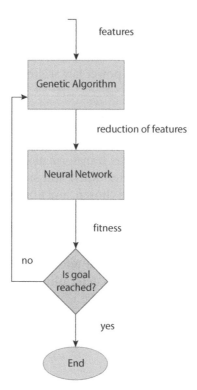

Figure 13.1 GA-based distinctive phonetic features recognition.

Fifteen frames are taken as input from each phoneme waveform. Each frame contains the feature vectors of 256 points spectrogram, 39-coeffificient MFCC, 15 values of Zero-crossing Rate, short time energy and voicing percentage per input vector. A total 4,456 points of feature vectors are available in each frame.

Not all these feature vectors are essential for classification model. GA-based approach helps to reduce these input entities. GA uses an encoding scheme for feature vector of length 61 bits. These 61 bits comprise of 15 bits for 15 spectrogram, 15 bits for 15 MFCC coefficients, 15 bits for 15 zero crossing values, 15 bits for 15 energy values and finally 1 bit for pitch percentage.

GA is applied to the feed forward neural network. Roulette wheel procedure is used for selection operator. Feature vector of size 3231 is sufficient to achieve good performance using GA.

13.2.4   GA in Phonetic Decoding

Phonetic decoding refers to mapping the acoustic signal into its possible phonemes. Each phoneme is represented as frame and has two vectors, the MFCC and linear prediction coefficients (LPC). They are denoted as $V_{V13k,mx}$ and $V_{V42k,mx}$ respectively. As GA is considered in phonetic decoding, each phoneme is separated as vocal sequence and vectors of reference. The initial population formed by the above vectors forms the problem space where solution need to be identified. The GA will solve for best solution by using its operators. The fitness function is to improve the Manhattan distance between the acoustic reference and acoustic vector of each phoneme given by [9],

$$Ff_{mx} = \sum_{m=1}^{m_x} (|V_{V42k,mx} - \mu v_{42k,mx}| + |V_{V13k,mx} - \mu v_{13k,mx}|)/2 \times \sigma \quad (13.12)$$

The distance are normalized by its standard deviation σ. GA does not stop its evolution in global solution always. It can be halted by predetermined iterations.

13.3   Genetic Algorithm in Speech Emotion Recognition

13.3.1   Speech Emotion Recognition

In academia and industry, SER is now a popular topic. In order to create an efficient SER, feature engineering is necessary. Despite the fact that academics have put in a lot of effort in this area, the difficulties of speech feature selection and the proper application of feature engineering remain unsolved in the SER domain. A feature optimization strategy based on a clustering-based genetic algorithm is proposed in this study. Instead of selecting the new generation at random, clustering is used at the fitness evaluation level to identify outliers that should be excluded from future generations.

While machines are presently quite bad at understanding human emotions, such an ability could be valuable in a variety of applications, such as improving the performance of spoken dialogue systems (SDSs) or evaluating the quality of contact centers. SER is a classification problem that can be solved using supervised learning approaches in a variety of ways. Speech wave forms can be used to extract a variety of numerical information.

A feature selection technique results in an exchange between the model's accuracy and the time-consuming feature extraction. But some qualities may be strongly correlated, or their variability may be quite low, hence some traits may not have a positive impact on the system, and may even degrade its performance. As a result, an effective feature set for the ER job (as well as for speech-based speaker identification (SI) and gender identification (GI) problems) should be both accurate and efficient. Furthermore, deleting extraneous features from speech-based ER, SI, and GI models could greatly improve their performance.

Speech is some of the most common and direct methods of expressing emotions and detecting others sentiments [10]. This is because voice emotion recognition is critical to the success of many applications such as auto-replies, chat bots, speaking humanoid robots, and other scenarios involving human-machine interaction.

13.3.2   Genetic Algorithms in Speech Emotion Recognition

GA is a popular topic in the research field . This system is often divided into two parts, the first stage is the front-end, which extracts feature vectors from voice utterance samples. The second stage is the back-end, which recognizes the emotion using a set of feature vectors, algorithms, and models and it is one of the best optimization techniques. For the past two decades, researchers have been studying the emotion interpretation of speech signals [11]. Numerous models for audio emotion identification that involve machine learning and deep learning is discussed in the study of Bhavan *et al.* [12]. The features are retrieved, and the categorization is carried out. The effectiveness of categorization is determined by the number and quality of characteristics employed. In this regard, feature engineering is a critical stage in the categorization effort.

The impacts of speech, reverberation, and their combined effects are investigated on spontaneous SER in the wild [13]. It shows that previous SER systems based on per-frame characteristics (calculated from the modulation spectrum) perform poorly for spontaneous speech, despite being useful for enacted/posed emotions. It also discovered that this method outperformed the baseline system utilized in the emotion challenge when it came to predicting arousal.

13.3.2.1   *Feature Extraction Using GA for SER*

In the first step, adaptive evolutionary algorithms are used to find the lowest performing features in terms of the likelihood of successful classification attained by the Bayes classifier. These characteristics are then removed from consecutive floating feature selection, which uses the Bayes classifier's likelihood of proper classification as a requirement. In a subsequent step, adaptive genetic algorithms look for the sentences that perform the poorest in terms of the same criterion. On the Danish emotional speech database, the consecutive use of both steps is proved to increase speech emotion identification [14].

Genes are referred to as a chromosomal elements with integer values (i.e. strings of genes encoding individuals). Instead of looking for the greatest genes, looking for the worst ones. It is defined an integer matrix P of dimensions $N_p \times N_w$, every element P_{ij} codes the feature index of the ith individual's jth worst gene (chromosome). P_{ij} accepts integer values between [1 and N], where N is the number of characteristics in the first stage or the number of statements in the second stage. N_p and N_w are pre-defined variables.

Now, let us define population diversity as the total of differences between any two distinct rows of the population matrix [15],

$$D = \frac{2}{N_p(N_p-1)} \sum_{i=1}^{N_p-1} \sum_{j=i+1}^{N_p} \sqrt{(p_i - p_j)(p_i - p_j)^T} \qquad (13.13)$$

where p_i represents the ith chromosome as a row vector. Inner products are used in equation (13.13) to avoid misunderstandings. The starting population is usually produced at random. A uniform random number generator fills P with integers in the necessary range to do this. Inside each chromosome, P_{ij} are tested for uniqueness. Np values of 50, 100, and 200 are common. N_p has a default value of 100. Experiments with Np = 50 and 200 yielded no meaningful results.

The number of iterations is denoted by Niter. Niter usually accepts the numbers 50, 100, and 200. The larger Niter, on the other hand, the better the possibility of finding the optimal value, but at the cost of more computational time. When Niter is big, it is more likely to get a null diversity if adaptive GAs are not used. This is because, after a few repetitions, the dominant chromosome will most likely occupy all rows of P. The selection approach is different from traditional selection in that it is cross-generational.

The fittest genes have a better chance of surviving via classic selection. Cross-generational selection, on the other hand, adds random chromosomes to P. N_p or a percentage of N_p could be the number of new chromosomes. In our trials, another N_p chromosomes are created at random, and the Np worst chromosomes out of the $2N_p$ worst chromosomes in terms of fitness are given a chance to survive in future generations.

Repeated ψ-fold cross validated prediction error is used to assess the population's fitness [16]. A basic multipoint crossover operator is used. For any pair of potential parents for crossover, the number of points and their places are determined at random. The level of population variety determines the likelihood of a crossover. Adaptive crossover is what we call it. A single-point binary mutation is executed at point k (the kth bit is toggled), integer-binary-integer conversion is considered.

13.3.2.2 Steps for Adaptive Genetic Algorithm for Feature Optimization

The outline of adaptive GA methodology is as follows.

1. For $N_p = 100$, create the matrix P of dimension $N_p \times N_w$. N_w can range from 1 to N_f for feature trimming, with N_f denoting the amount of features. $N_w = 10$ for feature trimming and $N_w = 3$ for noise trimming.
2. Double-check that there are no repeats inside each row or between rows.
3. Assess the first population's fitness.
4. Repeat steps 1 to 3 until all chromosomes in the population have been checked (i.e. the maximum generation is reached). Control the population's variety as well. If it hits zero, the loop should be terminated.
5. Begin a loop. In the selection step, make more N_p chromosomes and attach them to the preceding population. After that, assess their fitness. Choose the Np chromosomes that are the poorest.
6. Determine the population's diversity and the crossover and mutation operators' probabilities. If the diversity exceeds a certain threshold, give both probability a minimum value (e.g. 0.5 to crossover and 0.01 to mutation). T_{min} and T_{max} are two thresholds that can be defined. If $D< T_{min}$, then the chances of crossing and mutation will increase. If D exceeds T_{max}, lower them. Otherwise, leave them alone. T_{min} and T_{max} were set at 0.1 and 0.95, respectively, in our trials.
7. Apply crossover to pairs of parents chosen at random.
8. Apply the mutation to a set of parents chosen at random.
9. Repetition of the loop (i.e., jump to step 4).
10. Remove the poorest features/utterances from the data set after the GA has converged.

11. When the features are modeled by a multivariate Gaussian probability density function, evaluate the remaining features using the Sequential Forward Floating Selection (SFFS) method with the criterion of the probability of accurate classification attained by the Bayes classifier. If certain utterances are removed, SFFS is applied to the remaining utterances, and the Bayes classifier's probability of successful classification is evaluated using repeated ψ-fold cross validation.

Adaptive GAs yields an improvement in correct classification rate. The state of population variety, also known as adaptive mutation, influences the likelihood of mutation. When compared to the mutation likelihood, the crossover rate is unimportant. A high mutation probability will prevent the search from focusing on the better regions, forcing the GA to do a random search. A tiny amount, on the other hand, will prevent the search from escaping local minima. GA will be able to explore the most promising regions while avoiding being caught in local minima if the probability of mutation is chosen optimally.

13.4 Genetic Programming in Hate Speech Using Deep Learning

The evolution of technological era and widespread handling of social media, users will explicit their feelings and impression without any other constraints. In view of the fast growing of on-line content hate speech has become a standard issue which might influence collection of hate crimes. So there is a requirement to search out correct and proficient technique to identify on-line hate content and flag them significantly. Although all the most important social media platform try to expose and prevent hate speech, they principally have confidence reports of such actions from users. The most familiar definitions of hate speech is it is communication toward a particular person or cluster group with some aggressive content based on some aspects like gender, race, color, religion, or position [17].

13.4.1 Introduction to Hate Speech Detection

The hate speech detection may be outlined as either a binary or multiclass classification task. In the binary classification task, a document is divided into two categories. One is hate and another one is not hate. In the multi-classification work, a document is divided into three or n number of classes which will address the level of hate content or various types of hate [18, 19]. Different machine learning approaches have been employed to implement classifiers for hate speech detection, such as support vector machine (SVM), logistic regression (LR), random forest (RF), K-Nearest Neighbors (KNN), Naive Bayes (NB), decision trees (DT), natural language processing (NLP), recurrent neural networks (RNN), and convolutional neural network (CNN) [20].

Hate speech is regrettably frequent occurrence on the social media and in some cases terminates in server hazards to people. Social media sites, thus, face the issues of finding and prohibitory issuing posts while weighing the proper freedom of speech. The importance of detective work and moderating hate speech is obvious from the forceful link between hate speech and actual hate crimes. Early identification of users promoting hate speech might alter reaching programs that struggle to protect an escalation from speech to action. Sites, like Twitter and Facebook, are seeking to actively combat hate speech. Recently, facebook declared that they might request to combat racism and social phobia geared toward refugees. Presently much of these moderation needs manual review of questionable documents, that not only controls how much individual analyst can be judged, however, additionally introduces subjective notions of what constitutes hate speech.

In spite of those reasons, NLP analysis on hate speech has been delimited because of the shortage of a general definition of hate speech, an searching of its demographic influences and analysis of the foremost effective scopes.

The simple and parallelized NLP modeling that is not totally different but typically the foremost delayed step is deals with the information of developing scopes from the clean information [21]. GA's area units are evolution-inspired optimizations which behave well on advanced information, in order that they naturally lend well to NLP information.

The Ensemble deep learning approach detects hate speech on social media websites exploitation an efficient learning method that classifies the text into neutral, offensive and hate language [21]. The performance of the system is then evaluated exploitation overall accuracy, f-score, preciseness and recollect metrics.

13.4.2   GA Integrated With Deep Learning Models for Hate Speech Detection

Genetic programming (GP) is an growing approach that develops genetic algorithms to allow the exploration of the area of computer programs. Like other growing algorithms, by mimicking the basic rules of Darwinian evolution, GP works by telling a goal in the form of a quality criterion (or fitness) and using this criterion to evolve a set (or population) of candidate solutions (individuals). GP delivers the solutions to problems using an repetitious process involving the probabilistic selection of the fittest solutions and their variation by means of a set of genetic operators, usually crossover and mutation [22, 23]. In real-world problem domains, GP has been applied successfully.

The most suitable network architectures are RNN and CNN. CNN is a standard as an efficient network to act as feature extractors and RNN is used for modeling sequence learning issues within the context of hate speech classification, intuitively, CNN extracts word or character mixtures. CNN is the main technique of deep learning, and it has shown outstanding superiority in numerous real-world applications.

Genetic algorithm usually uses the fixed-length encryption strategy due to the crossover operators originally planned for the people having similar lengths. During this case, the length of the encryption should be specified beforehand. Classically, the length must be the optimal CNN depth that is largely unknown in leading. As a result, the stated number is also incorrectly calculable, leading to ineffective architecture planned. Several variable length encryption strategies have been developed by many scholars, as a result, CNN is not optimal because the crossover operator was not redesigned accordingly [24].

The largest accessible datasets for hate speech is considered for LR [25]. This utilized a multiclass classifier for detection of hate speech on their data set, using n-grams, sentiment lexicon, and Term Frequency-Inverse Document Frequency (TF-IDF) as scopes. Using LR 90% F1-score is obtained, however the confusion matrix displayed which the classifier biased to classify the tweet as not hateful. In LA, GA will be helpful and efficient for seeking a combination of variables for the most effective accomplishment (e.g., accuracy of diagnosis), particularly when the seek space is big, complex, or poorly understood, as within the case in prediction of AD development.

To classify the tweeted data into hate or not hate classes, we can use some of the techniques mentioned above. Nowadays, the most common GP model to perform the binary classification. The preprocessing step is utilized to eliminate the content that is not expected to contribute to the detection of hate speech and to organize the information for the next steps. The feature extraction step of our model uses the universal sentence encoder to represent every tweet as a high 512-dimensional vector. Within the projected general practitioner model, every individual could be a tree used for classifying the tweets.

An approach was developed for utilizing GP where trees are chosen by the Roulette wheel situated on the unfitness measure. Genetic operator gives a chance to these trees to evaluated themselves [26]. From different domains, the performance of this approach on five datasets could be measured. For evolution in the GP framework, modified mutation and crossover operations has been employed to increase the chances of unfit trees selected. Also, OR-ing and weight-based schemes was also introduced to optimize the multi-class classifiers achieving the optimal classifier in a single genetic programming run. The classifiers from both approaches produced satisfactory results.

13.5 Conclusion

GA integrated with neural networks led to robust models, also supported in input selection and model learning. Modified GA operators provided the best solution for feature selection and classification problems. This chapter gives an insight on GA integration in ASR, emotion recognition and hate speech detection in social media. GA-supported feed forward NN proves improved accuracy in phoneme recognition and 50% drop in feature size. VAD integrated with GA optimized the F1 score and showed 91.4% true positive rate for different male and female speakers under different noise conditions. SER along with GA had proved optimized classification for different datasets under both speaker-dependent and -independent conditions. Hybrid mutation in GA improved the binary classification problem in despise speech detection.

References

1. Katoch, S., Chauhan, S.S., Kumar, V., A review on genetic algorithm: Past, present, and future. *Multimed. Tools Appl.*, 80, 8091–8126, 2021.
2. Guo, P., Wang, X., Han, Y., The enhanced genetic algorithms for the optimization design. *2010 3rd International Conference on Biomedical Engineering and Informatics*, pp. 2990–2994, 2010.
3. Lin, C., An adaptive genetic algorithm based on population diversity strategy. *2009 Third International Conference on Genetic and Evolutionary Computing*, pp. 93–96, 2009.
4. Lezzoum, N., Gagnon, G., Voix, J., Voice activity detection system for smart earphones. *IEEE Trans. Consum. Electron.*, 60, 737–744, 2014.
5. Kawase, T., Okamoto, M., Fukutomi, T., Takahashi, Y., Speech enhancement parameter adjustment to maximize accuracy of automatic speech recognition. *IEEE Trans. Consum. Electron.*, 66, 125–133, 2020.

6. Stephan, J., Rasha, H., Ali, R., Speech recognition using genetic algorithm. *IJCET*, 5, 76–81, 2014.

7. Barman, T. and Deb, N., State of the art review of speech recognition using genetic algorithm. *IEEE International Conference on Power, Control, Signals and Instrumentation Engineering*, pp. 2944–2946, 2017.

8. Ibrahim, A.B., Seddiq, Y.M., Meftah, A.H., Alghamdi, M., Selouani, S.A., Qamhan, M.A., Alotaibi, Y.A., Alshebeili, S.A., Optimizing arabic speech distinctive phonetic features and phoneme recognition using genetic algorithm. *IEEE Access*, 8, 200395–200411, 2020.

9. Aissiou, M., A genetic model for acoustic and phonetic decoding of standard arabic vowels in continuous speech. *Int. J. Speech Technol.*, 23, 425–434, 2020.

10. Akçay, M.B. and Oğuz, K., Speech emotion recognition: Emotional models, databases, features, preprocessing methods, supporting modalities, and classifiers. *Speech Commun.*, 116, 56–76, 2020.

11. Song, P. and Zheng, W., Feature selection based transfer subspace learning for speech emotion recognition. *IEEE Trans. Affect. Comput.*, 11, 373–382, 2020.

12. Bhavan, A., Chauhan, P., Shah, R.R., Bagged support vector machines for emotion recognition from speech. *Knowl. Based Syst.*, 184, 104886, 2019.

13. Avila, A.R., Akhtar, Z., Santos, J.F., O'Shaughnessy, D., Falk, T.H., Feature pooling of modulation spectrum features for improved speech emotion recognition in the wild. *IEEE Trans. Affect. Comput.*, 12, 177–188, 2021.

14. Swain, M., Routray, A., Kabisatpathy, P., Databases, features and classifiers for speech emotion recognition: A review. *Int. J. Speech Technol.*, 21, 93–120, 2018.

15. Sedaaghi, M.H., Ververidis, D., Kotropoulos, C., Improving speech emotion recognition using adaptive genetic algorithms. *European Signal Processing Conference*, pp. 2209–2213, 2007.

16. Burman, P., A comparative study of ordinary cross-validation, ψ-fold cross-validation and the repeated learning-testing methods. *Biometrika*, 76, 503–514, 1989.

17. Aljero, M.K.A. and Dimililer, N., Genetic programming approach to detect hate speech in social media. *IEEE Access*, 9, 115115–115125, 2021.

18. Fortuna, P. and Nunes, S., A survey on automatic detection of hate speech in text. *ACM Comput. Surv.*, 51, 1–30, 2018.

19. Santoso, L., Babu, R., Rajest, S., Genetic programming approach to binary classification problem. *EAI Endorsed Trans. Energy Web*, 8, 1–8, 2020.

20. Waseem, Z. and Hovy, D., Hateful symbols or hateful people? Predictive features for hate speech detection on Twitter. *NAACL*, pp. 88–93, 2016.

21. Kuo, C.S., Hong, T.P., Chen, C.L., Applying genetic programming technique in classification trees. *Soft Comput.*, 11, 1165–1172, 2007.

22. Chaudhari, N., Tiwari, A., Purohit, A., Genetic programming for classification. *IJCEE*, 1, 69–76, 2009.

23. Al-Makhadmeh, Z. and Tolba, A., Automatic hate speech detection using killer natural language processing optimizing ensemble deep learning approach. *Computing*, 102, 501–522, 2020.

24. Sun, Y., Xue, B., Zhang, M., Yen, G.G., Lv, J., Automatically Designing CNN architectures using GA for image classification. *IEEE Trans. Cybern.*, 50, 9, 3840–3854, 2020.

25. Davidson, T., Warmsley, D., Macy, M., Weber, I., Automated hate speech detection and the problem of offensive language. *ICWSM*, pp. 15–18, 2017.

26. Muni, D.P., Pal, N.R., Das, J., A novel approach to design classifiers using genetic programming. *IEEE Trans. Evol. Comput.*, 8, 183–196, 2004.

14

Performance of P, PI, PID, and NARMA Controllers in the Load Frequency Control of a Single-Area Thermal Power Plant

Ranjit Singh* and L. Ramesh

Dr. M.G.R. Educational and Research Institute, Chennai, India

Abstract

This chapter investigates the load frequency control (LFC) based on a neural network for improving power system dynamic performance of a single-area thermal power plant. The performance of P, PI, PID, and NARMA-L2 controllers is studied in terms of their capability to reduce the frequency deviations to zero. NARMA-L2 controller is tuned with different epochs to best tune the system and with the application of PID controller, an error has been minimized quickly. NARMA-L2 controller is found to overcome the control problems of P, PI, and PID controllers due to the input multiplicities. Necessary graphs are drawn in order to prove the superiority of the NARMA-L2 controller. MATLAB/SIMULINK software is used in this chapter.

Keywords: Frequency deviations, NARMA-L2 controller, artificial neural network, load frequency control, automatic generation control

14.1 Introduction

Small signal stability is defined as that property of the power system which maintains its synchronism under small disturbances. Due to continuous variations in the power generation and load demand, disturbances occur in the power system [1].

Due to these disturbances, oscillations occur in the power system, which must be damped to maintain the system stability. Instability can be of two

---

Corresponding author: rsa.ranjit@gmail.com

Anita Khosla, Prasenjit Chatterjee, Ikbal Ali and Dheeraj Joshi (eds.) Optimization Techniques in Engineering: Advances and Applications, (231–242) © 2023 Scrivener Publishing LLC

forms: (i) steady increase in rotor angle due to lack of sufficient synchronizing torque that results in non-oscillatory instability. (ii) Rotor oscillations of increasing amplitude due to lack of sufficient damping torque that results in Oscillatory instability [2].

Oscillations can occur in two modes:

(i) Local plant mode oscillations: these are related to units at the generating station swinging with respect to the rest of the system. The range of frequencies of these oscillations lies in the range of (0.8 - 2) Hz.

(ii) Interarea oscillations: These are related to the swinging of many machines in one part of the system against machines in other parts. The range of frequencies of these oscillations lies in the range of (0.1–0.7 Hz) [8].

ACE is an important parameter of power system stability and is defined as the change in area frequency which when used with tuned PID controllers helped in bringing system frequency error to zero [3].

AGC helps in maintaining the equilibrium between the generation and demand of a particular power system [4–7]. In this chapter, fully, the frequency response in a single-area power system is observed, and the error is being minimized by tuning the NARMA-L2 controller. Also, with the introduction of the PID controller steady-state error is reduced to zero in a quick interval of time. The load demand change is also considered here.

14.2   Single-Area Power System

In a single-area power system, Narma-L2 Controller along with PID Controller is connected with a hydraulic amplifier and turbine of the power system. Load demand change and Regulation are both important parameters of the power system.

Tie lines are used to connect all the controlling units of the power system and the power flowing in these tie lines has to be constant so that the continuity of the power supply is maintained. The uniformity of the power flow in the tie lines must be maintained at any cost.

The frequency changes can be kept constant by load frequency control (LFC). Frequency, active powers, and rotor angle are being changed while the power system is being operated [8–11].

The change in the System frequency Δf_i, is observed and brought to null position in quick time, i.e., 7 seconds.

Even a small change in the single-area power system block diagram can upset the synchronism of the whole system.

14.3   Automatic Load Frequency Control (ALFC)

Automatic load frequency control (ALFC) is being introduced in the power system to allow an area to first meet its own load demand changes and to help in bringing the steady-state frequency of the system Δf to zero.

The frequency and power in the case of turbine governor can be related as

$$\Delta Pm = (\Delta Pref - 1/R^* \Delta f)$$

where

ΔPm = change in turbine mechanical power output.
$\Delta Pref$ = change in reference power setting
Δf = change in frequency
R = Regulation constant which identifies the sensitivity of the generator to a change in frequency.

14.4   Controllers Used in the Simulink Model

14.4.1   PID Controller

PID controller is defined as a control loop feedback mechanism that is being widely used in industrial control systems [12, 13]. It generally computes an error value as the difference between a measured process variable and the desired set point. The performance characteristics of the systems, such as rise time, overshoot, settling time, a steady-state error can be raised by tuning the value of parameters (K_p, K_i, and K_d) of PID controller as shown in Figure 14.1.

Mathematically PID is represented as:

$$y(t) = K_p \left[e(t) + T_d \frac{d(e)}{d(t)} + \frac{1}{T_i} \int_0^t e(t) d(t) \right]$$

$$y(t) = \left[K_p e(t) + K_d \frac{d(e)}{d(t)} + K_i \int_0^t e(t) d(t) \right]$$

$$K_i = \frac{K_p}{T_i} \quad \text{and} \quad K_{d=} K_p . T_d$$

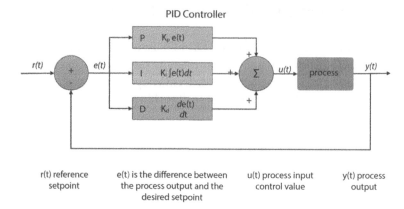

Figure 14.1 Block diagram of PI controller.

The controller should be responsive against changes in frequency and load. Rise time and overshoot are reduced by proportional and derivative control, whereas the integral control action will minimize the static frequency error to zero.

14.4.2 PI Controller

PI controller shown in Figure 14.2 is a feedback control loop that calculates an error signal by taking the difference between the output of a system, which in this case is the power being drawn from the battery, and the setpoint [14, 15].

14.4.3 P Controller

Proportional control shown in Figure 14.3 in engineering and process control is a type of linear feedback control system in which a correction is applied to the controlled variable, which is proportional to the difference between the desired value (setpoint [SP]) and the measured value (process variable [PV]) [16, 17].

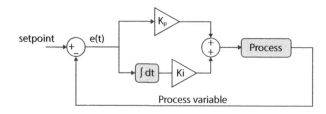

Figure 14.2 Block diagram of PI controller.

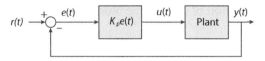

Figure 14.3 Block diagram of P controller.

14.5 Circuit Description

The following circuit diagram shows the single-area thermal power plant. Gain and time constant of hydraulic amplifier, turbine, and power system block have been modified and tuned so as to help the PID and NARMA-L2 controllers to reduce rise time, overshoot, and the error to zero in 3.6 seconds as evident from the graph.

Figure 14.4 shows the Simulink model for single-area power system with Narma-L2 controller and PID controller is given below.

The hydraulic amplifier is used to operate the steam valve for controlling the flow of steam and the transfer function is given as

$$G_{amp} = \frac{K_{amp}}{1 + sT_{amp}}$$

K_{amp} = Gain of the Amplifier block
K_{amp} = Gain of the Amplifier block

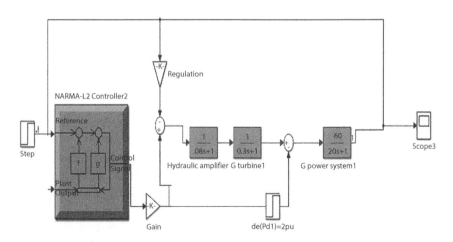

Figure 14.4 Simulink model of single-area thermal power plant.

The transfer function of the turbine block is given as:

$$G_t = \frac{K_t}{1+sT_t}$$

where
   K_t = Gain of turbine block
   T_t = Time constant of turbine block

14.6   ANN and NARMA L2 Controller

ANN, as the name suggests, is an information processing system. In this system, the element used for processing the information is called neurons [18–21]. The connecting links used for transmitting signals process an associated weight, which is multiplied along with the incoming signal (net input) for any typical neural net. The output signal is obtained by applying the activation function to the net input. Neural network architecture—the multilayer perceptron—as unknown function is shown in Figure 14.4. Parameters of the network are adjusted so that it produces the same response as the unknown function, if the same input is applied to both systems [22–25]. The unknown function could also represent the inverse of a system being controlled; in this case, the neural network can be used to implement the controller. ANN controller architecture employed here is a nonlinear autoregressive model reference adaptive controller [26–29]. It is simply a rearrangement of the neural network plant model. The plant output is forced to track the reference model output. NARMA L2 controller mainly consists of reference, plant output and control signal. The computation required for this type of controller is very less [30, 31]. NARMA-L2 is one of the important neural network architectures that has been implemented in the MATLAB for prediction and control of various systems.

NARMA-L2 controller: The ANN controller architecture employed here is nonlinear auto regressive moving average (NARMA) model is a representation of input-output behavior of a finite-dimensional and nonlinear discrete-time dynamic plant in neighborhood of the equilibrium state [32]. The nonlinearity property of the ANN controller makes its implementation for real-time control systems difficult. To overcome the computational complexity of ANN controllers, two classes of NARMA are introduced in reference [33]: NARMA-L1 and NARMA-L2.

The NARMAL2 is more convenient to practically implement using multilayer neural networks. This controller is simply a rearrangement of the neural network plant model, which is trained offline, in batch form. NARMA L2 controller mainly consists of reference, plant output, and control signal. The computation required for this type of controller is very less. The plant output is forced to track the reference model output, and the effect of controller changes on plant output is predicted for further calculations. The main quality of this controller is that it permits the updating of controller parameters design performed by two stages, i.e., system identification and control design. After a series of trial and error and modifications, the ANN architecture, which provides the best performance, is selected.

In this controller, the frequency deviations, tie-line power deviation, and load perturbation of the area are chosen as the neural network controller inputs. Control signals applied to the governors in the area act as the outputs of the neural network. The data required for the ANN controller training is obtained by designing the reference model neural network and apply it to the power system with step response load disturbance. NARMA-L2 is one of the important neural network architectures that has been implemented in the MATLAB for prediction and control of various systems. The NARMA-L2 controller design is performed by two stages, i.e., system identification and control design [34]. The outputs of the neural network are the control signals, which are applied to the speed governors in the corresponding area [35, 36]. After a series of trial and error and modifications, the ANN architecture, which provides the best performance, is selected. In this case, it is a three-layer perceptron with five inputs, 13 neurons in the hidden layer, and one output in the ANN controller that is selected. The activation function of the neurons of the network is trainlm function.

Three hundred training samples have been taken to train 300 epochs. The proposed network has been trained by using the learning performance.

In this chapter, it is a three-layer perceptron with two inputs, nine neurons in the hidden layer, and one output in the ANN controller that is selected. The activation function of the neurons of the network is trainlm function. 300 training samples have been taken to train 100 epochs.

14.7 Simulation Results and Comparative Analysis

The necessary graphs obtained after Simulink, the MATLAB Model, are discussed in this section. Also, with the introduction of Narma-L2

Controller, the error is being brought to zero in quick time. Regulation is also varied to get the best results.

Thus, simulation is performed, and keeping the load demand changes in the area, the error has been reduced to zero in 7 seconds with the help of NARMA-L2 controller along with PID controller.

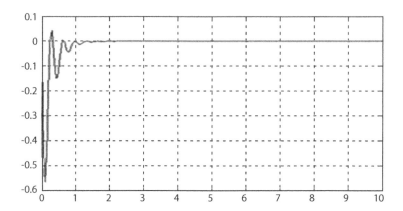

Graph 1 Frequency error minimization by NARMA-L2 controller.

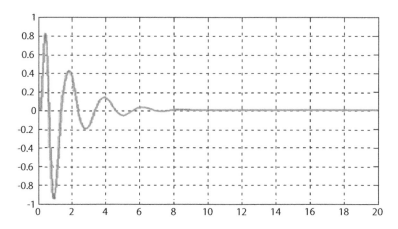

Graph 2 Frequency error minimization by PID controller.

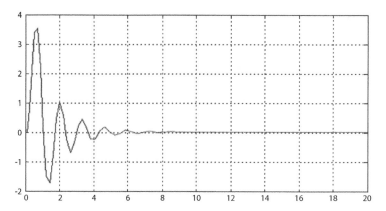

Graph 3 Frequency error minimization by PI controller.

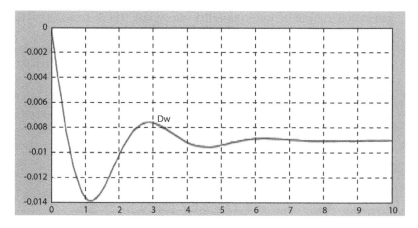

Graph 4 Frequency error minimization by P controller.

14.8   Conclusion

The load frequency control mechanism is applied to the single-area thermal power plant using NARMA-L2 controller and the performance analysis was compared with P, PI, and PID controllers. The graphs obtained show that the NARMA-L2 controller has a better response in reducing the frequency error to zero and that too in a quick time. Further, the research can be done on the larger interconnection of the power plants and studying the impact of different controllers and algorithms in the LFC analysis of the system.

References

1. Shariatzadeh, F., Kumar, N., Srivastava, A., Optimal control algorithms for reconfiguration of shipboard microgrid distribution system using intelligent techniques. *IEEE Trans. Ind. Appl.*, 53, 474–482, Aug. 18, 2016.

2. Salam, A.A., Mohamed, A., Hannan, M.A., Technical challenges on microgrids. *ARPN J. Eng. Appl. Sci.*, 3, 6, 64–69, December 2008.

3. Lal, D.K., Barisal, A.K., Tripathy, M., Load frequency control of multi area interconnected microgrid power system using grasshopper optimization algorithm optimized fuzzy PID controller. *2018 Recent Advances on Engineering, Technology and Computational Sciences (RAETCS)*, Allahabad, pp. 1–6, 2018.

4. Siti, M.W., Tungadio, D.H., Sun, Y., Mbungu, N.T., Tiako, R., Optimal frequency deviations control in microgrid interconnected systems. *IET Renewable Power Generation*, 13, 13, 2376–2382, October 07, 2019.

5. Xi, L. *et al.*, A virtual generation ecosystem control strategy for automatic generation control of interconnected microgrids. *IEEE Access*, 8, 94165–94175, 2020.

6. Ferraro, P., Crisostomi, E., Shorten, R., Milano, F., Stochastic frequency control of grid-connected microgrids. *IEEE Trans. Power Syst.*, 33, 5, 5704–5713, Sept. 2018.

7. Sahoo, S.K. and Kishore, N.K., Battery state-of-charge-based control and frequency regulation in the MMG system using fuzzy logic. *IET Generation, Transmission & Distribution*, 14, 14, 2698–2709, July 17, 2020.

8. Latif, A., Das, D.C., Barik, A.K., Ranjan, S., Illustration of demand response supported coordinated system performance evaluation of YSGA optimized dual stage PIFOD-(1+PI) controller employed with wind-tidal-biodiesel based independent two-area interconnected microgrid system. *IET Renewable Power Generation*, 14, 6, 1074–1086, April 27, 2020.

9. Fooladivanda, D., Optimal design and operation of a grid-connected microgrid. *Electrical Power & Energy Conference (EPEC)*, 2009, IEEE, Source IEEE Xplore, November 2009.

10. Barik, A.K. and Das, D.C., Proficient load-frequency regulation of demand response supported bio-renewable cogeneration-based hybrid microgrids with quasi-oppositional selfish-herd optimization. *IET Renewable Power Generation*, 13, 13, 2889–2898, July 09, 2019.

11. Malik, S.M., Sun, Y., Ai, X., Chen, Z., Wang, K., Cost-based droop scheme for converters in Interconnected hybrid microgrids. *IEEE Access*, 7, 82266–82276, 2019.

12. Tah, A. and Das, D., An enhanced droop control method for accurate load sharing and voltage improvement of isolated and interconnected DC microgrids. *IEEE Trans. Sustain. Energ.*, 7, 3, 1194–1204, July 2016.

13. Zhou, J., Zhang, H., Sun, Q., Ma, D., Huang, B., Event-based distributed active power sharing control for interconnected AC and DC microgrids. *IEEE Trans. Smart Grid*, 9, 6, 6815–6828, Nov. 2018.

14. Wang, H. and Huang, J., Incentivizing energy trading for interconnected microgrids. *IEEE Trans. Smart Grid*, 9, 4, 2647–2657, July 2018.

15. Zhang, C., Wang, X., Lin, P., Liu, P.X., Yan, Y., Yang, J., Finite-time feed-forward decoupling and precise decentralized control for DC microgrids towards large-signal stability. *IEEE Trans. Smart Grid*, 11, 1, 391–402, Jan. 2020.

16. Naderi, M., Khayat, Y., Shafiee, Q., Dragicevic, T., Bevrani, H., Blaabjerg, F., Interconnected autonomous AC microgrids via back-to-back converters— Part I: Small-signal modeling. *IEEE Trans. Power Electron.*, 35, 5, 4728–4740, May 2020.

17. Li, F., Qin, J., Wan, Y., Yang, T., Decentralized cooperative optimal power flow of multiple interconnected microgrids via negotiation. *IEEE Trans. Smart Grid*, 11, 5, 3827–3836, Sept. 2020.

18. Papadimitriou, C.N., Kleftakis, V.A., Hatziargyriou, N.D., Control strategy for seamless transition from islanded to interconnected operation mode of microgrids. *J. Mod. Power Syst. Clean Energy*, 5, 2, 169–176, March 2017.

19. Gan, L.K., Hussain, A., Howey, D.A., Kim, H., Limitations in energy management systems: A case study for resilient interconnected microgrids. *IEEE Trans. Smart Grid*, 10, 5, 5675–5685, Sept. 2019.

20. Hossain, M.J., Pota, H.R., Mahmud, M.A., Aldeen, M., Robust control for power sharing in microgrids with low-inertia wind and PV generators. *IEEE Trans.Sustain. Energ.*, 6, 3, 1067–1077, July 2015.

21. Fathi, M. and Bevrani, H., Statistical cooperative power dispatching in interconnected microgrids. *IEEE Trans. Sustain.Energ.*, 4, 3, 586–593, July 2013.

22. Zolfaghari, M., Abedi, M., Gharehpetian, G.B., Power flow control of interconnected AC–DC microgrids in grid-connected hybrid microgrids using modified UIPC. *IEEE Trans. Smart Grid*, 10, 6, 6298–6307, Nov. 2019.

23. Zou, H., Mao, S., Wang, Y., Zhang, F., Chen, X., Cheng, L., A survey of energy management in interconnected multi-microgrids. *IEEE Access*, 7, 72158–72169, 2019.

24. Nejabatkhah, F. and Li, Y.W., Overview of power management strategies of hybrid AC/DC microgrid. *IEEE Trans. Power Electron.*, 30, 12, 7072–7089, Dec. 2015.

25. Gan, L.K., Zhang, P., Lee, J., Osborne, M.A., Howey, D.A., Data-driven energy management system with gaussian process forecasting and MPC for interconnected microgrids. *IEEE Trans. Sustain. Energ.*, 12, 1, 695–704, Jan. 2021.

26. Hans, C.A., Braun, P., Raisch, J., Grüne, L., Reincke-Collon, C., Hierarchical distributed model predictive control of interconnected microgrids. *IEEE Trans. Sustain. Energ.*, 10, 1, 407–416, Jan. 2019.

27. Nunna, H. S. V. S. K., Sesetti, A., Rathore, A.K., Doolla, S., Multiagent-based energy trading platform for energy storage systems in distribution systems with interconnected microgrids. *IEEE Trans. Ind. Appl.*, 56, 3, 3207–3217, May-June 2020.

28. Shabib, G., Gayed, M.A., Rashwan, A.M., Optimal tuning of PID controller for AVR system using modified particle swarm optimization. *Proceedings of the 14th International Middle East Power Systems Conference*, Cairo University, Egypt, December 19–21, 2010, Paper ID 170, 2010.

29. Ozkop, E., Sharaf, A.M., Atlas, I.H., Load frequency control of four area power systems using fuzzy logic PI controller. *16th National Power Systems Conference*, DECEMBER 15th-17th, 2010.

30. Kundur, P., *Power System Stability & Control*, Tata Mcgraw Hill, New York, 1994.

31. Sadat, H., *Power System Analysis*, 2 Edition, Tata McGraw Hill, New Delhi, India, 2002.

32. Chang, C.S. and Fu, W., Area load frequency control using fuzzy gain scheduling of PI controllers. *Electr. Power Energy Syst.*, 42, 2, 145–152, 1997.

33. Ismail, A., Improving UAE power systems control performance by using combined LFC and AVR. *The seventh U.A.E University Research Conference, Eng*, pp. 50–60, 2006.

34. Mathur, H.D. and Ghosh, S., A comprehensive analysis of intelligent controllers for load frequency control. *IEEE Power India Conference*, 2006, doi: 10.1109/POWERI.2006.1632619.

35. Rani, P. and Jaswal, R., Automatic load frequency control of multi-area power system using ANN controller and Genetic algorithm. *IJETT*, 4, 9, 3777–3784, Sep. 2013.

36. Surjan, B.S. and Garg, R., Power system stabilizer controller design for SMIB stability study. *Int. J. Adv. Technol.*, 2, 1, 209–214, October 2012.

Part 2

DECISION SCIENCE AND SIMULATION-BASED OPTIMIZATION

Selection of Nonpowered Industrial Truck for Small Scale Manufacturing Industry Using Fuzzy VIKOR Method Under FMCDM Environment

Bipradas Bairagi

*Department of Mechanical Engineering, Haldia Institute of Techonology,
West Bengal, India*

Abstract

Nonpowered industrial truck selection plays an important role in material handling in a small-scale manufacturing organization. In order to meeting the low-cost and high-productivity target fulfillment, decision makers need to analyze the performance of different nonpowered industrial truck as material handling device to determine appropriate equipment with accurate functionalities. Suitable nonpowered industrial truck selection for a particular material handling intention is one of the critical tasks for the decision makers. This chapter exploits fuzzy VIKOR (multi criteria optimization compromise solution) for nonpowered industrial truck selection considering multiple conflicting criteria. Subjective judgment of weight of criteria and performance rating of alternatives is accomplished based on experience, perception, and opinion of experts/decision makers involved in the process. Normalization is carried out to restrict the magnitude and sense of ratings of alternatives. Weights of criteria are combined with normalized rating to calculate S, R, and Q values, which give ranking order of the alternatives. A suitable example on nonpowered industrial truck selection is illustrated using the present approach, which establishes the applicability and usefulness of the method.

Keywords: Industrial truck selection, Fuzzy VIKOR, FMCDM, decision making under uncertainty

Email: bipradasbairagi79@gmail.com

Anita Khosla, Prasenjit Chatterjee, Ikbal Ali and Dheeraj Joshi (eds.) Optimization Techniques in Engineering: Advances and Applications, (245–260) © 2023 Scrivener Publishing LLC

15.1　Introduction

Due to the industrial globalization over last few decades and ferocious competition among industrial organizations, the requirement of right selection and utilization of material handling equipment in industries considerably increases. It has been estimated that 30% to 75% of the overall cost of a manufactured goods is because of handling material. This cost can be reduced to 15 to 30 percent using well-organized material handling (MH) system [1]. This information regarding material handling cost highlights the significance of proper material handling equipment selection. In industry, where investment capital as well as handling volume is limited and building limitation precludes utilization of heavier devices, nonpowered industrial trucks (NPITs) are widely used. These limitations lead organizations to tender more weight to the procuring of NPITs and its interrelated decisions. These decisions involve a significant investment of capital.

Experts/decision makers consider several important criteria while selecting NPIT for industrial purpose. Hence, nonpowered industrial truck (NPIT) selection is a multi-criteria decision making problem that includes both quantitative and qualitative factors. However, proper selection of NPIT for industrial application is extremely essential, past researchers have not given sufficient attention to proper selection of NPIT. The following comprehensive literature survey in the broad areas of material handling equipment selection explores this deficiency of research work on performance evaluation and selection of NPITs.

Goswami and Behera made an investigation for the capability and applicability of two well-known MCDM (Multi Criteria Decision Making) approaches ARAS (Additive Ratio Assessment) and COPRAS (COmplex PRoportional ASsessment) for the evaluation and selection of conveyors, AGV (Automated Guided Vehicle) and robots as material handling equipment [2]. Soufi *et al.* introduced an AHP (Analytical Hierarchy Process) based MCDM methodology for the evaluation and selection of material handling equipment to be utilized in manufacturing systems [3]. Satyam *et al.* applied a multi attribute decision making approach for evaluation and selection of conveyors as material handling equipment [4]. Nguyen *et al.* advocated a combined multi criteria decision making model for the evaluation and selection of conveyor as the material handling equipment based on fuzzy analytical hierarchy process and fuzzy ARAS with vague and imprecision information [5]. Mathewa and Sahua made a comparison among the novel multi-criteria decision making approaches by solving a problem on material handling equipment selection [6].

Kahraman *et al.* proposed a fuzzy hierarchical TOPSIS (Technique for Order Preference by Similarity to Ideal Solution) model for selection of industrial robotic systems [7]. Chu and Lin suggested a fuzzy TOPSIS technique in which the values of objective criteria were transformed into indices without dimension to make certain matching between linguistic terms under subjective criteria and objective criteria values. Through fuzzy arithmetic, defuzzified weighted rating, mean of removals and closeness coefficient, the robots were ranked [8]. Parkan and Wu suggested a technique which explained the application and analyze some of the current MADM (Multi Attribute Decision Making) and performance assessment process through a robot selection problem [9].

Chittratanawat and Noble proposed a hybrid algorithm (a nonlinear mixed-integer program) for cracking MHE (Material Handling Equipment) selection problems minimizing the overall facility design costs [10]. Computer assisted models have been advocated by researchers to deal with the large number of robot attributes and available robots [11]. Hassan *et al.* presented an algorithm for material handling equipment selection to minimize entire costs associated with operation and investment on the equipment under consideration [12].

The above literature survey reveals that some of the past researchers have applied MCDM techniques in the broad areas of material handling equipment selection problems. However, this effort is inadequate for exhaustive and extensive decision making regarding proper selection of specific material handling device like nonpowered industrial truck (NPIT) from thousands of available alternatives under multiple conflicting criteria of diverse categories. Therefore an effort in the chapter is made to suggest a combined multi-criteria fuzzy AHP-based Fuzzy Grey Theory (FGT) approach for performance evaluation of conveyors under MCDM environment. The real life situation of conveyor evaluation is associated with vague, imprecise and ambiguous information. Hence imprecise data in a volatile environment deserves theory of fuzzy set in MCDM approaches. The present chapter uses fuzzy VIKOR approach in the evaluation and ranking of NPITs, which is found as an appropriate technique.

Due to the presence of large number of material handling devices with various criteria the suitable nonpowered industrial truck selection is a complicated process and time consuming task. There is a requirement of efficient and systematic approach for nonpowered industrial truck selection to find the best alternative material handling device for a particular material and condition.

Objectives of the research are listed below.

1. To evaluate and select the best industrial truck under consideration.

2. To apply fuzzy VIKOR techniques as decision-making process.
3. Short listing the key parameters of nonpowered industrial trucks (NPITs) evaluation and selection.

The rest part of the chapter is equipped as following manner. Section 15.2 gives a brief description basic concept of fuzzy set. Section 15.3 introduces the fuzzy VIKOR algorithms. Section 15.4 cites a decision making problem on nonpowered industrial truck selection. Section 15.5 presents the calculation along with discussion with some salient points of the chapter. Finally, Section 15.6 is dedicated for some essential conclusions and suggestion of future research.

15.2 Fuzzy Set Theory

Decision makers usually have a preference in subjective assessment to objective assessment of fuzzy information. Theory of fuzzy set is used to convert these subjective data into numerical (objective) values [13]. A number of important definitions on fuzzy set are presented in the following subsection 15.2.1.

15.2.1 Some Important Fuzzy Definitions

Definition 1: A fuzzy set $\tilde{A}$ is defined in a universe of discourse denoted by X specified by $\mu_{\tilde{A}}(x)$, called membership function, which connects every member x (a real number) in X in a interval where x belong to [0, 1] [14].

Definition 2: A Triangular Fuzzy Number (TFN) $\tilde{q}$ is defined as a triplet (q_1, q_2, q_3), where membership function is characterized as below [15].

$$\mu_{\tilde{q}}(x) = \begin{cases} 0, & x < q_1 \\ \dfrac{x - q_1}{q_2 - q_1}, & q_1 \leq x \leq q_2 \\ \dfrac{x - q_3}{q_2 - q_3}, & q_2 \leq x \leq q_3 \\ 0, & x > q_3. \end{cases} \tag{15.1}$$

Membership function of a TFN $\tilde{q} = (q_1, q_2, q_3)$ is graphically shown in Figure 15.1.

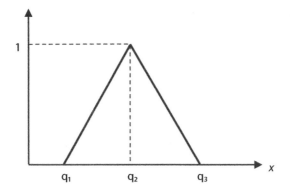

Figure 15.1 Membership Function of a TFN $\tilde{q} = (q_1, q_2, q_3)$.

Definition 3: Let $\tilde{q} = (q_1, q_2, q_3)$ and $\tilde{r} = (r_1, r_2, r_3)$ be two TFNs, then the distance between the two fuzzy numbers can be calculated as

$$d(\tilde{q}, \tilde{r}) = \sqrt{\frac{1}{3}\left[(q_1 - r_1)^2 + (q_2 - r_2)^2 + (q_3 - r_3)^2\right]} \qquad (15.2)$$

This method of calculating distance between two fuzzy numbers is termed as vertex method [16].

15.2.2 Fuzzy Operations

Let $\tilde{q} = (q_1, q_2, q_3)$ and $\tilde{r} = (r_1, r_2, r_3)$ are two triangular fuzzy numbers.

(a) Addition:

$$\tilde{q} \oplus \tilde{r} = (q_1 + r_1, q_2 + r_2, q_3 + r_3) \qquad (15.3)$$

(b) Multiplication of a fuzzy number $\tilde{q} = (q_1, q_2, q_3)$ with a real number k

$$k \otimes \tilde{q} = (kq_1, kq_2, kq_3) \quad \text{where} \quad k \geq 0 \,\&\, k \in R \qquad (15.4)$$

(c) Multiplication commutative property

$$k \otimes \tilde{q} = \tilde{q} \otimes k \text{ where } k \geq 0 \,\&\, k \in R \qquad (15.5)$$

(d) Division of a fuzzy number $\tilde{q} = (q_1, q_2, q_3)$ with a real number k

$$\tilde{q}(\div)k = \left(\frac{q_1}{k}, \frac{q_2}{k}, \frac{q_3}{k} \right) \quad \text{where} \quad k \geq 0 \,\&\, k \in R \qquad (15.6)$$

(e) A TFN $\tilde{q} = (q_1, q_2, q_3)$ can be defuzzified by the equation

$$BNP_i = \frac{\left[(q_3 - q_1) + (q_2 - q_1) \right]}{3} + q_1 \qquad (15.7)$$

BNP_i be the best nonfuzzy performance. When a fuzzy number is defuzzified then this value can be called best nonfuzzy performance value (BNP) [17]. Alpha-cut, center of area, mean of maximal are defuzzification method [18]. Each fuzzy data expressed by decision makers is transformed into equivalent TFN. In the current method, TFN is chosen for its capability of handing linguistic variables, simplicity, and ease of use.

15.2.3   Linguistic Variable (LV)

A linguistic term/variable (LV) is a word or a phrase or a sentence in a natural language or in an artificial language. Linguistic variables are used in intricate situation in which assessment is hard to define and hazardous to quantify with conventional methods [19]. In the current chapter, a set of five grades of linguistic terms has been used for capturing importance weights of criteria. The LVs are equally important, weakly important, essentially important, very important, and absolutely important. These linguistic terms are required to transform to fuzzy numbers to quantify the assessment. The respective fuzzy numbers are (1, 1, 2), (2, 3, 4), (4, 5, 6), (6, 7, 8) and (8, 9, 9) presented in Table 15.1.

To assess alternatives against criteria linguistic terms in five grades have been utilized in the chapter, namely, Exceptionally Low (EL), Low (L), Medium (M), High (H) and Exceptionally High (EH). These Linguistic terms will be converted to the respective fuzzy numbers (0, 1, 3), (1, 3, 5), (3, 5, 7), (5, 7, 9) and (7, 9, 10) arranged in Table 15.2. In cases of both weights and performance measures, every TFNs is described with exactly three values, viz. lower, middle, and upper values over the range of the function. In the present chapter, triangular fuzzy number is used due to its previously proven ability of proper conversion and quantification of subjective assessment.

15.3 FVIKOR

Visekriterijumsko KOmpromisno Rangiranje (VIKOR) was introduced by Zeleny [20]. It was later expanded by Opricovic and Tzeng to Fuzzy VIKOR [21]. VIKOR is a multicriteria compromise and optimization technique. The combination of FST with VIKOR is termed as FVIKOR. This method gives ranks to alternatives on the basis of ideal point method. In this approach, PIS and NIS are computed from the best value and the worst value, respectively, under every criterion.

$$\tilde{L}_{p,i} = \left[\left\{ \sum_{j=1}^{n} \tilde{w}_j \frac{(\tilde{x}_j^+ - \tilde{x}_{ij})}{(\tilde{x}_j^+ - \tilde{x}_j^-)} \right\}^p \right]^{\frac{1}{p}} \tag{15.8}$$

where $1 \le p \le \infty$, $i = 1, 2 \dots m$. $j = 1, 2 \dots n$. $\tilde{x}_{ij}$ denotes fuzzy performance rating of alternative i regarding criterion j. m is number of alternative. n is number of criteria. $\tilde{w}_j$ denotes fuzzy weight of criterion j. Fuzzy VIKOR method has the following steps.

Step 1: Decision matrix: Assess the alternatives for every subjective criterion with linguistic terms, construct a decision matrix with the linguistic terms.

Step 2: Transform the linguistic terms into related TFN, $\tilde{x}_{ij} = (a_{ij}, b_{ij}, c_{ij})$.

Step 3: Find PIS ($\tilde{x}_j^+$) and NIS ($\tilde{x}_j^-$) for every criterion.

$$\tilde{x}_j^+ = \left(\max_i \tilde{x}_{ij} \middle| j \in B, \quad \min_i \tilde{x}_{ij} \middle| j \in C \right) \quad j = 1, 2 \dots n. \tag{15.9}$$

$$\tilde{x}_j^- = \left(\min_i \tilde{x}_{ij} \middle| j \in B, \quad \max_i \tilde{x}_{ij} \middle| j \in C \right) \quad j = 1, 2 \dots n. \tag{15.10}$$

Step 4: Compute $\tilde{S}_i$ and $\tilde{R}_i$ values using following equations.

$$\tilde{S}_i = \tilde{L}_{1,i} = \sum_{j=1}^{n} \tilde{w}_j \left(\frac{\tilde{x}_j^+ - \tilde{x}_{ij}}{\tilde{x}_j^+ - \tilde{x}_j^-} \right) \tag{15.11}$$

$$\tilde{R}_i = \tilde{L}_{\infty,i} = \max_j \left\{ \tilde{w}_j \left(\frac{\tilde{x}_j^+ - \tilde{x}_{ij}}{\tilde{x}_j^+ - \tilde{x}_j^-} \right) \right\}$$ (15.12)

$\tilde{S}_i$ is optimal fuzzy solution derived by comprehensive assessment of the alternatives, R_i is the worst fuzzy solution of alternatives' comprehensive evaluation. w_j is the fuzzy weight of criterion j.

Step 5: Evaluate $\tilde{Q}_i$ for each alternative using following equation.

$$\tilde{Q}_i = \tilde{v} \left(\frac{\tilde{S}_i - \tilde{S}_i^+}{\tilde{S}_i^- - \tilde{S}_i^+} \right) + (\tilde{1} - \tilde{v}) \left(\frac{\tilde{R}_i - \tilde{R}_i^+}{\tilde{R}_i^- - \tilde{R}_i^+} \right)$$ (15.13)

where $i = 1,2...m.$ $\tilde{S}_i^+ = \min(\tilde{S}_i), \tilde{S}_i^- = \min (\tilde{S}_i), \tilde{R}_i^+ = \min(\tilde{R}_i), \tilde{R}_i^- = \max(\tilde{R}_i).$
v is the weight of decision making strategy "maximum group utility" or "majority of criteria."

Step 6: Rank the alternatives according to the ascending order of defuzzyfied $\tilde{S}_i$, $\tilde{R}_i$ and $\tilde{Q}_i$ values. The alternative with the least value corresponds to the best one and the alternative with the largest value is associated with the highest rank. Thus, three ranks of the alternatives are obtained.

Step 7: Consider the alternative a' with minimum value of $\tilde{Q}_i$ as the optimal solution if both of the following two conditions simultaneously satisfy. Acceptable advantage (C1): $Q(a'') - Q(a') \geq 1/(m - 1)$, m is the number of alternatives. a'' is the alternative with second minimum value of Q. Acceptable stability in decision-making (C2): An alternative has the first rank if at least one of the two ranking by S and R values. The stability in decision making can be obtained by "voting by majority rule" (when v>0.5) or "consensus" (when v 0.5) or "veto" (when v<0.5).
Propose a compromise solution: If only condition C2 does not satisfy both alternatives and are optimal solutions. If only condition C1 does not satisfy, are optimal solutions.

15.4   Problem Definition

An Eastern Indian company desires to select the best NPIT. After initial screening test, five different nonpowered industrial trucks are accepted for further evaluation. A decision making committee is formed, which decides to assess the alternative and considers six selection criteria. The alternative nonpowered industrials trucks are: dolly (T1), 4-wheel hand track (T2), hand lift truck (jack) (T3) semilive skid (T4), and trailer (T5). Six selection criteria under consideration are as follows, cost (C1), floor/aisle space requirement (C2), limitation (C3), load-carrying capacity (C4), traveling distance (C5), life period (C6) [22].

15.5   Results and Discussions

In this chapter, fuzzy VIKOR approach has been used for making right decision on a nonpowered industrial truck selection problem. Five alterative and six criteria have been considered. Decision matrix and weight matrix in terms of five degrees respective linguistic are presented in Table 15.1. Linguistic terms are transformed in related TFNs and accommodated in Table 15.2. Weighted decision matrix with normalization is decorated in Table 15.3.

BNP value of $\tilde{S}_i$ and corresponding ranking order of NPITs are shown in Table 15.4. $\tilde{R}_i$, BNP value of $\tilde{R}_i$ and corresponding ranking order of NPITs are shown in Table 15.5. $\tilde{Q}_i$, BNP value of $\tilde{Q}_i$ and respective ranking order of NPITs are in Table 15.6. BNP of fuzzy Q values are shown in Figure 15.2.

Comparison of ranking order based on BNP of fuzzy S, R, and Q values is graphically represented in Figure 15.3. FVIKOR approach provides ranking order to the alternatives on the basis of BNP of fuzzy S_i, fuzzy R_i, and fuzzy Q_i. The NPITs are ranked based on BNP of fuzzy Si values as T5 >T1>T3>T4>T2, whereas the ranking order of NPITs as per BNP of R_i values is T2>T1>T4>T3>T5. In line with FVIKOR, NPIT 2 attains the maximum BNP of fuzzy S_i, R_i, and Q_i values, which assures the conditions of acceptable advantage (C1) and acceptable stability (C2). This confirms closeness to the optimal solution. Hence, T2 (4-wheel hand track) is selected the best NPIT under consideration.

Table 15.1 Decision matrix and weight matrix.

Objective	Min	Min	Min	Max	Max	Max
Criteria	C1	C2	C3	C4	C5	C6
T1	450	High	High	Exceptionally High	Low	Medium
T2	79.5	Low	Medium	Exceptionally Low	Low	High
T3	520	Low	Exceptionally High	Low	Medium	Medium
T4	377	Low	Medium	Medium	Low	Medium
T5	502	Medium	Low	High	Medium	Medium
Weights	Very Important	Essentially Important	Weakly Important	Absolutely Important	Weakly Important	Weakly Important

Table 15.2 Decision matrix in TFNs.

	*Cost	Floor space	Limitation	Load capacity	Traveling distance	Life period
T1	(405,450,495)	(5,7,9)	(5,7,9)	(7,9,10)	(1,3,5)	(3,5,7)
T2	(71.5,79.5,87.4)	(1,3,5)	(3,5,7)	(0,1,3)	(1,3,5)	(5,7,9)
T3	(468,520,572)	(1,3,5)	(7,9,10)	(1,3,5)	(3,5,7)	(3,5,7)
T4	(339,377,415)	(1,3,5)	(3,5,7)	(3,5,7)	(1,3,5)	(3,5,7)
T5	(451,502,552)	(3,5,7)	(1,3,5)	(5,7,9)	(3,5,7)	(3,5,7)
Weights	(6,7,8)	(4,5,6)	(2,3,4)	(8,9,9)	(4,5,6)	(4,5,6)

*Cost data are transformed into TFNs by 10% expansion in both sides.

Table 15.3 Weighted normalized decision matrix.

	Cost (-)	Floor space req. (-)	Limitations (-)	Load capacity (+)	Traveling distance (+)	Life period (+)
T1	(0.30,0.49,0.72)	(0.24,0.48,0.78)	(0.04,0.18,0.42)	(0.44,0.75,1.0)	(0.06,0.24,0.49)	(0.08,0.24,0.48)
T2	(0.05,0.09,0.13)	(0.05,0.20,0.44)	(0.02,0.13,0.33)	(0, 0.08,0.3)	(0.06,0.24,0.49)	(0.13,0.33,0.61)
T3	(0.34,0.53,0.84)	(0.05,0.20,0.44)	(0.06,0.23,0.47)	(0.06,0.25,0.5)	(0.17,0.40,0.68)	(0.08,0.24,0.48)
T4	(0.29,0.42,0.61)	(0.05,0.20,0.44)	(0.02,0.13,0.33)	(0.19,0.42,0.7)	(0.06,0.24,0.49)	(0.08,0.24,0.48)
T5	(0.33,0.55,0.81)	(0.14,0.34,0.61)	(0.01,0.09,0.24)	(0.32,0.58,0.9)	(0.17,0.40,0.68)	(0.08,0.24,0.48)
PIS	(0,0,0)	(0,0,0)	(0,0,0)	(1,1,1)	(1,1,1)	(1,1,1)
NIS	(1,1,1)	(1,1,1)	(1,1,1)	(0,0,0)	(0,0,0)	(0,0,0)

Table 15.4 Ranking of NPITs based on BNP value of $\tilde{S}_i$.

NPITs	$\tilde{S}_i$	BNP value of $\tilde{S}_i$	Rank
T1	(1.72, 2.64, 3.60)	2.65	5
T2	(0.87, 1.20, 1.51)	1.19	1
T3	(1.30, 1.99, 2.70)	2.00	3
T4	(1.51,2.19,2.83)	2.18	4
T5	(1.08, 1.62,2.06)	1.59	2
$\tilde{S}_i$ Max	(1.72,2.64,3.60)	-	-
$\tilde{S}_i$ Min	(0.87, 1.20, 1.51)	-	-

Table 15.5 Ranking of NPITs based on BNP value of $\tilde{R}_i$.

NPITs	$\tilde{R}_i$	BNP $\tilde{R}_i$	Rank
T1	(0.58, 0.79,0.97)	0.78	2
T2	(0.63,0.84,1.00)	0.82	1
T3	(0.54,0.63,0.84)	0.67	4
T4	(0.58,0.79,0.97)	0.78	3
T5	(0.40,0.60,0.81)	0.60	5
$\tilde{R}_i$ Max	(0.63,0.84,1.00)	-	-
$\tilde{R}_i$ Min	(0.40,0.60,0.81)	-	-

Table 15.6 Ranking of NPITs based on BNF value of $\tilde{Q}_i$.

NPITs	$\tilde{Q}_i$	BNP of $\tilde{Q}_i$	Rank
T1	(0.8904, 0.8940, 0.9229)	0.9024	5
T2	(0.3904, 0.3940, 0.4229)	0.4024	1
T3	(0.6456, 0.6674, 0.7083)	0.6737	3
T4	(0.7690, 0.7375, 0.7394)	0.7486	4
T5	(0.5145, 0.5405, 0.5550)	0.5367	2

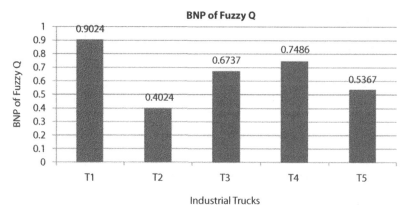

Figure 15.2 BNP of fuzzy Q value.

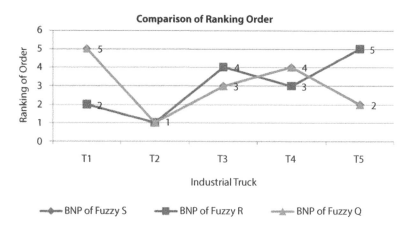

Figure 15.3 Comparison of ranking order based on BNP of fuzzy S, R, and Q values.

15.6 Conclusions

Application of Fuzzy VIKOR approach reveals the best NPIT. The consequence of the evaluation process found by the approach shows the conformity in finding the best solution. This method illustrated in the present chapter can be utilized in the future decision making procedures in the real life situation. The study of the outcome of the NPITs problem ensures that FMCDM approach is useful and effective in the evaluation and selection of NPITs. Utilization of different conversion scales, different fuzzy numbers, and incorporation of fuzzy performance values might be several significant aspects of future research.

References

1. Sule, D.R., *Manufacturing Facilities: Location, Planning, and Design*, PWS, Boston, 1994.
2. Goswami, S.S., Behera, D.K., Solving material handling equipment selection problems in an industry with the help of entropy integrated COPRAS and ARAS MCDM techniques. *Process Integr. Optim. Sustain.*, 5, 947–973, 2021.
3. Soufi, Z., David, P., Yahouni, Z., A methodology for the selection of material handling equipment in manufacturing systems. *IFAC-Papers Online*, 54, 122–127, 2021.
4. Satyam, F., Satywan, K., Avinash, K., *Application of Multi-Attribute Decision-Making Methods for the Selection of Conveyor*, Research Square, 2021,
5. Nguyen, H.-T., Siti, D., Nukman, Y., Hideki, A., An integrated MCDM model for conveyor equipment evaluation and selection in an FMC based on a fuzzy AHP and fuzzy ARAS in the presence of vagueness. *Plos One*, 11, 2016.
6. Mathewa, M. and Sahua, S., Comparison of new multi-criteria decision making methods for material handling equipment selection. *Manag. Sci. Lett.*, 8, 139–150, 2018.
7. Kahraman, C., Cevik, S., Ates, N.Y., Gulbay, M., Fuzzy multi-criteria evaluation of industrial robotic systems. *Comput. Ind. Eng.*, 52, 414–433, 2007.
8. Chu, T.C. and Lin, Y.C., A fuzzy TOPSIS method for robot selection. *Int. J. Adv. Manuf. Technol.*, 21, 284–290, 2003.
9. Parkan, C. and Wu, M.L., Decision-making and performance measurement models with application to robot selection. *Comput. Ind. Eng.*, 36, 503–523, 1999.
10. Chittratanawat, S. and Noble, J.S., An integrated approach for facility layout, P/D location and material handling system design. *Int. J. Prod. Res.*, 37, 683–706, 1999.
11. Boubekri, N., Sahoui, M., Lakrib, C., Development of an expert system for industrial robot selection. *Comput. Ind. Eng.*, 20, 119–127, 1991.
12. Hassan, M.M.D., Hogg, G.L., Smith, D., RA construction algorithm for the selection and assignment of materials handling equipment. *Int. J. Prod. Res.*, 23, 381–392, 1985.
13. Klir, J.G. and Yuan, B., *Fuzzy Sets and Fuzzy Logic: Theory and Applications*, Prentice Hall of India Private Limited, New Delhi, 2005.
14. Zimmermann, H.J., *Fuzzy Set Theory and Its Applications*, 2nd ed., Kluwer Academic Publishers, London, 1991.
15. Keufmann, A. and Gupta, M.M., *Introduction to Fuzzy Arithmetic: Theory and Application*, Van Nostrand Reinhold, New York, 1991.
16. Opricovic, S. and Tzeng, G.H., Extended VIKOR method in comparison with outranking methods. *Eur. J. Oper. Res.*, 17, 514–529, 2007.

17. Wu, H.Y., Tzeng, G.H., Chen, Y.H., A fuzzy MCDM approach for evaluating banking performance based on balanced scorecard. *Expert Syst. Appl.*, 36, 10135–10147, 2009.

18. Chen, Y.C., Lien, H.P., Tzeng, G.H., Yang, L.S., Fuzzy MCDM approach for selecting the best environment-watershed plan. *Appl. Soft Comput.*, 11, 1, 265–275, 2008.

19. Zadeh, L.A., The concept of a linguistic variable and its application to approximate reasoning. *Inf. Sci.*, 8, 199–249(I)-301-357(II), 1973.

20. Zeleny, M., *Multiple Criteria Decision Making*, McGraw-Hill, New York, 19821982.

21. Opricovic, S. and Tzeng, G.H., Extended VIKOR method in comparison with outranking methods. *Eur. J. Oper. Res.*, 17, 514–529, 2007.

22. Apple, J.M., *Material Handling Systems Design*, John Willy and Sons, New York, 1972.

## 16

Slightly and Almost Neutrosophic gsα*—Continuous Function in Neutrosophic Topological Spaces

P. Anbarasi Rodrigo and S. Maheswari*

Department of Mathematics, St. Mary's College (Autonomous), Thoothukudi. Registration number: 20212212092003 Affiliated by Manonmaniam Sundaranar University, Abishekapatti, Tirunelveli, India

Abstract

This study introduces the new concept on N_{eu} – closed set namely $N_{eu}gsα^*$ – closed set and study about the new concept of N_{eu} – continuous functions, namely Slightly $N_{eu}gsα^*$ – continuous function and Almost $N_{eu}gsα^*$ – continuous function. Additionally, we compare the properties and characterizations of these functions with already existing N_{eu} – functions. We also discussed about the separation axioms for $N_{eu}gsα^*$ – closed set and it is also used in theorems.

Keywords: $N_{eu}gsα^*$ – closed set, $N_{eu}gsα^*$ – open set, slightly $N_{eu}gsα^*$ – continuous function, almost $N_{eu}gsα^*$ – continuous function

16.1 Introduction

The intuitionistic fuzzy sets was first suggested by Atanassov [1]. Then, the concept of fuzzy sets was introduced by Zadeh [2]. In the continuation of fuzzy sets, Smarandache [3] has introduced the new concept called N_{eu} – set theory. It includes three components, truth, indeterminancy and false membership function. Dhavaseelan and Page [4] have discussed about the concept of almost N_{eu} – continuous function. The real-life application of $N_{eu}gsα^*$ – topology is applied in Information Systems, Applied

Corresponding author: mahma1295@gmail.com

Anita Khosla, Prasenjit Chatterjee, Ikbal Ali and Dheeraj Joshi (eds.) Optimization Techniques in Engineering: Advances and Applications, (261–274) © 2023 Scrivener Publishing LLC

Mathematics, etc. Here, we suggested some new ideas related to $N_{eu}gs\alpha^*$ – continuous function, namely slightly $N_{eu}gs\alpha^*$ – continuous function and almost $N_{eu}gs\alpha^*$ – continuous function.

16.2   Preliminaries

Definition 2.1: [5] Let P be a non-empty fixed set. A N_{eu} – set Ħ on the universe $\mathbb{P}$ is Ħ = {⟨đ, ($t_Ħ$ (đ), $i_Ħ$ (đ), $f_Ħ$ (đ))⟩ : đ ∈ $\mathbb{P}$}. Here, $t_Ħ$ (đ), $i_Ħ$ (đ), $f_Ħ$ (đ) represent the degree of membership, indeterminacy, and nonmembership function, respectively, for each element đ ∈ $\mathbb{P}$ to the set Ħ. Also, $t_Ħ$, $i_Ħ, f_Ħ$: $\mathbb{P}$ →] ⁻0, 1⁺ [and ⁻0 ≤ $t_Ħ$ (đ) + $i_Ħ$ (đ) + $f_Ħ$ (đ) ≤ 3⁺. Set of all N_{eu} – set over $\mathbb{P}$ is denoted by $N_{eu}(\mathbb{P})$.

Definition 2.2:[5] Let $\mathbb{P}$ be a non-empty set. Á = {⟨℘, (t_A (℘), i_A (℘), f_A (℘))⟩: ℘ ∈ $\mathbb{P}$} and B = {⟨℘, (t_B (℘), i_B (℘), f_B (℘))⟩ : ℘ ∈ $\mathbb{P}$} are N_{eu} – sets , then

(i)   Á ⊆ B if t_A (℘) ≤ t_B (℘), i_A (℘) ≤ i_B (℘), f_A (℘) ≥ f_B (℘) for all ℘ ∈ $\mathbb{P}$.

(ii)   Á ∩ B = {⟨ ℘, (min (t_A (℘), t_B (℘)), min (i_A (℘), i_B (℘)), max (f_A (℘), f_B (℘)))⟩ : ℘ ∈ $\mathbb{P}$}.

(iii)   Á ∪ B = {⟨ ℘, (max (t_A (℘), t_B (℘)), max (i_A (℘), i_B (℘)), min (f_A (℘), f_B (℘)))⟩ : ℘ ∈ $\mathbb{P}$}.

(iv)   Áᶜ = {⟨ ℘, (f_A (℘), 1 – i_A (℘), t_A (℘))⟩: ℘ ∈ $\mathbb{P}$}.

(v)   ($0_{N_{eu}}$ = {⟨℘,(0,0,1)⟩ : ℘ ∈ $\mathbb{P}$} and $1_{N_{eu}}$ = {⟨℘,(1,1,0)⟩ : ℘ ∈ $\mathbb{P}$}).

Definition 2.3: [5] A N_{eu} – topology (N_{eu}T) on a non-empty set $\mathbb{P}$ is a family $\tau_{N_{eu}}$ of N_{eu} – sets in $\mathbb{P}$ satisfying the following axioms,

(i) $0_{N_{eu}}, 1_{N_{eu}} \in \tau_{N_{eu}}$.

(ii) $Á_1 \cap Á_2 \in \tau_{N_{eu}}$ for any $Á_1, Á_2 \in \tau_{N_{eu}}$.

(iii) $\cap Á_i \in \tau_{N_{eu}}$ for every family $\{Á_1 / i \in \Omega\} \subseteq \tau_{N_{eu}}$.

Here, $(\mathbb{P}, \tau_{N_{eu}})$ or simply $\mathbb{P}$ is called a N_{eu} – topological space (N_{eu}TS). The elements of $\tau_{N_{eu}}$ is N_{eu} – open set (N_{eu} – OS) and $\tau_{N_{eu}}{}^c$ is N_{eu} – closed set (N_{eu} – CS).

Definition 2.4: [6] A N_{eu} – set Á in a N_{eu}TS $(\mathbb{P}, \tau_{N_{eu}})$ is called a neutrosophic generalized semi alpha star closed set ($N_{eu}gs\alpha^*$ – CS) if $N_{eu}\alpha – int(N_{eu}\alpha – cl(Á)) \subseteq N_{eu} – int(Ň)$, whenever Á ⊆ Ň and Ň is $N_{eu}\alpha^*$ – OS.

Definition 2.5: A N_{eu} – function $f_N \colon (\mathbb{P}, \tau_{N_{eu}}) \to (\mathbb{Q}, \sigma_{N_{eu}})$ is

1. N_{eu} – continuous [7] if f_N^{-1} of each N_{eu} – CS in $(\mathbb{Q}, \sigma_{N_{eu}})$ is a N_{eu} – CS in $(\mathbb{P}, \tau_{N_{eu}})$.
2. $N_{eu}gs\alpha^*$ – continuous [8] if f_N^{-1} of each N_{eu} – CS in $(\mathbb{Q}, \sigma_{N_{eu}})$ is a $N_{eu}gs\alpha^*$ – CS in $(\mathbb{P}, \tau_{N_{eu}})$.
3. $N_{eu}gs\alpha^*$ – irresolute map [8] if f_N^{-1} of each $N_{eu}gs\alpha^*$ – CS in $(\mathbb{Q}, \sigma_{N_{eu}})$ is a $N_{eu}gs\alpha^*$ – CS in $(\mathbb{P}, \tau_{N_{eu}})$.
4. $N_{eu}gsa^* - T_{\frac{1}{2}}$ space if every $N_{eu}gs\alpha^*$ – CS in $(\mathbb{P}, \tau_{N_{eu}})$ is a N_{eu} – CS in $(\mathbb{P}, \tau_{N_{eu}})$.
5. strongly $N_{eu}gs\alpha^*$ – continuous [9] if f_N^{-1} of every $N_{eu}gs\alpha^*$ – CS in $(\mathbb{Q}, \sigma_{N_{eu}})$ is a N_{eu} – CS in $(\mathbb{P}, \tau_{N_{eu}})$.
6. perfectly $N_{eu}gs\alpha^*$ – continuous [9] if f_N^{-1} of every $N_{eu}gs\alpha^*$ – CS in $(\mathbb{Q}, \sigma_{N_{eu}})$ is N_{eu} – OS and N_{eu} – CS (ie, N_{eu} – clopen set) in $(\mathbb{P}, \tau_{N_{eu}})$.
7. totally $N_{eu}gs\alpha^*$ – continuous [9] if f_N^{-1} of every N_{eu} – CS in $(\mathbb{Q}, \sigma_{N_{eu}})$ is $N_{eu}gs\alpha^*$ – OS and $N_{eu}gs\alpha^*$ – CS (ie, $N_{eu}gs\alpha^*$ – clopen set) in $(\mathbb{P}, \tau_{N_{eu}})$.

Definition 2.6: [10] Let $\tau_{N_{eu}} = \{0_{N_{eu}}, 1_{N_{eu}}\}$ is a N_{eu} TS over $\mathbb{P}$. Then $(\mathbb{P}, \tau_{N_{eu}})$ is N_{eu} – discrete topological space.

Definition 2.7: A N_{eu} TS $(\mathbb{P}, \tau_{N_{eu}})$ is N_{eu} – clopen set if it is N_{eu} – OS and $N_{eu}gs\alpha^*$ – CS in $(\mathbb{P}, \tau_{N_{eu}})$.

Definition 2.8: A N_{eu} –function $f_N \colon (\mathbb{P}, \tau_{N_{eu}}) \to (\mathbb{Q}, \sigma_{N_{eu}})$ is $N_{eu}\alpha^*$ –continuous [11] if f_N^{-1} of every N_{eu} – CS in $(\mathbb{Q}, \sigma_{N_{eu}})$ is a $N_{eu}\alpha^*$ – CS in $(\mathbb{P}, \tau_{N_{eu}})$.

16.3   Slightly Neutrosophic gsα* – Continuous Function

Definition 3.1: A N_{eu} –function $f_N \colon (\mathbb{P}, \tau_{N_{eu}}) \to (\mathbb{Q}, \sigma_{N_{eu}})$ is slightly $N_{eu}gs\alpha^*$ – continuous if f_N^{-1} of every N_{eu} – clopen set in $(\mathbb{Q}, \sigma_{N_{eu}})$ is a $N_{eu}gs\alpha^*$ – CS in $(\mathbb{P}, \tau_{N_{eu}})$. (ie) $f_N^{-1}(\mathbb{A})$ is a $N_{eu}gs\alpha^*$ – CS in $(\mathbb{P}, \tau_{N_{eu}})$ for every N_{eu} – clopen set $\mathbb{A}$ in $(\mathbb{Q}, \sigma_{N_{eu}})$.

Theorem 3.2: Every $N_{eu}gs\alpha^*$ – continuous function is slightly $N_{eu}gs\alpha^*$ – continuous, but not conversely.

Proof: Let $f_N \colon (\mathbb{P}, \tau_{N_{eu}}) \to (\mathbb{Q}, \sigma_{N_{eu}})$ be any neutrosophic function. Let $\mathbb{A}$ be any N_{eu} – clopen set in $(\mathbb{Q}, \sigma_{N_{eu}})$. Given f is $N_{eu}gs\alpha^*$ – continuous, then $f_N^{-1}(A)$ is $N_{eu}gs\alpha^*$ – CS and $N_{eu}gs\alpha^*$ – OS in $(\mathbb{P},\tau_{N_{eu}}) \Rightarrow f_N^{-1}(A)$ is a $N_{eu}gs\alpha^*$ – CS in $(\mathbb{P},\tau_{N_{eu}}) \Rightarrow f_N$ is slightly $N_{eu}gs\alpha^*$ – continuous.

Example 3.3: Let $\mathbb{P} = \{p\}$ and $\mathbb{Q} = \{q\}$. $\tau_{N_{eu}} = \{0_{N_{eu}}, 1_{N_{eu}}, A\}$ and $\sigma_{N_{eu}} = \{0_{N_{eu}}, 1_{N_{eu}}, B\}$ are $N_{eu}TS$ on $(\mathbb{P},\tau_{N_{eu}})$ and $(\mathbb{Q},\sigma_{N_{eu}})$, respectively. Also $A = \{\langle p, (0.7, 0.6, 0.5)\rangle\}$ and $B = \{\langle q, (0.2, 0.4, 0.6)\rangle\}$ are $N_{eu}(\mathbb{P})$ and $N_{eu}(\mathbb{Q})$. Define a map $f_N: (\mathbb{P},\tau_{N_{eu}}) \to (\mathbb{Q},\sigma_{N_{eu}})$ by $f_N(p) = q$. Let $C = \{\langle q, (0, 0, 1)\rangle\}$ be a N_{eu} – clopen set in $(\mathbb{Q},\sigma_{N_{eu}})$. Then $f_N^{-1}(C) = \{\langle p, (0, 0, 1)\rangle\}$. $N_{eu}\alpha^* - OS = N_{eu}\alpha - OS = \{0_{N_{eu}}, 1_{N_{eu}}, A, D\}$ and $N_{eu}\alpha - CS = \{0_{N_{eu}}, 1_{N_{eu}}, A^C, E\}$, where $D = \{\langle p, ([0.7,1], [0.6,1], [0,0.5])\rangle\}$, $E = \{\langle p, ([0,0.5], [0,0.4], [0.7,1])\rangle\}$. $N_{eu}\alpha$ – $cl(f_N^{-1}(C)) = E$. Now, $N_{eu}\alpha - int(N_{eu}\alpha - cl(f_N^{-1}(C))) = 0_{N_{eu}} \subseteq N_{eu} - int(A)$, N_{eu} – $int(D)$, $N_{eu} - int(1_{N_{eu}}) = A$, $1_{N_{eu}}$, whenever $f_N^{-1}(C) \subseteq A$, D, $1_{N_{eu}} \Rightarrow f_N^{-1}(C)$ is a $N_{eu}gs\alpha^*$ – CS in $(\mathbb{P},\tau_{N_{eu}})$. Hence, f_N is slightly $N_{eu}gs\alpha^*$ – continuous function. But f_N is not $N_{eu}gs\alpha^*$ – continuous function. Let $B^c = \{\langle q, (0.6, 0.6, 0.2)\rangle\}$ be a N_{eu} – CS in $(\mathbb{Q},\sigma_{N_{eu}})$. Then $f_N^{-1}(B^c) = \{\langle p, (0.6, 0.6, 0.2)\rangle\}$. Now, $N_{eu}\alpha - int(N_{eu}\alpha - cl(f_N^{-1}(B^c))) = 1_{N_{eu}} \not\subseteq N_{eu} - int(F) = A$, when $f_N^{-1}(B^c) \subseteq F$, where $F = \{\langle p, ([0.7,1], [0.6,1], [0,0.2])\rangle\} \Rightarrow f_N^{-1}(B^c)$ is not a $N_{eu}gs\alpha^*$ – CS in $(\mathbb{P},\tau_{N_{eu}})$.

Theorem 3.4: Let $f_N: (\mathbb{P},\tau_{N_{eu}}) \to (\mathbb{Q},\sigma_{N_{eu}})$ be slightly $N_{eu}gs\alpha^*$ – continuous and $(\mathbb{Q},\sigma_{N_{eu}})$ be a N_{eu} – discrete topological space, then f_N is $N_{eu}gs\alpha^*$ – continuous.

Proof: Let A be N_{eu} – CS in $(\mathbb{Q},\sigma_{N_{eu}})$. Since $(\mathbb{Q},\sigma_{N_{eu}})$ be a N_{eu} – discrete topological space, then A is N_{eu} – OS in $(\mathbb{Q},\sigma_{N_{eu}}) \Rightarrow A$ is a N_{eu} – clopen set in $(\mathbb{Q},\sigma_{N_{eu}})$. Given f_N is slightly $N_{eu}gs\alpha^*$ – continuous, then $f_N^{-1}(A)$ is a $N_{eu}gs\alpha^*$ – CS in $(\mathbb{P},\tau_{N_{eu}}) \Rightarrow f_N$ is $N_{eu}gs\alpha^*$ – continuous.

Definition 3.5: A $N_{eu}TS$ $(\mathbb{P},\tau_{N_{eu}})$ is called $N_{eu}gs\alpha^*$ – clopen set if it is both $N_{eu}gs\alpha^*$ – OS and $N_{eu}gs\alpha^*$ – CS in $(\mathbb{P},\tau_{N_{eu}})$.

Theorem 3.6: Let $f_N: (\mathbb{P},\tau_{N_{eu}}) \to (\mathbb{Q},\sigma_{N_{eu}})$ be any N_{eu} – function. Then the following statements are equivalent.

1. f_N is slightly $N_{eu}gs\alpha^*$ – continuous.
2. f_N^{-1} of every N_{eu} – clopen set A in $(\mathbb{Q},\sigma_{N_{eu}})$ is $N_{eu}gs\alpha^*$ – CS in $(\mathbb{P},\tau_{N_{eu}})$.
3. f_N^{-1} of every N_{eu} – clopen set A in $(\mathbb{Q},\sigma_{N_{eu}})$ is $N_{eu}gs\alpha^*$ – OS in $(\mathbb{P},\tau_{N_{eu}})$.

4. f_N^{-1} of every N_{eu} – clopen set $\mathbb{A}$ in $(\mathbb{Q}, \sigma_{N_{eu}})$ is $N_{eu}gs\alpha^*$ – clopen set in $(\mathbb{P}, \tau_{N_{eu}})$.

Proof: (1) $\Rightarrow$ (2), Proof follows from definition 3.1.

(2) $\Rightarrow$ (3), Let $\mathbb{A}$ be any N_{eu} – clopen set in $(\mathbb{Q}, \sigma_{N_{eu}})$. Then $\mathbb{A}^c$ is a N_{eu} – clopen set in $(\mathbb{Q}, \sigma_{N_{eu}})$. Then by (2), $f_N^{-1}(\mathbb{A}^c) = (f_N^{-1}(\mathbb{A}))^c$ is a $N_{eu}gs\alpha^*$ – CS in $(\mathbb{P}, \tau_{N_{eu}}) \Rightarrow f_N^{-1}(\mathbb{A})$ is a $N_{eu}gs\alpha^*$ – OS in $(\mathbb{P}, \tau_{N_{eu}})$.

(3) $\Rightarrow$ (4), By (2) & (3), $f_N^{-1}(\mathbb{A})$ is a $N_{eu}gs\alpha^*$ – CS and $N_{eu}gs\alpha^*$ – OS in $(\mathbb{P}, \tau_{N_{eu}}) \Rightarrow f_N^{-1}(\mathbb{A})$ is a $N_{eu}gs\alpha^*$ – clopen set in $(\mathbb{P}, \tau_{N_{eu}})$.

(4) $\Rightarrow$ (1), Let $\mathbb{A}$ be any N_{eu} – clopen set in $(\mathbb{Q}, \sigma_{N_{eu}})$. Then by (4) , $f_N^{-1}(\mathbb{A})$ is a $N_{eu}gs\alpha^*$ – clopen set in $(\mathbb{P}, \tau_{N_{eu}}) \Rightarrow f_N^{-1}(\mathbb{A})$ is a $N_{eu}gs\alpha^*$ – CS in $(\mathbb{P}, \tau_{N_{eu}}) \Rightarrow f_N$ is slightly $N_{eu}gs\alpha^*$ – continuou.

Theorem 3.7: Let $f_N : (\mathbb{P}, \tau_{N_{eu}}) \to (\mathbb{Q}, \sigma_{N_{eu}})$ and $g_N : (\mathbb{Q}, \tau_{N_{eu}}) \to (\mathbb{R}, \gamma_{N_{eu}})$ be slightly $N_{eu}gs\alpha^*$ – continuous. Then $g_N \circ f_N : (\mathbb{P}, \tau_{N_{eu}}) \to (\mathbb{R}, \gamma_{N_{eu}})$ is slightly $N_{eu}gs\alpha^*$ – continuous, if $(\mathbb{Q}, \sigma_{N_{eu}})$ is $N_{eu}gs\alpha^* - T_{1/2}$ space.

Proof: Let $\mathbb{A}$ be any N_{eu} – clopen set in $(\mathbb{R}, \gamma_{N_{eu}})$. Given g_N is slightly $N_{eu}gs\alpha^*$ – continuous, then $g_N^{-1}(\mathbb{A})$ is a $N_{eu}gs\alpha^*$ – clopen set in $(\mathbb{Q}, \sigma_{N_{eu}})$. Given $(\mathbb{Q}, \sigma_{N_{eu}})$ is $N_{eu}gs\alpha^* - T_{1/2}$ space, then $g_N^{-1}(\mathbb{A})$ is a N_{eu} – clopen set in $(\mathbb{Q}, \sigma_{N_{eu}})$. Given f_N is slightly $N_{eu}gs\alpha^*$ – continuous, then $f_N^{-1}(g_N^{-1}(\mathbb{A})) = (g_N \circ f_N)^{-1}(\mathbb{A})$ is a $N_{eu}gs\alpha^*$ – CS in $(\mathbb{P}, \tau_{N_{eu}})$. Hence, $g_N \circ f_N$ is slightly $N_{eu}gs\alpha^*$ – continuous.

Theorem 3.8: Let $f_N : (\mathbb{P}, \tau_{N_{eu}}) \to (\mathbb{Q}, \sigma_{N_{eu}})$ and $g_N : (\mathbb{Q}, \tau_{N_{eu}}) \to (\mathbb{R}, \gamma_{N_{eu}})$ be any neutrosophic functions. Then $g_N \circ f_N : (\mathbb{P}, \tau_{N_{eu}}) \to (\mathbb{R}, \gamma_{N_{eu}})$ is slightly $N_{eu}gs\alpha^*$ – continuous, if

1. f_N is $N_{eu}gs\alpha^*$ – irresolute and g_N is slightly $N_{eu}gs\alpha^*$ – continuous.
2. f_N is $N_{eu}gs\alpha^*$ – irresolute and g_N is $N_{eu}gs\alpha^*$ – continuous.
3. f_N is $N_{eu}gs\alpha^*$ – irresolute and g_N is N_{eu} – continuous.
4. f_N is $N_{eu}gs\alpha^*$ – continuous and g_N is N_{eu} – continuous.

Proof:

1. Let $\mathbb{A}$ be any N_{eu} – clopen set in $(\mathbb{R}, \gamma_{N_{eu}})$. Given g_N is slightly $N_{eu}gs\alpha^*$ – continuous, then $g_N^{-1}(\mathbb{A})$ is a $N_{eu}gs\alpha^*$ – CS in $(\mathbb{Q}, \sigma_{N_{eu}})$. Given f_N is $N_{eu}gs\alpha^*$ – irresolute, then $f_N^{-1}(g_N^{-1}(\mathbb{A})) = (g_N \circ f_N)^{-1}(\mathbb{A})$ is a $N_{eu}gs\alpha^*$ – CS in $(\mathbb{P}, \tau_{N_{eu}}) \Rightarrow g_N \circ f_N$ is slightly $N_{eu}gs\alpha^*$ – continuous.

2. Let A be any N_{eu} – clopen set in $(\mathbb{R}, \gamma_{N_{eu}})$. Given g_N is $N_{eu}gs\alpha^*$ – continuous, then $g_N^{-1}(A)$ is a $N_{eu}gs\alpha^*$ – OS and $N_{eu}gs\alpha^*$ – CS in $(\mathbb{Q}, \sigma_{N_{eu}})$. Given f_N is $N_{eu}gs\alpha^*$ – irresolute, then $f_N^{-1}(g_N^{-1}(A)) = (g_N \circ f_N)^{-1}(A)$ is a $N_{eu}gs\alpha^*$ – OS and $N_{eu}gs\alpha^*$ – CS in $(\mathbb{P}, \tau_{N_{eu}}) \Rightarrow (g_N \circ f_N)^{-1}(A)$ is a $N_{eu}gs\alpha^*$ – clopen set in $(\mathbb{P}, \tau_{N_{eu}}) \Rightarrow g_N \circ f_N$ is slightly $N_{eu}gs\alpha^*$ – continuous.

3. Let A be any N_{eu} – clopen set in $(\mathbb{R}, \gamma_{N_{eu}})$. Given g_N is neutrosophic continuous, then $g_N^{-1}(A)$ is a N_{eu} – clopen set in $(\mathbb{Q}, \sigma_{N_{eu}}) \Rightarrow g_N^{-1}(A)$ is a $N_{eu}gs\alpha^*$ – OS and $N_{eu}gs\alpha^*$ – CS in $(\mathbb{Q}, \sigma_{N_{eu}})$. Given f_N is $N_{eu}gs\alpha^*$ – irresolute , then $f_N^{-1}(g_N^{-1}(A)) = (g_N \circ f_N)^{-1}(A)$ is a $N_{eu}gs\alpha^*$ – OS and $N_{eu}gs\alpha^*$ – CS in $(\mathbb{P}, \tau_{N_{eu}}) \Rightarrow (g_N \circ f_N)^{-1}(A)$ is a $N_{eu}gs\alpha^*$ – clopen set in $(\mathbb{P}, \tau_{N_{eu}}) \Rightarrow g_N \circ f_N$ is slightly $N_{eu}gs\alpha^*$ – continuous.

4. Let A be any N_{eu} – clopen set in $(\mathbb{R}, \gamma_{N_{eu}})$. Given g_N is neutrosophic continuous, then $g_N^{-1}(A)$ is a N_{eu} – clopen set in $(\mathbb{Q}, \sigma_{N_{eu}})$. Given f_N is $N_{eu}gs\alpha^*$ – continuous , then $f_N^{-1}(g_N^{-1}(A)) = (g_N \circ f_N)^{-1}(A)$ is a $N_{eu}gs\alpha^*$ – OS and $N_{eu}gs\alpha^*$ – CS in $(\mathbb{P}, \tau_{N_{eu}}) \Rightarrow (g_N \circ f_N)^{-1}(A)$ is a $N_{eu}gs\alpha^*$ – clopen set in $(\mathbb{P}, \tau_{N_{eu}}) \Rightarrow g_N \circ f_N$ is slightly $N_{eu}gs\alpha^*$ – continuous.

Theorem 3.9: Let $f_N \colon (\mathbb{P}, \tau_{N_{eu}}) \to (\mathbb{Q}, \sigma_{N_{eu}})$ be slightly $N_{eu}gs\alpha^*$ – continuous and $g_N \colon (\mathbb{Q}, \tau_{N_{eu}}) \to (\mathbb{R}, \gamma_{N_{eu}})$ be perfectly $N_{eu}gs\alpha^*$ – continuous, then $g_N \circ f_N \colon (\mathbb{P}, \tau_{N_{eu}}) \to (\mathbb{R}, \gamma_{N_{eu}})$ is $N_{eu}gs\alpha^*$ – irresolute.

Proof: Let A be any $N_{eu}gs\alpha^*$ – CS in $(\mathbb{R}, \gamma_{N_{eu}})$. Given g_N is perfectly $N_{eu}gs\alpha^*$ – continuous, then $g_N^{-1}(A)$ is a N_{eu} – clopen set in $(\mathbb{Q}, \sigma_{N_{eu}})$. Given f_N is slightly $N_{eu}gs\alpha^*$ – continuous, then $f_N^{-1}(g_N^{-1}(A)) = (g_N \circ f_N)^{-1}(A)$ is a $N_{eu}gs\alpha^*$ – CS in $(\mathbb{P}, \tau_{N_{eu}}) \Rightarrow g_N \circ f_N$ is $N_{eu}gs\alpha^*$ – irresolute.

16.4   Almost Neutrosophic $gs\alpha^*$ – Continuous Function

Definition 4.1: A N_{eu} – function $f_N \colon (\mathbb{P}, \tau_{N_{eu}}) \to (\mathbb{Q}, \sigma_{N_{eu}})$ is almost $N_{eu}gs\alpha^*$ – continuous if f_N^{-1} of every $N_{eu}R$ – CS in $(\mathbb{Q}, \sigma_{N_{eu}})$ is a $N_{eu}gs\alpha^*$ – CS in $(\mathbb{P}, \tau_{N_{eu}})$. (ie) $f_N^{-1}(A)$ is a $N_{eu}gs\alpha^*$ – CS in $(\mathbb{P}, \tau_{N_{eu}})$ for every $N_{eu}R$ – CS A in $(\mathbb{Q}, \sigma_{N_{eu}})$.

Theorem 4.2: Every $N_{eu}gs\alpha^*$ – continuous function is almost $N_{eu}gs\alpha^*$ – continuous function, but not conversely.

Proof: Let $f_N: (\mathbb{P}, \tau_{N_{eu}}) \to (\mathbb{Q}, \sigma_{N_{eu}})$ be any N_{eu} – function. Let $\mathbb{A}$ be any $N_{eu}R$ – CS in $(\mathbb{Q}, \sigma_{N_{eu}})$. Then $\mathbb{A}$ is a N_{eu} – CS in $(\mathbb{Q}, \sigma_{N_{eu}})$ [9]. Given f_N is $N_{eu}gs\alpha^*$ – continuous, then $f_N^{-1}(\mathbb{A})$ is a $N_{eu}gs\alpha^*$ – CS in $(\mathbb{P}, \tau_{N_{eu}}) \Rightarrow f_N$ is almost $N_{eu}gs\alpha^*$ – continuous.

Example 4.3: Let $\mathbb{P} = \{\wp\}$ and $\mathbb{Q} = \{q\}$. $\tau_{N_{eu}} = \{0_{N_{eu}}, 1_{N_{eu}}, \mathbb{A}\}$ and $\sigma_{N_{eu}} = \{0_{N_{eu}}, 1_{N_{eu}}, \mathbb{B}\}$ are $N_{eu}TS$ on $(\mathbb{P}, \tau_{N_{eu}})$ and $(\mathbb{Q}, \sigma_{N_{eu}})$ respectively. Also $\mathbb{A} = \{\langle \wp, (0.6, 0.8, 0.4) \rangle\}$ and $\mathbb{B} = \{\langle q, (0.5, 0.7, 0.4) \rangle\}$ are $N_{eu}(\mathbb{P})$ and $N_{eu}(\mathbb{Q})$. Define a map $f_N: (\mathbb{P}, \tau_{N_{eu}}) \to (\mathbb{Q}, \sigma_{N_{eu}})$ by $f_N(\wp) = q$. Let $\mathbb{C} = \{\langle q, (0, 0, 1) \rangle\}$ be $N_{eu}R$ – CS in $(\mathbb{Q}, \sigma_{N_{eu}})$. Then $f_N^{-1}(\mathbb{C}) = \{\langle \wp, (0, 0, 1) \rangle\}$. $N_{eu}\alpha^* - OS = N_{eu}\alpha - OS = \{0_{N_{eu}}, 1_{N_{eu}}, \mathbb{A}, D\}$ and $N_{eu}\alpha - CS = \{0_{N_{eu}}, 1_{N_{eu}}, \mathbb{A}^C, E\}$, where $D = \{\langle \wp, ([0.6, \ 1], [0.8, \ 1], [0, \ 0.4]) \rangle\}$, $E = \{\langle \wp, ([0, \ 0.4], [0, \ 0.2], [0.6, \ 1]) \rangle\}$. Now, $N_{eu}\alpha - int(N_{eu}\alpha - cl(f_N^{-1}(\mathbb{C}))) = 0_{N_{eu}} \subseteq N_{eu} - int(0_{N_{eu}})$, N_{eu} – int $(\mathbb{A})$, $N_{eu} - int(D)$, $N_{eu} - int(1_{N_{eu}}) = 0_{N_{eu}}$, $\mathbb{A}$, $1_{N_{eu}}$, whenever $f_N^{-1}(\mathbb{C}) \subseteq 0_{N_{eu}}$, $\mathbb{A}$, D, $1_{N_{eu}} \Rightarrow f_N^{-1}(\mathbb{C})$, is a $N_{eu}gs\alpha^*$ – CS in $(\mathbb{P}, \tau_{N_{eu}})$. Hence, f_N is almost $N_{eu}gs\alpha^*$ – continuous function. But f_N is not $N_{eu}gs\alpha^*$ – continuous function . Let $\mathbb{B}^c = \{\langle q, (0.4, 0.3, 0.5) \rangle\}$ be N_{eu} – CS in $(\mathbb{Q}, \sigma_{N_{eu}})$. Then $f_N^{-1}(\mathbb{B}^c) = \{\langle \wp, (0.4, 0.3, 0.5) \rangle\}$. Now, $N_{eu}\alpha - int(N_{eu}\alpha - cl(f_N^{-1}(\mathbb{B}^c))) = 1_{N_{eu}} \subseteq N_{eu} - int(\mathbb{A})$, N_{eu} – int $(D) = \mathbb{A}$, whenever $f_N^{-1}(\mathbb{B}^c) \subseteq \mathbb{A}$, $D \Rightarrow f_N^{-1}(\mathbb{B}^c)$ is not a $N_{eu}gs\alpha^*$ – CS in $(\mathbb{P}, \tau_{N_{eu}})$.

Theorem 4.4: Every $N_{eu}gs\alpha^*$ – irresolute map is almost $N_{eu}gs\alpha^*$ – continuous function, but not conversely.

Proof: Let $f_N: (\mathbb{P}, \tau_{N_{eu}}) \to (\mathbb{Q}, \sigma_{N_{eu}})$ be any N_{eu} – function. Let $\mathbb{A}$ be any $N_{eu}R$ – CS in $(\mathbb{Q}, \sigma_{N_{eu}})$. Then $\mathbb{A}$ is a N_{eu} – CS in $(\mathbb{Q}, \sigma_{N_{eu}}) \Rightarrow \mathbb{A}$ is a $N_{eu}gs\alpha^*$ – CS in $(\mathbb{Q}, \sigma_{N_{eu}})$. Given f_N is $N_{eu}gs\alpha^*$ – irresolute, then $f_N^{-1}(\mathbb{A})$ is $N_{eu}gs\alpha^*$ – CS in $(\mathbb{P}, \tau_{N_{eu}}) \Rightarrow f_N$ is almost $N_{eu}gs\alpha^*$ – continuous.

Example 4.5: Let $\mathbb{P} = \{\wp\}$ and $\mathbb{Q} = \{q\}$. $\tau_{N_{eu}} = \{0_{N_{eu}}, 1_{N_{eu}}, \mathbb{A}\}$ and $\sigma_{N_{eu}} = \{0_{N_{eu}}, 1_{N_{eu}}, \mathbb{B}\}$ are $N_{eu}TS$ on $(\mathbb{P}, \tau_{N_{eu}})$ and $(\mathbb{Q}, \sigma_{N_{eu}})$ respectively. Also $\mathbb{A} = \{\langle \wp, (0.7, 0.6, 0.5) \rangle\}$ and $\mathbb{B} = \{\langle q, (0.4, 0.6, 0.8) \rangle\}$ are $N_{eu}(\mathbb{P})$ and $N_{eu}(\mathbb{Q})$. Define a map $f_N: (\mathbb{P}, \tau_{N_{eu}}) \to (\mathbb{Q}, \sigma_{N_{eu}})$ by $f_N(\wp) = q$. Let $\mathbb{C} = \{\langle q, (0, 0, 1) \rangle\}$ be $N_{eu}R$ – CS in $(\mathbb{Q}, \sigma_{N_{eu}})$. Then $f_N^{-1}(\mathbb{C}) = \{\langle \wp, (0, 0, 1) \rangle\}$. $N_{eu}\alpha^* - OS = N_{eu}\alpha - OS = \{0_{N_{eu}}, 1_{N_{eu}}, \mathbb{A}, D\}$ and $N_{eu}\alpha - CS = \{0_{N_{eu}}, 1_{N_{eu}}, \mathbb{A}^C, E\}$, where $D = \{\langle \wp, ([0.7, 1], [0.6, 1], [0, 0.5]) \rangle\}$, $E = \{\langle \wp, ([0, 0.5], [0, 0.4], [0.7, 1]) \rangle\}$. Now $N_{eu}\alpha - int(N_{eu}\alpha - cl(f_N^{-1}(\mathbb{C}))) = 0_{N_{eu}} \subseteq N_{eu} - int(0_{N_{eu}})$, $N_{eu}\alpha$ – $int(\mathbb{A})$, $N_{eu}\alpha - int(D)$, $N_{eu} - int(1_{N_{eu}}) = 0_{N_{eu}}$, $\mathbb{A}$, $1_{N_{eu}}$, whenever $f_N^{-1}(\mathbb{C}) \subseteq 0_{N_{eu}}$, $\mathbb{A}$, D, $1_{N_{eu}} \Rightarrow f_N^{-1}(\mathbb{C})$ is a $N_{eu}gs\alpha^*$ – CS in $(\mathbb{P}, \tau_{N_{eu}})$. Hence, f_N is almost

$N_{eu}gs\alpha^*$ – continuous function. But f_N is not $N_{eu}gs\alpha^*$ – irresolute. Let $E =$ $\{\langle q, (0.8, 0.4, 0.6)\rangle\}$ be $N_{eu}gs\alpha^*$ – CS in $(\mathbb{Q}, \sigma_{N_{eu}})$. Then $f_N^{-1}(E) = \{\langle p, (0.8, 0.4, 0.6)\rangle\}$. Now, $N_{eu}\alpha - int(N_{eu}\alpha - cl(f_N^{-1}(E))) = 1_{N_{eu}} \not\subseteq N_{eu} - int(F) = A$, whenever $f_N^{-1}(E) \subseteq F$, where $F = \{\langle p, ([0.8,1], [0.6,1], [0,0.5])\rangle\} \Rightarrow f_N^{-1}(E)$ is not a $N_{eu}gs\alpha^*$ – CS in $(\mathbb{P}, \tau_{N_{eu}})$.

Theorem 4.6: Every strongly $N_{eu}gs\alpha^*$ – continuous function is almost $N_{eu}gs\alpha^*$ – continuous function, but not conversely.

Proof: Let $f_N: (\mathbb{P}, \tau_{N_{eu}}) \to (\mathbb{Q}, \sigma_{N_{eu}})$ be any N_{eu} – function. Let A be any $N_{eu}R$ – CS in $(\mathbb{Q}, \sigma_{N_{eu}})$. Then A is a N_{eu} – CS in $(\mathbb{Q}, \sigma_{N_{eu}}) \Rightarrow A$ is a $N_{eu}gs\alpha^*$ – CS in $(\mathbb{Q}, \sigma_{N_{eu}})$. Given f_N is strongly $N_{eu}gs\alpha^*$ – continuous , then $f_N^{-1}(A)$ is a N_{eu} – CS in $(\mathbb{P}, \tau_{N_{eu}}) \Rightarrow f_N^{-1}(A)$ is a $N_{eu}gs\alpha^*$ – CS in $(\mathbb{P}, \tau_{N_{eu}}) \Rightarrow f_N^{-1}$ is almost $N_{eu}gs\alpha^*$ – CS continuous.

Example 4.7: Let $\mathbb{P} = \{p\}$ and $\mathbb{Q} = \{q\}$. $\tau_{N_{eu}} = \{0_{N_{eu}}, 1_{N_{eu}}, A\}$ and $\sigma_{N_{eu}} = \{0_{N_{eu}}, 1_{N_{eu}}, B\}$ are $N_{eu}TS$ on $(\mathbb{P}, \tau_{N_{eu}})$ and $(\mathbb{Q}, \sigma_{N_{eu}})$ respectively. Also $A = \{\langle p, (0.7, 0.8, 0.3)\rangle\}$ and $B = \{\langle q, (0.6, 0.7, 0.4)\rangle\}$ are $N_{eu}(\mathbb{P})$ and $N_{eu}(\mathbb{Q})$. Define a map $f_N: (\mathbb{P}, \tau_{N_{eu}}) \to (\mathbb{Q}, \sigma_{N_{eu}})$ by $f_N(p) = q$. Let $C = \{\langle q, (1, 1, 0)\rangle\}$ be $N_{eu}R$ – CS in $(\mathbb{Q}, \sigma_{N_{eu}}s)$. Then $f_N^{-1}(C) = \{\langle p, (1, 1, 0)\rangle\}$. $N_{eu}\alpha^* - OS = N_{eu}\alpha - OS = \{0_{N_{eu}}, 1_{N_{eu}}, A, D\}$ and $N_{eu}\alpha$ – CS $= \{0_{N_{eu}}, 1_{N_{eu}}, A^C, E\}$, where $D = \{\langle p, ([0.7,1], [0.8,1], [0,0.3])\rangle\}$, $E = \{\langle p, ([0,0.3], [0,0.2], [0.7,1])\rangle\}$. Now, $N_{eu}\alpha - int (N_{eu}\alpha - cl (f_N^{-1}(C))) = 1_{N_{eu}} \subseteq N_{eu}\alpha - int(1_{N_{eu}}) = 1_{N_{eu}}$, whenever $f_N^{-1}(C) \subseteq 1_{N_{eu}} \Rightarrow f_N^{-1}(C)$ is a $N_{eu}gs\alpha^*$ – CS in $(\mathbb{P}, \tau_{N_{eu}})$. Hence, f_N is almost $N_{eu}gs\alpha^*$ – continuous function. But f_N is not strongly $N_{eu}gs\alpha^*$ – continuous function. Let $E = \{\langle q, (0.2, 0.2, 0.7)\rangle\}$ be $N_{eu}gs\alpha^*$ – CS in $(\mathbb{Q}, \sigma_{N_{eu}})$. Then $f_N^{-1}(E) = \{\langle p, (0.2, 0.2, 0.7)\rangle\}$. Since, $N_{eu} - cl(f_N^{-1}(E)) = A^c \neq f_N^{-1}(E) \Rightarrow f_N^{-1}(E)$ is not a N_{eu} – CS in $(\mathbb{P}, \tau_{N_{eu}})$.

Theorem 4.8: Every perfectly $N_{eu}gs\alpha^*$ – continuous function is almost $N_{eu}gs\alpha^*$ – continuous function, but not conversely.

Proof: Let $f_N: (\mathbb{P}, \tau_{N_{eu}}) \to (\mathbb{Q}, \sigma_{N_{eu}})$ be any N_{eu} – function . Let A be any $N_{eu}R$ – CS in $(\mathbb{Q}, \sigma_{N_{eu}})$. Then A is a N_{eu} – CS in $(\mathbb{Q}, \sigma_{N_{eu}}) \Rightarrow A$ is a $N_{eu}gs\alpha^*$ – CS in $(\mathbb{Q}, \sigma_{N_{eu}})$. Given f_N is perfectly $N_{eu}gs\alpha^*$ – continuous, then $f_N^{-1}(A)$ is a N_{eu} – OS and N_{eu} – CS in $(\mathbb{P}, \tau_{N_{eu}}) \Rightarrow f_N^{-1}(A)$ is a $N_{eu}gs\alpha^*$ – CS in $(\mathbb{P}, \tau_{N_{eu}}) \Rightarrow f_N^{-1}$ is almost $N_{eu}gs\alpha^*$ – continuous.

Example 4.9: Let $\mathbb{P} = \{p\}$ and $\mathbb{Q} = \{q\}$. $\tau_{N_{eu}} = \{0_{N_{eu}}, 1_{N_{eu}}, A\}$ and $\sigma_{N_{eu}} = \{0_{N_{eu}}, 1_{N_{eu}}, B\}$ are $N_{eu}TS$ on $(\mathbb{P}, \tau_{N_{eu}})$ and $(\mathbb{Q}, \sigma_{N_{eu}})$

respectively. Also $A = \{\langle \wp, (0.8, 0.5, 0.2)\rangle\}$ and $B = \{\langle q, (0.9, 0.6, 0.1)\rangle\}$ are $N_{pu}(\mathbb{P})$ and $N_{eu}(\mathbb{Q})$. Define a map $f_N: (\mathbb{P}, \tau_{N_{eu}}) \to (\mathbb{Q}, \sigma_{N_{eu}})$ by $f_N(\wp) = q$. Let $C = \{\langle q, (1, 1, 0)\rangle\}$ be $N_{eu}R - CS$ in $(\mathbb{Q}, \sigma_{N_{eu}})$. Then $f_N^{-1}(C) = \{\langle \wp, (1, 1, 0)\rangle\}$. $N_{eu}\alpha^* - OS = N_{eu}\alpha - OS = \{0_{N_{eu}}, 1_{N_{eu}}, A, D\}$ and $N_{eu}\alpha - CS = \{0_{N_{eu}}, 1_{N_{eu}}, A^C, E\}$, where $D = \{\langle \wp, ([0.8,1], [0.5,1], [0,0.2])\rangle\}$, $E = \{\langle \wp, ([0,0.2], [0,0.5], [0.8,1])\rangle\}$. Now, $N_{eu}\alpha - int(N_{eu}\alpha - cl(f_N^{-1}(C))) = 1_{N_{eu}} \subseteq N_{eu}\alpha - int(1_{N_{eu}}) = 1_{N_{eu}}$, whenever $f_N^{-1}(C) \subseteq 1_{N_{eu}} \Rightarrow f_N^{-1}(C)$ is a $N_{eu}gs\alpha^* - CS$ in $(\mathbb{P}, \tau_{N_{eu}})$. Hence, f_N is almost $N_{eu}gs\alpha^* -$ continuous function. But f_N is not perfectly $N_{eu}gs\alpha^* -$ continuous function. Let $B^c = \{\langle \wp, (0.1, 0.4, 0.9)\rangle\}$ be $N_{eu}gs\alpha^* - CS$ in $(\mathbb{Q}, \sigma_{N_{eu}})$. Then $f_N^{-1}(B^c) = \{\langle \wp, (0.1, 0.4, 0.9)\rangle\}$. Since, $N_{eu} - int(f_N^{-1}(B^c)) = 0_{N_{eu}} \neq f_N^{-1}(B^c)$ and $N_{eu} - cl(f_N^{-1}(B^c)) = A^c \neq f_N^{-1}(B^c) \Rightarrow f_N^{-1}(B^c)$ is not both $N_{eu} - OS$ and $N_{eu} - CS$ in $(\mathbb{P}, \tau_{N_{eu}})$.

Theorem 4.10: Every totally $N_{eu}gs\alpha^* -$ continuous function is almost $N_{eu}gs\alpha^* -$ continuous function, but not conversely.

Proof: Let $f_N: (\mathbb{P}, \tau_{N_{eu}}) \to (\mathbb{Q}, \sigma_{N_{eu}})$ be any $N_{eu} -$ function. Let A be any $N_{eu}R - CS$ in $(\mathbb{Q}, \sigma_{N_{eu}})$. Then A is a $N_{eu} - CS$ in $(\mathbb{Q}, \sigma_{N_{eu}})$. Given f_N is totally $N_{eu}gs\alpha^* -$ continuous, then $f_N^{-1}(A)$ is a $N_{eu}gs\alpha^* - OS$ and $N_{eu}gs\alpha^* - CS$ in $(\mathbb{P}, \tau_{N_{eu}}) \Rightarrow f_N^{-1}(A)$ is a $N_{eu}gs\alpha^* - CS$ in $(\mathbb{P}, \tau_{N_{eu}}) \Rightarrow f_N$ is almost $N_{eu}gs\alpha^* -$ continuous.

Example 4.11: Let $\mathbb{P} = \{\wp\}$ and $\mathbb{Q} = \{q\}$. $\tau_{N_{eu}} = \{0_{N_{eu}}, 1_{N_{eu}}, A\}$ and $\sigma_{N_{eu}} = \{0_{N_{eu}}, 1_{N_{eu}}, B\}$ are $N_{eu}TS$ on $(\mathbb{P}, \tau_{N_{eu}})$ and $(\mathbb{Q}, \sigma_{N_{eu}})$ respectively. Also $A = \{\langle \wp, (0.4, 0.6, 0.2)\rangle\}$ and $B = \{\langle q, (0.5, 0.8, 0.2)\rangle\}$ are $N_{eu}(\mathbb{P})$ and $N_{eu}(\mathbb{Q})$. Define a map $f_N: (\mathbb{P}, \tau_{N_{eu}}) \to (\mathbb{Q}, \sigma_{N_{eu}})$ by $f_N(\wp) = q$. Let $C = \{\langle q, (1, 1, 0)\rangle\}$ be $N_{eu}R - CS$ in $(\mathbb{Q}, \sigma_{N_{eu}})$. Then $f_N^{-1}(C) = \{\langle \wp, (1, 1, 0)\rangle\}$. $N_{eu}\alpha^* - OS = N_{eu}\alpha - OS = \{0_{N_{eu}}, 1_{N_{eu}}, A, D\}$ and $N_{eu}\alpha - CS = \{0_{N_{eu}}, 1_{N_{eu}}, A^C, E\}$, where $D = \{\langle \wp, ([0.4,1], [0.6,1], [0,0.2])\rangle\}$, $E = \{\langle \wp, ([0,0.2], [0,0.4], [0.4,1])\rangle\}$. Now, $N_{eu}\alpha - int(N_{eu}\alpha - cl(f_N^{-1}(C))) = 1_{N_{eu}} \subseteq N_{eu} - int(1_{N_{eu}}) = 1_{N_{eu}}$, whenever $f_N^{-1}(C) \subseteq 1_{N_{eu}} \Rightarrow f_N^{-1}(C)$ is a $N_{eu}gs\alpha^* - CS$ in $(\mathbb{P}, \tau_{N_{eu}})$. Hence, f_N is almost $N_{eu}gs\alpha^* -$ continuous function. But f is not totally $N_{eu}gs\alpha^* -$ continuous function. Let $B^c = \{\langle q, (0.2, 0.2, 0.5)\rangle\}$ be a $N_{eu} - CS$ in $(\mathbb{Q}, \sigma_{N_{eu}})$. Then $f_N^{-1}(B^c) = \{\langle \wp, (0.2, 0.2, 0.5)\rangle\}$. Hence, $f_N^{-1}(B^c)$ is a $N_{eu}gs\alpha^* - CS$, but not a $N_{eu}gs\alpha^* - OS$ in $(\mathbb{P}, \tau_{N_{eu}})$.

Theorem 4.12: Every almost $N_{eu} -$ continuous function is almost $N_{eu}gs\alpha^* -$ continuous function, but not conversely.

Proof: Let $f_N : (\mathbb{P}, \tau_{N_{eu}}) \to (\mathbb{Q}, \sigma_{N_{eu}})$ be any N_{eu} – function. Let $\mathbb{A}$ be any $N_{eu}R$ – CS in $(\mathbb{Q}, \sigma_{N_{eu}})$. Given f_N is almost neutrosophic continuous, then $f_N^{-1}(\mathbb{A})$ is a N_{eu} – CS in $(\mathbb{P}, \tau_{N_{eu}}) \Rightarrow f_N^{-1}(\mathbb{A})$ is a $N_{eu}gs\alpha^*$ – CS in $(\mathbb{P}, \tau_{N_{eu}}) \Rightarrow f_N^{-1}$ is almost $N_{eu}gs\alpha^*$ – continuous.

Example 4.13: Let $\mathbb{P} = \{p\}$ and $\mathbb{Q} = \{q\}$. $\tau_{N_{eu}} = \{0_{N_{eu}}, 1_{N_{eu}}, \mathbb{A}\}$ and $\sigma_{N_{eu}} = \{0_{N_{eu}}, 1_{N_{eu}}, \mathbb{B}\}$ are N_{eu}TS on $(\mathbb{P}, \tau_{N_{eu}})$ and $(\mathbb{Q}, \sigma_{N_{eu}})$ respectively. Also $\mathbb{A} = \{\langle p, (0.4, 0.5, 0.7)\rangle\}$ and $\mathbb{B} = \{\langle q, (0.5, 0.3, 0.8)\rangle\}$ are $N_{eu}(\mathbb{P})$ and $N_{eu}(\mathbb{Q})$. Define a map $f_N : (\mathbb{P}, \tau_{N_{eu}}) \to (\mathbb{Q}, \sigma_{N_{eu}})$ by $f_N(p) = q$. Let $\mathbb{B}^c = \{\langle q, (0.8, 0.7, 0.5)\rangle\}$ be $N_{eu}R$ – CS in $(\mathbb{Q}, \sigma_{N_{eu}})$. Then $f_N^{-1}(\mathbb{B}^c) = \{\langle p, (0.8, 0.7, 0.5)\rangle\}$. $N_{eu}\alpha^* - OS = N_{eu}\alpha - OS = \{0_{N_{eu}}, 1_{N_{eu}}, \mathbb{A}\}$ and $N_{eu}\alpha - CS = \{0_{N_{eu}}, 1_{N_{eu}}, \mathbb{A}^c\}$. Now, $N_{eu}\alpha - int(N_{eu}\alpha - cl(f_N^{-1}(\mathbb{B}^c))) = 1_{N_{eu}} \subseteq N_{eu} - int(1_{N_{eu}}) = 1_{N_{eu}}$, whenever $f_N^{-1}(\mathbb{B}^c) \subseteq 1_{N_{eu}} \Rightarrow f_N^{-1}(\mathbb{B}^c)$ is a $N_{eu}gs\alpha^*$ – CS in $(\mathbb{P}, \tau_{N_{eu}})$. Hence, f_N is almost $N_{eu}gs\alpha^*$ – continuous function. But f_N is not almost neutrosophic continuous function , because $f_N^{-1}(\mathbb{B}^c)$ is not a N_{eu} – CS in $(\mathbb{P}, \tau_{N_{eu}})$. Since $N_{eu} - cl(f_N^{-1}(\mathbb{B}^c)) = 1_{N_{eu}} \ne f_N^{-1}(\mathbb{B}^c)$.

Theorem 4.14: Every almost $N_{eu}\alpha$ – continuous function is almost $N_{eu}gs\alpha^*$ – continuous function, but not conversely.

Proof: Let $f_N : (\mathbb{P}, \tau_{N_{eu}}) \to (\mathbb{Q}, \sigma_{N_{eu}})$ be any N_{eu} – function. Let $\mathbb{A}$ be any $N_{eu}R$ – CS in $(\mathbb{Q}, \sigma_{N_{eu}})$. Since f_N is almost $N_{eu}\alpha$ – continuous, then $f_N^{-1}(\mathbb{A})$ is a $N_{eu}\alpha$ – CS in $(\mathbb{P}, \tau_{N_{eu}}) \Rightarrow f_N^{-1}(\mathbb{A})$ is a $N_{eu}gs\alpha^*$ – CS in $(\mathbb{P}, \tau_{N_{eu}})$. Hence, f_N is almost $N_{eu}gs\alpha^*$ – continuous.

Example 4.15: Let $\mathbb{P} = \{p\}$ and $\mathbb{Q} = \{q\}$. $\tau_{N_{eu}} = \{0_{N_{eu}}, 1_{N_{eu}}, \mathbb{A}\}$ and $\sigma_{N_{eu}} = \{0_{N_{eu}}, 1_{N_{eu}}, \mathbb{B}\}$ are N_{eu}TS on $(\mathbb{P}, \tau_{N_{eu}})$ and $(\mathbb{Q}, \sigma_{N_{eu}})$ respectively. Also $\mathbb{A} = \{\langle p, (0.2, 0.4, 0.6)\rangle\}$ and $\mathbb{B} = \{\langle q, (0.3, 0.2, 0.8)\rangle\}$ are $N_{eu}(\mathbb{P})$ and $N_{eu}(\mathbb{Q})$. Define a map $f_N : (\mathbb{P}, \tau_{N_{eu}}) \to (\mathbb{Q}, \sigma_{N_{eu}})$ by $f_N(p) = q$. Let $\mathbb{B}^c = \{\langle q, (0.8, 0.8, 0.3)\rangle\}$ be $N_{eu}R$ – CS in $(\mathbb{Q}, \sigma_{N_{eu}})$. Then $f_N^{-1}(\mathbb{B}^c) = \{\langle p, (0.8, 0.8, 0.3)\rangle\}$. $N_{eu}\alpha^* - OS = N_{eu}\alpha - OS = \{0_{N_{eu}}, 1_{N_{eu}}, \mathbb{A}\}$ and $N_{eu}\alpha - CS = \{0_{N_{eu}}, 1_{N_{eu}}, \mathbb{A}^c\}$. Now, $N_{eu}\alpha - int(N_{eu}\alpha - cl(f_N^{-1}(\mathbb{B}^c))) = 1_{N_{eu}} \subseteq N_{eu} - int(1_{N_{eu}}) = 1_{N_{eu}}$, whenever $f_N^{-1}(\mathbb{B}^c) \subseteq 1_{N_{eu}} \Rightarrow f_N^{-1}(\mathbb{B}^c)$ is a $N_{eu}gs\alpha^*$ – CS in $(\mathbb{P}, \tau_{N_{eu}})$. Hence, f_N is almost $N_{eu}gs\alpha^*$ – continuous function. But f_N is not almost $N_{eu}\alpha$ – continuous function, because $f_N^{-1}(\mathbb{B}^c)$ is not a $N_{eu}\alpha$ – CS in $(\mathbb{P}, \tau_{N_{eu}})$. Since $N_{eu} - cl(N_{eu} - int(N_{eu} - cl(f_N^{-1}(\mathbb{B}^c)))) = 1_{N_{eu}} \not\subseteq f_N^{-1}(\mathbb{B}^c)$.

Theorem 4.16: If $(\mathbb{P}, \tau_{N_{eu}})$ is a N_{eu} – discrete topological space, then $N_{eu}gs\alpha^*$ – CS = $N_{eu}gs\alpha^*$ – OS = $N_{eu}R$ – OS = $N_{eu}R$ – CS.

Proof: Given $(\mathbb{P}, \tau_{N_{eu}})$ is a N_{eu} – discrete topological space, then $\tau_{N_{eu}} = \{0_{N_{eu}}, 1_{N_{eu}}\}$. Since $0_{N_{eu}}$ and $1_{N_{eu}}$ are N_{eu} – OS and N_{eu} – CS in $(\mathbb{P}, \tau_{N_{eu}})$, then $0_{N_{eu}}$ and $1_{N_{eu}}$ are $N_{eu}gs\alpha^{*}$ – OS and $N_{eu}gs\alpha^{*}$ – CS in $(\mathbb{P}, \tau_{N_{eu}})$. Also, $N_{eu} - int(N_{eu} - cl(0_{N_{eu}})) = 0_{N_{eu}}$ and $N_{eu} - int(N_{eu} - cl(1_{N_{eu}})) = 1_{N_{eu}} \Rightarrow 0_{N_{eu}}$ and $1_{N_{eu}}$ are $N_{eu}R$ – OS in $(\mathbb{P}, \tau_{N_{eu}})$. Also, $N_{eu} - cl(N_{eu} - int(0_{N_{eu}})) = 0_{N_{eu}}$ and $N_{eu} - cl(N_{eu} - int(1_{N_{eu}})) = 1_{N_{eu}} \Rightarrow 0_{N_{eu}}$ and $1_{N_{eu}}$ are $N_{eu}R$ – CS in $(\mathbb{P}, \tau_{N_{eu}})$. Hence, $N_{eu}gs\alpha^{*}$ – CS $= N_{eu}gs\alpha^{*}$ – OS $= N_{eu}R$ – OS $= N_{eu}R$ – CS.

Remark 4.17: Let $f_{N} : (\mathbb{P}, \tau_{N_{eu}}) \rightarrow (\mathbb{Q}, \sigma_{N_{eu}})$ and $g_{N} : (\mathbb{Q}, \tau_{N_{eu}}) \rightarrow (\mathbb{R}, \gamma_{N_{eu}})$ be almost $N_{eu}gs\alpha^{*}$ – continuous, then $g_{N}of_{N} : (\mathbb{P}, \tau_{N_{eu}}) \rightarrow (\mathbb{R}, \gamma_{N_{eu}})$ need not be almost $N_{eu}gs\alpha^{*}$ – continuous.

Example 4.18: Let $\mathbb{P} = \{p\}$ and $\mathbb{Q} = \{q\}$. $\tau_{N_{eu}} = \{0_{N_{eu}}, 1_{N_{eu}}, A\}$ and $\sigma_{N_{eu}} = \{0_{N_{eu}}, 1_{N_{eu}}, B\}$ are N_{eu}TS on $(\mathbb{P}, \tau_{N_{eu}})$ and $(\mathbb{Q}, \sigma_{N_{eu}})$ respectively. Also $A = \{\langle p, (0.6, 0.8, 0.4)\rangle\}$ and $B = \{\langle q, (0.4, 0.6, 0.8)\rangle\}$ are $N_{eu}(\mathbb{P})$ and $N_{eu}(\mathbb{Q})$. Define a map $f_{N} : (\mathbb{P}, \tau_{N_{eu}}) \rightarrow (\mathbb{Q}, \sigma_{N_{eu}})$ by $f_{N}(p) = q$. Let $E = \{\langle q, (1, 1, 0)\rangle\}$ be $N_{eu}R$ – CS in $(\mathbb{Q}, \sigma_{N_{eu}})$. Then $f_{N}^{-1}(E) = \{\langle p, (1, 1, 0)\rangle\}$ is a $N_{eu}gs\alpha^{*}$ – CS in $(\mathbb{P}, \tau_{N_{eu}})$. Hence, f_{N} is almost $N_{eu}gs\alpha^{*}$ – continuous function. Let $\mathbb{R} = \{r\}$. Also, $C = \{\langle r, (0.7, 0.3, 0.8)\rangle\}$ is $N_{eu}(\mathbb{R})$ and $\gamma_{N_{eu}} = \{0_{N_{eu}}, 1_{N_{eu}}, C\}$ is N_{eu}TS on $(\mathbb{R}, \gamma_{N_{eu}})$. Define a map $g_{N} : (\mathbb{Q}, \sigma_{N_{eu}}) \rightarrow (\mathbb{R}, \gamma_{N_{eu}})$ by $g_{N}(q) = r$ – 0.3. Let $C^{c} = \{\langle r, (0.8, 0.7, 0.7)\rangle\}$ be $N_{eu}R$ – CS in $(\mathbb{R}, \gamma_{N_{eu}})$. Then $g_{N}^{-1}(C^{c}) = \{\langle q, (0.5, 0.4, 0.4)\rangle\}$ is a $N_{eu}gs\alpha^{*}$ – CS in $(\mathbb{Q}, \sigma_{N_{eu}})$. Hence, g_{N} is almost $N_{eu}gs\alpha^{*}$ – continuous function. But $g_{N}of_{N}$ is not almost $N_{eu}gs\alpha^{*}$ – continuous function. Define a map $g_{N}of_{N} : (\mathbb{P}, \tau_{N_{eu}}) \rightarrow (\mathbb{R}, \gamma_{N_{eu}})$ by $g_{N}of_{N}(p) = r$ – 0.3. Also, $(g_{N}of_{N})^{-1}(C^{c}) = \{\langle p, (0.5, 0.4, 0.4)\rangle\}$. Now, $N_{eu}\alpha - int(N_{eu}\alpha - cl((g_{N}of_{N})^{-1}(C^{c}))) = 1_{N_{eu}} \not\subseteq N_{eu} - int(A) = A$, whenever $(g_{N}of_{N})^{-1}(C^{c}) \subseteq A \Rightarrow (g_{N}of_{N})^{-1}(C^{c})$ is not a $N_{eu}gs\alpha^{*}$ – CS in $(\mathbb{P}, \tau_{N_{eu}})$.

Theorem 4.19: Let $f_{N} : (\mathbb{P}, \tau_{N_{eu}}) \rightarrow (\mathbb{Q}, \sigma_{N_{eu}})$ and $g_{N} : (\mathbb{Q}, \sigma_{N_{eu}}) \rightarrow (\mathbb{R}, \gamma_{N_{eu}})$ be almost $N_{eu}gs\alpha^{*}$ – continuous. Then $g_{N}of_{N} : (\mathbb{P}, \tau_{N_{eu}}) \rightarrow (\mathbb{R}, \gamma_{N_{eu}})$ is almost $N_{eu}gs\alpha^{*}$ – continuous, if $(\mathbb{Q}, \sigma_{N_{eu}})$ is a N_{eu} – discrete topological space.

Proof: Let A be any $N_{eu}R$ – CS in $(\mathbb{R}, \gamma_{N_{eu}})$. Given g_{N} is almost $N_{eu}gs\alpha^{*}$ – continuous, then $g_{N}^{-1}(A)$ is a $N_{eu}gs\alpha^{*}$ – CS in $(\mathbb{Q}, \sigma_{N_{eu}})$. Given $(\mathbb{Q}, \sigma_{N_{eu}})$ is a N_{eu} – discrete topological space, then $g_{N}^{-1}(A)$ is a $N_{eu}R$ – CS in $(\mathbb{Q}, \sigma_{N_{eu}})$ (by theorem 4.16). Given f_{N} is almost $N_{eu}gs\alpha^{*}$ – continuous, then $f_{N}^{-1}(g_{N}^{-1}(A)) = (g_{N}of_{N})^{-1}(A)$ is a $N_{eu}gs\alpha^{*}$ – CS in $(\mathbb{P}, \tau_{N_{eu}}) \Rightarrow g_{N}of_{N}$ is almost $N_{eu}gs\alpha^{*}$ – continuous.

Theorem 4.20: Let $f_N \colon (\mathbb{P}, \tau_{N_{eu}}) \to (\mathbb{Q}, \sigma_{N_{eu}})$ be slightly $N_{eu}gs\alpha^{*}$ – continuous and $(\mathbb{Q}, \sigma_{N_{eu}})$ is N_{eu} – discrete topological space, then f_N is almost $N_{eu}gs\alpha^{*}$ – continuous.

Proof: Let $\mathbb{A}$ be any $N_{eu}R - CS$ in $(\mathbb{Q}, \sigma_{N_{eu}})$. Then $\mathbb{A}$ is a $N_{eu} - CS$ in $(\mathbb{Q}, \sigma_{N_{eu}})$. Given $(\mathbb{Q}, \sigma_{N_{eu}})$ is a N_{eu} – discrete topological space, then $\mathbb{A}$ is a $N_{eu} - CS$ in $(\mathbb{Q}, \sigma_{N_{eu}}) \Rightarrow \mathbb{A}$ is a N_{eu} – clopen set in $(\mathbb{Q}, \sigma_{N_{eu}})$. Given f_N is slightly $N_{eu}gs\alpha^{*}$ – continuous, then $f_N^{-1}(\mathbb{A})$ is a $N_{eu}gs\alpha^{*} - CS$ in $(\mathbb{P}, \tau_{N_{eu}}) \Rightarrow f_N$ is almost $N_{eu}gs\alpha^{*}$ – continuous.

Theorem 4.21: Let $f_N \colon (\mathbb{P}, \tau_{N_{eu}}) \to (\mathbb{Q}, \sigma_{N_{eu}})$ be almost $N_{eu}gs\alpha^{*}$ – continuous and $(\mathbb{P}, \tau_{N_{eu}})$ is $N_{eu}gs\alpha^{*} - T_{\frac{1}{2}}$ space, then f_N is almost N_{eu} – continuous.

Proof: Let $\mathbb{A}$ be any $N_{eu}R - CS$ in $(\mathbb{Q}, \sigma_{N_{eu}})$. Given f_N is almost $N_{eu}gs\alpha^{*}$ – continuous, then $f_N^{-1}(\mathbb{A})$ is a $N_{eu}gs\alpha^{*} - CS$ in $(\mathbb{P}, \tau_{N_{eu}})$. Given $(\mathbb{P}, \tau_{N_{eu}})$ is $N_{eu}gs\alpha^{*} - T_{\frac{1}{2}}$ space, then $f_N^{-1}(\mathbb{A})$ is a $N_{eu} - CS$ in $(\mathbb{P}, \tau_{N_{eu}}) \Rightarrow f_N$ is almost N_{eu} – continuous.

Theorem 4.22: Let $f_N \colon (\mathbb{P}, \tau_{N_{eu}}) \to (\mathbb{Q}, \sigma_{N_{eu}})$ be almost $N_{eu}gs\alpha^{*}$ – continuous and $(\mathbb{P}, \tau_{N_{eu}})$ is $N_{eu}gs\alpha^{*} - T_{\frac{1}{2}}$ space, then f_N is almost $N_{eu}\alpha$ – continuous.

Proof: Let $\mathbb{A}$ be any $N_{eu}R - CS$ in $(\mathbb{Q}, \sigma_{N_{eu}})$. Given f_N is almost $N_{eu}gs\alpha^{*}$ – continuous, then $f_N^{-1}(\mathbb{A})$ is a $N_{eu}gs\alpha^{*} - CS$ in $(\mathbb{P}, \tau_{N_{eu}})$. Given $(\mathbb{P}, \tau_{N_{eu}})$ is $N_{eu}gs\alpha^{*} - T_{\frac{1}{2}}$ space, then $f_N^{-1}(\mathbb{A})$ is a $N_{eu} - CS$ in $(\mathbb{P}, \tau_{N_{eu}}) \Rightarrow f_N^{-1}(\mathbb{A})$ is a $N_{eu}\alpha - CS$ in $(\mathbb{P}, \tau_{N_{eu}}) \Rightarrow f_N$ is almost $N_{eu}\alpha$ – continuous.

Theorem 4.23: Let $f_N \colon (\mathbb{P}, \tau_{N_{eu}}) \to (\mathbb{Q}, \sigma_{N_{eu}})$ be any N_{eu} – function. Then the following are equivalent.

(1) f_N is almost $N_{eu}gs\alpha^{*}$ – continuous.
(2) f_N^{-1} of every $N_{eu}R - OS$ in $(\mathbb{Q}, \sigma_{N_{eu}})$ is a $N_{eu}gs\alpha^{*} - OS$ in $(\mathbb{P}, \tau_{N_{eu}})$.

Proof: (1) $\Rightarrow$ (2), Let $\mathbb{A}$ be any $N_{eu}R - OS$ in $(\mathbb{Q}, \sigma_{N_{eu}})$. Then $\mathbb{A}^c$ is a $N_{eu}R - CS$ in $(\mathbb{Q}, \sigma_{N_{eu}})$. Given f_N is almost $N_{eu}gs\alpha^{*}$ – continuous, then $f_N^{-1}(\mathbb{A}^c) = (f_N^{-1}(\mathbb{A}))^c$ is a $N_{eu}gs\alpha^{*} - CS$ in $(\mathbb{P}, \tau_{N_{eu}}) \Rightarrow f_N^{-1}(\mathbb{A})$ is a $N_{eu}gs\alpha^{*} - OS$ in $(\mathbb{P}, \tau_{N_{eu}})$.

(2) $\Rightarrow$ (1), Let $\mathbb{A}$ be any $N_{eu}R - CS$ in $(\mathbb{Q}, \sigma_{N_{eu}})$. Then $\mathbb{A}^c$ is a $N_{eu}R - OS$ in $(\mathbb{Q}, \sigma_{N_{eu}})$. Then by hypothesis, $f_N^{-1}(\mathbb{A}^c) = (f_N^{-1}(\mathbb{A}))^c$ is a $N_{eu}gs\alpha^{*} - OS$ in $(\mathbb{P}, \tau_{N_{eu}}) \Rightarrow f_N^{-1}(\mathbb{A})$ is a $N_{eu}gs\alpha^{*} - CS$ in $(\mathbb{P}, \tau_{N_{eu}}) \Rightarrow f_N$ is almost $N_{eu}gs\alpha^{*}$ – continuous.

Theorem 4.24: Let $f_N: (\mathbb{P}, \tau_{N_{eu}}) \to (\mathbb{Q}, \sigma_{N_{eu}})$ be $N_{eu}gs\alpha^*$ – irresolute and $g_N: (\mathbb{Q}, \sigma_{N_{eu}}) \to (\mathbb{R}, \gamma_{N_{eu}})$ be almost $N_{eu}gs\alpha^*$ – continuous, then $g_N of_N: (\mathbb{P}, \tau_{N_{eu}}) \to (\mathbb{R}, \gamma_{N_{eu}})$ is almost $N_{eu}gs\alpha^*$ – continuous.

Proof: Let $\mathbb{A}$ be any $N_{eu}R$ – CS in $(\mathbb{R}, \gamma_{N_{eu}})$. Given g_N is almost $N_{eu}gs\alpha^*$ – continuous, then $g_N^{-1}(\mathbb{A})$ is a $N_{eu}gs\alpha^*$ – CS in $(\mathbb{Q}, \sigma_{N_{eu}})$. Given f_N is $N_{eu}gs\alpha^*$ – irresolute, then $f_N^{-1}(g_N^{-1}(\mathbb{A})) = (g_N of_N)^{-1}(\mathbb{A})$ is a $N_{eu}gs\alpha^*$ – CS in $(\mathbb{P}, \tau_{N_{eu}}) \Rightarrow g_N of_N$ is almost $N_{eu}gs\alpha^*$ – continuous.

Theorem 4.25: Let $f_N: (\mathbb{P}, \tau_{N_{eu}}) \to (\mathbb{Q}, \sigma_{N_{eu}})$ be strongly $N_{eu}gs\alpha^*$ – continuous and $g_N: (\mathbb{Q}, \sigma_{N_{eu}}) \to (\mathbb{R}, \gamma_{N_{eu}})$ be almost $N_{eu}gs\alpha^*$ – continuous, then $g_N of_N: (\mathbb{P}, \tau_{N_{eu}}) \to (\mathbb{R}, \gamma_{N_{eu}})$ is almost $N_{eu}gs\alpha^*$ – continuous.

Proof: Let $\mathbb{A}$ be any $N_{eu}R$ – CS in $(\mathbb{R}, \gamma_{N_{eu}})$. Given g_N is almost $N_{eu}gs\alpha^*$ – continuous, then $g_N^{-1}(\mathbb{A})$ is a $N_{eu}gs\alpha^*$ – CS in $(\mathbb{Q}, \sigma_{N_{eu}})$. Given f_N is strongly $N_{eu}gs\alpha^*$ – continuous, then $f_N^{-1}(g_N^{-1}(\mathbb{A})) = (g_N of_N)^{-1}(\mathbb{A})$ is a N_{eu} – CS in $(\mathbb{P}, \tau_{N_{eu}}) \Rightarrow (g_N of_N)^{-1}(\mathbb{A})$ is a $N_{eu}gs\alpha^*$ – CS in $(\mathbb{P}, \tau_{N_{eu}}) \Rightarrow g_N of_N$ is almost $N_{eu}gs\alpha^*$ – continuous.

Theorem 4.26: Let $f_N: (\mathbb{P}, \tau_{N_{eu}}) \to (\mathbb{Q}, \sigma_{N_{eu}})$ be perfectly $N_{eu}gs\alpha^*$ – continuous and $g_N: (\mathbb{Q}, \sigma_{N_{eu}}) \to (\mathbb{R}, \gamma_{N_{eu}})$ be almost $N_{eu}gs\alpha^*$ – continuous, then $g_N of_N: (\mathbb{P}, \tau_{N_{eu}}) \to (\mathbb{R}, \gamma_{N_{eu}})$ is almost $N_{eu}gs\alpha^*$ – continuous.

Proof: Let $\mathbb{A}$ be any $N_{eu}R$ – CS in $(\mathbb{R}, \gamma_{N_{eu}})$. Given g_N is almost $N_{eu}gs\alpha^*$ – continuous, then $g_N^{-1}(\mathbb{A})$ is a $N_{eu}gs\alpha^*$ – CS in $(\mathbb{Q}, \sigma_{N_{eu}})$. Given f_N is perfectly $N_{eu}gs\alpha^*$ – continuous, then $f_N^{-1}(g_N^{-1}(\mathbb{A})) = (g_N of_N)^{-1}(\mathbb{A})$ is a N_{eu} – OS and N_{eu} – CS in $(\mathbb{P}, \tau_{N_{eu}}) \Rightarrow (g_N of_N)^{-1}(\mathbb{A})$ is a $N_{eu}gs\alpha^*$ – CS in $(\mathbb{P}, \tau_{N_{eu}}) \Rightarrow g_N of_N$ is almost $N_{eu}gs\alpha^*$ – continuous.

Theorem 4.27: Let $f_N: (\mathbb{P}, \tau_{N_{eu}}) \to (\mathbb{Q}, \sigma_{N_{eu}})$ be totally $N_{eu}gs\alpha^*$ – continuous and $g_N: (\mathbb{Q}, \sigma_{N_{eu}}) \to (\mathbb{R}, \gamma_{N_{eu}})$ be almost $N_{eu}gs\alpha^*$ – continuous. Then $g_N of_N: (\mathbb{P}, \tau_{N_{eu}}) \to (\mathbb{R}, \gamma_{N_{eu}})$ is almost $N_{eu}gs\alpha^*$ – continuous, if $(\mathbb{Q}, \sigma_{N_{eu}})$ is $N_{eu}gsa^* - T_{1/2}$ space.

Proof: Let $\mathbb{A}$ be any $N_{eu}R$ – CS in $(\mathbb{R}, \gamma_{N_{eu}})$. Given g_N is almost $N_{eu}gs\alpha^*$ – continuous, then $g_N^{-1}(\mathbb{A})$ is a $N_{eu}gs\alpha^*$ – CS in $(\mathbb{Q}, \sigma_{N_{eu}})$. Given $(\mathbb{Q}, \sigma_{N_{eu}})$ is $N_{eu}gsa^* - T_{1/2}$ space, then $g_N^{-1}(\mathbb{A})$ is a N_{eu} – CS in $(\mathbb{Q}, \sigma_{N_{eu}})$. Since f_N is totally $N_{eu}gs\alpha^*$ – continuous, then $f_N^{-1}(g_N^{-1}(\mathbb{A})) = (g_N of_N)^{-1}(\mathbb{A})$ is a $N_{eu}gs\alpha^*$ – OS and $N_{eu}gs\alpha^*$ – CS in $(\mathbb{P}, \tau_{N_{eu}}) \Rightarrow (g_N of_N)^{-1}(\mathbb{A})$ is a $N_{eu}gs\alpha^*$ – CS in $(\mathbb{P}, \tau_{N_{eu}}) \Rightarrow g_N of_N$ is almost $N_{eu}gs\alpha^*$ – continuous.

16.5   Conclusion

We discussed the newly introduced idea, namely slightly $N_{eu}gs\alpha^*$ – continuous function and almost $N_{eu}gs\alpha^*$ – continuous function. Then we also established the relationship between these continuous functions with already existing $N_{eu}gs\alpha^*$ – continuous function. The future work of this concept is used in theoretical framework, such as decision making field.

References

1. Atanassov, K., Intuitionistic fuzzy sets. *Fuzzy Set. Syst.*, 20, 87–94, 1986.
2. Zadeh, L.A., Fuzzy sets. *Inf. Control*, 8, 338–353, 1965.
3. Smarandache, F., Neutrosophic set: A generalization of intuitionistic fuzzy set. *J. Def. Resour. Manag.*, 24, 107–116, 2010.
4. Dhavaseelan, R. and Page, M.H., Neutrosophic almost contra α-continuous functions, in: *Neutrosophic Sets And Systems, An International Journal in Information Science and Engineering, Neutrosophic Science International Association (NSIA)*, ISSN:2331-608X (online), vol. 29, pp. 71–77, University of New Mexico, 2019.
5. Sreeja, D. and Sarankumar, T., Generalized alpha closed sets in neutrosophic topological spaces. *J. Appl. Sci. Comput.*, ISSN: 1076-5131, 5, 11, 1816–1823, Nov-2018.
6. Rodrigo, P.A. and Maheswari, S., Neutrosophic generalized semi alpha star closed sets in neutrosophic topological spaces. *Proceedings of International Conference on Mathematics, Statistics, Computers And Information Sciences*, 2021.
7. Blessie, R.S. and Francina, S.A., Neutrosophic generalized regular contra continuity in neutrosophic topological spaces. *Int. J. Res. Advent Technol.*, 7, 2, 761–765, Feb 2019.
8. Rodrigo, P.A. and Maheswari, S., Functions related to neutrosophic gsα*-closed sets in neutrosophic topological spaces. *Proceedings of 24th FAI International Conference on Global Trends of Data Analytics in Business Management Social Sciences, Medical Sciences and Decision Making 24th FAI-ICDBSMD*, 2021.
9. Rodrigo, P.A. and Maheswari, S., More functions associated with neutrosophic gsα*- closed sets in neutrosophic topological spaces, in: *Advanced Topics of Topology*.
10. Karatas, S. and Cemil, K., Neutrosophic topology, in: *Neutrosophic Sets & Systems, An International Book Series in Information Science and Engineering*, ISBN: 978-1-59973-515-3 vol. 13, pp. 90–95, University of New Mexico, 2016.
11. Abbas, N.M.A. and Khalil, S.M., On new classes of neutrosophic continuous and contra mappings in neutrosophic topological spaces. *Int. J. Nonlinear Anal. Appl.*, 12, 1, 718–725, 2021.

## 17

Identification and Prioritization of Risk Factors Affecting the Mental Health of Farmers

Hullash Chauhan[1], Suchismita Satapathy[1]*, A. K. Sahoo[1] and Debesh Mishra[2]

*[1]School of Mechanical Engineering, KIIT Deemed to be University,
Bhubaneswar, Odisha, India*
[2]Mechanical Engineering Department, BEC, Bhubaneswar, Odisha, India

Abstract

There has been a global concern in recent times over mental health issues of farmers. These studies aim to close a significant gap in sympathetic of the possible key risk factor affect mental health of farmers throughout the world. In this study, based on the extensive review of literature and discussion with farmers, as well as experts in agriculture, the risk factors in agriculture leading to mental stress of farmers were identified. Then, by the use of ELimination and Choice Expressing REality (ELECTRE) technique, as one of the latest multicriteria decision-making technique are selected to solve the problems of the possible key risk factor affect mental health of farmers. The results show that the purpose of this technique is quite helpful for decision making and all the identified risk factors were ranked according to the method has succeed to get the best alternative from highest to low based on their preferences.

Keywords: Characteristics, ELECTRE, farmers, mental health, risk factors

17.1 Introduction

A number of working health-risks of the agri-farm community has been identified through different studies, and the farming has also been specified as a stressful-occupation by different researchers [2, 8–11]. As under challenging-conditions the farming activities are performed, so it is usually

---

*Corresponding author: suchismitasatapathy9@gmail.com

Anita Khosla, Prasenjit Chatterjee, Ikbal Ali and Dheeraj Joshi (eds.) Optimization Techniques in Engineering: Advances and Applications, (275–296) © 2023 Scrivener Publishing LLC

associated with a variety of psychological and physical health-related risks [9]. [31, 35] have suggested that the farming profession creates stress due to financial and climatic problems, work overload, social interaction and agricultural issues [32]. Comparing the stress management strategy of poultry and cassava farmers in Nigeria, financial, meteorological, occupational, physical condition and other, social and mental stress these dimension is taken into account for the study. In general, the nature of farming can be stressful for farming family: agriculture can be an isolated profession as farmer by tradition work for long hours outdoors, often in inclement weather and alone. In a study by Lesli *et al.* [33] of Mid Wales farmers, government policy, financial problems and time pressures were identified as the most stressful factors. Sainath [34] studied in his report that in five years from 1997 to 2001, there were 78,737 agricultural suicides in the country, averaging about 15,747 per year. The literature survey on agricultural injuries and accident in India is limited to a few. Many authors and researchers have report that the rate of agricultural accident is higher than that of industrial sector. The lack of infrastructure, medical facilities, training and infrequent use and maintenance of machines, and the inability to define occupation according to sex or age are the causes of accidents in agriculture [36, 37]. Around the world, the studies on mental health have identified several common risk factors in farming communities, such as *commodities* prices, debts, weather changes, droughts, overworks, government regulation, isolations, role conflicts, time pressures, and poor housings, respectively [12–16].

Whenever the work demands become high, the work-related stresses occur such that the workers get unable to control, manage, or cope with such stresses [17]. The advent of future climate changes may lead to more stressful jobs for farmers [18]. The chronic stress among farmers may lead to physical problem, like headache, sleep problem; mental problem like anxieties, angers, depressions, and cognitive issues, like memory losses, inability in making decisions [19]. The life of farmers has been reported as nonworthy than nonfarmers [9]. The major risk factor for suicide attempt along with farmers has been identified as mental disorders [20]. In several studies, a higher suicidal rate among farmer, farm managers, and agriworkers has been reported [21–23]. A number of working health-risk of the agri-farm community has been identified through different studies, and the farming has also been specified as a stressful-occupation by different researchers [2, 8, 9–11], [24, 25]. An integration of abnormal-thoughts, emotions, behaviours as well as associations with others are included in mental-disorders [24], which also includes depressions, anxieties, stresses, schizophrenias, bipolar-disorders, and psychological or emotional distresses [25, 31, 35] have suggested that the farming profession creates stress due to financial and climatic problems, work overload, social interaction and agricultural issues. A significant contribution to poor mental health has been reported through farming profession [1–4]. Although the farming industries play a vital role in reducing poverty levels, agriculture has been reported as a hazardous occupation that exposes the farm workers to a number of occupational risks like agricultural stressors [5–7]. In a study, 35% of "Canadian farmers" reported of depression symptoms [26]. Figueira *et al.* [27] were presented description of ELimination and Choice Expressing Reality (ELECTRE) family method, deliberate for various criterion decision aids. Govindan and Jepsen [29] have investigated how ELECTRE and ELECTRE base methods have been measured in different areas of application, modification to the methods, comparison with other techniques, and general studies of the ELECTRE techniques. Yu *et al.* [28] have suggested invent precise ELECTRE techniques for prioritize MCDM multicriteria decision making problem will promote the development of mutually ELECTRE and prioritize MCDM. These methods are used as a liking model, outranking relations in set of behavior. Therefore, an effort was complete in this study to analysis the possible risk factors in the agricultural sector in India that lead to the farmers' mental ill health affecting the farming systems as a whole.

17.2   Materials and Methods

Based on extensive review of literature and discussion with farmers and experts in agriculture, the risk factors leading to mental stress of farmers

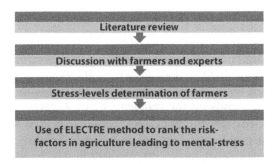

Figure 17.1 Steps in this research work.

in agriculture were identified. Then, by the use of ELECTRE method, all the identified risk factors were ranked based on their preferences. The steps followed in this research work were as summarized in Figure 17.1.

17.2.1 ELECTRE Technique

ÉLECTRE is a family unit of multicriteria decision making methods (MCDM) that originate in Europe in the mid-1960s. It was initially applied in 1965, the ELECTRE technique was to select the best action from a known set of actions, but it is soon useful to three main problems: choose, rank, and categories. ELECTRE technique has been extensively used for multiple criteria decision aiding (MCDA) in several real-world decisions trouble, range from farming to surroundings and water managing, from economics to plan selections, beginning employees recruit to shipping, and many other. The technique was initially projected by Bernard Roy and his equals at SEMA Advisory Corporation. A group at SEMA be an operational on the existing, various criterion, real-world problems of how firm can choose lying on new actions and have finished problem by a weighted sum method. Bernard Roy was known in as an advisor and the grouping devise the ELECTRE technique. Since it is initially applied during 1965, the ELECTRE technique was to prefer the top achievement from a given set of procedures; however, it is rapidly useful to three main problem: choose, rank and categorization. The technique become new broadly identified while a paper by B. Roy appear in a French operation journal study. It evolves into ELECTRE I (*ELECTRE one*) and the evolution contain continuous with ELECTRE 2, ELECTRE 3, ELECTRE 4, ELECTRE IS & ELECTRE (*ELECTRE TRI*), to reveal a hardly any. These are use in the field of commerce, growth, plan, and small power plant. Bernard Roy is broadly predictable as the priest of the ELECTRE technique, which was one of the initial approaches in at times identified as the French instruct of decision making. It is generally classified as an "outranking method" of decision making. The two most important parts to an ELECTRE applications: first, the creation of single or numerous outranking relation, which aim at evaluate in a complete way every pair of action; second, a utilization method that elaborates on the reference obtain in the initial phases. The character of the proposal depends on the problems being address: choose, rank or categorization. Generally, the ELECTRE technique is used to remove some alternative to the problems, which are undesirable. Further, the use MCDA to choose the most excellent one. The benefit by means of the ELECTRE technique previous to do so that we can be relevant a different MCDA with a constrained set of alternative and save a large amount of time (Figure 17.2).

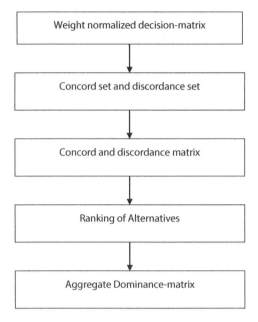

Figure 17.2 Procedural steps of ELECTRE method.

ELECTRE algorithm

Step 1: Weight normalized decision matrix

Here, a multicriteria decisions making (MCDM) problems by a lay m action, $X = [x\ 1, x\ 2, ..., x\ m]$, with a lay of n criterion, $C = [c\ 1, c\ 2, ..., c\ n]$, we constantly desire to choose the most excellent actions as of X throughout evaluate or rank all activities in the n criterion. [30] formulate an original form for MCDM as a vector optimizations problem:

$$\text{Max } c\{x\}$$
$$s.t.\ x \in X \tag{17.1}$$

Here, c; $X \to (0, 1)\ n$, $cr\ (x) = [cr\ 1\ (x), cr\ 2\ (x), ..., cr\ n\ (x)]$ are satisfaction of x in particular criterion. In point of view of [30] an actions x^* is chosen up as of X as the top one, after that $\_x \in X \setminus \{x^*\}$ in such wise $x \trianglerighteq x^*$, here "$\trianglerighteq$" is sign of dominance relations. $x \trianglerighteq x^*$ mean x is lead x^* or x^* is subject by x, i.e., $c\ i\ (x) \geq c\ i\ (x^*)\ \{i = 1, 2, ..., n\}$ and $c\ j\ (x) > c\ j\ (x^*)$ anyhow $j \in [1, 2, ..., n]$. Usually words, the dominance relations is too harsh to create the decisions outcome converge, because here generally are lot of action which should be subject by other.

Step 2: Concord set and discordance set

Significance: The known decision in order, $\forall\, x_j, x_k \in X$, if resolution maker or analyst have reason to consider x_j is better or unresponsive to x_k, after that there exist outranking relations among x_j and x_k, represent as $x_j\, S\, x_k$, meaning $x\,j$ is at least as superior as x_k.

Some outranking relations has to follow two property:

a) (*Weakly transitivity*) $\forall\, x_j, x_k, x_l \in X$,

$$\left.\begin{array}{c} x_j\, S\, x_k \\[6pt] x_k \trianglerighteq x_l \end{array}\right\} \Rightarrow x_j\, S\, x_l$$

And

$$\left.\begin{array}{c} x_k \trianglerighteq x_l \\[6pt] x_k\, S\, x_l \end{array}\right\} \Rightarrow x_j\, S\, x_l$$

b) (*Reflexivity*) $\forall\, x \in X \Rightarrow xSx$, i.e., every actions is outranking independently.

The followed two property, has simply assume a different assets, $x_j \trianglerighteq x_k \Rightarrow x_j\, Sx_k$ for $x_j, x_k \in X$. In further statement, the dominance relations is literal than outranking relations.

Until now, here numerous method for MCDM problem base on multiple outranking relation, call outranking method as a general name. Mainly ordinary outranking methods are ELECTRE.

Step 3: Concord and discordance matrix

ELECTRE I and its evolved version, the structure of an outranking relations is based on two main concepts:

1. *Concord*: an outranking $x_j Sx_k$ to be validating, an adequate greater part of criterion must be real in support of this assertions.
2. *Nondiscordance*: while the concordance situations hold, none of criterion in the alternative should be against too sturdily to the assertions $x_j Sx_k$.

On top of power of the concord combination ought to be dominant adequate to hold the assertions, $x_j Sx_k$. ELECTRE I define concord index to calculate the power of the concord coalitions.

Step 4: Ranking of Alternatives

Assume here a set of weight, $w_1, w_2, ..., w_n$, related to particular criterion by $\sum_{i \in N} w_i = 1$ ($N = \{1, 2, ..., n\}$), and a specified concordance level, α, whose values usually fall in the ranges $[0.5, 1 - \min_{i \in N} w_i]$. For every couple of action $x_j, x_k \in X$, can build three set of index underneath:

$$N_{jk}^+ = N^+(x_j, x_k) = \{i \in N \mid c_i(x_j) > c_i(x_k)\} \qquad (17.2)$$

$$N_{jk}^= = N = (x_j, x_k) = \{i \in N \mid c_i(x_j) > c_i(x_k)\} \qquad (17.3)$$

$$N_{jk}^- = N^-(x_j, x_k) = \{i \in N \mid c_i(x_j) > c_i(x_k)\} \qquad (17.4)$$

The concord index is defined:

$$I_{jk} = \sum_{i \in N_{jk}^+} w_i + \sum_{i \in N_{jk}^=} w_i \qquad (17.5)$$

If concord index is not as much of than concord level, i.e., $I_{jk} \geq \alpha$, it mean the assertions $x_j s x_k$ is validated by the concordance.

Step 5: Aggregate Dominance-matrix

Alternatively, no discordance adjacent to the affirmation "x_j is no less than as good as x_k" may arise. The discordance is calculated by a discordance index as follow:

$$D_{jk} = \max_{i \in N}\{\frac{c_i(x_k) - c_i(x_j)}{v}\} \qquad (17.6)$$

Here v represent a known veto threshold. If $D_{jk} \geq 1$, the affirmation $x_j S x_k$ is no extensive suitable; or else, discordant exert no power. If the assertion $x_j S x_k$ pass both the concord support & discordance support, i.e., $I_{jk} \geq \alpha$ and $D_{jk} < 1$, x_j determination outrank x_k and the outranking relations $x_j S x_k$ k exists.

17.3   Result and Discussion

From the demographic characteristics of agrifarm, it was observed that "household incomes from agriculture" was 20% to 50% for mostly number of farmer i.e. 18, while 48 farmers were not found of doing any off-farm jobs and 41 farmers were found of being the principal owners of farms (Table 17.1).

Table 17.1 Demographic characteristic of farmer (n = 53) shown.

Characteristics		Number of farmers (%)
Sex	Male	33 (62.26)
	Female	20 (37.74)
Age in years	≤35	42 (79.24)
	≥31	11 (20.75)
Educational levels	Nil	02 (3.77)
	High school	44 (83.01)
	College	06 (11.32)
	Graduate	01 (1.88)
Marital status	Married	32 (60.37)
	Unmarried	21 (39.62)
Roles on farm	Principal owner	41 (77.35)
	Partner owner	03 (5.66)
	Secondary owner	01 (1.88)
	Owner's child	00 (00)
	Others	08 (15.09)
Type of operation	Operating independently	22 (41.50)
	Operating with family	18 (33.96)
	Operating with nonfamily	13 (24.52)
Off-farming jobs	Nil	48 (90.56)
	Sometimes	03 (5.66)
	Part-time	02 (3.77)
	Full-time	00 (00)
Household incomes from agriculture	< 20%	12 (22.64)
	20–50%	18 (33.96)
	51–75%	17 (32.07)
	76–100%	06 (11.32)

˙n = Total number of farmers.

Table 17.2 Stress levels of farmers (n = 53) shown.

Stress domains	Stress levels	Anxieties (%)	Depressions (%)
Finance-related	Nil	01 (1.88)	08 (15.09)
	Very little	05 (9.43)	07 (13.20)
	Somewhat	13 (24.52)	02 (3.77)
	To a larger extent	11(20.75)	08 (15.09)
Time pressures	Nil	02 (3.77)	05 (9.433)
	Very little	04 (7.54)	02 (3.77)
	Somewhat	03 (5.66)	05 (9.433)
	To a larger extent	06 (11.32)	10 (18.86)
Climatic conditions	Nil	03 (5.66)	06 (11.32)
	Very little	06 (11.32)	07 (13.20)
	Somewhat	12 (22.64)	06 (11.32)
	To a larger extent	10 (18.86)	05 (9.433)
Hazardous conditions	Nil	02 (3.77)	04 (7.54)
	Very little	07 (13.20)	08 (15.09)
	Somewhat	10 (18.86)	12 (22.64)
	To a larger extent	11 (20.75)	13 (24.52)
Socially isolated	Nil	06 (11.32)	07 (13.20)
	Very little	05 (9.433)	08 (15.09)
	Somewhat	13 (24.52)	06 (11.32)
	To a larger extent	14 (26.41)	12 (22.64)

*n = Total number of farmers.

In Table 17.2, the stress levels of farmers are shown, where 53 farmers are taken. Along with stress domains are finance-related, time pressures, climatic conditions, hazardous conditions, and socially isolated to identify the stress levels of farmers with anxieties and depressions.

Table 17.3 shows the identification of risk factors affecting the mental stress of farmers. Stress domains are taken as criteria with a total of five

Table 17.3 Identification of risk factors and key objective shown.

Stress domains	Related risk factors	Key objective
Finance-related: C_1	General finance like input prices/incomes/profits/market conditions: A_1	Minimization
Time pressures: C_2	Regulations and policies of government/paper-related works/time pressures: A_2	Minimization
Climatic conditions: C_3	Uncertainty in weather including droughts and climate changes: A_3	Minimization
Hazardous conditions: C_4	Future farm concerns/animal diseases/breakdown of machinery: A_4	Minimization
	Poor physical health/previous injuries: A_5	Minimization
	General farming/heavy workloads/stresses/farming hazards: A_6	Minimization
	Exposure to harmful pesticides: A_7	Minimization
Socially isolated: C_5	Working with family only: A_8	Minimization
	Isolations/loneliness/lacking in social relationships: A_9	Minimization

criteria and nine alternatives. The criteria involved "finance-related, time pressures, climatic conditions, hazardous conditions and Socially isolated," along with the alternatives as general finance like input prices/incomes/profits/market conditions, Regulations and policies of government/paper related works/time pressures, Uncertainty in weather including droughts and climate changes, future farm concerns/animal diseases/breakdown of machinery, poor physical health/previous injuries, general farming/heavy workloads/stresses/farming hazards, exposure to harmful pesticides, working with family only and isolations/loneliness/lacking in social relationships, with the key objectives to minimize the mental stress of framers.

Here criterion denotes **C** and Alternative denotes **A**.

Table 17.4 illustrates the initial decision matrix with weight and kind of criterion of both alternatives and criteria. Further, Table 17.5 elaborates the normalized decision matrix.

After obtaining the value of (r) subsequently the weighting procedure is carry out the normalized matrix (v) by multiply w by r, the result are in Table 17.6.

Table 17.4 Initial decision matrix given away.

Weight of criterion	0.16	0.15	0.12	0.19	0.18
Kind of criterion	−1	−1	−1	−1	−1
	C-1	C-2	C-3	C-4	C-5
A-1	45	40	35	62	34
A-2	45	163	2	19	12
A-3	65	51	35	15	87
A-4	55	45	41	18	55
A-5	41	44	40	20	54
A-6	41	55	10	25	41
A-7	12	56	20	23	42
A-8	40	41	55	55	40
A-9	45	41	22	22	48
SUM OF SQUARE	18431	44254	9744	9817	22159
SQRT	135.76	210.36	98.71	99.080	148.85

Table 17.5 Normalized decision matrix given away.

Weight of criterion	0.16	0.15	0.12	0.19	0.18
Kind of criterion	−1	−1	−1	−1	−1
	C-1	C-2	C-3	C-4	C-5
A-1	0.3315	0.1901	0.3546	0.6258	0.2284
A-2	0.3315	0.7748	0.0203	0.1918	0.0806
A-3	0.4788	0.2424	0.3546	0.1514	0.5844
A-4	0.4051	0.2139	0.4154	0.1817	0.3695
A-5	0.3020	0.2092	0.4052	0.2019	0.3628
A-6	0.3020	0.2614	0.1013	0.2523	0.2754
A-7	0.0884	0.2662	0.2026	0.2321	0.2821
A-8	0.2946	0.1949	0.5572	0.5551	0.2687
A-9	0.3315	0.1949	0.2229	0.2220	0.3225

Table 17.6 Weighted normalized decision matrix given away.

Weight of criteria	0.16	0.15	0.12	0.19	0.18
Kind of criteria	−1	−1	−1	−1	−1
	C-1	**C-2**	**C-3**	**C-4**	**C-5**
A-1	0.0530	0.0285	0.0425	0.1189	0.0411
A-2	0.0530	0.1162	0.0024	0.0364	0.0145
A-3	0.0766	0.0364	0.0425	0.0288	0.1052
A-4	0.0648	0.0321	0.0498	0.0345	0.0665
A-5	0.0483	0.0314	0.0486	0.0384	0.0653
A-6	0.0483	0.0392	0.0122	0.0479	0.0496
A-7	0.0141	0.0399	0.0243	0.0441	0.0508
A-8	0.0471	0.0292	0.0669	0.1055	0.0484
A-9	0.0530	0.0292	0.0267	0.0422	0.0580

After getting the value of v, then calculate the set of concord and discordance index by equations (17.5) and (17.6), with the result as shown in Table 17.7.

It may be found that the cells containing positive values were the concord set (Table 17.8) and the cellcontaining negative values were the discordance set (Table 17.9).

Moreover, Table 17.10 and Table 17.11 show the concord dominance matrix and the discordance dominance matrix, respectively, for all the concerned nine alternatives.

Based on the aggregate dominance matrix as shown in Table 17.12, the final solutions are obtained from the sum of row and column and the subsequent ranking of alternatives are done (Table 17.13).

It is found that exposure to harmful pesticides ranked 1st, general farming/heavy workloads/stresses/farming hazards ranked 2nd, isolations/loneliness/lacking in social relationships ranked 3rd, regulations and policies of government/paper-related works/time pressures ranked 4th, poor physical health/previous injuries ranked 5th, general finance like input prices/incomes/profits/market conditions ranked 6th, future farm concerns/animal diseases/breakdown of machinery and working with family only ranked 7th, uncertainty in weather including droughts and climate changes ranked 8th.

Table 17.7 Concord set and discordance set given away.

Weight of criterion	0.16	0.15	0.12	0.19	0.18
Kind of criterion	−1	−1	−1	−1	−1
	C–1	C-2	C-3	C-4	C-5
A-1 to A-2	0.0000	0.0877	−0.0401	−0.0825	−0.0266
A-1 - A-3	0.0236	0.0078	0.0000	−0.0901	0.0641
A-1 - A-4	0.0118	0.0036	0.0073	−0.0844	0.0254
A-1 - A-5	−0.0047	0.0029	0.0061	−0.0805	0.0242
A-1 - A-6	−0.0047	0.0107	−0.0304	−0.0710	0.0085
A-1 - A-7	−0.0389	0.0114	−0.0182	−0.0748	0.0097
A-1 - A-8	−0.0059	0.0007	0.0243	−0.0134	0.0073
A-1 - A-9	0.0000	0.0007	−0.0158	−0.0767	0.0169
A-2 - A-1	0.0000	−0.0877	0.0401	0.0825	0.0266
A-2 - A-3	0.0236	−0.0799	0.0401	−0.0077	0.0907
A-2 - A-4	0.0118	−0.0841	0.0474	−0.0019	0.0520
A-2 - A-5	−0.0047	−0.0849	0.0462	0.0019	0.0508
A-2 - A-6	−0.0047	−0.0770	0.0097	0.0115	0.0351
A-2 – A-7	−0.0389	−0.0763	0.0219	0.0077	0.0363
A-2 – A-8	−0.0059	−0.0870	0.0644	0.0690	0.0339
A-2 - A-9	0.0000	−0.0870	0.0243	0.0058	0.0435
A-3 – A-1	−0.0236	−0.0078	0.0000	0.0901	−0.0641
A-3 - A-2	−0.0236	0.0799	−0.0401	0.0077	−0.0907
A-3 – A-4	−0.0118	−0.0043	0.0073	0.0058	−0.0387
A-3 - A-5	−0.0283	−0.0050	0.0061	0.0096	−0.0399
A-3 – A-6	−0.0283	0.0029	−0.0304	0.0192	−0.0556

(Continued)

Table 17.7 Concord set and discordance set given away. (*Continued*)

Weight of criterion	0.16	0.15	0.12	0.19	0.18
Kind of criterion	−1	−1	−1	−1	−1
	C–1	C–2	C–3	C–4	C–5
A-3 – A-7	−0.0625	0.0036	−0.0182	0.0153	−0.0544
A-3 - A-8	−0.0295	−0.0071	0.0243	0.0767	−0.0568
A-3 – A-9	−0.0236	−0.0071	−0.0158	0.0134	−0.0472
A-4 - A-1	−0.0118	−0.0036	−0.0073	0.0844	−0.0254
A-4 – A -2	−0.0118	0.0841	−0.0474	0.0019	−0.0520
A-4 – A-3	0.0118	0.0043	−0.0073	−0.0058	0.0387
A-4 – A-5	−0.0165	−0.0007	−0.0012	0.0038	−0.0012
A-4 - A-6	−0.0165	0.0071	−0.0377	0.0134	−0.0169
A-4 –A-7	−0.0507	0.0078	−0.0255	0.0096	−0.0157
A-4 – A-8	−0.0177	−0.0029	0.0170	0.0710	−0.0181
A-4 – A-9	−0.0118	−0.0029	−0.0231	0.0077	−0.0085
A-5 - A-1	0.0047	−0.0029	−0.0061	0.0805	−0.0242
A-5 – A-2	0.0047	0.0849	−0.0462	−0.0019	−0.0508
A-5 – A-3	0.0283	0.0050	−0.0061	−0.0096	0.0399
A-5 – A-4	0.0165	0.0007	0.0012	−0.0038	0.0012
A-5 - A-6	0.0000	0.0078	−0.0365	0.0096	−0.0157
A-5 – A-7	−0.0342	0.0086	−0.0243	0.0058	−0.0145
A-5 – A-8	−0.0012	−0.0021	0.0182	0.0671	−0.0169
A-5 – A-9	0.0047	−0.0021	−0.0219	0.0038	−0.0073
A-6 – A-1	0.0047	−0.0107	0.0304	0.0710	−0.0085
A-6 – A-2	0.0047	0.0770	−0.0097	−0.0115	−0.0351

(*Continued*)

Table 17.7 Concord set and discordance set given away. (*Continued*)

Weight of criterion	0.16	0.15	0.12	0.19	0.18
Kind of criterion	−1	−1	−1	−1	−1
	C–1	C–2	C–3	C–4	C–5
A-6 – A-3	0.0283	−0.0029	0.0304	−0.0192	0.0556
A-6 – A-4	0.0165	−0.0071	0.0377	−0.0134	0.0169
A-6 – A-5	0.0000	−0.0078	0.0365	−0.0096	0.0157
A-6 – A-7	−0.0342	0.0007	0.0122	−0.0038	0.0012
A-6 – A-8	−0.0012	−0.0100	0.0547	0.0575	−0.0012
A-6 – A-9	0.0047	−0.0100	0.0146	−0.0058	0.0085
A-7 - A-1	0.0389	−0.0114	0.0182	0.0748	−0.0097
A-7 – A-2	0.0389	0.0763	−0.0219	−0.0077	−0.0363
A-7 – A-3	0.0625	−0.0036	0.0182	−0.0153	0.0544
A-7 – A-4	0.0507	−0.0078	0.0255	−0.0096	0.0157
A-7 – A-5	0.0342	−0.0086	0.0243	−0.0058	0.0145
A-7 - A-6	0.0342	−0.0007	−0.0122	0.0038	−0.0012
A-7 – A-8	0.0330	−0.0107	0.0425	0.0614	−0.0024
A-7 – A-9	0.0389	−0.0107	0.0024	−0.0019	0.0073
A-8 - A-1	0.0059	−0.0007	−0.0243	0.0134	−0.0073
A-8 – A-2	0.0059	0.0870	−0.0644	−0.0690	−0.0339
A-8 - A-3	0.0295	0.0071	−0.0243	−0.0767	0.0568
A-8 – A-4	0.0177	0.0029	−0.0170	−0.0710	0.0181
A-8 - A-5	0.0012	0.0021	−0.0182	−0.0671	0.0169
A-8 – A-6	0.0012	0.0100	−0.0547	−0.0575	0.0012
A-8 - A-7	−0.0330	0.0107	−0.0425	−0.0614	0.0024

(*Continued*)

Table 17.7 Concord set and discordance set given away. (*Continued*)

Weight of criterion	0.16	0.15	0.12	0.19	0.18
Kind of criterion	−1	−1	−1	−1	−1
	C–1	C–2	C–3	C–4	C–5
A-8 – A-9	0.0059	0.0000	−0.0401	−0.0633	0.0097
A-9 - A-1	0.0000	−0.0007	0.0158	0.0767	−0.0169
A-9 – A-2	0.0000	0.0870	−0.0243	−0.0058	−0.0435
A-9 – A-3	0.0236	0.0071	0.0158	−0.0134	0.0472
A-9 – A-4	0.0118	0.0029	0.0231	−0.0077	0.0085
A-9- A-5	−0.0047	0.0021	0.0219	−0.0038	0.0073
A-9 – A-6	−0.0047	0.0100	−0.0146	0.0058	−0.0085
A-9 - A-7	−0.0389	0.0107	−0.0024	0.0019	−0.0073
A-9 – A-8	−0.0059	0.0000	0.0401	0.0633	−0.0097

Table 17.8 Concord matrix given away.

	A-1	A-2	A-3	A-4	A-5	A-6	A-7	A-8	A-9
A-1	---	0.3100	0.6100	0.6100	0.4500	0.3300	0.3300	0.4500	0.4900
A-2	0.6500	---	0.4600	0.4600	0.4900	0.4900	0.4900	0.4900	0.6500
A-3	0.3100	0.3400	---	0.3100	0.3100	0.3400	0.3400	0.3100	0.1900
A-4	0.1900	0.3400	0.4900	---	0.1900	0.3400	0.3400	0.3100	0.1900
A-5	0.3500	0.3100	0.4900	0.6100	---	0.5000	0.3400	0.3100	0.3500
A-6	0.4700	0.3100	0.4600	0.4600	0.4600	---	0.4500	0.3100	0.4600
A-7	0.4700	0.3100	0.4600	0.4600	0.4600	0.3500	---	0.4700	0.4600
A-8	0.3500	0.3100	0.4900	0.4900	0.4900	0.4900	0.3300	---	0.4900
A-9	0.4700	0.3100	0.6100	0.6100	0.4500	0.3400	0.3400	0.4600	---
TOTAL SUM	29.71								
Threshold Value	0.412								

Table 17.9 Discordance matrix given away.

	A-1	A-2	A-3	A-4	A-5	A-6	A-7	A-8	A-9
A-1	---	0.9402	1	1	1	1	1	0.5521	1
A-2	1	---	0.8806	1	1	1	1	1	1
A-3	0.7111	1	---	1	1	1	1	0.7409	1
A-4	0.3010	0.6180	0.1885	---	1	1	1	0.2556	1
A-5	0.3003	0.5985	0.2403	0.2324	---	1	1	0.2522	1
A-6	0.1507	0.4554	0.3448	0.3562	0.2629	---	1	0.1735	0.6843
A-7	0.1525	0.4755	0.2456	0.1892	0.2504	0.3557	---	0.1743	0.2750
A-8	1	0.7936	1	1	1	1	1	---	1
A-9	0.2207	0.5004	0.2846	0.3321	0.2154	1	1	0.1529	---
TOTAL SUM	49.85								
Threshold Value	0.69								

Table 17.10 Concord dominance matrix given away.

	A-1	A-2	A-3	A-4	A-5	A-6	A-7	A-8	A-9
A-1	---	0	1	1	1	0	0	1	1
A-2	1	---	1	1	1	1	1	1	1
A-3	0	0	---	0	0	0	0	0	0
A-4	0	0	1	---	0	0	0	0	0
A-5	0	0	1	1	---	1	0	0	0
A-6	1	0	1	1	1	---	1	0	1
A-7	1	0	1	1	1	0	---	1	1
A-8	0	0	1	1	1	1	0	---	1
A-9	1	0	1	1	1	0	0	1	---

Table 17.11 Discordance dominance matrix given away.

	A-1	A-2	A-3	A-4	A-5	A-6	A-7	A-8	A-9
A-1	---	0	0	0	0	0	0	1	0
A-2	0	---	0	0	0	0	0	0	0
A-3	0	0	---	0	0	0	0	0	0
A-4	1	1	1	---	0	0	0	1	0
A-5	1	1	1	1	---	0	0	1	0
A-6	1	1	1	1	1	---	0	1	1
A-7	1	1	1	1	1	1	---	1	1
A-8	0	0	0	0	0	0	0	---	0
A-9	1	1	1	1	1	0	0	1	---

Table 17.12 Aggregate dominance matrix given away.

	A-1	A-2	A-3	A-4	A-5	A-6	A-7	A-8	A-9	SUM
A-1	---	0	0	0	0	0	0	1	0	1
A-2	0	---	0	0	0	0	0	0	0	0
A-3	0	0	---	0	0	0	0	0	0	0
A-4	0	0	1	---	0	0	0	0	0	1
A-5	0	0	1	1	---	0	0	0	0	2
A-6	1	0	1	1	1	---	0	0	1	5
A-7	1	0	1	1	1	0	---	1	1	6
A-8	0	0	0	0	0	0	0	---	0	0
A-9	1	0	1	1	1	0	0	1	---	5
SUM	3	0	5	4	3	0	0	3	2	

Table 17.13 Ranking (higher value in final solutions have higher ranking) given away.

Alternative	Sum of row	Sum of column	Final solutions	Rank
A-1	1	3	−2	6
A-2	0	0	0	4
A-3	0	5	−5	8
A-4	1	4	−3	7
A-5	2	3	−1	5
A-6	5	0	5	2
A-7	6	0	6	1
A-8	0	3	−3	7
A-9	5	2	3	3

17.4 Conclusion

Based on the result and discussion, the risk factors affecting mental issues of farmers and its knowledge is essential in order to reduce the burdens of mental stress. Therefore, during this study, a significant step has been taken in synthesizing some of the important risk factors and their ranking, such that possible preventive measures can be initiated. The results from overall ranking of all the five criteria, namely finance-related, time pressures, climatic conditions, hazardous conditions, socially isolated and nine alternatives. The ELECTRE technique is quite efficiently useful as a study tool. Ranking conduct according to the technique has succeeded to get the best alternatives. So the purpose of this technique is quite helpful for decision making, and all the identified risk factors were ranked according to the method has succeeded to get the best alternative from highest to low based on their preferences were found as: exposure to harmful pesticides ranked, general farming/heavy workloads/stresses/farming hazards ranked, isolations/loneliness/lacking in social relationships ranked, regulations and policies of government/paper-related works/time pressures ranked, poor physical health/previous injuriesranked, general finance like input prices/incomes/profits/market conditions ranked, future farm concerns/animal diseases/breakdown of machinery and working with family only ranked, uncertainty in weather, including droughts and climate changes ranked.

Future research may attempt to appropriate the MCDM technique to decision support systems combined with mental health information system. Thus, this attribute and conceptual data can illustrate the study of an object with important risk factors and a more complex revelation.

References

1. Ellis, N.R. and Albrecht, G.A., Climate change threats to family farmers' sense of place and mental wellbeing: A case study from the Western Australian wheat belt. *Soc. Sci. Med.*, 175, 161–168, 2017.
2. Gregoire, A., The mental health of farmers. *Occup. Med.*, 52, 471–476, 2002.
3. Hounsome, B., Edwards, R.T., Hounsome, N., Edwards-Jones, G., Psychological morbidity of farmers and non-farming population: Results from a UK survey. *Community Ment. Health J.*, 48, 503–510, 2012.
4. Morgan, M.I., Hine, D.W., Bhullar, N., Dunstan, D.A., Bartik, W., Fracked: Coal seam gas extraction and farmers mental health. *J. Environ. Psychol.*, 47, 22–32, 2016.
5. Grovermann, C., Schreinemachers, P., Berger, T., Quantifying pesticide overuse from farmer and societal points of view: An application to Thailand. Elsevier *Crop Prot.*, 53, 161–168, 2013.
6. Suwanna, P., Pepijn, S., Piyatat, P., Prasnee, T., Pesticides, external costs and policy options for Thai agriculture. *Environ. Sci. Policy*, 27, 103–113, 2013.
7. Helitzer, D.L., Hathorn, G., Benally, J., Ortega, C., Culturally relevant model program to prevent and reduce agricultural injuries. *J. Agric. Saf. Health*, 20, 175–198, 2014.
8. Gregoire, A., The mental health of farmers. *Occup. Med.*, 52, 471–476, 2002.
9. Fraser, C.E., Smith, K.B., Judd, F., Humphreys, J.S., Fragar, L.J., Henderson, A., Farming and mental health problems and mental illness. *Int. J. Soc. Psychiatry*, 51, 340–349, 2005.
10. Roy, P., Tremblay, G., Olie, J.L., Jbilou, J., Robertson, S., Male farmers with mental health disorders: A scoping review. *Aust. J. Rural Health*, 21, 3–7, 2013.
11. Price, L. and Evans, N., From stress to distress: Conceptualizing the British family farming patriarchal way of life. *J. Rural Stud.*, 25, 1–11, 2009.
12. Mora, D.C., Quandt, S.A., Chen, H., Arcury, T.A., Associations of poor housing with mental health among North Carolina Latino migrant farm workers. *J. Agromedicine*, 21, 327–334, 2016.
13. Logstein, B., Farm-related concerns and mental health status among Norwegian farmers. *J. Agromedicine*, 21, 316–326, 2016.

14. Hanklang, S., Kaewboonchoo, O., Morioka, I., Plernpit, S.-A., Gender differences in depression symptoms among rice farmers in Thailand. *Asia Pac. J. Public Health*, 28, 83–93, 2016.

15. Ramos, A., Su, D., Lander, L., Rivera, R., Stress factors contributing to depression among Latino migrant farmworkers in Nebraska. *J. Immigr. Minor. Health*, 17, 1627–1634, 2015.

16. Wheeler, S.A., Zuo, A., Loch, A., Water torture: Unravelling the psychological distress of irrigators in Australia. *J. Rural Stud.*, 62, 183–194, 2018.

17. Lunner Kolstrup, C., Kallioniemi, M., Lundqvist, P., Kymäläinen, H.-R., Stallones, L., Brumby, S., International perspectives on psychosocial working conditions, mental health, and stress of dairy farm operators. *J. Agromedicine*, 18, 244–255, 2013.

18. Kearney, G.D., Raerty, A.P., Hendricks, L.R., Allen, D.L., Tutor-Marcom, R., A cross-sectional study of stressors among farmers in eastern North Carolina. *N. C. Med. J.*, 75, 384–392, 2014.

19. Williams, R., The ongoing farm crisis: Health, mental health and safety issues in Wisconsin. *Rural Ment. Health*, 26, 15–17, 2001.

20. Liu, B.-P., Qin, P., Liu, Y.-Y., Yuan, L., Gu, L.-X., Jia, C.-X., Mental disorders and suicide attempt in rural China. *Psychiatry Res.*, 261, 190–196, 2018.

21. Das, A., Farmers' suicide in India: Implications for public mental health. *Int. J. Soc. Psychiatry*, 57, 21–29, 2011.

22. Kunde, L., Kõlves, K., Kelly, B., Reddy, P., De Leo, D., Pathways to suicide in Australian farmers: A life chart analysis. *Int. J. Environ. Res. Public Health*, 14, 352, 2017.

23. Perceval, M., Kõlves, K., Reddy, P., De Leo, D., Farmer suicides: A qualitative study from Australia. *Occup. Med.*, 67, 383–388, 2017.

24. World Health Organization, *Depression and Other Common Mental Disorders: Global Health Estimates*, World Health Organization, Geneva, Switzerland, 2007a.

25. World Health Organization, *Promoting Mental Health: Concepts, Emerging Evidence, Practice: Summary Report*, World Health Organization, Geneva, Switzerland, 2007b.

26. Jones-Bitton, A., Best, C., MacTavish, J., Fleming, S., Hoy, S., Stress, anxiety, depression, and resilience in Canadian farmers. *Soc. Psychiatry Psychiatr. Epidemiol.*, 55, 2, 229–236, 2020. Retrieved from https://doi.org/10.1007/s00127-019-01738-2.

27. Figueira, J.R., Greco, S., Roy, B., Słowiński, R., ELECTRE methods: Main features and recent developments, in: *Handbook of Multicriteria Analysis*, pp. 51–89, Springer, Berlin, Heidelberg, 2010.

28. Yu, X., Zhang, S., Liao, X., Qi, X., ELECTRE methods in prioritized MCDM environment. *Inf. Sci.*, 424, 301–316, 2018.

29. Govindan, K. and Jepsen, M.B., ELECTRE: A comprehensive literature review on methodologies and applications. *Eur. J. Oper. Res.*, 250, 1, 1–29, 2016.

30. Kaliszewski, I., Miroforidis, J., Podkopaev, D., Interactive multiple criteria decision making based on preference driven evolutionary multiobjective optimization with controllable accuracy. *Eur. J. Oper. Res.*, 216, 188–199, 2012.

31. Ramesh, A.S. and Madhavi, C., Occupational stress among farming people. *J. Agric. Sci.*, 4, 3, 115–125, 2009.

32. Meludu, N.T. and Bajowa, O.M., Gender and stress coping strategies of poultry and cassava farmers in Nigeria. *J. Hum. Ecol.*, 23, 2, 159–164, 2008.

33. Lesli, P., Jennifer, D., Alice, G., Joyce, W., A preliminary study into stress in Welsh farmers. *J. Ment. Health*, 11, 2, 213–221, 2002.

34. Sainath, P., The farm crisis: Why have over one lakh farmers killed themselves in the past decade, in: *Speaker's Lecture Series: Parliament House*, 2007.

35. Ramesh, A.S. and Madhavi, C., Occupational stress among farming people. *J. Agric. Sci.*, 04, 3, 115–125, 2009.

36. Knapp, L.W., Agricultural injury prevention. *J. Occup. Med.*, 7, 11, 545–553, 1965.

37. Knapp, L.W., Occupational and rural accidents. *Archives of Environmental Health: An International Journal*, 13, 4, 501–506, 1966.

18

Multiple Objective and Subjective Criteria Evaluation Technique (MOSCET): An Application to Material Handling System Selection

Bipradas Bairagi

Department of Mechanical Engineering, Haldia Institute of Technology, West Bengal, India

Abstract

This chapter aims to propose a scientific and mathematical-based multiple objective and subjective criteria evaluation technique (MOSCET) to aid decision makers of industrial organization for the most appropriate decision, based on objective and subjective criteria, in those circumstances where human brain is incapable to find the right solution. The algorithm commences with the formation of a homogeneous decision making committee consisting of experts from different sections of the organization. The committee members unanimously choose required important criteria of both subjective and objective category with their depth knowledge and experience. A set of alternatives is primarily chosen through screening test of the alternatives based on sum minimum cut off value of the criteria. Performance ratings in terms of crisp number and linguistic variable are estimated. Fuzzy weighs of the criteria are evaluated with the experts' perception. Conversion of linguistic variables into crisp number, normalization of performance rating, and integration of rating of alternative with estimated weights of criteria are accomplished sequentially. A unique performance index via performance score for each alternative is computed with proposed exponential technique. The proposed MCDM technique MOSCET is demonstrated through a suitable material handling system selection problem and validated by existing method. The result shows that the proposed method is applicable and useful for decision-making process, considering both objective and subjective criteria under MCDM (Multi Criteria Decision Making).

Email: Bipradasbairagi79@gmail.com

Anita Khosla, Prasenjit Chatterjee, Ikbal Ali and Dheeraj Joshi (eds.) Optimization Techniques in Engineering: Advances and Applications, (297–312) © 2023 Scrivener Publishing LLC

Keywords: MCDM, objective criteria, subjective criteria, material handling system selection, MOSCET

18.1   Introduction

In performance evaluation of material handling systems, both objective and subjective criteria are considered by the decision makers and the researchers. Performance evaluation and selection of material handling system considering objective and subjective criteria is a very crucial decision making procedure in manufacturing industry. Objective criteria are those which are both measurable and quantitative such as cost, weight, speed, distance, lifecycles, reliability etc. Subjective criteria are those which are qualitative and not directly measurable nor quantifiable. Subjective criteria are associated to imprecision and vagueness and realized by human perception. Past researchers have some works on the material handling system selection. A brief literature review is furnished below.

Soufi *et al.* introduced an AHP (Analytical Hierarchy Process) based MCDM methodology for the evaluation and selection of material handling equipment to be utilized in manufacturing systems [1]. Goswami and Behera made an investigation for the capability and applicability of two well-known MCDM approaches ARAS (Additive Ratio Assessment) and COPRAS (Complex Proportional Assessment) for the evaluation and selection of conveyors, AGV (Automated Guided Vehicle) and robots as material handling equipment [2]. Satyam *et al.* applied a multi attribute decision making approach for evaluation and selection of conveyors as material handling equipment [3]. Nguyen *et al.* advocated a combined multi criteria decision making model for the evaluation and selection of conveyor as the material handling equipment based on fuzzy analytical hierarchy process and fuzzy ARAS with vague and imprecision information [4]. Mathewa and Sahua made a comparison among the novel multi-criteria decision making approaches by solving a problem on material handling equipment selection [5].

In last few decades, extensive researches on industrial material handling system selection have been executed. Hsu-Shih Shih (2008) [6] has evaluated performances of robots on their incremental benefit-cost ratio and in this work cost was shown in two representations. They have not demonstrated the effectiveness of their model. MCDM technique is widely used in ranking one or more alternatives from a set of available alternatives with respect to several criteria [7–12]. The study examine the modification in the most favorable result of a perturbation in a diversity of constraint or substitution rates, the criteria weights or the vagueness on performance procedures [13, 14].

Decision makers always like to know which option is best among a set of several feasible alternatives [15]. In order to determine the tactical decision-making about twofold market high machinery goods, a model on mixed integer goal programming is introduced to smooth the progress of the procedure of marketing media selection [16]. A framework is constructed using MCDM method for the sustainable technologies for generation of electricity in Greece to elaborate more realistic and transparent outcomes [17].

As per the global literature, the decision support framework formulation must be adequately flexible to consider variation in institutional settings, original capabilities and motivation as well as style of decision making [18, 19].

An integrated approach is introduced for considering the vendor selection procedure. In the beginning the authors formulated the vendor selection problem using multiple criteria decision-making methodology. Then the modified TOPSIS (Technique for Order Preference by Similarity to Ideal Solution) is used to select challenging products in terms of their general performances. TOPSIS is another constructive tool for working out multi criteria problems. In the concept of TOPSIS, the optimal alternative should be close to positive ideal solution and the maximum possible distant from the negative idea solution [20].

The above literature survey clearly shows that there is still absolute necessity of further investigation for proper selection of the robots considering variable decision making attitude with the objective of aiding managerial decision makers.

The above literature survey also reveals that some of the past researchers have applied MCDM techniques for material handling system (MHS) selection problem. However, this effort is insufficient for exhaustive and extensive decision making regarding proper selection MHS from thousands of available alternatives under multiple conflicting criteria of diverse categories. Therefore an effort in the chapter is made to propose a scientific and mathematical based Multiple Objective and Subjective Criteria Evaluation Technique (MOSCET) to aid decision makers of industrial organization for the most appropriate decision, based on objective and subjective criteria, in those circumstances where human brain is incapable to find the right solution.

The rest of the chapter is organized in the following manner. Section 18.2 is dedicated for describing the proposed algorithm. Section 18.3 cites a decision making problem on material handling system performance evaluation, and provides illustration, calculation and discussion. Section 18.4 makes some essential concluding remark.

18.2 Multiple Objective and Subjective Criteria Evaluation Technique (MOSCET): The Proposed Algorithm

Step 1: Form a decision making committee comprising of experts from different important sections of organization. Denote the decision makers as $D = [D_1, D_2, ..., D_p]$. p is number of total decision makers.

Step 2: Select the decision criteria. Denote the criteria as $C = [C_1, C_j, ... C_n]$. n is the number of criteria.

Step 3: Execute an initial screening test for selecting the set of alternative based on individual criterion cut off value. Denote the alternative as $A = [A_1 ... A_i ... A_m]^T$, m is the number of alternative to be considered, T stands for transpose matrix.

Step 4: Construct the decision matrix comprising of performance ratings in terms of crisp number or linguistic variable as applicable.

$$
A = \begin{array}{c} A_1 \\ ... \\ A_i \\ ... \\ A_m \end{array} \begin{bmatrix} a_{11} & ... & a_{1j} & ... & a_{1n} \\ ... & ... & ... & ... & ... \\ a_{i1} & ... & a_{ij} & ... & a_{in} \\ ... & ... & ... & ... & ... \\ a_{m1} & ... & a_{mj} & ... & a_{mn} \end{bmatrix} \tag{18.1}
$$

a_{ij} denotes the performance rating of ith alternative with respect to jth criterion.

Step 5: Convert the linguistic variable into respective fuzzy numbers.

$$
a_{ij} = \begin{cases} \tilde{a}_{ij}, & \text{if } j \in \text{Subjective criteria} \\ a_{ij}, & \text{if } j \in \text{Objective criteria} \end{cases} \quad \text{Where, } \tilde{a}_{ij} = (a_{ij(1)}, a_{ij(2)}, a_{ij(3)})
$$

$$\tag{18.2}$$

Step 6: Defuzzification: Transform the performance in terms of triangular fuzzy number into crisp number using the equation.

$$b_{ij} = \frac{1}{3}\sum_{k=1}^{3} a_{ij(k)} \qquad (18.3)$$

Step 7: Convert the entire performance ratings of the decision matrix in terms of crisp number only.

$$B = \begin{array}{c} A_1 \\ \cdots \\ A_2 \\ \cdots \\ A_m \end{array} \begin{bmatrix} b_{11} & \cdots & b_{1j} & \cdots & b_{1n} \\ \cdots & \cdots & \cdots & \cdots & \cdots \\ b_{i1} & \cdots & b_{ij} & \cdots & b_{in} \\ \cdots & \cdots & \cdots & \cdots & \cdots \\ b_{m1} & \cdots & b_{mj} & \cdots & b_{mn} \end{bmatrix} \qquad (18.4)$$

b_{ij} denotes the crisp performance rating of ith alternative and j^{th} criterion.

Step 8: Normalize the crisp performance rating using following normalization equation.

$$r_{ij} = \frac{b_{ij} - (b_j)_{min}}{(b_j)_{max} - (b_j)_{min}} \qquad (18.5a)$$

$$r_{ij} = ((b_{ij})_{max} - b_{ij})/((b_{ij})_{max} - (b_{ij})_{min}) \qquad (18.5b)$$

Equation (18.5a) and equation (18.5b) are for benefit criteria and cost criteria respectively.

Where, each normalized performance rating is restricted by $0 \leq r_{ij} \leq 1$.

Step 9: Construct weight matrix with linguistic variables assessed by the knowledge, experience and opinion of each of the experts involved in the decision making process.

$$C = \begin{array}{c} D_1 \\ \cdots \\ D_i \\ \cdots \\ D_m \end{array} \begin{array}{ccccc} C_1 & \cdots & C_j & \cdots & C_n \end{array} \\ \begin{bmatrix} u_{11} & \cdots & u_{1j} & \cdots & u_{1n} \\ \cdots & \cdots & \cdots & \cdots & \cdots \\ u_{i1} & \cdots & u_{ij} & \cdots & u_{in} \\ \cdots & \cdots & \cdots & \cdots & \cdots \\ u_{m1} & \cdots & u_{mj} & \cdots & u_{mn} \end{bmatrix} \qquad (18.6)$$

Step 10: Convert the linguistic variables of the weight matrix in fuzzy numbers as follows.

$$
D = \begin{matrix} & & C_1 & \cdots & C_j & \cdots & C_n \\ D_1 & \\ \cdots & \\ D_i & \\ \cdots & \\ D_m & \end{matrix}
\begin{bmatrix}
\tilde{v}_{11} & \cdots & \tilde{v}_{1j} & \cdots & \tilde{v}_{1n} \\
\cdots & \cdots & \cdots & \cdots & \cdots \\
\tilde{v}_{i1} & \cdots & \tilde{v}_{ij} & \cdots & \tilde{v}_{in} \\
\cdots & \cdots & \cdots & \cdots & \cdots \\
\tilde{v}_{m1} & \cdots & \tilde{v}_{mj} & \cdots & \tilde{v}_{mn}
\end{bmatrix}
\tag{18.7}
$$

where $\tilde{v}_{ij} = (v_{ij(L)}, v_{ij(M)}, v_{ij(U)})$ is a triangular fuzzy number.

Step 11: (a) Determine the mean weight in fuzzy number using the formula

$$
\tilde{v}_{j(Mean)} = \left(\frac{1}{p} \sum_{i=1}^{p} v_{ij(L)}, \quad \frac{1}{p} \sum_{i=1}^{p} v_{ij(M)}, \quad \frac{1}{p} \sum_{i=1}^{p} v_{ij(U)}, \right)
\tag{18.8}
$$

(b) Construct the mean weight matrix as follows

$$
\begin{bmatrix} \tilde{v}_{1(Mean)} & \cdots & \tilde{v}_{j(Mean)} & \cdots & \tilde{v}_{n(Mean)} \end{bmatrix}
\tag{18.9}
$$

Step 12: Defuzzify the mean fuzzy weight using the equation.

$$
\overline{v}_j = \frac{1}{3} \left(\frac{1}{p} \sum_{i=1}^{p} v_{ij(L)} + \frac{1}{p} \sum_{i=1}^{p} v_{ij(M)} + \frac{1}{p} \sum_{i=1}^{p} v_{ij(U)} \right)
\tag{18.10}
$$

Step 13: Evaluate the weight (w_j) for each criterion Cj using the equation (18.11).

$$
w_j = \frac{\overline{v}_j}{\sum_{j=1}^{n} \overline{v}_j}
\tag{18.11}
$$

Step 14: Calculate the weighted normalized performance rating applying the following proposed equation (18.12).

$$x_{ij} = EXP(r_{ij} + w_j) \tag{18.12}$$

Step 15: Determine the performance score of each alternative by using the following proposed exponential equation (18.13).

$$PS_i = \sum_{j=1}^{n} EXP(r_{ij} + w_j) \tag{18.13}$$

Step 16: Measure the Relative Performance Index (RPI) for each alternative by using the following equation (18.14).

$$RPI_i = \frac{\sum\limits_{j=1}^{n} EXP(r_{ij} + w_j)}{\sum\limits_{i=1}^{m} \sum\limits_{j=1}^{n} EXP(r_{ij} + w_j)} \tag{18.14}$$

Step 17: Arrange the alternatives in decreasing order of their relative performance indices. Select the best alternative having the highest relative performance index.

18.3   Illustrative Example

18.3.1   Problem Definition

A manufacturing company desires to select the best robot for its new automotive factory to accomplish a specific task. For this purpose a decision making committee is formed with four members (D_1, D_2, D_3 and D_4) who are experts of different sections of the organization. The committee unanimously selects six decision criteria viz. velocity (C_1), Load carrying capacity (C_2), Costs (C_3), Repeatability (C_4), Vendors Service Quality (VSQ) (C_5) and Programming Flexibility (PF) (C_6). Of these four (Velocity, Load carrying capacity, Costs, Repeatability) are objective (quantitative) criteria whereas the remaining two criteria, service quality and programming flexibility are subjective (qualitative) criteria. From the benefit and non-benefit angle of view, four criteria viz. velocity, Load carrying capacity, Vendors service quality and programming flexibility are of benefit category and the remaining two criteria, that is, cost and repeatability are non-benefit criteria. The decision making committee chooses a set of four material handling systems (MHS_1, MHS_2, MHS_3 and MHS_4) through preliminary screening for further process. The performance ratings of the alternative MHSs under the objective criteria are obtained from different sources like the operating manuals, specifications, design handbook and catalog, vendors, manufacturers, experts. The performance ratings of the alternative MHSs under objective criteria as well as the importance weights of the criteria (objective and subjective) are assessed by the experience, knowledge and valuable opinion of the members of the decision making committee in term of linguistic variables. The linguistic variables for the assessment of alternatives with respect to subjective criteria and weight of both categories of criteria are shown in Table 18.1 and Table 18.2, respectively. The decision making committee constructs a decision matrix in combination of crisp numbers and linguistic variables and is

Table 18.1 Linguistic variables, acronyms and TFN for performance rating.

Linguistic variables	Acronyms	TFNs
Extremely Low	EL	(0, 1, 3)
Low	L	(1, 3, 5)
Medium	M	(3, 5, 7)
High	H	(5, 7, 9)
Extremely High	EH	(7, 9, 10)

Table 18.2 Linguistic variables, acronym and TFNs for criteria weights.

Linguistic variables	Acronym	TFNs
Equally important	EI	(1, 1, 2)
Inadequately important	II	(2, 3, 4)
Moderately important	MI	(4, 5, 6)
Strongly important	SI	(6, 7, 8)
Absolutely Important	AI	(8, 9, 9)

Table 18.3 Decision matrix in terms of both crisp numbers and linguistic variables.

MHS$_i$	Velocity (m/s)	Load capacity (kg)	Costs ($)	Repeatability (mm)	VSQ	PF
MHS$_1$	1.8	90	9500	0.45	L	L
MHS$_2$	1.4	80s	5500	0.35	M	H
MHS$_3$	0.8	70	4500	0.20	EH	EL
MHS$_4$	0.8	60	4000	0.15	H	EH
max	1.8	90	9500	0.45	EH	EH
Min	0.8	60	4000	0.15	L	EL

shown in Table 18.3. The proposed method has been applied for finding the ranking order of the material handling system selection problems under consideration.

18.3.2   Calculation and Discussions

The material handling system selection problem is formulated in the decision matrix that consists of both subjective measure in linguistic variables and objective measure in crisp numbers and is summarized in Table 18.3. The decision making committee is comprised of the four homogeneous decision makers from different sections of the organization. The decision makers are denoted by D_1, D_2, D_3 and D_4. The six criteria under consideration have been designated by C_1, C_2, C_3, C_4, C_5 and C_6. The set of alternatives under assessment are denoted by MHS$_1$, MHS$_2$, MHS$_3$ and MHS$_4$. The decision matrix representing the performance rating in terms of crisp and fizzy numbers is represented in Table 18.4.

The conversion process of the linguistic variables into corresponding triangular fuzzy numbers is accomplished according to Table 18.1. The fuzzy numbers of the decision matrix are defuzzified and converted into crisp numbers using the suggested equation (18.3) and shown in Table 18.5. Maximum and minimum values of the crisp performance rating has been identified for each criterion and tabulated in the same column. Normalization process of crisp performance rating is accomplished to restrict the rating in [0, 1] by employing the equation (18.5) suggested in step 8 of the proposed algorithm and is depicted in Table 18.6.

Table 18.4 Decision matrix in terms of both crisp and fuzzy numbers.

MHS_i	Velocity (m/s)	Load capacity (kg)	Costs ($)	Repeatability (mm)	VSQ	PF
MHS_1	1.8	90	9500	0.45	(1, 3, 5)	(1, 3, 5)
MHS_2	1.4	80	5500	0.35	(3, 5, 7)	(5, 7, 9)
MHS_3	0.8	70	4500	0.2	(7, 9, 10)	(0, 1, 3)
MHS_4	0.8	60	4000	0.15	(5, 7, 9)	(7, 9, 10)
Max	1.8	90	9500	0.45	(7, 9, 10)	(7, 9, 10)
Min	0.8	60	4000	0.15	(1, 3, 5)	(0, 1, 3)

Table 18.5 Decision matrix in terms of crisp numbers.

MHS_i	Velocity (m/s)	Load capacity (kg)	Costs ($)	Repeatability (mm)	VSQ	PF
MHS_1	1.8	90	9500	0.45	3	3
MHS_2	1.4	80	5500	0.35	5	7
MHS_3	0.8	70	4500	0.2	8.66	1.33
MHS_4	0.8	60	4000	0.15	7	8.66
Max	1.8	90	9500	0.45	8.66	8.66
Min	0.8	60	4000	0.15	3	1.33

Table 18.6 Decision matrix in terms of normalized performance ratings.

MHS_i	Velocity	Load capacity	Costs	Repeatability	VSQ	PF
MHS_1	1.00	1.00	0.00	0.00	0.00	0.23
MHS_2	0.60	0.67	0.73	0.33	0.35	0.77
MHS_3	0.00	0.33	0.91	0.83	1.00	0.00
MHS_4	0.00	0.00	1.00	1.00	0.71	1.00

Weight matrix is formed by the decision makers for estimating importance weight of the different criteria in terms of linguistic variables is given in Table 18.7. The linguistic variables of the weight matrix are transformed in terms of triangular fuzzy numbers using indicated manner in the algorithm and shown in Table 18.8.

Mean fuzzy weights and mean crisp weights of the criteria under consideration are computed and furnished in Table 18.9. Weighted normalized decision matrix comprising of weights of criteria and performance

Table 18.7 Fuzzy weights matrix in terms of TFNs by decision makers.

D_k	C_1	C_2	C_3	C_4	C_5	C_6
D_1	EI	MI	II	SI	EI	II
D_2	MI	AI	MI	SI	SI	MI
D_3	MI	SI	AI	MI	MI	AI
D_4	II	MI	MI	SI	MI	SI

Table 18.8 Fuzzy weight matrix in terms of TFNs.

D_k	C_1	C_2	C_3	C_4	C_5	C_6
D_1	(1, 1, 2)	(4, 5, 6)	(2, 3, 4)	(6, 7, 8)	(1, 1, 2)	(2, 3, 4)
D_2	(4, 5, 6)	(8, 9, 9)	(4, 5, 6)	(6, 7, 8)	(6, 7, 8)	(4, 5, 6)
D_3	(4, 5, 6)	(6, 7, 8)	(8, 9, 9)	(4, 5, 6)	(4, 5, 6)	(8, 9, 9)
D_4	(2, 3, 4)	(4, 5, 6)	(4, 5, 6)	(6, 7, 8)	(4, 5, 6)	(6, 7, 8)

Table 18.9 Mean weights of criteria.

Weights	C_1	C_2	C_3	C_4	C_5	C_6
Fuzzy numbers	(2.75, 3.5, 4.5)	(5.5, 6.5, 7.25)	(4.5, 5.5, 6.25)	(5.5, 6.5, 7.5)	(3.75, 4.5, 6.5)	(5, 6, 6.75)
Crisp numbers	3.58	6.42	5.42	6.5	4.92	5.92
Normalized weight	0.11	0.2	0.17	0.2	0.15	0.18

rating of alternative in suitable combination is presented in Table 18.10. Performance score for each individual alternative material handling system is computed by using the prescribed equation in given algorithm and is shown in Table 18.11.

Relative Performance Index (RPI) of every alternative material handling system is measured by the equation (18.14) described in step 16 and accommodated in Table 18.11. It is observed that MHS1, MHS2, MHS3 and MH14 have the performance indices 0, 0.4548, 0.4904 and 1 respectively. Relative performance index of each of the alternative material handling systems is represented in Figure 18.1.

At last, the alternative material handling systems are arranged in decreasing order of their relative performance indices as MHS4>MHS3>MHS2>MHS1. The ranking order of the alternative material handling systems is graphically depicted in Figure 18.2. Therefore, MHS4 is selected as the best robot having the highest relative performance index.

Table 18.10 Weighted normalized performance ratings.

MHS$_i$	C$_1$	C$_2$	C$_3$	C$_4$	C$_5$	C$_6$
MHS$_1$	3.03	3.32	1.19	1.22	1.16	1.50
MHS$_2$	2.03	2.38	2.45	1.70	1.65	2.59
MHS$_3$	1.12	1.70	2.94	2.81	3.16	1.20
MHS$_4$	1.12	1.22	3.22	3.32	2.36	3.25

Table 18.11 Performance score, relative performance index and ranking order.

MHS$_i$	Performance score	Relative performance index	Rank
MHS$_1$	11.43	0.0000	4
MHS$_2$	12.82	0.4548	3
MHS$_3$	12.93	0.4904	2
MHS$_4$	14.49	1.0000	1

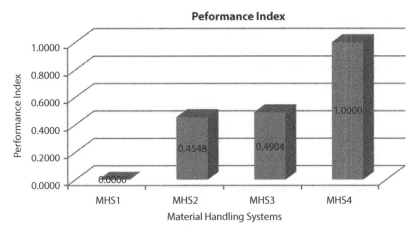

Figure 18.1 Relative performance index of the alternative material handling systems.

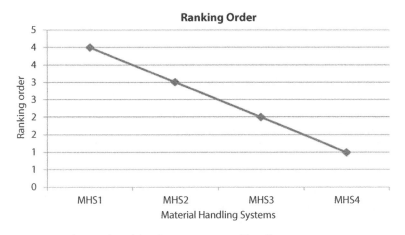

Figure 18.2 Ranking order of the alternative material handling systems.

18.4   Conclusions

Material handling system selection in manufacturing industry is a very critical decision making procedure, and it is an imperative responsibility of the concerned managerial decision makers of any organization. The decision making process involves significant capital investment and time. The success and survival of any automotive manufacturing company in many cases depend on proper decision making regarding selection of proper material handling systems that takes a key role in future growth. Naturally, decision making committee considers multiple conflicting criteria in combination of subjective, objective, benefit and nonbenefit category. In such a situation, the solution process of such a complex decision making problem deserves novel and suitable MCDM model. The present investigation has developed and proposed a novel decision making algorithm namely Multiple Objective and Subjective Criteria Evaluation Technique (MOSCET), with 18 steps capable of consideration subjective, objective, benefit, and nonbenefit criteria. The solution of the material handling system selection problems clearly shows that proposed method MOSCET is effective and useful for selection of material handling system with respect to subjective and objective criteria. Heterogeneous group decision making process may be a direction of future research.

References

1. Soufi, Z., David, P., Yahouni, Z., A methodology for the selection of material handling equipment in manufacturing systems. *IFAC-Papers Online*, 54, 122–127, 2021.
2. Goswami, S.S. and Behera, D.K., Solving material handling equipment selection problems in an industry with the help of entropy integrated COPRAS and ARAS MCDM techniques. *Process Integr. Optim. Sustain.*, 5, 947–973, 2021.
3. Satyam, F., Satywan, K., Avinash, K., Application of multi-attribute decision-making methods for the selection of conveyor. *Res. Sq.*, 1–18, 2021.
4. Nguyen, H.-T., Siti, D., Nukman, Y., Hideki, A., An integrated MCDM model for conveyor equipment evaluation and selection in an FMC based on a fuzzy AHP and fuzzy ARAS in the presence of vagueness. *PloS One*, 11, 2016.
5. Mathewa, M. and Sahua, S., Comparison of new multi-criteria decision making methods for material handling equipment selection. *Manage. Sci. Lett.*, 8, 139–150, 2018.
6. Shih, H.-S., Incremental analysis for MCDM with an application to group TOPSIS. *Eur. J. Oper. Res.*, 186, 720–734, 2008.
7. Wang, T.-C. and Lee, H.-D., Developing a fuzzy TOPSIS approach based on subjective weights and objective weights. *Expert Syst. Appl.*, 36, 8980–8985, 2009.
8. Ding, J.-F. and Liang, G.-S., Using fuzzy MCDM to select partners of strategic alliances for liner shipping. *Inf. Sci.*, 173, 197–225, 2005.
9. Belton, V. and Stewart, T.J., *Multiple Criteria Decision Analysis: An Integrated Approach*, Kluwer Academic Publishing, Boston, 2002.
10. Dyer, J.S., Fishburn, P.C., Steuer, R.E., Wallenius, J., Multiple criteria decision making, multiattribute utility theory: The next ten years. *Manage. Sci.*, 38, 645–654, 1992.

11. Gal, T., Stewart, T.J., Hanne, T. (Eds.), *Multicrteria Decision Making: Advances in MCDM Models, Algorithms, Theory, and Applications*, Kluwer Academic Publishing, Norwell, MA, 1999.

12. Liu, D. and Stewart, T.J., Integrated object-oriented framework for MCDM and DSS modeling. *Decis. Support Syst.*, 38, 421–434, 2004.

13. Steuer, R.E., *Multiple Criteria Optimization: Theory Computation and Application*, John Wiley, 1986.

14. Taha, H.A., *Operations Research: An Introduction*, Pearson, Upper Saddle River, NJ, 2003.

15. Hwang, C.L. and Yoon, K., *Multiple Attribute Decision Making*, Springer-Verlag, Berlin, 1981.

16. Kwak, N.K., Lee, C.W., Kim, J.H., An MCDM model for media selection in the dual consumer/industrial market. *Eur. J. Oper. Res.*, 166, 255–265, 2005.

17. Doukas, H., Patlitzianas, K.D., Psarras, J., Supporting sustainable electricity technologies in Greece using MCDM. *Resour. Policy*, 31, 129–136, 2006.

18. Romero, C., Determination of the optimal externality: Efficiency versus equity. *Eur. J. Oper. Res.*, 113, 183–192, 1999.

19. Ehtamo, H., Kettunen, E., Hamalainen, R.P., Searching for joint gains in multi-party negotiations. *Eur. J. Oper. Res.*, 130, 54–69, 2001.

20. Shyura, H.-J. and Shih, H.S., A hybrid MCDM model for strategic vendor selection. *Math. Comput. Model.*, Taiwan, 44, 749–761, 2006.

19

Evaluation of Optimal Parameters to Enhance Worker's Performance in an Automotive Industry

Rajat Yadav[1], Kuwar Mausam[1]*, Manish Saraswat[2] and Vijay Kumar Sharma[3]

[1]Department of Mechanical Engineering, G L A University, Mathura, India
[2]Department of Mechanical Engineering, Lloyd Institute of Engineering and Technology, Grater Noida, Uttar Pradesh, India
[3]Department of Mechanical Engineering, ABES Engineering College Ghaziabad, Uttar Pradesh, India

Abstract

In an automotive industry or manufacturing plant, there are several environmental factors that influence the performance of workers. Some of them include relative humidity, temperature, lighting, etc. In order to achieve the best efficiency, there is a need to determine the optimized parameters. In this study, a data set was obtained by performing the experiments in a virtual Indian field. The problem is subjected to following a repetitive process by downloading it manually. The productivity is measured every 10 minutes, and the factors including relative humidity; temperature and lightning are monitored continuously. In order to predict the best parameters to get the optimum efficiency, the data is evaluated by using Taguchi method. The ideal values obtained from this analysis give the values as 555 lux of brightness factor, 240°C of ideal temperature, and around 45 % of relative humidity. This experiment will help in making the automotive industry work more efficiently.

Keywords: Humidity, luminance, optimum, productivity, brightness factor, relative humidity

*Corresponding author: kuwar.mausam@gla.ac.in

Anita Khosla, Prasenjit Chatterjee, Ikbal Ali and Dheeraj Joshi (eds.) Optimization Techniques in Engineering: Advances and Applications, (313–322) © 2023 Scrivener Publishing LLC

19.1 Introduction

The automotive industry is one of the most important contributors to the national economy's income. As a result, healthy competition is essential in the industry in order to succeed in the global market. Time is a factor that has a significant impact on an industry's efficiency. Various analysis techniques have been discovered and applied to improve industrial efficiency and product quality. Several factors have been listed as the cause of the decline in labor productivity, according to the report. As a result, the parameters for the workstation setting must be obtained not only to maximize efficiency but also to ensure the comfort, health, and safety of the staff involved [1, 2]. The environment and a pleasant atmosphere are critical because they can help employees stay focused and work well over long periods of time. If their disability is the subject of their impairment, this is what has contributed to a decrease in productivity, or even worse, injuries. As a result, the principles should be implemented in an ergonomic working atmosphere to ensure a secure and high-quality working environment. Ergonomics analysis is not only useful for detecting and preventing occupational accidents but it can also be used to boost productivity [3–5]. According to report on the effect of lighting level on productivity, higher illumination levels (1200 lux vs. 800 lux) result in increased productivity. The results of this study indicate that changing and improving lighting can have an effect on productivity. It is also discovered that increasing illumination levels would improve a person's productivity [6]. This finding is consistent with that of who those found that at higher levels of illuminance, people were more satisfied with the climate [6]. The research found that as illuminance rises, human alertness rises proportionally. The main objective due to which this study is carried out was to identify and quantify the amount of radiance (illuminance levels) required to elicit. Casual relation between the changes occurred due to induced light during brain imaging consequences, assuring effects in humans and endocrinology [7–9]. As the body is subjected to thermal stress, the system controlling temperature adjusts its state to keep the core temperature within the range as given by Parsons [14]. The analysis of the thermal comfort temperature range for factory workers in warm humid tropical climates was conducted [10]. The findings of the work described here revealed that the capability of operating factory buildings involving free running would prove to be extremely beneficial if we consider the terms of reducing the energy amount which is required to provide sufficient thermal comfort for employees in hot, humid tropical climates. The water vapor pressure of the air at a given temperature is referred to as relative humidity [11]. It is one of the environmental factors that could have an effect on workers' productivity. In their previous studies already mentioned that in mucous membranes and facial skin, symptoms occur more often and this is due to lower value of relative humidity [12, 13]. In these symptoms, runny nose, irritation in eyes, throat and mouth dryness, etc. are also included. In the study, it is mentioned that western people are not that much susceptible to the humidity as the citizens of Japan are. Taking this in view, if we need to perform thermal studies for the environment during humid summer and hot weather, then the methods used must be different for Japan and the western countries [14, 15]. The study performed illustrates that when there occurs the temperature change to the cooler one from the warm and humid then how this will show the effect of humidity on the comfort and efficiency of the humans. In all the situations the efficiency of workers was observed at the constant line, but they were feeling a little more exhausted at RH value of around 70 percent, when there happens a phase shift in humidity, despite the fact that there will be the extra release of sweat from the body of the humans if the value of relative humidity decreases [16, 17]. The aim of this study was to see whether environmental variables including lighting, humidity, and WBGT had a significant impact on worker output in an Indian manufacturing plant.

19.2 Methodology

Figure 19.1 depicts the experimental setup. This research was carried out in a room measuring 4.91 × 3.53 m, which was designed to resemble a field of work in various industries. As a result, the research can be carried out in a controlled environment. This room will hold one subject at a time and has space for study observation equipment. Three male staff have been chosen as study subjects. Calibration of measurement equipment was required prior to the start of the analysis. The goal is to figure out how accurate a data device is. Coordination calibration is carried out with the aid of computer equipment to ensure that the calibration is carried out in accordance with defined standards. The installation will be done in the stands by the subjects, and the total output will be recorded every 10 minutes. The observation equipment will be checked every 10 minutes to ensure that the room remains in the regulated environment that was established at the start of the analysis. Two other workers can replicate the same set of criteria in order to achieve a more precise reading. The study was performed for 8 days in order to achieve the L8 Taguchi nature of an experiment.

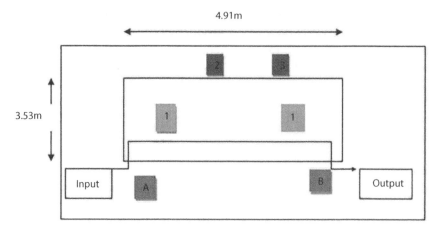

1- Dimmable fluorescent lamp

2- Air conditioner

3- Humidity

4- Quest thermal environmental monitor(A)

5- Heavy duty light meter(B)

Figure 19.1 Experimental layout.

19.3   Results and Discussion

The average productivity of three workers can be seen in Table 19.1 as a result of the research and revenue data obtained. For the purpose of analyzing the hypothesis, Minitab 15.0 software was used. This program can calculate the importance of optimization using the Taguchi Method. The Taguchi method is a good way to design an experiment for an engineering process that requires combining multiple experimental parameters to get the best results. After that, the data will be analyzed using an ANOVA measure of the signal-to-noise ratio (S/N ratio). The signal-to-noise ratio definition is a quality-improvement metric. The higher the signal-noise ratio, the better for calculating the data collected. This is due to the fact that the higher the efficiency, the better. This demonstrates increasing demand and high-quality production. The results of the productivity ratio S/N are shown in Table 19.1. The difference between the average value of each levels 1 and 2 can be seen by mapping the data graph. The greater the disparity, the greater the effect on productivity. The graph's Y-axis represents the value of the parameter, while the X-axis represents the S/N ratio (see Figures 19.2, 19.3, 19.4, 19.5). When it comes to things like temperature,

Table 19.1 Results of average worker productivity study and S/N ratio.

Experiment no.	WBGT temperature	Relative humidity (%)	Illuminance (lx)	Productivity of worker (1)	Productivity of worker (2)	Productivity of worker (3)	Average productivity (unit)	S/N ratio (dB)
1	25	45	250	.90	.86	.86	.873	1.21
2	25	45	550	1.32	1.13	1.42	1.29	1.90
3	25	45	250	.88	.87	.93	.89	1.06
4	25	45	550	1.01	1.19	1.2	1.13	.95
5	33	75	250	.86	.87	.85	.86	-1.42
6	33	75	550	.90	1.09	.89	.96	-.501
7	33	75	250	.72	.72	.70	.71	-3.31
8	33	75	550	.80	.76	.82	.793	-2.05

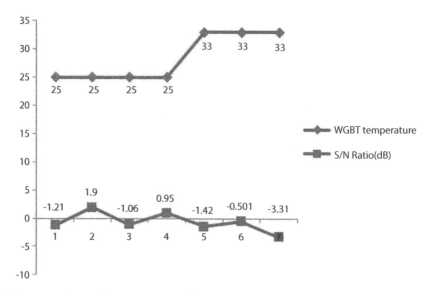

Figure 19.2 Figure showing variation of WBGT temperature with S/N ratio.

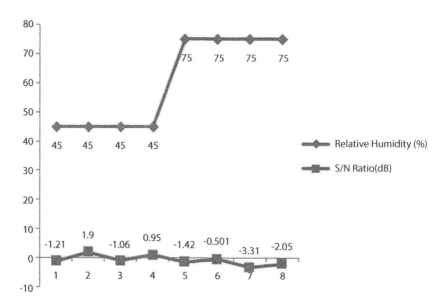

Figure 19.3 Figure showing variation of relative humidity with S/N ratio.

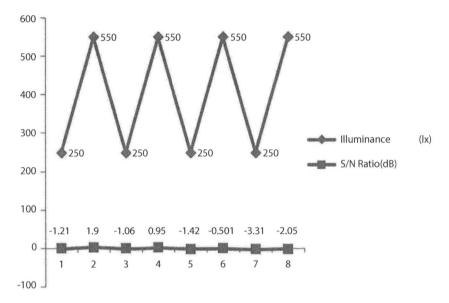

Figure 19.4 Figure showing variation of illuminance with S/N ratio.

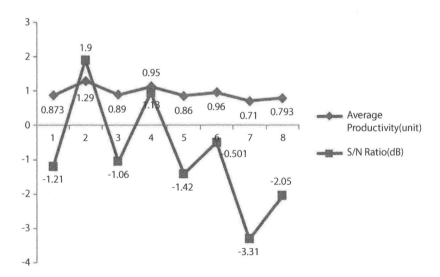

Figure 19.5 Figure showing variation of average productivity with S/N ratio.

level 1 means that the value is higher than level 2. Level 1 has a value of 0.118, while level 2 has a value of −1687. The two levels have a range of 1805. The relative humidity factor is the second factor, and level 1 has a higher value than level 2. Level 1 gives you an S/N ratio of −0.291, while level 2 gives you a range of −1.321 and a value of 1.047. The brightness factor is also a factor; level 1 has a value of −1.716, while level 2 has a value of 0.071. The two tiers have a total range of 1.792. As a result of the S/N ratio range obtained, it can be concluded that temperature factors have the greatest effect on productivity, whereas brightness and relative humidity are the second and third most important factors influencing productivity. This can be demonstrated by considering the location of field experiments in a private room where the three variables to be tested will be monitored during the analysis. As a result, each parameter is set for the duration of the research. As a result, none of the variables are affecting one another.

The ideal temperature was 240°C. The most optimal relative humidity value is 45%, and the most optimum brightness value for workers is 555 lux. This parameter is correct, as are the ISO 7730 guidelines, which state that the best temperature for employee comfort is from 220°C to 28°C. The best range of relative humidity is approximately from 38% to 48 %, as suggested by Tsutsumi et al. [16]. As a result, the Taguchi method of analysis indicates that the relative humidity range for this study is close to what he found in his studies. The brightness of 555 lux meets the specifications defined by the European Standard (EN 12464-1:2002), which specifies that brightness 555 lux is best used for installation work in the automotive industry.

19.4   Conclusions

Overall, the analysis reached the target's goals and scope. The Taguchi method of data analysis is used in this work in order to establish the relationship between environmental factors and productivity. The ideal temperature was 240°C. The most optimal relative humidity value is 45%, and the most optimum brightness value for workers is 555 lux. This research was conducted, so that it will provide the back up to the already assumed research works which usually takes the effect caused by human behavior on the environmental factors. The results of tests conducted on different sample sizes, sectors, and countries can differ. However, the results of the study are limited to the Indian workplace, where worker knowledge of how to improve productivity is still poor.

References

1. Singh, P.K., Chaturvedi, R., Islam, A., Description on analyzing of forces acting on connection rod for various composite materials. *Mater. Today Proc.*, 45, 2856–2860, 2021.

2. Hakkak, M., Nawaser, K., Vafaei-Zadeh, A., Hanifah, H., Determination of optimal leadership styles through knowledge management: A case from the automotive industry. *Int. J. Innov. Technol. Manag.*, 18, 04, 2150012, 2021.

3. Cajochen, C., Alerting effects of light. *Sleep Med. Rev.*, 11, 6, 453–464, 2007.

4. Gavhed, D. and Klasson, L., Perceived problems and discomfort at low air humidity among office workers. 3, 225–230, 2005.

5. Verma, S.K., Sharma, K., Gupta, N.K., Soni, P., Upadhyay, N., Performance comparison of innovative spiral shaped solar collector design with conventional flat plate solar collector. *Energy*, 194, 116853, 2020.

6. Jain, J.K., Dangayach, G.S., Agarwal, G., Banerjee, S., Supply chain management: Literature review and some issues. *J. Stud. Manufacturing*, 1, 1, 11–25, 2010.

7. Chaturvedi, R., Islam, A., Sharma, A., Analysis on manufacturing automated guided vehicle for MSME projects and its fabrication, in: *Computational and Experimental Methods in Mechanical Engineering*, pp. 357–366, Springer, Singapore, 2022.

8. Pradhan, S., Das, S.R., Dhupal, D., Performance evaluation of recently developed new process HAJM during machining hardstone quartz using hot silicon carbide abrasives: An experimental investigation and sustainability assessment. *Silicon*, 13, 9, 2895–2919, 2021.

9. Juslén, H., Wouters, M., dan Tenner, A., The influence of controllable task-lighting on productivity: A field study in a factory. *Appl. Ergon.*, 38, 39–44, 2006.

10. Juslén, H.T., Verbossen, J., Wouters, M.C.H.M., Appreciation of localised task lighting in shift work-a field study in the food industry. *Int. J. Ind. Ergon.*, 37, 5, 433–443, 2007.

11. Sharma, A. and Dwivedi, V.K., Effect of spindle speed, feed rate and cooling medium on the burr structure of aluminium through milling. *IOP Conf. Ser. Mater. Sci. Eng.* IOP Publishing, 998, 1, 012028, December 2020.

12. Araujo, T.R. d., Jugend, D., Pimenta, M.L., Jesus, G.M.K., Barriga, G.D.D.C., Toledo, J.C. d., Mariano, A.M., Influence of new product development best practices on performance: An analysis in innovative Brazilian companies. *J. Bus. Ind. Mark.*, 37, 2, 266–281, 2022.

13. Nicol, F., Wilson, M., Chiancarella, C., Using field measurements of desktop illuminance in European offices to investigate its dependence on outdoor conditions and its effect on occupant satisfaction, and the use of lights and blinds. *Energy Build.*, 38, 7, 802–813, 2006.

14. Parsons, K.C., Environmental ergonomics: A review of principles, methods and models. *Appl. Ergon.*, 31, 581–594, 2000.

15. Tiwari, M., Mausam, K., Sharma, K., Singh, R.P., Investigate the optimal combination of process parameters for EDM by using a grey relational analysis. *Procedia Mater. Sci.*, 5, 1736–1744, 2014.
16. Tsutsumi, H., Tanabea, S.I., Harigayaa, J., II, Guchib, Y., Nakamura, G., Effect of humidity on human comfort and productivity after step changes from warm and humid environment. *Build. Environ.*, 42, 4034–4042, 2007.
17. Wijewardane, S. and Jayasinghe, M.T.R., Thermal comfort temperature range for factory workers in warm humid tropical climates. *Renew. Energy*, 33, 9, 2057–2063, 2008.

## 20

Determining Key Influential Factors of Rural Tourism—An AHP Model

Puspalata Mahaptra[1], RamaKrishna Bandaru[1], Deepanjan Nanda[2] and Sushanta Tripathy[2]*

[1]*School of Commerce and Economics, KIIT deemed University, Bhubaneshwar, Odisha, India*
[2]*School of Mechanical Engineering, KIIT deemed University, Bhubaneshwar, Odisha, India*

Abstract

The Indian tourism industry has emerged as one of the engines of the country growth. Travel and tourism sector have been contributing around 10% to the Indian GDP. The Indian government has been putting lot of efforts to enhance the revenue from the tourism sector. In order to promote the country as a 365-day tourist destination, the ministry proposed the Niche tourism products development scheme. Under the niche tourism products, wellness, adventure, cruise, adventure, medical, golf, polo, meeting incentives conferences & exhibition, film tourism, ecotourism, sustainable tourism, and rural tourism were identified by the Indian Tourism Department. Therefore, the present study focused on rural tourism and aimed to identify the key factors in order to push up the rural tourism as India has almost 68% rural villages. Further, subfactors of the top 3 main factors also ranked to know more contributing subfactors by allotting both local and global weights toward the success of rural tourism. The study identified nine factors with 33 subfactors and ranked the nine factors using Analytic Hierarchy Process (AHP) model. The primary data has collected from the 206 rural tourists and 25 tourism experts and the results reveal that the cultural factor (CF) has ranked at top 1 position followed by heritage and local quality factors. The study is an aid to the ministry of the tourism in order to recognize the key factors as ranked by the respondents and framing the policies to attract the many tourists to the rural destination.

Keywords: Niche tourism product, rural tourism, Indian tourism ministry, cultural factor, AHP model

*Corresponding author: sushant.tripathy@gmail.com

Anita Khosla, Prasenjit Chatterjee, Ikbal Ali and Dheeraj Joshi (eds.) Optimization Techniques in Engineering: Advances and Applications, (323–344) © 2023 Scrivener Publishing LLC

20.1   Introduction

Tourism is one of the important sectors and is the economic power for majority of the countries in the Globe [1]. Before the COVID-19 pandemic, travel and tourism accommodated for 1 in 4 of all new jobs opened all over the world as per WTTC's annual report—2020. The tourism sector has provided an employment opportunity both directly or indirectly to around 334 million of the people in the Globe. Further, the sector has been contributing 10.4% to Global GDP, which equal to US$ 9.2 trillion. It is also clear that some of the county's economy like Singapore, Thailand, etc. has depended only on tourism revenue. India perspective, tourism is one of the driving forces of the economy. The tourism industry in India has emerged as one of the engines of the country growth. This sector has been contributing around 10% to the Indian GDP [2]. Foreign exchange earnings during the 2016 to 2019 registered at a CAGR of 7% is a witness of the potential of the sector. The Indian Government has been putting lot of efforts to enhance the revenue from the tourism sector. As a part, Ministry of Indian tourism extends support to various Agencies at the Central level like Indian Tourism Development Corporation, Port Trust of India, Archaeological Survey of India etc. to build up the potential tourist destinations under their control. The amount of Rs. 40 crore has allocated to different organization to strengthening the tourist destinations by the Ministry. The Tourism Ministry has recognized 19 iconic destinations in the country for enlargement under "Iconic Tourist sites Development Project" and proposed to carry out the enrichment of these sites in connection with certain communities. According to Ministry of Tourism annual report—2020 [2], the Tourism Ministry's initiative to conquer the characteristic of "seasonality" and promote India as a 365-day tourist destination, to attract tourists with specific interests, and to ensure repeat visits for the unique products in which India has a comparative advantage is to identify, diversify, develop, and promote. Under the niche tourism products, wellness, adventure, cruise, adventure, medical, golf, polo, meeting incentives conferences & exhibition, film tourism, ecotourism, sustainable tourism, and rural tourism were identified by the Indian Tourism Department. The tourism ministry has established board for the promotion of the niche tourism products. The ministry also has designed guidelines to support golf, polo, medical, and wellness tourism. The Tourism ministry also initiating to formulate the developing models for the remaining niche tourism products, namely rural tourism, sustainable tourism, etc. Rural tourism is a destination where the tourists use to spend his time engaging in leisure activities on a farm or in a rural areas and its environment [3]. The present study focused on one of the niche tourism products proposed by the central government, i.e., rural tourism and aimed to identify the critical success factors in order to develop the rural tourism destinations. The study used the analytic hierarchical process (AHP), which are most powerful tools of multicriteria decision making (MCDM), to examine the most critical success factors keeping in view of the tourism organizers (experts). The result of the study is an aid to the ministry of the tourism in order to develop the rural destinations.

20.2   Rural Tourism

Rural tourism is one of the tourism products and it reflects art, culture and heritage, rural life, at rural areas, in that way helping the local communities who are socially and economically back word [4]. Past decade, peoples are interesting toward "experiential tourism" to experiencing new traditions, cuisine, cultures, etc. Today, the discriminating traveler is prepared to travel to previously unknown places to acquire the inimitable experience. The traveler is aimed at being an accountable traveler and about giving back to the crowd communities. The rural and villages economies also have practitioners of exclusive arts and crafts in their novel forms that are solid to come by in the cities. The rural tourism displaying the exceptional experiences of villages of India and associated niche areas of tourism such as ecotourism, adventure tourism, farm tourism, etc. offers a gigantic occasion to promote responsible and sustainable tourism in the country. In a single line, rural tourism has been creating many more semiskilled opportunities for the local communities in not only local hotels and catering trades but also in different fields, like transport, heritage, retailing, etc.

Rural tourism generally spotlights on cheeping into the life of rural. True or real life of village can be a tourist attraction. Particularly, this tourism is multidimensional and involves cultural tourism, agricultural tourism, adventure tourism, nature tourism, and ecotourism, which are all directly united. The ministry of tourism has identified around 153 rural locations all over the country under its rural tourism schemes and 36 rural sites are also recognized by the United Nations enlargement program for competence building.

20.3   Literature Review

There are numerous critical factors that influence the success of the rural tourism. Some of the past studies have used different dimensions in order to evaluate the critical success factors of other tourism products like leisure tourism, heritage tourism, entertain tourism, etc. are stated in the following part of this chapter.

The study by Sarma [5] explored the factors that influence the tourist while choosing the rural destination are like suitable accommodation, local people, recommendation of tour operators, price suitability of accommodation, weather condition, infrastructure, and cost of transportation. The authors [6] examined some of the factors which effects the tourist decision making. The author came to the conclusion that the location's environment, culture and history, trip distance, entertainment, children's activities, lodging facilities, and understanding of the local language are the most influential elements. Food is a primary travel preference for tourists [7], and other elements such as local cuisines, delicacies, high-level service quality, and so on are the most influencing aspects for the tourism sector. The study [8], investigated the elements that encourage foreign tourists to travel, including culture, food quality and testing, investigation of new things, escape from daily life, pleasure of recreational activities, and the weather of that location. Deepak [9] studied tourism in Jammu and Kasmir and found that the tourist point, culture, tradition, way of life, and hospitality of a particular region are the most important aspects that attract visitors. Mukesh and Priyanka [1] did a study and found that numerous motivating elements influence a tourist's decision to travel to a given destination, including destination image, incentive to visit, food quality, and taste. Tourism destination marketing 33 CSFs in four categories: strategy, destination image and identity, stakeholder involvement, implementation monitoring and review [10]. Marais *et al.* [11] have identified financial support, human resources, product and customer-related pieces like infrastructure, security, etc. are as the key factors of tourism in South Africa. The authors determined the key success factors of the wine tourism destination are land protection, branding, and lifestyle [12]. Freeman and Thomlinson [13] have found that resources, guidance and strategies are the CSFs of mountain bike tourism. Lin [14] determined that the CSFs for a travel application service provider selection by travel intermediaries in Taiwan are technology, organization, and environment. Singh and Hsiung [15] identified 13 CSFs of Napa's wine tourism industry from the perspective of demand, among which brand quality and satisfactory experience are the most important factors. Further identified seven CSFs for the management of 4 × 4 ecotrails, namely, facilities and accommodation, accessibility, nature and wildlife, trail planning and challenging experience, interpretation, accessibility, value and quality [16]. Kozak and Buhalis [17] examined the CSFs of Turkey-Greece cross border tourism destination marketing, including trust, politics, product, marketing, distribution, accessibility, organizational cooperation, facilitation, planning, education, economic benefits, and socio-cultural benefits. Traveler choices were convenience, curisines, environmental conditions and tourism infrastructure and destination festivals are the key factors for the rural tourism [18]. The traditional festivals, variety activates, cost, infrastructure and environmental conditions are the key factors [19]. Luan et al. [20] has used the AHP method in his study and identified that tourism activates, infrastructures and tourist guides quality were the key factors to decide the tourist destination. The pricing mechanism is the deciding factors for the success of the Indian Rural Tourism Industry. Price should not high which is not affordable and should not be that much low which will not generate any revenue [21]. Xue and Kerstetter [22] suggested that Local people's willingness to adapt to new tourism avenue, community support, local government initiative and tourist budget influence the tourist to choose a particular destination. Kachniewska [23] highlighted the factors like growing environmental conscience among people and funds available with the government for developing the infrastructure of rural destinations which are key influential for success of rural tourism. Tourist age and typology, tourist travel motives, recommendation of others, publicity and advertisement, plays an important role in the promotion of rural tourism [24]. The celebrity as brand ambassador and exclusively their age popularity, reputation, image, and trustworthiness play a crucial role for the success of rural tourist [25]. The study focused [26] on several challenges for the growth of rural tourism and found the resources diminution and urbanization adversely affects the rural tourism. The local people should behave properly and they need to improve the hospitality to attract more and more tourist [27]. Further, the study [28] suggested about the introduction of family business models in rural tourism industry and establishment of local community support will boost the industry development. Shekhar and Kumar [29] suggested that though there many factors conductive for the development of Indian rural tourism, but the factors like infrastructure, growing environmental conscience, local government support and participation of private sectors are very much influential for the success of the rural tourism of India. Kumar and Shekhar [30] carried out a systematic literature review based on rural tourism and tried to find out the link between technology and development of rural tourism.

His study found out that there is significant and positive impact of technology on the way the rural tourism is being conducted. Modern technology has helped in customization of tourism activities and proved to be a key factor for the inclusive growth of the rural tourism industry.

Though few of the studies conducted on growth and development of rural tourism, its impact on employability and economic growth of rural people, rural sustainability, etc. but no substantial study focused on the key success factors of the rural tourism with respect to Indian rural destinations. Keeping in view of the research gap, various key factors for the success of tourism products have been evolved as a result of the literature survey taken up in this study. This research study identifies nine major factors and 33 subfactors that are vital to success of rural tourism. The identified factors are shown in Table 20.1 and Figure 20.1.

20.4   Objectives

Based on the above-discussed factors along with the subfactors, which are essential for the success of the rural tourism, this research work attempts

1. To identify the ranking position of the identified factors.
2. To examine the ranking position of the subfactors under top 3 ranked factors.

20.5   Methodology

The analytical hierarchical method (AHP), which was developed by Prof. Thomas Saaty, is one of popular multi criteria decision-making method that has been used by many researchers in different areas to choose the best results due to its ease of use. This well-accepted method considering both qualitative and quantitative factors supposed to calculate the weights of the multiple criteria among many alternatives according to its relative importance to optimize decision making process. Here, in this study, AHP technique is used to identify and rank the critical influencing factors responsible for the success of the rural tourism.

This study attempts to identify key influential factors that influence the success of the Indian Rural Tourism Industry. This study uses AHP for multifactor analysis and to get the best result, the weight of main factors and weight of subfactors of top ranked factor like cultural factor. The factor and subfactor, which get the highest weight, is having the strong

Table 20.1 Identified key influencing factors of the rural tourism.

Dimension	Subvariables
Cultural Factors	Music, dance, theater of the village (CF1)
	Art and craft of the village (CF2)
	Celebration and cuisine (CF3)
	Spiritual beliefs and life style (CF4)
	Food habits\ Varieties of dishes (CF5)
Heritage Factors	Architecture of the village (HF1)
	Archaeological sites of the village (HF2)
	Rural monuments (HF3)
	Village level activities and games (HF4)
Natural Factors	Rural life style (NF1)
	Climate of the village (NF2)
	Hunting, fishing and Foraging (NF3)
	Forestry and wood (NF4)
Value Added Factors	Parks & children's play grounds (VAF1)
	Shopping & Recreational facilities (VAF2)
	Restaurant & Entertainment services (VAF3)
Promotional Factors	Advertising & Publicity (PF1)
	Establishment of the brand of the village (PF2)
	Tour packages & marketing to positional tourists (PF3)
Infrastructure Factors	Construction of Guest houses\ accommodation (IF1)
	Basic amenities & Parking space (IF2)
	Transport, Water & power availability (IF3)
	Internet service and other services (IF4)

(Continued)

Table 20.1 Identified key influencing factors of the rural tourism. (*Continued*)

Dimension	Subvariables
Safety & Security Factors	Appointment of Security staff & safety symbols (SF1)
	Primary health centers (SF2)
	Local people involvement in security (SF3)
Service & Hospitality	Receptivity of the local residence (SHF1)
	Cleaning and neatness of the village (SHF2)
	Tourism information centers (SHF3)
	Availability of food and beverages & Payment system (SHF4)
Local Quality Factors	Fairs, festivals and wine routes (LQF1)
	Community Support(LQF2)
	Availability of Local products (LQF3)

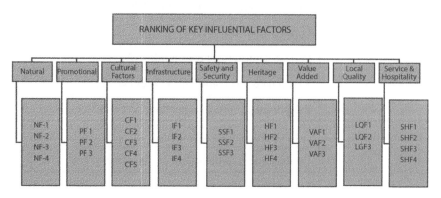

Figure 20.1 AHP-based model for ranking the key influential factors for sustainable growth of rural tourism.

importance for the success of the Industry. Finally, a global score has been determined for ranking each factors and subfactors. There are nine main dimensions, and each of these dimensions include some subdimensions, resulting a total of 33, which have been chosen based on the interviewing with expert of tourism. Based on simple random sample method, the number of 206 tourists and 25 experts of the tourism industry were selected, and the questionnaire delivered and filled up from them and the response rate was 100%. AHP method used here is based on numbers of pairwise comparison, which start with the formation of a hierarchy tree by the decision maker. This formulated tree displays various levels and each factors compared with other factors for which weight age is to be assigned for each factor. Finally, through the hierarchical process, integrated matrix will be formulated on the basis of which optimal decision will be attained.

This specific MCDM Method (AHP) gets going with the following Steps for the Analysis:

Step 1 a decision problem is defined & Development of Hierarchical Framework
The hierarchical structure is developed with the help of survey technique which is divided into three levels. The top level represents the goal, followed by various criteria and next level where criteria further divided into subcriteria, which highlight the details of main criteria.

Step 2 Perform Judgement for Pair wise Comparison
Judgment matrix has been derived from the above pair wise comparison matrix. The above two steps same as a pair wise comparison matrix have been followed to obtain the score vectors. The vector *si* containing the scores of the evaluated option with respect to (*j*) the criteria.

Step 3 Checking of Consistency
To know the consistency test there is a need to calculate the Principal Eigen value (λmax), Consistency Index (CI) and Consistency Ratio (CR). Here, the consistency ratio is calculated by dividing the Consistency Index for the set of judgments by the Index for the corresponding random matrix. According to Saaty if that ratio exceeds 0.1 then the decision based on judgement may be too inconsistent and not reliable. So on the other hand where value of CR is "0," then the judgement are perfectly consistent and acceptable. In nonacceptable CR value, judgement based on surveyed respondents requires to revise again. Consistency Table (Saaty scale for Random index).

Step 4 Development of Overall Priority Ranking
After the pair wise comparison, then weights are assigned by making comparisons between different alternatives under each criteria by following relative preference of Saaty's table (1-9). The formula followed for that, if the total number of alternatives is "n" a total of comparisons to be made is

n (n-1)/2 among all the alternative criteria. The overall priorities are highly influenced by weights given to the respective criteria for which it is necessary to undergo as if analysis to get the best result. For ranking the factors and subfactors in this study the local ranking and global ranking have been referred.

Step 5 Based on ranking selection of Best alternatives
Then on the basis of result of the priorities and what if analysis, an overall ranking will be made, and final recommendation or final decision for criteria can be made.
    Global weights can be calculated with the following formula:

Global weight = Σ {Local weight for criterion (I) x local weight of subcriterion (j) with respect to criterion (i)}

20.6   Analysis

On the basis of extensive literature review and respondents perception, an AHP model has emerged to find out the key influential factors, which lead the success of the tourism Industry. Considering the requirements of the study, Key influencing factor is placed at the top followed by nine dimensions of influential factors in the 2nd level and 32 subdimensions are placed in the 3rd called as criteria level of the Hierarchy Tree. Here, Figure 20.1 is the conceptual model of the proposed research. After formation of the hierarchy tree based on AHP model, a questionnaire was prepared, and the required data was collected from the respondents.

20.7   Results and Discussion

As it is earlier mentioned, the key influential factors are very much required for the success of Indian Rural Tourism, so in this study, it has been attempted to identify and prioritize them through application of AHP method. As significant research has not been done for prioritizing key success factors of rural tourism, this paper attempts to apply AHP method to determine the critical influential factors of the Indian rural tourism. Here under the study nine relevant factors like cultural, heritage, natural, local quality, infrastructure, safety & security, service & hospitality, promotional and value added factors and its 32 subfactors have been identified from detailed literature review and evident from current practices followed in tourism Industries. This study finds that cultural factor is highly important and got the highest rank (1st) as per the expert opinion through the use of AHP analysis with consistency Index followed by heritage and local quality. The findings (from Tables 20.1 to 20.9) provide the ranking of all

Table 20.2 The fundamental scale developed by Saaty (AHP).

The Fundamental Scale of Absolute Numbers Scale	Bases of Ranking	Clarification
1	Equally important	Both criteria contribute equally for objective
3	Moderately important	Based on calculation and judgment, reasonable preference is given to one criteria over the other
5	Strongly important	Based on experience and circumstances, comparatively one criteria is preferred over the other
7	Very strongly important	One criteria or alternative is strictly preferred over the other due to its proven dominance.
9	Extremely important	One criterion is strongly preferred over the other one on the basis of one's strict confidence.
2,4,6 & 8		Mid-values between the respective points

Table 20.3 Saaty Scale for Random Index.

(N)	1	2	3	4	5	6	7	8	9	10
R.I Value	0	0	.52	.89	1.11	1.25	1.35	1.4	1.45	1.49

Source: Saaty, T.L., 1994.

Table 20.4 Pair wise comparison matrix of factors.

Factors	Natural	Promotional	Heritage	Safety & security	Service & hospitality	Cultural	Local quality	Value added	Infrastructure
Natural	1	2	0.3333	4	3	0.25	0.5	5	6
Promotional	0.5	1	0.25	3	2	0.2	0.3333	4	5
Heritage	3	4	1	6	5	0.5	2	7	8
Safety & security	0.25	0.3333	0.1666	1	0.5	0.1429	0.2	2	3
Service & hospitality	0.3333	0.5	0.2	2	1	0.1667	0.25	3	4
Cultural	4	5	2	7	6	1	3	8	9
Local quality	2	3	0.5	5	4	0.3333	1	6	7
Value added	0.2	0.25	0.1428	0.5	0.3333	0.125	0.1666	1	2
Infrastructure	0.1666	0.2	0.125	0.3333	0.25	0.1111	0.1428	0.5	1

Table 20.5 Criteria weightage and ranking of factors.

Natural	0.10888162	4
Promotional	0.076442363	5
Heritage	0.218203759	2
Safety & security	0.037028328	7
Service & hosp.	0.053308698	6
Cultural	0.306952599	1
Local quality	0.154322576	3
Value added	0.025945969	8
Infrastructure	0.018914088	9

λmax -9.407994218, C.I- 0.050999277, C. R-0.035171915, Random Index (9)-1.45.

Table 20.6 Pairwise comparison matrix of subfactors (cultural factors).

Subfactors	CF-1	CF-2	CF-3	CF-4	CF-5	Criteria weights	Ranking
CF-1	1	0.2	0.14286	0.33333	0.11111	0.034820809	5
CF-2	5	1	0.33333	3	0.2	0.134350441	3
CF-3	7	3	1	5	0.33333	0.260231588	2
CF-4	3	0.33333	0.2	1	0.14286	0.067777667	4
CF-5	9	5	3	7	1	0.502819496	1

λmax 5. 242606918, C.I- 0.060651729, C.R-0.05415333, Random Index (5)-1.12.

influential key factors and subfactors of only top 3 ranked factors, which are crucial for the success of rural tourism industry. The finding is also found consistent with the annual report published by Ministry of Tourism of India. Again, subfactors like rural monuments (1st), archaeological sites of the village (2nd), and architecture of the village (3rd) are top 3 ranked subfactors through having the highest global ranking among all subfactors taken into consideration under this study. All these top 3 ranked subfactors are coming under the heritage factors but subfactors of cultural factors (1st) are ranked as 4th, 5th, 6th, and 11th during the study. It is further found that the CI of all the factors <1 indicate the robustness of the results.

Table 20.7 Pairwise comparison matrix of subfactors (heritage factor) with ranking.

Subfactors	HF-1	HF-2	HF-3	HF-4	Criteria Weights	Ranking
HF-1	1	0.2	0.33333	0.33333	.012334510	4
HF-2	5	1	0.33333	3	.45268332	1
HF-3	3	3	1	2	.38654322	2
HF-4	3	0.33333	0.5	1	.1288543	3

Consistency Index-Lambda- 4.013, C.R.-.007695, N-4, CI- 0.013044.

Table 20.8 Pair wise comparison matrix of subfactor (local quality factor).

Subfactors	LQF-1	LQF-2	LQF-3	Criteria Weights	Ranking
LQF-1	1	.2	.1666	.2321887	3
LQF-2	5	1	.3333	.3886754	2
LQF-3	6	3	1	.4867433	1

Consistency Index--Lambda- 3.011, C.R-.007695, N-3, C.I- 0.00346.

Table 20.9 Ranking through global and local weight of factors and subfactors.

Criteria	Description	Local Weight	Local Ranking	Global Weight	Global Ranking
NF	Natural Factor	0.10888162	4	0.10888162	4
PF	Promotional Factor	0.076442363	5	0.076442363	5
HF	Heritage Factor	0.218203759	2	0.218203759	2
SSF	Safety & Security Factor	0.037028328	7	0.037028328	7
SHF	Service & Hospitality Factor	0.053308698	6	0.053308698	6
CF	Cultural Factor	0.306952599	1	0.306952599	1
LQF	Local Quality Factor	0.154322576	3	0.154322576	3
VAF	Value Added Factor	0.025945969	8	0.025945969	8
IF	Infrastructure Factor	0.018914088	9	0.018914088	9
Subcriteria					
With respect to Cultural factors (CF)					
CF1	Music, dance, theater of the village	0.502819496	1	0.013687189	12
CF2	Art and craft of the village	0.134350441	3	0.092501919	5
CF3	Celebration and cuisine	0.034820809	5	0.013687189	6

(Continued)

Table 20.9 Ranking through global and local weight of factors and subfactors. (*Continued*)

Criteria	Description	Local Weight	Local Ranking	Global Weight	Global Ranking
CF4	Spiritual beliefs and life style	0.067777667	4	0.111536342	4
CF5	Food habits\ Varieties of dishes	0.034820809	2	0.064258544	9
With respect to Heritage factor (HF)					
HF1	Architecture of the village	.012334510	4	0.023498351	10
HF2	Archaeological sites of the village	.45268332	1	0.187060637	2
HF3	Rural monuments	.38654322	2	0.224414367	1
HF4	Village level activities and games	.1288543	3	0.139620551	3
Local Quality factor (LQF)					
LQF1	Fairs, festivals and wine routes	.2321887	3	0.018190336	11
LQF2	Community Support	.3886754	2	0.05319861	7
LQF3	Availability of Local products	.4867433	1	0.040555898	8

R.I of (12) = 1.53, λmax= 13799.45339, C.I= 1253.404854, C.R= 819.2188587.

20.8   Conclusions

This study has identified the critical success factors of the runral tourism using AHP methods. The data for this AHP model came from a question-naire survey of 206 respondents who visited rural tourist locations in India during the month of October 2021. The findings shows that cultural fac-tor has been the most preferred factors, followed by heritage factors, local quality factors, natural factors, promotional factors, service & hospitality factors, safety & security factors, value-added factors and Infrastructure factors. According to the results, the culture of the rural village is the most important factor for the success of the rural tourism. Under the cultural factors, art and craft of the village, village life style, food habits, and cel-ebrations are the key element to attract the tourists. The results of the investigation confirm the accuracy and dependability of the AHP model used in this study. According to the findings, the government should rec-ognize communities that meet the aforementioned requirements. Further, it is concluded that respondents have given low ranks to the infrastructure factors and valued added factor. It means the natural beauty of the village should not disturb by constructing guesthouses, parks etc. Therefore, it is suggested that the tourism organizations have to operate the caravans for the accommodation of the rural tourists with out distributing the natural beauty of the village.

20.9   Managerial Implications

Rural tourism is the one which has a huge potential in India as rural population formed 68.84% of the total population (Census of India—2011). India has almost 6, 38,000 villages where most of the rural peoples are primarily depended on agricultural and its allied acclivities. In the past decade, the urban population has been increasing and is requiring the natural and village level environment. This is one of the reasons for increasing the rural tourism contribution for the last 5 years. Keeping in view of this, the Ministry of Tourism has been initiating to identify the new rural destination and promoting them under the Niche tourism project (Annual Report—2020). The present study mainly focused on examination of the critical success factor for the success of the rural des-tinations. The study also examined the ranking position of the identified factors and subfactors of the top 1 factor. The analysis outcomes confirm the accuracy as well as the reliability of the AHP model employed in this study. The results reveals that cultural factor (CF) is the top most ranked factor followed by heritage factors, local quality factors, natural factors, promotional factors, service & hospitality factors, safety & security factors, value added factors and infrastructure factors. There fore, the ministry of the tourism has to recognize the culture of the destination to attract the rural tourists. Based on the art and craft of the village, village lifestyle, food habits, and celebrations the ministry has to recognize the villages to develop under the niche project. The results of this study will be highly helpful to the ministry of the tourism as the inputs to draft the policy matters. The present study would provide to enrich the current literature by recognizing and hierarchizing the different influential factors of rural tourism, which have noteworthy impact on the overall growth of Indian rural tourism industry.

References

1. Ranga, M. and Pradhan, P., Terrorism terrorizes tourism: Indian Tourism effacing myths? *Int. J. Saf. Secur. Tour.*, 5, 26–39, 2014.

2. Ministry of Tourism, *Annual Report, Indian Ministry of Tourism*, Ministry of Tourism, India, 2020, Retrieved from https://tourism.gov.in/sites/default/files/2021-03/Annual%20Report%202021%2021%20English.pdf.

3. Fisher, G. and Beatson, A., The impact of culture on self-service on technology adoption in the hotel industry. *Int. J. Hosp. Tour. Adm.*, 3, 3, 59–77, 2002. https://doi.org/10.1300/J149v03n03.

4. Ministry of Tourism, *Ministry of Tourism Policy Paper-2020*, Ministry of Tourism, India, 2019, Retrieved from https://hrani.net.in/Files/News/167263796_Draft-NTP-for-Consultation-Au.pdf.

5. Sarma, M.K., Influence of information sources on tourists: A segment-wise analysis with special focus on destination image. *Vision J. Bus. Perspect.*, 11, 1, 35–45, 2007.

6. Pars, S.R. and Gulsel, C., The effects of brand image on consumers' choice. *Int. J. Bus. Soc. Sci.*, 2, 20, 227–238, 2011.

7. Amuquandoh, F.E. and Asafo-Adjei, R., Traditional food preferences of tourists in Ghana. *Br. Food J.*, 116, 6, 987–1002, 2013.

8. Yiamjanya, S. and Wongleedee, K., International tourists' travel motivation by push-pull factors and the decision making for selecting Thailand as destination choice. *Int. J. Social Behavioral Educational Economic Business Ind. Eng.*, 8, 5, 1348–1353, 2014.

9. Jain, D., Visitor's perception of destination image- A case study of J&K tourism. *Prestig. Int. J. Manag. IT- Sanchayan*, 2, 1, 91–113, 2013.

10. Baker, M.J. and Cameron, E., Critical success factors in destination marketing. *Tour. Hosp. Res.*, 8, 2, 79–97, 2008. https://doi.org/10.1057/thr.2008.9.

11. Marais, M., Du Plessis, E., Saayman, M., A review on critical success factors in tourism. *J. Hosp. Tour. Manag.*, 31, 6, 1–12, 2017a. https://doi.org/10.1016/j.jhtm.2016.09.002.

12. Jones, M.F., Singh, N., Hsiung, Y., Determining the critical success factors of the wine tourism region of Napa from a supply perspective. *Int. J. Tour. Res.*, 17, 3, 261–271, 2015. https://doi.org/10.1002/jtr.1984.

13. Freeman, R.A.Y. and Thomlinson, E., Mountain bike tourism and community development in British Columbia: Critical success factors for the future. *Tour. Rev. Int.*, 18, 1, 9–22, 2014. https://doi.org/10.3727/154427214X13990420684400.

14. Lin, S.W., The critical success factors for a travel application service provider evaluation and selection by travel intermediaries. *Tour. Manag.*, 56, 10, 126–141, 2016. https://doi. org/10.1016/j.tourman.2016.03.028.

15. Singh, N. and Hsiung, Y., Exploring critical success factors for Napa's wine tourism industry from a demand perspective. *Anatolia*, 27, 4, 1–11, 2016. http://dx.doi.org/10.1080/ 13032917.2016.1160414.

16. Saayman, M. and Klaibor, C.A., Critical success factors for the management of 4x4 ecotrails. *South Afr. J. Bus. Manag.*, 47, 3, 45–54, 2016. https://doi.org/10. 4102/sajbm.v47i3.67.

17. Kozak, M. and Buhalis, D., Cross–border tourism destination marketing: Prerequisites and critical success factors. *J. Dest. Mark. Manage.*, 14, 12, 100392, 2019. https://doi.org/10.1016/j.jdmm.2019.100392.

18. Dahiya, K.S. and Batra, D.K., Tourist decision making: Exploring the destination choice criteria. *Asian J. Manag. Res.*, 7, 2016.

19. Debski, M. and Nasierowski, W., Criteria for the selection of tourism destinations by students from different countries. *Found. Manag.*, 9, 317–330, 2017.

20. Chen, L., Ng, E., Huang, S.-C., Fang, W.-T., A self-evaluation system of quality planning for tourist attractions in Taiwan: An integrated AHP-delphi approach from career professionals. *J. Sustain. Tour.*, 9, 1–18, 2017.

21. Viteri Mejía, C. and Brandt, S., Managing tourism in the Galapagos Islands through price incentives: A choice experiment approach. *Ecol. Econ.*, 117, 1–11, 2015.

22. Xue, L. and Kerstetter, D., Rural tourism and livelihood change: An emic perspective. *J. Hosp. Tour. Res.*, 43, 3, 416–437, 2019. https://doi.org/10.1177/1096348018807289.

23. Kachniewska, M.A., Tourism development as a determinant of quality of life in rural areas. *Worldw. Hosp. Tour. Themes*, 7, 5, 500–515, 2015. https://doi.org/10.1108/WHATT-06- 2015-0028.

24. Panda, B. and Thakkar, A., Celebrity endorsement in tourism advertisement: A study of Gujarat tourism. *J. Content Community Commun.*, 6, 3, 67–70, 2017.

25. Ahmad, A., Jamaludin, A., Zuraimi, N.S.M., Valeri, M., Visit intention and destination image in post-Covid-19 crisis recovery. *Curr. Issues Tour.*, 1–6, 2020. https://doi.org/10.1080/13683500.2020.1842342.

26. Barbieri, C., Agritourism research: A perspective article. *Tour. Rev.*, 75, 1, 149–152, 2019. https://doi.org/10.1108/TR-05-2019-0152.

27. Hadinejad, A., Moyle, B.D., Scott, N., Kralj, A., Nunkoo, R., Residents' attitudes to tourism: A review. *Tourism Rev.*, 74, 2, 157–172, 2019. https://doi.org/10.1108/TR-01-2018-00.

28. Wilson, S., Fesenmaier, D.R., Fesenmaier, J., Van Es, J.C., Factors for success in rural tourism development. *J. Travel Res.*, 40, 2, 132–138, 2001. https://doi.org/10.1177/004728750104000203.

29. Asthana, S. and Kumar, S., Understanding the relationship among factors influencing rural tourism: a hierarchical approach. *J. Organ. Change Manage.*, 32, 2, 21–38, 2021. DOI 10.1108/JOCM-01-2021-0006.

30. Kumar, S. and Asthana, S., Technology and innovation: Changing concept of rural tourism–a systematic review. *Open Geosci.*, 12, 1, 737–752, 2020. https://doi.org/10.1515/geo-2020-0183.

Solution of a Pollution-Based Economic Order Quantity Model Under Triangular Dense Fuzzy Environment

Partha Pratim Bhattacharya[1]*, Kousik Bhattacharya[2], Sujit Kumar De[2],
Prasun Kumar Nayak[2], Subhankar Joardar[3] and Kushankur Das[3]

[1]Department of Computer Science and Engineering, MAKAUT, W.B., India
[2]Department of Mathematics, Midnapore College (Autonomous), India
[3]Department of Computer Science & Engineering, Haldia Institute of Technology,
W.B., India

Abstract

In this chapter, the main issue is environmental pollution, which considers pollution-sensitive economic order quantity (EOQ) model for several items under so many styles of organized via triangular dense fuzzy environment. Here, we constructed a new pollution function via this model, then we have discussed about a substantive case study in a sponge iron industry. We have proposed an EOQ model where we applied the cost minimization technique depending on environmental pollution. The fuzzy model parameters develop a triangular dense fuzzy mathematical model by stirring the demand rate and all cost items of the inventory management system as triangular dense fuzzy numbers. We reorganized the introduced model and analyzed it with an old methodology. This model has been investigated using crisp and triangular dense fuzzy. Finally, we get numerical results when the inventory cost function reaches its minimum. LINGO software and MATLAB software have been used to draw various graphs and numerical illustrations. At last, we support our model using sensitivity analysis with graphical presentations.

Keywords: Modeling, pollution function, triangular dense fuzzy set, optimization

*Corresponding author: partha.bhattacharya1@gmail.com

Anita Khosla, Prasenjit Chatterjee, Ikbal Ali and Dheeraj Joshi (eds.) Optimization Techniques in Engineering: Advances and Applications, (345–362) © 2023 Scrivener Publishing LLC

21.1   Introduction

The introduction section can be split into two subsections; overview and motivation and specific study.

21.1.1   Overview

Carbon emission generated due to production and various way of transportation controls the modern pollution system. Due to globalization, the manufacturing of iron, steel, aluminum, and chemicals plays a substantial role in the environment that we have created. This impact is related to total energy use and different pollution levels coming from various stages in the industrial process. The contribution of ferroalloys production in this severe pollution is minor compared with the base materials such as steel and aluminum. Severe environmental effects of silicon and ferroalloy contribute a considerable portion of this complete man-made pollution. Taking consideration of the by-products of the production of alloy, the daily increment in use of common assets like electrical, as well as electronic products, chemical materials, iron, and steel items is alarming contents. Also, the considerable amount of daily exhausted baby food products, lapsed drugs are a burning issue for our environment. The manufacturers have extensively marketed for updated items to remain in contention of the global game. With the upgradation of commodities, old stocks become meaningless for consumption and thus generate various liabilities causing a severe impact on our surroundings.

We have to control and minimize the surrounding pollution linked with the manufacturing process. To consider the environmental impact in alloy production from a broad view is a real issue. The inclusion of the LCA study dishes out an integrated analysis of resources, substantial, and health effects on the system. Also, it paves the way for environmental advancements by carrying out significant opportunities. In a complete LCA, the total environmental impact consists of all material sources and energy resources inducted in the process start from raw materials to production and transportation.

21.1.2   Motivation and Specific Study

In recent years, a great thrust has been put into the research related to pollution and controlling cost minimization. De *et al.* [1] investigated the pollution mechanism using the triangular dense fuzzy set. Giri *et al.* [2]

reported a price-dependent multi-item inventory model using intuition-istic fuzzy numbers. Also, in recent years, Sarkar *et al.* [3] De and Mahata *et al.* [4], and Karmakar *et al.* [5, 6] provided the outcome of an uneven lot size model for changeable establishment cost and carbon discharge cost in an SC problem and cloudy fuzzy set.

The existence of some nonrandom uncertain parameters in the system triggers the utilization of the Fuzzy system. After the invention of triangu-lar dense lock fuzzy sets by De [7], De and Mahata [8] developed a supply chain back-ordering model under the triangular lock fuzzy environment. Bhattacharya *et al.* [9, 10] demonstrated pollution, sensitive inventory models, with the effect of corruption and global warming and solved these via the fuzzy system. After Zadeh [11] developed the fuzzy set theory, there were multiple reports by renowned scientists across the globe [Kumar *et al.* [12], De and Sana [13], De *et al.* [14]].

Madadi *et al.* [15] came about a multi-tiered inventory management settlement with shipment cost. In 2016, Sarkar *et al.* [16] reported the consequence of changing shipment and outpouring of carbon in their three-echelon SC model. Bryan *et al.* [17] proposed a model that depends on electrical energy on railway shipment. Sithole *et al.* [18] introduced novel mechanization for carbon combustion. For Ferromanganese and steel industry, Sjoqvist *et al.* [19] reported the outcome of carbon excretion during cleaning. The alarming environmental contamination is involved in the Ferro industry-related conveying problem. There is a strong cor-relation between manufacturing, shipment, and carbon release. Recent works suggest the severe knock-on our surrounding by the transport sec-tor, this setback forces us to reconsider the environmental effect due to the transport organizing and operations. The rising environmental awareness, enormous competition, strict policies from the government enforce the manufacturer to minimize this severe pollution for mankind. The different oxides of carbon and nitrogen, and different organic chemicals [20] are the serious culprits. The important model by Benjaafar *et al.* [21] describes the way of controlling carbon footprint in supply chains. Aarthi [22], Chen *et al.* [23], Mancini *et al.* [24], Akten & Akyol [25] suggest a different model (like the EOQ model) and methods to combat the rising carbon footprint. Grzywiński *et al.* [26, 27] analyzed various optimization techniques using metaheuristic algorithm and Jaya algorithm. Eirgash *et al.* [28] described a multiobjective inventory model with trade credit. Bera *et al.* [29] studied the impacts of air pollution in COVID situations in urban areas. A risk assessment of bankrupt cases in European Countries was reported by Misu and Madaleno [30]. Abualigah *et al.* [31] developed an arithmetic optimi-zation algorithm to solve supply chain management problems. Although the major works measure carbon emission through production, transportation plays a major role.

The above-mentioned literature shows no one has investigated the industrial supply chain (SC) problem that includes pollution. Indeed, methodology over fuzzy learning theory was not popularly utilized yet. In our study, we include cost minimization SC problem with pollution under learning fuzzy environment.

The organization of this article is developed as follows: section one is introduction followed by motivation and specific study. Section 21.2 includes preliminaries that focus pollution function and definition of triangular dense fuzzy sets and their defuzzification techniques. Section 21.3 describes notations, assumptions and a case study. Section 21.4 indicates formulation of mathematical model and includes the triangular dense fuzzy mathematical model and its defuzzification method; section 21.5 and 21.6 indicates numerical illustration and sensitivity analysis, respectively. Sections 21.7 develops graphical illustrations; section 21.8 represents the merits and demerits of the article and finally section 21.9 keeps a conclusion followed by scope of future work.

21.2 Preliminaries

In this section, we shall give some definitions and basic formulae that are used to formulate and solve the proposed model.

21.2.1 Pollution Function

From the report by Bhattacharya *et al.* [32], we have taken the differential equation, which governed the production-pollution-production model [the model diagram is displayed in Figure 21.1] given by:

$$\begin{cases} \dfrac{dJ_i(t)}{dt} + \varphi J_i(t) = \gamma p^i, 0 \le t < \infty \\ \text{Subject to } J_i(0) = \gamma' p_0^{i-1}, i = 1, 2, 3, \ldots n \end{cases} \tag{21.1}$$

Solving (21.1) we get

$$J_i(t) = \gamma' p_0^{i-1} e^{-\varphi t} + \gamma p^i (1 - e^{-\varphi t}) \tag{21.2}$$

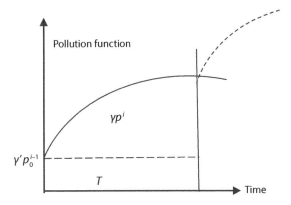

Figure 21.1 Pollution generating model at ith production process.

Now utilizing (21.2) the total amount of pollution after n cycles is given by

$$W_n = \sum_{i=1}^{n} \int_0^{nT} J_i(t) \, dt = \int_0^{nT} \left\{ \gamma' e^{-\varphi t} \sum_{i=1}^{n} p_0^{i-1} + \gamma(1-e^{-\varphi t}) \sum_{i=1}^{n} p^i \right\} dt$$

So average amount of cumulative pollution per cycle over n cycles is

$$\bar{w} = \frac{W_n}{n} = \left[\left\{ T - \frac{(1-e^{-\varphi nT})}{n\varphi} \right\} \frac{\gamma p(p^n-1)}{p-1} + \frac{(1-e^{-\varphi nT})}{n\varphi} \frac{\gamma'(p_0^n-1)}{p_0-1} \right]$$

$$(21.3)$$

21.2.2   Triangular Dense Fuzzy Set (TDFS)

From De *et al.* [1], in this section, we introduce different definitions of dense fuzzy set and triangular dense fuzzy set with their graphic representations and examples for subsequent use.

Definition 2.1. Consider the fuzzy set A whose components are sequence of functions generating from the mapping of natural numbers with a crisp number x. Now if all the components converge to the crisp number x as $n{\to}\infty$ then the fuzzy sets under considerations are called dense fuzzy set (DFS).

Definition 2.2. Let a fuzzy number $\tilde{A} = <a_1, a_2, a_3>$ with $a_1 = a_2 f_n$ and $a_3 = a_2 g_n$ where f_n and g_n are the sequence of functions. If f_n and g_n. In this section, we introduce different definitions are both converge to 1 as $n \to \infty$ then the fuzzy set $\tilde{A} = <a_1, a_2, a_3>$ converges to a crisp singleton $\{a_2\}$. Then we call the fuzzy set $\tilde{A} = <a_1, a_2, a_3>$ as a Triangular dense fuzzy set (TDFS).

Example 2.6. As per definitions (1–4) let us assume the TDFS as follows

A fuzzy number $\tilde{A} = <a_1, a_2, a_3>$ is called triangular dense fuzzy number if, after an infinite time, the set converges to a singleton crisp set. That is, if the time $n \to \infty$, the set $\tilde{A}$ becomes $A = \{a_2\}$. For example, we consider the fuzzy number

$$\tilde{A} = \left\langle a_2\left(1-\frac{\rho}{1+n}\right), a_2, a_2\left(1+\frac{\sigma}{1+n}\right)\right\rangle, \text{ for } 0 < \rho, \sigma < 1 \quad (21.4)$$

Here we see that both $\lim\limits_{n \to \infty} a_2\left(1-\dfrac{\rho}{1+n}\right)$ and $\lim\limits_{n \to \infty} a_2\left(1+\dfrac{\sigma}{1+n}\right)$ converges to a_2. Then its membership function for $n \geq 0$ is given by

$$\mu(x,t) = \begin{cases} 0 & \text{if } x \langle a_2\left(1-\dfrac{\rho}{1+n}\right) \text{ and } x \rangle a_2\left(1+\dfrac{\sigma}{1+n}\right) \\[4mm] \dfrac{x-a_2\left(1-\dfrac{\rho}{1+n}\right)}{\dfrac{\rho a_2}{1+t}} & \text{if } a_2\left(1-\dfrac{\rho}{1+n}\right) \leq x \leq a_2 \quad (21.5) \\[8mm] \dfrac{a_2\left(1+\dfrac{\sigma}{1+n}\right)-x}{\dfrac{\sigma a_2}{1+t}} & \text{if } a_2 \leq x \leq a_2\left(1+\dfrac{\sigma}{1+n}\right) \end{cases}$$

For the left and right α – cuts $L^{-1}(\alpha,t) = a_2\left(1-\dfrac{\rho}{1+n}+\dfrac{\rho\alpha}{1+n}\right)$ and $R^{-1}(\alpha,t) = a_2\left(1+\dfrac{\sigma}{1+n}-\dfrac{\sigma\alpha}{1+n}\right)$ respectively.

21.3 Notations and Assumptions

In this section, we consider the pollution-sensitive EOQ model discuss the notations and assumptions that are used throughout the proposed model. The assumptions and notations for developing an imperfect pollution-sensitive EOQ model by Bhattacharya *et al.* [32].

Notations

h: Holding cost per unit per unit time ($)
s: Set-up cost ($)
c_p: Pollution cost per unit industrial pollution ($)
T: Total cycle time (year) (a decision variable)
D: Demand rate per year
Q: Optimum order quantity (MT) (a decision variable)
z: Total average inventory cost ($)

Assumptions

1. Replenishments are instantaneous.
2. No deterioration and backlog are allowed.
3. Lead time is zero.

21.3.1   Case Study

We visited a sponge iron industry, Rohit Ferro, situated in Bishnupur, Bankura, West Bengal-722122, India [(Latitude, Longitude) = (24.75° N, 87.75° E)] established on 2004. After long discussion with the General Manager, we came to know that they are manufacturer and supplier of refractories items like alumina bricks, mortar etc. Their capacity of producing bricks is 420 metric ton (MT) per month and their major markets in India are situated at the states like West Bengal, Orissa, Bihar Jharkhand, and Chhattisgarh etc. Total number of employees including labors are up to 100 to 150 people in this plant. Also, the plant is running with a marginal profit and the management is always trying to minimize their monthly expenditure. Here some pollution generates during production are running, the produced items are stored and is being exhausted due to regional demand. The monthly regional needs of yarn are 50 metric tons (MT) (Batches).

The research problem is

(i)   Is it possible to control the contamination and reach the least annual average expenditure in our proposed SI production?
(ii)   What is the ideal quantity of order numbers which results in a minimum inventory cost?
(iii) What will be the optimum cycle time so as to minimize the system cost?
(iv)   Whether our triangular dense fuzzy system is more effective to reduce the pollution of the supply chain, as well as average inventory cost than the crisp.

21.4   Formulation of the Mathematical Model

In this section, we discuss the crisp and fuzzy mathematical models via different subsections.

21.4.1   Crisp Mathematical Model

We consider the above assumptions and notations for developing an imperfect pollution-sensitive EOQ model by Bhattacharya *et al.* [32]. Thus, in the proposed mathematical model, we have the average inventory cost of the pollution-sensitive EOQ model as

$$
\left\{
\begin{aligned}
& Minimize\ Z = \frac{1}{2}\,hDT + \frac{s}{T} + c_p\frac{\overline{w}}{T} \\
& \overline{w} = \left[\left\{T - \frac{(1-e^{-\varphi nT})}{n\varphi}\right\}\frac{\gamma p(p^n-1)}{p-1} + \frac{(1-e^{-\varphi nT})}{n\varphi}\frac{\gamma'(p_0^n-1)}{p_0-1}\right] \\
& Q = DT
\end{aligned}
\right.
$$

$$(21.6)$$

21.4.2   Formulation of Triangular Dense Fuzzy Mathematical Model

With dense type flexibility, all our cost parameters $(\tilde{h},\tilde{s},\widetilde{c_p})$ with demand rate $(\tilde{D})$ connected with the model represented as:

$$
\left\{
\begin{aligned}
& \widetilde{\widetilde{h}} = \langle h_1,h_2,h_3\rangle = \left\langle h_2\left(1-\frac{\rho_c}{1+n}\right),h_2,h_2\left(1+\frac{\sigma_c}{1+n}\right)\right\rangle \\
& \tilde{D} = \langle D_1,D_2,D_3\rangle = \left\langle D_2\left(1-\frac{\rho_d}{1+n}\right),D_2,D_2\left(1+\frac{\sigma_d}{1+n}\right)\right\rangle
\end{aligned}
\right.
\quad (21.7)
$$

$$\widetilde{c}_p = \langle c_{p1}, c_{p2}, c_{p3}\rangle = \left\langle c_{p2}\left(1 - \frac{\rho_c}{1+n}\right), c_{p2}, c_{p2}\left(1 + \frac{\sigma_c}{1+n}\right)\right\rangle$$

$$\tilde{q} = \langle q_1, q_2, q_3\rangle = \langle D_1\tau_1, D_2\tau_1, D_3\tau_1\rangle$$

where ρ_c, σ_c, ρ_d, σ_d are fuzzy system deviation parameters for cost vector and demand rate, respectively.

Then the triangular dense fuzzy problem using equation (21.4), our fuzzy problem (21.7) whose dense fuzzy cost parameters $(\tilde{h}, \tilde{s}, \widetilde{c}_p)$ and fuzzy demand rate $(\tilde{D})$ follow the membership function as per subsection 2.2. Simultaneously, the fuzzy order quantity, fuzzy holding cost, setup cost, and fuzzy pollution level are of the form given in (21.8).

$$\left\{ \begin{array}{c} \overline{Minimize\ \tilde{Z}} \cong \dfrac{1}{2}\tilde{h}\tilde{D}T + \dfrac{\tilde{s}}{T} + \widetilde{c}_p\dfrac{\overline{w}}{T} \\[3mm] \overline{w} = \left[\left\{T - \dfrac{(1-e^{-\varphi nT})}{n\varphi}\right\}\dfrac{\gamma\, p(p^n - 1)}{p-1} + \dfrac{(1-e^{-\varphi nT})}{n\varphi}\dfrac{\gamma'(p_0^n - 1)}{p_0 - 1}\right] \\[3mm] \tilde{Q} \cong \tilde{D}T \end{array} \right. \qquad (21.8)$$

21.4.3   Defuzzification of Triangular Dense Fuzzy Model

From equation (21.7), our fuzzy problem has been transformed into a similar Crisp problem using equation (21.6). All our fuzzy components are represented in (21.7, 21.8). We have replaced the respective index parameter with mentioned constraints and might be presented as

$$Minimize\ I(\tilde{z}) \cong \frac{1}{2}\,\tilde{h}\tilde{D}T + \frac{\tilde{s}}{T} + \widetilde{c}_p\frac{\overline{w}}{T} \qquad (21.9)$$

subject to the constraints

$$
\left\{
\begin{array}{l}
I(\tilde{D}) = d_2 + \dfrac{d_2}{4}(\sigma_d - \rho_d)\dfrac{\log(1+t_1)}{t_1}, \\[3mm]
I(\tilde{q}) = t_1\{d_2 + \dfrac{d_2}{4}(\sigma_d - \rho_d)\dfrac{\log(1+t_1)}{t_1}\}, \\[3mm]
I(\tilde{h}) = h_2 + \dfrac{h_2}{4}(\sigma_c - \rho_c)\dfrac{\log(1+t_1)}{t_1} \\[3mm]
I(\tilde{s}) = s_2 + \dfrac{s_2}{4}(\sigma_c - \rho_c)\dfrac{\log(1+t_1)}{t_1} \\[3mm]
I(\tilde{c_p}) = c_{p2} + \dfrac{c_p}{4}(\sigma_c - \rho_c)\dfrac{\log(1+t_1)}{t_1}
\end{array}
\right.
\tag{21.10}
$$

(for details, see Appendix A.1)

21.5 Numerical Illustration

In this section we obtain the minimize optimal cost using the pollution function From the data set mentioned in Table 21.1 and using the pollution function, the obtained minimized results. Also, the computed results using crisp and triangular dense fuzzy of the problem related to SC cost have been shown in Table 21.2. We have considered fuzzy system parameters $(\rho_c, \sigma_c, \rho_d, \sigma_d) = (0.35, 0.3, 0.13, 0.1)$ for our calculation.

Table 21.1 Observed data set.

Set up cost/cycle $s = \$500$	Unit holding cost/ unit item $h = \$2.5$	Unit pollution cost $c_p = \$3$	Demand (MT) $D = 50$
Scale parameter of current pollution $\gamma = 10$	Scale parameter of initial pollution $\gamma' = 5$	Pollution absorbance rate by the nature $\varphi = 0.001$	Threshold amount of pollution rate $P_0 = 1.5$
Rate of current pollution input $p = 2.5$	Production cycle $n = 1$		

Table 21.2 Optimal solution of the SC model under various approaches.

Model/ Approaches	T^* (Year)	$\overline{w}^{*}$ (Year)	q^* (MT)	Z^* ($)	$\dfrac{Z^{*} - Z_{crisp}}{Z_{crisp}} \times 100\%$	$\dfrac{\overline{w}^{*} - \overline{w}_{*}}{\overline{w}_{*}} \times 100\%$
Crisp	2.828	16.22	141.39	368.64	0	0
Triangular Dense Fuzzy	3.295	14.58	158.85	343.43	−6.78	−10.11

Table 21.2 shows that, in crisp model, the average SC cost is $368.64 with respect to optimum pollution rate 16.22% and order quantity 141.39MT and optimum cycle time 2.828 years exclusively. The triangular dense fuzzy approach gives the optimum average SC cost $ 343.43, which is 6.78% less than that of crisp value having optimal pollution rate 14.58%, order quantity 158.85MT and cycle time 3.295 years.

21.6   Sensitivity Analysis

For the above fuzzy game problem, we take the change of fuzzy system parameters $(\rho_c, \sigma_c, \rho_d, \sigma_d)$ with the variation on and from −50% to +50% each. To see the variability of the average inventory cost over the optimal cycle time, order quantity the optimal results are shown in Table 21.3.

Table 21.3 explores that the average inventory cost and corresponding pollution level are the moderately sensitive as a whole with respect to the crisp minimum. The cycle time, the order quantity, the average inventory cost and the pollution index are lie within the bounds [3.12, 3.26] year, [155.92, 162.52] units, $ [341.26, 344.81], and [13.34, 14.86]%, respectively throughout the whole study. Thus, it is seen that the demand parameter is more responsible for reducing the system pollution level exclusively. Moreover, the triangular dense fuzzy model gives the average inventory cost almost 7% lesser than crisp model, which is much significant in any industrial decision-making problem.

21.7   Graphical Illustration

Here we shall draw several graphs obtained from the numerical results taken from Tables 21.2 to 21.3 for justification of our proposed model.

Table 21.3 Sensitivity Analysis on fuzzy deviation parameters of the proposed model.

Fuzzy parameters	% Change	T^* (Year)	q^* (MT)	Z^* ($)	$\overline{w}^*$	$\dfrac{Z^* - Z_{crisp}}{Z_{crisp}} \times 100\%$
P_c 0.35	+50	3.214	157.65	343.21	14.22	−6.73
	+30	3.254	157.92	343.54	14.18	−6.80
	−30	3.142	160.42	342.25	14.26	−7.16
	−50	3.141	162.52	343.61	14.24	−6.78
σ_c 0.3	+50	3.125	160.34	341.56	14.72	−7.34
	+30	3.126	159.28	344.28	14.53	−6.60
	−30	3.251	155.92	342.46	14.61	−7.10
	−50	3.231	156.52	341.26	13.43	−7.42
P_d 0.13	+50	3.217	160.56	344.43	13.62	−6.56
	+30	3.263	159.39	341.27	13.34	−7.42
	−30	3.258	160.27	342.64	14.52	−7.05
	−50	3.271	160.81	343.56	14.46	−6.80
σ_d 0.1	+50	3.215	160.26	345.27	14.57	−6.33
	+30	3.235	160.23	344.19	14.34	−6.63
	−30	3.246	160.14	344.73	14.86	−6.48
	−50	3.264	160.29	344.81	14.57	6.46

Figure 21.2 expresses the variation of order quantity with the variation of cycle time in different kinds of models. We see that the minimum order quantity (156 units) occurs at the cycle time 3.251 years and the maximum order quantity (161 units) occurs at 3.271 years. As the cycle time increases, sometimes, the order quantity curve is also increasing.

Figure 21.3 expresses the variation of average inventory cost with the variation of pollution rate in different kinds of models. We see that the minimum average inventory cost (341) occurs at the pollution rate 13.34%, and the maximum average inventory cost (345.5) occurs at the pollution 14.86%. As the average inventory cost increases, sometimes, the pollution curve is also increasing.

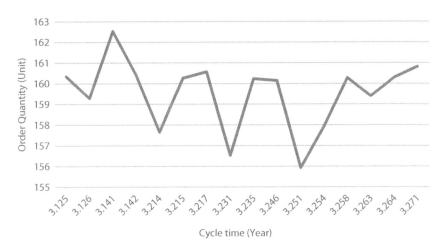

Figure 21.2 Variation of order quantity with respect to cycle time.

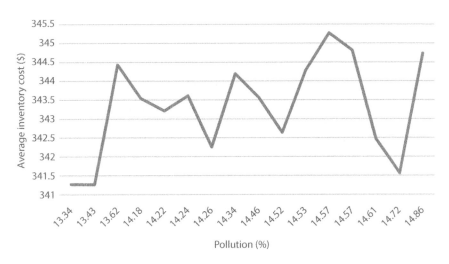

Figure 21.3 Variation of average inventory cost due to pollution index.

Figure 21.4 expresses the variation of order quantity with the variation of pollution rate in different kinds of models. We see that the minimum order quantity (156 units) occurs at the pollution rate 13.43% and the maximum order quantity (163 units) occurs at pollution rate 14.26%. As the cycle time increases, sometimes, the order quantity curve is also increasing.

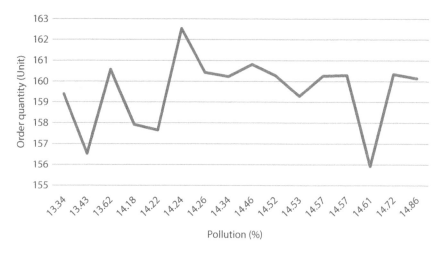

Figure 21.4 Variation of order quantity with respect to pollution index.

21.8   Merits and Demerits

In this section, we shall discuss the merits and demerits of the article.
  Merits

1. Pollution-sensitive SC model has been analyzed.
2. Triangular dense fuzzy number has been utilized for explaining the learning experience of any industrial set up.
3. Numerical illustrations are done over the data collected by a real case study.
4. Sensitivity analysis and graphical illustrations are made to justify the model.

Demerits
The article is silent about three or more layer supply chain modeling, which is more appropriate to study the industrial set ups. Also, the comparative study may be done for different fuzzy systems like monsoon fuzzy, neutrosofic fuzzy systems.

21.9   Conclusion

In this study, we have developed a pollution-sensitive EOQ model under triangular dense fuzzy environment. Here, we developed a new pollution function that measures actual pollution index locally in the environment at the manufacturing site. The model has been developed according to the needs of a case study in a Ferro industry. We compare the proposed methodology with respect to the triangular dense fuzzy approach. Our study reveals that this pollution-sensitive EOQ model gives the minimum average system cost, order quantity, and also optimized pollution index. By applying this approach, the decision makers will have been able to get 6.78% cost benefit than any other models. Under this study, the decision makers could be able to order 158.85 MT for sustainability in the environment with respect to minimum pollution index 14.58 throughout the optimum cycle time duration of 3.295 months alone. Here, triangular dense fuzzy approach is most appropriate than crisp models.

Scope of future work

1. Different kinds of pollution function may be developed.
2. Various model can be studied using different fuzzy systems like Monsoon fuzzy set, Fuzzy approximate reasoning, Doubt fuzzy, Neutrosofic fuzzy set etc.

Acknowledgement

The authors are thankful to the honourable associate editor and the respected anonymous reviewer for their constructive comments for improving this chapter.

Appendix

A.1 Adding left and right α- cuts of membership function of cloudy fuzzy demand $\tilde{d}$ we get,

$$L^{-1}(\alpha,t) + R^{-1}(\alpha,t) = d_1 + d_3 + \alpha(-d_1 + 2d_2 - d_3)$$

Now,

$$
\begin{aligned}
I(\tilde{d}) &= \frac{1}{2t_1} \int\int_{\alpha=0}^{\alpha=1} \{d_1 + d_3 + \alpha(-d_1 + 2d_2 - d_3)\} d\alpha dt \\
&= \frac{1}{2t_1} \int_{t=0}^{t_1} \left[\{(d_1 + d_3)\alpha\}_0^1 - \left\{(d_1 - 2d_2 + d_3)\frac{\alpha^2}{2}\right\}_0^1 \right] dt \\
&= \frac{1}{2t_1} \int_{t=0}^{t_1} \left[(d_1 + d_3) - \frac{1}{2}(d_1 - 2d_2 + d_3) \right] dt \\
&= \frac{1}{2t_1} \int_{t=0}^{t_1} \frac{1}{2}[(d_1 + d_3 + 2d_2)] dt \\
&= \frac{1}{2t_1} \int_{t=0}^{t_1} \frac{1}{2}\left[d_2\left\{\left(1 - \frac{\rho}{1+t}\right) + \left(1 + \frac{\sigma}{1+t}\right)\right\} + 2d_2 \right] dt \\
&= \frac{1}{2t_1} \int_{t=0}^{t_1} \frac{d_2}{2}\left[4 + \frac{\sigma - \rho}{1+t} \right] dt \\
&= \frac{1}{2t_1} \left[\frac{d_2}{2}\{4t_1 + (\sigma - \rho)\log(1 + t_1)\} \right] \\
&= \left(\frac{1}{2t_1} \times \frac{d_2}{2} \times 4t_1 \right) + \frac{1}{2t_1} \times \frac{d_2}{2} \times (\sigma - \rho)\log(1 + t_1) \\
&= d_2 + \frac{d_2}{4}(\sigma - \rho)\frac{\log(1 + t_1)}{t_1} \\
&= d_2\left[1 + \frac{\sigma - \rho}{4}\frac{\log(1 + t_1)}{t_1} \right]
\end{aligned}
$$

References

1. De, S.K. and Beg, I., Triangular dense fuzzy sets and new defuzzification methods. *Int. J. Intell. Fuzzy Syst.*, 31, 469–477, 2017.
2. Giri, S.K., Garai, T., Garg, H., Possibilistic mean of generalized non-linear intuitionistic fuzzy number to solve a price and quality dependent demand multi-item inventory model. *Comput. Appl. Math.*, 40, 4, 1–24, 2021.
3. Sarkar, B., Saren, S., Sinha, D., Hur, S., Effect of unequal lot size, variable set up cost and carbon emission cost in a supply chain model. *Math. Probl. Eng.*, 13, 469–486, 2015.

4. De, S.K. and Mahata, G.C., Decision of a fuzzy inventory with fuzzy backorder model under cloudy fuzzy demand rate. *Int. J. Appl. Comput. Math.*, 3, 2593–2609, 2017.

5. Karmakar, S., De, S.K., Goswami, A., A pollution sensitive dense fuzzy economic production quantity model with cycle time dependent production rate. *J. Clean. Prod.*, 154, 139–150, 2017.

6. Karmakar, S., De, S.K., Goswami, A., A pollution sensitive remanufacturing model with waste items: Triangular dense fuzzy lock set approach. *J. Clean. Prod.*, 187, 789–803, 2018.

7. De, S.K., Triangular dense fuzzy lock sets. *Soft Comput.*, 22, 7243–7254, 2018.

8. De, S.K. and Mahata, G.C., A production inventory supply chain model with partial backordering and disruption under triangular linguistic dense fuzzy lock set approach. *Soft Comput.*, 24, 5053–5069, 2019.

9. Bhattacharya, K., De, S.K., Khan, A., Nayak, P.K., Pollution sensitive global crude steel production–transportation model under the effect of corruption perception index. *Opsearch*, 58, 636–660, 2020.

10. Bhattacharya, K., De, S.K., Nayak, P.K., A robust fuzzy decision making on global warming. *J. Fuzzy Logic Modeling Eng.*, 1, 1–20, 2022.

11. Zadeh, L.A., Fuzzy sets. *Inf. Control*, 8, 338–356, 1965.

12. Kumar, R.S., De, S.K., Goswami, A., Fuzzy EOQ models with ramp type demand rate partial backlogging and time dependent deterioration rate. *Int. J. Math. Oper. Res.*, 4, 473-502, 2012.

13. De, S.K. and Sana, S.S., Fuzzy order quantity inventory model with fuzzy shortage quantity and fuzzy promotional index. *Econ. Model.*, 31, 351–358, 2013.

14. De, S.K., Goswami, A., Sana, S.S., An interpolating by pass to Pareto optimality in intuitionistic fuzzy technique for an EOQ model with time sensitive backlogging. *Appl. Math. Comput.*, 230, 664–674, 2014.

15. Madadi, A., Kurz, M.E. and Ashayeri, J., Multilevel inventory management decision with transportation cost consideration. *Transport. Res. E Log.*, 46, 719–734, 2010.

16. Sarkar, B., Ganguly, B., Sarkar, M., Pareek, S., Effect of variable transportation and carbon emission in a three–echelon supply chain model. *Transport. Res. E*, 91, 112–128, 2016.

17. Bryan, J., Weisbrod, G., Martland., C.D., Rail freight as a means of reducing roadway congestion: Feasibility considerations for transportation planning. *Transp. Res., Transportation Res. Board Natl. Academies, Washington, D.C.*, 2008, 75–83, 2007.

18. Sithole, N.A., Bam, W.G., Steenkamp, J.D., Comparing electrical and carbon combustion-based energy technologies for the production of high carbon ferromanganese: A literature review. *Proceedings of INFACON XV*, Cape Town, South Africa, pp. 25–28, 2018.

19. Sjoqvist, T., Jonsson, P., Berg, H., The effect of ferro manganese cleanness on inclusions in steel. *Proceedings of INFACON IX*, pp. 411–420, 2001.

20. Nouira, I., Hammami, R., Frein, Y., Temponi, C., Design of forward supply chains: Impact of a carbon emissions-sensitive demand. *Int. J. Prod. Econ.*, 173, 80–98, 2016.

21. Benjaafar, S., Li, Y., Daskin, M., Carbon footprint and the management of supply chains: Insights from simple models. *IEEE Trans. Autom. Sci. Eng.*, 10, 99–116, 2010.

22. Aarthi, H.T., Review on mitigation of air pollution in sponge iron industries. *Int. J. Civ. Eng. Technol.*, 8, 8, 1353-1356, 2017.

23. Chen, X., Benjaafar, S., Elomri, A., The carbon-constrained EOQ. *Oper. Res. Lett.*, 41, 2, 172–179, 2013.

24. Mancini., M.S., Galli, A., Niccolucci, V., Lin, D., Bastianoni, S., Wackernagel, M., Marchettini, N., Ecological footprint: Refining the carbon footprint calculation. *Ecol. Indic.*, 61, 390–403, 2016.

25. Akten, M. and Akyol, A., Determination of environmental perceptions and awareness towards reducing carbon footprint. *Appl. Ecol. Environ. Res.*, 16, 4, 5249–5267, 2018.

26. Grzywiński, M., Selejdak, J., Dede, T., Shape and size optimization of trusses with dynamic constraints using a metaheuristic algorithm. *Steel Compos. Struct.*, 33, 5, 747–753, 2019a.

27. Grzywiński, M., Dede, T., Özdemir, Y.I., Optimization of the braced dome structures by using Jaya algorithm with frequency constraints. *Steel Compos. Struct.*, 30, 1, 47–55, 2019b.

28. Eirgash, M.A., Togan, V., Dede, T., A multi-objective decision-making model based on TLBO for the time-cost trade-off problems. *Struct. Eng. Mech.*, 71, 2, 139–151, 2019.

29. Bera, B., Bhattacharjee, S., Shit, P.K., Sengupta, N., Saha, S., Significant impacts of COVID-19 lockdown on urban air pollution in Kolkata (India) and amelioration of environmental health. *Environ. Dev. Sustain.*, 23, 5, 6913–6940, 2020.

30. Misu, N.B. and Madaleno, M., Assessment of bankruptcy risk of large companies: European countries evolution analysis. *J. Risk Financ. Manag.*, 13, 3, 1–28, 2020.

31. Abualigah, L., Diabat, A., Mirjalili, S., Elaziz, M.A., Gandomi, A.H., The arithmetic optimization algorithm. *Comput. Methods Appl. Mech. Eng.*, 376, 113609, 2021.

32. Bhattacharya, K. and De, S.K., Solution of a pollution sensitive EOQ model under fuzzy lock leadership game approach. *Granul. Comput.*, 7, 673–689, 2021.

Common Yet Overlooked Aspects Accountable for Antiaging: An MCDM Approach

Rajnandini Saha[1], Satyabrata Aich[2], Hee-Cheol Kim[3] and Sushanta Tripathy[1*]

[1]KIIT Deemed to be University, Bhubaneswar, Odisha, India
[2]Wellmatix Corporation Limited, Changwon, South Korea
[3]College of AI Convergence/Institute of Digital Anti-aging Healthcare/u-AHRC,
Inje University, Gimhae, South Korea

Abstract

Aging is a complicated organic process concerning a couple of cellular pathways and biochemical activities, which are prompted via way of means of each environmental and inherited factor. A decline in practical ability and strain tolerance with age is related to an expanded chance of contamination and mortality. Nonetheless, the invention that genetic or nutritional interventions can expand existence in a numerous spectrum of evolutionary distinct creatures demonstrates that loss of life may be deferred. Increased self-confidence is one of the most significant benefits of antiaging. When a person looks well, but rather feels great. Maintaining a youthful, appealing appearance can help a person live life to the utmost. Instead of worrying about facial wrinkles or a double chin, they can spend more time enjoying life and attempting new, interesting things. Scopus, Nature Medicine, IEEE, Google Scholar, Wiley Library, and PubMed were used to research and analyze the literature. "Anti-aging," "genetics," "lifestyle," "hormones," and other terms were used in the search. Using the Analytical Hierarchy Process (AHP) method, we utilized a total of 10 factors responsible for aging, we segregated and chose the best out of these factors according to their priority ranking, which are extremely, strongly, and least accountable for aging.

Keywords: Antiaging, metabolism, genetics, healthcare, analytical hierarchy process

*Corresponding author: sushant.tripathy@gmail.com

Anita Khosla, Prasenjit Chatterjee, Ikbal Ali and Dheeraj Joshi (eds.) Optimization Techniques in Engineering: Advances and Applications, (363–376) © 2023 Scrivener Publishing LLC

22.1   Introduction

Why do we become older and fully fledged? When do we start to age? Is there an inherent limit to how aged we can get? These are concerns that humanity has frequently pondered over the last few hundred years. Despite recent advances in molecular biology and genetics, the mysteries of human longevity remain unresolved [1]. Gradually, becoming old throughout the lifetime is aging, which comprises a number of modifications throughout the course of one's life. Individuals' bodily and intellectual capacities degrade as they age, and they are now not capable of manipulate their lives as efficaciously as they formerly did [2]. Transitions consist of retirement, migration, the loss of life of a partner or friend, geriatric symptoms and symptoms which include frailty, a decline in bodily activity, reminiscences difficulties, and so on.

Active Aging is the process of increasing opportunities for health, participation, and security as individuals age in order to improve quality of life. The process of aging is the accumulation of structural and functional changes in an organism as time passes. The changes show as a decline in peak fertility and physiological functions till death [2, 3]. Growing older is both tough and rewarding. There were several hypotheses provided to provide an explanation for the growing old process, however, none seem absolutely adequate. Traditional views on growing old keep that it is miles neither an edition nor a genetically programmed process. Modern biology hypotheses on humans growing old are divided into categories: programmed theories and broken or defective thoughts [1, 4]. According to the programmed hypothesis, growing old adheres to an organic timetable that is a continuation of the only one that governs youth boom and development. This manipulate might be primarily based totally on modifications in gene expression, which might have an impact on structures liable for maintenance, repair, and defense responses. Environmental attacks on dwelling organisms that create cumulative harm at several tiers are highlighted because of the reason for growing old withinside the harm or mistakes hypothesis [5].

Aging theories are classified into two types: programmed theories and erroneous theories. According to programmed views of aging, it is like puberty, is a natural developmental phase. Here are a few examples:

- Programmed aging (phenoptosis)
- Endocrine (hormone) theory
- Immunological theory (and "inflammaging")

Aging erroneous theories contend that aging is the result of a succession of "accidents" rather than a predetermined process. These are so "me" examples:

- Wear and tear theory
- Rate of living theory
- Free radical theory
- Protein cross-linking theory
- Somatic DNA damage theory

These kinds of theories are certainly diametrically opposed, as programmed theories see growing old as a herbal manner that follows a „good" cycle withinside the body, while inaccurate theories see growing old as an twist of fate and a trouble that should be addressed [2, 6]. Because programmed theories describe growing old as a herbal manner that follows a "healthy" cycle withinside the body, those factors of view are diametrically opposed.

22.2   Literature Review

Aging is influenced by a variety of variables. Biological, behavioral, social, psychological, spiritual, and cognitive effects, as well as diseases related with aging, are among these aspects. These factors may not only contribute to aging but also to a variety of disorders associated with the aging process.

There are several other factors that are responsible for aging, however, we have enlisted some of the major factors.

Genetics	Human genes are genetically predisposed to aging. Rapamycin, a protein found in human genes, has been implicated in the regulation of aging and growth. Human longevity and healthy aging are influenced by a fortunate combination of hereditary and nongenetic variables [7]. According to family research, genetic variables account for around 25% of the variation in human longevity.

(Continued)

(*Continued*)

Metabolism	The regulation of aging and growth is heavily influenced by metabolism [3, 8]. Metabolism generates reactive chemicals, also known as oxidising agents, which can hasten the aging process by causing cell damage.
Sleep	Your body is aging beneath the surface as well, and lack of sleep can hasten the process. Most people find that as they become older, they have a harder time falling asleep [9]. They are more likely to wake up during the night and early in the morning. The overall amount of sleep time stays the same or decreases dramatically (6.5 to 7 hours per night). Falling asleep may be more difficult, and you may spend longer time in bed overall.
Nutrition	Changes in your body as you become older can predispose you to deficit in calcium, vitamin D, vitamin B12, iron, magnesium, and a variety of other critical minerals [7, 10]. It could also affect how you perceive physiological symptoms like hunger and thirst.
Lifestyle	Behaviors and lifestyle choices that can have a substantial impact on overall health and well-being, such as fertility, are examples of modifiable lifestyle factors. Sun exposure and smoking were the most significant external factors determining the degree of aging [11]. Alcohol intake, stress, food, exercise, disease, and medicine are all potentially contributing lifestyle factors.
Disorders	Hearing loss, cataracts, and refractive errors, in addition to lower back and neck ache and osteoarthritis, COPD, diabetes, depression, and dementia, are all common worries the various elderly [12–14]. Basically, the psychological, physical & nonsecular diseases.
Decreased cellular functions	As cells age, all of them revel in modifications. They develop in length and lose their cap potential to cut up and multiply. Inside the cell, there is a surge in pigments and fatty compounds, amongst different things (lipids). Many cells both stop to feature or start to characteristic improperly [15, 16].

(*Continued*)

(*Continued*)

Hormones	Changes in the way our bodies are controlled occur naturally as we age. Some target tissues become less receptive to the hormone that controls them. The number of hormones generated may also vary. Other hormone levels in the blood rise, some fall, and some remain steady. Most hormone levels decline as we become older [17–19]. This can have varied impacts depending on the individual. Menopause is caused by a decrease in oestrogen production in women. Men's sexual function and bone density suffer when their testosterone levels fall.
Immunologiocal deterioration	Many modifications arise withinside the immune machine as we age, along with reduced synthesis of B and T cells withinside the bone marrow and thymus, in addition to reduced interest of mature lymphocytes in secondary lymphoid organs [20, 21]. As a result, older humans do now no longer reply as fiercely to immunological attacks as younger humans do [22].
Age	Even if the variety of molecular layers stays constant, the outer pores and skin layer (epidermis) thins with age [23]. Melanocytes (pigment-containing cells) are getting scarce. The last melanocytes develop in size. Aged pores and skin appears thinner, paler, and clearer (translucent).

22.3   Analytic Hierarchy Process (AHP)

It is a method based on mathematics and psychology for organizing and evaluating complex decisions.

It was created in the 1970s by Thomas L. Satty and has been widely researched and refined since then.

It is specifically beneficial for organization decision-making, and it is employed in an extensive variety of decision-making situations across the world, inclusive of government, business, industry, healthcare, and education.

Table 22.1 Satty preference scale.

Intensity of importance	Definition	Explanation
1	Equal importance	Two activities contribute equally to the objective
3	Weak importance of one over another	Experience and judgment slightly favor one activity over another
5	Essential or strong importance	Experience and judgment strongly favor one activity over another
7	Demonstrated importance	An activity is strongly favored and its dominance is demonstrated in practice
9	Absolute importance	The evidence favoring one activity over another is of the highest possible order of affirmation
2, 4, 6, 8	Intermediate values between the two adjacent judgments	When compromise is needed

Calculation based on AHP method.

Table 22.2 Pairwise comparison matrix of the criterion.

	Genetics	Lifestyle	Hormones	Nutrition
Genetics	1	2.1	3.5	4.7
Lifestyle	0.476	1	0.384	0.303
Hormones	0.285	2.6	1	0.344
Nutrition	0.212	3.3	2.9	1
Sum	1.973	9	7.784	6.347

Table 22.3 Normalized matrix.

	Genetics	Lifestyle	Hormones	Nutrition	Row sum	Priority
Genetics	0.506	0.233	0.449	0.740	1.928	0.482
Lifestyle	O.241	0.111	0.049	0.047	0.448	0.112
Hormones	0.144	0.288	0.128	0.054	0.614	0.153
Nutrition	0.107	0.366	0.372	0.157	1.002	0.250
					= 3.99 ~ 4	

Repeating the earlier steps for alternative providers for each criterion. Here we are considering 3 alternative providers i.e., age (A), metabolism (M) and disorder (D).

For Genetics (G),

Table 22.4 Pairwise matrix of the alternate providers w.r.t G.

	A	M	D
A	1	0.38	0.188
M	2.6	1	2.5
D	5.3	0.4	1
Sum	8.9	1.78	3.68

Table 22.4.1 Normalised matrix.

	A	M	D	Row sum	Priority
A	0.11	0.213	0.051	0.374	0.124
M	0.292	0.561	0.679	1.532	0.510
D	0.59	0.224	0.271	1.085	0.361
				= 2.991 ~ 3	

For Lifestyle (L),

Table 22.5 Pairwise matrix of the alternate providers w.r.t L.

	A	M	D
A	1	3.5	2.8
M	0.285	1	0.434
D	0.357	2.3	1
Sum	1.642	6.8	4.23

Table 22.5.1 Normalized matrix.

	A	M	D	Row sum	Priority
A	0.609	0.514	0.661	1.784	0.594
M	0.173	0.147	0.102	0.422	0.140
D	0.217	0.338	0.236	0.791	0.263
				= 2.99 ~ 3	

For Hormones (H),

Table 22.6 Pairwise matrix of the alternate providers w.r.t H.

	A	M	D
A	1	0.263	2.3
M	3.8	1	3
D	0.434	0.33	1
Sum	5.234	1.593	6.3

Table 22.6.1 Normalized matrix.

	A	M	D	Row sum	Priority
A	0.191	0.165	0.365	0.721	0.240
M	0.726	0.627	0.476	1.829	0.609
D	0.082	0.207	0.158	0.447	0.149
				= 2.99 ~ 3	

For Nutrition (N),

Table 22.7 Pairwise matrix of the alternate providers w.r.t N.

	A	M	D
A	1	0.285	4.8
M	3.5	1	4.5
D	0.208	0.222	1
Sum	4.708	1.507	10.3

Table 22.7.1 Normalized matrix.

	A	M	D	Row sum	Priority
A	0.212	0.189	0.466	0.867	0.289
M	0.743	0.663	0.436	1.842	0.614
D	0.044	0.147	0.097	0.288	0.096
				= 2.99 ~ 3	

Calculation of final provider priorities

Criteria wise priority matrix × Criteria priority matrix = Final priorities

Table 22.8 Calculation of final provider priorities.

	G	L	H	N		0.482		
A	0.124	0.594	0.240	0.289		0.112		0.235
M	0.510	0.140	0.609	0.614	×	0.153	=	0.508
D	0.361	0.263	0.149	0.096		0.25		0.250
								= 0.993 ~ 1

Since Metabolism (M) is having the greater priority value, this proves to be the best alternate provider.

22.4   Result and Discussion

All the 10 factors we have introduced are responsible for aging of an individual. However, we have selected four most appropriate factors which best describes the function of aging in an individual. These are genetics (G), lifestyle (L), hormones (H), nutrition (N). After the analysis through AHP method, we found out, among these four factors we used as criteria the priority wise ranking came out be (refer Table 22.3):

    i.   Genetics(G) proves to be the extremely responsible factor for aging with the priority of 0.482.

    ii.   Lifestyle (L) with the priority of 0.250 being very strongly responsible.

    iii.   Hormones (H) is strongly responsible with the priority of 0.153.

    iv.   Nutrition (N), moderately responsible for aging with the priority of 0.112.

Alternatives or the subcriteria, such as age (A), metabolism (M), and disorder (D), serve to be the driving factors of each of the main criteria we have used, i.e., genetics, lifestyle, hormones & nutrition. After the AHP analysis of each subcriteria alone w.r.t the main criteria we found that,

    i.   For genetics (refer Table 22.4.1), Metabolism is extremely accountable with the priority 0.510. Disorder is moderately accountable with the priority of 0.361. Age is least accountable with the priority of 0.124.

    ii.   For Lifestyle (refer Table 22.5.1), Age is extremely accountable with the priority 0.594. Disorder is moderately accountable with the priority of 0.263. Metabolism is least accountable with the priority of 0.140.

    iii.   For Hormones (refer Table 22.6.1), Metabolism is extremely accountable with the priority 0.609. Age is moderately accountable with the priority of 0.240. Disorder is least accountable with the priority of 0.149.

    iv.   For Nutrition (Table 22.7.1), Metabolism is extremely accountable with the priority 0.614. Age is moderately accountable with the priority of 0.289. Disorder is least accountable with the priority of 0.096.

After the calculation of final provider priorities, we found out that metabolism (M) is having the greater   priority value 0.508 (refer Table 22.8), this proves to be the best alternate provider or the subcriteria which is accountable for all the main criteria.

22.5   Conclusion

Our analysis suggests that all the factors are in one way or other relatable toward aging, these are either extremely, strongly or least accountable to slow the process of aging of an individual. Metabolism proves to be the best subcriteria accountable for all the main cafeterias used and genetics as a factor to be extremely responsible for aging.

The backside line is that all of us age, irrespective of which getting older concept is accurate or whether or not getting older is the sum of numerous theories. Even if we can not keep away from the "one hundred twenty years" cited in Genesis, a sure lifestyle conduct can be capable of putting off our dying through a considerable amount, or at least provide us with a better first class of lifestyles in percentage to the range of years we live. There is not any regulation pointing out that with the intention to be healthy, you should be bored stupid with a pastime, or eat dull food.

References

1. Aliper, A.M., Csoka, A.B., Buzdin, A., Roumiantsev, S., Moskalev, A. *et al.*, Signaling pathway activation drift during aging: Hutchinson-Gilford progeria syndrome fibroblasts are comparable to normal middle-age and old-age cells. *Aging*, 7, 26–37, 2015.
2. Lozano, R., Naghavi, M., Foreman, K., Lim, S., Shibuya, K., Aboyans, V. *et al.*, Global and regional mortality from 235 causes of death for 20 age groups in 1990 and 2010: A systematic analysis for the global burden of disease study 2010. *Lancet*, 380, 2095–2128, 2013.
3. Makarev, E., Cantor, C., Zhavoronkov, A., Buzdin, A., Aliper, A., Csoka, A.B., Pathway activation profiling reveals new insights into age-related macular degeneration and provides avenues for therapeutic interventions. *Aging (Albany. NY)*, 6, 1064–1075, 2014.
4. Moskalev, A.A., Aliper, A.M., Smit-McBride, Z., Buzdin, A., Zhavoronkov, A., Genetics and epigenetics of aging and longevity. *Cell Cycle*, 13, 1063–1077, 2014.
5. Moskalev, A., Chernyagina, E., de Magalhães, J.P., Barardo, D., Thoppil, H., Shaposhnikov, M. *et al.*, Geroprotectors.org: A new, structured and curated

database of current therapeutic interventions in aging and age-related disease. *Aging (Albany. NY)*, 7, 616–628, 2015.

6. Murray, C.J.L. and Lopez, A.D., *The Global Burden of Disease: A Comprehensive Assessment of Mortality and Disability from Diseases, Injuries, and Risk Factors in 1990 and Projected to 2020*, Harvard School of Public Health on behalf of the World Health Organization and the World Bank, Boston, MA, 1996.

7. Pew Research Center, *Living to 120 and Beyond: Americans' Views on Aging, Medical Advances and Radical Life Extension*, Pew Research Center Religion and Public Life Project, Washington, DC, 2013.

8. Tacutu, R., Budovsky, A., Yanai, H., Fraifeld, V.E., Molecular links between cellular senescence, longevity and age-related diseases-a systems biology perspective. *Aging (Albany. NY)*, 3, 1178–1191, 2011.

9. Zhavoronkov, A., *The Ageless Generation: How Advances in Biomedicine Will Transform the Global Economy*, Palgrave Macmillan, New York, NY, 2013.

10. Zhavoronkov, A., Longevity expectations in the pension fund, insurance, and employee benefits industries. *Psychol. Res. Behav. Manage.*, 8, 27–39, 2015.

11. Zhavoronkov, A. and Cantor, C.R., Methods for structuring scientific knowledge from many areas related to aging research. *PloS One*, 6, e22597, 2011.

12. Zhavoronkov, A., Debonneuil, E., Mirza, N., Artyuhov, I., Evaluating the impact of recent advances in biomedical sciences and the possible mortality decreases on the future of healthcare and social security in the United States. *Pensions Int. J.*, 17, 241–251, 2012.

13. Zhavoronkov, A. and Litovchenko, M., Biomedical progress rates as new parameters for models of economic growth in developed countries. *Int. J. Environ. Res. Public Health*, 10, 5936–5952, 2013.

14. Jin, K., Simpkins, J.W., Ji, X., Leis, M., Stambler, I., The critical need to promote research of aging and aging-related diseases to improve health and longevity of the elderly population. *Aging Dis.*, 6, 1, 1–5, 2015.

15. Stambler, I., Jin, K., Lederman, S., Barzilai, N., Olshansky, S.J., Omokaro, E., Barratt, J., Anisimov, V.N., Rattan, S., Yang, S., Forster, M., Byles, J., Aging health and R&D for healthy longevity must be included into the WHO work program. *Aging Dis.*, 9, 2, 331–333, 2018.

16. World Health Organization (WHO), United Nations, Department of Economic and Social Affairs, Population Division, *World Population Prospects: The 2019 Revision*, 2019, Accessed December 2019.

17. Stambler, I., Life extension: Opportunities, challenges, and implications for public health policy, in: *Anti-Aging Drugs: From Basic Research to Clinical Practice*, A. Vaiserman, (Ed.), pp. 537–56, Royal Society of Chemistry, London, 2017.

18. Goldman, D.P., Cutler, D.M., Rowe, J.W., Michaud, P.C., Sullivan, J., Peneva, D., Olshansky, S.J., Substantial health and economic returns from delayed aging may warrant a new focus for medical research. *Health Aff.*, 32, 10, 1698–1705, 2013.

19. Chang, E.S. *et al.*, Global reach of ageism on older persons' health: A systematic review. *PloS One*, 15, e0220857, 2020.

20. Hamel, M.B. *et al.*, Patient age and decisions to withhold life-sustaining treatments from seriously Ill, hospitalized adults. *Ann. Intern. Med.*, 130, 116–125, 1999.

21. Limpawattana, P., Phungoen, P., Mitsungnern, T., Laosuangkoon, W., Tansangworn, N., A typical presentations of older adults at the emergency department and associated factors. *Arch. Gerontol. Geriatr.*, 62, 97–102, 2016.

22. Lavan, A.H. and Gallagher, P., Predicting risk of adverse drug reactions in older adults. *Ther. Adv. Drug Saf.*, 7, 11–22, 2016.

23. American Geriatrics Society Beers Criteria Update Expert Panel, American Geriatrics Society 2019 Updated AGS Beers Criteria® for Potentially Inappropriate Medication Use in Older Adults. *J. Am. Geriatr. Soc.*, 67, 674–694, 2019.

## 23

E-Waste Management Challenges in India: An AHP Approach

Amit Sutar, Apurv Singh, Deepak Singhal, Sushanta Tripathy*
and Bharat Chandra Routara

*School of Mechanical Engineering, KIIT Deemed to be University, Bhubaneswar,
Odisha, India*

Abstract

E-waste or waste electrical and electronic equipment (WEEE) can refer to any electrical or electronic appliance or device or a sub-assembly or component of the same which is regarded as not useful or obsolete by the user and hence discarded. The growing quantity of generated electronic and electrical waste in India is a pressing concern for the government and the citizens. Domestic generation, as well as foreign imports, is stressing the already overburdened waste management system. Lack of government regulation and strict enforcement of such regulation is complicating the issue. E-waste contains many toxic substances and its improper handling can cause harm to human health and the environment. Environmentally sustainable e-waste management in India is very limited due to a number of factors like the lack of technology, lack of funds, inadequate number of players in the sector, ignorance among recyclers, etc. The challenges in environmentally sound management (ESM) in India are many, and this chapter aims to identify and rank the same on the basis of their importance using the analytic hierarchy process (AHP). The factors or challenges were identified and sent to experts who ranked them according to their importance. Then, we performed the AHP and calculated the relative weightages of the different factors and also calculated the consistency ratio.

Keywords: E-waste, India, MCDM, AHP

*Corresponding author: sushant.tripathy@gmail.com

Anita Khosla, Prasenjit Chatterjee, Ikbal Ali and Dheeraj Joshi (eds.) *Optimization Techniques in Engineering: Advances and Applications*, (377–392) © 2023 Scrivener Publishing LLC

23.1 Introduction

The first great concern for the Indian scenario is the enormous volume of e-waste generated every year and the number is ever-increasing. This is due to the decreasing lifespan of electronic and electrical devices because of the high rate of obsolescence of present technology and the increased adoption of new technologies [1]. As India's economic engine is gaining pace, the size of the middle class is also increasing which is translating into more disposable income-buying more consumer goods of which a significant portion comprises of electrical and electronics. Also, the rapid rate of urbanization fuelled by the search of a better life and livelihood is putting increasing pressure on urban waste management systems, including e-waste management systems [2]. Another concern is the shortcomings of the local, state, and the central government in managing this problem of e-waste. The lack of government enthusiasm to enforce the regulations against import of e-waste from foreign countries is adding to the problem of increasing volumes of WEEE [3]. The country lacks an adequate framework of legislation dictating the exact way of handling e-waste. The ignorance among municipal waste handlers leads them to employ untrained individuals to "handle" all sorts of waste, most of which ultimately end up burned or in landfills or being sold to local electronics repair shops [4]. Lack of proper technology to handle e-waste effectively is a major factor in effective e-waste management. E-waste recycling can be a profitable business but it is also very expensive and requires advanced technologies not easy to acquire [5]. And then, there is the lack of interest and incentives to turn WEEE recycling into a profitable business [6]. Most of India's waste handling takes place at the local level. These local handlers have practiced the old method of "segregation-selling-burning-burying" for decades and are resistant to change. They do not see the e-waste the collect as a means to a profitable end because they lack the vision, the technology, and the organizational structure to make a profitable venture out of it. True, there are a number of new, small startups in India seeking to exploit the potential of e-waste, but they are very few considering volume e-waste generated. The absence of proper e-waste collection systems is another hindrance [7]. Every kind of waste—household, biological, electrical, electronic—goes into the same bin. Extraction of e-waste becomes more complicated when it is mixed up with other waste, some of which may be soiled. Untrained rag pickers segregate the waste they have collected into those which can be sold locally and those which cannot be sold. The latter are more often than not burned for volume reduction. This causes the release of toxic elements usually present in WEEE into the atmosphere and environment causing air and soil pollution and present serious health hazards for the rag pickers [8]. Municipal corporations usually lack the funds needed to really make a difference in the management of e-waste [9].

23.2   Literature Review

Table 23.1 presents a comprehensive review on e-waste mmanagement.

23.3   Methodology

The main objective of this chapter is to find out all there is to know about the generation and management of e-waste in India in order to have a better understanding of the situation, which will help us in the identification and prioritization of the various barriers or challenges to proper, eco-friendly e-waste management in India by the application of the analytical hierarchy process (AHP). Hence, we have read a number of relevant papers written by different scholars about WEEE management and control in India.

23.4   Results and Discussion

Based on the exhaustive literature review and expert opinions, we have finalized the nine challenges for e-waste management in India, as shown in Table 23.2. Next, experts were consulted to construct a pairwise comparison matrix. Experts have used the following scale (see Table 23.3) of relative importance to establish the pairwise comparison matrix. Pairwise comparison matrix is shown in the Tables 23.4 and 23.5.

The following pairwise comparison matrix gives the relative importance of the various factors (challenges) with respect to the ultimate objective. We have also included the sum of the column elements in each column. Next, we generated the normalized pairwise comparison matrix by dividing each element of the pairwise comparison matrix with the sum of the elements of the respective column to which that element belongs. We have also calculated the weightage of each factor by calculating the average of all the elements in each row in the normalized pairwise comparison matrix.

Table 23.1 Review of literature on e-waste mmanagement.

Author Reference No.	Year	Industry	Country	Key Findings
[10]	2017	E-waste recycling sites in Bangalore	India	Harmful effects of e-waste chemicals on hair, soil and air. Its harmful effects on human health due to unskilled way of e-waste management.
[7]	2016	General	Global	Several tools like PRO and EPS are introduced to control E-waste management. This can help to develop jobs and business also E-Friendly procedure are followed for management of E-waste
[11]	2006	General	Africa	As Africa is not capable of making high quality of electronic devices it has started importing these from developed country at low cost, which gets dumped easily and hence causes E-waste. But Africa has no capacity to deal with E-Waste properly which causes harm to many residents of Africa.
[4]	2017	IT Sector	India	India is the second greatest exporter of E-Waste from created nations but, most of the E-Waste administration is done in incompetent path by needy individuals which prompts release of numerous harmful synthetic concoctions in nature and furthermore influences human wellbeing in different ways. The E- waste is expanding day-by- day. Hence, it is critical to oversee it as quickly as time permits.

(*Continued*)

Table 23.1 Review of literature on e-waste mmanagement. (*Continued*)

Author Reference No.	Year	Industry	Country	Key Findings
[3]	2017	General	Global	Here we found about the scenario of E-Waste in different countries and how they have tried to control them in various ways by seating up companies or by making laws for consumers, manufactures and transporters.
[12]	2015	General	Northern Vietnam	It provided information about the concentration of different types of PDES in various sites of Northern Vietnam and how it is increasing day- by-day. Also, the effect of these types of alternatives on human health and the food chain.
[13]	2016	General	India	An investigation in Bangalore, India demonstrated that casual reusing of e-waste is the explanation behind substantial metal defilement of close-by soil and human tissues. As indicated by a study, the defilement because of reusing of e-squander in India and China is 80% higher than whatever remains of the world. Thus, we investigated the different methods for e-squander reusing on soil, water, air, flora and fauna close to the e-squander reusing zones.

(*Continued*)

Table 23.1 Review of literature on e-waste mmanagement. (*Continued*)

Author Reference No.	Year	Industry	Country	Key Findings
[14]	2012	IT Sector	India	In case of recycling of e-waste is not undertaken properly. The risks and harmful effects poised by improper e-waste treatment in developing countries should be properly addressed. Normally the discarded electronic items lie untouched in Indian households and offices due to inadequate knowledge regarding management of e-waste
[9]	2004	Computer and television industry.	India	It has been assessed that 75% of hardware are put away in homes because of absence of satisfactory information with respect to its appropriate disposal. Developing nations like India should wake up and stop the imposing business model of certain created nations who dump
[15]	2012	Computer Industry	United States	E-waste management system in US is also improper. A certain study shows approx. 40 million used computers (scrap computers) entered the e-waste management system in the year 2010, from which approx. 30% were used again in domestic areas,6-29% of the scrap were exported to developing countries,17-21% were dumped in landfills domestically and the remaining 20-47% of the computer e- waste were collected from houses for the purpose of recycling. This shows that even in a well-developed country like the United States, the proper e- waste management system is not present.

(*Continued*)

Table 23.1 Review of literature on e-waste mmanagement. (*Continued*)

Author Reference No.	Year	Industry	Country	Key Findings
[16]	2010	General	Switzerland, India	Here we found out about the developed way of recycling of e-waste Switzerland and compared it with Indian e-waste management system and also how it can become a proper business if maintained in a proper way.
[17]	2008	Guiyu (area in Guangdong province in China) industrial area	Guiyu, Guangdong China	Guiyu City in Chaoyang locale, Southeast China, is a rice developing district and the business here is being overwhelmed by the reusing of e-squander since the late 20th century; it has also been found that soil in this area is highly contaminated with harmful heavy metals. Testing of soil of a particular area in Guiyu city was done. Results showed us that at certain sites where e-waste recycling process was carried out, there the level of contamination was considerably higher than that of those areas where other kind of wastes were dumped or burnt, such as clothes and other household wastes. People are unaware about the danger posed by the improper e-waste treatment in this area.

(Continued)

Table 23.1 Review of literature on e-waste mmanagement. (*Continued*)

Author Reference No.	Year	Industry	Country	Key Findings
[18]	2005	General	India and Switzerland	Switzerland has become the 1st country across the globe to establish a formal system for management of e-waste. Switzerland even crossed the target set by the Swiss government of collection of e-waste of 4 kg/capita by reaching a high of 9 kg/capita. Swiss law on management of waste concentrates on "polluter pays principle" and has adopted 3Rs—reduce, reuse, recycle. However, in case of India, the situation of e-waste management is poor. India produces approximately 1.38 million obsolete PCs which is one of the biggest contributors to e-waste. The proper treatment of e-waste is not present in India as it depends on the earning factors, in India, a e-waste recycler earns approximately CHF 4.1/day while in Switzerland, this figure rises up to CHF 150/day. Another reason for proper recycling method not being adopted in a country like India is that the knowledge regarding the harmful effects the improper disposal of e- waste was not available to Indian people, it came into picture recently

(Continued)

Table 23.1 Review of literature on e-waste mmanagement. (*Continued*)

Author Reference No.	Year	Industry	Country	Key Findings
[19]	2010	General	China	There is a need for China to concentrate on dealing with the e-waste imported from foreign countries; a bigger matter of concern is to deal with domestically generated e-waste. As study of e-waste production in China in the year 2003 forecasts that the number will increase drastically by the end of the decade. The Chinese government do have the knowledge regarding the harmful effects of improper treatment of e-waste on environment, thus they have implemented various environmental laws, norms etc. in order to minimize the harmful effects. The general environmental law of China implements rules considering "pollution prevention" principle and "polluter pays" principle.

Table 23.2 List of challenges.

Serial no.	Factor code	Challenge
1.	F1	Enormous volume of e-waste generated.
2.	F2	Ignorance among consumers.
3.	F3	Ignorance among municipal waste handlers.
4.	F4	Lack of strict enforcement of Government regulations.
5.	F5	Lack of interest and incentives to make e-waste management a profitable venture.
6.	F6	Lack of proper technology to handle e-waste.
7.	F7	Lack of proper e-waste collection systems.
8.	F8	Improper handling of e-waste.
9.	F9	Lack of funds.

Table 23.3 Scale of relative importance.

Serial no	Importance level	Numerical rating
1.	Equal importance	1
2.	Moderate importance	3
3.	Strong importance	5
4.	Very strong importance	7
5.	Extreme importance	9
6.	Intermediate values	2, 4, 6, 8
7.	Values for inverse comparison	(1/2), (1/3), (1/4), (1/5), (1/6), (1/7), (1/8), (1/9)

The different factors or challenges have been ranked in the descending order of their importance based on their calculated weightage as as shown in Table 23.6.

From the results, it is clear that the biggest challenge faced by the Indian e-waste management systems is the huge volume of e-waste that is being generated annually and the fact that the quantity is increasing. No matter

Table 23.4 Pairwise comparison matrix.

Factor	F1	F2	F3	F4	F5	F6	F7	F8	F9
F1	1	7	5	2	3	4	2	3	2
F2	0.143	1	0.2	0.167	0.250	0.250	0.167	0.143	0.5
F3	0.2	5	1	0.25	1	0.5	0.25	1	2
F4	0.5	6	4	1	5	3	4	2	7
F5	0.333	4	1	0.2	1	0.5	0.5	0.167	0.5
F6	0.250	4	2	0.333	2	1	3	1	0.25
F7	0.5	6	4	0.25	2	0.333	1	4	2
F8	0.333	7	1	0.5	6	1	0.25	1	5
F9	0.5	2	0.5	0.143	2	4	0.5	0.2	1
Sum	3.759	42	18.7	4.843	22.25	14.583	11.667	12.51	20.25

Table 23.5 Normalized pairwise comparison matrix.

Factor	F1	F2	F3	F4	F5	F6	F7	F8	F9	Weightage
F1	0.2660	0.1670	0.2674	0.4130	0.1348	0.2743	0.1714	0.2398	0.0988	0.2258
F2	0.0380	0.0238	0.0107	0.0345	0.0112	0.0171	0.0143	0.0114	0.0247	0.0206
F3	0.0532	0.1190	0.0535	0.0516	0.0449	0.0343	0.0214	0.0799	0.0988	0.0620
F4	0.1330	0.1429	0.2139	0.2065	0.2247	0.2057	0.3428	0.1599	0.3457	0.2195
F5	0.0886	0.0833	0.0535	0.0413	0.0449	0.1029	0.0429	0.0133	0.0247	0.0550
F6	0.0665	0.0833	0.1070	0.0688	0.0899	0.0686	0.2571	0.0799	0.0123	0.0926
F7	0.1330	0.1429	0.2139	0.0516	0.0899	0.0228	0.0857	0.3197	0.0988	0.1287
F8	0.0886	0.1670	0.0535	0.1032	0.2697	0.0686	0.0214	0.0799	0.2469	0.1221
F9	0.1330	0.0476	0.0267	0.0295	0.0899	0.2743	0.0429	0.0160	0.0494	0.0788

Table 23.6 Ranking of the challenges.

Rank	Factor code	Factor/challenge	Weightage
1	F1	Enormous volume of e-waste generated.	0.2258
2	F4	Lack of strict enforcement of Government regulations.	0.2195
3	F7	Lack of proper e-waste collection systems.	0.1287
4	F8	Improper handling of e-waste.	0.1221
5	F6	Lack of proper technology to handle e-waste.	0.0926
6	F9	Lack of funds.	0.0788
7	F3	Ignorance among municipal waste handlers.	0.0620
8	F5	Lack of interest and incentives to make e-waste management a profitable venture.	0.0550
9	F2	Ignorance among consumers.	0.0206

how well organized the system is or what technologies we have at hand, this is and always will be a major hurdle because adapting the existing system to handle more and more at such a fast rate is a lot to ask. Contributing to this problem is the lack of enforcement of government rules, especially those banning or limiting the import of WEEE from other countries. Lax on the part of the government automatically means freedom to do anything with e-waste in India. The absence of a proper, segregated waste collection system is another important challenge for the e-waste recycling industry. Proper collection is the first step to proper management of any form of waste, especially e-waste. Improper handling of e-waste by untrained individuals is also of great concern since this may potentially endanger the health of the same as well as the health of the people living in the surrounding areas as the number of toxic materials contained in e-waste is many and have already been discussed. The next challenges include unavailability of proper resources and funds, which is really a challenge in almost any sector. From the analysis, we can conclude that ignorance among municipal handlers and consumers and the lack of interest in pursuing e-waste management as a business opportunity is the least of all concerns. Indian consumers are known to spend judiciously and almost all WEEE, especially mobiles and computers, that have any resell value are exchanged for newer things at a discounted price. As for the lack of adequate number of WEEE management companies, e-waste management is still a pretty nascent sector in India, considering the fact that normal waste management systems are well below the adequate or required standards. And statistics show that young entrepreneurs are taking notice of this gap and looking to exploit it thanks to their 'can create a successful Start-up' mindset and the encouragement and incentives offered by the Indian Government to promote such a mindset.

23.5   Conclusion

Hence, we can conclude that to ensure proper, environmentally sustainable e-waste management in India, we must start with addressing the issue of quantity. Of equal importance is the need for strict enforcement of proper legislation by appropriate bodies. Proper guidelines regarding the management of WEEE by competent bodies are a must and so is training workers in the sector. Improper handling of e-waste by untrained individuals is also of great concern since this may potentially endanger the health of the same as well as the health of the people living in the surrounding areas as the number of toxic materials contained in e-waste is many and have already been discussed. Private companies are the key to future e-waste management solutions since they are better capable of managing this business efficiently and ensure a profitable outcome. As for the lack of adequate number of WEEE management companies, e-waste management is still a pretty nascent sector in India, considering the fact that normal waste management systems are well below the adequate or required standards. And statistics show that young entrepreneurs are taking notice of this gap and looking to exploit it thanks to their "can create a successful start-up" mindset and the encouragement and incentives offered by the Indian Government to promote such a mindset. The government can help by bringing about collaborations with experienced foreign e-waste management bodies to ensure essential transfer of technical know-how related to WEEE management. With luck and a lot of dedication on various ends, India will emerge from being a dumping ground of e-waste for the entire world to a nation that adds to its economy by capitalizing on what others throw away.

References

1. Ikhlayel, M., An integrated approach to establish e-waste management systems for developing countries. *J. Clean. Prod.*, 170, 119–130, 2018.
2. Cucchiella, F., D'Adamo, I., Koh, S.L., Rosa, P., Recycling of WEEEs: An economic assessment of present and future e-waste streams. *Renew. Sust. Energ. Rev.*, 51, 263–272, 2015.
3. Zeng, X., Duan, H., Wang, F., Li, J., Examining environmental management of e-waste: China's experience and lessons. *Renew. Sust. Energ. Rev.*, 72, 1076–1082, 2017.
4. Borthakur, A. and Singh, P., Electronic waste in India: Problems and policies. *Int. J. Environ. Sci.*, 3, 1, 353–362, 2012.
5. Kumar, A., Holuszko, M., Espinosa, D.C.R., E-waste: An overview on generation, collection, legislation and recycling practices. *Resour. Conserv. Recy.*, 122, 32–42, 2017.
6. Zeng, X., Song, Q., Li, J., Yuan, W., Duan, H., Liu, L., Solving e-waste problem using an integrated mobile recycling plant. *J. Clean. Prod.*, 90, 55–59, 2015.
7. Garlapati, V.K., E-waste in India and developed countries: Management, recycling, business and biotechnological initiatives. *Renew. Sust. Energ. Rev.*, 54, 874–881, 2016.
8. Ha, N.N., Agusa, T., Ramu, K., Tu, N.P.C., Murata, S., Bulbule, K.A., Tanabe, S., Contamination by trace elements at e-waste recycling sites in Bangalore, India. *Chemosphere*, 76, 1, 9–15, 2009.
9. Ramachandra, T.V. and Saira, V.K., Environmentally sound options for e-wastes management. *Envis J. Hum. Settlements*, 5, 2004.
10. Zeng, X., Yang, C., Chiang, J.F., Li, J., Innovating e-waste management: From macroscopic to microscopic scales. *Sci. Total Environ.*, 575, 1–5, 2017.
11. Schmidt, C.W., Unfair trade e-waste in Africa. *Environ. Health Perspec.*, 114, 4, a232–5, 2006.
12. Matsukami, H., Tue, N.M., Suzuki, G., Someya, M., Viet, P.H., Takahashi, S., Takigami, H., Flame retardant emission from e-waste recycling operation in northern Vietnam: Environmental occurrence of emerging organophosphorus esters used as alternatives for PBDEs. *Sci. Total Environ.*, 514, 492–499, 2015.
13. Awasthi, A.K., Zeng, X., Li, J., Relationship between e-waste recycling and human health risk in India: A critical review. *Environ. Sci. Pollut. Res.*, 23, 12, 11509–11532, 2016.
14. Borthakur, A. and Govind, M., Emerging trends in consumers' e-waste disposal behaviour and awareness: A worldwide overview with special focus on India. *Resour. Conserv. Recy.*, 117, 102–113, 2017.
15. Kahhat, R. and Williams, E., Materials flow analysis of e-waste: Domestic flows and exports of used computers from the United States. *Resour. Conserv. Recy.*, 67, 67–74, 2012.

16. Wath, S.B., Dutt, P.S., Chakrabarti, T., E-waste scenario in India, its management and implications. *Environ. Monit. Assess.*, 172, 1-4, 249–262, 2011.

17. Xiezhi, Y., Markus, Z., Magnus, E., Anna, R., Maria, L., Hung, W.M., Roland, W., E-waste recycling heavily contaminates a Chinese city with chlorinated, brominated and mixed halogenated dioxins. *Organohalogen Compd.*, 70, 813–816, 2008.

18. Khetriwal, D.S., Kraeuchi, P., Widmer, R., Producer responsibility for e-waste management: Key issues for consideration–learning from the Swiss experience. *J. Environ. Manage.*, 90, 1, 153–165, 2009.

19. Yu, J., Ju, M., Williams, E., Waste electrical and electronic equipment recycling in china: practices and strategies. *Sustain. Syst. Technol.*, 1–1, 2009.

24

Application of k-Means Method for Finding Varying Groups of Primary Energy Household Emissions in the Indian States

Tanmay Belsare[1]*, Abhay Deshpande[1], Neha Sharma[2] and Prithwis De[3]

[1]*Symbiosis Statistical Institute, Symbiosis International University, Pune, India*
[2]*Analytics and Insights, Tata Consultancy Services, Pune, India*
[3]*MBU, Tata Consultancy Services, London, United Kingdom*

Abstract

Household emissions being one of the major types of emissions and GHG being the reason behind climate change, it is necessary to find out the regions with dominant emissions. The taxonomic approach to group things characterized by different attributes with the k-means is used in this chapter. As various Indian states contribute to primary energy household emissions in varying levels, knowing group of states that contributes significantly can be useful for policymakers, therefore, the purpose of the study is to cluster Indian states, such that they are similar within groups and dissimilar between groups. The study objects for the analysis are 35 Indian states, including the union territories and 11 variables relating to the primary energy household emissions of GHG and different fuel types for the year 2015. The primary energy household emissions can be related to the residential emissions defined by the IPCC. In this chapter, particularly k-means clustering method was used to find the groups of the Indian States and agglomerative hierarchical method to find the initial clusters. LPG and Kerosene are two of the major fuels primarily used in the households of India for cooking purposes. The performed analysis is based on the phase III emission estimates from GHG Platform India.

Keywords: GHG, residential emissions, HCEs, k-means method

Corresponding author: tanmaybelsare123@gmail.com

Anita Khosla, Prasenjit Chatterjee, Ikbal Ali and Dheeraj Joshi (eds.) Optimization Techniques in Engineering: Advances and Applications, (393–408) © 2023 Scrivener Publishing LLC

24.1 Introduction

The pace at which the climate is changing is a matter of concern and greenhouse gases (GHG) being the reason behind it. The warming of the earth's atmosphere occurs when the balance of GHG in the atmosphere increases, leading to climate change [1]. In June 1992, the first international convention for controlling GHG emissions and tackling climate change was adopted and called the United Nations Framework Convention on Climate Change (UNFCCC) [2]. The Kyoto Protocol, an extension of UNFCCC, was adopted in 1997, sets a limit on GHG emissions by committed developed nations and targets to reduce it [3]. Subsequently, the developing countries also started making commitments to reduce emissions through the Delhi Declaration (2002), Bali Roadmap (2007), and the Copenhagen Accord (2009) [2]. The latest movement in this direction started in December 2015 in the form of Paris Agreement, which is signed by 196 nations as a legally binding international treaty. The Paris Agreement works on a goal to put a limit on global warming to 2°C and aims to restrict the increase to 1.5°C [2, 3]. Detailed information concerning about the GHG and its calculation from different sources, such as energy, industrial processes, land-use, agriculture, residential, waste, etc. are given in guidelines issued by Intergovernmental Panel on Climate Change (IPCC). According to the IPCC 2006 guidelines, the gases responsible for the greenhouse effect are carbon dioxide (CO_2), methane (CH_4), nitrous oxide (N_2O), chlorofluorocarbons (CFCs) [4]. Among these, the contribution of CO_2 in the climate change is of utmost importance. An older study in India says that total household energy consumption contributes around 75% of total energy consumption [5]. Most used fuels in India for the household purposes are LPG, kerosene, animal dung, and crop residue [6].

The aim of this paper is

1. Establishing the resemblance between residential emissions and primary energy household emissions
2. Identifying trend in the direction of primary energy household emissions from LPG, Kerosene and Diesel in India
3. Classifying the Indian states according to their varying primary energy household emissions, finding out the important fuel sources, the factor behind the formation of cluster and suggesting how can India control its primary energy household emissions.

"Emissions from fuel combustion in the households" are defined as "residential emissions" by IPCC. With reference to the definition, the resemblance between residential CO_2 emissions and household carbon emissions (HCEs) lies in the emissions from household due to different fuel usages. The GHG emissions from the consumption of fuels and electricity in the household usage are interchangeably termed as household/domestic/residential emissions. Because of the limitation of a globally standardized rule on account of the HCEs, this issue of different terminologies arises besides there are numerous expressions which causes confusion [2, 7].

In this paper, gases CO_2, CH_4, and N_2O were considered, as these are the gases with the most threat. As per the availability of fuel types for all the states in GHG Platform India, fuels, namely LPG, diesel, and kerosene, was used for analysis. This paper is divided into six sections. The next section will discuss about the methodologies used in calculating HCEs, various literature related to HCEs. Following, the section 24.3 will cover materials and methods used for the problem statement. Section 24.4 consists of the exploratory data analysis (EDA). Various important results were briefed in the section 24.5, respectively. The findings were discussed and concluded in the section 24.6 and the references are mentioned at the end.

24.2   Literature Review

This section will summarize HCEs, methods that are used for calculating HCEs and numerous studies associated with it. The HCEs can be generalized into three different types. Primary energy HCEs are emissions from the usage of gas, coal, oil and other fuels. The indirect combustion of energy usage like heat and electricity would be considered in secondary energy HCEs. The household consumption HCEs comprises of emissions from the indirect household energy consumption of clothing, food, housing, medical care, culture, transportation, communication, household equipments, entertainment, education, and other services [2].

HCEs are partitioned into different types in literature, and there are a variety of methods for the calculation of HCEs. Emission coefficient method (ECM) is predominantly used for primary energy HCEs and secondary energy HCEs (direct emissions), whereas methods like input-output method (IOM), life-cycle analysis (LCA), and consumer lifestyle approach (CLA) are used for household consumption HCEs (indirect emissions). These quantification methodologies are described briefly by Zhang *et al.* (2015) [8]. Wang *et al.* (2018) used the ECM and CLA for calculating energy carbon emissions and products carbon emissions from 30 provinces of China, deducing that heat and electricity are the primary reasons for the energy carbon emissions in households and products HCEs are majorly due to high carbon emission categories like food, residences, transport, and communication [7]. Huang *et al.* [9] applied ECM for direct CO_2 emissions and used IOM to calculate indirect CO_2 emissions from urban and rural households of the Beijing, Tianjin, Shanghai, and Chongqing in China, concluding that electricity accounts for a larger proportion of direct HCEs. Ahmad *et al.* (2015) analyses per capita HCEs from the direct usage of energies like cooking fuels, electricity and private transportation in the Indian cites for the period 2009 to 2010. Authors used random effects and fixed effects model for identifying the important factors, interpreting that household size and income are the most important factors for household emissions [10]. Úrsula *et al.* (2021) measured the energy usage relating to the households and their GHG emissions for the years 2007 to 2015 in Lima City; furthermore, analysis was performed on districts using multiple regression. The authors concluded that LPG was the main source of energy in lower income households, whereas increase in population and affluence to be the reasons behind household related energy usage and emissions [11]. Ramchandra *et al.* [12] estimates GHG from different sectors like domestic, transportation, industrial, energy, waste, agriculture, and livestock managements from Delhi, Greater Bangalore, Greater Mumbai, and Chennai of India using equations provided in the IPCC 1996 GHG inventories guidelines. Jingjing *et al.* (2021) identified the trend in the direction of HCEs, deducing the increasing studies due to the arising awareness of HCEs in global warming. The authors also found out that USA and China are the countries with most active researches on HCEs. Additionally, the major theme of the HCEs research is focused on explanation of household consumption, the emissions and its persuading factors [13].

Kijewska & Bluszcz [14] applied the clustering approach to group the 28 European countries with respect to their GHG emissions and GHG emissions per capita for the year 2012, resulting into forming four clusters. Ghanbari *et al.* (2021) carried out the study of cluster analysis with 18 variables including the total GHG emissions in the Middle East and Central Asia for the period 1994 to 2014, which resulted in the formation of five main clusters [15].

Much of the household emissions literature is either focused on calculating, analyzing the emissions, and finding significant factors, also household emissions sector is not much explored in India. GHG platform India uses the guidelines of IPCC for measuring and tracking GHG data of India, considering different states and sectors [16]. As, the clustering approach for forming groups of states in India based on their primary energy household emissions is not yet addressed, this paper will focus on finding suitable groups of Indian states for the primary energy household emissions of CO_2, CH_4, and N_2O.

24.3   Materials and Methods

24.3.1   Data Preparation

The GHG Platform India (GHGPI) estimates the emissions from different sectors using the standard guidelines issued by IPCC 2006. The energy sector emission estimates were between 2005 and 2015 and comprising of the fuel combustion emissions from electricity, energy production, transportation, and others, including residential, agriculture, fisheries, commercial etc. The residential emission data of Phase III emission estimates from the energy sector is used in this paper [16]. Before using the data, pre-processing included deleting rows with NA values, dropping unneeded columns, filtering emissions from residential sector and renaming them to primary energy household emissions using Python. The primary energy household emissions from 2015 were used to form the clusters, as this was the latest data available and were standardized before performing cluster analysis. 35 objects including the states and union territories were used for performing cluster analysis considering the primary energy household CO_2, CH_4, and N_2O emissions from the fuel types like LPG, Kerosene, Diesel and Fuelwood. In 2015, the primary energy household emissions were subzero for Delhi, hence were replaced as zero. The population data for 2015 was taken from Census of India (Census India) [17].

24.3.2   Methods and Approach

24.3.2.1   Cluster Analysis

Cluster analysis is one of the unsupervised learning algorithms. The goal of cluster analysis is to form a group of observations that are similar within and different between. To create such clusters, several methods exist, such as the agglomerative method in hierarchical clustering and k-means method of nonhierarchical clustering. At times, a combination of both is used to form the clusters [14]. Determining number of clusters is a drawback of hierarchical clustering, whereas predetermining number of clusters is a problem in k-means clustering.

24.3.2.2   Agglomerative Hierarchical Clustering

Each observation is considered as a separate cluster in the first step of agglomerative method. With the help of distance metric (Euclidean) and linkage method (average linkage) similar observations and clusters are grouped, eventually ending in a single cluster of all observation.

Dendrogram

The hierarchical clustering results in the formation of dendrogram which helps in summarizing the process of clustering. Dendrogram helps in getting an idea about choosing number of clusters and also records in those clusters can be identified.

24.3.2.3   K-Means Clustering

In the k-means algorithm, knowledge regarding initial number of clusters (k) present is required. k-means algorithm depends on the value of k. It is an iterative algorithm, which segregates the data into nonoverlapping groups of k such that there is a similarity in within-cluster data points and difference in between-cluster data points. The cluster points are assigned such that sum of squared distance between the points and centroid of the cluster is as minimum as possible. The following are the four steps involved in k-means algorithm.

    i.   Choose initial clusters (k) to start with
    ii. Each data point is allocated to the cluster with the nearest centroid at every step
    iii. Cluster centroids are recalculated when the data points in the clusters are lost or gained and perform step 2 again
    iv. Stop at the instant when moving the data points causes to increase the cluster variance.

Approach

    1. Finding initial number of clusters using agglomerative hierarchical clustering.
    2. To find and interpret the clusters using k-means algorithm.

24.4   Exploratory Data Analysis

Uttar Pradesh, Maharashtra, Tamil Nadu, West Bengal, and Karnataka were the top 5 highest contributors of primary energy HCEs from LPG, Kerosene and Diesel in the year 2015, while the smallest emitter was Lakshadweep (Figure 24.1). Considering all the fuel types, the highest

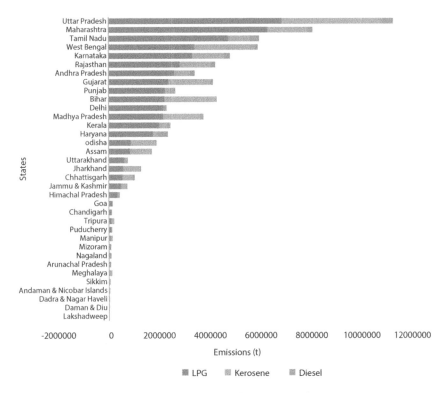

Figure 24.1 Primary energy HCEs of states by fuel type (2015).

total primary energy HCEs from Uttar Pradesh were 10879412.05 (t) and the lowest total primary energy HCEs were 2064993.62 (t) from Lakshadweep.

Considering all the 35 States and Union territories (Figure 24.2), the primary energy HCEs from LPG substantially increased from 28413897 (t) in 2005 to 48565070 (t) in 2015 i.e., 171% increase, whereas HCEs from Kerosene decreased from 29191188 (t) in 2005 to 20706423 (t), i.e., 141% decrease. The primary energy HCEs from Diesel saw a rise too, but compared to the emissions from LPG and Kerosene, Diesel emissions are less. The total primary energy household CH_4 and N_2O emissions from LPG, Kerosene and Diesel over the period 2005 to 2010 are described in Figure 24.3. Initially, the CH_4 emissions increased from 6531 (t) in 2005 to 7058 (t) in 2010, following a decline and again increased to 7133 (t) in 2015. A slight rise in the emissions from CH_4 can be seen, whereas the N_2O emissions were constant. The emissions from CH_4 and N_2O are quite less as compared to the emissions from CO_2.

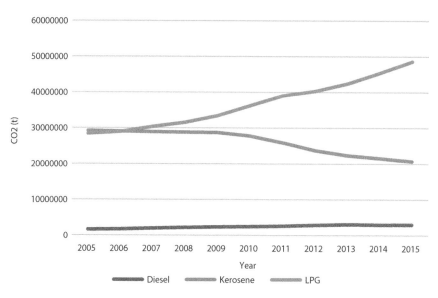

Figure 24.2 Total primary energy HCEs by fuel type.

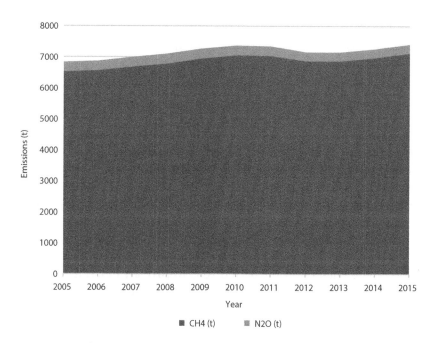

Figure 24.3 Total primary energy household emissions of LPG, kerosene, diesel by CH_4 and N_2O.

24.5   Results and Discussion

Before performing the cluster analysis, for comparability, each source of primary household emissions was standardized as,

$$z_i = \frac{x_i - \overline{x}}{S_x}$$

where $\overline{x}$ and S_x are mean and standard deviation of each of the emission source.

The clustering analysis used in this study was performed using SPSS software. Figure 24.4 represents dendrogram, which is an important output from agglomerative hierarchical clustering. It can be clearly seen that three or four clusters of the states can be formed. Using k = 3 and k = 4, the k-means is performed to confirm the value and the one with the best formation of clusters is chosen. When k = 4, not much difference was observed between the distances of the two clusters centroids, hence value of k = 3 is chosen, as it showed sufficient distance between the cluster centroids.

Table 24.1 describes analysis of variance. The F-value describes the importance of variables in the formation of clusters. The F-value of kerosene (49.051) and LPG (F = 48.880) are higher; hence, these fuel types have

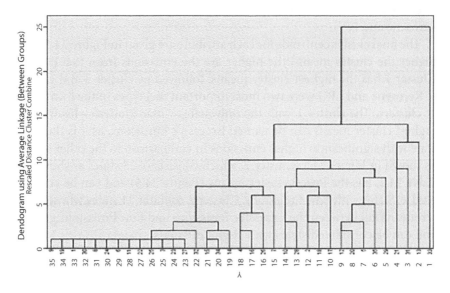

Figure 24.4 Dendrogram.

Table 24.1 Analysis of variance.

Variables	Cluster sum of squares	df	Error sum of squares	df	F	p-value
LPG_CO$_2$	12.808	2	0.262	32	48.880	0.000
Kerosene_CO$_2$	12.819	2	0.261	32	49.051	0.000
Diesel_CO$_2$	10.314	2	0.418	32	24.683	0.000
LPG_CH$_4$	12.808	2	0.262	32	48.880	0.000
Kerosene_CH$_4$	12.819	2	0.261	32	49.051	0.000
Diesel_CH$_4$	10.314	2	0.418	32	24.683	0.000
Fuelwood_CH$_4$	8.925	2	0.505	32	17.683	0.000
LPG_N$_2$O	12.808	2	0.262	32	48.880	0.000
Kerosene_N$_2$O	12.819	2	0.261	32	49.051	0.000
Diesel_N$_2$O	10.314	2	0.418	32	24.683	0.000
Fuelwood_N$_2$O	8.925	2	0.505	32	17.683	0.000

an important role in the formation of clusters. The diesel ($F = 24.683$) and Fuelwood ($F = 17.683$) fuel types are of less importance compared to the kerosene and LPG.

The final cluster centroids for each attribute are given in Figure 24.5. The higher the cluster means, the higher are the emissions from that cluster. Cluster 1 has the highest cluster means, followed by cluster 3 and cluster 1. Kerosene and LPG were two most important fuel types in the formation of clusters. The cluster 1 with the only state—Uttar Pradesh—having the highest cluster means can be named Excessive Emissions, as it is the only state with significantly higher emissions in comparison to the other states, as shown in Figure 24.1. Cluster 2, which consists of 23 states as shown in Table 24.2, has the lowest cluster means (Figure 24.5) and can be considered as States with Low Emissions. Cluster 3 contains 11 states whose cluster means fall between the Excessive Emissions and Low Emissions groups and can be considered states with High Emissions.

Figure 24.6 depicts bubbles of clusters on the India map, where the size of the bubble is proportional to the population. The low emissions group has a lower population, the high emission group has a higher population

Table 24.2 Clusters and distances of the states from the centroids.

Cluster 1	Distance from cluster 1	Cluster 2	Distance from cluster 2	Cluster 3	Distance from cluster 3
Uttar Pradesh	0	Andaman & Nicobar	0.85482	Andhra P	1.32613
		Arunachal P	0.77853	Bihar	2.80199
		Assam	1.75045	Gujarat	1.87528
		Chandigarh	3.31893	Haryana	4.47546
		D&N Haveli	0.83945	Karnataka	1.02376
		Daman & Diu	0.87958	Kerala Madhya P	2.19354 1.44246
		Delhi	2.40225	Maharashtra	3.19035
		Goa	0.79606	Rajasthan	2.44881
		Himachal P	0.23150	Tamil Nadu	3.25075
		Jammu & Kashmir	0.52204	West Bengal	2.61677
		Jharkhand	1.13479		
		Lakshadweep	0.89472		
		Manipur	0.73903		
		Meghalaya	0.67174		
		Mizoram	0.82467		
		Nagaland	0.76779		
		Odisha	2.86973		
		Puducherry	0.75332		
		Punjab	3.02798		
		Sikkim	0.86601		
		Tripura	0.54622		
		Uttarakhand	0.55384		

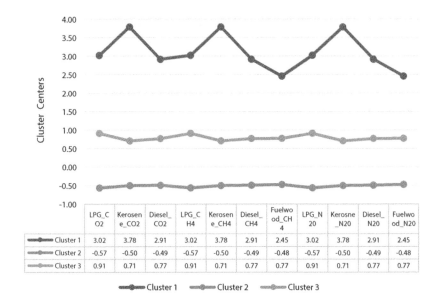

	LPG_C O2	Kerosen e_CO2	Diesel_ CO2	LPG_C H4	Kerosen e_CH4	Diesel_ CH4	Fuelwo od_CH 4	LPG_N 20	Kerosne _N20	Diesel_ N20	Fuelwo od_N20
Cluster 1	3.02	3.78	2.91	3.02	3.78	2.91	2.45	3.02	3.78	2.91	2.45
Cluster 2	-0.57	-0.50	-0.49	-0.57	-0.50	-0.49	-0.48	-0.57	-0.50	-0.49	-0.48
Cluster 3	0.91	0.71	0.77	0.91	0.71	0.77	0.77	0.91	0.71	0.77	0.77

Cluster 1   Cluster 2   Cluster 3

Figure 24.5 Cluster centers by fuel type and gas type.

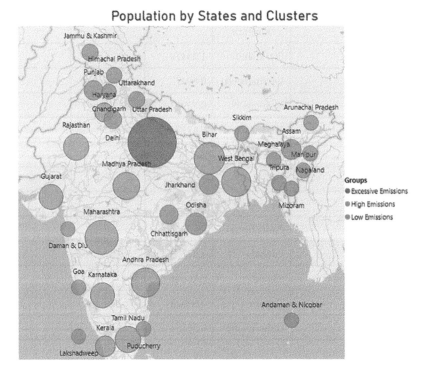

Figure 24.6 Population (2015) by states and clusters.

than the lower emission group, and the excessive emission group, which includes only Uttar Pradesh, has the highest population among the other groups and among other Indian states. It demonstrates that population is one of the variables that explains the above cluster formation. With the formation of clusters, needed restrictions can be imposed on high emissions and excessive emissions states, particularly Uttar Pradesh. The purpose for which the fossil fuels are used in household can be electrified. Fuels used for the cooking purpose can be substituted with electric induction or magnetic induction stoves. Many experts have suggested for a substantial shift to electrify the processes, and then generating the increased electricity needs through hydropower, solar and wind as they are zero or low carbon sources (EcoWatch) [18]. As the literature for this paper focuses on Primary Energy HCEs, the future scope for India in this field would be developing a framework for calculating Secondary Energy HCEs and Household Consumption HCEs, also known as Indirect Carbon Emissions in some literature, as well as identifying important factors affecting HCEs. Furthermore, this study excludes emissions from other sectors, and the clustering algorithm to be used may be a point of contention.

24.6 Conclusion

Household emissions from primary energy are among the most significant contributors to GHG. Residential emissions as defined by the IPCC and primary energy household emissions as defined in the literature have similar meanings. Between 2005 and 2015, majority of the Indian states saw an increase in primary energy HCEs from LPG and a consistent decrease in primary energy HCEs from kerosene. When compared to HCEs and household CH_4 emissions, the contribution of primary energy household N_2O emissions is quite negligible across all states. As, the aim was to find groups of Indian States based on their primary energy HCEs from LPG, kerosene, diesel, and primary energy N_2O and CH_4 from LPG, kerosene, diesel, and Fuelwood using the k-means method, the Indian states formed three clusters that are homogeneous within and different between. However, it should be noted that k-means may not be the perfect method for the formation of clusters in this problem statement, therefore which clustering method to be used can be an area for the future research, also the study was limited to primary energy household emissions. Excessive emissions, high emissions, and low emissions are the three clusters formed, consisting of 1, 11, and 23 states, respectively. To reduce the workload, and for being effective in reducing the emissions, policymakers can focus on specific groups such as excessive emissions and high emissions group instead of focusing on every state for emission reduction. Kerosene and LPG are the two fuel types that have been crucial in the formation of clusters. It tends to be seen that the population of the states is one of the reasons for such conduct of the cluster's arrangement. Most Indian States has seen a decrease in primary energy HCEs from kerosene. The primary energy HCEs from the LPG are on an increment during 2005 to 2015 as its utilization is expanding with the population. The most elevated contributing state to the primary energy HCEs was the Uttar Pradesh, and furthermore, it was the state with a solo cluster. Certain the findings of the paper, it is recommended that when determining GHG emission limitations, consider the membership of a given state in a particular cluster on the one hand, and the criterion for determining emission limits on the other. To reduce the emissions from the excessive and high emissions group, the following measures can be undertaken by the policymakers

1. Taking population control measures in future, to further control the year-by-year increase in the primary energy household emissions.
2. Although expensive but encouraging the use of electric induction or magnetic induction stoves in the households would not contribute to any GHG emissions, if the generation of the electricity in a nation is based on zero-carbon goal.
3. Motivating further research in India relating to the household emissions domain by developing an updated and recent framework for emissions, finding more important factors behind the emissions and controlling them.

References

1. National Academy of Sciences, *An Overview from the Royal Society and the US National Academy of Sciences*, 2020, Available at: https://royalsociety. org/~/media/royal_society_content/policy/projects/climate-evidence-causes/climate-change-evidence-causes.pdf
2. Liu, L., Qu, J., Maraseni, T.N., Niu, Y., Zeng, J., Zhang, L., Xu, L., Household CO2 emissions: Current status and future perspectives. *Int. J. Environ. Res. Public Health*, 17, 19, 7077, 2020. https://doi.org/10.3390/ijerph17197077.

3. United Nations Framework on Climate Change (UNFCCC), *What is Kyoto Protocol?*, UNFCCC, Available at: https://unfccc.int/kyoto_protocol (Accessed: 17 November 2021).

4. Intergovernmental Panel on Climate Change (IPCC), *Guidelines for National Greenhouse Gas Inventories*, 2006, Available at: https://www.ipcc-nggip.iges.or.jp/public/2006gl/

5. Pachauri, S. and Spreng, D., Direct and indirect enrgy requirements of households in India. *Energy Policy*, 30, 6, 511–523, 2002. https://doi.org/10.1016/s0301-4215(01)00119-7.

6. Ministry of Environment and Forests Government of India, India, Greenhouse gases emissions 2007. *Atmos. Pollut. Res.*, 7, 5, 935–944, 2010. https://www.iitr.ac.in/wfw/web_ua_water_for_welfare/water/WRDM/MOEF_India_GHG_Emis_2010.pdf.

7. Wang, Y., Yang, G., Dong, Y., Cheng, Y., Shang, P., The scale, structure and influencing factors of total carbon emissions from households in 30 provinces of China-based on the extended STIRPAT model. *Energies*, 11, 5, 1125, 2018. https://doi.org/10.3390/en11051125.

8. Zhang, X., Luo, L., Skitmore, M., Household carbon emission research: an analytical review of measurement, influencing factors and mitigation prospects. *J. Clean. Prod.*, 103, 873–883, 2015. https://doi.org/10.1016/j.jclepro.2015.04.024.

9. Huang, R., Zhang, S., Liu, C., Comparing urban and rural household CO2 emissions—case from China's four megacities: Beijing, Tianjin, Shanghai, and Chongqing. *Energies*, 11, 5, 1257, 2018. https://doi.org/10.3390/en11051257.

10. Ahmad, S., Baiocchi, G., Creutzig, F., CO2 emissions from direct energy use of urban households in India. *Environ. Sci. Technol.*, 49, 19, 11312–11320, 2015. https://doi.org/10.1021/es505814g.

11. Cárdenas-Mamani, Ú., Kahhat, R., Vázquez-Rowe, I., District-level analysis for household-related energy consumption and greenhouse gas emissions: A case study in Lima, Peru. *Sustain. Cities Soc.*, 77, 103572, 2022. https://doi.org/10.1016/j.scs.2021.103572.

12. Ramachandra, T.V. and Sridevi, H., Comparative analysis of greenhouse gas emissions from major cities of India. *Int. J. Renew. Energy Environ. Eng.*, 02, 38–43, 2014. https://www.researchgate.net/publication/297716139_Comparative_analysis_of_greenhouse_gas_emissions_from_major_cities_of_India.

13. Zeng, J., Qu, J., Ma, H., Gou, X., Characteristics and Trends of household carbon emissions research from 1993 to 2019: A bibliometric analysis and its implications. *J. Clean. Prod.*, 295, 126468, 2021. https://doi.org/10.1016/j.jclepro.2021.126468.

14. Kijewska, A. and Bluszcz, A., Research of varying levels of greenhouse gas emissions in European countries using the k-means method. *Atmos. Pollut. Res.*, 7, 5, 935–944, 2016, https://doi.org/10.1016/j.apr.2016.05.010.

15. Ghanbari, S. and Daneshvar, M.R.M., Urban and rural contribution to the GHG emissions in the MECA countries. *Environ. Dev. Sustain.*, 23, 6418–6452, 2021. https://doi.org/10.1007/s10668-020-00879-8.

16. Mohan, R.R., Dharmala, N., Ananthakumar, M.R., Kumar, P., Bose, A., *Greenhouse Gas Emission Estimates from the Energy Sector in India at the Sub-national Level*, 2.0, GHG Platform India Report, New Delhi, 2019, http://www.ghgplatform-india.org/data-and-emissions/energy/GHGPI-PhaseIII-Methodology%20Note-Energy-Sep%202019.pdf.

17. Census of India, Population Projections for India and States 2001-2026, New Delhi, India, 2006, Available at: http://statehealthsocietybihar.org/survey_reports/Population_Projection_Report_2006.pdf

18. EcoWatch, *Magnetic Induction Cooking Can Cut Your Kitchen's Carbon Footprint*, EcoWatch, Ohio, United States, 2020, https://www.ecowatch.com/magnetic-induction-cooking-carbonemissions-2649690738.html

## 25

Airwaves Detection and Elimination Using Fast Fourier Transform to Enhance Detection of Hydrocarbon

Garba Aliyu[1]*, Mathias M. Fonkam[1], Augustine S. Nsang[1], Muhammad Abdulkarim[2], Sandip Rakshit[1] and Yakub K. Saheed[1]

[1]American University of Nigeria, Yola, Nigeria
[2]Ahmadu Bello University, Zaria, Nigeria

Abstract

Exploration of hydrocarbons in the sea is particularly expensive because it is best done by supplying a transmitter with a strong current, which is hazardous to the lives of marine life. A steady supply of voltage and current to the transmitter is normally used to determine the strength of electromagnetic waves. The mineral deposition has been detected using different techniques, both offshore and onshore. Detection of minerals by employing a controlled source electromagnetics (CSEM) has recently proved to be extremely effective with yielding promising results. Due to noise, both the transmitted and received signals may differ. The signal received from the subsurface in marine settings is generally limited by a variety of noise. The frequency spectrum of frequency signals and waveforms change when they interact with physical objects. Understanding how the frequency spectrum is altered allows us to examine how the signal and waveforms change. To accurately evaluate and eradicate these noises, they must be researched and taken into consideration. One of the most challenging problems employing Marine CSEM (MCSEM) in the detection of hydrocarbon is airwaves. When an electromagnetic (EM) is passed over a conductive surface, the affected signal is frequently influenced by the resistive body with high resistivity distribution. The signal is recorded by some electromagnetic (EM) fields scattered by subsurface with electric and magnetic sensors. Furthermore, the signal recorded is noise, often known as airwaves. This, however, occurs in shallow water. Hence, this work proposes to use Fast Fourier Transform (FFT) to detect and remove the

Corresponding author: garba.aliyu@aun.edu.ng

Anita Khosla, Prasenjit Chatterjee, Ikbal Ali and Dheeraj Joshi (eds.) Optimization Techniques in Engineering: Advances and Applications, (409–422) © 2023 Scrivener Publishing LLC

noise from the transmitted signal to reduce misinterpretation in the exploration of hydrocarbon in shallow water environments. Moreover, the simulated results obtained from the CST EM studio shows that when an EM signal is subjected to FFT, airwaves can be detected and removed, which enhances and reduces the uncertainty in the deposition of the hydrocarbon layer in a shallow water environment.

Keywords: Hydrocarbon, airwaves, Fast Fourier Transform, signal processing, minerals

25.1   Introduction

Exploration of hydrocarbons in the sea is particularly costly since it requires supplying a transmitter with a high current, which is dangerous to marine life. The voltage and current supplied to the transmitter are the sole determinants of electromagnetic wave power. A man-made electric and magnetic field is used to charge the earth in order to discover underlying minerals. Mineral deposition has been detected using different techniques, both offshore and onshore. Detection of minerals by employing a Controlled Source Electromagnetic (CSEM) has recently proved to be extremely effective with yielding promising results [1]. Moreover, Sea Bed Logging (SBL) is an application of the Marine Controlled Source Electromagnetic (MCSEM) system that is striving to discover contrast in subsurface resistivity in a deep-water ecosystem [2]. Electromagnetic Seabed Logging (EM-SBL) has been found to be an effective technology for identifying hydrocarbons. Seismic surveying, on the other hand, employs sound waves to discover and identify the structure of a possible reservoir [3]. The transmitter design system determines the effectiveness of MCSEM, which tows transmitters with several static receivers [4] to detect the presence of mineral deposition and measure both the amplitude and signal received [5]. Due to noise, both the transmitted and received signals may differ. The signal received from the subsurface in offshore settings is generally limited to a variety of noise. When frequency signals and waveforms interact with physical objects, their frequency spectrum is altered. We can observe how the signal and waveforms are changed by understanding how the frequency spectrum is altered. The different types of noise must be investigated and brought into attention to precisely quantify and eliminate them. One of the most challenging issues in employing MCSEM for the detection of hydrocarbons is known as airwaves. When an Electromagnetic (EM) passes through a conductive surface, the affected signal is frequently influenced by the resistivity distribution. When sediments are filled with saltwater and exposed to seawater environments, they act as a good conductor. Hydrocarbons that have been filled with sediments, on the other hand, form resistant substances that disperse the electromagnetic field. The signal is recorded by some EM field scattered by subsurface with electric and magnetic sensors. Furthermore, the signal recorded is noise, often known as airwaves. This, however, occurs in shallow water. According to Khairuddin *et al.* (2012), airwaves begin to dominate at 600 meters of water depth and are increasingly significant at 300 meters and below. It should be observed that the airwaves may overwhelm the EM results being collected, making the existence of the light resistive body very hard to detect [3]. Hence this work proposed to use Fast Fourier Transform (FFT) to detect and correct the transmitted signal to reduce mislead in the exploration of hydrocarbon in shallow environments. FFT is used to do real-time computations on acquired data and is the best with an efficient method, therefore it is used to analyze, monitor, and control various systems [6]. It allows detection of noise in the frequency domain that cannot be possible in the time domain. The EM signal transmitted is prone to noise also known as airwaves. According to Gilbert Strong of Massachusetts Institute of Technology (MIT), FFT is the most relevant mathematical algorithm in our lifetime. It has proven to be the best mathematical operation in the field of many applications such as signal processing, data analysis, communications, medical imaging, imaging video compression, differential equation solver, noise filtration and other applications that need spectral analysis [7]. FFT has emerged as one of the most effective methods for Electronic Warfare (EW) receiver construction due to a loss of prior understanding of the signal properties and the demand for real-time processing [8]. Fourier Discrete in Speech, image, and seismic processing all rely on transform. DFT aids in spectrum analysis and correlation analysis. Spectral analysis is used in speech bandwidth reduction systems, radar systems for determining target velocity, and surface vessels and subsurface [9].

25.1.1   Airwaves

A key components of airwaves is energy that diffuses from a source inside the seawater and travels upwards to the sea surface. Before reflecting down into the seabed to the receiver, this airwave diffuses at the speed of light with no attenuation [10]. In shallow water, this airwave obscures the signal that indicates the existence of hydrocarbons because it is runty attenuated, reflected, and recorded by the receiver, which misinforms the existence of hydrocarbon. The airwaves can be

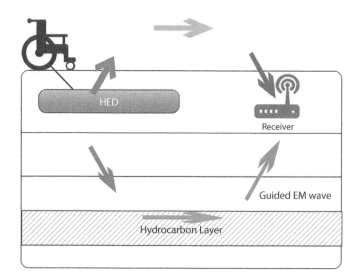

Figure 25.1 CSTM experimental setup.

measured using simulations or mathematical models found in the literature. Mathematical models have been used to estimate the airwaves [11]. However, direct wave is missing in this computation. The direct wave is a significant part of the recorded signal that must be measured and eliminated. Because of the paucity of communication bandwidth, researchers are looking into algorithms to identify congested channels over the airwaves so that they can be avoided and communication quality is not disrupted [12, 13]. Figure 25.1 shows the experimental setup in the CSTM environment.

25.1.2   Fast Fourier Transform

Fourier transform is a mathematical operation that allows the conversion of a signal from a time domain to a frequency domain. The model states that the signal is a decomposition of many sinusoidal representations of functions with a noted frequency, amplitude, and phase. The Fourier series is based on a periodic signal, which represented by the equation below:

$$x(t) = \frac{A_0}{2} + \sum_{n=1}^{N}\left(A_n \sin\left(\frac{2\pi nt}{P} + \phi_n\right)\right) = \sum_{n=-N}^{N}\left(C_n e^{2\pi \mathrm{int}\frac{1}{P}}\right) \quad (25.1)$$

The P represents the period of the signal and C_n is the Fourier coefficient of the signal $x(t)$. The coefficients can be determined by:

$$C_n = \frac{1}{P} \int_0^P e^{\frac{-i2\pi nt}{P}} x(t)dt \qquad (25.2)$$

The Fast Fourier Transform is a method for computing DFT that uses the supremacy of the unique features of complex roots of unity in time $\theta(n \log n)$ in comparison to the DFT, which has a time complexity of $\theta(n^2)$. Because the DFT represents a finite-duration sequence in the frequency domain as a discrete frequency representation, it is worth looking at its potential applications in linear system analysis and, in particular, linear filtering. When an input signal with a spectrum $X(\omega)$ is excited by a system with a frequency response $H(\omega)$, the output spectrum $Y(\omega) = X(\omega)H(\omega)$ is produced. The inverse Fourier transform is used to obtain the output sequence $Y(\omega)$. The problem with this frequency-domain method in terms of computation is that $X(\omega)$, $H(\omega)$ and $Y(\omega)$ are functions of the continuous variable ω. As a result, a digital computer cannot do the computations, which can exclusively store and make computations on discrete-frequency values. The DFT, on the other hand, lends itself to digital computer processing. DFT can be used to accomplish frequency-domain linear filtering. It offers, in particular, a computational approach that can be used instead of time-domain convolution. In fact, due to the advent of efficient algorithms for calculating the DFT, the frequency-domain method based on the DFT is computationally more effective than the time-domain convolution. These algorithms are FFT algorithms. The values of the signal for all time are necessary to compute the spectrum of either a continuous-time or discrete-time signal. In actuality, though, we only monitor signals for a limited time. As a result, a signal's spectrum can only be approximated using a finite data set. FFT can be used to examine how a finite data record affects frequency analysis.

25.2   Related Works

In offshore environments, the signal received from the subsurface is primarily associated with a range of noises. The diffused electromagnetic signal part, which propagates vertically up in the form of a wave at the air or sea surface at the speed of light often without attenuation before diffusing back down over the water layer and being recorded by EM receivers, is essentially what generates the airwaves. This research Ansari *et al.* [10] focused on the use of electromagnetic techniques to discover hydrocarbon layers beneath the seabed and to demonstrate the relationship between hydrocarbon thickness and resistivity contrast. The receiver response generated by installed receivers in seabed logging is dominated by airwaves, which makes it difficult to analyze the measured data and establish the presence of hydrocarbons. However, Ansari *et al.* [14] identified and applied the independent component analysis (ICA) statistical approach for filtering the airwaves from the signal response and described and filtered the airwaves within the signal response received from the receiver. This noise must be considered in order to accurately measure and eliminate it [15]. Lack of effective noise management will lead to erroneous interpretation of the absence or presence of a hydrocarbon deposit, resulting in millions of dollars in costs and time spent drilling or misinforming of its existence. One of the most challenging issues employing MCSEM for the detection of hydrocarbons is airwaves [16]. Abdulkarim *et al.* [16] used a mathematical model to describe the pattern of airwaves, which is considered a predictive model. This provides a curve fitting method that identifies a mathematical representation that adequately explains the pattern or forms of airwaves data. The presence of hydrocarbon in the survey environment is difficult to determine due to obstruction of airwaves with the EM field and encountered resistive body variation in shallow water. Khairuddin *et al.* [3] intensively discussed the effect of airwaves in SBL for shallow water environments. For various water depths, it starts from deep-water of 1000 m to the shallow water of 100 m. EM data was obtained through simulation using CST EM Studio with and without hydrocarbon deposits. It is was found that airwaves began to dominate around 600 meters and became more critical at 300 meters and below, according to the findings. The Fast Fourier Transform is the basis of the frequency domain method. It only requires a little expense of computing and can be used in real-time. For sinusoidal signals, it also has a large Signal-to-Noise Ratio (SNR) increase. As a result, the frequency domain method has become prominent [17]. A new approach for estimating the frequency of sinusoidal signals based on interpolation of FFT and Discrete-Time Fourier Transform (DTFT) was proposed in the study of Liu *et al.* [17]. To begin, A-point FFT was used to locate the highest FFT spectrum line and provide an approximate frequency estimate.

Fast Fourier transform (FFT) is, however, widely acknowledged as the most efficient numerical algorithm in signal processing. It is used to detect life forms or track signals emitted from the depths of the earth. Furthermore, the algorithm is widely employed in all fields of science and engineering [18]. As a result, it is recommended for use because of its superior processing capacity over the Discrete Fourier Transform (DFT).

25.3   Theoretical Framework

Gaussian noise has corrupted the system's output measurements in operation. Because the bi-spectrum of a Gaussian signal is zero, the bi-spectrum of the observed and true outputs must be the same. As a result, working with the bi-spectrum has the advantage of being resistant to measurement of noise. In terms of the bi-coherence function, the noise effect will be negligible as long as the noise power is substantially lower than the signal power, i.e. in high SNR settings, or the noise effect can be fully eradicated if its covariance (or power spectrum) is identified. However, Liu *et al.* [17], focused on a novel frequency estimation method based on FFT and DTFT interpolation, where a single frequency signal is modelled against a white Gaussian noise, it is represented by the equation:

$$x(t) = Ae^{i(2\pi f_0 t + \theta_0)} + w(t)$$

where f_0 is the frequency, A, is the amplitude from the complex sinusoid, θ_0 is the phase, and $w(t)$ is the noise.

Moreover, $w(t)$ can be detected and removed using FFT if the signal is converted to frequency domain. However, when the above equation is sampled, we have

$$x(n) = Ae^{i(2\pi \frac{f_0}{f_s} n + \theta_0)} + w(n), n = 0,1,2,...,N-1$$

where N is the number of sampling and it is based on the Nyquist Shannon theorem and f_s is the sampling frequency.

A divide-and-conquer strategy is used in the FFT method. The halving lemma provides the motivation, as it suggests that for even n, we may only need half of the points for evaluation. The concept to explain the two distinct polynomials $A^e(x)$ and $A^o(x)$, use the even-index and odd-index coefficients of $A(x)$ separately as shown below:

$$A^e(x) = a_0 + a_2 x + a_4 x^2 + ... + a_{n-2} x^{n/2-1}$$
$$A^o(x) = a_1 + a_3 x + a_5 x^2 + ... + a_{n-1} x^{n/2-1}$$

A^e, has all of A's even-index coefficients (the index's binary representation ends in 0), whereas A^o, has all of A's odd-index coefficients (the index's binary representation ends in 1). Hence, we can deduce that:

$$A(x) = A^e(x^2) + xA^o(x^2)$$

The problem of computing $A(x)$ at w_n^0, w_n^1,.... w_n^{n-1} is now reduced to the divide-and-conquer strategy. Where $w_n = e^{2\pi i/n}$.

The degree-bound $n/2$ polynomials $A^e(x)$ and $A^o(x)$ are recursively computed at the $n/2$ complex ($n/2$)th roots of unity. Because each of the small problems have, the same pattern as the initial problem but is half the size. Hence, FFT is very efficient and presumed to play a significant role in the detection of hydrocarbons. The Fourier Transform itself is not restricted to digital signal processing. In reality, the Fourier Transform helps speed up the training of convolutional neural networks [19]. Consider how a convolutional layer applies a kernel to a segment of an image and conducts bit-wise multiplication on all of the values in that area. The kernel is subsequently relocated to a different part of the image, and the procedure is repeated until the entire image has been traversed.

25.4   Methodology

The experiment was conducted on a simulation model, which includes air, seawater, sediments, and hydrocarbons, using computer simulation technology (CST) software. The CST software makes it simple to construct a 3D seabed logging simulation [14]. The data for the investigation was collected by simulating the seabed environment with the CST Simulation software. The Fast Fourier Transform model was used to detect the existence of noise in the form of airwaves. The simulation was first conducted without airwaves and overburden (hydrocarbon). The second phase introduced airwaves, and the results were collected and recorded. The third phase deposited a resistive object based on the specification as indicated in Table 25.1. The transmitter is normally towed 20 to 50 m above the seabed, while the receivers are situated on the seabed, and the frequencies mostly used in marine CSEM are in the range of 0.1 to 10 Hz [20].

Table 25.1 Parameter value settings.

Parameter	Value
Transmitter depth range	100m – 300m
Frequency range	0.1 – 10 Hz
Receiver depth	100m – 300m
Receiver depth	50000m

25.5   Results and Discussions

Outliers altered the periodogram estimates by changing the amplitude and phase of the Fourier series. Furthermore, in the frequency domain, detection of measurements of outliers is innumerably more precise than in the time domain [21]. Electrical and magnetic fields make up EM waves, which give useful information about varying resistive layers. The resistivity contrast can be discerned by graphing the EM field against the source-receiver offset [22]. Figures 25.2(a), 25.2(b), and 25.2(c) show a difference

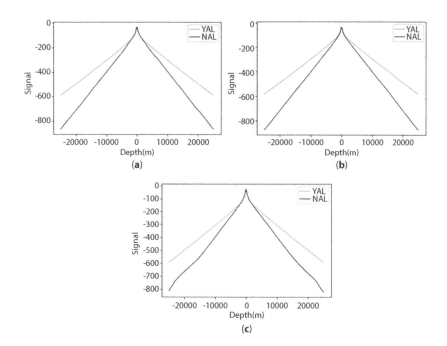

Figure 25.2 Air layer and without air layer.

in the "tails" of the two graphs, which could indicate the presence of hydrocarbons (HC). However, it is actually not a HC but airwaves. The graphs show how the presence of the air layer rises above as compared to the one simulated without an air layer with varied receiver depth of 100 m to 300 m (on typical shallow seawater). This shows that as the depth of the receiver increases so the lesser the effect of airwaves. This gives an idea of how pattern the airwave looked before we subjected it to FFT for detection and removal to avoid detecting hydrocarbon in place of the noise.

As it can be observed from Figure 25.3 below, when the depth decreases, the noise increases. The YHC100 indicates there is the presence of hydrocarbons deposited on the reservoir at a 100m depth. Similarly, NHC100, represents results of the simulation without hydrocarbons. Generally, the results show that there is a high electric magnetic signal when there is a resistive body (hydrocarbons) under shallow water, which normally starts at 100m depth and decreases as the depth increases.

FFT is used to do real-time computations on acquired data and is the most effective method known; as a result, it is used to analyze, monitor, and control a variety of systems. It detects noise in the frequency domain that is impossible to detect in the time domain. The transmitted EM signal is susceptible to noise, often known as airwaves. Figure 25.4 shows that there is high frequency due to the presence of airwaves while Figure 25.5 shows how the frequency significantly reduced in the absence of airwaves.

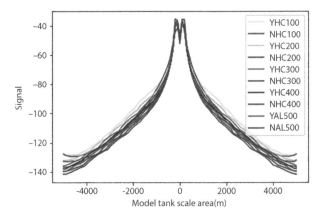

Figure 25.3 Electric field against the offset with and without hydrocarbon for a 100-m to 500-m depth of seawater.

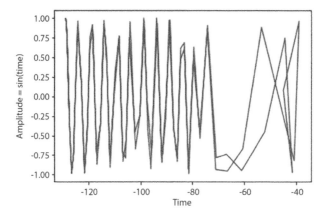

Figure 25.4 Hydrocarbon with airwaves.

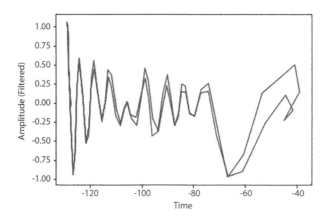

Figure 25.5 Hydrocarbon without airwaves.

FFT can be used to investigate the impact of a finite data record on frequency analysis. The frequency spectrum of frequency signals and waveforms are affected when they interact with physical objects (hydrocarbon). Understanding how the frequency spectrum is adjusted allows us to examine how signals and waveforms change. The change in the waveforms from the two figures justified the existence of noise known as airwaves. After observing the nature of the noise, the FFT was able to detect and remove the presence of airwaves as shown in Figure 25.6.

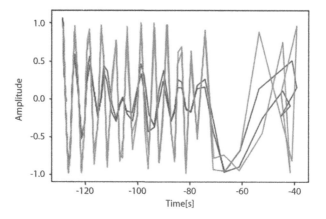

Figure 25.6 Hydrocarbon with filtered airwaves.

25.6   Conclusion

FFT has proven to be the best mathematical operation in the field of many applications such as signal processing, data analysis, communications, medical imaging, imaging video compression, differential equation solver, noise filtration, and other applications that need spectral analysis. Moreover, in this chapter, the simulated results obtained from the CST EM studio shows that when an EM signal is subjected to FFT, noise can be detected and removed, which enhances and reduces the uncertainty in the deposition of the hydrocarbon layer in a shallow water environment. The optimum depth for each antenna type will be changed in the future, from 400 meters to the point when EM waves are no more reflected upward and iteratively apply FFT to detect and remove the noise at every stage.

References

1. Passalacqua, H. and Strack, K., *Integrated Geophysical Reservoir Monitoring for Heavy Oil*, Kuwait City, Kuwait, Day 3 Thu, December 08, 2016, p. D031S013R003, Dec. 2016.
2. Mukhtar, S.M., Daud, H., Dass, S.C., *Squared Exponential Covariance Function for Prediction of Hydrocarbon in Seabed Logging Application*, Kuala Lumpur, Malaysia, p. 020012, 2016.
3. Khairuddin, M.K., Zaid, H.M., Shafie, A., Yahya, N., Airwaves effect in Sea Bed Logging for shallow water environment, in: *2012 IEEE Business, Engineering & Industrial Applications Colloquium (BEIAC)*, Kuala Lumpur, Malaysia, pp. 199–203, Apr. 2012.

4. Wang, M., Deng, M., Wu, Z., Luo, X., Jing, J., Chen, K., The deep-tow marine controlled-source electromagnetic transmitter system for gas hydrate exploration. *J. Appl. Geophys.*, 137, 138–144, Feb. 2017.

5. Niaz Akhtar, M., Yahya, N., Nasir, N., New EM transmitter with Y3Fe5O12 based magnetic feeders potentially used for seabed logging application. *Adv. Mater. Res.*, 667, 10–23, Mar. 2013.

6. Mohapatra, B.N. and Mohapatra, R.K., FFT and sparse FFT techniques and applications, in: *2017 Fourteenth International Conference on Wireless and Optical Communications Networks (WOCN)*, Mumbai, India, pp. 1–5, Feb. 2017.

7. Elshafiy, A., El-Motaz, M.A., Farag, M.E., Nasr, O.A., Fahmy, H.A.H., On optimization of mixed-radix FFT: A signal processing approach, in: *2019 IEEE Wireless Communications and Networking Conference (WCNC)*, Marrakesh, Morocco, pp. 1–6, Apr. 2019.

8. Durga, M., Chauhan, A.M., Kulkarni, A.S., Paranjape, H.V., Parallel higher point FFT for improving continuous wave threat resolution using minimal FPGA resources, in: *2020 IEEE International Conference on Electronics, Computing and Communication Technologies (CONECCT)*, Bangalore, India, pp. 1–6, Jul. 2020.

9. Angeline, T. and Narain Ponraj, D., A survey on FFT processors. *Int. J. Sci. Eng. Res.*, 4, 3, 1–5, Mar. 2013. Accessed: Aug. 21, 2021. [Online]. Available: https://www.ijser.org/paper/A-Survey-on-FFT-Processors.html.

10. Ansari, A. *et al.*, Subsurface exploration of seabed using electromagnetic waves for the detection of hydrocarbon layers, in: *2014 International Conference on Computer and Information Sciences (ICCOINS)*, Kuala Lumpur, Malaysia, pp. 1–5, Jun. 2014.

11. Nyamasvisva, T.E., Hasbullah, H.B., Yahya, N., Nayan, Y.B., Rostami, A., Rauf, M., Computer algorithm for airwave prediction in marine controlled source electromagnetics data, in: *2016 3rd International Conference on Computer and Information Sciences (ICCOINS)*, Kuala Lumpur, Malaysia, pp. 386–390, Aug. 2016.

12. Edwards, G., Identifying unwanted signal in a spread spectrum band, in: *2019 SoutheastCon*, Huntsville, AL, USA, pp. 1–4, Apr. 2019.

13. Daud, H., Yahya, N., Asirvadam, V., Talib, K., II, Air waves effect on sea bed logging for shallow water application, in: *2010 IEEE Symposium on Industrial Electronics and Applications (ISIEA)*, Penang, Malaysia, pp. 306–310, Oct. 2010.

14. Ansari, A. *et al.*, Infomax and FASTICA using principle component analysis as preprocessor for airwave removal in seabed logging, in: *2014 International Conference on Computer and Information Sciences (ICCOINS)*, Kuala Lumpur, Malaysia, pp. 1–5, Jun. 2014.

15. Nyamasvisva, T.E., Yahya, N., Hasbullah, H.B., Rauf, M., Rostami, A., Dahy, E., Estimating direct waves with respect to receiver offset, antenna current and frequency in MCSEM, in: *2016 International Conference on Computer*

and Communication Engineering (ICCCE), Kuala Lumpur, Malaysia, pp. 480–484, Jul. 2016.

16. Abdulkarim, M., Shafie, A., Ahmad, W.F.W., Razali, R., Airwaves prediction model for shallow water marine control source electromagnetic data. *AASRI Procedia*, 4, 173–181, 2013.

17. Liu, J., Fan, L., Jin, J., Wang, X., Xing, J., He, W., An Accurate and efficient frequency estimation algorithm by using FFT and DTFT, in: *2020 39th Chinese Control Conference (CCC)*, Shenyang, China, pp. 2913–2917, Jul. 2020.

18. Shayan, U., FFT: Equations and history. *EDN*, Apr. 13, 2016. https://www.edn.com/fft-equations-and-history/ (accessed Jun. 16, 2021).

19. Maklin, C., Fast fourier transform. *Medium*, Dec. 29, 2019. https://towards-datascience.com/fast-fourier-transform-937926e591cb (accessed Oct. 10, 2021).

20. Sconstable, Scripps Institution of Oceanography Marine EM Laboratory, *Resources, Web Hosted Active-Source Modeling*, 2021, https://marineemlab.ucsd.edu/wham/wham_form.html (accessed Nov. 16, 2021).

21. Shittu, O.I. and Shangodoyin, D.K., Detection of outliers in time series data: A frequency domain approach. *Asian J. Sci. Res.*, 1, 2, 130–137, 2008.

22. Shafie, A., Yahya, N., Abdulkarim, M., A simulation study to verify the effects of air waves in Sea Bed Logging for shallow water, in: *2012 International Conference on Electromagnetics in Advanced Applications*, Cape Town, WP, South Africa, pp. 626–629, Sep. 2012.

## 26

Design and Implementation of Control for Nonlinear Active Suspension System

Ravindra S. Rana* and Dipak M. Adhyaru

Instrumentation and Control Department, Nirma University, Ahmedabad, India

Abstract

In this chapter, linear and nonlinear parts of an active suspension system using quarter car model have been investigated. Due to the presence of nonlinearities in spring, damper, and tire, it is impossible to achieve desired performance using linear control techniques. To ensure robustness of designated control technique in different operating conditions, nonlinearity in plant has to be considered. Nonlinear model is linearized around equilibrium point and represented in state space form. The performance of proposed quarter car model has been investigated using proportional-integral derivative (PID) and state feedback strategies. Comparison of simulation results for passive, active, and linearized model of quarter car system is discussed.

Keywords: Active suspension system, quarter car model, state feedback, PID, nonlinear system

26.1   Introduction

There has been a huge interest in robust control design in automobile. Antilock braking, active steering, active suspension systems are of prime focus for researchers. The robust controls that use system states can give better performance compared to passive suspension systems. Primary function of a suspension is to isolate passengers sitting in vehicle from different road profiles. In order to provide isolation in a vehicle, vehicle wheels must follow the vertical profile of the road, while sprung mass of the body remains as fixed height. In practical scenario, sprung mass of body cannot remain at fixed height, which contradict with limitation of available

---

*Corresponding author: ranaravindra08@gmail.com

Anita Khosla, Prasenjit Chatterjee, Ikbal Ali and Dheeraj Joshi (eds.) Optimization Techniques in Engineering: Advances and Applications, (423–436) © 2023 Scrivener Publishing LLC

suspension travel. Hence, degree of isolation provided by suspension is a function of the amount of suspension travel available.

In automotive vehicle, to give ride comfort, a suspension system must isolate the car sprung mass from the irregular, rough road profile. A passive suspension system uses spring and dampers with fixed value coefficient, which unable to provide comfort in all road conditions. Instead of passive suspension, active suspension system provide better ride comfort by activating actuator force in different rough road conditions and cornering and braking. It is to be considered that while providing ride comfort, a firm contact of tyre with the road have to be maintained all time and this must be done within limits of rattle space. Hence, it is always a trade between ride comfort and handling different road conditions in limited rattle space. Nonlinear behavior of the parameters of the suspension spring, dampers and unknown road conditions, creates difficulty to achieve ride comfort.

Springs and dampers are used in passive suspension to absorb vibrations and shocks. Characteristic of springs and dampers of suspension system is defined, passive suspension system can provide its best performance for a specified load and for a defined type of road profile. Whereas, one step further, in a semiactive suspension system, the behavior of the damper can be adjusted with the use of actuator activating it to give better comfort for more number of road conditions. Last but not the list, an active suspension system actuator can be placed between the unsprung mass and the sprung mass to produce actuating force to provide comfort in variety of road conditions, cornering and braking in real time. We can give assurance that an active suspension systems considered here employ an actuator over and above the passive suspension components. Active suspension systems can give potentially superior ride comfort compared to semiactive and passive suspension systems.

Suspension systems main objectives are to minimize suspension deflection, increase ride comfort and robustness to road disturbances, corning, and braking [1]. Furthermore, ride comfort can be improved by minimizing effects of external disturbances, such as cornering, braking. It may be dangerous situation, if tyre loses contact with road while riding on higher speed. Hence, it is necessary to maintain tyre grip on road and limiting the vehicle body vibration [2, 3]. Currently, there are passive, semiactive, and active kind of suspension systems. Among these systems, passive suspension system is easy to fit in a vehicle and it has inherent advantages. Whereas disadvantage of passive suspension system is unable to provide ride comfort by nonadapting to different conditions, such as rough road and cornering and braking [4]. During normal operating conditions, passive suspension system performance is perfect as it includes predefined behavior of spring and damper and also its efficiency depend on the fixed standard of certain automobile parameters. Thus, to achieve better ride comfort results, semi-active suspension system adjusting damper force is introduced in automotive system. When we compare passive and semi-active systems, the later one uses considerably less control force and it is less complex system also. Hence, it can provide significantly improved in ride comfort. Karnopp introduced method to control skyhook model, which is widely used control approach for semi-active suspension systems as it can reduce the 'resonant peak' to achieve better ride comfort [5]. Magneto-rheological dampers (MR) are more popular approach in semi-active suspension system, because it uses low control force and safer system [6]. What if the power fails, Magneto-rheological dampers (MR) work as passive suspension systems, so in case of power failure performance of Magneto-rheological damper (MR) is limited. So instead of using flexi dampers, a new approach so-called active suspension systems using actuator is introduced. Active suspension system uses computerized brain to generate control force and adjust actuator to provide ride comfort. Its nature to consume less energy while producing actuator forces which minimizes suspension deflection [7]. Passive and semiactive suspension systems are not capable to provide dynamic compensation, whereas active suspension is able [8]. In active suspension system, actuators majorly can be placed between sprung and unsprung mass. Ride comfort can be achieved by hydraulic, pneumatic, or electromagnetic actuators [9]. Pneumatic actuators are simplest in nature among pneumatic, hydraulic, and electromagnetic, but limited application due to its bulky and required more space. For heavy applications, hydraulic actuators are very useful for their performance. Electromagnetic kind of actuators is accurate among all three [10]. In application of forest machines, active suspension using pneumatic actuators is controlled using cascading approach. It proposes parallel mechanical structure to achieve goal [11]. The hydraulic actuator dynamics are used to apply control force to suspension system in Dong et al. [12]. In suspension system, application of hydraulic actuators has limitation of oil leakage and dampers and forming of spring, which is overcome by the electromagnetic actuator in Khan et al. [13]. Skyhook model of active suspension system is developed in Xia et al. [14]. A new control approach for active suspension system using electromagnetic and hydraulic actuators is presented in Hasbullah and Faris [15]. An active damping suspension is an efficient way to enhance the suspension performance to achieve ride comfort is presented in Khan et al. [16]. A new robust adaptive law for adaptive control of vehicle active suspensions with unknown dynamics is proposed to improve ride performance. This adaptive law is designed to minimize parameter estimation error and exponential convergence of tracking error and parameter estimation error is proved [17]. An active suspension control using a feedback control scheme and an input decoupling transformation is proposed for a full-vehicle suspension system. Cascade control approach is used to provide better ride comfort [18]. Fuzzy sliding mode control, which embedded with skyhook surface method, is proposed for the ride comfort of a vehicle semi-active suspension in [19], H_∞ control is designed for the system to minimize the effect of road disturbances and achieve better ride comfort in Rizvi *et al.* [20], and back-stepping control is proposed for a seven degrees of freedom (DoF), nonlinear full vehicle model in Yagiz and Hacioglu [21]. The practical applicability of electromagnetic active suspension is presented in Martins *et al.* [22]. Feasibility of the H_∞-LMI technique to deal with backlash nonlinearity in the actuator is presented in Pujol and Acho [23]. Modified energy-saving skyhook consisting of active control, energy regeneration, and switch is presented in Ding *et al.* [24]. An application of new signal differentiation technique for the online estimation of disturbance trajectories due to irregular road surfaces and velocity state variables is described in Beltran-Carbajal *et al.* [25].

The organization of the chapter is as follows: In section 26.2, mathematical model of active suspension quarter-car model is derived. Linearizing nonlinearity of model. Active control strategies: state feedback and proportional–integral–derivative (PID) are briefly proposed in section 26.3. The comparative analysis of the proposed controllers along with traditional control strategy is compared in section 26.4. Section 26.5 summarizes the conclusion and future work of the chapter.

26.2 Mathematical Model of Quarter Car Suspension System

26.2.1 Mathematical Model

We have considered quarter car model of suspension system as shown in Figure 26.1 as described in Kim and Ro [26]. Here, both linear and non-linear model of the quarter car suspension system are introduced and time responses of two models are compared to demonstrate the limitation of the linear suspension model to develop active suspension system.

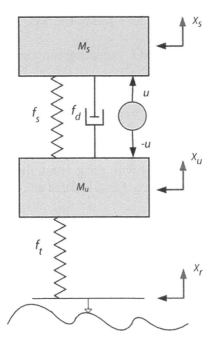

Figure 26.1 Quarter car suspension system.

The vertical forces on sprung and un-sprung masses are considered. It is assumed that vehicle moves with a constant speed. In a passive suspension system, the sprung mass and unsprung mass are connected by springs and dampers having constant force coefficients. In active suspension system, an actuator is placed in parallel with the springs and dampers between the sprung and un-sprung mass.

The suspension system is described by

$$m_s \ddot{x}_s = -f_s - f_d + u \tag{26.1}$$

$$m_u \ddot{x}_u = f_s + f_d - f_t - u \tag{26.2}$$

where m_s is nominal sprung mass, m_u is nominal unsprung mass, x_s is displacement of sprung mass relative to its static position, x_u is displacement of unsprung mass relative its static position, z_r is uneven road profile relative to plane ground, f_s is nonlinear spring force, f_d is nonlinear damping force, f_t is tyre force, u is control force generated by actuator. The spring force f_s and damping force f_d are given by [26].

$$f_s = k_1 \Delta x + k_2 \Delta x^2 + k_3 \Delta x^3 \qquad (26.3)$$

where the coefficients k_1, k_2 and k_3 are spring constants and $\Delta x = (x_s - x_u)$ is the suspension deflection,

$$f_d = c_1 \Delta \dot{x} + c_2 \Delta \dot{x}^2 \qquad (26.4)$$

where the coefficients c_1 and c_2 are damping constants.

When the tyre loses contact with the ground, the force exerted by the tyre becomes zero. The tyre force f_t is calculated as

$$f_t = \begin{cases} k_t (x_u - z_r) & \text{if} \quad (x_u - z_r) < \dfrac{(m_s + m_u)\, g}{k_t} \\[3mm] 0 & \text{if} \quad (x_u - z_r) \geq \dfrac{(m_s + m_u)\, g}{k_t} \end{cases} \qquad (26.5)$$

where g is the acceleration due to gravity and k_t tyre spring constant. Here spring force f_s and damper force f_d are considered as unknown. The road profile z_r is also unknown.

Let the state variables be denoted as shown in Table 26.1, $x_1 = x_s$; $x_2 = \dot{x}_s$; $x_3 = x_u$ and $x_4 = \dot{x}_u$. The dynamics represented by (26.1) and (26.2) can be expressed in the state variable form as follows:

Table 26.1 Quarter car suspension system syllables.

F_c control action
Z_r The road surface position
x_1 tire displacement with (unsprung mass in quarter car model)
x_2 vehicle body displacement (sprung mass in the quarter car model)
m_s sprung mass
m_u unsprung mass
K_s sprung mass spring coefficient
B_s sprung mass damping coefficient
K_u unsprung mass spring coefficient
B_u unsprung mass damping coefficient

$$\dot{x}_1 = x_2 \qquad (26.6)$$

$$\dot{x}_2 = \frac{1}{m_s}(- f_s - f_d + u) \qquad (26.7)$$

$$\dot{x}_3 = x_4 \qquad (26.8)$$

$$\dot{x}_4 = \frac{1}{m_u}(f_s + f_d - f_t - u) \qquad (26.9)$$

26.2.2   Linearization Method for Nonlinear System Model

One common way to approach analysis and synthesis of linear controllers for nonlinear systems is to use such controllers, based upon linearization about known operating points. This has the advantage of allowing the
application of linear system methods, and often the resulting constraints on
system operation are conservative enough that the methods are adequate.

In practice, we have observed that almost majority of systems are nonlinear in nature, hence, the differential equations governing the system
behavior are nonlinear. However, majority of research work is concentrat-
ing on linear systems. So, in this section, we developed a "Jacobian linearization of a nonlinear system," about a specific operating point, called an
equilibrium point.

Now rewriting equations 26.6, 26.7, 26.8 and 26.9 in following form:

$$\dot{x} = f(x) + g(x)u \qquad (26.10)$$

$$f_1(x) = x_2 \qquad (26.11)$$

$$f_2(x) = \frac{1}{m_s}[-k_1(x_1 - x_3) - k_2(x_1 - x_3)^3 - c_1(x_2 - x_4) - c_2(x_2 - x_4)^2] \qquad (26.12)$$

$$f_3(x) = x_4 \qquad (26.13)$$

$$f_4(x) = \frac{1}{m_u}[k_1(x_1 - x_3) + k_2(x_1 - x_3)^3 + c_1(x_2 - x_4) + c_2(x_2 - x_4)^2 - k_t x_3 \qquad (26.14)$$

$$
J = \begin{bmatrix}
\dfrac{\partial f_1}{\partial x_1} & \dfrac{\partial f_1}{\partial x_2} & \dfrac{\partial f_1}{\partial x_3} & \dfrac{\partial f_1}{\partial x_4} \\[2mm]
\dfrac{\partial f_2}{\partial x_1} & \dfrac{\partial f_2}{\partial x_2} & \dfrac{\partial f_2}{\partial x_3} & \dfrac{\partial f_2}{\partial x_4} \\[2mm]
\dfrac{\partial f_3}{\partial x_1} & \dfrac{\partial f_3}{\partial x_2} & \dfrac{\partial f_3}{\partial x_3} & \dfrac{\partial f_3}{\partial x_4} \\[2mm]
\dfrac{\partial f_4}{\partial x_1} & \dfrac{\partial f_4}{\partial x_2} & \dfrac{\partial f_4}{\partial x_3} & \dfrac{\partial f_4}{\partial x_4}
\end{bmatrix}
= \begin{bmatrix}
0 & 1 & 0 & 0 \\[2mm]
\dfrac{-k_1}{m_s} & \dfrac{-c_1}{m_s} & \dfrac{k_1}{m_s} & \dfrac{c_1}{m_s} \\[2mm]
0 & 0 & 0 & 1 \\[2mm]
\dfrac{k_1}{m_u} & \dfrac{c_1}{m_u} & \dfrac{-k_1-k_t}{m_u} & \dfrac{-c_1}{m_u}
\end{bmatrix} ;
$$

$$
g(\mathrm{x}) = \begin{bmatrix}
0 & 0 & 0 \\
-1 & 1 & 0 \\
0 & 0 & 0 \\
-1 & 1 & k_t
\end{bmatrix} \begin{bmatrix}
g \\
u \\
z_r
\end{bmatrix}
$$

Solving for $f_1(x), f_2(x), f_3(x), f_4(x)$, we observe that equilibrium points are $[0\,0\,0\,0]$

Table 26.2 Parameters of the quarter car suspension system.

Parameter	Value
m_s	240 Kg
m_u	50 Kg
k_1	12394 Nm^{-1}
k_2	3170400 Nm^{-1}
k_t	150000 Nm^{-1}
c_1	1385.4 Nm^{-1}s
c_2	524.28 Nm^{-1}s^2
z_r	0.1 m

26.2.3 Discussion of Result

The efficacy of the method is verified through simulations of the model shown in Figure 26.1. This section presents simulation results to show the effectiveness of the control methods applied. Simulation based on mathematical model active control algorithms, such as PID and state feedback laws are implemented using MATLAB/SIMULINK. Performance of the suspension system in terms of ride comfort and vehicle handling is observed under different road conditions. Active suspension system simulation parameter values are considered as shown in Table 26.2. The main objective is to minimize vehicle body displacement, suspension travel and tyre deflection.

Figures 26.2 and 26.3 show the comparison performance of proposed PID controllers in terms of sprung mass velocity and suspension deflection.

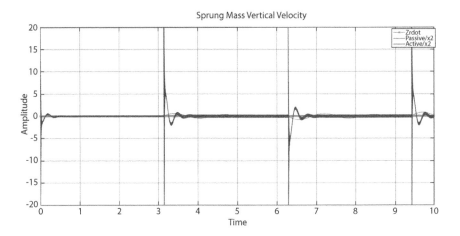

Figure 26.2 Sprung mass velocity.

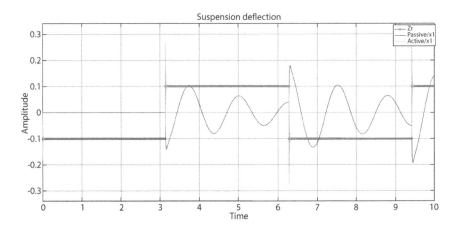

Figure 26.3 Suspension deflection.

Figures 26.4 and 26.5 show the comparison performance of proposed state feedback controllers in terms of sprung mass velocity and suspension deflection.

Figures 26.6 and 26.7 show the comparison performance of proposed state feedback controllers in terms of sprung mass velocity and suspension deflection for proposed linearized model.

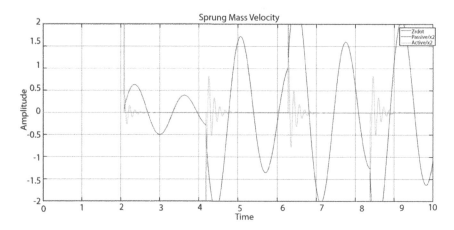

Figure 26.4 Sprung mass velocity.

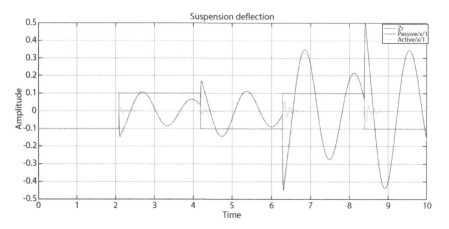

Figure 26.5 Suspension deflection.

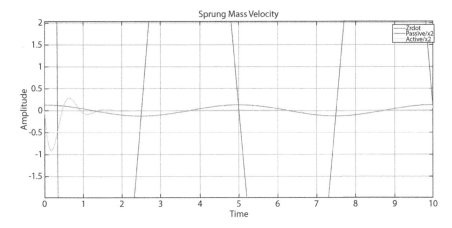

Figure 26.6 Sprung mass velocity.

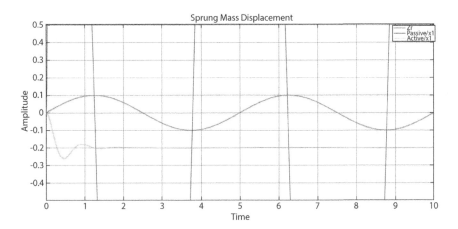

Figure 26.7 Suspension deflection.

26.3   Conclusion

In this chapter, PID control and State feedback control are developed for the quarter-car model to improve the performance parameter of active suspension system. The linearized quarter car model performance is compared with linear active suspension model and traditional passive suspension system. The performance of each control strategy is analyzed in terms of vertical displacement, suspension travel and wheel deflection by the execution of simulations using MATLAB/Simulink on the quarter car suspension model. The comparative analysis verifies that the active suspension system has the ability to diminish the external road disturbances that effects the vehicle stability and provides better control performance to PID, State feedback and passive suspension system. In future work, this research study can be expanded to design observer-based adaptive control of vehicle suspension to improve the ride ease and vehicle stability.

References

1. Du, M., Zhao, D., Yang, B., Wang, L., Terminal sliding mode control for full vehicle active suspension systems. *J. Mech. Sci. Technol.*, 32, 2851–2866, 2018.
2. Wang, H., Mustafa, G.I., Tian, Y., Model-free fractional-order sliding mode control for an active vehicle suspension system. *Adv. Eng. Softw.*, 115, 452–461, 2018.
3. Daniyan, I., Mpofu, K., Daniyan, O., Adeodu, A., Dynamic modelling and simulation of rail car suspension systems using classic controls. *Cogent Eng.*, 6, 1602927, 2019.
4. Gao, H., Xue, S., Yin, S., Qiu, J., Wang, C., Output feedback control of multirate sampled-data systems with frequency specifications. *IEEE Trans. Control Syst. Technol.*, 25, 1599–1608, 2016.
5. Han, S.Y., Zhong, X.F., Chen, Y.H., Tang, G.Y., Discrete approximate optimal vibration control nonlinear vehicle active suspension. *J. Vibro Eng.*, 19, 1287–1300, 2017.
6. Harrag, A. and Messalti, S., PSO-based SMC variable step size P & O MPPT controller for PV systems under fast changing atmospheric conditions. *Int. J. Numer. Model. Electron. Netw. Devices Fields*, 32, 5, e2603, 2019.
7. M'Sirdi, N., Rabhi, N., Fridman, A., Davila, L., Delanne, J., Second order sliding-mode observer for estimation of vehicle dynamic parameters. *Int. J. Veh. Des.*, 48, 190–207, 2008.
8. Kashem, S.B.A., Ektesabi, M., Nagarajah, R., Comparison between different sets of suspension parameters and introduction of new modified skyhook control strategy incorporating varying road condition. *Veh. Syst. Dyn.*, 50, 1173–1190, 2012.
9. M'Sirdi, N., Rabhi, N., Fridman, A., Davila, L., Delanne, J., Load-dependent observer design for active suspension systems. *Int. J. Veh. Des.*, 68, 163–190, 2015.
10. Bai, R. and Guo, D., Sliding-mode control of the active suspension system with the dynamics of a hydraulic actuator. *Complexity*, 2018, Article ID 5907208, 6, 2018.
11. Li, M., Zhang, Y., Geng, Y., Fault-tolerant sliding mode control for uncertain active suspension systems against simultaneous actuator and sensor faults

via a novel sliding mode observer. *Opt. Control Appl. Methods*, 39, 1728–1749, 2018.

12. Dong, X., Zhao, D., Yang, B., Han, C., Fractional-order control of active suspension actuator based on parallel adaptive clonal selection algorithm. *J. Mech. Sci. Technol.*, 30, 2769–2781, 2016.

13. Khan, L., Qamar, S., Khan, M.U., Comparative analysis of adaptive neuro-fuzzy control techniques for full car active suspension system. *Arab. J. Sci. Eng.*, 39, 2045–2069, 2014.

14. Xia, G., Hua, Y., Tang, X., Zhao, L., Chen, W., Internal-model control of vehicle chassis based on wavelet-network dynamic inversion method. *Int. J. Veh. Auton. Syst.*, 14, 170–195, 2018.

15. Hasbullah, F. and Faris, W.F., Simulation of disturbance rejection control of half-car active suspension system using active disturbance rejection control with decoupling transformation. *J. Phys. Conf. Ser.* IOP Publ., 949, 012025, 2017.

16. Khan, L., Qamar, S., Khan, U., Adaptive PID control scheme for full car suspension control. *J. Chin. Inst. Eng.*, 39, 169–185, 20162016.

17. Huang, Y., Na, J., Wu, X., Gao, G.B., Guo, Y., Robust adaptive control for vehicle active suspension systems with uncertain dynamics. *Trans. Inst. Meas. Control*, 40, 1237–1249, 2018.

18. Ikenaga, S., Lewis, F.L., Campos, J., Davis, L., Active suspension control of ground vehicle based on a full-vehicle model, in: *Proceedings of the 2000 American Control Conference, ACC (IEEE Cat. No. 00CH36334)*, Chicago, IL, USA, vol. 6, pp. 4019–4024, June 28–30, 2000.

19. Chen, Y., Wang, Z.L., Qiu, J., Huang, H.Z., Hybrid fuzzy skyhook surface control using multi-objective microgenetic algorithm for semi-active vehicle suspension system ride comfort stability analysis. *J. Dyn. Syst. Meas. Control*, 134, 041003, 2012.

20. Rizvi, S.M.H., Abid, M., Khan, A.Q., Satti, S.G., Latif, J., H$_\infty$ control of 8 degrees of freedom vehicle active suspension system. *J. King Saud. Univ. Eng. Sci.*, 30, 161–169, 2018.

21. Yagiz, N. and Hacioglu, Y., Backstepping control of a vehicle with active suspensions. *Control Eng. Pract.*, 16, 1457–1467, 2008.

22. Martins, I., Esteves, J., Marques, G.D., Da Silva, F.P., Permanent-magnets linear actuators applicability in automobile active suspensions. *IEEE Trans. Veh. Technol.*, 55, 86–94, 2006.

23. Pujol, G. and Acho, L., Stabilization of the furuta pendulum with backlash using H-LMI technique: Experimental validation. *Asian J. Control*, 12, 460–467, 2010.

24. Ding, R., Wang, R., Meng, X., Chen, L., A modified energy-saving skyhook for active suspension based on a hybrid electromagnetic actuator. *J. Vib. Control*, 25, 286–297, 2019.

25. Beltran-Carbajal, F., Valderrabano-Gonzalez, A., Favela-Contreras, A., Hernandez-Avila, J.L., Lopez-Garcia, I., Tapia-Olvera, R., An active vehicle

suspension control approach with electromagnetic and hydraulic actuators, in: *Actuators*, vol. 8, p. 35, Multidisciplinary Digital Publishing Institute, Basel, Switzerland, 2019.

26. Kim, C. and Ro, P., II, A sliding mode controller for vehivle active suspension systems with non-linearities. *Proc. Inst. Mech. Eng. D J. Automob. Eng.*, 212, 79–92, 1998.

## 27

A Study of Various Peak to Average Power Ratio (PAPR) Reduction Techniques for 5G Communication System (5G-CS)

Himanshu Kumar Sinha, Anand Kumar and Devasis Pradhan*

Department of Electronics & Communication Engineering, Acharya Institute of Technology, Bangalore, Karnataka, India

Abstract

Interest in interactive media information administrations has exploded in recent years. Orthogonal frequency division multiplexing (OFDM), one of the most promising multitransporter frameworks, is the foundation for all 5G remote correspondence frameworks due to its enormous ability to allow a large number of subcarriers, high information rate, and universal inclusion with high versatility. OFDM is altogether impacted by the top to-average power proportion (PAPR). Tragically, the high PAPR inborn to OFDM signal envelopes will infrequently drive high power intensifiers (HPAs) to work in the nonlinear district of their trademark bend. The fundamental downside of the OFDM framework is the high top to average power proportion (PAPR) of the communicated signal. OFDM comprises an enormous number of autonomous subcarriers because of which the abundance of such a sign can have high pinnacle valves. The Diverse PAPR decrease strategies are accessible, like clipping, companding, selective mapping (SLM), interleaving, tone reservation (TR) tone injection (TI), and partial transmit sequence (PTS) and made examination between them.

Keywords: 5G, OFDM, peak-to-average power reduction (PAPR), intercarrier interference (ICI), high power amplification (HPA), selective mapping (SLM), PTS

27.1 Introduction

Fourth-generation wireless communication systems are now in use in a vast number of countries around the world. Nonetheless, there are still

---

Corresponding author: devasispradhan@acharya.ac.in

Anita Khosla, Prasenjit Chatterjee, Ikbal Ali and Dheeraj Joshi (eds.) Optimization Techniques in Engineering: Advances and Applications, (437–454) © 2023 Scrivener Publishing LLC

a few difficulties like a blast of remote cell phones and administrations, which cannot be obliged even by 4G, like the range shortage and high-energy utilization. 5G innovation represents fifth-age versatile innovation, which is the norm past 4G and LTE-progressed. Filter bank multicarrier is a strategy wherein a bank of channels are utilized on the transmitter and beneficiary side. The transmitter channel is known as the combination channel bank, and the collector channel is known as the investigation channel bank. Strangely, FBMC is the multicarrier procedure, which was created preceding OFDM.

Despite the fact that thrilling examination is in progress to upgrade channel execution of OFDM with insignificant intercarrier interference (ICI), better range use, and negligible intersymbol interference (ISI) utilizing a cyclic prefix (CP), it displays a few inborn downsides. First of all, due to rectangular pulse leakage, frequency discrepancy is encountered. Besides, misfortune in the range happens because of CP add-on to destroy blurring in a multipath environment [8–10]. Third, tough recurrence and time synchronization neglect to safeguard the symmetry in subtransporters despite the fact that it helps protect obstructions inside and among cells. Fourthly, focused on exponential increment of PAPR. Fifthly, high out-of-band radiations, as OFDM sends square heartbeats for the baseband. Finally, high bit error rate (BER) expansion with respect to regulation levels.

Fifth-Generation (5G) portable correspondence standard is en route to being industrially functional in a couple of years and is expected to achieve a significant transformation in different market domains, for example, logical, business, industry, public, to make reference to a couple [12, 13]. It would give improved energy proficiency, throughput, information inclusion, and inertness contrasted and the present 4G construction. The predominant 4G standard is without a skilled foundation that would empower it to be forward viable with the approaching 5G network. Quite possibly the most basic concern for carrying out 5G correspondence is choosing the best waveform that is the most ideal for that specific application. On the off chance that we pick the appropriate channel then obstruction is just between adjoining channels and there is no impedance between non-contiguous channels. Hence UMFC procedure is more appropriate for high versatility applications and here symmetry might be obliterated which will not deliver ICI, in contrast to OFDM. Additionally, huge side flaps in OFDM is an issue that makes it troublesome in intellectual radio application [18, 19]. To stifle the side flaps there would be up to half misfortune in data transfer capacity. So UMFC is an appropriate possibility for 5G correspondence.

27.2   Literature Review

The PAPR is among a couple of hindrances to its regularization. PAPR hampers the display of the system in light of the fact that the use of the OFDM transmission schemes at the source of the structure PAPR is viewed as one of the huge worries in planning the FBMC structure. An acceleration in PAPR diminishes the greatness of the framework by expanding the PAPR and spot mistake rate (BER) of FBMC. The plan of FBMC is underlying channels; Inverse Fast Fourier changes (IFFTs) and, FFTs. The bunch of channels lessens the range surge and further develops the data transfer capacity forming [1, 2]. BFA is viewed as the most recent improvement streamlining agent calculation, focused on the scavenge conduct of the *E. coli* microorganisms. The vital diligence of BFA is to create an ideal stage factor for SLM [3]. The creators of [4] described that the FBMC waveform cannot utilize OFDM's moderate PAPR rehearses as a result of its exceptional arrangement.

The symmetrical recurrence division multiplexing (OFDM) is the most widely used regulation scheme in fourth-generation (4G) frameworks [5–7]. OFDM can viably battle the multiway blurring channel to give dependable transmission and increment the framework limit. Along these lines, OFDM utilizes a cyclic prefix (CP) and a guard interval between the OFDM images to stay away from the interchannel interference (ICI) and the intersymbol interference (ISI), attributable to the nearby subtransporters and images, individually. As of late, numerous options in contrast to OFDM innovation were proposed for the 5G air interface. These incorporate sifted OFDM (F-OFDM) [14], filtered bank multicarrier (FBMC) [3], universal filtered multicarrier (UFMC) [1], and generalized frequency division multiplexing (GFDM) [15]. In the UFMC framework, the sub-transporters are stuffed and separated as sub-groups. This diminishes the channel length, making UFMC more appropriate for dynamic range designation methods in intellectual radio (CR) networks [16, 17]. Moreover, UFMC gives lower side flap radiation, low inactivity, and capacity of supporting recurrence division and multiadministration applications [15]. Regardless, UFMC experiences high PAPR emerging from the utilization of multitransporter transmission [11].

A few methods for PAPR decrease were proposed in the writing [20, 21]. These procedures can be named either signal bending [22, 23], encoding [24], or probabilistic techniques [25, 26]. The first technique utilizes cutting or separating to restrict the greatest level of the sign, thus lessening the PAPR. This presents contortions in the communicated signal, which considers the framework bit error rate (BER) execution [21]. Moreover, the encoding plans cause low information rate productivity [27, 28]. On the opposite side, the probabilistic strategies, like the chose planning (SLM) [29–31] and incomplete communicate succession (PTS) [28, 32], present irregular stage shifts on the sent images as a pre-coding step without causing critical mutilations.

27.3   Overview of 5G Cellular System

5G is a confounded cell network as well, so it needs to construct a few different strategies, which can be of mm wave correspondence, MIMO, increased piddling cells, and grouped organizations. There are likewise 5G execution markers that are liable for the exhibition given by the organization for example are association thickness, reliability, and energy viability [24–26]. Subsequently, growing the assignment of 5G systems to millimeter-wave (mm-Wave) bunches is fundamental due to the openness of immense proportions of move speed. In any case, prior to loosening up 5 G structures to mm-Wave gatherings, it is indispensable to make exact mm-Wave inciting models and survey them insensible framework circumstances [27]. There are a couple of continuous assessments in the composition on mm-Wave channel showing. Figure 27.1 discusses the various application of 5G.

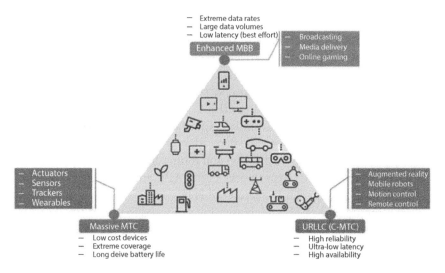

Figure 27.1 Application of 5G Cellular System (Source: Ericsson white-papers/5g-wireless-access-an-overview).

It will give speeds quicker than any past age—up to 3000 Mbps (3 Gbps) in reality, contingent upon the conditions and the tech being utilized—contending even with those conveyed through fiber-optic links. Motion pictures that required minutes to download with 4G will require seconds with 5G. In 2020, there were an expected 12B IoT associations internationally, as indicated by IoT Analytic. By 2025, it is guessed that there will be more than 30B IoT associations all over the planet, multiple IoT gadgets for each individual on Earth. Independent vehicles, automated medical procedures, and basic framework observing are only a couple of the possible utilization of 5G-empowered IoT.

27.4   PAPR

The PAPR is the basic component though which performance of the system with respect to data rate can be monitored toward efficient usage of communication system in 5G technology. PAPR happens when the diverse sub-transporters in a multicarrier framework are out of stage with one another. In a multicarrier framework, there are countless freely tweaked subcarriers, which are out of stage as for one another. In the event that multiple subcarriers accomplish the greatest worth simultaneously, the resulting envelope will build causing a top in the yield, and when these pinnacles are accumulated for transmission, enormous pinnacle esteem arrives at that is extremely huge contrasted with the normal worth of the example [6]. PAPR is characterized by the accompanying condition:

$$PAPR = \frac{\max\{x[n]\}^2}{E\{x[n]\}^2} \qquad (27.1)$$

where the amplitude of $x[n]$ and E is the assumption for the signal. If PAPR value is high then the power intensifier act in the immersion district, prompting expansions in blunders and furthermore increments in out of band radiation.

27.4.1   Continuous Time PAPR

It is extent among the most elevated momentary power and ordinary force of base-band signal $x(t)$.

$$PAPR\ [x(t)] = \frac{\max\{x(t)\}^2}{P_{av}} \tag{27.2}$$

where the normal power of x(t) is P_{av}

27.4.2   Continuous Time PAPR

The discrete-time succession's PAPR ordinarily chooses the inconvenience of advanced hardware as far as the number of bits vital to achieving a necessary sign to quantization commotion for both advanced activity and the DAC. The PAPR is used to find the best approximation for OFDM tests are accomplished by L time over inspecting. The oversampled IFFT yield is displayed as:

$$x[n] = \frac{1}{\sqrt{N}} \sum_{k=0}^{N-1} X_k e^{j\left(\frac{2\pi nk}{LN}\right)},\ 0 \le n \le LN - 1 \tag{27.3}$$

27.5   Factors on which PAPR Reduction Depends

While applying various techniques for PAPR diminishment we need to keep up with the brilliant working of the framework with reference to different elements such as:

- While picking the PAPR diminishment technique, the variable ought to be remembered that it has the least damaging issues. For instance inside band and outside band twisting.
- PAPR has diminished yet the ordinary force of the framework is improved, which brings about a decrease in the BER execution of the framework.
- Normally, complex plans give better PAPR decreasing. In any case, time and equipment prerequisites ought to be least.
- Assuming that there is an extension in transfer speed then it brings about information rate misfortune on account of side data. So it ought to be stayed away from or ought to be pretty much as least as could really be expected.

27.6   PAPR Reduction Technique

There are different PAPR decrease procedures that can be utilized to work on the exhibition of multicarrier modulation systems. These procedures are separated into two gatherings - signal scrambling methods and signal distortion.

27.6.1   Scrambling of Signals

The essential rule of these systems is to scramble each OFDM signal with different scrambling plans likewise select one which has the most diminutive PAPR as an impetus for transmission. Clearly, this technique does not guarantee the decline of PAPR regard under a particular breaking point, be that as it may, it can reduce the appearance probability of high PAPR to an uncommon degree.

a. SLM: In the SLM method, the entire arrangement of the signal address a similar sign however most good sign is picked connected with PAPR sent. The side data should be sent with the picked signal. This plan is entirely dependable yet has a downside hat is side data should be sent alongside the picked signal. The SLM-OFDM transmitter is portrayed in Figure 27.2.

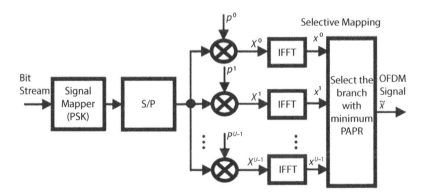

Figure 27.2 SLM-OFDM transmitter.

Here $X = [X(0), X(1), ... X(N - 1)]$ is multiplied with U different phase sequences

$$P^u = [P_1^u, P_2^u, P_3^u ....P_{N-1}^u] \tag{27.4}$$

where $P_v^u = e^{j\emptyset} \epsilon (0, 2\pi)$,
for $v = 0,1,2,......N - 1$, and $u = 1,2,3,4,5 .... U$ which produce a modified data block

$$X^u = [x^u[0], x^u[1], x^u[2], x^u[3]... ... ..x^u[N - 1]]^T \tag{27.5}$$

SLM the technique needs U IFFT action and the quantity of required pieces as side information is for each data block. As such, the limit of PAPR decline in SLM depends upon the quantity of stage factors and the arrangement of the stage factors.

b. PTS: It is likewise one of the Probabilistic based methods. The primary thought of this plan is information block partition into uncovering sub-blocks with autonomous pivot factors. This revolution factor creates time area information with the most reduced sufficiency. This is the adjusted method of the SLM plan and gives preferred execution over SLM. Due to differential balance, no requirements to send the side data. The PTS-OFDM transmitter is shows in Figure 27.3.

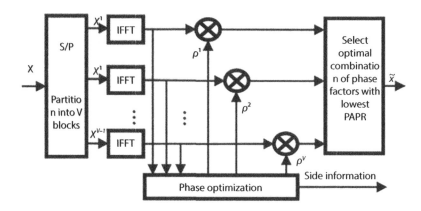

Figure 27.3 PTS-OFDM transmitter.

PTS is one more exceptionally successful way to deal with lessen the PAPR, here the info information square of N images is apportioned into V disjoint subblock as follows

$$X = [X^1, X^2 \ldots \ldots \ldots X^V]^T$$

Then, at that point, each parceled subblock is increased by a relating complex stage factor $\rho^v = e^{j\varnothing v}$, v = 1,2,3 … ….. V, subsequently taking its IFFT to yield

$$x = IFFT\left[\sum\nolimits_{v=1}^{V} \rho^v x^v\right] = \sum\nolimits_{v=1}^{V} \rho^v IFFT\left[x^v\right] = \sum\nolimits_{v=1}^{V} \rho^v x^v \quad (27.6)$$

Where is alluded to as a PTS. The stage vector is picked with the goal that the PAPR can be limited, which is displayed as

$$\left[\rho^{\sim 1}, \rho^{\sim 2}, \rho^{\sim 3} \ldots \rho^{\sim V}\right] = arg\ min(max_{n=0,1,2\ldots\ldots N-1})\left|\sum\nolimits_{(v=1)}^{V} \rho^v x^v(n)\right|$$
$$(27.7)$$

Then, at that point, the comparing time-area signal with the least PAPR vector can be communicated as

$$x^{\sim} = \sum\nolimits_{v=1}^{V} \rho^{\sim V} x^v \qquad (27.8)$$

The PTS technique requires U IFFT operations for each data block and $[\log_2 U^V]$ bits of side information.

c. Linear Block Code (LBC): This technique is generally called the standard exhibit of direct block codes. In this arrangement, a specific U sign is sent close by the conveyed gathering. U specific sign is by and large created using genuine co–set words. Using scrambling codes, no prerequisites to send side information, and the got sign can be adequately decoded. Strangely, they select a standard group of codes to diminish the PAPR. This strategy discusses the sign with the least PAPR using scrambling code. This technique has ideal execution over the SLM strategy.

d. Interleaving: In this method, a limit component is utilized which additionally decreases the intricacy. Versatile interleaving is to build up an early ending limit. So the looking through the process is ended when the worth of PAPR comes to underneath the limit esteem.

e. Tone Reservation (TR): The guideline thought about this system is to save a little course of action of tones for PAPR decline. This can be begun as an angled issue and this issue can be tended to unequivocally. The tone reservation strategy relies upon adding a data square and time-region signal. A data block is a dependent time region sign to the first multicarrier sign to restrict the high top. This time-space sign not really settled basically at the transmitter of the structure and stripped off at the recipient. The amount PAPR decline depends upon specific factors like number of held tones, proportion of unpredictability, space of the saved tones, and allowed power on saved tones This method explains an additional substance plot for restricting PAPR in the multicarrier correspondence system [22, 23].

f. Tone Injection (TI): This strategy is for the most part utilized as an added substance technique for PAPR decrease. Utilizing this technique information rate misfortune is extremely less. This technique utilizes the arrangement of dynamic star grouping focuses for a unique heavenly body highlight to decrease the PAPR. In this unit, all unique groups of stars are planned on a few comparable heavenly bodies focuses and this additional focuses opportunity can be handily used to diminish the PAPR.

27.6.2 Signal Distortion Technique

a. Peak Widowing Technique: Here top windowing technique is fundamentally equivalent to the segment procedure yet it will give better execution by adding some self-impedance and extending in the BER (bit error rate). The OFDM signal is expanded with a couple of these windows; the ensuing reach is a convolution of the primary OFDM range with the scope of the applied window. This suggests the windows should be limited as could be anticipated [23].

b. Envelope Scaling: This technique is associated with scaling suggests before OFDM signals are delivered off the IFFT, all subcarriers are scaled the information envelope. In this strategy, 256 subcarriers are used so all subcarriers will remain same. The essential idea is that the information envelopes in some subcarriers are scaled to achieve the tiniest proportion of PAPR at the aftereffect of the IFFT. Here recipient should not mess around with any side information at the authority end for deciphering [24].

c. Clipping & Filtering: These techniques are the best methods to diminish the high PAPR in the OFDM system. Here cutting is the nonlinear cycle that forms the band upheaval bending, also, a development in the piece goof rate reduces the supernatural usefulness. Filtering resulting to removing will diminish of-band radiation. This methodology will diminish the PAPR without range improvement. Here accepting the OFDM signal is over-tried then the arrangement of cure is suitable with the removed so each subcarrier is made with the impedance [24, 25].

27.6.3 High Power Amplifier (HPA)

The OFDM authority area capability is astoundingly sensitive to the non-direct contraptions used as a piece of its sign taking care of circle, for instance, progressed to the straightforward converter (DAC) and high power enhancer. This may truly block structure execution due to introduced spooky regrowth and recognizable proof capability debasement. For example, most radio structures delegate the HPA in the transmitter to get satisfactory communicates power and the HPA are by and large worked at or near the drenching locale which achieved the most noteworthy yield power usefulness and consequently the memoryless non-straight reshaping due to the high PAPR of the data signs will be brought into the correspondence channel. HPA is not worked in the straight region with significant power ease off [25, 26].

27.7 Limitation of OFDM

OFDM has specific imperatives like cyclic-prefix overhead, Sensitivity to recurrence offset CFO, Spectral re-development and High PAPR make it not the most sensible waveform for every one of the engaged utilizations of 5G. In OFDM to ride with ICI on account of multipath blurring, the cyclic prefix is the best ever strategy utilized. Be that as it may, the cyclic prefix acquaints extra pieces with the communicating information so information excess expanded. The symmetry in OFDM depends on the ideal synchronization transporters of transmitter and collector [28].

In OFDM the symmetry is guaranteed with the ideal synchronization of transmitter and beneficiary for data enough said. For this, the OFDM data will be out of nowhere limited the transmission after each image duration. This abrupt intermittence will cause spikes in the recurrence area. This out-of-band radiation will influence by the adjoining transporters. The high PAPR in an OFDM framework basically emerges as a result of IFFT activity. In OFDM the communicated tests are IFFT tests of information symbols [27, 28].

27.8   Universal Filter Multicarrier (UMFC) Emerging Technique to Reduce PAPR in 5G

The new waveform ought to accomplish offbeat gathering and transmission, non-orthogonal waveform for better unearthly proficiency and low inactivity. And yet, you can without much of a stretch tune the subcarriers dispersing and a number of tones contingent on the band reach and transfer speed of the application that we are managing. Intending to the adaptable waveform on a similar organization, we can acquaint separating with the OFDM images that we can really have diverse numerology conjunction on a similar organization. Some new waveform plans are more drawn in by businesses just as exploration associations which are less perplexing in the plan, UFMC is generally satisfactory for 5G [29, 30].

UFMC is the strategy that joins the benefits of symmetry OFDM and channel bank in FBMC. Rather than separating every carrier like in FBMC, we have to filter a block of a carrier called a sub-band. Each sub-band contains various carriers; channel length will be contingent on the width of the sub-band. In the UFMC framework, the perplexing symbol is created from the base-band modulator. The length of N point IFFT result will be serialized block-wise and that result will be separated with a molding channel of length L. The information stream X will be changed over to B disjoint blocks [31].

27.8.1   Transmitter of UMFC

In the UFMC structure, the information image is changed over to take after streams, achieving squares of streams and given as a commitment

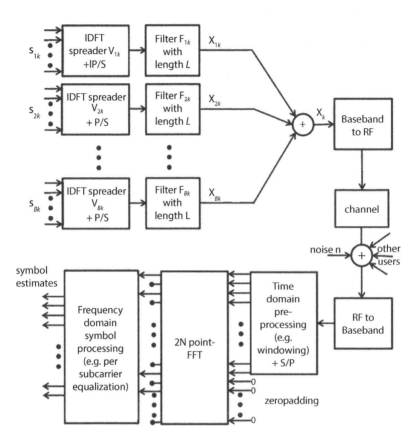

Figure 27.4 Basic block diagram for UMFC transceiver.

to the IFFT block which changes the commitment from repeat region to time-space. The N point IFFT result will be serialized block-wise and the outcome will be filtered with a heartbeat molding channel of length L. Finally, the filtered signals are consolidated to shape the imparted signal. This collaboration is shown in Figure 27.4. For the ith sub-band ($1 \leq i \leq B$), the data blocks are addressed with $X_{i,k}$, IFFT matrix $V_{i,k}$ and pulse shaping filter with $F_{i,k}$. The final signal transmitted in the channel is represented as

$$x_k = \sum_{i=1}^{B} F_{i,k} V_{i,k} X_{i,k} \qquad (27.9)$$

27.8.2   Receiver of UMFC

The recipient a piece of UFMC is shown in Figure 27.4. After the RF-associate section, the sign will go through the time region pre-dealing with window to smother deterrent. Resulting to windowing, the sign will change over into "2N" equal streams; here "N" is the quantity of sub-carriers. The demodulated signal is transported off the demapper, which is the QPSK demodulator to recuperate the data bits from the information images. Other demodulation strategies, for a model, Zero Forcing (ZF), Matched Filtering (MF) and Least Mean Square Error (LMSE) have moreover been evaluated.

UFMC is a potential multicarrier framework for cutting edge cell frameworks advancing toward a 5G organization, which gives low inertness, repeat offset power, and diminished out-of-band (OOB) transmission. Regardless, UFMC encounters the issue of high PAPR, which might influence the limit of high power enhancers causing a nonlinear bending.

27.9   Comparison Between Various Techniques

The comparison is done on the basis of BER, distortionless, power utilization, and data rate loss while using the different PAPR Reduction Techniques. Table 27.1 discusses the comparative effectiveness of the techniques.

27.10   Conclusion

OFDM is comprehensively passed on in remote 5G frameworks due to its phantom capability and power of the channel. Yet high PAPR is an issue in OFDM. In this chapter, we examined different PAPR diminishment strategies, which have both benefits and bad marks (misfortune in information rate, corrupted BER, increase in signal influence, expanded complexity). These strategies ought to be used by the application. In this way, UFMC can be one of the most potential applicant waveforms for 5G, which can supplant OFDM, utilized already in LTE 4G interchanges.

Table 27.1 Comparison of the parameter.

Sl. No.	Techniques PAPR Reduction	Parameter					
		Complexity of implementation	Band width expansion	BER degradation	Distortionless	Power Utilization	Data Rate Loss
		Signal Scrambling					
1	SLM	Low	Yes	Yes	Yes	No	Yes
2	PTS	High	Yes	No	No	Yes	No
3	LBC	Low	Yes	No	Yes	Yes	Yes
4	TR	Quasi-optimal	No	No	Yes	Yes	Yes
5	TI	Low	Yes	No	Yes	Yes	No
		Signal Distortion Technique					
1	PWT	High	No	No	Yes	Yes	No
2	ES	Low	Yes	No	No	Yes	No
3	Clipping	Low	No	No	No	No	No
4	Filtering	High	No	Yes	Yes	Yes	No
5	HPA	Low	Yes	No	No	Yes	No

References

1. Na, D. and Choi, K., Low PAPR FBMC. *IEEE Trans. Wirel. Commun.*, 17, 1, 182–193, 2018.

2. Liang, H. and Jiang, H., The modified artificial bee colony-based SLM scheme for PAPR reduction in OFDM systems, in: *2019 Int. Conf. on Artificial Intelligence in Information and Communication (ICAIIC)Okinawa, Japan*, pp. 504–508, 2019.

3. Zhang, Q., Chen, H., Luo, J., Xu, Y., Wu, C. *et al.*, Chaos enhanced bacterial foraging optimization for global optimization. *IEEE Access*, 6, 64905–64919, 2018.

4. Sandoval, F., Poitau, G., Gagnon, F., Hybrid peak-to-average power ratio reduction techniques: Review and performance comparison. *IEEE Access*, 5, 27145–27161, 2017.

5. Arun, K., Novel hybrid PAPR reduction technique for NOMA and FBMC system and its impact in power amplifiers. *IETE J. Res.*, 65, 5, 1–17, 2019.

6. Cho, Y.S., Kim, J., Yang, W.Y., Kang, C.G., *MIMO-OFDM Wireless Communications with MATLAB*, John Wiley & Sons, Hoboken, NJ, USA, 2010.

7. Dai, L., Wang, Z., Yang, Z., Time-frequency training OFDM with high spectral efficiency and reliable performance in high-speed environments. *IEEE J. Sel. Areas Commun.*, 30, 695–707, 2012.

8. Fathy, S.A., Ibrahim, M., El-Agooz, S., El-Hennawy, H., Low-complexity SLM PAPR reduction approach for UFMC systems. *IEEE Access*, 8, 68021–68029, 2020.

9. Almutairi, A.F., Al-Gharabally, M., Krishna, A., Performance analysis of hybrid peak to average power ratio reduction techniques in 5G UFMC systems. *IEEE Access*, 7, 80651–80660, 2019.

10. Wang, Y., Zhang, R., Li, J., Shu, F., PAPR reduction based on parallel tabu search for tone reservation in OFDM systems. *IEEE Wirel. Commun. Lett.*, 8, 576–579, 2019.

11. Kamurthi, R.T., Review of UFMC technique in 5G, in: *Proceedings of the 2018 International Conference on Intelligent Circuits and Systems (ICICS)*, Phagwara, India, pp. 115–120, April 19–20, 2018.

12. Valluri, S. and Mani, V., A novel approach for reducing complexity in the SLM-GFDM system. *Phys. Commun.*, 34, 188–195, 2019.

13. Barba-Maza, L.M. and Dolecek, G.J., Papr reduction of GFDM system using xia pulse and OPTS scheme. *2020 IEEE 63rd International Midwest Symposium on Circuits and Systems (MWSCAS)*, IEEE, pp. 774–777, 2020.

14. Zhao, Y., Wu, C., Wu, L., Li, C., GFDM system PAPR reduction based on MCT method. *International Conference in Communications, Signal Processing, and Systems*, Springer, pp. 923–934, 2017.

15. Kishore, G.S. and Rallapalli, H., Towards 5G: A survey on waveform contenders, in: *Advances in Decision Sciences, Image Processing, Security and*

Computer Vision, pp. 243–250, Springer, Cham, Springer Nature Switzerland AG, 2020.

16. Redana, S. (Ed.), Bulakci, Ö. (Ed.), Zafeiropoulos, A., Gavras, A., Tzanakaki, A., Albanese, A., Kousaridas, A., Weit, A., Sayadi, B., Jou, B. T., Bernardos, C. J., Benzaid, C., Mannweiler, C., Camps-Mur, D., Breitgand, D., Estevez, D. G., Navratil, D., Mi, D., Lopez, D., ... Zhang, Y., 5G PPP Architecture Working Group: View on 5G Architecture. European Commission, White Paper from European Commission, 2019.

17. Sim, Z.A., Reine, R., Zang, Z., Juwono, F.H., Gopal, L., Reducing the PAPR of GFDM systems with quadratic programming filter design. *2019 IEEE 89th Vehicular Technology Conference (VTC2019-Spring)*, IEEE, pp. 1–5, 2019.

18. Laabidi, M. and Bouallegue, R., Three implementations of the tone reservation PAPR reduction scheme for the FBMC/OQAM system. *IET Commun.*, 13, 7, 918–925, 2019.

19. Nambi, S.A. and Giridhar, K., Lower order modulation aided BER reduction in OFDM with index modulation. *IEEE Commun. Lett.*, 22, 8, 1596–1599, 2018.

20. Na, D. and Choi, K., Low PAPR FBMC. *IEEE Trans. Wirel. Commun.*, 17, 1, 182–193, 2018.

21. Liang, H. and Jiang, H., The modified artificial bee colony-based SLM scheme for PAPR reduction in OFDM systems, in: *2019 Int. Conf. on Artifificial Intelligence in Information and Communication (ICAIIC)*, Okinawa, Japan, pp. 504–508, 2019.

22. Zhang, Q., Chen, H., Luo, J., Xu, Y., Wu, C. *et al.*, Chaos enhanced bacterial foraging optimization for global optimization. *IEEE Access*, 6, 64905–64919, 2018.

23. Pradhan, D. and Priyanka, K.C., RF-energy hHarvesting (RF-EH) for sustainable ultra-dense green network (SUDGN) in 5G green communication. *Saudi J. Eng. Technol.*, 5, 6, 258–264, 2020.

24. Pradhan, D., Sahu, P., Dash, A., Tun, H., Sustainability of 5G green network toward D2D communication with RF-energy techniques. *IEEE International Conference on Intelligent Technologies (CONIT 2021)*, K.L.E.I.T, Hubbali, Karnataka, IEEE Bangalore Section, IEEE, pp. 1–10, 2021June 25, 2021.

25. Pradhan, D. and Rajeswari, 5G-green wireless network for communication with efficient utilization of power and cognitiveness, in: *International Conference on Mobile Computing and Sustainable Informatics, ICMCSI 2020. EAI/Springer Innovations in Communication and Computing*, Springer, Cham, 2021, https://doi.org/10.1007/978-3-030-49795-8_32.

26. Devasis, P. and Priyanka, K.C., Effectiveness of spectrum sensing in cognitive radio toward 5G technology. *Saudi J. Eng. Technol.*, 4, 12, 473–785, Dec 2019.

27. Patil, P., Pawar, P. R., Jain, P. P., K.V., M., Pradhan, D., Performance analysis of energy detection method in spectrum sensing using static & variable threshold level for 3G/4G/VoLTE. *Saudi J. Eng. Technol.*, 5, 4, 173–178, 2020.

28. Tao, Y., Liu, L., Liu, S., Zhang, Z., A survey: Several technologies of non-orthogonal transmission for 5G. *China Commun.*, 12, 1–15, 2015.

29. Rani, P.N. and Rani, C.S., UFMC: The 5G modulation technique, in: *Proceedings of the 2016 IEEE International Conference on Computational Intelligence and Computing Research (ICCIC)*, Chennai, India, pp. 1–3, December 15–17, 2016.

30. Kamurthi, R.T., Review of UFMC technique in 5G, in: *Proceedings of the 2018 International Conference on Intelligent Circuits and Systems (ICICS)*, Phagwara, India, pp. 115–120, April 19–20, 2018.

31. Luo, F.L. and Zhang, C., *Signal Processing for 5G: Algorithms and Implementations*, John Wiley & Sons, Hoboken, NJ, USA, 2016.

## 28

Investigation of Rebound Suppression Phenomenon in an Electromagnetic V-Bending Test

Aman Sharma[1]*, Pradeep Kumar Singh[1], Manish Saraswat[2] and Irfan Khan[2]

[1]Department of Mechanical Engineering, GLA University, Mathura, India
[2]Department of Mechanical Engineering, Lloyd Institute of Engineering and Technology, Greater Noida, India

Abstract

Electromagnetic forming (EMF) is a highly advanced technique. The time developments and spatial distributions of EMF in the body and die-induced limitations are key elements affecting the dynamical behavior of sheets metal. The immense power generated by the sheet and die colliding at fast speeds allows the sheet to recover from the die. In this chapter, the phenomenon of rebound is investigated for an electromagnetic V-bending test based on the time-bearing contrast between the sheet metal displacement and the power amplitude. Collision encourages deformation, causing a dramatic shift in plane geometry, in which the component fits with die is aided by an innovative distribution of EMF. As the force reduced by the increasing distance is formed into a not-so-deep die, EMF retains sufficient strength to effectively eliminate a rebound and contribute to the calibration about the shape of the section, which is "V." Increase the length of the spindle current pulses contributes to a shallow die to suppress the rebounding effect of sheet metal.

Keywords: Electromagnetic forming, V-bend, calibration, aluminum alloy, duration, rebound

28.1 Introduction

Low forming at room temperature is restricted to the application of aluminum alloys. However, there are advantages like corrosion resistance, high ratio of strength-to-weight, and weldability. Electromagnetic forming

---

**Corresponding author*: aman.sharma@gla.ac.in

Anita Khosla, Prasenjit Chatterjee, Ikbal Ali and Dheeraj Joshi (eds.) *Optimization Techniques in Engineering: Advances and Applications*, (455–468) © 2023 Scrivener Publishing LLC

(EMF) is a technology with high speed that enables formability to improve without costly and long thermal treatment. In the aerospace and automotive sectors, EMF has been used extensively. An important approach is "the finite element method," which is used in the sheet metal to investigate its dynamic characteristics [1–4]. For a numerical model of EMF, two majorly used strategies are sequential & lose coupling. For the electromagnetic calculation, the influence of structure deformation is not considered in the loose coupling strategy. According to G. Bartels, for both the strategies the deviation will increase with time. For relatively fast deformation processes, the only strategy which can be used for good approximation is the loose coupling strategy. For small displacement, it is also useful for the numerical simulation of tube forming. For the research area, the loose coupling strategy is widely adopted and it is a fast process with a lower cost of calculation, although some accuracy is lost. The nodal electric power, measured without deforming the workpiece in the electromagnetic field, is transferred in the loose coupling strategy directly into the workpiece in the structural field as the input load [5, 6]. The constraints of electromagnetic body forces on the sheet metal exerted and the temporal & spatial distribution are important factors affecting the dynamic behavior of the plate deformation. During deformation when the distance between sheet and coil is increased, there occurs the decay in EMF. This led to the overestimation of EMF for loose coupling strategy and this in turn results in a more violent collision. The target shape of parts is not achieved due to the rebound phenomenon which is caused due to undesirable violent impact. To calculate the EMF, in sinusoid coil current's quarter-circle between half and quarter of a sinusoid coil current pulse. For calculating EMF, a portion of time is neglected and in structure field, their compensation in overestimated force, for a flat sheet free- bulging, the impact of several pulses on deformation is investigated and for this, both the above-mentioned strategies are compared. The reason for the lower flow stress and overly transmitted energy, the value of the estimated rebound is more than the experimental outcome as observed. To represent physical characteristics of die [7–9]. To investigate the rebound effect, the appropriate geometrical stiffness of the workpiece is introduced in combination with damping coefficient and stiffness. A V-bending experiment is conducted in this chapter and for loose coupling strategy, the numerical model is established. In a numerical model of V-bending, it is observed that the rebound phenomenon is higher than the experimental result. The impact of pulse duration can be seen for the rebound suppression by studying the time relationship for the amplitude of EMF in the sheet and displacement of the sheet. There is also the analysis on how the forces will be distributed on the final shape of the part and to get the desired shape of the part there is the need for a better understanding of all these factors. The calculated force is generated by a uniform pressure actuator using half of the coil current pulse. The EMF process is another high-speed forming method. By discharging a capacitor bank, a high-density electric current is routed through a conductive coil, resulting in a transient magnetic field that induces eddy currents in an adjacent metal sheet. The metal sheet can be deformed or accelerated by the mutually repelling electromagnetic pressure created by the stationary coil and the metal sheet [10–12]. There are a lot of benefits to this method. This method applies forming a force to the workpiece without making contact with it, allowing semi-finished pieces to be formed without damaging the surface layer. There is no need for lubricant, and the process is non-toxic. In addition, excellent reproducibility may be accomplished by modifying the shaping machine [13, 14].

In comparison to explosive forming, the advantages of the EHF are its exact control over the amount and rate of released energy, as well as its capabilities for multi-pass forming [15]. The electrodes, on the other hand, corrode with time in the electrohydraulic forming process, and the distance between electrodes increases as a result of corrosion. As a result, the electrodes must be adjusted regularly [16–18]. During the procedure, the electrodes are consumed, and after many usages, they need to be changed with fresh electrodes. Furthermore, particles discharged into the fluid as a result of electrode corrosion can hit the produced portion quickly in subsequent explosions, scraping and injuring it. Furthermore, any change in the liquid volume may need the design and fabrication of a new die in the forming process [19, 20]. To investigate the electromagnetic and mechanical fields, [21] ANSYS/EMAG and LS-DYNA were used to create a loose coupling numerical model. The loose coupling technique, on the other hand, neglected to account for the influence of sheet deformation, which shows results in deviations [22–24]. For tube compression, ANSYS software was used to create a transient electromagnetic/mechanical/thermal numerical model that took deformation effects into account, However, air mesh difficulties frequently plague researchers when utilizing the Finite Element Analysis (FEA) approach, regardless of coupling method, because air elements deform As the mechanical field changes, particularly in the EMF approach due to the tiny starting spacing between the sheet and the coil [25–27]. To solve this problem, we developed a novel electromagnetism (EM) module that allows us to do coupled electromagnetic-mechanical simulations. Using the Boundary Element Method (BEM), the EM module reduced air mesh, potentially improving the numerical model's accuracy significantly [28–31]. The EHFQ technique increases the mechanical precision of the 5A90 Al-Li alloy U-shaped parts. The precipitate behavior and matched relationship of δ' phase is explored, which affect the mechanical properties of parts. A mechanical model is developed to characterize the hardening mechanisms and the contribution of each mechanism is studied [32].

28.2   Investigation

Bend is one of the common modes of deformation in the shaping of sheets. V-bend experiment is performed to gain insight into the local aluminum sheet metal bending deformation behavior during electromagnetic forging.

28.2.1   Specimen for Tests

In this experiment, the samples of the aluminum alloy 2024-T3 having 100 mm/40 mm as the dimension of a plane, and 1.8 mm thickness will be considered. Table 28.1 shows the fundamental physical and mechanical characteristics of 2024-T3.

28.2.2   Design of Die and Tool

The flat spiral coil is well known to be widely used in research. An improved flat spiral coil with four layers is used here in the experiment, providing greater forming strength than the coil having only one layer. Table 28.2 shows the geometrical and electrical parameters. Figure 28.1 shows the die used for experiments.

Table 28.1 Characteristics of al alloy (2024-T3).

Parameter	Poisson's ratio	Density (kg·m⁻³)	Specific heat (J/(g·K))	Tensile strength (MPa)	Yield strength (MPa)	Heat conductivity (W/(m·K))	Elastic modulus (GPa)
Value	0.33	2.68×10^3	0.875	483	345	121	73.1

Table 28.2 Coil parameters.

Parameters	No. of layers	No. of Turns	Gap b/w layers (mm)	Gap b/w turns (mm)	Res. (Ω)	Ind. (H)	Cross sectional-area (mm²)
Value	4	16	0.4	0.8	0.001	2×10^{-6}	2×4

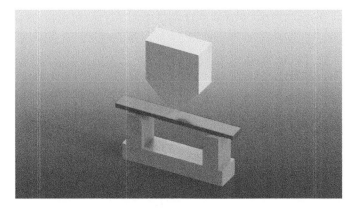

Figure 28.1 Figure showing schematic of die.

28.2.3   Configuration and Procedure

The coil is mounted on the lower part and the die-cavity is pressed towards the top of the coil. The coil is pressed. For the experimental setup, in Figure 28.2(a), the top profile and 28.2(b) the side profile is shown. The condenser loading voltage is set at 18 kV. Figure 28.3 illustrates the shaped section.

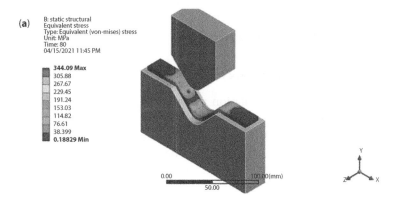

Figure 28.2 Schematic showing forming result of part.

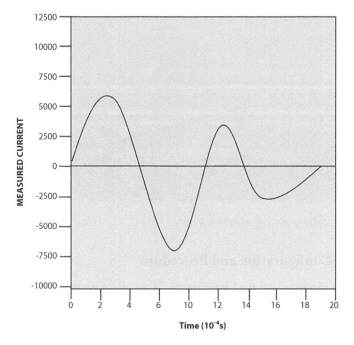

Figure 28.3 Figure showing variation of measured coil current.

28.3   Mathematical Evaluation

28.3.1   Simulation Methodology

In this chapter, a numerical simulation method for the study is selected for the loose coupling strategy. Initially, an EMF simulation is performed and in an electromagnetic field, the source of excitement is measured pulse current which is used to solve the sheet's nodal electromagnetic and, as a direct driving charge, the EMF is input into the structural field. Figure 28.3 shows the estimated belt current used for simulation, and Figure 28.4

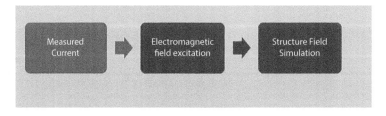

Figure 28.4 Figure showing flowchart for the strategy.

illustrates the connecting approach. The simulation only uses the first pulse of the coil current.

28.4 Modeling for Material

The constructive rate-dependent model of Cowper-Symonds is shown in Expression (28.1). The rate-dependent parameters taken in this model are P=4 and C=6500 s^{-1} [10]. For calculating the dynamic flow stress, we can use equation (28.1), here the stress is taken at plastic strain rate.

$$\sigma_Y = \left[1 + \left\{\frac{\epsilon}{C}\right\}^{\frac{1}{P}}\right]\sigma_{ys} \tag{28.1}$$

where σ_{yz} denotes quasi-static flow stress.

28.4.1 Suppressing Rebound Phenomenon

The EMF in the sheet is still overestimated. This is because there is decay in EMF when the distance between coil and sheet is increased, and this has not been taken into consideration. With the removal of EMF at 1.3 × 10^{-4} seconds, the over-input energy is compensated. In the die cavity, if the sheet has not been pushed down, it will continuously move in the initial state with field velocity for this moment. In Figure 28.5, it is shown that the sheet is slowed down, recoils, and stops. The film energy currently contained in the sheet is sufficiently high to remove the sheet from the die, but some energy was dispersed in a collision.

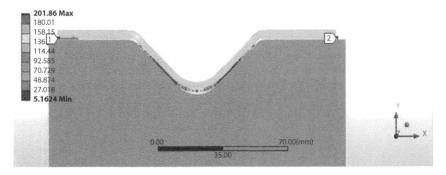

Figure 28.5 Showing the final shape of part (EMF removal).

During the experiment, the sheet will be in contact with the die and it reveals that EMF can strongly suppress the rebound. The sheet will still undergo this EMF after 1.3×10^{-4} seconds. For a complete excitation of this current pulse, the final shape of the part is shown in Figure 28.7. In Figures 28.3 and 28.6, the gaps shown are not that significant as the gaps which are between both the left and right sides of the part and die. A rebound is causing the difference on the left side. The comparatively largely asymmetric electromagnet force on the right side of the plate is responsible for

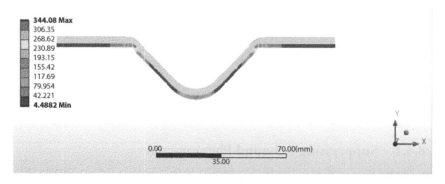

Figure 28.6 Current pulse excitation showing the final shape of the part.

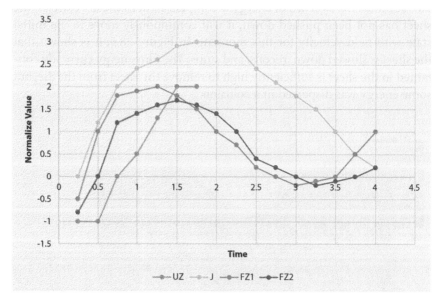

Figure 28.7 Graph depicting the fluctuation of current, displacement, and EMF over time.

the comparable greater gap in the die radius. Figure 28.7 seems to have a longer period of force than in Figure 28.6.

Figure 28.7 depicts the relationship between several normalized physics quantities. U_z represents the sheet's displacement in the Z-axis, while J represents the coil's current. In Figure 28.6, Nodal EMF is shown in correspond to position 1 and 2 elements where Fz1 and Fz2 denote nodal EMF. The sequential evolution of absolute value is the primary concern in this experiment. For evaluating the comparison easily, there is some normalization in values, which is as follows (Table 28.3).

When the displacement tracking process is stopped, the sheet will reach its deepest position at 1.5×10^{-4} seconds in its deformation history. The graph shows that the current pulse has wider than the force pulse.

The increase in distance between the sheet and dying causes a substantial reduction of strength due to unfettered sheet movement and a longer deformation duration, a flat sheet-free bulging phase. In this article, however, a shallow die limits the distance between the sheet and the spiral where the force attenuation is comparatively smaller. As shown in Figure 28.8, Fz1, Fz2, and EMF have reached their peak values ahead of the current in the coil. The forces maintain enough intensity near their peaks when the sheet will reach its deepest position. The electromagnetic force's distance-dependent decaying curve against time was already analyzed [7]. The schematic curve of EMF sequence coupling is shown in Figure 28.10. Its amplitude in the simulation for loose coupling is rather less than the electromagnetic control. The time axis is represented by the x-axis, and the normalized force amplitude is represented by the y-axis. The plate hits full depth on t1 and then bounds out of the die before t2 when the plate for the second time suits the die.

Figure 28.9 depicts the of electromagnetic strength and sequence strategy for coupling, which assuming in the second collision the majority of cinematic energy has been used up, the force from t1 to t2 is used to prevent the plate from rebounding from its internal surface. In Figure 28.10

Table 28.3 Depiction of values of various parameters.

Parameters	Maximum normalized value
J	3
Uz	2
Fz1	2
Fz2	2

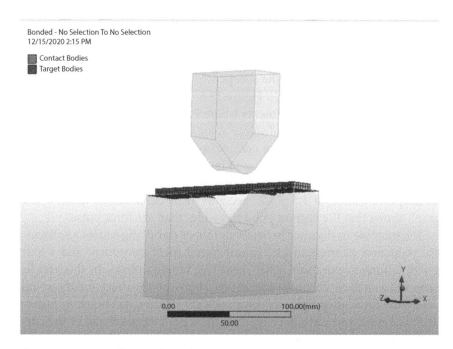

Figure 28.8   Figure showing Fz1 and Fz2 positioning.

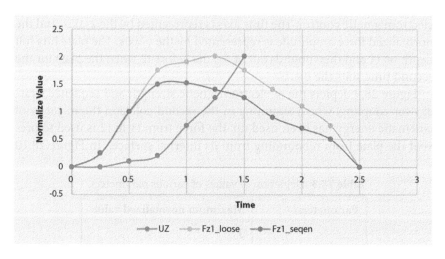

Figure 28.9   Electromagnetic strength and sequence strategy for coupling.

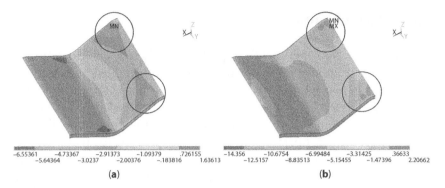

| -6.55361 | -4.73367 | -2.91373 | -1.09379 | .726155 | | -14.356 | -10.6754 | -6.99484 | -3.31425 | .36633 |
| | -5.64364 | -3.0237 | -2.00376 | -.183816 | 1.63613 | -12.5157 | -8.83513 | -5.15455 | -1.47396 | 2.20662 |

(a)   (b)

Figure 28.10 (a) Depiction of X-component of EMF. (b) Depiction of Z-component of EMF.

shaded area shows the force which is the impulse on the sheet between time duration t1 and t2. The result of the formation is influenced by the dispersion of electromagnetic forces and the function of precision calculation by contrasting the technique of loose coupling to the sequential strategy of coupling [7]. The next equation determines the EMF.

$$F = J * B \qquad (28.2)$$

where F-EMF, J-current, B-intensity of the flux.

The plane of J and B is normal to F, according to the geometric meaning of equation (28.2). The component of force is always normal to the sheet's surface because the flow of only in the geometrical region of a sheet can an induced Eddy current occur. Figure 28.10 depicts the contour plot of the EMF component in another mathematical model's deformation region in which the sheet is of V-shape. The sheet is pushed to the die by these two components. In Figure 28.10 (a) and 28.10 (b), the circles depict the region where the amplitude of force is highest along the X and Z axes, respectively. In Figure 28.7 and Figure 28.3, it is shown that the force in the circles will aid in reducing gaps for the right die radius. It does so by not allowing the right part of the sheet to move toward the die's cavity. The sheet is pressed towards the sidewall of the V-shaped die with the help of a new direction of EMF. This process is like calibration but the accuracy of estimation for loose coupling strategy is limited. Due to a lack in alteration of force distribution, there is limited forecasting of forming process with die.

28.5 Conclusion

By examining the experiment's impact on workpiece deformation and motional electromotive force, this research has constructed finite element models to investigate the EMF process, the electromagnetic and structural coupling processes. It is shown in this research that the larger pulse duration of the electromagnetic force increases the acting force time. For this purpose, a more exact part can be made by suppressing the rebound phenomenon and this can be done by extending the width of the electromagnetic pulse to a flawless die in which the small gap between the sheet and the spinal cord led to a weaker attenuation of the EMF. To transfer the sheet to the die the new force distribution will help us and thus keep the parts in V form. In addition, to achieve a more accurate prediction, the sequential combinations strategy to update amplitude and power distribution is essential.

References

1. Stiemer, M., Unger, J., Svendsen, B. *et al.*, An arbitrary Lagrangian Eulerian approach to the three-dimensional simulation of electromagnetic forming. *Comput. Methods Appl. Mech. Eng.*, 198, 1535–1547, 2009.
2. Cui, X., Mo, J., Xiao, S., Du, E., Magnetic force distribution and deformation law of sheet using uniform pressure electromagnetic actuator. *Trans. Nonferrous Met. Soc. China*, 21, 11, 2484–2489, 2011.
3. Demir, O.K., Psyk, V., Tekkaya, A.E., Simulation of wrinkle formation in free electromagnetic tube compression. *4th International Conference on High-Speed Forming-2010*, Ohio, USA, pp. 181–188, 2010.
4. Cui, X., Mo, J., Xiao, S., Du, E., Numerical simulation of electromagnetic sheet bulging based on FEM. *Int. J. Adv. Manuf. Technol.*, 57, 1–4, 127–134, 2011.
5. Li, L., Han, X., Peng, T., Ding, H., Ding, T., Qiu, L., Zhou, Z., Xiong, Q., Space-time-controlled multi-stage pulsed magnetic field forming and manufacturing technology. *The 5th International Conference on High Speed Forming*, Dortmund, Germany, pp. 53–58, 2012.
6. Li, L., Han, X., Cao, Q., Chen, Q., Lai, Z., Zhou, Z., Xiong, Q., Zhang, X., Li, X., Fu, J., Liu, Y., Development of space-time-controlled multistage pulsed magnetic field forming and manufacturing technology at the WHMFC. *The 6th International Conference on High Speed Forming*, Daejeon, Korea, pp. 353–362, 2014.
7. Kumar, A., Sharma, K., Dixit, A.R., Role of graphene in biosensor and protective textile against viruses. *Med. Hypotheses*, 144, 110253, 2020.

8. Weddeling, C., Hahn, M., Daehn, G.S., Tekkaya, A.E., Uniform pressure electromagnetic actuator—An innovative tool for magnetic pulse welding. *Proc. Int. Conf. Manuf. Lightweight Components*, vol. 18, pp. 156–161, 2014.

9. Kiliclar, Y., Demir, O.K., Vladimirov, I.N., Kwiatkowski, L., Brosius, A., Reese, S., Tekkaya, A.E., Combined simulation of quasi-static deep drawing and electromagnetic forming by means of a coupled damage–viscoplasticity model at finite strains. *The 5th International Conference*, 2012.

10. Wang, L., Chen, Z.Y., Li, C.X., Huang, S.Y., Numerical simulation of the electromagnetic sheet metal bulging process. *Int. J. Adv. Manuf. Technol.*, 30, 395–400, 2006.

11. Singh, P.K., Singh, P., Sharma, K., Saraswat, M., Effect of sonication parameters on mechanical properties of *in-situ* amine functionalized multiple layer graphene/epoxy nanocomposites. *J. Sci. Ind. Res.*, 79, 11, 985–989, 2020.

12. Mausam, K., Sharma, A., Singh, P.K., Calculating stress, temperature in brake pad using ANSYS composite materials. *Mater. Today Proc.*, 45, 2, 3547–3550, 2021. https://doi.org/10.1016/j.matpr.2020.12.991.

13. Bartels, G., Schätzing, W., Scheibe, H.P., Leone, M., Comparison of two different simulation algorithms for the electromagnetic tube compression. *Int. J. Mater. Form.*, 2, 693–6, 2009.

14. Imbert, J. and Worswick, M., Electromagnetic reduction of a pre-formed radius on AA 5754 sheet. *J. Mater. Process. Technol.*, 211, 896–908, 2011.

15. Singh, P.K. and Sharma, V., Analysis on the safety factor of corrugated tubes having predicted deformation patterns, 988, 012074, 2020. https://doi.org/10.1088/1757-899X/988/1/012074.

16. Cui, X.-H., Mo, J.-H., Xiao, S.-J., Du, E.-H., Magnetic force distribution and deformation law of sheet using uniform pressure electromagnetic actuator. *Trans. Nonferrous Met. Soc. China*, 21, 2484–9, 2011.

17. Imbert, J., Worswick, M., L'eplattenier, P., Effects of force distribution and rebound on electromagnetically formed sheet metal, in: *Fourth International Conference on High Speed Forming*, pp. 169–80, 2010.

18. Singh, P.K., Chaturvedi, R., Sharma, A., Implementation of finite element model in compound propeller blades for using in aircraft. *Mater. Today Proc.*, 45, 2, 2747–2750, 2021. https://doi.org/10.1016/j.matpr.2020.11.604.

19. Beerwald, C., Beerwald, M., Dirksen, U., Henselek, A., Impulse hydroforming method for very thin sheets from metallic or hybrid materials. *4th International Conference on High Speed Forming*, pp. 150–158, 2010.

20. Gillard, A.J., Golovashchenko, S.F., Mamutov, A.V., Effect of quasi-static pre-strain on the formability of dual phase steels in electrohydraulic forming. *J. Manuf. Process.*, 15, 2, 201–218, 2013.

21. Sonia, P., Jain, J.K., Saxena, K.K., Influence of ultrasonic vibration assistance in manufacturing processes: A Review. *Mater. Manuf. Process.*, 36, 1–25, 2021.

22. Singh, P.K. and Singh, P.K., Synthesis of silicon nanofibrous structures using femtosecond laser radiation. *Mater. Today: Proc.*, 37, 2959–2960, 2021, https://doi.org/10.1016/j.matpr.2020.08.705.

23. Wielage, H., Niehoff, H.S., Vollertsen, F., Niehoff, S., Forming behaviour in laser shock drawing. *3rd International Conference on High Speed Forming*, pp. 213–222, 2008.

24. Zhang, X., Cui, J.J., Xu, J.R., Li, G.Y., Microstructure investigations on 2A10 aluminum alloy bars subjected to electromagnetic impact upsetting. *Mater. Eng.*, 702, 142–52, 2017.

25. Xu, J.R., Cui, J.J., Lin, Q.Q., Li, Y.R.S., Magnetic pulse forming of AZ31 magnesium alloy shell by uniform pressure coil at room temperature. *Int. J. Adv. Manuf. Technol.*, 77, 289–304, 2015.

26. Karch, C. and Roll, K., Transient simulation of electromagnetic forming of aluminium tubes. *Adv. Mater. Res.*, 6, 8, 639–48, 2005.

27. L'Eplattenier, P., Cook, G., Ashcraft, C., Burger, M., Imbert, J., Worswick, M., Introduction of an electromagnetism module in LS-DYNA for coupled mechanical thermal-electromagnetic simulations. *Steel Res. Int.*, 80, 5, 351–8, 2009.

28. Noh, H.G., Song, W.J., Kang, B.S., Kim, J., Two-step electromagnetic forming process using spiral forming coils to deform sheet metal in a middle-block die. *Int. J. Adv. Manuf. Technol.*, 76, 1691–703, 2015.

29. Su, H.L., Huang, L., Li, J.J., Ma, F., Huang, P., Feng, F., Two-step electromagnetic forming: A new forming approach to local features of large-size sheet metal parts. *Int. J. Mach. Tool Manuf.*, 124, 99–116, 2018.

30. Neugebauer, R., Bouzakis, K.-D., Denkena, B., Klocke, F., Sterzing, A., Tekkaya, A.E. *et al.*, Velocity effects in metal forming and machining processes. *CIRP Ann. Manuf. Technol.*, 60, 627–50, 2011.

31. Rohatgi, A., Stephens, E.V., Soulami, A., Davies, R.W., Smith, M.T., Experimental characterization of sheet metal deformation during electro-hydraulic forming. *J. Mater. Process. Technol.*, 211, 11, 1824–33, 2011.

32. Liu, Y., Lai, X., Gu, Y., Wang, B., Wang, G., Liu, Q., Investigation on the ageing behaviour and hardening mechanisms of 5A90 Al–Li alloy U-shaped parts formed by electric resistance heating forming-quenching process. *J. Alloys Compd.*, 869, 159120, 2021.

Quadratic Spline Function Companding Technique to Minimize Peak-to-Average Power Ratio in Orthogonal Frequency Division Multiplexing System

Lazar Z. Velimirovic

Mathematical Institute SANU, Belgrade, Serbia

Abstract

High peak-to-average power ratio (PAPR) represents one of the biggest problems in orthogonal frequency division multiplexing (OFDM) systems. Therefore various methods for PAPR reduction are proposed in the literature. In this chapter, a PAPR reduction method based on the new class of compandors is proposed. Nonlinear compandors are applied to the OFDM signals at the transmitter in order to attenuate the high signals' peaks more than the other parts of the signal, thus decreasing the PAPR. In order to reduce the complexity of the compandor model, a compandor model based on quadratic spline technique is proposed. Simulation results show that OFDM system performances improve by reducing PAPR, which is performed by using the suggested compandor model.

Keywords: Companding, quadratic spline, OFDM, PAPR reduction

29.1 Introduction

The rapid growth and development of wireless and wired communication systems has led to a significant increase in researchers' interest in a technique called orthogonal frequency-division multiplexing (OFDM) [1–5]. OFDM, or multicarrier transmission, or discrete multitone (DMT), which was developed relatively long ago, has again come into

Email: lazar.velimirovic@mi.sanu.ac.rs

Anita Khosla, Prasenjit Chatterjee, Ikbal Ali and Dheeraj Joshi (eds.) Optimization Techniques in Engineering: Advances and Applications, (469–482) © 2023 Scrivener Publishing LLC

the spotlight due to the possibility of efficient application in digital signal processing technology. OFDM technology is an integral part of many international standards that define high-speed wireless communications, such as IEEE 802.11, IEEE 802.16, and IEEE 802.20 [6–8]. The features of OFDM-based system, which are reflected in high resistance to multipath fading and impulse noise and reducing the need for equalizers, are very useful for wireless applications. Additionally, the use of fast Fourier transform (FFT) techniques is very useful for efficient hardware implementation.

The high peak-to-average power ratio (PAPR) is one of the major drawbacks of OFDM. High PAPR leads to lower power efficiency which results in great difficulties in implementing OFDM. Namely, lower power efficiency directly influences the range of multicarrier transmission. With a high-power amplifier (HPA) that would work with a large input backoff, this problem could be partially overcome. However, the very high cost of HPA with a large linear range, their complexity of production, as well as the size that makes up almost half of the size of a transmitter lies, eliminate HPA as a solution to this problem [9, 10].

In order to solve this problem, a number of approaches or techniques to reduce PAPR have been proposed and implemented. The reduction of PAPR in these approaches is reflected in the increase of computational complexity, bit error rate (BER), and transmit signal power, and loss of data rate, etc. These techniques include amplitude clipping [11], clipping and filtering [12], coding [13, 14], tone reservation (TR) [15], tone injection (TI) [15], active constellation extension (ACE) [16], and multiple signal representation techniques such as partial transmit sequence (PTS) [17, 18], selected mapping (SLM) [19], and interleaving [20].

Nonlinear companding transform (NCT) based on the speech processing algorithm μ-law is the first developed companding algorithm for PAPR reduction [21]. In μ-law companding transform, the aim is to keep peak signals unchanged while increasing small amplitude signals. In this way, it is possible to increase the average power of the transmitted signals. The performance obtained by this algorithm is significantly better than the performance obtained using the clipping technique.

Exponential companding technique is described in [22]. If the transform parameters are selected in the right way, it is possible to achieve a uniform distribution of the output signals, by adjusting both small and large input signals provided that the average power is not changed. This technique very successfully reduces PAPR for different subcarrier sizes and various modulation shapes. Compared to the μ-law companding scheme, this technique achieves better performance in terms of BER, power spectrum, phase error, and PAPR reduction. Also, less spectrum side-lobes is achieved by exponential companding schemes than μ-law companding.

PAPR reduction using the square rooting companding (SQRT) technique was discussed in [23]. With this method, PAPR reduction is achieved by changing the statistical characteristics of the output signals. Changing the statistical characteristics of the output signals is enabled by applying the square rooting companding (SQRT) technique. The application of this technique also affects the change of parameters that affect the average and peak power values, which actually initiates a decrease in the value of PAPR.

The companding technique based on the μ-companding transform and hadamard transform technique is given in [24]. The results obtained by applying this technique in terms of reducing the value of PAPR of OFDM signal show that this technique improves the performance of the system compared to when only μ-companding transform would be used. Also, using this technique does not worsen the BER value.

The obtained numerical results of the hybrid clipping-companding techniques described in [25] show that these techniques may be a good choice for PAPR reduction. The performance of the observed system, in case *tanh* or *erf* companding functions are used as companding functions, is almost the same. The performance of the hybrid PAPR reduction scheme based on the log companding function is significantly better than the performance achieved using the *tanh* or *erf* companding function.

In this chapter, a PAPR reduction using the quadratic spline function companding technique is proposed. The chapter is organized as follows: in Section 29.2 a description of the OFDM system and PAPR of OFDM signal is given. Section 29.3 describes an OFDM system based on the quadratic spline technique. Numerical results and discussion are in Section 29.4. Finally, Section 29.5 is the conclusion.

29.2 OFDM System

The number of active mobile devices and the needs of users make the development of high speed communication a priority. One of the ways to solve this problem is the development and implementation of various multicarrier modulation techniques, among which OFDM and Code Division Multiple Access (CDMA) stand out [26].

The OFDM technique is based on the principle of parallel transmission a number of lower data rate streams, which are obtained by dividing high data rate streams. Parallel transmission in this case allows to increase the symbol duration. This causes the prorated amount of dispersion in time to decrease. OFDM technique meets all the conditions to be classified on the one hand in the modulation technique, while on the other hand it can be classified in the multiplexing technique [26].

Increasing symbol rates in order to achieve higher data rates does not affect OFDM communication systems, which significantly simplifies the management of Inter Symbol Interference (ISI). Due to parallel transmission data instead of serially, at the same transmission rate, symbols on single carrier systems are much shorter OFDM symbols [26].

Compared to frequency division multiplexing (FDM), to which OFDM is very similar, the process of sending multiple messages using a single radio channel is much more precisely controlled, resulting in significantly better spectral efficiency [26]. In FDM, overall spectral efficiency is significantly lower because carrier frequencies are nonorthogonal in nature, i.e., a large band gap is needed to avoid interchannel interference.

Compared to multiple-access techniques, OFDM has significant advantages, which are reflected primarily in high spectral efficiency, easy adaptation for broadband data transmission, impedance to ISI, provide Multiple Input Multiple Output (MIMO) schemes and frequency-selective scheduling [26].

The orthogonality of OFDM signals can be observed by observing its spectrum. Every OFDM subcarrier has frequency response, in the frequency domain [26]. The fact that in the frequency domain it is possible to overlap subcarriers, allows a very efficient use of the frequency band, which is a great advantage of OFDM systems [9, 26].

The extension of OFDM, called orthogonal frequency-division multiple access (OFDMA), is a technique used for a multi-user communication system. The OFDMA technique is used as a solution in the Long-Term Evolution (LTE) downlink.

The design of the time-frequency representation of OFDM to provide high levels of flexibility in allocation of each of the time frames for transmission and the spectra. Variety of frequency bands and scalable set of bandwidths are supported due to the spectrum flexibility in LTE. In order to reduce latency, small frame size is enabled in LTE. Due to the short frame sizes, appropriate link adaptation to the base station is enabled, which significantly improves the channel estimation to be carried out of the mobile [27].

29.2.1   PAPR of OFDM Signal

The complexity of the realization of the digital circuitry is directly dependent on the PAPR value of the discrete time OFDM signal because the value of the signal to quantization noise ratio to be realized is directly dependent on the number of bits needed to achieve that value [28]. To better approximate the PAPR of a continuous time OFDM signal, the discrete time OFDM signal is to be obtained by L times oversampling. The oversampled discrete time OFDM signal can be obtained by performing LN point IFFT on the data block with $(L-1)\,N$ zero padding as follows:

$$[x(n)]=\frac{1}{\sqrt{N}}X_k e^{\left(\frac{j2\pi kn}{LN}\right)},0\leq n\leq NL-1. \tag{29.1}$$

PAPR of the oversampled OFDM signal of becoming

$$PAPR[x(n)]=\frac{\underset{0\leq n\leq NL-1}{MAX}[|x(n)|^2]}{E[|x(n)|^2]}. \tag{29.2}$$

In the previous expression, the expectation operator is denoted by $E\,[.]$ while the total number of sub-carriers is denoted by N.

The PAPR of baseband PAPR OFDM signal is approximately twice as small that of passband PAPR.

Complementary cumulative distribution function (CCDF) for an OFDM signal is:

$$P(PAPR>PAPR_0)=1-\left(1-e^{PAPR_0}\right)^2, \tag{29.3}$$

where the clipping level marked with $PAPR_0$.

The cumulative distribution function (CDF) of the PAPR of the amplitude of a signal sample is given by:

$$F(z)=1-exp(z). \tag{29.4}$$

Determining CCDF of the PAPR of the data block enables comparing outputs of different companding techniques for PAPR reduction:

$$Pr(PAPR>z)=1-Pr(PAPR\leq z)=1-F(z)^N=1-(1-exp(-z))^N, \tag{29.5}$$

where, the given reference level is z.

29.3   Companding Technique

A special clipping technique, called the nonlinear companding technique, is a technique that can achieve significant PAPR reduction with better BER performance, which reduces implementation complexity, and does not require bandwidth expansion [29].

In clipping technique, it is not possible to reconstruct the signal because clips the large amplitude signals occur. In companding technique, it is possible to reconstruct the signal because the large amplitude signals do not clips. In a companding technique, large amplitude signals are compressed, while small amplitude signals are enlarged. No changes are made over small amplitude signals in clipping technique. Due to these features, a large number of different companding techniques have been developed. A common feature of a large number of companding techniques is that the Rayleigh distributed OFDM signal transforms into a uniformly distributed signal [21].

The μ-law companding technique can achieve better system performance than the clipping method. Unlike the clipping method, the μ-law companding method is based on enlarging small amplitude signals, keeping peak signals unchanged. This causes the average power of the transmitted signals to increase. This can result in exceeding the saturation region of the HPA which can adversely affect system performance. In order to overcome the problem reflected in increasing average power and achieve better PAPR reduction, several different companding techniques have been developed [30–33].

In this chapter, a quadratic spline function companding technique is proposed. OFDM system model with quadratic spline function companding technique is shown in Figure 29.1.

29.3.1   Quadratic Spline Function Companding

The essence of the companding technique is that the large amplitude signals are compressed and the small amplitudes of the signals are increased. In this chapter, we propose a companding method inspired by the nonlinear companding transform used in the LTE system [34].

The quadratic spline function companding is given by [35]:

$$g(x) = (a_i + b_i |x| + c_i |x|^2) \, \text{sgn}(x), \qquad (29.6)$$

where $x \in [x_{i-1}, x_i]$, $i = 1, \ldots, L$, L is the number of segments.

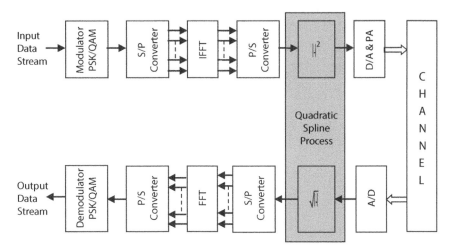

Figure 29.1 Block diagram of an OFDM system using quadratic spline technique.

The quadratic spline, also called a second-degree spline, is a continuously differentiable piecewise quadratic function. When determining the coefficients of the quadratic spline, it is necessary to meet the pre-set conditions. The system of linear equations to be solved to determine the value of the quadratic spline coefficients is equal to the product of the number of coefficients observed in the quadratic spline and the number of subintervals [35].

The quadratic spline decompanding function at the receiver side is given by:

$$g^{-1}(x) = \left| \left(\frac{-b_i + \sqrt{b_i^2 - 4a_i c_i + 4c_i \,|\,x\,|}}{2c_i} \right) \right| \mathrm{sgn}(x), \qquad (29.7)$$

Figure 29.2 shows one example of the approximation of a nonlinear optimal compressor function using the quadratic spline function [36].

29.4   Numerical Results and Discussion

The performance of the considered system in this chapter was evaluated by determining the values of PAPR, CCDF, and BER and comparing it with similar systems. Using CCDF, a statistical estimate of PAPR was performed. The probability of exceeding a given threshold $PAPR_0$ is expressed

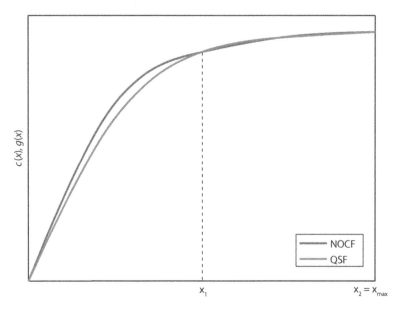

Figure 29.2 Approximation of the nonlinear optimal compressor function (NOCF) using the quadratic spline function (QSF).

depending on the ratio of the CCDF of PAPR. For the transmitted OFDM, PAPR is determined by:

$$PAPR = 10 \log R \frac{\max |x|^2}{E |x|^2}. \tag{29.8}$$

Also, the BER was determined for all cases considered. Simulation parameters for which PAPR, CCDF, and BER values for the considered models are shown in Table 29.1. The obtained numerical results for these quantities, which describe the performance of the considered system, were first compared for the case of OFDM system without any PAPR reduction techniques, and then with the A companding model, μ-law companding, and absolute exponential companding (AEXP).

For the case OFDM system without any PAPR reduction techniques the value of PAPR is equals to 25.6015 dB, while CCDF of PAPR is equals to 10.28 dB. In this case, SNR at BER (10^{-4}) is equal to 11.4314 dB.

The proposed model was considered for the values of parameter c from -1.8 to -1.0, because testing showed that the best system performance is achieved for these values of parameter c. The influence of parameter values on the PAPR value is shown in Table 29.2. The table shows the values only

Table 29.1 Simulation parameters.

Parameter	Description
FFT size	128
Spacing frequency	15 KHz
System bandwidth	1.25MHz
CP length	32
No symbol	1000
Sampling frequency	192MHz
Modulated type	QPSK

Table 29.2 PAPR for various b and c parameter.

Parameter		PAPR [dB]	Parameter		PAPR [dB]
$a = 0$ $b = 0.5$	$c = 0.5$	29.0503	$a = 0$ $b = 2.5$	$c = 0.5$	24.6984
	$c = -0.5$	19.6331		$c = -0.5$	23.7362
	$c = 1.5$	32.3371		$c = 1.5$	26.4635
	$c = -1.5$	7.1473		$c = -1.5$	23.7243
	$c = 2.5$	35.9959		$c = 2.5$	27.4646
	$c = -2.5$	31.3853		$c = -2.5$	19.8726
	$c = 3.5$	32.9952		$c = 3.5$	28.2563
	$c = -3.5$	48.7428		$c = -3.5$	17.3173
$a = 0$ $b = 1.5$	$c = 0.5$	25.3247	$a = 0$ $b = 3.5$	$c = 0.5$	27.5488
	$c = -0.5$	24.2285		$c = -0.5$	24.7060
	$c = 1.5$	28.4373		$c = 1.5$	26.5416
	$c = -1.5$	20.5167		$c = -1.5$	21.9512
	$c = 2.5$	30.3387		$c = 2.5$	27.5881
	$c = -2.5$	14.8627		$c = -2.5$	21.2542
	$c = 3.5$	29.9652		$c = 3.5$	26.6602
	$c = -3.5$	10.0751		$c = -3.5$	19.7492

for the case when values of parameter b is positive (because similar values are obtained for the case when values of parameter b is negative).

Figure 29.3 shows the CCDF dependence of PAPR (i.e., CCDF Pr (PAPR > $PAPR_0$)) of the considered quadratic spline companding PAPR reduction techniques, for various values of c parameter.

Figure 29.4 shows BER dependence of SNR of the quadratic spline companding for various values of c parameter.

Based on the presented results, it can be noticed that the proposed model in this chapter significantly improves the performance of the observed system. For the parameter value $c = -1.0$, the improvement in PAPR by 13.4159 dB, and CCDF of PAPR = (4.58 dB), while the SNR at BER (10^{-4}) deteriorated by -1.4686 dB, with respect to OFDM system without PAPR reduction method. For SNR at BER (10^{-4}) ≤ 17.5 dB, the percentage of improvement in PAPR is much higher than the degradation in BER. The best one improvement in PAPR and CCDF of PAPR is at $c = -1.8$.

Generally, for range $c = [-1.8, -1.0]$, and for SNR at BER (10^{-4}) ≤ 25 dB, the proposed model with respect to OFDM system without PAPR

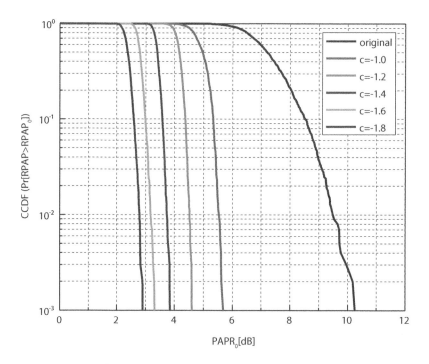

Figure 29.3 CCDF of PAPR OFDM system the quadratic spline companding for various values of c parameter.

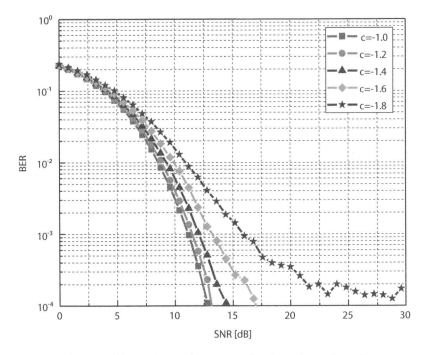

Figure 29.4 The BER of the quadratic spline companding for various values of c parameter.

reduction method achieves the following: PAPR improved by (13.4159–20.1026 dB), CCDF of PAPR improved by (4.58–7.38 dB), and the amount of SNR at BER (10^{-4}) degradation is (1.4686–5.5586 dB).

Comparing the obtained numerical results of the proposed model ($c = -1.0$) with the A companding model ($A = 10$), it can be seen that the proposed model achieves better system performance, namely the improvement in PAPR by 2.5061 dB, and CCDF of PAPR deteriorated by -0.97 dB, while the SNR at BER (10^{-4}) improvement by 3.22 dB.

In relation to the μ-law companding technique ($\mu = 20$), the proposed model achieves the following performances ($c = -1.0$): the improvement in PAPR by 5.0717 dB, and CCDF of PAPR deteriorated by -0.622 dB, while the SNR at BER (10^{-4}) improvement by 3.35 dB.

The performance of the system based on absolute exponential companding (AEXP) for various values of d parameter [37], compared to the performance of the system based on quadratic spline companding are as follows ($c = -1.0$): for SNR at BER (10^{-4}) $\leq$ 17.5 dB, and $d = 0.9$, using AEXP improvement in PAPR by 5.4356 dB is achieved, and CCDF of PAPR = (2.508 dB), while the SNR at BER (10^{-4}) improvement by 3.40 dB. Although AEXP achieves better system performance in terms of PAPR and

CCDF of PAPR, the advantage of quadratic spline companding is reflected in the realization of SNR at BER (10^{-4}) values and much less complexity in the implementation of digital circuits.

29.5 Conclusion

In this chapter, a companding scheme based on the quadratic spline function is proposed. Based on the obtained results, it can be concluded that the proposed quadratic spline function companding technique provides better PAPR reduction compared to similar models and OFDM system without PAPR reduction method. Also, the proposed model achieves better CCDF of PAPR and BER performance compared to other companding methods. The advantage of the proposed model is reflected in its low complexity. Unlike PTS and SLM techniques, this model does not require any additional side information to be transmitted. Due to all the above, the proposed companding method can be used very successfully for PAPR reduction of OFDM system. Also, in future research, the proposed companding method can be used in hybrid PAPR techniques to improve system performance.

Acknowledgment

This work was supported by the Serbian Ministry of Education, Science and Technological Development through Mathematical Institute of the Serbian Academy of Sciences and Arts.

References

1. Lassalle, R. and Alard, M., Principles of modulation and channel coding for digital broadcasting for mobile receivers. *EBU Tech. Rev.*, 224, 1, 68–190, 1987.
2. Reimers, U., Digital video broadcasting. *IEEE Commun. Mag.*, 36, 6, 104–110, 1998.
3. Chang, R.W. and Gibby, R., A theoretical study of performance of an orthogonal multiplexing data transmission scheme. *IEEE Trans. Commun. Technol.*, 16, 4, 529–540, 1968.
4. Cimini, L., Analysis and simulation of a digital mobile channel using orthogonal frequency division multiplexing. *IEEE Trans. Commun.*, 33, 7, 665–675, 1985.

5. Bingham, J.A.C., Multicarrier modulation for data transmission: An idea whose time has come. *IEEE Commun. Mag.*, 28, 5, 5–14, 1990.

6. Hiertz, G.R. *et al.*, The IEEE 802.11 universe. *IEEE Commun. Mag.*, 48, 1, 62–70, 2010.

7. Wongthavarawat, K. and Ganz, A., Packet scheduling for QoS support in IEEE 802.16 broadband wireless access systems. *Int. J. Commun. Syst.*, 16, 1, 81–96, 2003.

8. Bolton, W., Xiao, Y., Guizani, M., IEEE 802.20: Mobile broadband wireless access. *IEEE Wirel. Commun.*, 14.1, 84–95, 2007.

9. Hill, G., *Peak Power Reduction in Orthogonal Frequency Division Multiplexing Transmitters*, Diss., Victoria University, 2011.

10. Cho, Y.S. *et al.*, *MIMO-OFDM Wireless Communications with MATLAB*, John Wiley & Sons, Singapore, 2010.

11. O'Neill, R. and Lopes, L.B., Envelope variations and spectral splatter in clipped multicarrier signals. *Proceedings of 6th International Symposium on Personal, Indoor and Mobile Radio Communications*, vol. 1, IEEE, 1995.

12. Armstrong, J., Peak-to-average power reduction for OFDM by repeated clipping and frequency domain filtering. *Electron. Lett.*, 38, 5, 246–247, 2002.

13. Tarokh, V. and Jafarkhani, H., On the computation and reduction of the peak-to-average power ratio in multicarrier communications. *IEEE Trans. Commun.*, 48, 1, 37–44, 2000.

14. Chong, C.V. and Tarokh, V., A simple encodable/decodable OFDM QPSK code with low peak-to-mean envelope power ratio. *IEEE Trans. Inf. Theory*, 47, 7, 3025–3029, 2001.

15. Tellado-Mourelo, J., *Peak to Average Power Reduction For Multicarrier Modulation*, Diss., Stanford University, 1999.

16. Krongold, B.S. and Jones, D.L., PAR reduction in OFDM via active constellation extension. *IEEE Trans. Broadcast.*, 49, 3, 258–268, 2003.

17. Jayalath, A.D.S. and Tellambura, C., Adaptive PTS approach for reduction of peak-to-average power ratio of OFDM signal. *Electron. Lett.*, 36, 14, 1226–1228, 2000.

18. Han, S.H. and Lee, J.H., PAPR reduction of OFDM signals using a reduced complexity PTS technique. *IEEE Signal Process. Lett.*, 11, 11, 887–890, 2004.

19. Breiling, H., Muller-Weinfurtner, S.H., Huber, J.B., SLM peak-power reduction without explicit side information. *IEEE Commun. Lett.*, 5, 6, 239–241, 2001.

20. Hill, G.R., Faulkner, M., Singh, J., Reducing the peak-to-average power ratio in OFDM by cyclically shifting partial transmit sequences. *Electron. Lett.*, 36, 6, 560–561, 2000.

21. Wang, X., Tjhung, T.T., Ng, C.S., Reduction of peak-to-average power ratio of OFDM system using a companding technique. *IEEE Trans. Broadcast.*, 45, 3, 303–307, 1999.

22. Jiang, T., Yang, Y., Song, Y.-H., Companding technique for PAPR reduction in OFDM systems based on an exponential function. *GLOBECOM'05, IEEE Global Telecommunications Conference*, 2005, vol. 5, IEEE, 2005.

23. Al-Azzo, W.F. *et al.*, Time domain statistical control for PAPR reduction in OFDM system. *2007 Asia-Pacific Conference on Communications*, IEEE, 2007.

24. Wang, Z., Zhang, S., Qiu, B., PAPR reduction of OFDM signal by using Hadamard transform in companding techniques. *2010 IEEE 12th International Conference on Communication Technology*, IEEE, 2010.

25. Singh, M.K. *et al.*, Hybrid clipping-companding schemes for peak-to-average power reduction of OFDM signal. *Int. J. Adv. Eng. Sci. Technol.*, 2, 1, 114–119, 2013.

26. Ray, P.K. and Sklar, B., *Digital Communications: Fundamentals & Applications*, 2nd ed, Dorling Kindersley Pvt. Ltd., India, 2014.

27. Zarrinkoub, H., *Understanding LTE with MATLAB: From Mathematical Modeling to Simulation and Prototyping*, John Wiley & Sons, Chichester, West Sussex, United Kingdom, 2014.

28. Han, S. and Lee, J.H., An overview of peak-to-average power ratio reduction techniques for multicarrier transmission. *IEEE Wirel. Commun.*, 12, 2, 56–65, 2005.

29. Foomooljareon, P. and Fernando, W.A.C., Input sequence envelope scaling in PAPR reduction of OFDM. *The 5th International Symposium on Wireless Personal Multimedia Communications*, vol. 1, IEEE, 2002.

30. Dhok, P. and Rathkantiwar, S.V., Performance improvement in BER and PAPR reduction in OFDM system using companding. *Int. J. Appl. Innov. Eng. Manage.*, 2, 1, 232–235, January 2013.

31. Aburakhia, S.A., Badran, E.F., Mohamed, D.A.E., Linear companding transform for the reduction of peak-to-average power ratio of OFDM signals. *IEEE Trans. Broadcast.*, 55, 1, 155–160, 2009.

32. Liu, S.-H. *et al.*, Threshold-based piecewise companding transform for PAPR reduction in OFDM systems. *J. China Univ. Posts Telecommun.*, 20, 2, 1–18, 2013.

33. Ragini, B., Babu, M.S., Kalitkar, K.R., Companding technique for reducing peak-to-average power ratio in OFDM linear coded systems. *Int. J. Power Syst. Oper. Energy Manage.*, 1, 2, 48–53, 2011.

34. Velimirovic, L.Z. and Maric, S., New adaptive compandor for LTE signal compression based on spline approximations. *ETRI J.*, 38, 3, 463–468, 2016.

35. Cheney, E.W. and Kincaid, D.R., *Numerical Mathematics and Computing*, Thomson, Belmont, 2008.

36. Velimirović, L. *et al.*, Design of compandor quantizer for Laplacian source for medium bit rate using spline approximations. *FU Elec. Energ.*, 25, 1, 81–92, 2012.

37. Shaheen, I.A., Zekri, A., Newagy, F., Ibrahim, R., Absolute exponential companding to reduced PAPR for FBMC/OQAM. *Palestinian International Conference on Information and Communication Technology*, 2017.

30

A Novel MCGDM Approach for Supplier Selection in a Supply Chain Management

Bipradas Bairagi

Department of Mechanical Engineering, Haldia Institute of Technology, Haldia, India

Abstract

This research work aims to explore a novel multicriteria group decision making approach for supplier selection in supply chain management. This approach is capable of considering multiple conflicting subjective criteria and their subcriteria. In this technique, performance ratings of alternatives and weights of subjective criteria and associated subcriteria are extracted from the experience and unanimous opinion of a group of experts. The performance ratings are normalized to squeeze and transform into required sense. Normalized ratings of alternatives are integrated with the weights of criteria and subcriteria. Absolute weighted ratings are defined and expressed in terms of integration of arithmetic and geometrical mean of their weighted performance ratings. Absolute weighted rating is used for measuring performance indices of the alternatives. Alternatives are arranged in the descending order of their performance indices. The alternative with the highest performance index is selected as the best alternative. The proposed approach is illustrated with a suitable supplier selection problem considering multiple subjective criteria and subcriteria. The result shows that the proposed method is effective and useful for selection of the best supplier under multicriteria decision making environment.

Keywords: Supplier selection, unanimous group decision making, MCDM, performance index

Email: bipradasbairagi79@gmail.com

Anita Khosla, Prasenjit Chatterjee, Ikbal Ali and Dheeraj Joshi (eds.) Optimization Techniques in Engineering: Advances and Applications, (483–500) © 2023 Scrivener Publishing LLC

30.1 Introduction

Proper supplier selection procedure is one of the most significant aspects of production management for many organizations. Improper selection of a supplier could be sufficient to disturb the company's operational and financial situation. Selection of the appropriate suppliers considerably improves competitiveness in the market, reduces purchasing costs, and increases satisfaction of end users. Selection procedure of supplier chiefly deals with the performance evaluation of diverse alternative supplier with respect to multiple conflicting criteria. Supplier selection procedure is basically considered as a multicriteria decision-making (MCDM) problem which considers multiple subjective as well as objective criteria including quality, performance, price, delivery, technical capability and many more.

Supply chain management has occupied an important position of research interest for last few decades. Melih and Gul [1] applied integrated BMW-TODIM in atmosphere of interval type-2 fuzzy set for supplier selection strategies. Ilyas *et al.* [2] designed a strategies for supplier selection under the COVID-19 environment for industrial purpose. Naqvi and Amin [3] performed a detailed literature review on supplier selection with order allocation highlighting the recent improvements in the domain. Dao *et al.* [4] solved green supplier selection problem with a novel combined generalized multiple criteria decision making approach capable of considering decision makers view and opinion. Javad *et al.* [5] used BWM and TOPSIS integrated with fuzzy for the purpose of green supplier selection. Haeri and Rezaei [6] applied a grey-based MCDM model for green supplier selection under uncertain environment.

The most important objective of green supply chain management is to decrease pollution along with other impact to environment. Tseng [7] assessed linguistic preference based on green supply chain management criteria and applied a grey based fuzzy set theory for specific industry. Bai and Sarkis [8] stated that supplier selection is the critical decision in a supply chain management. Supplier selection is a three-stage procedure: selection, evaluation, and then development.

Bai and Sarkis [9] have used rough set theory, which employs an incomplete information method. Some practical managerial issues and limitations are there in MCDM methods. The number of rules may be very large that depend on quantity of the data to be evaluated. Zhu *et al.* [10] employed analytical networking process (ANP) for supplier selection. The authors stated that analytical networking process is not complex even while both qualitative and quantitative factors are integrated for decision making procedure rather it acts as an aiding tool to attain a common resolution for several parties.

Lee *et al.* [11] employed fuzzy analytical hierarchy process combined with Delphi technique to evaluate green suppliers. In this chapter, the Delphi method has been primarily applied to distinguish the criteria important for evaluation of conventional and green selection of suppliers. The purchasing process become more complex while it is compared to environment related issues. Green purchasing ought to judge environmental responsibility of suppliers with conventional factors such as quality, cost, flexibility lead-time, etc. Fuzzy analytical hierarchy process is utilized to unravel green selection process of suppliers. The authors elucidate that, because of the rising government regulation and civic consciousness in environmental concern, organizations have to execute green environment practice to exist in modern worldwide marketplace.

Lu *et al.* [12] states that it is required to help the suppliers to know the value of solving environmental problems that supports them in establishing their individual initiatives. Vachon and Klassen [13] illustrated that a large number of manufacturing companies build up and employ solution to challenges related to environment by supervising relations between customers and suppliers. Zhang *et al.* [14] concluded that management of environmental supplier integrates the manufacturer with the supplier.

Humphreys *et al.* [15] mentioned that in a few supplier selection processes, multiattribute analysis and case-based reasoning are applied. Humphreys *et al.* [16] observed that the knowledge-based system is combined with environmental issues for the purpose of selection of suppliers. Presently, owing to outsourcing scheme, business organizations become more and more dependent on their suppliers. Consequently, Bhutta and Huq [17] claimed that it is more important to select and assess performance of suppliers. Evaluation and selection of supplier need the consideration of multiconflicting criteria.

Handfield *et al.* [18] have applied environmental oriented criteria in analytical hierarchy process and demonstrated the concept of analytical hierarchy process as a decision support framework to aid managerial decision makers to comprehend the trade-off amongst the environmental parameters. Bowen *et al.* [19] suggested that organizations will execute green supply chain management practices provided that the organizations would attain effective and financial benefits. Enarsson [20] assessed the suppliers' environmental features by using fish bone diagram. Noci [21] introduced an analytical hierarchy process based technique which has been applied for evaluation of environmental efficiency of vendors. The technique has also been used to estimate capabilities of suppliers to attain towering performance related to environment.

Although past researchers have developed and implemented a number of mathematical models to solve the supplier selection problems, yet there is an absolute necessity to introduce new tools to aid the decision makers for making appropriate decisions with simple computational work, ease of understanding, less time consumption and having robustness.

The objective of the current research work is to improve evaluation and selection approaches and to advocate an alternative method by introducing a suitable technique. This chapter aims to justify the applicability of the proposed technique to unravel diverse supplier evaluation and selection problems in supply chain management.

This entire chapter is divided into four sections. Section 30.1 is dedicated to introduction and literature survey, Section 30.2 introduces the proposed algorithm, Section 30.3 gives an illustrative example with solution and discussions. Section 30.4 presents some important concluding remarks with direction of further research.

30.2   Proposed Algorithm

Step 1: The proposed algorithm starts with the formation of a homogeneous group decision making committee. The committee is homogeneous in the sense that every member bears equal importance. It is expected that the members of the committee posses required knowledge in the relevant field. The selection criteria and their subcriteria to be considered are listed. Main criteria can be denoted by $[C_1 \ldots C_j \ldots C_n]$ and subcriteria under j^{th} criteria can be indicated by C_{j1}, $C_{j2} \ldots$ etc. where C_{j1} stands for subcriteria 1 under j^{th} main criterion and n is the total number of criteria. An approximate and minimum value per criterion or its subcriterion should be set for screening test. Every feasible alternative must pass this initial standard to be further evaluated in the final selection. The provisional list of alternative supplier can be represented by $[A_1 \ldots A_i \ldots A_m]^T$. T stands for transpose matrix and m denotes total number of alternatives passed the initial screening test and entered into the final selection procedure. At the end of the first step the set of criteria should be placed in the topmost rows and the initial list of alternative suppliers should occupy the leftmost column of a matrix.

Step 2: Form a decision matrix consisting of performance rating of the alternatives with respect to each criteria and subcriteria. It is assumed that all the decision makers agree to assign performance rating on the basis of discussion, interaction and exchange of opinion as well as experience. Subcriteria are assessed in 1 to 5 scale as advocated and accommodated in a matrix. In the following matrix, x_{ij1} denotes performance rating of ith alternative with respect jth criterion and its first subcriterion. It is a unanimous objective measure of subjective criterion. All the $m \times n$ entries in the matrix have the similar meanings.

$$M_d = \begin{array}{c} \\ \\ S_1 \\ \cdots \\ S_i \\ \cdots \\ S_m \end{array} \begin{array}{ccccccccc} & C_1 & & & C_j & & & C_n & \\ C_{11} & C_{12} & \cdots & C_{j1} & C_{j2} & \cdots & C_{n1} & C_{n2} & \cdots \\ \left[\begin{array}{c} x_{111} \\ \cdots \\ x_{i11} \\ \cdots \\ x_{m11} \end{array}\right. & \begin{array}{c} x_{112} \\ \cdots \\ x_{i12} \\ \cdots \\ x_{m12} \end{array} & \begin{array}{c} \cdots \\ \cdots \\ \cdots \\ \cdots \\ \cdots \end{array} & \begin{array}{c} x_{1j1} \\ \cdots \\ x_{ij1} \\ \cdots \\ x_{mj1} \end{array} & \begin{array}{c} x_{1j2} \\ \cdots \\ x_{ij2} \\ \cdots \\ x_{mj2} \end{array} & \begin{array}{c} \cdots \\ \cdots \\ \cdots \\ \cdots \\ \cdots \end{array} & \begin{array}{c} x_{1n1} \\ \cdots \\ x_{in1} \\ \cdots \\ x_{mn1} \end{array} & \begin{array}{c} x_{1n2} \\ \cdots \\ x_{in1} \\ \cdots \\ x_{mn2} \end{array} & \left.\begin{array}{c} \cdots \\ \cdots \\ \cdots \\ \cdots \\ \cdots \end{array}\right] \end{array}$$

Step 3: Form the weight matrix consisting of relative importance of the criteria and subcriteria. In MCDM, multiple conflicting criteria are considered. In a particular decision making process each individual criterion does not have equal importance. Some criteria have more importance and the other has less importance. Thus, relative importance of the criteria under consideration should be measured by the rational judgement of expert or decision making committee formed for the purpose. The weights of criteria are assigned in such a way that the sum of the weights is necessarily unity. The weights of each set of subcriteria are allocated in such a way that the sum of the weights is equal to the individual weight the original criterion. In the following weight matrix w_j denotes the weight of jth original criterion whereas w_{11}, w_{12}, w_{13} etc denotes the weights of its subcriteria, where $w_j = w_{j1} + w_{j2} + wj_3 \ldots$

Criteria	C_1			C_j			C_n		
Subcriteria	C_{11}	C_{12}	$\cdots$	C_{j1}	C_{j2}	$\cdots$	C_{n1}	C_{n2}	$\cdots$
Weight	$[w_{11}$	w_{12}	$\cdots$	w_{j1}	w_{j2}	$\cdots$	w_{n1}	w_{n2}	$\cdots]$

Step 4: Normalize the performance rating of the decision matrix. A decision matrix is composed of performance rating in terms of objective measurement (numerical value) of different level. In normalization process, performance ratings are transformed in a desired range. The

transformation process is carefully carried out so that original rating and newly transformed rating are rationally correlated. In the current research work, normalization of performance rating under benefit criteria and cost criteria have been carried out by separate individual formula. The normalized value of ratings under benefit criteria have positive correlation, while normalized value of ratings under cost criteria have negative correlation. Normalization of rating under benefit criteria and cost criteria are calculated using equation (30.1) and equation (30.2) respectively.

$$y_{ijk} = EXP\left(\dfrac{x_{ijk}}{\dfrac{1}{m}\sum\limits_{i=1}^{m} x_{ijk}}\right), \text{ For benefit criteria} \qquad (30.1)$$

$$y_{ijk} = EXP\left(\dfrac{\dfrac{1}{m}\sum\limits_{i=1}^{m} x_{ijk}}{x_{ijk}}\right) \text{ For cost criteria} \qquad (30.2)$$

Here, y_{ijk} denotes the normalized value of initial performance rating of ith alternative with respect to jth criterion. In case of the benefit criteria, higher values are always desirable before and after the normalization. Lower value of cost criteria is desirable before normalization; however, the normalization of the cost criteria is executed in such a manner that it turns into benefit sense. It implies that higher normalized vale is desirable irrespective of the category of criteria. Normalized performance rating of the alternatives with respect to each criterion and subcriterion are expressed in the following matrix form.

$$M_{nd} = \begin{array}{c} \\ S_1 \\ \cdots \\ S_i \\ \cdots \\ S_m \end{array} \begin{array}{c} \overset{\displaystyle C_1}{\overbrace{C_{11} \quad C_{12}}} \\ \end{array} \cdots \begin{array}{c} \overset{\displaystyle C_j}{\overbrace{C_{j1} \quad C_{j2}}} \\ \end{array} \cdots \begin{array}{c} \overset{\displaystyle C_n}{\overbrace{C_{n1} \quad C_{n2}}} \\ \end{array} \cdots$$

	C_1			C_j			C_n		
	C_{11}	C_{12}	$\cdots$	C_{j1}	C_{j2}	$\cdots$	C_{n1}	C_{n2}	$\cdots$
S_1	y_{111}	y_{112}	$\cdots$	y_{1j1}	y_{1j2}	$\cdots$	y_{1n1}	y_{1n2}	$\cdots$
$\cdots$	$\cdots$	$\cdots$	$\cdots$	$\cdots$	$\cdots$	$\cdots$	$\cdots$	$\cdots$	$\cdots$
S_i	y_{i11}	y_{i12}	$\cdots$	y_{ij1}	y_{ij2}	$\cdots$	y_{in1}	y_{in1}	$\cdots$
$\cdots$	$\cdots$	$\cdots$	$\cdots$	$\cdots$	$\cdots$	$\cdots$	$\cdots$	$\cdots$	$\cdots$
S_m	y_{m11}	y_{m12}	$\cdots$	y_{mj1}	y_{mj2}	$\cdots$	y_{mn1}	y_{mn2}	$\cdots$

Step 5: Calculate the weighted normalized rating for each subcriterion. The performance of each alternative is affected by each subcriterion. The contribution of subcriterion to the performance of the alternative is a function of performance rating and the weight of the subcriterion. Proper weighted technique should be introduced to capture combined effect and contribution of rating as well as weight of subcriteria. In this chapter, exponential function has been introduced instead of linear one with a view to distinguish alternatives on the basis of their measured performance rating. The following equation has been introduced for the calculation of weighted normalized rating for each subcriterion.

$$z_{ijk} = \left(y_{ijk} \right)^{EXP(10w_{jk})} \tag{30.3}$$

Here z_{ijk} denotes the weighted normalized rating of ith alternative with respect kth subcriterion under jth criterion. y_{ijk} denotes the normalized value of initial performance rating of ith alternative with respect to jth criterion. w_{jk} is the weight of kth subcriterion under jth original criterion. Calculated weighted rating of each alternative with respect each subcriterion is expressed in the following matrix format.

$$
M_{wnd} =
\begin{matrix}
 & & \begin{matrix} C_1 & & & C_j & & & C_n & \\ C_{11} & C_{12} & \cdots & C_{j1} & C_{j2} & \cdots & C_{n1} & C_{n2} & \cdots \end{matrix} \\
\begin{matrix} S_1 \\ \cdots \\ S_i \\ \cdots \\ S_m \end{matrix} &
\begin{bmatrix}
z_{111} & z_{112} & \cdots & z_{1j1} & z_{1j2} & \cdots & z_{1n1} & z_{1n2} & \cdots \\
\cdots & \cdots & \cdots & \cdots & \cdots & \cdots & \cdots & \cdots & \cdots \\
z_{i11} & z_{i12} & \cdots & z_{ij1} & z_{ij2} & \cdots & z_{in1} & z_{in1} & \cdots \\
\cdots & \cdots & \cdots & \cdots & \cdots & \cdots & \cdots & \cdots & \cdots \\
z_{m11} & z_{m12} & \cdots & z_{mj1} & z_{mj2} & \cdots & z_{mn1} & z_{mn2} & \cdots
\end{bmatrix}
\end{matrix}
$$

Step 6: Compute the weighted performance rating for each criterion. It is the combined weighted effect of all subcriteria under each individual criterion. This combined weighted effect is obtained from the weighted performance rating of subcriterion of the previous step. Calculation of weighted performance rating for jth criterion can be carried out using the following simple equation (30.4).

$$z_{ij} = \sum_{k \in Subcriteria} y_{ijk}^{EXP(10w_{jk})} \tag{30.4}$$

Here, z_{ij} is the weighted performance rating of ith alternative. Weighted performance rating of each alternative is expressed in the following matrix form.

$$M_{wnd(C)} = \begin{array}{c} \\ S_1 \\ \cdots \\ S_i \\ \cdots \\ S_m \end{array} \begin{array}{ccccc} C_1 & \cdots & C_j & \cdots & C_n \\ \left[\begin{array}{ccccc} z_{11} & \cdots & z_{1j} & \cdots & z_{1n} \\ \cdots & \cdots & \cdots & \cdots & \cdots \\ z_{i1} & \cdots & z_{ij} & \cdots & z_{in} \\ \cdots & \cdots & \cdots & \cdots & \cdots \\ z_{m1} & \cdots & z_{mj} & \cdots & z_{mn} \end{array} \right] \end{array}$$

Step 7: Determine the absolute weighted rating (AWR): AWR is the weighted performance rating of each individual alternative. This is the combination of normalized performance rating weighed by all criteria importance. Higher AWR is better. The current research work proposes a unique technique which is the sum of arithmetic mean and geometric mean of the weighted ratings under the homogeneous decision making attitude towards the different mean values.

$$AWR_i = \frac{1}{2n} \sum_{j=1}^{n} \sum_{k \in Subcriteria} y_{ijk}^{EXP(10w_{jk})}$$
$$+ \frac{1}{2} \sqrt[n]{\left(\sum_{k \in subcriteria} y_{i1k}^{EXP(10w_{jk})} \times \ldots \times \sum_{k \in subcriteria} y_{ink}^{EXP(10w_{jk})} \right)} \tag{30.5}$$

AWR_i denotes the absolute weighted rating for ith alternative.

Step 8: Measure the performance score for each alternative. Performance score is the indicator for measurement of performance of individual alternative. Higher performance score is desirable. Performance score of each individual alternative is computed using the equation (30.6).

$$PS_i = \frac{AWR_i}{\max(AWR_i)} \qquad (30.6)$$

The alternatives are arranged in the descending order their performance score. Rank 1 is awarded to the alternative with the highest performance score, rank 2 is given to the alternative associated with second highest performance score and so on. Now select the best alternative having the highest performance score because maximum performance score ensures the maximum benefit.

30.3 Illustrative Example

30.3.1 Problem Definition

A south Indian company decides for evaluation and selection of raw material suppliers for its plants. For the purpose, the company forms an expert committee consisting of experienced personnel from different important sections of the company for appropriate decision making. Through a long and effective discussion and based on a unanimous opinion, they choose six important subjective criteria. The criteria are C1: quality C2: cost C3: transportation and delivery time C4: product packaging C5: minimum order quantity, and C6: customer relations. There are three benefit criteria viz. quality, product packaging and customer relation. The remaining three criteria namely cost, transportation and delivery time and minimum order quantity are of cost category.

The experts also divided each criterion into several subcriteria. In initial screening they set a cutoff score for each candidate of supplier to be considered for final selection. A set of five suppliers passed the cutoff score and entered into the final selection process. Then the expert committee award performance rating to each of the alternative supplier in a scale of 1 to 5. For benefit criteria, grade 5 is preferred and for cost criteria 1 is preferred. The expert committee assesses the alternatives with respect each subcriteria and forms a decision matrix presented in Table 30.1. The expert committee also unanimously distributes weights to the criteria and subcriteria based on their experience and expertise. The criteria, different subcriteria and the respective weights are presented in Table 30.2.

30.3.2   Calculation and Discussions

Step 1. Formation of decision making committee, identification of important criteria and carrying out the screening test for the initial section of the set of feasible alternative suppliers is regarded as the step 1. This step involves listing the criteria, subcriteria and names of the suppliers.

Step 2. Decision making committee assesses the alternative with respect to each criteria and subcriteria in a grade of five by assigning a value of 1, 2, 3, 4, or 5. This assessment is presented in Table 30.1.

Step 3. The members of the expert committee are expected to have sufficient knowledge and experience to judge the importance the criteria and subcriteria. The weights to the criteria or to the subcriteria are distributed in such a way that the sum of the weights is always unity. Weight matrix is shown in Table 30.2.

Step 4. Normalization of performance rating is conducted by using Equation (30.1) and Equation (30.2) for benefit criteria and cost criteria respectively. The normalized values are presented in Table 30.3.

Step 5. Weighted normalized ratings of the subcriteria are calculated by using equation (30.3). The corresponding values are shown in Table 30.4.

Step 6. Weighted normalized ratings of the individual criteria are computed using equation (30.4). The corresponding values of weighted normalized performance rating are decorated in Table 30.5.

Step 7. Absolute weighted ratings of each alternative supplier are measured by equation (30.5) and the associated values are presented in Table 30.6.

Step 8. Performance score of individual supplier is computed by using the equation (30.6). The alternative suppliers are arranged in the descending order of their performance score. It is observed that S4 has the highest performance score, therefore, supplier S4 is selected as the best alternative. The ranking order of the suppliers is shown in Table 30.7.

Table 30.1 Decision matrix comprising of performance ratings of the alternative suppliers.

Suppliers	C1 (+) quality			C2(-) cost			C3 (-) transportation & delivery time			C4 (+) product packaging		C5(-) min. order Qty		C6(+) customer relations	
	C_{11}	C_{12}	C_{13}	C_{21}	C_{22}	C_{23}	C_{31}	C_{32}	C_{33}	C_{41}	C_{42}	C_{51}	C_{52}	C_{61}	C_{62}
S1	3	5	3	5	3	4	3	4	5	5	5	5	4	4	5
S2	4	4	3	3	3	3	5	2	4	2	3	1	1	1	3
S3	3	1	2	5	5	5	2	4	4	3	3	2	4	3	5
S4	5	5	3	3	1	1	4	5	3	4	4	3	2	2	5
S5	2	1	5	4	4	3	5	4	5	3	5	5	5	5	1
Avg.	3.4	3.2	3.2	4	3.2	3.2	3.8	3.8	4.2	3.4	4	3.2	3.2	3	3.8

Table 30.2 Weight matrix consisting the weights of the criteria and subcriteria.

	C1 (0.25)			C2 (0.15)			C3 (0.12)			C4 (0.20)		C5 (0.10)		C6 (0.18)	
	C11	C12	C13	C21	C22	C23	C31	C32	C33	C41	C42	G51	C52	C61	C62
wi	0.06	0.01	0.09	0.06	0.03	0.06	0.06	0.03	0.03	0.08	0.06	0.06	0.04	0.1	0.08
Ei	1.82	1.11	2.46	1.82	1.35	1.82	1.82	1.35	1.35	2.23	1.82	1.82	1.49	2.72	2.23

Table 30.3 Normalized performance rating of the alternative suppliers.

Si	C1			C2			C3			C4		C5		C6	
	C11	C12	C13	C21	C22	C23	C31	C32	C33	C41	C42	G51	C52	C61	C62
S1	0.88	1.56	0.94	0.80	1.07	0.80	1.27	0.95	0.84	1.47	1.25	0.64	0.80	1.33	1.32
S2	1.18	1.25	0.94	1.33	1.07	1.07	0.76	1.90	1.05	0.59	0.75	3.20	3.20	0.33	0.79
S3	0.88	0.31	0.63	0.80	0.64	0.64	1.90	0.95	1.05	0.88	0.75	1.60	0.80	1.00	1.32
S4	1.47	1.56	0.94	1.33	3.20	3.20	0.95	0.76	1.40	1.18	1.00	1.07	1.60	0.67	1.32
S5	0.59	0.31	1.56	1.00	0.80	1.07	0.76	0.95	0.84	0.88	1.25	0.64	0.64	1.67	0.26

Table 30.4 Weighted normalized performance ratings for suppliers with respect to subcriteria.

Si	C1			C2			C3			C4		C5		C6	
	C_{11}	C_{12}	C_{13}	C_{21}	C_{22}	C_{23}	C_{31}	C_{32}	C_{33}	C_{41}	C_{42}	C_{51}	C_{52}	C_{61}	C_{62}
S1	0.80	1.64	0.85	0.67	1.09	0.67	1.54	0.93	0.79	2.36	1.50	0.44	0.72	2.19	1.84
S2	1.34	1.28	0.85	1.69	1.09	1.12	0.61	2.38	1.07	0.31	0.59	8.33	5.67	0.05	0.59
S3	0.80	0.28	0.31	0.67	0.55	0.44	3.22	0.93	1.07	0.76	0.59	2.35	0.72	1.00	1.84
S4	2.02	1.64	0.85	1.69	4.81	8.33	0.91	0.69	1.57	1.44	1.00	1.12	2.02	0.33	1.84
S5	0.38	0.28	3.00	1.00	0.74	1.12	0.61	0.93	0.79	0.76	1.50	0.44	0.51	4.01	0.05

Table 30.5 Weighted normalized performance ratings of the suppliers for each criteria.

Suppliers	C1	C2	C3	C4	C5	C6
S1	3.29	2.42	3.26	3.86	1.16	4.03
S2	3.48	3.90	4.05	0.90	14.00	0.64
S3	1.39	1.66	5.22	1.35	3.07	2.84
S4	4.51	14.82	3.18	2.44	3.14	2.17
S5	3.65	2.86	2.33	2.26	0.96	4.06

Table 30.6 Absolute weighting ratings (AWR) for the alternative suppliers.

Supplier	AM	GM	AWR
S1	3.00	2.79	2.90
S2	4.50	2.76	3.63
S3	2.59	2.28	2.44
S4	5.04	3.90	4.47
S5	2.69	2.45	2.57

Table 30.7 Performance score and ranking order of the suppliers.

Suppliers	Performance score	Ranking order
S1	0.65	3
S2	0.81	2
S3	0.54	5
S4	1.00	1
S5	0.57	4

30.4 Conclusions

Proper supplier selection under multicriteria decision making environment is always a hard task (Figures 30.1 and 30.2). This task becomes harder while multiple subjective criteria along with multiple subcriteria are considered. Therefore, there exists absolute necessity for introducing a new and suitable approach capable of considering alternative, subjective criteria along with subcriteria, expert opinion under MCDM. The present research work proposed a novel multicriteria decision making approach, which is illustrated using a suitable example on supplier selection. It shows that the proposed technique is effective and useful for solving decision making problem in the field of supplier selection. The proposed method considers that the group decision making is homogeneous and unanimous. Consideration of heterogeneous group decision making along with interdependent criteria may be a direction of future research in this regard.

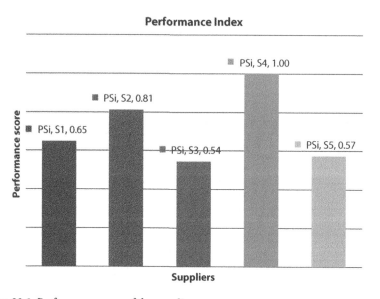

Figure 30.1 Performance score of the suppliers.

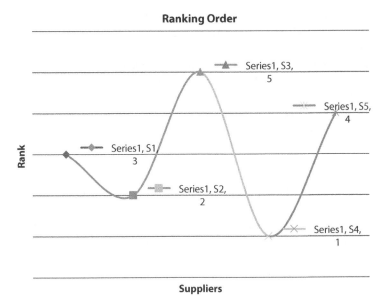

Figure 30.2 Ranking order of the suppliers.

References

1. Melih, C.E. and Gul, Y.M., Green supplier selection for textile industry: A case study using BWM-TODIM integration under interval type-2 fuzzy set. *Environ. Sci. Pollut. Res.*, 28, 64793–64817, 2021.
2. Ilyas, M., Carpitella, S., Zoubr, E., Designing supplier selection strategies under COVID-19 constraints for industrial environments. *31st CIRP Design Conference 2021(CIRP Design 201) Procedia CIRP*, vol. 100, pp. 589–594, 2021.
3. Naqvi, M.A. and Amin, S.H., Supplier selection and order allocation: A literature review. *JDIM*, 3, 125–139, 2021.
4. Doa, A.D., Ta, V.L., Canhc, C.D., Tad, Q.T., Luub, H.V., A new integrated generalized multi-criteria group decision making approach for green supplier selection. *Uncertain Suppl. Chain Manage.*, 8, 813–820, 2020.
5. Javad, M.O.M., Darvishi, M., Javad, A.O.M., Green supplier selection for the steel industry using BWM and fuzzy TOPSIS: A case study of Khouzestan steel company. *Sustain. Futures*, 2, 100012, 2020.
6. Haeri, S.A.S. and Rezaei, J., A grey-based green supplier selection model for uncertain environments. *J. Clean. Prod.*, 221, 768–784, 2019.
7. Tseng, M.L., Green supply chain management with linguistic preferences and incomplete information. *Appl. Soft Comput.*, 11, 4894–4903, 2011.
8. Bai, C. and Sarkis, J., Green supplier development: Analytical evaluation using rough set theory. *J. Clean. Prod.*, 18, 1200–1210, 2010.

9. Bai, C. and Sarkis, J., Integrating sustainability into supplier selection with grey system and rough set methodologies. *Int. J. Prod. Econ.*, 124, 252–264, 2010.

10. Zhu, Q., Dou, Y., Sarkis, J., A portfolio-based analysis for green supplier management using the analytical network process. *Int. J. Supply Chain Manag.*, 15, 306–319, 2010.

11. Lee, A.H.I., Kang, H.Y., Hsu, C.F., Hung, H.C., A green supplier selection model for high-tech industry. *Expert Syst. Appl.*, 36, 7917–7927, 2009.

12. Lu, L.Y.Y., Wu, C.H., Kuo, T.C., Environmental principles applicable to green supplier evaluation by using multi-objective decision analysis. *Int. J. Prod. Res.*, 45, 4317–4331, 2007.

13. Vachon, S. and Klassen, R.D., Green project partnership in the supply chain: The case of the package printing industry. *J. Clean. Prod.*, 14, 661–671, 2006.

14. Zhang, H.C., Li, J., Merchant, M.E., Using fuzzy multi-agent decision-making in environmentally conscious supplier management. *CIRP Ann. Manuf. Technol.*, 52, 385–388, 2003.

15. Humphreys, P., McIvor, R., Chan, F.T.S., Using case-based reasoning to evaluate supplier environmental management performance. *Expert Syst. Appl.*, 25, 141–153, 2003.

16. Humphreys, P.K., Wong, Y.K., Chan, F.T.S., Integrating environmental criteria into the supplier selection process. *J. Mater. Process. Technol.*, 138, 349–356, 2003.

17. Bhutta, K.S. and Huq, F., Supplier selection problem a comparison of total cost of ownership and analytical hierarchy process approach. *Int. J. Supply Chain Manag.*, 7, 2002.

18. Handfield, R., Walton, S.V., Sroufe, R., Melnyk, S.A., Applying environmental criteria to supplier assessment: A study in the application of the analytical hierarchy process. 141, 70–87, 2002.

19. Bowen, F.E., Cousins, P.D., Lamming, R.C., Faruk, A.C., The role of supply management capabilities in green supply. *Prod. Oper. Manag.*, 10, 174–189, 2001.

20. Enarsson, L., Evaluation of suppliers: How to consider the environment. *Int. J. Phys. Distrib. Logist. Manag.*, 28, 5–17, 1998.

21. Noci, G., Designing "green" vendor rating systems for the assessment of a suppliers environmental performance. *Eur. J. Purch. Supply Manag.*, 3, 103–11, 1997.

Index

Also of Interest

Check out these published and forthcoming titles in "Sustainable Computing and Optimization" series from Scrivener Publishing

Optimization Techniques in Engineering
Advances and Applications
Edited by Anita Khosla, Prasenjit Chatterjee, Ikbal Ali and Dheeraj Joshi
Published 2023. ISBN 978-1-119-90627-8

Computational Intelligence in Sustainable Reliability Engineering
Edited by S. C. Malik, Deepak Sinwar, Ashish Kumar, S. R. Gadde, Prasenjit Chatterjee and Bui Thanh Hung
Published 2023. ISBN 978-1-119-86501-8

Decision Support Systems for Smart City Applications
Edited by Loveleen Gaur, Vernika Agarwal and Prasenjit Chatterjee
Published 2023. ISBN 978-1-119-89643-2

Fuzzy Computing in Data Science
Applications and Challenges
Editors: Sachi Nandan Mohanty, Prasenjit Chatterjee and Bui Thanh Hung
Published 2022. ISBN 978-1-119-86492-9

Handbook of Intelligent Computing and Optimization for Sustainable Development
Edited by Mukhdeep Singh Manshahia, Valeriy Kharchenko, Elias Munapo, J. Joshua Thomas and Pandian Vasant
Published 2022. ISBN 978-1-119-79182-9

Machine Learning Algorithms and Applications
Edited by Mettu Srinivas, G. Sucharitha and Anjanna Matta
Published 2021. ISBN 978-1-119-76885-2

Smart Sustainable Intelligent Systems
Edited by Namita Gupta, Prasenjit Chatterjee and Tanupriya Choudhury
Published 2021. ISBN 978-1-119-75058-1

www.scrivenerpublishing.com

.

Printed and bound by CPI Group (UK) Ltd, Croydon, CR0 4YY

27/10/2024

14580178-0005